Economic Report
of the President

OCT 1 9 2009

Transmitted to the Congress
January 2009

together with
THE ANNUAL REPORT
of the
COUNCIL OF ECONOMIC ADVISERS

UNITED STATES GOVERNMENT PRINTING OFFICE

WASHINGTON : 2009

For sale by the Superintendent of Documents, U.S. Government Printing Office
Internet: bookstore.gpo.gov   Phone: (202) 512-1800   Fax: (202) 512-2104
Mail Stop: IDCC, Washington, DC 20402-0001

ISBN-13: 978-0-16-082221-6

CONTENTS

* For a detailed table of contents of the Council's Report, see page 11

ECONOMIC REPORT
OF THE PRESIDENT

ECONOMIC REPORT OF THE PRESIDENT

To the Congress of the United States:

The American economy has consistently proven its strength and resilience in the face of shocks such as natural disasters, high energy prices, and the terrorist attacks of September 11. The economy experienced 6 years of uninterrupted expansion, which included a record stretch of 52 consecutive months of job creation. The past year saw this growth cease as several forces that developed over many years in the credit and housing markets converged. The combination of these factors, coupled with a sustained period of rising energy prices, was sufficient to threaten the entire financial system and generated a shock so large that its effects have been felt throughout the global economy.

Under ordinary circumstances, it would be preferable to allow the free market to take its course and correct over time. But the Government has a responsibility to safeguard the broader health and stability of our economy. Under the extraordinary circumstances created by the financial crisis, the potential damage to American households and businesses was so severe that a systemic, aggressive, and unprecedented Government response was the only responsible policy option.

The actions taken by my Administration in response to the financial crisis have laid the groundwork for a return to economic growth and job creation, and they are beginning to show some early results. A measure of stability has returned to the financial system. There will, of course, continue to be challenges. Temporary Government programs must remain temporary and be unwound in an orderly manner as soon as conditions warrant. Financial regulations must be modernized to reflect the realities of the 21st century, and these efforts should ensure that the objective of protecting consumers and investors does not come at the expense of the flexibility required for innovations to come to the market. We must also continue to trust

Americans with the responsibility of homeownership and empower them to weather turbulent times in the market by helping creditworthy homeowners avoid foreclosure.

As the country navigates through this trying period, we must never lose sight of the enormous benefits delivered by the free enterprise system. Americans have good reasons to be confident about the long-term health of our economy. Despite the current difficulties, there are a number of positive economic factors. Inflationary pressures have moderated as record high prices for oil and gasoline have retreated. Productivity growth, which helps to increase our standard of living and improve our international competitiveness, remains solid. The American economy continues to be the largest and most dynamic in the world, and its solid foundation of flexible labor markets, low tax rates, and open trade and investment policies all contribute to its ability to recover fairly quickly from shocks. Over the past 8 years, my Administration has worked to strengthen this foundation by adopting pro-growth, market-oriented policies, and our policies will position the economy for a strong rebound and continued long-run growth.

Sound economic policy begins with keeping taxes low. The tax relief enacted by my Administration was the largest in a generation. Tax rates have been lowered for every American who pays income taxes. More than 13 million Americans had their Federal income tax liability completely eliminated, and individuals and businesses have kept $1.7 trillion of their own hard-earned money. Raising taxes at any time reduces our international competitiveness and further distorts the decisions of individuals and businesses; doing so in the current environment would have serious consequences for the economy. This tax relief has been a key factor in promoting the economic growth and job creation of recent years, and it should be made permanent. Unless the Congress acts, most of the tax relief that we have delivered over the past 8 years will be taken away, and 116 million American taxpayers will see their taxes rise.

The Government also has a responsibility to spend the taxpayers' money wisely. Over the course of my Administration, the rate of growth in nonsecurity discretionary spending has steadily decreased from more than 16 percent in 2001 to below the rate of inflation today. While the financial crisis has required significant taxpayer investments that will increase the budget deficit, we expect that most or all of those investments will be paid back to taxpayers over time. The greatest challenge to the fiscal health of the country remains the unsustainable growth in entitlement programs such as Social Security,

Medicare, and Medicaid. I have laid out responsible, innovative solutions to address these challenges, which will otherwise only grow more difficult to solve over time. The Congress has an obligation to confront these issues.

Government does have a role to play in health care, but a robust private market is critical to ensuring that health care is affordable and accessible for all Americans. My Administration has sought to balance public and private roles in health care with market-oriented policies that increase the efficiency of health care delivery, encourage competition, and leave decisions in the hands of individuals and their doctors. For example, enactment of the Medicare prescription drug benefit program has provided more than 40 million Americans with better access to prescription drug coverage, expanded competition in Medicare, trusted consumers to make their own health care decisions, and the costs have been much lower than originally estimated. The introduction of Health Savings Accounts has also provided consumers with greater access to affordable health care plans. There is much more that can be done to improve health care, such as adopting medical liability reform, eliminating the bias in the tax code against those who do not receive health insurance through their employers, and increasing the power of small employers, civic groups, and community organizations to negotiate lower-priced health premiums. These policies would help reduce frivolous lawsuits that increase patients' costs, promote the use of health savings accounts, and encourage competition among health plans across State lines.

To be competitive in the global marketplace, the United States must remain open to international trade and investment and reject the false promise offered by protectionist policies. American workers and businesses can compete with anyone in the world, as evidenced by the remarkable performance of American exports in recent years. When I took office, the United States had free trade agreements (FTAs) in force with only three countries. Today, we have FTAs in force with 16 countries. I thank the Congress for its approval of these agreements and strongly encourage prompt approval of the agreements with Colombia, Panama, and South Korea that will benefit our country. These agreements will provide greater access for our exports, support good jobs for American workers, and promote America's strategic interests. We also have an unprecedented opportunity to reduce barriers to global trade and investment through a successful conclusion to the World Trade Organization Doha Round negotiations. In addition, the Congress should reauthorize and reform trade adjustment assistance so that we can help those workers whose jobs are displaced to learn new skills and find new jobs.

The rapid increase in energy prices in the past year exposed just how dependent our economy is on oil. We must continue taking steps to increase our energy security. The Energy Policy Act of 2005 and the Energy Independence and Security Act of 2007 were major steps toward this goal, but in the short term, our country will continue to rely on fossil fuels for most of its energy supply. I am pleased that the Congress recognized this reality and agreed to remove restrictions that will allow responsible oil and gas exploration on the Outer Continental Shelf and expanded access to oil shale to help meet America's energy needs. In the long run, our energy security will require advances in clean and renewable energy technologies. My Administration has worked to reduce gasoline consumption and promote alternative fuels to transform the way Americans power their cars and trucks. We have also worked to develop cleaner energy sources to power Americans' homes and places of work, such as clean coal, nuclear, solar, and wind power. At home, we are on the path to slow, stop, and eventually reverse the growth of greenhouse gas emissions, but substantial reductions in global greenhouse gas emissions are only possible with the concerted action of all countries. The Major Economies Process launched by my Administration in 2007 has brought all major economies together to discuss a common approach to a global climate agreement that includes the meaningful participation of all major economies.

The creativity, ingenuity, and resourcefulness of the American people is our country's greatest strength, and a vibrant education system is key to maintaining our Nation's competitive edge and extending economic opportunity to every citizen. Workers who invest in their education and training enjoy higher incomes and greater job security. The No Child Left Behind Act has succeeded in bringing greater accountability to schools, and the results are clear; as one example, African American and Hispanic students are posting all-time high scores in a number of categories. The Congress should reauthorize this vital law, and our Nation must continue to demand results and accountability from our educational system. To be competitive in the global economy, American workers also need to continually update their skills. To that end, my Administration has invested nearly $1 billion in new job training initiatives to ensure our workforce has the skills required of 21st century jobs. We have also nearly doubled support for Pell Grants to help millions of low-income Americans afford college tuition. The technological innovation that drives our global economic leadership depends on continued scientific discoveries and advancements, and I am pleased that the Congress authorized the doubling of basic research in key physical science and engineering agencies as I proposed in my American Competitiveness Initiative (ACI). I urge the Congress to appropriate these ACI funds promptly to help sustain our economy's long-term competitive position.

Many of these issues are discussed in the 2009 *Annual Report of the Council of Economic Advisers*. The Council has prepared this *Report* to help policymakers understand the economic conditions and issues that underlie my Administration's policy decisions. Free market policies have lifted millions of people out of poverty and given them the opportunity to build a more hopeful life. By continuing to trust the decisions of individuals and markets and pursuing pro-growth policies, Americans can be confident that the economy will emerge stronger than ever from its current challenges, with greater opportunity for prosperity and economic growth.

THE WHITE HOUSE
JANUARY 2009

THE ANNUAL REPORT
OF THE
COUNCIL OF ECONOMIC ADVISERS

LETTER OF TRANSMITTAL

COUNCIL OF ECONOMIC ADVISERS
Washington, D.C., January 16, 2009

MR. PRESIDENT:

The Council of Economic Advisers herewith submits its 2009 Annual Report in accordance with the provisions of the Employment Act of 1946 as amended by the Full Employment and Balanced Growth Act of 1978.

Sincerely,

Edward P. Lazear
Chairman

Donald B. Marron
Member

CONTENTS

LIST OF BOXES

Overview

The U.S. economy has proven itself remarkably resilient over the past 8 years, having withstood a number of major shocks throughout the period. During the last few months of 2008, however, the economy encountered major shocks in the financial sector that it could not shake off. Those financial shocks combined with other factors—record high commodity prices earlier in the year, natural disasters, and continued weakness in the housing market—to cause the economy to contract modestly in the third quarter and what appears to be a sharp decline in the fourth quarter (see Chapters 1 and 2). The contraction will likely last into early- or mid-2009. Despite rapid fiscal and monetary policy action in response to weakening economic conditions, the economy entered into recession at the end of 2007, ending 6 years of expansion and a record 52 months of uninterrupted job growth. Several factors contributed over many years to create the credit difficulties that reached crisis proportions late in the year. The magnitude of the crisis required unprecedented policy responses to reduce the extent of the damage to the economy. These policy actions have laid a foundation for a strong economic recovery early in the term of the next Administration. Most market forecasts suggest the weakness will continue in the first half of 2009, followed by a recovery beginning in the second half of 2009 that will gain momentum in 2010 and beyond.

Despite the risk that recent events may overshadow the many positive developments of the past 8 years, there have been major policy advances that have improved the long-term prospects of our economy and strengthened its foundation. Much of this *Report* examines the effects of pro-growth economic policies and market-based reforms adopted during the Administration, as well as policy considerations that will further improve the long-term position of our economy and allow more Americans to realize the benefits of economic expansion in the future.

Record-high energy prices in 2008 highlighted our economy's dependence on fossil fuels and underscored the need to diversify our national energy portfolio. Although it will take time and major technological breakthroughs to substantially reduce our dependence on fossil fuels, the Administration has invested unprecedented levels of Federal resources and adopted a number of policies that have helped advance the economy's transition to new sources of energy while reducing local and regional pollutants in responsible ways that do not threaten our economic well-being (see Chapter 3).

Export performance was one of the bright spots in the economy over the past several years, and played an important role in offsetting other areas of weakness in the economy. The United States's continued commitment to open trade and investment policies will be an important factor in maintaining the international competitiveness and the dynamic nature of our economy (see Chapter 4). Lower tax rates have also contributed to economic performance by easing the burden on labor and capital and enabling firms, investors, and consumers to allocate resources more efficiently (see Chapter 5). These policies, which contribute to the increased flexibility of the economy, will be important in facilitating the economic recovery going forward. There remains considerable opportunity to strengthen our economic position by eliminating the uncertainty surrounding tax relief that is scheduled to expire. In addition, rising health care costs and spending on entitlement programs are ongoing areas of concern, and the Administration has offered reforms that could substantially lower costs and improve our fiscal position (see Chapters 6 and 7). Education is essential to future prosperity, and the Administration has taken several steps to improve kindergarten through twelfth-grade education and to make college more affordable (see Chapter 8). Finally, as highlighted by the recent financial crisis, there are several areas in which regulatory reforms are necessary and appropriate to address market failures. The Administration has pursued market-oriented regulatory reforms that favor individual choice over Government decision making wherever appropriate, and this approach has proven effective in addressing market failures without imposing excessive costs on society or the economy (see Chapter 9).

Chapter 1: The Year in Review and the Years Ahead

Following 6 consecutive years of expansion of the U.S economy, the pace of real GDP expansion slowed in the first half of 2008 and turned negative in the second half. The Business Cycle Dating Committee of the National Bureau of Economic Research declared that the economy peaked in December of 2007, then began a recession that continued throughout 2008. Falling house prices initiated a cascade of problems that threatened the solvency of several major financial institutions and resulted in a major decline in the stock market. To respond to these problems, policymakers undertook a wide range of fiscal and monetary policy actions. Chapter 1 reviews the economic developments of 2008 and discusses the Administration's forecast for the years ahead. The key points of Chapter 1 are:

- Real GDP likely declined over the four quarters of 2008, ending a 6-year run of positive growth, as the slow growth in the first half of the year was eclipsed by what appears to be a sharp decline in the fourth quarter.
- Financial distress, which first became evident in mid-2007 in the market for mortgage-backed securities (MBS), continued through 2008 and affected a variety of markets. In the wake of the failure and near-failure of several major financial institutions in September 2008, financial stresses increased sharply to levels not seen during the post–World War II era.
- Payroll jobs declined during 2008, having peaked in December of 2007. Employment losses averaged 82,000-per-month during the first 8 months of 2008, before accelerating to a 420,000-per-month pace during the next 3 months. The unemployment rate was at 5 percent rate though April—a low rate by historical standards—but increased to 6.7 percent in November. Initial and continued claims for unemployment insurance moved up sharply over the course of the year.
- Energy prices dominated the movement of overall inflation in the consumer price index (CPI), with large increases through July, followed by a sharp decline during the latter part of the year. Core consumer inflation (which excludes food and energy inflation) edged down from 2.4 percent during the 12 months of 2007 to a 1.9 percent annual rate during the first 11 months of 2008. Food prices rose appreciably faster than core prices.
- Nominal hourly compensation increased 2.8 percent during the 12 months through September 2008 (according to the employment cost index), a gain that was undermined by the rise in food and energy prices, so that real hourly compensation fell 2 percent. In the long run, real hourly compensation tends to increase with labor productivity, although the correlation can be very loose over shorter intervals. Nonfarm business productivity has grown at an average annual rate of 2.6 percent since the business cycle peak in 2001.
- An economic stimulus was proposed by the President in January and passed by Congress in February, authorizing about $113 billion in tax rebate checks to low- and middle-income taxpayers and allowing 50 percent expensing for business equipment investment. The stimulus likely boosted GDP growth in the second and third quarters above what it might have been otherwise, but its influence faded by the end of the year.
- The Administration's forecast calls for real GDP to continue to fall in the first half of 2009, with the major declines projected to be concentrated in the fourth quarter of 2008 and the first quarter of 2009. An active monetary policy and the Treasury's injection of assets into financial institutions are expected to ease financial stress and to lead to a

rebound in the interest-sensitive sectors of the economy in the second half of 2009. Also supporting growth during 2009 is the substantial recent drop in petroleum prices, which offsets some of the effects of the recent decline in household wealth. The unemployment rate is expected to increase to an average of 7.7 percent for 2009. The expansion in 2010–11 is projected to be vigorous, bringing the unemployment rate down to 5 percent by 2012.

Chapter 2: Housing and Financial Markets

In the summer of 2008, the disruptions in credit markets that began in 2007 worsened to the point that the global financial system was in crisis. The magnitude of the crisis required an unprecedented response on the part of the Government to limit the extent of damage to the economy and restore stability to the financial system. Chapter 2 reviews the origins of the crisis, its consequences, the Government's response, and discusses several policy challenges going forward. The key points of Chapter 2 are:

- The roots of the current global financial crisis began in the late 1990s. A rapid increase in saving by developing countries (sometimes called the "global saving glut") resulted in a large influx of capital to the United States and other industrialized countries, driving down the return on safe assets. The relatively low yield on safe assets likely encouraged investors to look for higher yields from riskier assets, whose yields also went down. What turned out to be an underpricing of risk across a number of markets (housing, commercial real estate, and leveraged buyouts, among others) in the United States and abroad, and an uncertainty about how this risk was distributed throughout the global financial system, set the stage for subsequent financial distress.

- The influx of inexpensive capital helped finance a housing boom. House prices appreciated rapidly earlier in this decade, and building increased to well-above historic levels. Eventually, house prices began to decline with this glut in housing supply.

- Considerable innovations in housing finance—the growth of subprime mortgages and the expansion of the market for assets backed by mortgages—helped fuel the housing boom. Those innovations were often beneficial, helping to make home ownership more affordable and accessible, but excesses set the stage for later losses.

- The declining value of mortgage-related assets has had a disproportionate effect on the financial sector because a large fraction of mortgage-related assets are held by banks, investment banks, and other highly levered financial institutions. The combination of leverage (the use of borrowed funds) and, in particular, a reliance on short-term funding made these institutions (both in the United States and abroad) vulnerable to large mortgage losses.

- Vulnerable institutions failed, and others nearly failed. The remaining institutions pulled back from extending credit to each other, and inter-bank lending rates increased to unprecedented levels. The effects of the crisis were most visible in the financial sector, but the impact and consequences of the crisis are being felt by households, businesses, and governments throughout the world.
- The U.S. Government has undertaken a historic effort to address the underlying problems behind the freeze in the credit markets. These problems, the subject of much of this chapter, are a sudden increase in the desire for liquidity, a massive reassessment of risk, and a solvency crisis for many systemically important institutions. The Government has worked to preserve the stability of the overall financial system by preventing the disorderly failures of important financial institutions; taken unprecedented action to boost liquidity in short-term funding markets; provided substantial new protections for consumers, businesses, and investors; and cooperated closely with its international partners.
- Looking forward, the global financial crisis presents several additional challenges for the U.S. Government. Among them are the need to modernize financial regulation, unwind temporary programs in an orderly fashion, and develop long-term solutions for the government-sponsored enterprises (privately-owned, publicly-chartered entities) Fannie Mae and Freddie Mac.

Chapter 3: Energy and the Environment

Although fossil fuels will continue to constitute a large share of the Nation's energy portfolio for some time, the Administration has taken major steps to increase and diversify the Nation's energy supply and to improve the environment. Since 2001, significant investments have been made to develop cleaner and more reliable energy sources, and several regulatory changes are expected to deliver dramatic improvements in air quality nationwide. Chapter 3 reviews recent advances in energy and environmental policy and discusses several challenges associated with efforts to diversify the Nation's energy portfolio, to increase energy security, and to reduce emissions related to fossil-fuel based energy use. The key points of Chapter 3 are:

- Because of innovative regulations promulgated under this Administration, there should be substantial improvements in air quality over the next few decades. Two rules that implemented cap-and-trade programs in the electricity sector represent a significant step in using cost-effective, market-oriented policy instruments to dramatically reduce power plants' emissions of sulfur dioxide, nitrogen oxide, and mercury.
- Despite widespread support for using market-based approaches to achieve our environmental and energy policy goals going forward, challenges remain in realizing the full potential of these approaches.
- There is an increasing need to reassess how well existing laws can address the environmental problems associated with fossil fuel use in more cost-effective ways. For example, it may become increasingly costly to make additional reductions in traditional air pollutants, and existing statutes that focus on local or regional pollutants were not designed to address global problems such as greenhouse gas (GHG) emissions.
- Substantial reductions in global GHG emissions will require participation by all large emitters (countries and sectors within countries).

Chapter 4: The Benefits of Open Trade and Investment Policies

The United States has one of the most open economies in the world, ranking very high in common measures of openness to trade and investment. In the long run, the benefits that open economic policies generate far outweigh the narrow, short-run perceived benefits of protectionist or isolationist policies. The more diffuse but larger benefits of open trade and investment policies to the general economy are often difficult to discern, especially in the short run, and are sometimes obscured by the more visible effects of protectionist policies on favored groups. This chapter discusses several key facts about trade and investment in the United States, the benefits of free trade and open investment, and the policies that the United States has taken to enhance both. The key points of Chapter 4 are:

- Openness to trade and investment has boosted U.S. economic growth. Openness can also reduce the impact of shocks and increase the resilience of the U.S. economy.
- The number of U.S. free trade agreements has increased greatly during this Administration, and these agreements have contributed to the growth in U.S. exports.

- Portfolio and direct investments into the United States reached historic levels over the past decade, in part due to the depth, diversity, and openness of U.S. financial markets and the competitiveness of U.S. firms.
- The United States has maintained an open investment policy, facilitating foreign direct investment flows between the United States and the world while addressing legitimate national security concerns.
- U.S. development and trade initiatives, as well as U.S. engagement in multilateral institutions such as the World Trade Organization and the World Bank, have helped increase growth and foster political and economic stability in developing countries throughout the world.
- Continued commitment to open economic policies throughout the world will help ensure continued economic gains for the United States and the rest of the world.

Chapter 5: Tax Policy

Several policy changes over the past 8 years have resulted in lower tax rates for both individuals and businesses, and specific incentives have been established to reduce the adverse tax consequences of certain desirable activities, such as running a small business or buying an alternative-fuel vehicle. Lower tax rates have increased the benefit of working and investing; in particular, lower tax rates on dividends and capital gains helped business investment expand, thereby helping firms increase worker productivity. Tax relief has contributed to the solid economic growth and job creation that prevailed over most of the past several years. The expiration of these tax reductions would have serious consequences for the U.S. economy. An additional challenge is to further reduce business tax burdens to encourage business investment in the United States in order to develop new jobs for U.S. workers and to continue improving our standard of living. The key points of Chapter 5 are:

- Taxes alter individual and business incentives and thus have the potential to distort their behavior. This Administration consistently fought to reduce tax burdens on individuals and businesses; tax rates are now much lower than they were just 8 years ago.
- Tax reductions over the past 8 years have improved incentives to work, save, and invest.
- Globally, nations compete for businesses and the associated jobs; the United States may need to reduce tax rates on businesses to remain competitive in today's world.

- Future goals should include permanently extending the tax relief of the past 8 years and reforming the Alternative Minimum Tax.

Chapter 6: The Long-Run Challenges of Entitlement Spending

Federal spending on entitlement programs is expected to increase dramatically in the coming decades, particularly for Social Security, Medicare, and Medicaid. Taken together, these programs currently constitute 45 percent of Federal non-interest spending, and assuming no major changes to these programs, this share is projected to rise dramatically in coming decades. An aging population and rising health care spending per person are major reasons for these projected increases. The primary objective of this chapter is to highlight the budgetary challenges facing each of the three major entitlement programs and to outline possible strategies for addressing these challenges. The key points of Chapter 6 are:

- Federal entitlement spending is on an unsustainable path. Spending on the three major entitlement programs—Social Security, Medicare, and Medicaid—is projected to increase much faster than tax revenues or than the overall economy over the coming decades. Paying all scheduled benefits would eventually require substantial reductions in other Government spending, or major tax increases, or both.
- The aging population is a major cause of the expected increase, especially for Social Security, representing a permanent, as opposed to temporary, shift in the entitlement landscape. Currently, one out of six adults is age 65 or older; by 2020, one out of five adults will be 65 or older; and, by 2030, one out of four adults will be age 65 or older.
- The pay-as-you-go financing structure of Social Security, coupled with the aging population, creates a sizeable structural imbalance that will cause current and future generations of workers to bear increasing costs or receive smaller benefits than now scheduled, or both.
- Over the past 30 years, real per capita health care spending has grown considerably faster than real gross domestic product (GDP) per capita. Real growth in Medicare spending is being driven by increasing enrollment, greater utilization of more expensive high-technology medical treatments, and expansion of the goods and services covered by the program.
- Long-term care expenditures for low-income elderly and disabled persons represent a large and growing share of total Medicaid spending. The demand for long-term care is expected to grow in the United States

as a result of the aging population. In turn, this will place even greater financial strain on Federal and State budgets.

Chapter 7: Balancing Private and Public Roles in Health Care

Health care is one of the largest and fastest-growing sectors of the U.S. economy. While modern health care provides substantial benefits, there are growing concerns that its rising cost poses a threat to Americans' access to health insurance and medical care. The Administration has pursued several initiatives to encourage the efficient provision of health care through private markets and to improve access to affordable health care for individuals in the United States. This chapter provides an overview of U.S. performance with respect to the population's health status and spending on health care and discusses key efforts by the Administration to address issues of health care quality, cost, and access. The key points of Chapter 7 are:

- Health care spending is expected to grow rapidly over the next several decades, a trend that is driven by the increased use of high-technology medical procedures, comprehensive health insurance that decreases consumer incentives to shop for cost-effective care, rising rates of chronic disease, and the aging of the population in the United States.
- Markets for health care services can function more efficiently when payers, providers, and consumers have more complete information as well as incentives to use medical care that is clinically effective and of high value.
- Health insurance improves individuals' well-being by providing financial protection against uncertain medical costs and by improving access to care. Market-based approaches and innovative benefit designs can enable people to select coverage that best fits their preferences and to more actively participate in their own health care decision making.
- The Federal Government has an important role in investing in public health infrastructure, particularly with respect to improving the availability of community-based health care for the underserved, preparing for possible public health crises, supporting health-related research and development, and promoting global health improvement.

Chapter 8: Education and Labor

Long-term economic growth requires a productive workforce with the skills necessary to compete in a global labor market. The Administration's commitment to maintaining the high productivity of American workers is evident in successful education and training policies. A continued commitment to broader access to quality education and training will be required to meet the increasing worldwide demand for highly skilled labor. A workforce with better and more widely dispersed skills will ensure that workers enjoy higher incomes and will be a force in reducing income inequality in the United States. The United States also needs comprehensive reform of its immigration policies. The key points of this chapter are:

- Education benefits individuals through higher earnings, and it benefits society as a whole. Administration initiatives to improve kindergarten through twelfth-grade education, most notably the No Child Left Behind Act, are demonstrating clear, measureable results.

- Access to higher education was maintained through an expanded Pell Grant program and proactive efforts that helped protect Federally subsidized student loans from recent credit issues faced elsewhere in the economy.

- Despite a small decline in real median household income, which had begun prior to the Administration taking office, hourly earnings of workers outpaced inflation, and real per capita disposable income rose substantially during the past 8 years. Median household income increased steadily after the recovery began in earnest in 2004. Also, pension reforms were enacted to help protect retirement income.

- Income inequality and immigration reform must still be addressed. Strong support for education and a focus on workers' skills can help close income gaps. Reform of immigration policies must provide border security while allowing the economic benefits that immigrant labor provides to the economy.

Chapter 9: Economic Regulation

The private enterprise system, supported by consistent enforcement of laws protecting property and contracts, has been at the heart of the American economy's tremendous prosperity and growth. Although free markets produce the most efficient outcome in most cases, there are instances where government intervention can increase economic efficiency. Government regulation can improve economic outcomes where there are specific market failures that, for example, create negative externalities that impose costs on society or create harm from natural monopolies. At the same time, the Government's ability to create efficient regulation is limited and may create significant costs, which must be weighed against the potential benefits of addressing market failures. This chapter reviews several areas in which markets have been affected by Government policy in the past 8 years. The key points of this chapter are:

- Regulation is appropriate when, and only when, there is an important market failure that can be effectively addressed by the Government. For example, the Administration has taken steps to reduce restrictive regulation of broadband markets, preserving an environment conducive to innovation and new investment. Conversely, the Administration supported new rules for financial reporting when it became clear that existing laws did not adequately reduce information asymmetries between investors and management.

- When the Government intervenes to address market failures, it should attempt to take advantage of market-based incentives whenever possible. The Administration has helped ensure that scarce spectrum licenses are allocated more efficiently by increasing the amount of bandwidth allocated through auctions rather than through arbitrary allotments. In transportation, the Administration has supported market-based approaches to financing infrastructure such as roads and the air traffic control system.

- The Administration has endeavored to ensure that, when the government does intervene in markets, it does so in a way that supports the operation of competitive markets. When the market for terrorism insurance was disrupted following the attacks of 9/11, the Administration supported a temporary program of Federal support for terrorism insurance, and the Administration has insisted that subsidies be phased out as private insurers adapt and return to the market. By supporting tort reform, the Administration has helped reduce the scope for class action lawsuits that create costs that outweigh their social benefits.

C H A P T E R 1

The Year in Review and the Years Ahead

Following 6 consecutive years of expansion of the U.S economy, the pace of real GDP expansion slowed in the first half of 2008 and turned negative in the second half. Payroll jobs began to decline in January, following a record 52 months of continuous growth. The observed pattern of output, employment, and other key indicators led the Business Cycle Dating Committee of the National Bureau of Economic Research to declare that the economy peaked in December of 2007, beginning a recession that continued throughout 2008. The reorientation of the U.S. economy—which had been underway in 2006 and 2007—away from housing investment and consumer spending and toward exports and investment in business structures continued through the first three quarters of 2008. However, the reorientation was neither smooth nor graceful, as falling house prices initiated a cascade of problems beginning with mortgage delinquencies and falling prices of mortgage-backed securities. This eventually threatened the solvency of several major financial institutions and ultimately resulted in several failures and forced mergers along with a major decline in the stock market beginning in late September. To respond to these problems, policymakers have undertaken a wide range of actions during the year, including: personal tax rebates and bonus depreciation allowances for business (the Economic Stimulus Act of 2008, enacted in February); support for the housing market (the Housing and Economic Recovery Act of 2008 in July); large-scale investment in financial assets (the Emergency Economic Stabilization Act of 2008 in October); a reduction in the Federal funds rate from 5¼ percent in August 2007 to almost zero by December 2008; and the implementation of a variety of programs by the Treasury, the Federal Reserve, the Federal Deposit Insurance Corporation (FDIC), and other agencies to provide liquidity to financial institutions and to mitigate strains impairing the functioning of the overall financial system.

In the wake of mounting problems with the performance of *subprime* (higher risk) mortgages, financial markets became stressed beginning about August 2007 and became substantially more stressed after mid-September 2008. After a slight decline in real gross domestic product (real GDP, the total value of all goods and services produced in the United States after adjusting for inflation) in the fourth quarter of 2007, policy actions—including the enactment of a fiscal stimulus program and the initial round of Federal Reserve rate cuts—helped maintain positive real GDP growth in the first half of 2008. These actions likely delayed the downturn in output but were not sufficient to prevent the steep falloff in employment, production, and aggregate spending that appears to have begun in mid-September. After the mid-September failure of Lehman Brothers (an investment bank), the emergency loans to AIG (an insurance company with extensive involvement in insuring mortgage-related securities), and the takeover of Washington Mutual (a savings bank with extensive mortgage-related assets), the global financial markets showed a sharp increase in perceived risk, and the stock market tumbled.

Inflation figures were mixed, with notable rises through mid-year in indexes that included food and imported energy products such as the consumer price index (CPI) and the price index for gross domestic purchases. A sharp decline in petroleum prices brought these prices down substantially by the end of the year. In contrast, inflation was less volatile for the broadest index of the goods and services produced in the United States (the GDP price index) and for most measures of wages and hourly compensation.

This chapter reviews the economic developments of 2008 and discusses the Administration's forecast for the years ahead. The key points of this chapter are:

- Real GDP likely declined over the four quarters of 2008, ending a 6-year run of positive growth, as the slow growth in the first half of the year was eclipsed by what appears to be a sharp decline in the fourth quarter.
- Financial distress, which first became evident in mid-2007 in the market for mortgage-backed securities (MBS), continued through 2008 and affected a variety of markets. In the wake of the failure and near-failure of several major financial institutions in September 2008, financial stresses increased sharply to levels not seen during the post–World War II era.
- Payroll jobs declined during 2008, having peaked in December of 2007. Employment losses averaged 82,000-per-month during the first 8 months of 2008 before accelerating to a 420,000-per-month pace during the next 3 months. The unemployment rate was at 5 percent though April—a low rate by historical standards—but increased to 6.7 percent in November. Initial and continued claims for unemployment insurance moved up sharply over the course of the year.
- Energy prices dominated the movement of overall inflation in the consumer price index (CPI), with large increases through July, followed by a sharp decline during the latter part of the year. Core consumer inflation (which excludes food and energy inflation) edged down from 2.4 percent during the 12 months of 2007 to a 1.9 percent annual rate during the first 11 months of 2008. Food prices rose appreciably faster than core prices.
- Nominal hourly compensation increased 2.8 percent during the 12 months through September 2008 (according to the employment cost index), a gain that was undermined by the rise in food and energy prices,

so that real hourly compensation fell 2 percent. In the long run, real hourly compensation tends to increase with labor productivity, although the correlation can be very loose over shorter intervals. Nonfarm business productivity has grown at an average annual rate of 2.6 percent since the business-cycle peak in 2001.

• An economic stimulus package was proposed by the President in January and passed by Congress in February, authorizing about $113 billion in tax rebate checks to low- and middle-income taxpayers and allowing 50 percent expensing for business equipment investment. The stimulus likely boosted GDP growth in the second and third quarters above what it might have been otherwise, but its influence faded by the end of the year.

• The Administration's forecast calls for real GDP to continue to fall in the first half of 2009, with the major declines projected to be concentrated in the fourth quarter of 2008 and the first quarter of 2009. An active monetary policy and Treasury's injection of assets into financial institutions are expected to ease financial stress and to lead to a rebound in the interest-sensitive sectors of the economy in the second half of 2009. Also supporting growth during 2009 is the substantial recent drop in petroleum prices, which offsets some of the effects of the recent decline in household wealth. The unemployment rate is expected to increase to an average of 7.7 percent for 2009. The expansion in 2010–11 is projected to be vigorous, bringing the unemployment rate down to 5 percent by 2012.

Developments in 2008 and the Near-Term Outlook

During the first three quarters of 2008, the economy continued the rebalancing that began in 2006, with strong growth in business structures investment and exports offsetting pronounced declines in homebuilding, while consumer spending edged lower by 0.6 percent at an annual rate. By the fourth quarter of 2008, however, most major indicators became sharply negative.

Consumer Spending and Saving

Real consumer spending stagnated in the first half of 2008 and then fell sharply in the third quarter in what was the largest quarterly decline since 1980. This was a major deceleration after the 2.8 percent average annual rate during the 2001–07 expansion. During these three quarters, motor vehicle purchases fell to 12.9 million units at an annual rate, a drop of 19 percent at an annual rate, having fluctuated around a 16-17 million unit average annual pace during the expansion. Energy purchases (which had edged up at a 0.7 percent annual rate) declined at a 9 percent annual rate, finally reacting to the enormous increase in energy prices (relative to the price of the overall consumer basket) during the preceding 3 years. Other consumer spending (that is, outside of motor vehicles and energy) slowed to only a 1 percent annual rate of growth following a 3 percent average rate of growth during the preceding expansion. Consumer spending has continued to fall in the fourth quarter. Key factors influencing the evolution of consumer spending during the past year were the response to the multiyear increase in energy prices, the February stimulus package (see Box 1-1), and most importantly, the decline in household wealth during 2008.

Box 1-1: The Economic Stimulus Act of 2008

Policymakers moved quickly to address the slowing economy early in the year. The Federal Reserve cut the target Federal funds rate by 1¼ percentage points in January (following 1 percentage point of earlier cuts from August through December of 2007). The economic effects of monetary policy emerge more gradually then those of tax rebates, and so some fiscal stimulus from rebates was judged to be useful in supporting the economy in the short term. The Congress passed and the President signed the Economic Stimulus Act of 2008 in early February, only a few weeks after the President proposed it. The Act was designed to place money in the hands of those individuals and households who were most likely to spend it. The amount to be dispensed was about $113 billion, or about 0.8 percent of GDP. Most of the money was dispensed between late April and early July, with the bulk of the disbursements ($78 billion) in the second quarter.

Under this Act, the Treasury mailed checks ranging between $300 and $600 to taxpayers filing as individuals. Individuals who earned $3,000 (the minimum amount under this Act) received a $300 check; those who earned between $3,000 and $75,000 received a check for up to $600. The formula phased out the payments at a rate of $50 for every $1000 of income in excess of $75,000. (The figures for those filing as married couples were doubled.) Social Security and veterans payments were counted as earned income. The Act also included an allowance of $300 for each child (under the age of 17 as of the end of 2007). Those who did not qualify for payments based on their 2007 income could qualify based on their 2008 income, with the benefit to be paid in early 2009.

Some academic studies, however, suggest that individuals would realize that these checks were a one-time event and that they would choose to spend this windfall over many years. Other studies suggest that individuals, especially those who were credit-constrained, would

continued on the next page

Box 1-1 — continued

spend most of the money as it came in. A macroeconomic model simulated the expected boost to the profile of real GDP on the estimate that about 70 percent of the funds would be considered temporary income (to be spent over a long time) and the remaining funds would be regarded as immediately spendable. The profile from that simulation, which also showed the boost from bonus depreciation (discussed below), is shown in chart 1-1. The model simulation suggests a 2¼ percentage point boost to the annual rate of real GDP growth in the second quarter. Because many of the rebate checks were delivered late in the second quarter, however, some of the second-quarter stimulus shown in the chart was considered likely to spill over into the third quarter.

Boost to Quarterly Real GDP Growth from the 2008 Fiscal Stimulus

The Economic Stimulus Act of 2008 was expected to boost second- and possibly third-quarter growth.

Percentage point difference from baseline GDP growth at an annual rate

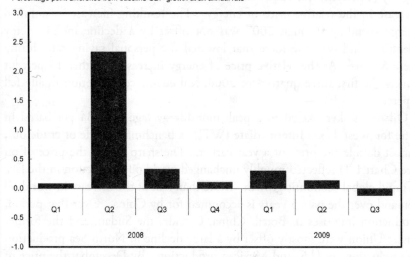

Note: The nominal Federal Funds rate was held constant at baseline for the simulation.
Source: Council of Economic Advisers.

The Act also authorized businesses to deduct 50 percent of the cost of investment equipment installed during 2008 from their 2008 taxes, a policy that is often referred to as *bonus depreciation*. The Act also expanded the limits for small business expensing, a policy that was expected to boost real GDP growth by about 0.2 percentage point during 2008. Bonus depreciation is valuable only to firms with positive profits,

continued on the next page

however, and so the fourth-quarter plunge in output will likely reduce the ability of firms to take advantage of this program.

Whether or not the fiscal stimulus produced the intended effect cannot be determined from observed macroeconomic data alone because the path that GDP would have taken without the stimulus remains unknown. However, a recent study that examined the nondurable purchases of a large sample of consumers found that the spending of individuals rose at the time rebate checks were received. The study concluded that the stimulus checks had a significant effect on purchases and that these effects were more pronounced among low-income consumers.

Energy Expenditures

Real energy consumption (that is, adjusted for increases in prices) increased slightly (4 percent) from 2001 through 2007, despite a cumulative 66 percent increase in the relative price of energy. The resulting increase in nominal energy spending through 2007 was not offset by a decline in nonenergy spending, and was one force that lowered the personal saving rate during these 6 years. As the relative price of energy increased another 15 percent during the first three quarters of 2008, real energy consumption finally fell 7 percent.

Oil prices skyrocketed to a peak monthly average of $134 per barrel in June for West Texas Intermediate (WTI) (a benchmark grade of crude oil), almost double the price of a year earlier. The sharp rise in the price of oil (see Chart 1-1) reflected roughly unchanged world oil production in the face of rapid global economic growth. More than half of the increase in world oil demand over the past 5 years is accounted for by China. Over that period, production increases in Brazil, China, Canada, the Sudan, and the former Soviet Union were mostly offset by a large decline in North Sea production and reductions in U.S. and Mexican production. By December the price of WTI oil had fallen to about $41 per barrel.

Because the U.S. imports about 3.7 billion barrels of oil per year, each $10-per-barrel increase adds about $37 billion to the national oil import bill. However, the economic consequences of the higher oil import bill during 2003–07 (when the price of WTI crude oil increased from a $31-per-barrel annual average to a $72-per-barrel annual average) were partially offset by an increase in demand for our exports (which grew at an average of 9 percent per year over this period). This increase in exports was partly a consequence of the same rise in foreign economic growth that caused the price of oil to increase. The additional $66-per-barrel increase in the price of oil from June

Chart 1-1 **Oil Prices: West Texas Intermediate**

Real oil prices reached record levels during the summer of 2008 before falling dramatically in the fall.

Dollars per barrel

Note: Nominal oil prices were deflated with the PCE chain-type price index to arrive at real oil prices.
Sources: Wall Street Journal and Department of Commerce (Bureau of Economic Analysis).

2007 to June 2008 was larger than the entire increase during the preceding 4 years and added roughly $245 billion to the national import bill. This rise in cost was reversed by an even larger decline from June through December, with the price decline attributable to the drop in energy demand due to a worldwide decline in economic activity.

Wealth Effects on Consumption and Saving

The decline in value for housing wealth and, even more importantly, stock-market wealth were among the most important influences on consumer behavior during 2008. Changes in real wealth and real consumer spending are correlated, as can be seen in Chart 1-2. The interrelationship between wealth and consumer spending is far from perfect (at least in part because many other factors influence spending). The relationship is nevertheless statistically significant whether or not other related factors such as income and lagged values are included. Household wealth peaked in the second quarter of 2007, when it reached a level that was worth 6.3 years of disposable income. Housing and stock market wealth fell over the next five quarters; by the end of the third quarter of 2008 (the most recent official data available), the wealth-to-income ratio had fallen by 1.0 year of income. The continued stock market declines in October and November, together with the downward trend in house prices, suggest that the wealth-to-income ratio dropped a further 0.5 year in the fourth quarter. As a result, the cumulative decline in the wealth-to-income ratio now appears to be about 1.5 years of income.

Most of the drop in household wealth is related to the stock market decline. In dollar terms, household net worth fell about $7 trillion between the second quarter of 2007 and the third quarter of 2008. Most of this decline was accounted for by the stock market, while the erosion of housing wealth was about one-half as large as that of the stock market. Other components of wealth (a category that includes consumer durables, credit market instruments, and equity in nonfinancial business, among others) were roughly unchanged over this five-quarter period.

Projected Consumer Spending

Consumer spending tends to rise and fall along with wealth (as illustrated in chart 1-2). A statistical analysis of the relationship between consumer spending, income, wealth, and other variables suggests that about 5 percent of wealth is spent every year. If this is so, the recent decline in the wealth-to-income ratio (of about 1.5 years of income) appears likely to reduce the consumption-to-income ratio and to raise the saving rate by roughly 7 percentage points over time. During the three years from 2005 to 2007, the saving rate averaged 0.5 percent, and so it appears that the saving rate will

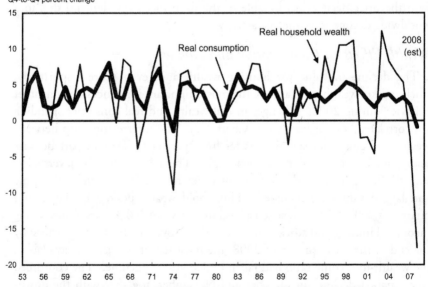

Chart 1-2 **Real Consumption and Real Wealth**
Real consumer spending fluctuates with real wealth.
Q4-to-Q4 percent change

Notes: Data for the fourth quarter of 2008 are CEA estimates. Household wealth deflated by the PCE price index.
Sources: Department of Commerce (Bureau of Economic Analysis) and Federal Reserve Board.

probably move up gradually towards 7 percent—barring any sizable recovery in the stock market. A saving rate at this level would return the saving rate to the same level as for the 10-year period through 1985 (that is, before the run-up in the stock market in the late 1990s). To get there from the third quarter saving rate of 1.1 percent, however, would require substantially slower growth in consumer spending than in income. Thus, it seems likely that real consumer spending will continue to fall during the fourth quarter of 2008 and early in 2009. A rebound in the stock market would, of course, make this adjustment easier, as the saving rate would not have to rise by the full 7 percentage points. If a stock market rebound does not occur, consumption growth will likely remain weak into 2010.

Residential Investment

Residential investment continued into its third year of decline in 2008. Major measures of housing activity moved lower over the course of the year, with housing starts falling to an average annual rate of 740,000 units during the three months through November, a huge decline from the 2.1 million unit annual rate at its peak in the first quarter of 2006. The drop in home construction now appears to have subtracted an average of 0.75 percentage point from the annual rate of growth of real GDP, similar to the subtraction during 2006 and 2007.

Housing prices peaked in the second quarter of 2007, as measured by the purchase-only index published by the Federal Housing Finance Authority (FHFA, formerly the Office of Federal Housing Enterprise Oversight). From that peak through the latest available data (the third quarter of 2008), housing prices have declined 6.5 percent (see Chart 1-3). According to the S&P/Case-Shiller index, which peaked earlier (in the second quarter of 2006) and subsequently declined 21 percent, the recent decline, as well as the earlier run-up, is more accentuated. (See Box 1-2 on the relative merits of the two house price indexes).

Further declines in home construction seem likely through at least the first half of 2009, as builders' confidence has fallen to the lowest level on record and the secondary market for housing-related securities continues to be thin. The Administration forecasts a steady uptrend in housing starts during the next 5 years, with the annual rate of starts gradually increasing so that by 2013 starts would reach 1.8 million units. This reflects, among other factors, a return to steady income growth, an easing of lending standards, and improved credit availability. The pace of the expected housing recovery has some upside risk. The number of unsold new houses has fallen to about 400,000 units, about the level of 2003 and 2004, even though the ratio of unsold new homes to the current selling pace remains near its record high. If and when aggregate demand accelerates, housing starts would easily be pulled upward.

Chart 1-3 **FHFA versus S&P/Case-Shiller Home Price Index**
Both house price indexes increased at an average rate of 5.5% per year from 2000 to 2008, but the Case-Shiller Index increased faster during 2000–06 and fell faster thereafter.

Index (1991:Q1 = 100)

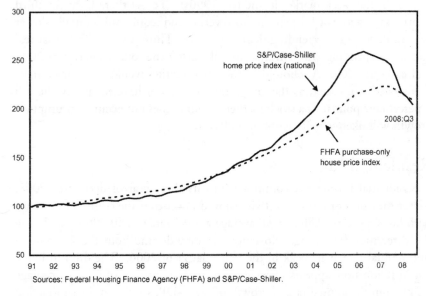

Sources: Federal Housing Finance Agency (FHFA) and S&P/Case-Shiller.

Box 1-2: Different Measures of House Prices

Both the FHFA purchase-only index and the S&P/Case-Shiller index have merit and use similar methods, but they cover different types of mortgages and have different regional coverage. As a result, each may have advantages in different contexts. Both are based on a methodology of observing pairs of sales of the same house over a span of years. The FHFA index is limited to homes purchased with conforming mortgages (that is, mortgages that conform to the maximum size and minimum downpayment standards set by Fannie Mae or Freddie Mac). In contrast, the S&P/Case-Shiller index collects data from a sample of homes that includes nonconforming as well as conforming mortgages. Each house gets an equal weight in the FHFA index, while more expensive houses are assigned larger weights in the S&P/Case-Shiller index. Of the two indexes, the FHFA index has the broadest national geographic distribution, while the Case-Shiller index has no data for 13 States and incomplete data for another 29 States.

continued on the next page

The contrasting path of house prices as measured by these two indexes during the past decade is informative. By relying on conforming mortgages only, the FHFA index may provide a more stable picture of house prices during a period when the mix of mortgages changed toward the nonconforming types (subprime and jumbo, for example) and then back again. (This may be relevant if the type of mortgage is correlated with the price of the house.) On the other hand, the S&P/Case-Shiller index better illustrates the price path of all houses regardless of mortgage type and mortgage size. The contrast between the two indexes suggests that the runup in housing prices may have been larger for homes purchased with nonconforming mortgages and perhaps with jumbo mortgages. As the share of nonconforming mortgages fell sharply over the past 2 years, the two indexes are likely relying on more similar samples in 2008, and as a result, the recent larger decline in the S&P/Case-Shiller index may partly reflect a falling back to earth after having been temporarily elevated by higher prices for homes purchased with nonconforming mortgages. One study suggests that the inclusion of subprime mortgages in the S&P/Case-Shiller index accounts for a substantial share of the index's deeper decline. The larger increase and subsequently larger decline in the S&P/Case-Shiller index may also reflect larger price movements among more expensive homes.

Business Fixed Investment

During the first three quarters of 2008, real business investment in equipment and software fell 4.4 percent at an annual rate, down from 2.8 percent growth in 2007. Growing categories included software (2.4 percent), communication equipment (5.2 percent), and agricultural equipment (27 percent), while investment in industrial equipment fell 4.0 percent. Investment in transportation equipment (which includes motor vehicles and aircraft) was particularly weak, falling 37 percent at an annual rate through the third quarter, with the sharpest drop seen in the light trucks category.

In contrast to residential investment, real business investment in nonresidential structures grew at a strong 12 percent annual rate through the third quarter of 2008. The gains during 2008 made it the third consecutive year of strong growth, which was a marked reversal from the weakness during the period from 2001 to 2005. Nearly 65 percent of total growth in nonresidential structures was accounted for by manufacturing structures and petroleum and natural gas exploration and wells.

Access to the credit markets to support investment became more difficult for nonfinancial corporations during 2008. The flow of new external funds (credit market instruments such as bond issues, commercial paper, and bank loans) in the fourth quarter of 2007 was about $1.9 trillion (the positive bars in Chart 1-4); it then fell by $1.3 trillion by the third quarter of 2008. Despite this drop in the flow of external funds, firms were able maintain solid investment by cutting back on programs to buy stock in their own company (by $700 billion, the negative bars in Chart 1-4) so that the total funds raised in all capital markets fell only $600 billion (the solid line in Chart 1-4). These share buyback programs had reached record levels during the period from 2004 through 2007. However, by the third quarter of 2008—when the major financial stress began—share buybacks had diminished to only $410 billion, so that this "source" of internal funds had been mostly exhausted.

Business investment growth is projected to decline in 2009, a projection that is based partially on the high level of interest rates on corporate bonds. It is also partially based on the pattern of business investment reacting to the change in output growth. That is, following the decline in output in late 2008, investment in 2009 is likely to fall. Later, the expected acceleration of real GDP in late 2009 and 2010 is expected to result in rapid growth of business investment. In the longer run, real business investment is projected to grow at about the same rate as real GDP.

Chart 1-4 **Nonfinancial Corporate Sector Net Borrowing by Type**
Loans and other credit market issues to nonfinancial corporations declined during 2008, but firms were able to cushion the effect on investment by scaling back their share buyback programs.

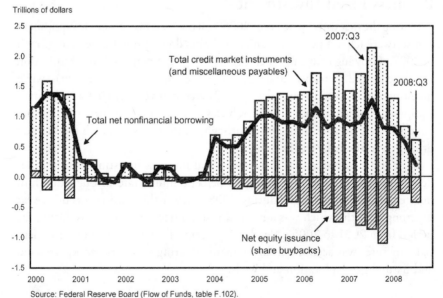

Source: Federal Reserve Board (Flow of Funds, table F.102).

Business Inventories

Inventory investment fell during the first three quarters of 2008 and had a noticeable influence on quarter-to-quarter fluctuations in real GDP, subtracting 1½ percentage points from growth in the second quarter. Inventories of motor vehicles on dealer lots were an important contributor to these fluctuations as these inventories were liquidated during the first half of 2008 and were increased slightly in the third quarter. Inventories of other goods outside of the motor vehicle sector were liquidated in each of the first three quarters of the year.

The overall ratio of inventories to sales has come down substantially since 2001. The inventory-to-sales ratio for manufacturing and trade (in current dollars) fell in the first half of 2008 before rising during the 3 months through October. Firms could soon find themselves with more inventory than they need if (as expected) sales continue to fall over the next few months. As a consequence, inventories are likely to be liquidated in the near term. Even so, a drop in inventory investment is not likely to be as dominant in the current downturn as it was in most of the post–World War II recessions because of the fairly lean inventory position relative to sales at the outset of this recession. In the long term, inventory investment is projected to be fairly stable, and the overall inventory-to-sales ratio is expected to continue to trend lower.

Government Purchases

Nominal Federal revenues (that is, in current dollars) fell 2 percent in fiscal year (FY) 2008, following 7 percent growth in FY 2007. The decline in revenues can be attributed partly to slowing economic growth (a key determinant of tax receipts), as well as reduced Federal tax revenues due to the tax rebate provisions of the Economic Stimulus Act of 2008. Coupled with declining revenues, a 9 percent increase in outlays resulted in an increase in the Federal budget deficit to 3.2 percent of GDP in FY 2008, up from 1.2 percent in FY 2007.

Through several appropriations acts, the Congress provided a total of $192 billion for the wars in Iraq and Afghanistan in FY 2008. One of these acts, the Supplemental Appropriations Act of 2008, also provided $68 billion in bridge funding for FY 2009.

Real State and local government purchases rose at a 1.2 percent annual rate during the first three quarters of 2008, down from 2.4 percent in 2007. State and local tax revenues slowed in 2008, as receipts from personal income taxes, sales taxes, and property taxes decelerated, while corporate tax receipts fell. Notably, property tax revenue, which had grown at a 6 percent annual rate each year in 2004, 2005, and 2006, slowed to a 2.6 percent annual rate of growth through the third quarter of 2008. Over the same period, receipts from sales taxes edged up only 0.1 percent at an annual rate.

The State and local government sector fell into deficit during 2008, reaching $109 billion or 0.8 percent of GDP, by the third quarter, the largest operating deficit on record. On average, State and local government operating budgets have been in surplus during the post–World War II period. In 2009 and 2010, only slow growth—if any—can be anticipated for this sector's consumption and gross investment. This decline results from the deterioration in their tax base, as reflected in falling home prices, declining consumer spending, and slowing growth in personal income. Property tax receipts and sales tax revenues each represent slightly more than 20 percent of State and local government revenues: Federal grants constitute another 20 percent; personal income tax receipts account for about 15 percent, while corporate tax collections constitute only 3 percent. A variety of fees, transfers, and incomes account for the remaining 18 percent.

Exports and Imports

Real exports of goods and services grew at a 7 percent annual rate during the first three quarters of 2008, following solid growth of at least 7 percent over the preceding 4 years. The rapid pace of export expansion over the past 5 years coincided with strong foreign growth from 2003 to 2007, as well as changes in the terms of trade between 2002 and mid-2008 that made American goods cheaper relative to those of some other countries. Recently, however, economic growth among our major trading partners has slowed considerably, with the Euro zone, Japan, and Canada posting negative growth. Because foreign growth and U.S. exports are closely related, the global economic slowdown will likely weigh on U.S. exports in the future.

By region, export growth during 2008 was strongest to Latin American countries, rising at a 24 percent annual rate through the third quarter. The European Union (EU) remains the major overseas destination for U.S. products and services, consuming about 25 percent of our exports. By country, Canada accounts for the largest share of U.S. exports, at about 16 percent. Mexico purchases 10 percent of our exports; Japan, 6 percent; and China, 5 percent.

Real imports fell at a 3.9 percent annual rate during the first three quarters of 2008; the last year of decline before that was 2001. The decline in real imports was especially pronounced among petroleum products, which fell 12 percent at an annual rate, pushed down by high prices and slowing domestic economic activity over this period. Due to rapidly rising petroleum prices through the first half of the year, nominal imports of petroleum products rose at a 46 percent annual rate. Oil prices have since receded dramatically, which will greatly reduce growth in nominal petroleum imports in coming quarters. Nonpetroleum import prices also increased substantially

(6.6 percent during the four quarters through the third quarter of 2008), which may also have restrained the level of imports.

The current account deficit (the excess of imports and income flows to foreigners over exports and foreign income of Americans) averaged 5.0 percent of GDP during the first three quarters of 2008, down from its 2007 average of over 5.3 percent. The decline in the current account deficit reflects faster growth in exports relative to imports, although domestic investment continues to exceed domestic saving, with foreigners financing the gap between the two.

Employment

The employment situation deteriorated during 2008, mirroring weakness in other sectors. The pace of job growth appears to have had two phases: a period of moderate job losses, at an average rate of 82,000 per month from January through August, followed by a steeper decline at an average rate of 420,000 per month in September, October, and November. Nonfarm payroll employment fell 1.9 million jobs during the first 11 months of the year. The unemployment rate rose 1.7 percentage points over the same period, reaching 6.7 percent. Initial claims for unemployment insurance rose to an average of about 550,000 per week in December, up from the 2007 average of 320,000 per week.

Job losses during the first 11 months of 2008 were concentrated in construction, manufacturing, and temporary help services. Although manufacturing and construction account for only about 15 percent of total employment, they accounted for nearly 60 percent of the overall decline in nonfarm jobs during 2008. Construction employment has been declining as a result of continued weakness in the housing market, and manufacturing employment has been on a downward trend as a share of overall employment for the past five decades. Temporary help services, which account for only 2 percent of employment, accounted for 21 percent of the year's job losses. Retailing also posted a notable decline. One bright spot in the employment picture has been education and health services, which added 505,000 jobs through November.

Changes in unemployment differed by education level, race, and gender over the year. Through November, the unemployment rate had risen for workers of all education levels; it increased 0.9 percentage point for those holding at least a bachelor's degree, 1.8 percentage points for those with some college, 2.1 percentage points for those whose education ended with a high school degree, and 2.9 percentage points among those who did not finish high school. By race and ethnicity, the unemployment rate for African Americans rose by 2.2 percentage points and was about 5 percentage points above the rate for Caucasians, a smaller margin than during most of the past 35 years. The unemployment rate among Caucasians rose 1.7 percentage point, among Hispanics rose 2.3 percentage points, and among Asian Americans rose 1.1 percentage points. By gender, the jobless rate for adult men rose 2.1 percentage points to 6.5 percent, and the rate for adult women rose by 1.1 percentage point to 5.5 percent. The median duration of unemployment increased to 10.0 weeks in November from 8.4 weeks at the end of 2007. The number of long-term unemployed (those who are jobless for 15 weeks or more) rose by 1.4 million over the same period.

The Administration projects that employment will decline during the four quarters of 2009, with the job losses likely to be largest early in the year. As the expected recovery strengthens in 2010, job growth is anticipated to pick up to 222,000 jobs per month. In the longer run, the pace of employment growth will slow, reflecting diminishing rates of labor force growth due to the retirement of the baby-boom generation. The Administration also projects that the unemployment rate will increase from 2008 to a 7.7 percent annual average in 2009 as a whole, before returning to roughly 5 percent in 2012, the middle of the range consistent with stable long-run inflation.

Productivity

Nonfarm productivity growth has averaged 2.5 percent at an annual rate since 1995 (see Chart 1-5). The best estimate of the productivity growth rate over the next 6 years is 2.4 percent, which is slightly below the 2.5 percent long-term (that is, post-1995) rate. Different measures of recent productivity growth are discussed in Box 1-3. Compared with last year's projection, this projected rate of growth has been revised down 0.1 percentage point. The downward revision is a consequence of the downward adjustment to output and productivity in the annual revision to the national income and product accounts.

Prices and Wages

Headline inflation rose and then fell during 2008, although key indicators of inflation trends were fairly stable. As measured by the overall consumer price index (CPI), the 12-month rate of inflation moved up to 5.6 percent for the 12 months through July, up from the 4.1 percent during the 12 months of 2007 (Chart 1-6). The acceleration was due to increases in food and energy price inflation. By November, however, the 12-month rate of overall CPI inflation had fallen to 1.1 percent. The 12-month change in the core CPI (which excludes the volatile food and energy components) fluctuated in a more narrow range, peaking at 2.5 percent during the third quarter, but edging down to 2.0 percent by November.

Chart 1-5 **Output per Hour in the Nonfarm Business Sector**
Productivity has trended up at an average annual rate of 2.5% since 1995.
Real output per hour (constant $2000, ratio scale)

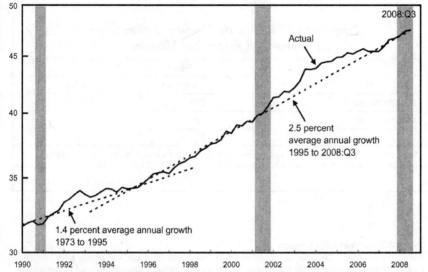

Note: Shading indicates recessions.
Sources: Department of Commerce (Bureau of Economic Analysis) and Department of Labor (Bureau of Labor Statistics).

Box 1-3: Alternate Measures of Productivity Growth

   Productivity growth can be projected by extrapolating its behavior over the recent past. But using which measure? According to the official index, which measures output from the product-side (spending) components of GDP, productivity growth picked up slightly from the 1995–2001 period (2.4 percent) to the 2001–08 period (2.6 percent at an annual rate), as shown in the following table. In contrast, an alternative measure of nonfarm output, derived from the income side of the national income and product accounts, shows a deceleration in productivity between the two periods to a 2.1 percent annual rate of increase over the period 2001–08. The income- and product-side measures of GDP differ by measurement error only, and the truth is likely to be somewhere in between. Both measures show a 2.5 percent annual average growth rate over the entire 1995–2008 interval.

continued on the next page

Box 1-3 — continued

Productivity Growth in the Nonfarm Busines Sector: Income- and Supply-Side Measures

Interval	Average Annual Percent Change	
	Product-Side (official)	Income-Side
1995:Q2 to 2001:Q1	2.4%	3.1%
2001:Q1 to 2008:Q3	2.6%	2.1%
1995:Q2 to 2008:Q3	2.5%	2.5%

Sources: Department of Commerce (Bureau of Economic Analysis), Department of Labor (Bureau of Labor Statistics), income-side calculations by the Council of Economic Advisers.

Chart 1-6 **Consumer Price Inflation**
The increase in overall CPI inflation through mid-2008 was due to rising food and energy price inflation. A late 2008 drop in energy prices reversed much of the earlier increase. Core inflation was more stable.

12-month change (percent)

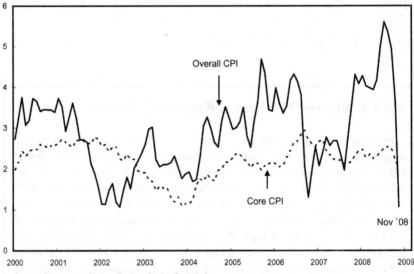

Source: Department of Labor (Bureau of Labor Statistics).

Energy prices increased rapidly in the second half of 2007 and in the early part of 2008 before peaking in July, when the 12-month rate of change reached 29 percent. Among the various energy products, prices of gasoline and heating oil increased the most rapidly during this period (reflecting the price of crude oil on world markets), but prices of electricity and natural gas also moved up sharply. Energy prices came down sharply during the 4 months from July to November, when consumer prices of petroleum products fell 41 percent (not at an annual rate). The rapid decline reflects the sharp fall in the price of crude oil; prices of West Texas Intermediate plunged from an average of $134 per barrel in June to roughly $41 per barrel in December.

Rapidly rising import prices were another factor boosting inflation early in the year and also holding it down later. Nonpetroleum import prices rose nearly 8 percent during the twelve months though July, before falling during the next 4 months. The pattern reflects the exchange value of the dollar, which depreciated in 2006, 2007, and during the first 3 months of 2008 before rebounding later in the year.

The effect of import prices appears clear in the contrast between the rate of inflation for the goods and services that Americans buy and the rate of inflation for what Americans produce (see Chart 1-7). The rate of inflation for the goods and services that Americans buy (measured by the price of gross domestic purchases) moved up from the year-earlier pace, in contrast to the less volatile rate of inflation for gross domestic product.

Chart 1-7 Gross Domestic Product and Gross Domestic Purchases Price Indexes
The price index for gross domestic purchases has increased more rapidly than the price index for gross domestic product over the past year due to rising prices for imported food and energy products.

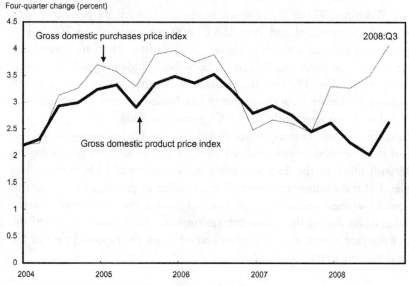

Four-quarter change (percent)

Source: Department of Commerce (Bureau of Economic Analysis).

Food prices advanced notably faster than core prices for the second consecutive year. During the first 10 months of 2008, food prices increased 6.5 percent at an annual rate following a 5 percent increase during the 12 months of 2007. The increase was a worldwide phenomenon and likely reflects several factors, including rapid growth in developing countries in the first half of 2008, crop shortages and increased production of biofuels as well as higher energy prices being passed through to consumers.

Growth in nominal hourly compensation edged down slightly. Private-sector hourly compensation increased at a 2.6 percent annual rate during the first 9 months of 2008, down slightly from 3.1 percent during 2007. Slightly diminished gains in benefits as well as wages and salaries account for the deceleration. Gains in real hourly wages of production workers rose 3.4 percent at an annual rate during the first 11 months of the year, following a 0.7 percent decline during the 12 months of 2007, when nominal wage gains were undermined by rapidly rising food and energy prices.

Despite the relative stability of several key measures of inflation (hourly compensation, the core CPI, and the GDP price index), a measure of consumers' inflation expectations moved up and down during the year in a way that suggests that it was influenced by volatile energy and nonpetroleum import prices. One-year-ahead median inflation expectations (as measured by the Reuters-University of Michigan survey) rose from 3.4 percent at the end of 2007 to about 5 percent in midyear, before falling to 1.7 percent in December. Longer-term inflation expectations were less volatile but also moved up and then down in a similar fashion in the 2.6 to 3.4 percent range.

Financial Markets

The Wilshire 5000 (a broad stock market index) fell 39 percent during 2008, and the Standard and Poor (S&P) 500 (an index of the 500 largest corporations) suffered a similar decline. This decline erased the cumulated increases over the preceding 5 years. The Wilshire index slipped 16 percent through September 16, but then tumbled another 40 percent through November 20, before recovering a bit in late November and December. The S&P index of financial stocks fell by 57 percent in 2008.

Yields on 10-year Treasury notes ended 2007 at 4.10 percent—at the low end of the historical range—and fell another 170 or so basis points during 2008 with much of the decline coming in November and December. The low level of these long-term interest rates was due in part to a likely flight to the quality of these secure assets relative to others in the private and international markets during the recent market turmoil. Rates also fell toward the end of the year as market participants revised down the expected path of the Federal Reserve's target rate.

The Administration's forecast of short-term interest rates was roughly based on the expected path of Federal funds rates in the futures market (where participants place "bets" on future rates) as of November 10, the date that the forecast was developed. The near-term interest rate forecast has been overtaken by more recent events as interest rates have fallen notably since the forecast was finalized. Whatever the starting point, the Administration projects the rate on 91-day Treasury bills to edge up gradually to 3.9 percent by 2012 and then remain at that level. At that level, the real rate (that is, the nominal rate less the rate of inflation) on 91-day Treasury bills would be close to its historical average.

The yield on 10-year Treasury notes on November 10 was 3.8 percent. The decline in this yield during the subsequent month means that this near-term forecast has also been overtaken by events. The Administration expects the 10-year rate to increase, eventually reaching a normal spread of about 1.2 percentage points over the 91-day Treasury-bill rate by 2012. Market participants also appear to expect an increase in yield as evidenced by the higher-than-average spread between the rate on 20-year Treasury notes over rates on notes with 10-year maturities. As a result, yields on 10-year notes are expected to increase, to 5.1 percent by 2012 and then to plateau at this rate for the remainder of the forecast.

One measure of increasing financial stress is the premium that private borrowers have had to pay relative to the rates on 10-year government notes (see Chart 1-8). This premium began rising around August of 2007. Rates on the highest-quality corporate bonds have increased 170 basis points since August 2007. Rates on BAA-rated corporate borrowers have increased more than 400 basis points, while rates on high-risk ("junk") bonds have skyrocketed.

Financial stress also became evident in other ways. The rate that international banks lend to each other (as measured by the London interbank offered rate, LIBOR) soared to an unprecedented premium over Treasury rates beginning in September. For 3-month maturities, this premium that had averaged 114 basis points during the first 8 months of the year jumped to 273 basis points in the second half of September and remained high in October and November, but fell to 135 basis points by year-end. The Federal Reserve's survey of senior loan officers also shows a tightening of lending standards for all private borrowers.

One consequence of the rising spreads for corporate debt is that the sharp drop in the target Federal funds rate (from 5.25 percent in August 2007 to a range of 0 to 0.25 percent in December 2008) has not translated into lower rates for corporate borrowers. The rising rates for corporate bonds and the troubled market for interbank lending means that two major channels for monetary policy (lower interest rates to encourage investment and lower rates

Chart 1-8 **Corporate Bond Spreads**
Corporate bond yields have risen dramatically relative to 10-year Treasury-notes as a result of the credit crunch.

Basis points

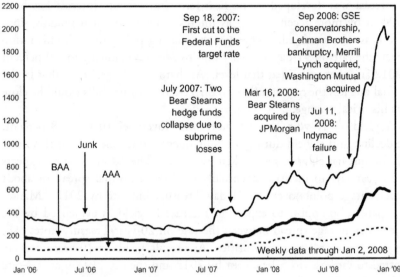

Sources: Moody's, Merrill Lynch, and the Treasury Department.

to boost consumer spending indirectly by raising the value of fixed income and equity assets) are not working as they have in the past. Chapter 2 of this *Report* discusses financial market developments in greater detail.

In view of how the stress in financial markets has interfered with the Federal Reserve's primary policy tool (the Federal funds rate), the Federal Reserve has responded by developing a range of programs to provide liquidity to support market functioning, thereby improving credit conditions for businesses and households. These include programs to provide liquidity directly to nondepository financial institutions (such as the Primary Dealer Credit Facility and the Term Securities Lending Facility) and programs to support the functioning of particular financial markets (such as the Asset-backed Commercial Paper Money Market Mutual Fund Liquidity Facility, the Commercial Paper Funding Facility, and the Term Asset-Backed Securities Loan Facility). These programs are allowed under section 13-3 of the Federal Reserve Act, which authorizes the Federal Reserve banks to make secured loans to entities under "unusual and exigent circumstances," provided that these entities are not able to secure funding from other banking institutions. In addition, the Federal Reserve has announced programs to buy substantial quantities of securities, including direct obligations of, and mortgage-backed securities issued by, the housing-related government-sponsored enterprises (GSEs). The Federal Reserve has also indicated that it is evaluating the potential benefits of purchasing longer-term Treasury securities.

The Long-Term Outlook Through 2014

After 6 years, the expansion ended in December 2007, and real GDP fell in the second half of 2008. Real consumer spending—a sector that constitutes two-thirds of GDP—is in the process of reacting to the substantial declines in wealth that began earlier in the year and cascaded in the fourth quarter. As a result, the Administration projects that after recording modest growth in the first half of 2008, real GDP contracted in the second half, with a sharp decline in the fourth quarter. The contraction is projected to continue into the first half of 2009, followed by a recovery in the second half of 2009 that is expected to be led by the interest-sensitive sectors of the economy. The overall decline, from the second-quarter level of GDP to the quarter with the lowest real GDP, is projected to slightly exceed the depth of the average post–World War II recession. This pattern translates into a small decline during the four quarters of 2008, followed by a small increase during 2009 (see Table 1-1). Reflecting the drop in real GDP, the unemployment rate is projected to increase to an annual average rate of 7.7 percent in 2009. The higher-than-normal level of slack is expected to put some downward pressure on the rate of inflation. Overall CPI inflation is projected at 1.7 percent in 2009 and 2010, a rate that appears plausible in view of the 2.0 percent change for the core CPI over the 12 months through November. Payroll employment is projected to fall during 2009 before rebounding in 2010. The 2009 forecasts for real GDP and inflation are similar to the consensus forecasts for those variables.

Downturns are eventually followed by recoveries, and historically the strength of a recovery appears to be loosely correlated with the depth of the preceding recession (see Chart 1-9). Moreover, the slope of the regression line in the scatter diagram indicates that—to the extent that a recession is deeper than the average—most of the excess depth is offset within the first four quarters of the recovery. During the 2 years following a recession, real GDP growth has averaged almost 5 percent, similar to the recovery anticipated in the Administration forecast for 2010 and 2011. The 5 percent growth rates in 2010 and 2011 would lower the unemployment rate from its projected 2009 peak to 5 percent, the center of the range consistent with stable inflation, in 2012.

TABLE 1-1.—*Administration Economic Forecast*[1]

Year	Nominal GDP	Real GDP (chain-type)	GDP price index (chain-type)	Consumer price index (CPI-U)	Uemploy-ment rate (percent)	Interest rate, 91-day Treasury bills[2] (percent)	Interest rate, 10-year Treasury notes (percent)	Nonfarm payroll employ-ment (average monthly change, Q4-to-Q4, thou-sands[3]
	Percent change, Q4-to-Q4				Level, calendar year			
2007 (actual)..........	4.9	2.3	2.6	4.0	4.6	4.4	4.6	104
2008......................	2.4	-0.2	2.5	2.8	5.7	1.4	3.8	-114
2009......................	2.2	0.6	1.7	1.7	7.7	0.7	4.2	-235
2010......................	6.6	5.0	1.5	1.7	6.9	2.0	4.6	222
2011......................	6.5	5.0	1.5	1.8	5.8	3.5	4.9	269
2012......................	5.1	3.4	1.6	1.9	5.0	3.9	5.1	261
2013......................	4.5	2.7	1.7	2.0	5.0	3.9	5.1	121
2014......................	4.5	2.7	1.8	2.1	5.0	3.9	5.1	115

[1] Based on data available as of November 10, 2008.

[2] Secondary market discount basis.

[3] The figures do not reflect the upcoming BLS benchmark which is expected to reduce 2007 and 2008 job growth by a cumulative 21,000 jobs.

Sources: Council of Economic Advisers, Department of Commerce (Bureau of Economic Analysis and Economics and Statistics Administration), Department of Labor (Bureau of Labor Statistics), Department of the Treasury, and Office of Management and Budget.

Chart 1-9 Recessions and Recession Recoveries
GDP growth over the eight quarters following a recession tends to be higher after more severe recessions.

Growth over the eight quarters subsequent to GDP trough (percent)

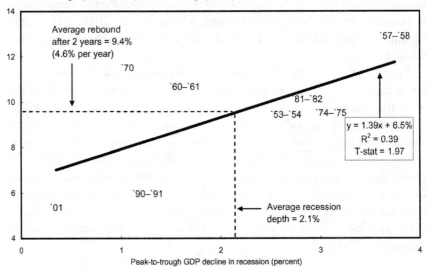

Note: Datapoint labels indicate year of recession. The depth of recession is meausured from the peak GDP quarter to the minimum GDP quarter. The recovery is the eight-quarter growth from that minimum-GDP quarter.
Source: Department of Commerce (Bureau of Economic Analysis).

Growth in GDP over the Long Term

The Administration forecast is based on a projection that sees the U.S. economy fluctuating around a long-run potential rate of growth of 2.7 percent. (*Potential real* GDP growth is a measure of the sustainable rate of growth of productive capacity.) The path of real GDP growth in the current downturn and projected recovery fluctuates around this long-term trend.

Over the next 6¼ years, real GDP growth is projected to increase 2.9 percent (see Table 1-2), a growth rate that is faster than the 2.7 percent long-term rate because the current level of the unemployment rate has considerable room to fall before the economy is again operating at its potential. Real GDP growth in 2013 and 2014, at 2.7 percent, is almost identical to the consensus projection of long-run growth.

The growth rate of the economy over the long run is determined by its supply-side components, which include population, labor force participation, the ratio of nonfarm business employment to household employment, the length of the workweek, and labor productivity. The Administration's forecast for the contribution of the growth rates of different supply-side factors to real GDP growth is shown in Table 1-2.

Over the next 6 years, the working-age population (line 1) is projected to grow 1.0 percent, the rate set in the Census Bureau's newly revised projection. The labor force participation rate (line 2), which edged down at a 0.2 percent annual rate during the past 8 years, is expected to decline even faster (0.3 percent per year) during the projection period. The further projected deceleration is a consequence of the aging baby-boom generation (born between 1946 and 1962) entering their retirement years. For example, the 1946 birth cohort reached the early-retirement age of 62 in 2008. Over long periods of time the employment rate (defined as 100 less the unemployment rate) is usually stable, but the elevated jump-off level of the unemployment rate makes room for some growth in this component (line 4). The ratio of nonfarm business employment to household employment (line 6), which has accounted for a puzzling subtraction from real GDP growth since 2001, is projected to edge down only slightly (0.1 percent per year) over the projection interval. The workweek (line 8) is projected to edge up slightly, in contrast to its general decline over the past 50 years. The slight upward tilt is projected to be a labor market reaction to buffer labor supply against the projected falling rates of labor force participation. Productivity growth (line 10) is projected to grow 2.4 percent, our best estimate of the trend rate of growth during the recent business cycle (accounting for some measurement issues, as noted earlier). The ratio of real GDP to nonfarm business (line 12) is expected to continue to subtract from overall growth as it has over most long periods.

TABLE 1-2.—*Supply-Side Components of Real GDP Growth, 1953-2014*
[Average annual percent change]

Item	1953 Q2 to 1973 Q4	1973 Q4 to 1995 Q2	1995 Q2 to 2001 Q1	2001 Q1 to 2008 Q3	2008 Q3 to 2014 Q4
1) Civilian noninstitutional population aged 16+[1]	1.6	1.4	1.2	1.2	1.0
2) PLUS: Civilian labor force participation rate	0.2	0.4	0.1	-0.2	-0.3
3) EQUALS: Civilian labor force[2]	1.8	1.8	1.4	1.0	0.8
4) PLUS: Civilian employment rate	-0.1	0.0	0.3	-0.2	0.2
5) EQUALS: Civilian employment[2]	1.7	1.8	1.6	0.7	0.9
6) PLUS: Nonfarm business employment as a share of civilian employment[2,3]	-0.1	0.1	0.4	-0.6	-0.1
7) EQUALS: Nonfarm business employment[4]	1.6	1.9	2.0	0.1	0.8
8) PLUS: average weekly hours (nonfarm business)	-0.3	-0.3	-0.2	-0.3	0.1
9) EQUALS: Hours of all persons (nonfarm business)[4]	1.3	1.6	1.9	-0.1	0.9
10) PLUS: Output per hour (productivity, nonfarm business)[4]	2.5	1.5	2.4	2.6	2.4
11) EQUALS: Nonfarm business output[4]	3.8	3.1	4.3	2.5	3.3
12) PLUS: Ratio of real GDP to nonfarm business output[5]	-0.2	-0.2	-0.5	-0.2	-0.4
13) EQUALS: Real GDP	3.6	2.8	3.8	2.3	2.9

[1] Adjusted by CEA to smooth discontinuities in the population series since 1990.

[2] BLS research series adjusted to smooth irregularities in the population series since 1990.

[3] Line 6 translates the civilian employment growth rate into the nonfarm business employment growth rate.

[4] Nonfarm employment, workweek, productivity, and output sourced from the BLS productivity and cost database.

[5] Line 12 translates nonfarm business output back into output for all sectors (GDP), which includes the output of farms and general government.

Note: 1953 Q2, 1973 Q4, and 2001 Q1 are NBER business-cycle peaks.

Detail may not add to total because of rounding.

Sources: Council of Economic Advisers, Department of Commerce (Bureau of Economic Analysis) and Department of Labor (Bureau of Labor Statistics).

A Perspective on the Past Eight Years

The past 8 years began with a mild recession and then shifted into a slow-growth recovery that only gradually gained momentum. Throughout the first 7 years, consumer spending provided a solid base for economic growth, and that base was fortified by housing investment. As residential construction fell in 2006 and 2007, it was replaced by export growth as a major contributor to overall GDP growth. In 2008, the combination of falling construction, losses in housing-related securities, rising oil prices, and a falling stock market eventually tipped the economy into recession. Inflation as measured by the four-quarter change in the price index for GDP fluctuated between 1.6 and 3.5 percent, a fairly narrow range in a broad historical context.

The economy showed signs of slowing in 2000: the dot-com bust was already underway, and GDP growth in the third quarter of 2000 was negative. In response to the incipient downturn, the Federal Reserve slashed its target rate early in January 2001. The economy began to shed jobs steadily in March 2001. The Administration and Congress responded proactively with EGTRRA (The Economic Growth and Tax Relief Reconciliation Act of 2001) which delivered about $36 billion of stimulus checks in 2001 and phased in cuts in marginal tax rates over several years. The recession of 2001 was particularly severe in business investment, a demand component that had been particularly strong in preceding years. Low interest rates during this period boosted demand for housing and consumer durables, both of which were substantially stronger than during an average recession. The recession of 2001 was exacerbated by the terrorist attacks of September 11, and several widely publicized accounting scandals also contributed to the economic uncertainty of the time. All told, however, the 2001 recession turned out to be the shallowest of the post–World War II period (the most that real GDP declined in a single quarter during the recession was 0.4 percent), with some of the credit attributable to the quick action of monetary and fiscal policy.

The unemployment rate continued to rise following the official end of the recession. To address the lagging recovery, the Administration and Congress instituted JCWAA (the Job Creation and Worker Assistance Act), which allowed firms to expense 30 percent of their equipment investment and extended unemployment compensation to laid-off workers, and JGTRRA (the Jobs and Growth Tax Relief Reconciliation Act), which boosted the expensing rate on investment to 50 percent and extended the duration of this provision. JGTRRA also cut the tax rate on dividends and capital gains. These Acts helped speed up economic growth soon after their implementation. The relative strength of the U.S. economy, evident in the demand for imports and in foreigners' desire to invest in the United States, helped maintain world demand during this early-recovery period. It also resulted in a large increase in the U.S. current account deficit.

Late in 2003, the economy shifted from a period of slow recovery to a period of broad economic expansion, marked by a decline in the unemployment rate and rapid growth in economic activity. The recovery was led by robust growth in consumer spending, equipment and software investment, exports, and residential construction, and coincided with spectacular house price appreciation. With the benefit of hindsight, house prices climbed too high. As home prices began to recede beginning in early 2006, so did the pace of housing starts. Housing starts continued to decline over the next 2½ years, eventually reaching an all-time low in November 2008.

During 2006 and 2007, rapid export growth and growth in investment of nonresidential structures replaced residential investment as the main drivers of aggregate demand. The economies of our trading partners, especially those in developing countries, picked up and boosted the demand for our exports—and also boosted the demand for petroleum. The rise in petroleum prices, which moved up again toward the end of 2007, added to the cascade of problems caused by falling house prices.

Although growth slowed to a crawl in early 2008 and employment edged down, fiscal stimulus and monetary policy actions held real GDP growth in generally positive territory through the first half of the year. The sharp declines in consumer spending in the third quarter and the stock market drop in September and October finally confirmed that the decline was a recession.

Until the second half of 2008, the economy was resilient, weathering many shocks including the 2001 recession, the terrorist attacks of September 11, some widely publicized accounting scandals, and the 2005 and 2008 hurricanes. The most damaging event was the decline in the housing market that began in early 2006. Even after the onset of the housing market decline, however, real GDP growth remained positive until the fourth quarter of 2007.

The business-cycle expansion lasted 73 months, the fourth longest post-World War II expansion. The growth rate of real GDP per labor force participant averaged 1.5 percent at an annual rate from the business-cycle peak in 2001 to the business-cycle peak in the fourth quarter of 2007, identical to its average growth over the period from 1953 to 2001.

Conclusion

The economy was weakening as it entered 2008, but was temporarily sustained at generally positive growth by the 2008 fiscal stimulus package and monetary policy actions. Consumer spending declined sharply in the third quarter, and mounting stress in financial markets reached a crescendo in September, triggering a decline in stock market wealth that further reduced consumer spending. Because of the large declines in wealth from September to December, the saving rate is likely to rise in 2009, which will continue to cause a decline or slow growth in consumer spending. The large September to December declines in wealth imply that an upward movement of the saving rate is likely in 2009, with further constraint on consumer spending as the increase plays out. The monetary and financial agencies of the Government have recently been particularly active with the Federal Reserve implementing a variety of new programs to provide liquidity to financial institutions and to support the functioning of financial markets. The Treasury, empowered by the recently passed Emergency Economic Stabilization Act, has also been active over this period and has strategically allocated funds to support financial sector solvency and liquidity (discussed in more detail in Chapter 2). These vigorous measures are expected to increase confidence in the financial sector over the next several months, leading to a rebound in output sometime in 2009.

Beyond the next few years, the economy is projected to settle into a steady state in which real GDP grows at about 2.7 percent per year, the unemployment rate stays around the level consistent with stable inflation (about 5.0 percent) and inflation remains moderate and stable (about 2.1 percent on the CPI). Economic forecasts are subject to error, and unforeseen positive and negative developments will affect the course of the economy over the next several years. Given the economy's strong basic structure (that is, free mobility of labor, relatively low taxes, and openness to trade), prospects for a resumption of steady growth in the years ahead remain good. Later chapters of this *Report* explore how market-based reforms and pro-growth policies such as tax reform and open commerce can enhance our economic performance.

CHAPTER 2

Housing and Financial Markets

In the summer of 2008, the disruptions in credit markets that began in 2007 worsened to the point that the global financial system was in crisis. The crisis was sparked by substantial declines in house prices, rising default rates on residential mortgages, and a resulting sharp decline in the value of mortgages and mortgage-backed securities, in part created by excesses in the mortgage market. These assets were held by institutions that play a vital role in the functioning of financial markets.

Many of those institutions were vulnerable to these losses because they were highly levered and, in particular, were highly dependent on short-term funding. In other words, those institutions had borrowed extensively against their long-term assets, and a large part of their debt was short-term, so that their existing debt needed to be paid off and replaced with new short-term debt with some frequency. As their losses mounted, those firms attempted to deleverage by selling assets or raising new capital. But several major firms failed in these efforts, either because their losses made them fundamentally insolvent or because their reliance on short-term funding did not give them enough time and flexibility to strengthen their financial positions.

The failure and near-failure of these firms, combined with broad-based declines in asset prices, including assets with little or no relationship to the mortgage market, placed enormous stress on world financial markets. Credit markets froze, and confidence in the financial system eroded. The Federal Reserve and the Administration acted aggressively to restore stability to the U.S. financial system; the Federal Reserve injected massive amounts of liquidity into the markets through existing and new facilities, and the Administration took several actions, including the creation of new authorities under the Emergency Economic Stabilization Act of 2008 (EESA). These unprecedented efforts laid the foundation for a recovery in credit markets.

The key points of this chapter are:

- The roots of the current global financial crisis began in the late 1990s. A rapid increase in saving by developing countries (sometimes called the "global saving glut") resulted in a large influx of capital to the United States and other industrialized countries, driving down the return on safe assets. The relatively low yield on safe assets likely encouraged investors to look for higher yields from riskier assets, whose yields also went down. What turned out to be an underpricing of risk across a number of markets (housing, commercial real estate, and leveraged buyouts, among others) in the United States and abroad, and an uncertainty about how this risk was distributed throughout the global financial system, set the stage for subsequent financial distress.

- The influx of inexpensive capital helped finance a housing boom. House prices appreciated rapidly earlier in this decade, and building increased to well-above historic levels. Eventually, house prices began to decline with this glut in housing supply.
- Considerable innovations in housing finance—the growth of subprime mortgages and the expansion of the market for assets backed by mortgages—helped fuel the housing boom. Those innovations were often beneficial, helping to make home ownership more affordable and accessible, but excesses set the stage for later losses.
- The declining value of mortgage-related assets has had a disproportionate effect on the financial sector because a large fraction of mortgage-related assets are held by banks, investment banks, and other highly levered financial institutions. The combination of leverage (the use of borrowed funds) and, in particular, a reliance on short-term funding made these institutions (both in the United States and abroad) vulnerable to large mortgage losses.
- Vulnerable institutions failed, and others nearly failed. The remaining institutions pulled back from extending credit to each other, and inter-bank lending rates increased to unprecedented levels. The effects of the crisis were most visible in the financial sector, but the impact and consequences of the crisis are being felt by households, businesses, and governments throughout the world.
- The U.S. Government has undertaken a historic effort to address the underlying problems behind the freeze in the credit markets. These problems, the subject of much of this chapter, are a sudden increase in the desire for liquidity, a massive reassessment of risk, and a solvency crisis for many systemically important institutions. The Government has worked to preserve the stability of the overall financial system by preventing the disorderly failures of important financial institutions; taken unprecedented action to boost liquidity in short-term funding markets; provided substantial new protections for consumers, businesses, and investors; and cooperated closely with its international partners.
- Looking forward, the global financial crisis presents several additional challenges for the U.S. Government. Among them are the need to modernize financial regulation, unwind temporary programs in an orderly fashion, and develop long-term solutions for the government-sponsored enterprises (privately-owned, publicly-chartered entities) Fannie Mae and Freddie Mac.

Origins of the Crisis

The roots of the global financial crisis can be traced back to before the beginning of this decade and were, in part, caused by a rise in saving by developing economies.

The Global Saving Glut

Countries in Asia and the Middle East started saving enormous sums in the late 1990s. This increase in saving was primarily due to two factors. First, a number of developing countries experienced financial crises in the 1990s. As these crises abated, these countries began accumulating extensive savings as a buffer against any future crises. Second, sharp increases in oil prices over the past few years generated large revenues for oil exporters, including Russia, Nigeria, Venezuela, and countries in the Middle East. With productive economies and strong legal regimes, the United States and other industrialized countries attracted a good portion of that saving, and foreign investors purchased low-risk assets such as Treasury bonds, debt issued by government-sponsored enterprises Fannie Mae and Freddie Mac, and mortgage-backed securities, as well as riskier assets. From 1996 to 2007, industrialized countries went from a current account surplus (recording a surplus in net trade in goods and services, and net income and transfers from abroad) of $14 billion to a current account deficit of almost $500 billion. At the same time, developing countries went from a current account deficit of $82 billion to a surplus of $760 billion.

As this influx of capital became available to fund investments, interest rates fell broadly. The return on safe assets was notably low: the 10-year Treasury rate ranged from only 3.1 percent to 5.3 percent from 2003 to 2007, whereas the average rate over the preceding 40 years was 7.5 percent. While to some extent the low rates reflected relatively benign inflation risk, the rate on risky assets was even lower relative to its historical average: the rate on a 10-year BAA investment-grade (medium-quality) bond ranged from only 5.6 percent to 7.5 percent from 2003 to 2007, whereas the average over the preceding 40 years was 9.3 percent. The net effect was a dramatic narrowing of *credit spreads*. A credit spread measures the difference between the yield on a risky asset, such as a corporate bond, and the yield on a riskless asset, such as a Treasury bond, with a similar maturity. Risky assets pay a premium for a number of reasons, including liquidity risk (the risk that it will be difficult to sell at an expected price in a timely manner) and default risk (the risk that a borrower will be unable to make timely principal and interest payments).

Credit spreads declined as these premiums shrank. From 2003 to mid-2007, for example, credit spreads on junk bonds fell by 5.5 percentage points, to a historical low of 2.4 percent. Credit spreads on AAA (high-quality) and BAA investment-grade bonds also fell over this time period. (See Chart 1-9 in Chapter 1.) While some market participants may have argued that declining credit spreads reflected an actual decline in the level of risk, we see in hindsight that many of these assets continued to be quite risky. Declining spreads reflected, at least in part, a temporary increase in demand for risky but higher-yielding assets. The underpricing of risk across a number of markets—including housing, commercial real estate, and lever-aged buyouts—in the United States and abroad set the stage for a subsequent financial crisis.

The Global Credit Boom and the Housing Market

The underpricing of risk made loans readily available to borrowers, especially to riskier borrowers, and gave rise to a global credit boom. At the epicenter of the global credit boom was the U.S. residential housing market. During the credit boom, the ease of credit financing encouraged rapid increases in demand for housing, leading to extraordinary house price increases. According to the S&P/Case-Shiller National Index, house prices increased by 11 percent in 2002, 11 percent in 2003, 15 percent in 2004, and 15 percent in 2005—stunning rates by historical standards. The Federal Housing Finance Agency (FHFA) purchase-only price index, which covers only homes purchased with conforming mortgages (that is, it excludes both subprime and large "jumbo" mortgages), rose more moderately but still climbed an impressive 9 percent in 2004 and 9 percent in 2005 (see Chart 2-1).

Measures of long-term balance in the housing market, such as the ratio of home prices to rents, reached record highs over this period. The compo-nents of this ratio are shown in Chart 2-1. As home prices rose much faster than rents after 2000, the ratio (not shown) of the two lines climbed beyond its historical range. This ratio had remained relatively stable from 1982 to 1999, but as house prices began to climb, the ratio of prices to rents soared to unprecedented heights, suggesting that owner-occupied housing became more expensive relative to rental housing.

In addition to expanded credit availability, the price increases reflected a number of other factors, such as income growth and extremely optimistic expectations about future house price gains. All of these factors likely increased demand for housing, which put upward pressure on house prices. Dramatic house price increases encouraged well-above-average residential investment and a decline in underwriting standards in the mortgage market.

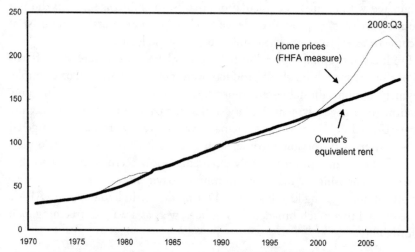

Index (1990=100)

Note: Before 1991, the FHFA purchase-only index was spliced with the FHFA total index. Before 1983, the CPI-U owner's equivalent rent of primary residence was spliced with the PCE price index for owner-occupied dwellings.
Sources: Federal Housing Finance Authority, Department of Labor (Bureau of Labor Statistics), and Federal Reserve Board.

Excesses in the Primary Mortgage Market

Over the past decade, there has been tremendous innovation and expansion in the market in which borrowers obtained loans from mortgage originators, also known as the *primary mortgage market.* Some innovation was beneficial, increasing mortgage affordability and structuring payment terms that fit borrowers' individual circumstances. For example, the increase in *subprime lending,* defined as lending to higher-risk groups, usually at interest rates high enough to imply a large risk premium, opened up new opportunities for borrowers with weaker or limited credit histories to purchase a home. Subprime lending expands access to credit to previously underserved households—albeit at restrictive and expensive terms.

The very competitive lending environment encouraged and intensified myopia among both lenders and borrowers, both of whom took on too much risk. For example, both likely assumed that risky mortgages could be easily refinanced or that homes could be easily sold if borrowers found themselves unable to afford their mortgage payments. Underwriting standards were loosened, even for subprime borrowers, and terms became less restrictive. In some cases, down payment requirements were relaxed to the point that borrowers' mortgages were greater than the value of their homes, as apparently both lenders and borrowers expected near-term house price appreciation. Furthermore, increasing numbers of mortgage loans were originated with limited documentation; that is, the mortgage lenders did not require borrowers to provide evidence (such as previous years' tax returns) of income or assets to affirm their ability to repay the loans.

Products appropriate for a limited group of borrowers were also offered to borrowers for whom these products were not well suited. For example, payment-option adjustable-rate mortgages ("option ARMs"), which allow monthly mortgage payments to vary so that the payment may cover only the interest owed or some of the principal owed as well, were initially targeted to borrowers with variable income, such as the self employed. Most option ARMs allowed minimum monthly payments below accrued interest so that borrowers choosing to make the minimum payment would have negative amortization, or rising loan balances. During the credit boom, option ARMs were offered to a much broader class of borrowers as a way of stretching loan affordability.

Excesses in the Market for Mortgage-Related Assets

Other developments helped set the stage for mortgage defaults. The rise of mortgage securitization, led both by government-sponsored enterprises (GSEs) Fannie Mae and Freddie Mac as well as private institutions, reduced the incentive for originators (which increasingly included non-bank mortgage specialists) to properly evaluate risk.

For many years, lenders followed an "originate-to-hold" model in which they kept the loans they originated. Securitization allowed lenders to move to an "originate-to-distribute" model by transforming collections of individual mortgages into *mortgage-backed securities* (MBS)—tradable securities backed by the loans—and selling the MBS to other investors. (Box 2-1 defines "mortgage-backed securities" and other financial terms.) Lenders that sold MBS used the cash to originate more loans and create new MBS, benefiting themselves as well as borrowers and investors. Securitization under the originate-to-distribute model seemed to work well. Borrowers benefited from lower mortgage rates, and investors benefited from being able to diversify their investments across a wider set of assets.

Lost in the frenzy of lending, borrowing, and securitization was the fact that the benefits of securitization come with a cost. In an originate-to-hold model, the loan originator will lose if the borrower defaults, and so the originator has the incentive to gather information on the borrower to be sure the borrower can afford to pay the mortgage. In contrast, in an originate-to-distribute model, the private-label MBS investor, not the originator, bears the default risk. Because originators do not expect to bear the risk, they do not have as much incentive to make sure the borrowers can pay. Moreover, the incentive for lenders to originate excessively risky loans becomes tempting. Because

Box 2-1: Definitions of Select Financial Terms

Asset-backed security (ABS): A security whose cash flows are backed by the principal and interest payments of a collection of loans, such as credit cards, automobile loans, and student loans.

Auction rate security (ARS): A long-term debt instrument whose interest rate is reset periodically (typically every 7, 28, or 35 days) through an auction process.

Collateralized mortgage obligation (CMO): A complex mortgage-backed security in which cash flows from the mortgage payments are split into tranches (slices), and each tranche is sold as a separate security.

Commercial mortgage-backed security (CMBS): A mortgage-backed security backed by mortgages on commercial property.

Commercial paper (CP): Short-term loans issued by corporations. CP terms range from 1 day ("overnight") to 270 days. Asset-backed commercial paper (ABCP) is commercial paper that is secured by assets. Commercial paper can be issued by financial institutions as well as non-financial institutions.

Government-sponsored enterprise mortgage-backed security (GSE MBS): A mortgage-backed security that includes a credit guarantee from a government-sponsored enterprise (Fannie Mae or Freddie Mac).

London interbank offered rate (LIBOR): The interest rate at which banks offer to lend unsecured funds to other banks. The 3-month LIBOR, the rate at which banks offer to lend for a 3-month term, is a key reference rate used for many financial contracts.

Mortgage-backed security (MBS): security whose cash flows are backed by the principal and interest payments of a collection of mortgage loans.

Mortgage-related asset: Any original mortgage loan or MBS.

Non-agency mortgage-backed security (non-agency MBS): A mortgage-backed security that does not include a credit guarantee from a government agency or government-sponsored enterprise. Also known as private-label MBS.

Residential mortgage-backed security (RMBS): A mortgage-backed security backed by mortgages on residential property.

Secured debt: A loan that is backed by collateral. If the borrower defaults on repayment, the lender can seize the collateral, sell it, and use the proceeds to repay the debt.

TED spread: The difference between the 3-month LIBOR and the 3-month Treasury Bill rate, a commonly used indicator of financial market distress.

Unsecured debt: A loan that is not backed by collateral. The loan is supported only by the borrower's creditworthiness.

MBS are complex securities, many investors relied on credit rating agencies to provide them with information on default risk rather than conducting their own due diligence. For their part, credit rating agencies made initial assessments that, in hindsight, used faulty assumptions and led to a significant number of downgrades. To their detriment, many market participants relied heavily on ratings that turned out to be overly optimistic.

Chart 2-2 shows the fraction of total mortgages outstanding that are securitized by private institutions (private-label MBS) as well as the share of total mortgage originations accounted for by subprime mortgages. Data on subprime mortgages have a limited history, which is perhaps not surprising given how recently this market became important. While a number of factors led to the surge in subprime lending, the increase in privately-issued MBS, and the increase in securitization more generally, likely played an important role.

Mortgage-backed securities were often repackaged into even more complex securities, reflecting an increased demand from investors for customized investment products called structured products. A *collateralized mortgage obligation* (CMO), for example, is a mortgage-backed security in which cash flows from the mortgage payments are ordered into "tranches" (slices), and each tranche is sold as a separate security. The tranches are typically ranked in descending order of repayment from highest (super senior) to lowest (equity). Senior tranches have a priority claim on the cash flow from the underlying

Chart 2-2 **Privately Securitized Mortgages and Subprime Mortgage Loans**
Privately securitized mortgages and subprime loans have become a larger share of the market since 2003.
Percent

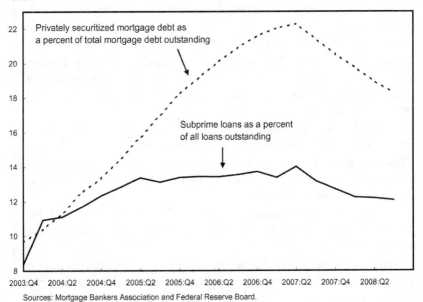

Sources: Mortgage Bankers Association and Federal Reserve Board.

collateral and must be paid before junior tranches. The middle tranches of a CMO could be repackaged yet again into even more complex securities.

A combination of overreliance on credit rating agencies' assessments of complex securities and flaws in the assumptions underlying those assessments, along with insufficient risk management at financial firms and regulatory policies that failed to mitigate risk-management weaknesses, created a situation in which many financial firms held mortgage-related assets that turned out to be far more risky than anticipated.

The Credit Crunch

Eventually, the number of houses on the market began rising faster than sales, and prices started to fall. Nationally, home price appreciation began to slow in 2005, and price levels began to fall in the third quarter of 2007, according to the FHFA purchase-only house price index. In some mortgage markets and in some regions, prices began their decline a year before the national average. The inventory of new homes for sale rose rapidly relative to the pace of new home sales, contributing to price declines. The residential construction industry reacted to a decline in housing demand, and by 2006, this sector experienced job losses as new housing starts plunged (Chart 2-3).

Chart 2-3 **Single-Family Housing Starts**
Housing starts have fallen more than 75 percent from their peak in 2006 to the lowest level on record.
Millions of units

Source: Department of Commerce (Bureau of the Census).

As house prices faltered, borrowers with little or no equity in their homes quickly found that they owed more to lenders than their homes were now worth in the market. Such borrowers are often referred to as being "underwater." Some borrowers were unable to afford their mortgage payments either because of financial circumstances or because their mortgage payments rose, as their mortgage contract included a sizable increase in monthly payments over the life of the loan. If these borrowers were also underwater, they were not able to refinance, making them likely to default. In fact, among subprime loans that were securitized in the second half of 2006, over 7 percent of these loans were at least 60 days past due within the first 6 months, exposing the weakening in underwriting standards over time and the effect of house prices faltering. By way of comparison, among subprime loans securitized in the first half of 2005, less than 3 percent of these loans were at least 60 days past due within the first 6 months.

Chart 2-4 shows that the rates of serious delinquency (defined as 90 days past due or in default) for both prime and subprime mortgages have risen since 2005. Rates for both fixed-rate mortgages (FRMs) and adjustable-rate mortgages (ARMs) have increased. Delinquency rates are considerably higher in the subprime market than in the prime market; however, rates of serious delinquency in both the subprime and prime mortgage markets have reached their highest levels since the Mortgage Bankers Association began collecting these data in 1979.

Chart 2-4 **Percent of Mortgages 90 Days Past Due or in the Process of Foreclosure**
Subprime adjustable-rate mortgages (ARMs) have performed particularly poorly over the past year.
Percent of loans

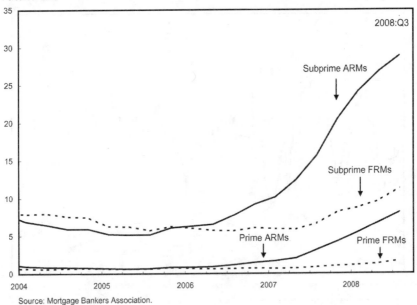

Source: Mortgage Bankers Association.

Lenders and investors that held mortgages and mortgage-backed securities, particularly risky subprime mortgages, incurred losses as default rates rose. Lenders demanded higher risk premiums in the form of higher mortgage spreads (mortgage interest rates charged in excess of long-term Treasury rates), and the supply of mortgage credit—at any given spread—decreased. In fact, new subprime lending began to dry up altogether beginning in 2007. With the unexpected increase in default rates, the value of the mortgages declined, and uncertainty over the future value of the complex securities that were backed by, or derived from, these mortgages increased. Demand for mortgage-related assets plummeted, particularly for subprime mortgages held as whole loans (original mortgage loans) and non-agency mortgage-backed securities for which uncertainty was the greatest. As a result, the market price for these assets fell dramatically.

Mortgage-related assets are very widely held. Domestic and international banks hold about three-fourths of the whole loans held outside of the GSEs, and banks hold about one-half of mortgage-related securities held outside of the GSEs. Insurance companies hold some whole loans and hold almost one-fourth of mortgage-related securities. Pensions and hedge funds also have substantial positions in mortgage-related securities. As of the end of 2008, global financial institutions that invested in these assets reported over $1 trillion in losses.

Leverage and Reliance on Short-Term Funds

The declining value of mortgages and mortgage-backed securities threatened the ability of systemically important financial institutions to meet their financial obligations (that is, their "solvency") because portions of the financial system are highly exposed to shocks. That exposure takes two basic forms: high *leverage* and reliance on *short-term funding*. Leverage is the use of borrowed funds (debt), as opposed to investment capital (equity), to finance assets. Short-term funding is the use of debt financing that must be paid back within a short period of time.

Before the financial crisis, the major investment banks were levered roughly 25 to 1. This means that every $100 in assets was funded by $96 in debt, leaving only $4 in equity. In other words, investment banks owned complex investment portfolios with only 4 percent down. Such leverage was a fundamental source of fragility—the capital base of those institutions would be eliminated by just a 4 percent decline in asset values. (Commercial banks, in contrast, were levered about 12 to 1.)

In addition, many major financial firms rely on short-term funding, requiring them to continually replace existing debt with new debt (a process called "rolling over" debt) and thereby putting them at the mercy of changes in the availability of liquidity. Put another way, if a bank is levered using long-term debt, it can survive as long as it can make debt service payments; if a bank is levered using short-term debt, it has to pay off the entire debt every few weeks, which it typically does by taking out new short-term debt. During the credit boom, liquidity was easily available, and firms could roll over enough debt to satisfy their short-term funding needs. Firms began to rely even more heavily on short-term debt and created financial innovations, such as auction rate securities (ARS) and structured investment vehicles (SIVs), to address those demands. But, when doubts arose about the availability of liquidity, those financing methods broke down, and firms faced a considerable risk of not being able to roll over their financing.

The collapse of Bear Stearns in March 2008 provides an example of how high leverage, combined with a heavy reliance on short-term term funding, can make a financial institution more fragile than it ought to be. In 2007, Bear Stearns was one of the largest global investment banks. Bear Stearns's assets were highly concentrated in mortgage-backed securities. In fact, two of Bear Stearns's managed hedge funds collapsed in June 2007 because of subprime mortgage losses.

During the week of March 10, 2008, rumors spread about liquidity problems at Bear Stearns, resulting in a "run." As the rumors spread, Bear Stearns was unable to borrow funds from other financial institutions, despite the fact that Bear Stearns pledged high-quality financial assets as collateral to secure repayment of many of its short-term loans. In a secured funding arrangement, the borrower agrees to forfeit the collateral if it defaults on the loan. However, possibly because the legal process of transferring ownership of collateral is quite lengthy, many of Bear Stearns's secured lenders refused to continue ("roll over") their short-term lending arrangements. As a result, Bear Stearns could not meet its short-term funding needs.

On Friday, March 14, 2008, the Federal Reserve Bank of New York (FRBNY) provided emergency funding to Bear Stearns. However, the FRBNY funding could not stop Bear Stearns's downward spiral, and Bear Stearns concluded that it would need to file for bankruptcy protection, unless another firm purchased it. On Sunday, March 16, 2008, Bear Stearns announced that it would be acquired by JP Morgan Chase, with financing support from the FRBNY.

Macroeconomic Consequences of the Crisis

The effects of the crises in the housing and financial markets were most visible for Wall Street firms like Bear Stearns, but their impact has been felt by businesses, consumers, and governments throughout the world. The precipitous drop in the stock market has drastically eroded the value of Americans' stock portfolios, 401(k) accounts, and other retirement accounts. The tightening of credit has made it more expensive and difficult for many families to borrow money for cars, homes, and college tuition. Many healthy businesses have found it harder to get loans to expand their operations and to create jobs.

Banks Reduced Lending to Consumers and Businesses

As default rates for household debt rose, lenders became increasingly reluctant to make any but the least risky loans. Many banks and other creditors tightened standards on mortgages and consumer debt. The Federal Reserve's Senior Loan Officer Survey on Bank Lending Practices reports changes in the supply of bank loans to businesses and households. As Chart 2-5 shows, the net percent of domestic lending institutions reporting that they tightened lending standards began rising at the end of 2007. Tighter standards reduce the availability of credit for households and, as a result, hinder households' ability to maintain spending in difficult economic times.

Chart 2-5 **Domestic Banks Tightening Lending Standards**
Banks have been tightening lending standards on a variety of loan products since the end of 2007.

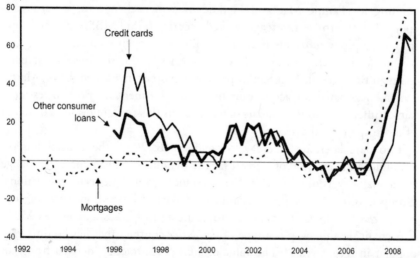

Note: "Net percent" refers to the percent of respondents tightening less the percent of respondents loosening. The values for mortgages for the second quarter of 2007 through the fourth quarter of 2008 were calculated as a weighted average of prime, subprime, and nontraditional loans using weights estimated by the Council of Economic Advisers. Source: Federal Reserve Board.

Similar survey responses on banks' standards for commercial and industrial loans show that banks tightened lending standards for business loans starting in mid-2007. The weakness in the business sector seen in business investment and outlays reflects, in part, this reduced access to credit from banks and other lenders, forcing businesses to tap cash reserves to fund investment and expenditures.

The Onset of the Crisis

Within a 9-day period in September 2008, the crisis deepened abruptly with a series of stunning events. On Sunday, September 7, 2008, the Federal Housing Finance Authority (FHFA) placed the ailing mortgage giants Fannie Mae and Freddie Mac into conservatorship because the FHFA determined that the values of Fannie Mae's and Freddie Mac's mortgage-related assets had deteriorated to the point that these institutions could no longer operate safely and soundly. Conservatorship gave the FHFA powers typically associated with Fannie Mae's and Freddie Mac's directors, officers, and shareholders, including all actions necessary and appropriate to put each company in a sound and solvent condition, carry on each company's business, and conserve the property and assets of each company. In addition to the FHFA conservatorship, the Treasury Department entered into commitments to inject up to $100 billion in capital into each firm in exchange for preferred stock and warrants (options to buy equity shares at a predetermined price) for common stock, created a temporary lending facility to provide secured funding for Fannie Mae and Freddie Mac in exchange for government-sponsored enterprise mortgage-backed security (GSE MBS) collateral, and initiated a program to purchase GSE MBS in the open market.

One week later, on Sunday, September 14, 2008, the investment bank Lehman Brothers filed for bankruptcy, and another investment bank, Merrill Lynch, negotiated an acquisition by Bank of America. Both investment banks suffered billions of dollars of writedowns (losses from declines in value) of mortgage-related assets.

Two days later, on Tuesday, September 16, 2008, the Federal Reserve announced the creation of a credit facility (lending arrangement) in exchange for a majority equity stake in the insurance giant American International Group (AIG). AIG suffered billions of dollars of losses from entering into *credit default swap* (CDS) contracts to insure against losses on complex MBS.

A credit default swap is a type of *derivative* contract that has become very popular in recent years. The value of a CDS contract is "derived from" an underlying credit instrument, such as a bond or an MBS, where one party— say a borrower—owes money to another party. The buyer of a CDS contract agrees to make a series of payments (similar to an insurance premium) to the seller over time. If the borrower who owes money according to the underlying credit instrument defaults, the seller of the CDS agrees to make a pre-specified payoff to the buyer. Essentially, the buyer of the CDS has taken out insurance on the default risk of a credit instrument, and the seller of the CDS is the insurance provider.

In the case of AIG, most of its CDS counterparties were banks that bought CDS contracts because they wanted to hedge against declines in the MBS held on their balance sheets. Contractual features in AIG's CDS required AIG to post cash collateral to their counterparties as the values of the MBS declined. The collateral calls were so large that AIG did not have the cash to post, and AIG faced a liquidity crisis. The increased burden to honor CDS contracts also undermined AIG's solvency.

Credit Market Investors Reduced Lending to Businesses

Following these events, reassessments of risk led to a flight to quality. This flight to quality extended beyond mortgage-related assets and affected a number of non-bank institutions and assets that businesses use to pledge as collateral for secured funding. For long-term debt funding (and equity funding), businesses rely on *capital markets,* where mutual funds, hedge funds, and pension funds, for example, invest in long-term bonds issued by corporations and State and local governments. For short-term funding, businesses rely on the *money market.* An important source of lending in the short-term credit markets are *money market mutual funds* (or money funds), which often invest in instruments called "paper." *Commercial paper* (CP) is short-term funding used by corporations, and it is often issued as asset-backed commercial paper (ABCP), which is secured by collateral. Other money market instruments include Treasury bills and *repurchase agreements* (or repos), where a borrower agrees to sell securities to a lender for cash and simultaneously agrees to buy back those securities at a later date at a higher price. A repo is economically similar to a secured loan, with the buyer/lender receiving securities as collateral to protect against default.

As lenders sacrificed yield for the safety of Treasury securities, interbank lending rates rose to unprecedented levels. Financial institutions pulled back from extending credit to each other, except at the very shortest maturities, because of an aversion to counterparty risk or concerns about their own liquidity needs. As shown in Chart 2-6, the *TED spread* increased dramatically in September 2008 above already elevated levels. The TED spread is the difference between the 3-month *London Interbank Offered Rate* (LIBOR) and the 3-month Treasury Bill rate. LIBOR is the rate at which banks offer unsecured loans to other banks. The dramatic increase in the TED spread indicates considerable distress in interbank lending.

Chart 2-6 **The TED Spread**
The spread between the 3-month London Interbank Offered Rate (LIBOR) and yields on 3-month
Treasury bills grew to historic highs during 2008, indicating distress in interbank lending.

Interest rate spread (basis points)

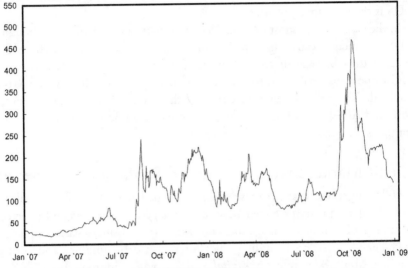

Sources: British Bankers Association and the Treasury Department.

When large financial institutions faced perceptions of insolvency, creditors became less willing to lend to them, even in the very short term. Companies that relied on what had been perceived as low-risk secured funding, such as ABCP and repos, were also affected by the freeze in lending. Left unchecked, the progression would have led to "runs." Institutions that were not able to obtain funding due to perceptions of insolvency would have faced a liquidity crisis. Without the ability to roll over their short-term debt, institutions that relied heavily on short-term financing would have to sell their assets at "fire sale" prices to meet their financial obligations. Such actions can lead to an actual (rather than perceived) insolvency crisis, which would likely have led to widespread financial and economic failure.

Money funds themselves can face a run if investors lose confidence in the fund's ability to protect them from a loss of principal. Principal protection is most visible in the fact that money funds seek to maintain a stable $1.00 net asset value (NAV). While money funds are required by law to invest in short-term low-risk securities, investment losses are possible. In September 2008, money market funds that had invested in Lehman Brothers commercial paper faced losses when Lehman Brothers declared bankruptcy. Over time, investment gains in other securities held in the diversified portfolios of money funds are usually big enough to offset the rare loss in an individual security. However, if an increase in investor anxiety causes a run in the form of large-scale redemptions, the money fund may be forced to liquidate other assets at below-market prices. If that happens, the fund may be unable to support a $1.00 NAV and thus "break the buck."

The Effect of the Crisis on the Non-Financial Economy

The financial crisis spread beyond financial institutions. It also affected households and non-financial businesses in the non-financial ("real") economy.

The Effect of the Crisis on Households

The financial crisis has affected households through a number of channels, including a sharp loss in stock market wealth (as discussed in Chapter 1), a further tightening in household credit markets, prospects for a slower recovery in the housing market, and increased pessimism regarding current and future economic conditions.

In the wake of the financial crisis, banks also began to further restrict households' access to credit. As mentioned earlier and shown in Chart 2-5, banks began tightening standards on household loans by the end of 2007. As the financial crisis deepened in September 2008, credit became even more expensive and less available. For example, interest rates on 30-year fixed-rate mortgages rose 0.7 percentage point by the end of October 2008 from their September weekly low of 5.8 percent. Continued tightness in mortgage credit markets could reduce demand for housing and could slow the recovery in this market.

Chart 2-7 shows measures of consumer confidence from both the Reuters/ University of Michigan survey and the Conference Board survey, which reveal substantial pessimism among consumers in the recent data. In fact, in October 2008 the Conference Board measure of confidence reached the lowest level ever seen in the index's 51-year history.

The Effect of the Crisis on Businesses

The financial crisis has also affected non-financial businesses through a number of channels, including a tightening in business credit markets and weaker demand both domestically and abroad. As mentioned above, businesses on the whole have had a difficult time raising funds in private debt and equity markets because of more expensive financing terms and reduced access. As a result, businesses' ability to finance ongoing operations, to invest, and to increase hiring has been curtailed, particularly beginning in the fall of 2008.

Chart 2-7 Consumer Confidence

Consumer confidence has declined sharply since the start of credit market disruptions in August 2007.

Index

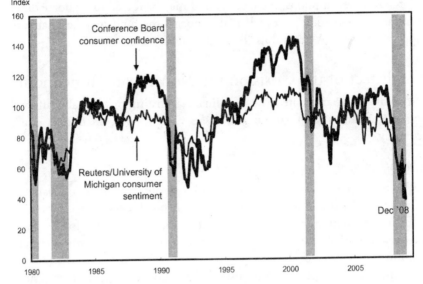

Note: Grey shading indicates recession.
Sources: Reuters/University of Michigan and Conference Board.

However, businesses have also reduced their demand for funds to expand operations. As consumer demand has weakened, businesses have become less willing to make investments to expand production. In addition, the crisis in credit markets has made it more difficult for consumers to finance some purchases, especially of "big ticket" durable goods such as automobiles. These difficulties result from disruptions in the market for asset-backed securities (ABS). Like mortgage-backed securities, asset-backed securities are tradable financial instruments that are backed by pools of individual loans—in this case, consumer loans. Since the financial crisis deepened in the fall of 2008, the demand for ABS has notably declined. These consumer credit market disruptions have led to a decline in consumer purchasing that has further reduced business demand for credit.

Businesses also have faced weaker demand abroad as the financial crisis has worsened the outlook for global economic growth. As a result of all these factors, business confidence has fallen notably since the fall of 2008.

Policy Responses to the Crisis

The global financial crisis is massive in scale and far-reaching in scope. The complexity of the financial system, as well as the financial instruments that are traded in various markets, has meant that the Government has had to take many new and drastic actions very quickly to limit further turmoil. While many different responses have been undertaken by different Government agencies, all of the responses have been designed to achieve the overarching goals of preserving the stability of financial institutions and boosting liquidity in financial markets.

Policy Responses in 2007

After the disruption in credit markets in the summer of 2007, the Administration and the Federal Reserve responded through a series of coordinated actions aimed at providing liquidity to financial markets and stabilizing housing markets. In the second half of 2007, for example, the Federal Reserve lowered interest rates and injected liquidity into financial markets by taking the following steps:

- Lowering the target for the Federal Funds rate (the interest rate at which U.S. banks lend to other banks overnight) by a total of 1 percentage point between September 2007 and December 2007 to reduce banks' funding costs.
- Expanding the Federal Reserve's lending through the discount window (the lending facility of last resort for depository institutions such as banks) to provide term financing for periods as long as 90 days, and establishing a Term Auction Facility (TAF) to further increase the availability of liquidity for depository institutions. Longer financing terms allow borrowers to roll over debt less frequently.
- Establishing reciprocal currency arrangements ("swap lines") with the European Central Bank (ECB) and the Swiss National Bank (SNB) to facilitate those banks' provision of dollar liquidity to institutions in their jurisdictions.

The Administration also took several steps to address difficulties in the housing market:

- In August 2007, the Administration launched a new program at the Federal Housing Administration (FHA) called *FHASecure*. The FHA insures (but does not originate) mortgages for qualified low- and moderate-income borrowers who have less-than-perfect credit and little savings for a down payment. The *FHASecure* initiative offers homeowners who have adjustable-rate mortgages, current or delinquent, the ability to refinance into a fixed-rate FHA-insured mortgage.

- In August 2007, the Administration repeated its call for Congress to pass a reform package for the GSEs Fannie Mae and Freddie Mac. Congress ultimately passed the Housing and Economic Recovery Act of 2008 (HERA) in July 2008 to strengthen the regulator charged with overseeing the GSEs.
- In October 2007, HOPE NOW, a private sector alliance of mortgage industry participants, was launched to encourage servicers, housing counselors, and investors to work together to help streamline the process of modifying mortgages for borrowers with adjustable-rate mortgages who can afford their current mortgage payments but will have trouble when their interest rates rise.

Policy Responses in 2008

As the crisis worsened over the course of 2008, the Administration and the Federal Reserve took additional and extraordinary steps to prevent systemwide failures in financial markets, provide protections for households' savings, and encourage the renegotiations of mortgages to prevent unnecessary foreclosures.

Intervention in Troubled Institutions

The Government has focused on preserving the stability of the overall financial system and acted to prevent disorderly failures of several large, interconnected firms—and did so in a way that protects taxpayers. For example, the failure of Fannie Mae and Freddie Mac would have materially exacerbated financial market turmoil and added to the disruptions in the mortgage market, putting more downward pressure on house prices. Examples of interventions in other troubled institutions are discussed above.

Injecting Liquidity

The Government has taken unprecedented action to inject liquidity—the grease that keeps the gears of the financial system turning. The Federal Deposit Insurance Corporation (FDIC) has temporarily guaranteed most new unsecured debt issued by insured banks; that is, the FDIC has agreed to make scheduled principal and interest payments in the event the issuer fails to make those payments. As a result, banks have found it easier to borrow.

The Federal Reserve has used a variety of tools to inject hundreds of billions of dollars in new liquidity into the financial system. The Federal Reserve has expanded the availability of term financing provided to depository institutions through the discount window and the Term Auction Facility (TAF). To support the liquidity of primary dealers, the Federal Reserve expanded its securities lending program by broadening the securities that can be used as collateral as well as extending the terms of the loans. More information on the securities lending program is on the Federal Reserve Bank of New York's website. In addition, the Federal Reserve established a Primary Dealer Credit Facility (PDCF) to meet the short-term funding needs of primary dealers, which are banks and securities broker-dealers that are authorized to trade directly with the Federal Reserve. Over the course of 2008, the Federal Reserve further reduced the target for the Federal Funds rate by over 4 percentage points. Moreover, it expanded its swap lines with foreign central banks and established a number of special programs designed to address strains in financial markets, including facilities structured to provide support to money market mutual funds, the commercial paper market, and the asset-backed securities markets.

Protecting Consumers, Businesses, and Investors

The Government has provided substantial new protections for consumers, businesses, and investors. The FDIC has temporarily expanded the amount of money insured in bank and thrift checking accounts, savings accounts, and certificates of deposit from $100,000 to $250,000 per depositor. The FDIC has also temporarily removed insurance limits for non-interest-bearing transaction accounts, which are used by many small businesses to finance daily operations. The Treasury has offered temporary government insurance for money market mutual funds. The Securities and Exchange Commission is vigorously investigating fraud, manipulation, and abuse in the securities markets, with an emphasis on abusive practices involving "short sales" (see Box 2-2). The programs being undertaken by Federal agencies are aimed at providing greater stability for the financial system.

Box 2-2: Short Sales

A short sale involves the sale of a stock by an investor who does not own it. To deliver the stock to the purchaser, the short seller must borrow the stock from a broker or from another investor. Later, the short seller closes out the position by purchasing the stock on the open market. Short sales are profitable if the stock price declines, because the short seller can buy the stock at the lower price. But if the price rises, the short seller will need to buy the stock at a higher price and, therefore, incur a loss.

Short sales are a part of many useful investment and trading strategies. Short sales are valuable to an investor who believes that the stock price will fall because the stock is overvalued. In this case, the short sale is used in the same way that an investor who believes that a security is currently undervalued will buy the stock. Short sales can be used

continued on the next page

Box 2-2 — continued

by market-makers in response to buyer demand for a stock that they do not currently own. Market-makers provide liquidity to other market participants by quoting buying prices (bids) and selling prices (asks) on stocks. They hope to profit on the difference, or spread, between the bid and ask prices, rather than on any price movement. Thus, short sales provide the market with an important benefit—liquidity. Short sales also provide the market with a second benefit—pricing efficiency—because efficient markets are characterized by prices that fully reflect both buying and selling interests.

Although short selling serves useful market purposes, in some rare instances it may be used to illegally manipulate stock prices (just as stock purchases may, in rare instances, be used to manipulate stock prices). One example is the "bear raid" in which a trader engages in heavy short selling in an attempt to drive down prices in the hope of triggering a cascade of sell orders from others that depresses prices further. The Securities and Exchange Commission (SEC), the primary overseer of U.S. securities markets, has promulgated many rules to prevent stock price manipulation and has aggressively pursued abusive short-selling practices that involve insider trading and other federal securities law violations.

At the same time, the SEC has adopted a balanced approach in pursuit of its mission to protect investors; maintain fair, orderly, and efficient markets; and facilitate capital formation. For example, the SEC has suspended short sale price restriction rules (for example, the uptick rule, which requires that a short sale must occur at a price above the most recent different transaction price) after carefully considering the solid empirical evidence based on research conducted by the SEC and independent academic economists that shows that the purported benefits of the rules no longer justify the costs. Also, the SEC has enacted rules that govern short sales immediately before stock offerings in an effort to maintain the integrity of the capital-raising process.

Stabilizing the Housing Market

The Administration continued its efforts to mitigate effects of the declining housing market and to help responsible homeowners in danger of defaulting on their mortgages. The FHA has provided countercyclical support for the mortgage market as conventional financing has partly withdrawn from the market. Between the time *FHASecure* was launched in August 2007 and December 2008, FHA helped more than 450,000 families, many of whom were facing the loss of their homes, refinance into a more affordable FHA-insured mortgage. In the midst of all of this, the FHA has been a leader in contacting FHA-insured homeowners in trouble to work out solutions. In 2008, FHA servicers completed more than 100,000 loss-mitigation actions. The Department of Housing and Urban Development (HUD) also launched the Neighborhood Stabilization Program in September 2008, which provides emergency assistance to State and local governments to acquire and redevelop foreclosed properties that might otherwise be abandoned and become blight.

In September 2008, the Treasury began purchasing GSE MBS and related products to support the mortgage financing market, as authorized by the Housing and Economic Recovery Act of 2008 (HERA). More recently, the Federal Reserve announced its intentions to purchase large volumes of agency debt and MBS backed by Fannie Mae, Freddie Mac, and Ginnie Mae (a government-owned corporation within HUD) in an effort to lower mortgage rates and increase the availability of mortgage credit.

In October 2008, additional mortgage assistance for homeowners at risk of foreclosure was introduced. The HOPE for Homeowners program, also authorized by HERA, refinances mortgages for borrowers who are having difficulty making their payments but can afford a new fixed-rate mortgage insured by the FHA. That refinancing is available, however, only if lenders are willing to write down the existing mortgage to below the new appraised value of the home, creating home equity for a borrower who may have been underwater. Some lenders may be willing to do so in order to avoid foreclosures that might be even costlier. In return, the borrower agrees to share the equity created at the beginning of this new mortgage and any future appreciation in the value of the home if the home is sold or refinanced. Unfortunately, some limitations of the program that were written into the law have limited the program's flexibility and made it less attractive to participants than it otherwise might be.

The HOPE NOW Alliance launched a new program in November 2008 that will make it easier and faster for the most at-risk homeowners to modify their mortgages and stay in their homes. The Streamlined Modification Plan expands upon the existing efforts of many lenders. Under the plan, lenders use an expedited process to modify, or restructure, a mortgage so that the homeowner can afford the monthly payments. The streamlined process will apply to at-risk borrowers who are at least 90 days late on their existing mortgages and whose loans are owned by a lender or servicer in the HOPE NOW alliance or are owned by Freddie Mac or Fannie Mae. The Streamlined Modification Plan also applies to all mortgage types.

In November 2008, HUD published a final rule reforming the regulations for the Real Estate Settlement Procedures Act (RESPA) to simplify the mortgage settlement process and improve consumers' ability to knowledgeably shop for mortgage loans. Included in the RESPA reform, which will become fully effective in January 2010, is a new uniform Good Faith Estimate (GFE) form that will inform borrowers of the charges they should expect at loan settlement and identify key features of the loan being offered, including whether the interest rate, monthly amount owed, and loan balance can rise, and if so, by how much. These disclosures will inform borrowers about potentially risky features of loan offers and vastly improve consumers' ability to compare loan offers, which should lead to improved loan terms and lower origination fees.

International Cooperation

The United States has also been at the forefront of a number of international reform efforts. U.S. Government officials have played leading roles in advancing reform measures that are being undertaken at the Financial Stability Forum, the Basel Committee on Banking Supervision, the Committee on Payment and Settlement Systems, and the International Organization of Securities Commissions. Since the onset of the global crisis, the Administration and the Federal Reserve have been cooperating even more closely with overseas partners. For example, in October 2008, the Federal Reserve and other central banks around the world enacted a remarkable coordinated cut in interest rates, which will help ease the pressure on credit markets around the world. In addition, starting at the end of 2007, the United States bolstered U.S. dollar liquidity in European financial markets by setting up dollar *swap facilities* (or *swap lines*) with European central banks, including the Bank of England, the European Central Bank, and the Swiss National Bank, among others. A dollar swap facility allows a foreign central bank to swap its currency for U.S. dollars from the Federal Reserve at a predetermined exchange rate. European central banks use swap lines to provide dollars to European commercial banks to help them meet their dollar-denominated funding needs during a period when investors are unwilling to be counterparties to dollar-denominated liabilities. European central banks swapped local currency for dollars with the Federal Reserve in order to limit disruptions to financial and currency markets. Starting in October 2008, the Federal Reserve removed the limits on swap lines for a number of foreign central banks and provided limited swap lines to other countries, including new $30 billion swap facilities for Brazil, Mexico, Singapore, and South Korea.

On November 15, 2008, the United States hosted the first of what is expected to be a series of summits of leaders of major developed and developing countries to move forward in addressing the financial crisis in its international dimensions. These efforts build on the ongoing international efforts to better coordinate financial disclosure and regulation standards. To this end, the United States has participated fully in the efforts of a special working group of the Financial Stability Forum (FSF) formed in 2007. (For an explanation of the FSF, see "Looking Forward" below.)

Recapitalizing the Financial Sector

The Government has undertaken a historic effort to address the underlying problem behind the freeze in the credit markets. In October 2008, Congress passed bipartisan legislation, the Emergency Economic Stabilization Act of 2008 (EESA), authorizing the Treasury Department to use up to $700 billion in a Troubled Asset Relief Program (TARP) to stabilize financial markets. Under its authority, the Treasury Department announced that it would purchase up to $250 billion in non-voting preferred stock (a stock that represents ownership in a corporation with a higher claim on assets and earnings than common stock) in Federally regulated banks and thrifts in a Capital Purchase Program (CPP). In addition to stock, the Treasury would also receive warrants (options to buy additional shares of stock at a predetermined price) from the participating institutions. By the end of December 2008, Treasury had invested $177.5 billion in 215 U.S. financial institutions through the CPP. The new capital will help banks fill the gaps created by losses during the financial crisis, so that the banks can resume lending to businesses and consumers. In addition to banks, the Treasury has purchased preferred stock in systemically important non-bank financial institutions, which have also experienced large losses. For example, $40 billion of the $700 billion TARP fund has been used to purchase preferred shares in insurance giant AIG.

Results So Far

Although it is much too soon to be able to conduct a complete evaluation of the results of government responses to the global financial crisis, some signs of improvement in financial conditions are already emerging. The first, and perhaps most important, sign is that the financial system is noticeably more stable than just a few months ago. Ongoing capital injections under the TARP are providing necessary capital as banks begin to decrease their reliance on financial leverage, a process called "deleveraging."

TARP-provided capital is also addressing concerns about the potential insolvency of systemically important financial institutions. Government guarantee programs are providing confidence in money funds and FDIC-insured deposit accounts. As a result, the uncertainty that led to runs has abated and financial institutions now can rely on a more secure deposit base.

The increased confidence in a more stable financial system has laid the foundation for credit market improvements. Although conditions are still strained, banks are beginning to lend to each other again. Interbank lending rates, while still elevated, have fallen dramatically since mid-October (see Chart 2-6). Credit spreads on bank debt are declining from their recent peaks. Federal Reserve credit facilities are providing the necessary liquidity for money funds to invest in commercial paper. Chart 2-8 shows that commercial paper spreads have been decreasing and that volumes are beginning to recover. These trends suggest that firms relying on access to short-term funding are able to borrow at reasonable rates again.

As shown in Chart 2-9, mortgage rates have also declined from their recent peaks. Rates on *conforming mortgages,* which are mortgages that conform to loan purchasing guidelines set by Fannie Mae and Freddie Mac, have benefited the most from recent actions such as the Federal Reserve's announced intentions to purchase large volumes of agency debt and MBS backed by agencies. Rates on non-conforming mortgages, such as "jumbos" (mortgages that exceed the conforming loan limits), have also benefited. However, rates still appear high relative to long-term Treasury rates, suggesting that investors continue to attach a substantial risk premium to risky assets, such as mortgage-related assets.

Improvements in long-term capital markets have been slower. The stock market is still volatile. However, highly rated corporate and municipal bond issuers have been able to issue bonds at slightly lower interest rates than before the crisis came to a head in the summer of 2008.

Chart 2-8 **Commercial Paper**
Oustanding commercial paper fell dramatically as asset-backed commercial paper (ABCP) spreads spiked in the summer of 2007 and the early fall of 2008 before recovering in late fall.

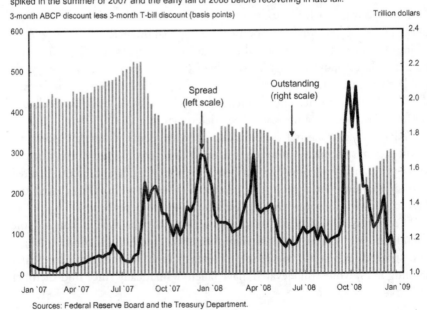

Sources: Federal Reserve Board and the Treasury Department.

Chart 2-9 Conforming and Jumbo Mortgage Rates
Interest rates on jumbo and conforming 30-year fixed-rate mortgages fell at the end of 2008.

Percent annual rate

Source: Bankrate.com.

Looking Forward

The current global financial crisis will create challenges for some time to come. These challenges include developing a new regulatory structure for financial markets, carefully unwinding programs put in place to stem the crisis, and developing a sustainable framework for mortgage financing.

Developing a New Regulatory Structure for Financial Markets

The current financial system has outgrown its supervisory and regulatory structures, which were designed decades ago. The new structure requires balancing the need to encourage vital innovation with the need to deter excessive risk taking. The new structure also requires the flexibility to adapt to market innovations.

The Treasury Blueprint for a Modernized Financial Structure

In March 2007, the Treasury convened a panel to discuss the competitiveness of U.S. capital markets. Industry leaders and policymakers alike agreed that the competitiveness of our financial services sector is constrained by an outdated financial regulatory framework. The panel released its blueprint in March 2008, which presents a series of recommendations for reforming the U.S. regulatory structure. These recommendations include merging of some of the regulatory agencies that oversee banks with some of the agencies that oversee other financial institutions, taking into account the blurring distinctions between types of financial products; creating an optional Federal charter for insurance to encourage a more competitive U.S. insurance industry; and creating an objectives-based regulatory approach. More information on these recommendations is on the Treasury's website.

PWG Initiatives to Strengthen Oversight and the Infrastructure of the OTC Derivatives Market

The President's Working Group on Financial Markets (PWG), which consists of the Secretary of the Treasury, the Chair of the Board of Governors of the Federal Reserve System, the Chair of the Securities and Exchange Commission, and the Chair of the Commodity Futures Trading Commission, announced a series of initiatives to strengthen oversight and the infrastructure of the *over-the-counter* derivatives market. Many derivatives are traded over the counter (OTC), which means that they are privately negotiated and traded between counterparties, without going through an organized exchange or intermediary. One type of derivative contract that has become very popular in recent years is the *credit default swap* (CDS). (See the section "The Onset of the Crisis" earlier in this chapter for an explanation of CDS contracts.) While appropriate use of CDS contracts can help market participants manage some risks, these contracts bring with them exposure to additional firms and additional risks.

On November 14, 2008, the PWG established four specific policy objectives for the OTC derivatives market, with a primary focus on credit default swaps. The first objective is to improve market transparency and integrity for CDS so regulators and investors can access information that could help them effectively monitor the CDS market and make efficient investment decisions. The second objective is to enhance risk management of OTC derivatives by encouraging market participants to adopt standard best practices, including public reporting, liquidity management, senior management oversight, and counterparty credit risk management. The third objective is to strengthen the derivatives market infrastructure. For example, the PWG is supporting industry efforts to establish a central counterparty clearing facility for derivatives that would help to reduce systemic risk and make clear how a major participant's failure would be addressed. The fourth objective is to continue cooperation among regulatory authorities by expanding existing frameworks for cooperation, coordination, and information sharing among U.S. regulatory agencies, as well as international jurisdictions with significant OTC derivatives activity.

Developing Common International Principles

Leaders from the United States and other major nations are holding a series of summits to discuss efforts to strengthen economic growth, respond to the financial crisis, and lay the foundation for reform to help ensure that a similar crisis does not happen again. The initial "Summit on Financial Markets and the World Economy" took place on November 15, 2008, in Washington, D.C., and the leaders from the participating countries agreed on common principles for reforming financial markets and keeping international markets open to trade and investment. The leaders agreed to implement financial market reforms that include addressing weaknesses in accounting and disclosure standards for "off-balance-sheet vehicles" (explained in the next section); ensuring that credit rating agencies avoid conflicts of interest, provide greater disclosure to investors, and differentiate ratings for complex products; ensuring that firms maintain adequate capital; developing enhanced guidance to strengthen banks' risk-management practices; establishing processes whereby national supervisors that oversee globally active financial institutions meet and share information; and expanding the Financial Stability Forum (FSF) to include a broader membership of emerging economies.

The Financial Stability Forum is an organization whose members are senior representatives from national financial authorities (Australia, Canada, France, Germany, Hong Kong, Italy, Japan, the Netherlands, Singapore, Switzerland, the United Kingdom, and the United States), international groups (for example, the International Monetary Fund and the World Bank), and central bank committees. The FSF's stated mandate is to assess vulnerabilities affecting the international financial system, to identify and oversee action needed to address these, and to improve coordination and information exchange among the various authorities responsible for financial stability. Leaders at the November 15, 2008, financial summit called upon the FSF to take an active role in drawing lessons from the current crisis, improving transparency in accounting standards, and strengthening prudential regulatory standards.

Unwinding Temporary Programs

The Government's efforts to restore stability and provide liquidity to the financial system introduced many programs whose continued existence the Government must evaluate as the crisis abates. Some programs should be phased out according to a preannounced schedule, while others should be phased out naturally as the costs of participation come to outweigh the benefits.

One program that is set to end in less than 1 year is the Treasury temporary guarantee program for money market funds that were deposited before September 19, 2008. This program was set up with an initial term of several months, after which the Secretary of the Treasury would review the need and terms for the program and the costs to provide the coverage. If the program is extended, funds will have the opportunity to renew their purchase of ongoing coverage. The Secretary has the option to extend the program until September 2009 at the latest.

Two programs that will likely be phased out over the next 5 years are the Federal Reserve's new credit facilities and the Treasury's Capital Purchase Program (CPP). Aside from the Federal Reserve's term auction facility, the new credit facilities' preannounced termination dates are all within the next 2 years, unless the Federal Reserve determines that conditions warrant postponing these dates. The Treasury's authority to make additional capital purchases expires at the end of 2009. In addition, the CPP provides a strong incentive for participants to raise private capital to pay off the Government capital injection within 5 years, as the cost of these funds rises over time. That is, the senior preferred shares issued to the U.S. Treasury in the program carry a 5 percent dividend for the first 5 years, rising to 9 percent thereafter.

The FDIC has several programs with preannounced end dates in 2009. The Temporary Liquidity Guarantee Program is a new program that guarantees the unsecured medium-term debt of all FDIC-insured institutions and grants unlimited insurance for non-interest-bearing transaction accounts used by many small businesses. Another program is the expansion of the existing deposit insurance program for savings accounts, checking accounts, and certificates of deposits from $100,000 to $250,000.

Modernizing Financial Regulation

The global financial crisis revealed that current financial regulation standards and practices, in the United States and throughout the world, are ineffective in preventing a major financial crisis that spans countries and different institutions. While no practical system of regulation could likely have prevented such a crisis altogether, a number of important lessons are clear.

Addressing Innovation and Restructuring in Financial Markets

First, financial regulation must be adapted to account for the major innovations and restructuring in financial markets in recent decades. The current U.S. financial regulatory framework is fraught with redundancies and gaps, in part produced by more than one regulator overseeing individual institutions.

Depository institutions, such as commercial banks and savings associations, are overseen by five Federal regulators as well as State regulators. Large holding companies with depository institutions, investment banks, and insurance companies may face a complex system of multiple regulators.

While it is clear that an overhaul of financial regulation is necessary, what is less clear is exactly how a new regulatory framework should be structured. The new financial regulatory framework needs to balance several objectives. Protecting investors and consumers and establishing a stable financial system are two necessary requirements for any successful regulatory system, but regulators must be careful to balance these goals against potential detrimental effects on capital formation and the desire to promote beneficial innovation.

Strengthening Disclosure Requirements

Second, regulators need to strengthen disclosures related to complex financial instruments, particularly those that are held "off balance sheet." A firm's balance sheet is one of many financial statements the firm prepares to provide useful information to investors, creditors, and regulators. The purpose of a balance sheet is to present a snapshot of the firm's financial position. The basic components of a balance sheet are assets, liabilities, and equity. *Assets* are things that provide probable future economic benefit to the firm. *Liabilities* are claims on those assets, such as debt issued to finance the purchase of assets. *Equity* is the residual interest in the assets that remains after deducting the liabilities.

While the above definitions appear straightforward, many questions and issues arise regarding whether certain items should be reported as liabilities or as equity. In addition, questions arise in determining which items should be reflected on the balance sheet at all. The formal accounting standards that are used to distinguish between on- and off-balance-sheet items are very complicated and are open to judgment. As a result, some companies may hold large amounts of off-balance-sheet items that do indeed affect a company's health and stability. For example, at the outset of the financial crisis, some large financial institutions had *structured investment vehicles* (SIVs) holding billions of dollars in mortgage-related assets that were not reflected on their balance sheets.

SIVs are investment funds that issue short-term debt, such as commercial paper, to finance the purchase of long-term assets, such as mortgage-backed securities. Leading up to the financial crisis, SIVs were often highly levered with a great deal of debt relative to their capital. In fact, some SIVs were used to circumvent regulatory capital requirements that restricted the amount of leverage that could be used by the parent financial institutions. In the end, the SIVs' combination of leverage and reliance on short-term funding made their parent financial institutions vulnerable to large mortgage losses. Many investors were surprised because institutions had disclosed little about the risks posed by the off-balance-sheet SIVs.

The challenge for financial market regulators is to address weaknesses in accounting and disclosure standards for off-balance-sheet items. Once complete and accurate information on the financial condition of firms is disclosed, regulators can more effectively measure firm-specific and system-wide risks. Then regulators can prudently manage those risks as appropriate.

Addressing the Pro-Cyclicality of Regulatory Capital Requirements

Third, problems with pro-cyclical regulatory capital requirements need to be addressed. During good economic times, values of financial assets increase, thus increasing a firm's capital and its ability to increase its liabilities, which helps to feed credit booms. During difficult times, values of financial assets decline. The firm's capital declines in value, and it is forced to reduce its liabilities or somehow increase its capital to satisfy regulatory requirements, which feeds the economic downturn.

The combination of mark-to-market accounting, illiquid markets, and forced sales to satisfy regulatory capital requirements during a downturn can lead to a vicious cycle. *Mark-to-market* accounting is one method for determining an asset's fair value. A *fair value* is the price that would be received if an asset were sold in an orderly transaction between market participants. The mark-to-market approach uses observable market prices to calculate an asset's fair value. An alternative valuation method is the *mark-to-model* approach, which relies on standard financial models that use factors such as interest rates, the probability of default, and related cash flows to calculate an asset's fair value.

Some observers have blamed mark-to-market accounting for driving asset prices well below the values determined by the asset's underlying fundamentals, such as interest rates and probabilities of default. These observers argue that understated asset values undermine investor confidence and have forced many firms to raise capital or sell assets to satisfy regulatory requirements. However, as discussed previously, problems at many financial institutions today are due less to their asset values being undervalued and more to the firms having too many troubled assets (such as MBS), engaging in poor risk management, and becoming too dependent on short-term borrowing. Mark-to-market accounting has helped bring attention to these problems by exposing which firms were very heavily invested in these troubled assets, but it did not cause them.

Investors and regulators can best evaluate a firm when they are aware of the market value of a firm's assets. Transparency is vital to the healthy functioning of financial markets. To effectively address the pro-cyclicality problem, in which firms may be forced to undertake actions in a downturn that worsen the downturn, financial accounting rules should be distinguished from the regulatory policies that establish standards for capital requirements. The purpose of financial accounting is to provide reliable information about a firm's financial situation so that investors and creditors can make sound economic decisions. From that perspective, mark-to-market accounting is useful because it improves the quality of information in the marketplace.

As noted earlier, some observers have argued that falling asset prices in acutely distressed markets have led firms to report reduced levels of capital. Then, in order to comply with regulatory capital requirements, firms have sold assets, thus driving prices lower. Even if this selling of assets in order to comply with requirements is responsible for the subsequent asset price declines, mark-to-market accounting is not the root cause. Instead, the problem lies with a regulatory policy that is too rigid in determining capital requirements. When most asset values are falling, massive sales of assets to meet the required ratio of capital to assets are likely to be destabilizing. To reduce this problem, regulators could maintain more flexible and forward-looking standards in distressed markets, so that capital requirements themselves do not create unhealthy firms.

The Future of Mortgage Financing and Fannie Mae and Freddie Mac

Over the first half of 2008, investors became increasingly concerned about the capital positions of the GSEs Fannie Mae and Freddie Mac, following a string of quarterly losses by both firms due to reductions in the value of their portfolio holdings of MBS and mortgage loans, and because of greater-than-expected credit losses. Eroding investor confidence in the GSEs endangered not only the U.S. mortgage market but the global financial system more generally, given the central role the GSEs play in mortgage financing and how broadly their debt and MBS are held around the world. At the recommendation of the Administration, Congress passed a bill in July 2008 that, among other things, created a new and stronger regulator for the GSEs, the Federal Housing Finance Agency (FHFA), and provided the Treasury with powers to purchase GSE debt and equity.

In September 2008, Fannie Mae and Freddie Mac were placed under conservatorship of the FHFA as serious concerns surfaced about the financial stability of these systemically important financial institutions. (See "Onset of the Crisis" above.) While conservatorship can provide necessary stability over a period of months, a long-term plan to reestablish the link between mortgage lenders and financial markets is critical to the future of the mortgage market.

Any plan for the long-term restructuring of Fannie Mae and Freddie Mac should have at its core at least three goals: to promote the efficient functioning of the mortgage market, even during periods of systemwide financial stress; to minimize systemic risk, which likely implies that government support should be either explicit or absent; and to protect the taxpayer.

Liquidation of the GSEs and Replacement by a Fully Private Market

One approach is to liquidate the GSEs and allow the private market alone to handle mortgage financing, maximizing the benefits of private market competition. The structure would be one in which private banks and other financial institutions securitize mortgages as a part of their business model, but no single firm would be a dominant player in this market, and the mortgage securitization business would make up only a fraction of the total business of each institution. This solution would dramatically reduce taxpayer risk, maintain a functioning mortgage market in most situations, and eliminate distortions. The elimination of any implicit or explicit government guarantee would, however, increase mortgage interest rates somewhat. This is one reason that the full privatization of mortgage financing may not be the best option in the near term, despite its attractive features.

Importantly, recent experience suggests that fully private financing may not be viable under stressed financial conditions. As an example, the recent financial crisis led to a near-halt in private mortgage securitization in the United States. In contrast, Fannie Mae and Freddie Mac continued to produce and sell large quantities of MBS throughout 2008, with private demand remaining somewhat secure. Apparently, investors valued GSE MBS because of the instruments' implied government support, suggesting that some form of backstop provided by the Government or widely dispersed private reinsurers may be necessary to maintain mortgage financing during periods of systemwide financial stress.

Government-Provided Insurance of MBS

The Government could sell insurance to GSEs and other financial institutions that apply for a charter to create MBS from conforming mortgages. This structure would foster competition among institutions, as the GSEs would have no institutional advantage over private institutions. Such a structure, with its explicit but limited role for government involvement, may be a good near-term solution for mortgage financing. Taxpayers would bear risk, but would be compensated by the insurance premiums paid by participating institutions. Depending on where the price of the insurance is set, the private sector could eventually compete with the Government by offering alternative mortgage products that could replace the Government insurance.

Nationalizing the GSEs

Another GSE structure that has been proposed by some but poses many challenges is nationalization. In this alternative, the GSEs could be taken out of conservatorship and be fully nationalized. As government corporations, they would be set up to guarantee conforming mortgages or MBS directly. What is less clear is how nationalization would be accomplished: Would the GSEs' debt become the Government's debt? What would happen to the equity held by existing shareholders? In addition, if Government prices for this guarantee were below the costs incurred by private markets, private competition for securitization would be precluded. Although systemic risk would be eliminated and the GSEs would have little incentive to engage in excessively risky behavior for short-run profits without shareholders, taxpayers could bear substantial risk. Finally, the terms of mortgage financing would be set by the Government, a role that can be fulfilled by the private sector.

Turning the GSEs into a Public Utility

Alternatively, Fannie Mae and Freddie Mac could be combined and turned into one public utility. This regulated private corporation would directly issue MBS, presumably with some government backing. Prices of the MBS and their rates of return would be set by a commission, and regulations would place tight limits on the company's investment portfolio. Public utilities are generally established in natural monopoly settings (because, for example, building duplicate telephone or power lines is inefficient) as a second-best solution to prevent monopoly pricing and guarantee public service. The mortgage market is not a natural monopoly, however, and can be easily served by many firms without duplicative inefficiency. As a consequence, a public utility would result in many distortions and disadvantages without significant offsetting positives.

Implicit Guarantees

The issue of distortions arising from implicit government guarantees is not limited to Fannie Mae and Freddie Mac. An increasingly important source of financing for depository institutions in recent years has been the Federal Home Loan Banks (FHLBs). As of the third quarter of 2008, the FHLBs had granted nearly $1 trillion in loans. These loans, often backed by real estate–related collateral, have been extended to the majority of depository institutions in the United States. The FHLBs raise funds at below-market rates because they have advantages over other debt issuers, such as certain exemptions from State and local taxes and an assumed implicit government guarantee even though the FHLBs are private member-owned cooperatives. Some of these savings are passed along to member banks, who, as a result, rely—in some cases very heavily—on financing from the FHLBs. Any long-term plan for mortgage financing must eliminate the distortions in credit markets created by implicit guarantees of this nature.

Conclusion

The United States experienced a crisis in both financial markets and housing markets in 2008. One factor that led to this crisis was an abundance of inexpensive capital that helped finance a housing boom. This boom was fueled by the growth of subprime mortgages and expanded mortgage securitization. As the boom proved unsustainable, the crisis was exacerbated by unprecedented declines in house prices, rising default rates on residential mortgages, and a resulting sharp decline in the value of mortgage-related assets. The assets were held by a wide range of institutions, some of which were highly levered and highly dependent on short-term funding. The resulting failure and near-failure of some of these firms, combined with broad-based declines in asset prices, placed enormous stresses on world financial markets. Credit markets froze, and confidence in the financial system eroded.

The Administration and the Federal Reserve aggressively responded to restore stability to the U.S. financial system and support the functioning of financial markets and firms. The Government has taken unprecedented action to boost liquidity in short-term funding markets; provided substantial new protections for consumers, businesses, and investors; and cooperated closely with its international partners. Looking ahead, the global financial crisis presents several challenges for the United States. Among them are the need to improve financial regulation, unwind temporary programs in an orderly fashion, and develop long-term solutions for Fannie Mae and Freddie Mac.

CHAPTER 3

Energy and the Environment

Although fossil fuels will continue to compose a large share of the U.S. energy portfolio for some time, the Federal Government has taken major steps to increase and diversify the Nation's energy supply and improve the environment. Since 2001, the Government has made significant investments to develop cleaner and more reliable energy sources. Several regulatory changes are expected to deliver dramatic improvements in air quality nationwide. The President has signed two major pieces of energy legislation, the Energy Policy Act (EPACT) of 2005 and the Energy Independence and Security Act of 2007 (EISA). EISA was enacted in response to the President's "Twenty in Ten" goal, issued in the 2007 State of the Union Address, of reducing U.S. gasoline usage by 20 percent in the next 10 years by improving fuel economy and increasing the production of alternative fuels. EISA also includes numerous energy efficiency mandates that are projected to result in substantial reductions in greenhouse gas (GHG) emissions. In addition, the Nation is on track to meet—and currently projected to exceed—the President's 2002 goal of reducing U.S. GHG intensity (emissions per unit of GDP) by 18 percent by 2012. This spring, the President set a new goal of stopping the growth in total U.S. GHG emissions by 2025 and to begin decreasing them thereafter. The Administration has also recently led efforts to encourage wider international action on addressing GHGs, including action in developing countries.

Despite these steps by the Administration to address the problems associated with the country's reliance on fossil fuel–based energy sources, major challenges remain. For public health and environmental reasons, the United States must continue to improve air quality by ensuring that State and local areas come into compliance with Clean Air Act (CAA) requirements. Additional steps should be taken to mitigate the global problem of rising GHG emissions associated with fossil fuel–based energy consumption. Furthermore, diversifying the Nation's portfolio of energy sources and increasing domestic production may reduce vulnerabilities associated with the U.S. dependence on imported fossil fuels.

This chapter discusses policies for addressing the Nation's energy needs in the context of both global climate change and the reduction of local and regional pollution associated with fossil fuel–based energy use. It reviews some of the steps this Administration has taken to advance the transition to new sources of energy with fewer environmental and security concerns, and to find cleaner, more efficient methods of using existing energy sources. It also identifies some of the overarching challenges that lie ahead in developing any comprehensive energy policy.

The key points in this chapter are:

- Because of innovative regulations promulgated under this Administration, there should be substantial improvements in air quality over the next few decades. Two rules that implemented cap-and-trade programs in the electricity sector represent a significant step in using cost-effective, market-oriented policy instruments to dramatically reduce power plants' emissions of sulfur dioxide, nitrogen oxide, and mercury.

- Despite widespread support for increased use of market-based approaches to achieve our environmental and energy policy goals going forward, challenges remain in realizing the full potential of these approaches.

- There is an increasing need to reassess how well existing laws can address the environmental problems associated with fossil fuel use in more cost-effective ways. For example, it may become increasingly costly to make additional reductions in traditional air pollutants, and existing statutes were not meant to regulate global problems such as GHG emissions.

- Substantial reductions in global GHG emissions will require participation by all large emitters (countries and sectors within countries).

U.S. Energy Use and Policy Goals

Fossil fuels continue to satisfy the majority of the Nation's demand for energy. Petroleum accounts for about 40 percent of total energy consumption; 70 percent of this petroleum is used for transportation. Coal and natural gas are the next most commonly used fuel types, representing 22 percent and 23 percent of consumption, respectively. Coal is used almost exclusively for electricity production; approximately a third of natural gas consumption is also used in electricity production, with the remaining two-thirds being used directly by residential, commercial, and industrial sources. Finally, nuclear power and renewable energy sources such as hydropower, biomass, geothermal, wind, and solar power remain a small but growing share of our energy consumption, with nuclear power accounting for approximately 8 percent of U.S. energy consumption in 2007 and renewable energy accounting for approximately 7 percent. (See the 2008 *Economic Report of the President* for more details on U.S. energy sources.)

The Nation's current patterns of energy use pose a number of problems that warrant government involvement in energy markets. One is the concern over the public health and environmental effects of fossil fuel–based energy production and use. In particular, the emission of many common air pollutants that are created by the combustion of fossil fuels increases the risk of premature mortality and numerous acute and chronic health conditions. Additionally, these emissions damage ecosystems, impair visibility, and have a substantial impact on water and soil quality. In this chapter, "common air pollutants" refers to the so-called *criteria pollutants* (particulate matter (PM), ozone, nitrogen oxides (NO_x), sulfur dioxide (SO_2), carbon monoxide (CO), and lead), although much that is written about the criteria pollutants also applies to hazardous air pollutants or air toxics.

As in many other countries, anthropogenic (human-made) U.S. GHG emissions continue to increase. Because of the environmental risks posed by climate change and the national security implications of events like droughts and rising sea levels, many countries have grown more aware of the need to slow and reverse the growth of global emissions of carbon dioxide (CO_2) and other greenhouse gases. In 2007, total U.S. GHG emissions were 7,282 million metric tons of CO_2 equivalent (MMTCO2e), a 3-percent increase over 2000 levels; this increase is mainly attributable to energy use. Energy-related CO_2 emissions account for 98 percent of U.S. CO_2 emissions and more than 80 percent of total U.S. GHG emissions. The United States represented about 17 percent of world GHG emissions in recent years.

For energy security reasons, concerns also remain about the U.S. reliance on imported fossil fuels. Net oil imports to the United States account for a substantial share of national oil consumption, which many argue makes the United States economy more vulnerable to oil price shocks that are the result of supply disruptions in unstable exporting regions. However, as economists have pointed out, it is important to remember that it is primarily U.S. oil dependence, rather than U.S. dependence on imported oil, that exposes the country to turmoil in world oil markets. Given the integrated nature of the oil market, a supply disruption in one region still removes oil from the world market causing the price of oil to rise regardless of where it was produced.

Despite a weak economic outlook for 2009, projections indicate that energy consumption in the United States and around the world will continue to grow in the long run. Thus, we will need to continue to determine how to meet these needs while both addressing energy security concerns and improving environmental protection. It is clear that long-term policies aimed at reducing the Nation's overall reliance on fossil fuels can help to advance both goals. However, taking intermediate steps that help us use fossil fuels in more responsible ways during the transition to alternative sources of energy is still consistent with this long-term objective. For example, this Administration has supported removing regulatory impediments to bringing domestic energy sources, including fossil fuels, to market, to advance energy security objectives. It has also supported finding cleaner ways of using fossil fuels. Some of the Administration's efforts on each of these fronts are covered later in this chapter. Before that, the next section provides a brief overview of policy approaches for addressing these objectives.

The Promise of Market-Oriented Policy Approaches

This section reviews the advantages of market-oriented policies, while noting some of the challenges that must be overcome to use them most effectively in tackling some policy objectives such as climate change. This section also discusses the role for policies supporting research and development and widespread adoption of new technologies that pose fewer environmental or security concerns.

Market-Oriented Environmental Regulation

Regulatory approaches for addressing the policy goals outlined above are often grouped roughly into two categories: conventional, or *command and control* approaches, and market-oriented approaches. Conventional approaches to reducing pollution, for example, tend to involve policy instruments that mandate the amount individual entities can emit or prescribe which abatement behaviors or technologies should be adopted. These types of policies are often called command and control approaches because they offer little flexibility about how a particular environmental goal may be met (although, among command and control approaches, performance-based standards can offer a bit more flexibility in achieving abatement goals than do technology-based standards). Market-oriented approaches, by contrast, encourage behavior through price signals rather than with explicit standards on pollution-control levels or methods. Policy tools such as tradeable permits or taxes, for example, offer firms an incentive to reduce their pollution by placing a price on each ton of pollutant emitted.

The primary advantage of market-oriented policies is that, if they are designed well and properly implemented, they have the potential to achieve environmental goals at a lower cost to society than traditional command and control policies. This is because of the greater flexibility they offer in determining how to reduce emissions. If emitters can choose the method of pollution reduction, they have an incentive to find the lowest-cost way to meet the regulatory requirement. For example, policymakers could require producers and consumers to take into account the environmental and public health effects of a criteria pollutant like sulfur dioxide by imposing a tax on emissions that is equal to the incremental damage caused by a unit of emissions or by establishing a *cap-and-trade* program, under which policymakers set an overall cap on emissions but allow regulated entities to trade rights (called *allowances*) to those limited emissions. Since the cost of reducing emissions may vary across firms and sectors, what may be the least expensive approach for one firm may be a relatively high-cost approach for another firm. Emitters that can reduce emissions most inexpensively will do so and then sell allowances to those who face much higher abatement costs. As a result, the most economically efficient allocation of the pollution-control burden among emitters can be achieved without requiring the policymaker to make assumptions about how compliance costs may vary across firms.

Another significant advantage of market-oriented approaches is that they can provide a greater incentive to develop new ways to reduce pollution than can command and control approaches. Command and control policies often offer incentives to abate only to the level of the standard, whereas a pricing approach encourages emitters to continue to innovate as long as they find it relatively cheap to do so. Well-designed pricing of CO_2 emissions through a tax or cap-and-trade program, for example, would give firms a direct incentive to invest in developing new low- or zero-carbon technologies based on their expectations of the increases in the costs of emissions. It would also encourage competition in making incremental innovations in existing emission reduction options. Of course, it will be important to address hurdles in providing the infrastructure necessary to allow large-scale deployment of new technologies, a point to which we return below.

Both of these advantages have created widespread support among economists for greater use of emission pricing policies to address environmental problems, including those problems associated with fossil fuel–based energy use. However, it is important to emphasize that challenges remain in realizing the full potential of market-oriented policy approaches. This is especially true in the context of climate change. Carbon pricing through a cap-and-trade system or, closely related, by taxing fossil fuels in proportion to their carbon content, will require broad-based participation to be effective in addressing global GHG concentrations. Limited action that does not result in emissions reductions from countries that contribute a significant share of world emissions will not lead to significant progress on climate change goals, since the majority of the future growth in emissions will come from developing nations. Absent action by all major emitting countries, it will be impossible to have a meaningful impact on the problem. Also, without similar policies across these countries, firms in energy-intensive industries that face high regulatory costs in the U.S. could have an incentive to move their operations to unregulated foreign markets. These issues and other challenges in implementing more economically efficient policies are discussed in greater detail below.

The Role for Technology Inducement Policies

Another method policymakers often use to give incentives for taking into account the environmental or security consequences of a particular behavior is to subsidize behavior that poses fewer environmental or security concerns.

For example, similar to the way a business reacts to a price signal such as an emissions tax, a profit-maximizing business will abate pollution or invest in research and development (R&D) in cleaner technologies up to the point where the cost is more than the subsidy or reward earned for doing so. This is not to imply that a tax and subsidy are equivalent policies. A tax generates revenue that can be used to offset other preexisting distortionary taxes (such as payroll taxes) in the economy, whereas a subsidy requires that revenue be raised by increasing existing taxes or requires reducing spending in other areas. Still, many economists maintain that, as a complement to any pricing policy, governments will need to support R&D for alternative energy sources and ensure that any R&D support is managed efficiently and effectively. These policies may be justified on economic grounds primarily because the process of generating and diffusing new energy technologies is characterized by imperfect market outcomes. The most significant of these is the general underinvestment in innovation due to the pure public-good nature of R&D. Because devoting a firm's resources to innovation may yield *knowledge spillovers*—benefits to society that do not translate into profits for the innovating firm—there may be an inefficient, low level of R&D in alternative energy technologies. This problem has long been recognized in all industries, and there are numerous policies in place to help innovators reap the rewards of their innovations (for example, patents, copyright laws, funding for general science research).

In assessing the desirability of public sector support for research and development, one might consider the extent to which private sector incentives for R&D already exist. Private incentives for R&D investment may vary across categories of prospective R&D:

- *Emission control for currently regulated pollutants.* In this case, there are regulatory incentives for the private sector to develop technologies that control emissions, but there will only be incentives to develop technologies that reduce emissions in ways captured by regulation.
- *Energy efficiency, new energy sources, and alternative energy.* Since energy is an expensive input, there are strong private sector incentives to develop new or improved technologies even without any government regulation. Support for public sector R&D in this area would be specifically justified if individual producers and consumers do not account for the broader value of energy security or of positive spillovers to others from the technology that goes with the new alternative.
- *Emissions from pollutants that are not currently regulated.* In this case, the incentive for private sector R&D is very limited, because prospective developers are not only uncertain about whether their new invention will work, but also must consider if or when the pollutant will be regulated, and whether their technology will be acceptable under future regulations.

Technologies to reduce emissions of non-CO_2 greenhouse gases are among those that are not currently regulated, as are technologies that would capture and store such gases to prevent them from entering the atmosphere.

It is important to highlight that domestic R&D support for alternative technologies may also help create incentives for action on climate change by other major emitting countries that are unwilling or unable to adopt GHG-reducing regulations. For example, investment in developing low-cost, low-carbon technologies could lead to inventions that such countries would adopt voluntarily. Additionally, it is often argued that production costs of new, unproven technologies fall as manufacturers gain production experience. If the gains from such "learning by doing" experience can be captured by other producers without compensating the early adopters, then there may be inefficient, low deployment of new technologies.

The difficulty in promoting technology adoption through subsidies and other tools lies in designing policies that are neutral across all alternative technologies. Weighting the size of a subsidy by the degree to which each technology reduces environmental and security concerns would help to ensure that the Government is not in the position of picking winners. In April 2008, the President called for a reform of the existing low-carbon technology deployment tax incentives into a single, expanded incentive with such features. We return to this issue below. Overall, there is less agreement among economists about the justification for these types of policies that target the commercial use of a technology than those that target the R&D stage of the technology innovation process. Many argue that once fundamental research is no longer necessary, the market should decide how widely a new technology is adopted.

Increasing Use of Alternative Energy Sources

There are many alternatives to fossil fuels available for meeting our energy needs in the electricity, transportation, and other sectors. Electricity may be generated using renewable sources (such as wind, solar, geothermal, biomass, and hydropower) or nuclear power. In the transportation sector, solutions range from finding new fuels for traditionally gas-powered vehicles to designing different types of vehicles such as those that run on electricity or hydrogen. Policy tools used under this Administration to promote the transition to some of these alternatives can be grouped into two categories: technology policies that provide incentives to encourage R&D and deployment of new technologies, and mandates that require increases in alternative energy use.

Generating Electricity

In the electricity sector, the Administration has supported development of alternative energy technologies through a mix of incentives, including both basic research investment and technology deployment policies. Department of Energy funding for electricity-related R&D, for example, totaled $11.5 billion (2007 dollars) from fiscal year 2002 through fiscal year 2007. This section reviews some of the existing incentives for promoting electricity generation from renewable energy sources and nuclear power.

Renewable Energy

Renewable sources of energy such as wind, solar, and geothermal power are desirable for generating electricity because, despite their high initial fixed costs, they are domestic sources of power with no fuel costs or emissions except those involved in building the infrastructure required to generate the power. Biomass-fired electricity, which is derived from sources such as wood, waste, and alcohol fuels, is also a renewable source. While not technically a zero-emission process, biomass energy produces fewer common air pollutants than coal and, depending on the feedstock and firing process, has the potential to create fewer GHG emissions than either conventional coal or natural gas. This Administration has encouraged deployment of renewable energy technologies in electricity generation primarily through tax incentives. For example, the renewable energy production tax credit (PTC) has been important in encouraging the growing market for wind power. Although wind still provides only 1 percent of the United States's electricity, wind generation has grown by about 400 percent since 2001 and, in 2007, made up 10 percent of electricity generation from renewable energy sources (see Chart 3-1). This growth is in part because, in some areas, the PTC makes the cost of wind more competitive with other energy sources such as natural gas. Incentives and requirements for renewable energy use in numerous States are also contributing to the increase. The Federal PTC has been renewed and expanded several times since its original enactment in 1992, including by EPACT 2005 and again in October 2008. It is currently available for a broad range of renewable sources such as solar power; certain geothermal, landfill-gas, and biomass projects; ocean energy; and livestock methane-based power.

Renewable energy deployment is also encouraged through tax credits for investments in renewable energy equipment and property. For example, the Energy Policy Act of 2005 (EPACT) increased the solar investment tax credit (ITC), which offers businesses a tax credit for investments in solar energy equipment and installations. The 21-percent increase in solar powered electricity generation capacity between 2006 and 2007 may indicate that the solar ITC is having some effect. In order to provide clear and consistent incentives for technology investment, policies such as the PTC should be maintained for a

Chart 3-1 **U.S. Wind Power Generation, 1995–2007**

U.S. wind power generation has soared in recent years and capacity grew further in 2008.

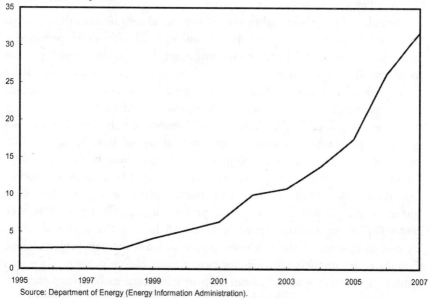

Billions of kilowatthours generated

Source: Department of Energy (Energy Information Administration).

reasonable length of time but be phased out once they are no longer warranted to address barriers associated with the early commercialization of a technology.

It is worth noting that renewable energy sources, especially wind and solar, face infrastructure obstacles because many large-scale renewable energy installations are most likely to be built in remote areas. Also, neither wind nor solar can currently be relied on as a consistent means to produce energy 24 hours a day. The challenges of bringing these resources to market and finding better ways to store energy are discussed in more detail later in the chapter.

Nuclear Power

In addition to renewable energy sources, the Administration has promoted increased use of nuclear power as a clean, efficient energy source to meet the Nation's growing need for electricity. Nuclear power is not a new technology. Currently, 104 commercial nuclear generating units (reactors) in the United States supply approximately 20 percent of the country's electricity. Nuclear power generation makes no contribution to global CO_2 emissions and produces no notable emissions of SO_2, NO_X, and particulates. In addition, nuclear plants have low operating costs and are able to operate at close to full capacity all the time, thus providing a reliable, constant supply of electricity. Despite these advantages, high construction costs, investment risks, long-term management of spent fuel generated by nuclear plants, and regulatory hurdles have deterred any new commercial reactors from being ordered and approved for construction since 1978. The last new nuclear plant came on line in 1996.

The Administration has taken several steps to address some of the concerns that are barring greater use of nuclear energy. EPACT 2005 provided a new production tax credit to reward investments in the latest developments in advanced nuclear power generation. Since then, the Nuclear Regulatory Commission has received 17 applications for combined construction permit and operating licenses for 26 new nuclear generating units.

As part of EPACT, the President also authorized the creation of loan guarantee programs to encourage commercial use of new or significantly improved energy related technologies, including nuclear power. In 2008, Congress authorized loan guarantees worth over $18 billion to support construction of new plants and enable nuclear plant owners to reduce their interest costs. A loan guarantee is a promise by the Government to take responsibility for a certain portion of a loan in case the debtor defaults. By assuming some of the risk associated with loans for new projects, these guarantees are implicit subsidies for new nuclear energy projects. If priced appropriately, loan guarantees can help to encourage early commercial use of new technologies that had been hampered by informational asymmetries between project developers and lenders. However, such guarantees should be used with caution. If the Government assumes too much of the financial or political risk associated with a new project, investors may attempt to embark on speculative projects that could end up being costly for taxpayers. This same caution applies to loan guarantee programs available to support other energy sources such as renewable and/or energy-efficient systems, cleaner coal-based power, and other technologies.

Alternative Transportation Fuels

Petroleum use in road travel dominates energy consumption in transportation. In recent years, tax incentives have increased the use of some alternatives to petroleum, especially corn-based ethanol, but there has been an increasing emphasis on promoting alternatives that do not rely on food crops and have greater promise for significantly reducing GHG emissions. The Administration's efforts in this area have focused on providing incentives and funding to develop new vehicle technologies and reliable, low-cost alternative fuels to conventional gasoline and on mandating increased use of renewable fuels, including biofuels from non-food sources.

Incentive-Based Promotion of Alternative Fuels

Federal R&D support for alternative fuels has been led by a $1.2 billion investment (over 5 years) in hydrogen-based fuel cell vehicles and about

$1 billion since 2001 in cellulosic ethanol—an ethanol produced from wood, grasses, or the nonedible parts of plants. These fuels face significant cost hurdles which currently prevent them from being commercially viable. The benefits of R&D in hydrogen vehicles will take a long time to be realized because the vehicles still face formidable technological obstacles that may take decades to resolve. The projected cost of cellulosic ethanol, however, has dropped by more than 60 percent since 2001. If these cost reductions continue, cellulosic ethanol may become a viable transportation fuel more quickly than alternatives like hydrogen. Aided by the Corporate Average Fuel Economy (CAFE) credit given to manufacturers for producing "flex-fuel" vehicles that can run on either all gasoline or up to 85 percent ethanol, the number of light-duty vehicles that can accommodate large amounts of ethanol has grown by more than 5 million since 2001 (see Chart 3-2). However, as with other types of biofuels, significant economic, scientific, environmental, and logistical challenges remain with incorporating nationally significant volumes of cellulosic ethanol into the market. Fuel distributors and gas station owners will need to make significant investments in the infrastructure for new fuel distribution and manufacturers will need to make changes to vehicles to accommodate substantially larger biofuel volumes; existing gas station infrastructure and non-flex-fuel vehicles are currently only compatible with gasoline blends consisting of up to 10 percent ethanol.

Chart 3-2 **Alternative Fuel Light-Duty Vehicles in the U.S. Fleet**
Flex-fuel vehicles, capable of burning up to 85% ethanol, have led U.S. growth in alternative-fuel vehicles.
Millions of vehicles

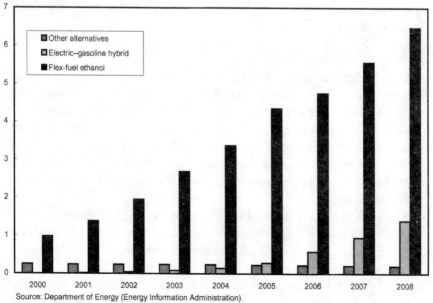

Source: Department of Energy (Energy Information Administration).

Another alternative technology that shows more near-term promise in reducing gasoline consumption is electricity for powering vehicles. The consumer tax credits created under EPACT in 2005 for purchasing electric—gasoline hybrid vehicles have helped to encourage hybrid sales, and there are now more than 1 million hybrid vehicles on the road. The so-called "plug-in hybrid" design takes this technology a step further by using the gas engine only for back-up status and letting the electric motor do most of the work. This is possible because the large battery pack of the plug-in hybrid can be recharged using a standard household outlet. The cost of the battery pack is a major hurdle to widespread commercialization of these vehicles. Between 2001 and 2008, the Department of Energy helped to advance battery technology with about $230 million in funding for energy storage R&D.

Replacing gasoline with electric power helps address energy security concerns by increasing the use of domestic, non-petroleum energy sources to meet our transportation needs. It does not eliminate GHG concerns or emissions of many local pollutants if the electricity is generated using fossil fuels, but it does reduce these concerns as well. Electric vehicles with more efficient alternating current systems would produce fewer CO_2 emissions per mile than most conventional gasoline vehicles if powered by electricity from a coal-fired power plant. CO_2 emissions per mile driven would be significantly lower than with gasoline if the electricity were generated with natural gas. This would also result in fewer emissions than powering a car directly with natural gas, which has shown greater use as an alternative to diesel in heavier trucks or buses. It will still be necessary to modernize and expand the electricity grid to accommodate substantial increases in electric power usage in the transportation sector. The challenge of expanding electricity transmission is discussed in more detail below.

Renewable Fuels Standard

In addition to using incentives to promote alternative fuels, the Administration has also acted to mandate increased use of alternatives to petroleum in transportation. In 2007, the President announced the Twenty in Ten goal to reduce U.S. gasoline use by 20 percent in 10 years. The passage of the Energy Independence and Security Act of 2007 (EISA) represents a major step toward this goal by requiring substantial increases in light-duty vehicle fuel economy standards and an increase in the production of renewable fuels.

The renewable fuels standard (RFS) portion of EISA is an expansion of the first RFS the President signed into law as part of Energy Policy Act of 2005 (EPACT), which required a minimum volume of renewable fuel to be sold or blended with gasoline in the United States. EISA raises the 2008 standard from 5.4 billion gallons to 9 billion gallons and increases the requirement each year thereafter, until reaching 36 billion gallons of renewable fuel by 2022. Beginning in 2009, about 5 percent of the RFS must be met with advanced biofuels—such as cellulosic ethanol made from switchgrass or wood chips or biodiesel made from leftover restaurant grease. By 2022, nearly 60 percent of the RFS-mandated volume must come from advanced biofuels. These advanced biofuels hold greater potential for reducing GHG emissions than current U.S. biofuels and are also less likely to affect future food prices because they are not reliant on food crops as feedstock, although some advanced biofuels may compete for land and other inputs with food crops. However, minimizing the negative environmental impacts (for example, on soil, water quality, forest cover, habitat diversity, and increased GHG emissions from land-use changes) of biofuel production is likely to remain a significant challenge regardless of the type of feedstock. Furthermore, while the RFS will lead to an increase in the use of biofuels, the expected reduction in gasoline consumption (and associated emissions) will likely be dampened due to unintended consequences. For example, gasoline consumption may increase in other countries due to a rebound effect from lower demand in the United States.

The risk of food-price spikes resulting from a binding RFS mandate could be mitigated by establishing a "safety valve" mechanism that would effectively cap the cost of meeting the mandate. With such a mechanism, a refiner or fuel blender would be allowed to purchase credits from the Government to satisfy its RFS requirement if biofuel prices exceeded a predetermined safety-valve price. This would prevent drastic shocks in food prices and also offer more regulatory certainty to refiners, blenders, and biofuel producers. Despite the Administration's support for a safety valve in the RFS mandate, the final version of EISA did not include such a provision.

Harnessing Existing Energy Sources More Responsibly

Given the economy's overwhelming reliance on fossil fuels, it is reasonable to assume that it will take some time to transition to alternative sources of energy. Therefore, in addition to supporting the development of alternatives described above, the Administration has led a parallel effort to promote cleaner, more efficient, and more reliable use of existing sources, including fossil fuels.

Increasing Efficiency

Efforts to use existing energy sources more efficiently have focused on improving efficiency in vehicle fuel use and in electric energy consumption through fuel economy standards on new cars and light trucks and through various lighting and appliance standards.

Vehicle Fuel Economy Standards

The EISA Vehicle Fuel Economy Mandate builds on the Department of Transportation's 2003 and 2006 fuel economy rules for light-duty trucks and requires that the light-duty vehicle fleet (new cars and light trucks) meet a Corporate Average Fuel Economy (CAFE) standard average of 35 miles per gallon (mpg) by 2020. The 2003 rulemaking increased fuel economy standards of new light trucks by 7 percent between 2004 and 2007 model-years, and the 2006 rulemaking required an additional 8 percent increase, bringing fuel economy of new light trucks to 24 mpg by model year 2011. The 2020 requirement represents approximately 40-percent increase in miles per gallon over 2008 standards: 27.5 mpg for passenger cars, and 22.5 mpg for light trucks. Several new credit trading and banking provisions will help reduce the cost to manufacturers of meeting the new standards and are an example of the use of market-based mechanisms. Under EISA, manufacturers whose vehicles exceed minimum CAFE standards can sell credits to other manufacturers below the standards, and companies can transfer credits between their car and light truck fleets. Companies are also permitted to carry credits forward for 5 years (instead of the current 3 years), which should encourage earlier introduction of new technologies and overcompliance in the initial years. In addition, EISA provides $25 billion in loans to the auto industry to assist in meeting the new CAFE standards. In April 2008, the Department of Transportation issued a proposal to raise fuel economy standards more rapidly than required by EISA.

In addressing potential energy security concerns, the advantage of CAFE over some other policies is that it encourages reductions in gasoline consumption, thus reducing not only oil imports but also the economy's overall reliance on oil. However, increased CAFE standards do nothing to reduce externalities related to miles driven (congestion, accidents, noise, local pollution) and will in fact increase these slightly as the per mile cost of driving falls. In addition, since regulations like CAFE standards that differentiate based on a vehicle's age make new vehicles less attractive than existing vehicles, the regulation may delay the turnover of the vehicle fleet and reduce the realized environmental benefits of the tighter standards. For such reasons, many economic analyses suggest that higher fuel taxes may be a more efficient solution to the negative externalities related to fuel consumption. As noted in Chapter 9, congestion pricing may also be a better way than CAFE to address many of the negative externalities associated with driving.

In the absence of other policies, increasing fuel economy standards will help reduce gasoline consumption and greenhouse gas emissions. It is also likely, as recent trends suggest, that higher fuel prices may persuade consumers to buy more fuel-efficient vehicles even before the higher mileage standards take full effect.

In addition to increasing the fuel economy of our vehicles, fuel efficiency may be increased by targeting inefficiencies at other points in the transportation network. For example, municipalities have saved millions of gallons of fuel and abated associated CO_2 emissions by monitoring and retiming their traffic signals and have seen significant returns on their signal-management investments (see Chapter 9).

Electric Energy Efficiency

The final set of mandates included in EISA is aimed at improving energy efficiency in electricity use. The Lighting Efficiency Mandate will essentially phase out the sale of incandescent light bulbs by 2014 and improve lighting efficiency by more than 65 percent by 2020. The Appliance Efficiency Mandate sets over 45 new standards for appliances. The Federal Government Operations Mandate requires Federal agencies to reduce the energy intensity of their facilities by 30 percent from 2003 levels by 2015 (an increase over the 20 percent reduction requirement set by EPACT 2005). EISA also revised the Federal Building Energy Efficiency Performance Standards so that fossil fuel-generated energy use is phased out of new Federal building designs by 2030. While these requirements will undoubtedly deliver efficiency improvements, reductions in fossil fuel use through these and other types of efficiency standards will be dampened by population and economic growth. In fact, the Energy Information Administration projects that net electricity consumption will still increase nearly 30 percent by 2030 even after accounting for the EISA efficiency standards. Furthermore, as in the case of vehicles, it is important to remember that improvements in electric efficiency will reduce energy cost per kilowatthour, resulting in some increased use of lighting, air conditioning, and other electricity-using activities. This rebound effect thus dampens somewhat the overall impact of the EISA mandates.

There are numerous other promising opportunities to make our electricity generation, distribution, and consumption more efficient and reliable. According to the Energy Information Administration, the U.S. electricity-generation system converts only one-third of total energy inputs into usable electricity, and about 9 percent of this electricity is lost during transmission and distribution. One way to increase the efficiency of the system would be through the use of a so-called "smart electricity grid." A smart grid could be able to receive power back from clients. It would thereby allow greater integration of renewable generation resources and facilitate distributed electricity generation from small-scale sources such as home photovoltaic panels and micro-turbines during peak demand times. Using a two-way communications system, a smart grid would also allow consumers in areas where electricity prices rise and fall based on real-time demand to shift energy consumption from high-priced peak demand periods to low-priced off-peak periods. Finally, by enabling near real-time monitoring of electricity use, a smart grid would give utility companies more time to detect faults and take steps to prevent the possibility of a blackout. These steps could include alerting consumers about reducing energy consumption during emergency periods of peak energy usage. Recent estimates suggest that deployment of smart-grid technologies could potentially reduce America's annual electricity usage by up to 4.3 percent by 2030.

The Department of Energy is undertaking many smart-grid planning, implementation, and awareness activities. EISA also authorized up to $100 million per year over the next 5 years for a smart-grid demonstration initiative to demonstrate the potential benefits of advanced grid technologies; to facilitate commercial transition from the current system to advanced technologies; and to improve system performance, power flow control, and reliability.

Cleaner Use of Fossil Fuels

The recent mandates for increased energy efficiency have been further supported by policies promoting cleaner use of fossil fuels, including numerous regulations targeting local and regional air pollution and technology deployment incentives, such as tax incentives for advanced coal technologies.

Regulating Local and Regional Air Pollutants

Regulations directed at local and regional air quality problems are and will continue to be linked to policies to reduce GHG emissions. These policies often provide co-benefits to each other. For example, to the extent that regulations that target common air pollutants in the transportation sector lower fossil fuel use and make fossil energy cleaner, they also contribute to more secure energy with less environmental harm. Similarly, significant air quality benefits can be expected from climate change mitigation policies. (Note that the reverse may not be true, since pollution-control equipment consumes power, which requires greater fossil fuel use (and CO_2 emissions) to generate the same amount of usable energy.) There may be additional savings from reduced investment in local air pollution controls (such as equipment to reduce the amount of nitrous oxide (NO_x) and sulfur dioxide (SO_2) released into the air from coal-burning power plants) under a future GHG emission pricing policy that reduces the use of fossil fuels.

According to a number of indicators, air quality has improved dramatically over the past few decades. As shown in Chart 3-3, emissions of many common air pollutants have decreased, and these trends have continued through this Administration. For example, between 2000 and 2007, NO_x and volatile organic compounds (VOC) emissions (the primary precursors to ground-level ozone) fell by 23 percent and 12 percent, respectively, and SO_2 emissions fell by 19 percent.

Chart 3-3 **Emissions Levels over Time**
Emissions of common air pollutants have declined substantially since 1980.

Percentage change since 1980

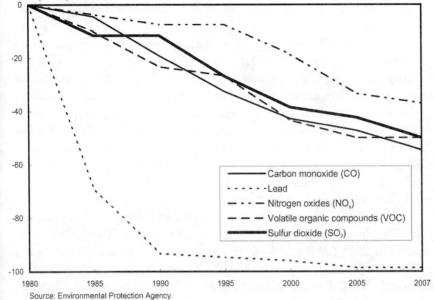

Source: Environmental Protection Agency.

Over the past decade, the Environmental Protection Agency (EPA) has finalized—and is implementing—a suite of regulations on light- and heavy-duty vehicles and engines and nonroad mobile sources (such as construction, agricultural, industrial equipment, locomotives, and marine engines) that are transforming the diesel engine. The 2004 Clean Air Nonroad Diesel Rule, for example, is expected to reduce emissions from new nonroad diesel equipment (such as tractors and bulldozers) by over 90 percent from 2004 levels by 2014 and to reduce sulfur levels in nonroad diesel fuel by 99 percent from 2004 levels by 2010. The Administration has also strengthened the National Ambient Air Quality Standards (NAAQS) for three out of the six common air pollutants: fine particulate matter (PM2.5), ground-level ozone (the primary component of smog), and lead. Emissions of these pollutants stem from a wide range of sources and State plans for complying with the new standards will vary. Unfortunately, several areas, such as parts of California, remain grossly out of compliance with current NAAQS, and it will be difficult for some of them to reach compliance within the next couple of decades.

The President's 2002 Clear Skies Initiative called for using cost-effective, market-based policy instruments to dramatically reduce power plants' emissions of sulfur dioxide, nitrogen oxide, and mercury. Although Clear Skies legislation did not pass the Congress, in 2005 the EPA took a major step toward a more efficient multipollutant policy in the electricity sector by finalizing two rules, the Clean Air Interstate Rule (CAIR) and the companion Clean Air Mercury Rule (CAMR), which echoed many features of the Clear Skies Initiative.

The Clean Air Interstate Rule (CAIR) received broad support from economists, environmental groups, states, policymakers, and the regulated industry for promoting significant environmental improvements at a lower cost to society than a traditional command and control type of regulation. CAIR was designed to provide states with a solution to the problem of pollution that crosses State boundaries. Covering 28 eastern States and the District of Columbia, the rule requires the steepest emissions cuts from coal-fired power plants required in over a decade implemented in two phases by 2015. When fully implemented, caps on annual NO_X and SO_2 emissions would permanently reduce NO_X and SO_2 from coal-fired power plants in the eastern United States by more than 60 percent and 70 percent, respectively, from 2003 levels. The rule is projected to achieve over $100 billion in net benefits by 2015 (see Table 3-1). In addition to the cost savings from using a more market-based approach, CAIR's cap-and-trade program has other beneficial effects. For example, the cap on NO_X would prevent any increases in aggregate NO_X emissions in the East that might otherwise arise from electricity sector restructuring.

In February 2008, the United States Court of Appeals ruled CAMR to be unlawful because the EPA had not taken the appropriate steps to regulate mercury emissions from power plants under a more flexible portion of the Clean Air Act (CAA) that allows for a cap-and-trade program. Then in July 2008, the Court ruled that the CAIR rule was fundamentally flawed, and it vacated the entire rule. The ruling was based on several issues, including that the cap-and-trade program was too focused on regionwide emission reductions and did not adequately factor in each State's significant contribution to air pollution issues. For example, the Court deemed that CAIR did not provide adequate protection for downwind areas. While both rulings have been appealed through the courts and contested and debated on many fronts, their invalidation would have substantial consequences because the underlying requirements of the Clean Air Act remain in place. For example, all States would have to redo their State Implementation Plans (SIPs) to demonstrate compliance with CAA requirements and would not be able to rely on the cost-effective controls built into CAIR. The thousands of premature deaths avoided annually and other significant health and environmental gains would come at a higher price, if at all, in the absence of a fix for these rules that retains their trading provisions. After receiving petitions from a range of industry groups, States, and the Administration, in December 2008 a Federal appeals court reversed the earlier decision on CAIR, allowing for the

TABLE 3-1—*Projected Net Benefits from Selected 2001-08 EPA Clean Air Regulations*

Rule Name	Year Enacted	Primary Pollutants Targeted*	Net Benefits in 2020** (billions of 2006 dollars)	
			3% Discounting	7% Discounting
Electricity Sector................................				
Clean Air Interstate Rule (CAIR)................................	2005	SO₂, NOₓ Cobenefits: Mercury	$119.2	$100.7
Clean Air Mercury Rule (CAMR)................................	2005; Revised 2006	Mercury Cobenefits: PM	–$0.8 to –$0.7	—
Transportation Sector................................				
Nonroad Diesel Engines and Fuel................................	2004	NOₓ, PM	$49.2	$48.0
Locomotive and Marine Diesel Engines........................	2008	NOₓ, PM	$3.6 to $8.5	$3.3 to $7.7
Small Spark Ignition Engines and Equipment................	2008	Hydrocarbon (HC) + NOₓ, CO	$1.0 to $3.9	$0.9 to $3.7
Emission Sources in Multiple Sectors........................				
Clean Air Visibility Rule (CAVR)................................	2005	SO₂, NOₓ	$2.7 to $14.5	$2.3 to $11.3
National Ambient Air Quality Standards (NAAQS)........				
Particulate matter (PM2.5)................................	2006	PM2.5, SO₂, NOX	$4.2 to $84.7	$2.9 to $71.4
Ozone................................	2008	NOₓ, VOC Cobenefits: PM	–$6.8 to $11	–$7.0 to $9.9
Lead................................	2008	Lead Cobenefits: PM	$0.9 to $6.8	–$2.6 to $2.4

*Lists pollutants whose reductions are monetized in the benefit calculations. There may be additional cobenefits resulting from reductions in other pollutants that are not quantified in the rulemaking analysis.
** The table shows net benefits expected in 2015 for CAIR and CAVR and 2016 for lead NAAQS.
   Note: Consistent with OMB and EPA guidelines, net benefits are calculated using both a 3 percent and 7 percent discount rate for valuing future impacts (although net benefits using the 7 percent discount rate are not available from the revised 2006 CAMR analysis). Note that the assumptions and methods used in each of the Regulatory Impact Analyses (RIAs) are not necessarily consistent across the rules listed.
   Source: Environmental Protection Agency (Regulatory Impact Analyses).

reinstatement of the rule until EPA crafts a replacement. This reversal helps to avoid a prolonged period of regulatory uncertainty that may result in the reduction or elimination of pollution-control construction projects.

Developing Cleaner Fossil Fuel Technology

In addition to regulating local and regional air pollutants, the Administration has promoted cleaner ways to use our domestic fossil fuels through the use of tax incentives. For example, EPACT broadened the scope of the investment tax credits (ITCs) for renewable energy production to apply to investments in certain clean coal facilities, such as Integrated Gasification Combined Cycle (IGCC) power plants, which rely on a two-stage process in which pollutants are removed before combustion occurs. Recent research shows that the 20 percent ITC for new IGCC plants potentially could make this technology cost-competitive with new conventional coal plants. Because of their inherently higher operating efficiency, IGCC plants are estimated to produce up to 8 percent fewer CO_2 emissions per megawatt hour (mWh) than conventional coal plants. Furthermore, capturing and store the CO_2 emissions underground (known as carbon capture and sequestration, or CCS) would be less expensive in an IGCC plant than in a conventional power plant. Also, the IGCC process produces very low levels of common air pollutants (NO_X, SO_2, and PM) and volatile mercury, which reduces the cost of compliance with regulations of these emissions. To date, two 260–290 megawatt (mW) IGCC power plants are in operation in the United States and others are in the pipeline. A third, larger facility (with 630 mW capacity) received approval in January 2008.

Removing Regulatory Impediments to Domestic Production

Finally, the Administration has worked to remove regulatory impediments to bringing domestic energy sources, including fossil fuels, to market. In July 2008, the President lifted the Executive restriction on offshore exploration and requested that the Congress also lift its ban. On September 30, 2008, the ban on offshore domestic exploration of natural gas and oil was allowed to expire, a decision that would allow open access to an estimated 14 billion barrels of oil and nearly 55 trillion cubic feet of gas off the Atlantic and Pacific coasts. These previously restricted areas represent a sizable portion of the estimated 101 billion barrels of oil and 480 trillion cubic feet of natural gas untapped on the outer continental shelf. While we strive toward the long-term goal of reducing the economy's overall reliance on oil for environmental and security reasons, expanded domestic oil and gas production in these areas will help reduce the $300 billion Americans spend each year on net petroleum imports.

Overarching Challenges

Despite widespread support for increasing the use of market-oriented approaches to achieve our environmental and energy policy goals going forward, numerous challenges remain in realizing the full potential of these types of policies.

Balancing Local, Regional and Global Goals

First, any future comprehensive national energy policy will need to address potential tradeoffs between environmental and security goals, as well as tradeoffs between competing environmental goals. As noted earlier, policies aimed at mitigating local air pollution can at times reduce GHG and vice versa. For example, the clean diesel programs may provide climate change benefits by reducing black carbon (soot), the climate change effects of which require further study but many argue could be quite substantial. (The clean diesel rules will also likely become more significant if there is an increase in the number of diesel vehicles due to policies aimed at improving fuel economy and reducing GHG emissions from mobile sources.) However, some air quality policies may result in "technology lock-in" that could cause major delays in the implementation of GHG control technologies because of the investment in capital and other resources to meet the air quality control requirements. Policies aimed at GHG mitigation may also at times increase emissions of traditional pollutants. For example, technology standards that require increasing the thermal efficiency of engines may lead designers to achieve the regulatory objective by raising combustion temperatures, a strategy that would tend to increase NO_x emissions unless countered by other control methods. The challenge going forward will be to design comprehensive policies that enhance synergies and reduce the degree to which policies may work at odds with one another.

There are additional conflicts that will continue to arise in achieving long term environmental goals. For example, in the transition to alternative energy sources, where will new facilities and transmission infrastructure for different types of electricity generation be built? This issue is especially contentious when talking about new nuclear facilities, large scale CCS facilities, and renewable sources such as off-shore wind turbines. Renewable energy facilities generally face greater siting hurdles than their conventional counterparts because they can only be located at certain sites. The most highly valued renewable resources are often in pristine, isolated parts of the country (like mountain ridges, open plains, and coastal waters) with significant environmental and aesthetic value. Siting hurdles are compounded by the additional transmission and distribution infrastructure that is needed to bring the electricity from remote generation sites to population centers. States will have to balance renewable energy goals with other environmental concerns in deciding whether to support investment in new transmission infrastructure, such as new regional transmission corridors. Similarly, there are significant challenges that must be faced in expanding or reconfiguring existing fuel distribution systems to accommodate the large volumes of ethanol and other biofuels required by EISA.

Obstacles to increased nuclear power generation extend beyond the hurdles of siting power plants. There is also a concern about the lack of long-term storage for the spent fuel generated by nuclear plants. To reduce the amount of spent fuel that must be properly contained for centuries, efforts may also be made to increase recycling of this fuel within the generation process, but without producing weapons-grade material. The Administration has laid the groundwork for tackling this issue through efforts such as the Global Nuclear Energy Partnership (GNEP) and the Nuclear Power 2010 joint government–industry effort to develop advanced nuclear plant technology and reduce technical, regulatory, and institutional barriers to nuclear deployment.

Efficient R&D Support for Alternative Energy Sources

Technology policies will continue to be an important component of any energy policy portfolio going forward. Many economists maintain that, as a complement to any pricing policy directed at environmental problems, governments will need to support R&D for alternative energy sources. The challenge will be to ensure that any R&D support is managed efficiently and effectively.

As discussed above, an emission pricing policy is a key step in inducing technological change at low cost because the emissions price provides the private sector with a direct incentive to invest in and deploy new environment-friendly innovations. Well-targeted technology policy can reinforce these incentives for private R&D and thus reduce future costs. Basic and applied energy-related research as well as the education of the next generation of researchers will continue to be in particular need of government support, because these areas are the least likely to be undertaken by the private sector. It will also be crucial to expand the use of more flexible research policy instruments that allow the market, rather than government, to pick technology winners. For example, the Government could award prizes for basic research advancements in energy storage, which would help to spur innovation in a wide range of low-carbon technologies. Efforts are already underway to expand the use of prizes in some areas. EISA provided authorization for an L-prize for high-efficiency solid-state lighting products and an H-prize for advancements in hydrogen technology.

Current policies that target the adoption or deployment phase of the technological development process also need reviewing. Many of the existing tax credits have been found to be costly ways of making renewable sources competitive with fossil fuel sources. However, if technology deployment incentives are needed, they should be applied in a way that is neutral across all alternatives. Existing subsidies such as the ethanol blender's tax credit, flex-fuel vehicle credits, and subsidies for alternative electricity generation, in combination with the growing use of existing residential deductions and credits for energy-efficient home improvements, have created a patchwork of incentives that send an inconsistent message about how much the abatement of a ton of carbon is worth. In addition, there are opportunity costs associated with resources devoted to any area of research or deployment support. For example, in the context of renewable fuels, additional support for first-generation biofuels such as corn ethanol reduces the amount of funding available for the development of other alternatives and could make it more difficult for second-generation biofuels (with potentially significantly lower GHG emissions) to become viable.

Going forward, it will be important to reform these subsidies so as to minimize market distortions. One way existing tax incentives could be simplified is to offer a single subsidy in which the payment is weighted by the extent to which petroleum consumption and/or carbon is reduced relative to a baseline technology. In April 2008, the President voiced strong support for such a reform of the current complicated mix of incentives to make the commercialization and use of new, lower emission technologies more competitive. Another policy instrument that could encourage commercial use of new energy-efficient technology at a lower cost to the taxpayer is the reverse auction, in which would-be subsidy recipients (such as a renewable energy project developer) submit proposals for new projects and bid the minimum price they would accept for zero- or low-carbon electricity generation. However, such technology adoption policies may still favor what are currently the least expensive technologies, rather than technologies that may have greater potential to reduce cost and improve environmental performance through learning by doing.

Economically Efficient Regulation Under Existing Statutes

Another significant challenge in realizing the full potential of market-oriented policy approaches is likely to be the ability of existing laws to address old and new environmental problems in more efficient ways.

Local and Regional Air Pollutants

Although there have been great gains in reducing common air pollutants under the Clean Air Act, air pollution will continue to be a problem in the future, and the importance of finding economically efficient ways to further improve air quality will only increase. As seen in the 2008 National Ambient Air Quality Standard (NAAQS) for ozone, stricter standards have moved the private sector up the marginal cost-of-control curve. That is, it is becoming more costly to reduce each additional ton of NO_x and VOC emissions (the precursors to ground-level ozone). Upcoming reviews of the NAAQS for other pollutants will undoubtedly reveal a similar trend. These trends do not shed light on the relative cost of controlling one pollutant over others, due to the sequential nature of the individual NAAQS reviews. However, it is likely to spark debate about the benefits of moving either toward a more integrated multipollutant approach to controlling emissions of pollutants that pose the most significant risks or toward a more goal-oriented standard setting, as there may be no level that adequately protects human health and the environment for some pollutants (for example, lead), and currently costs cannot be considered in setting a NAAQS.

A multipollutant approach can help reduce the costs of meeting standards in regulated industries, such as the electricity sector, in which power plants face an increasingly complex set of requirements under the current Clean Air Act (CAA) (see Chart 3-4). The President's Clear Skies Initiative was an important first step in establishing a multipollutant approach. It is important that the market-oriented aspects of the CAIR and CAMR rules not be lost upon being remanded to the EPA for revision. The Administration has also made efforts to reform the complex requirements for upgrading or building new power plants under the New Source Review provisions of the Clean Air Act. Such age differentiated regulations can create a disincentive to invest in energy efficiency improvements, thus slowing turnover in the capital stock (equipment and facilities) and pollution abatement. The debate over how best to reduce such counterproductive incentives will undoubtedly continue in the future.

Chart 3-4 **Clean Air Act Requirements for New Electric Generating Units, 2004–2022**
Power plants face a complex set of requirements under the current Clean Air Act.

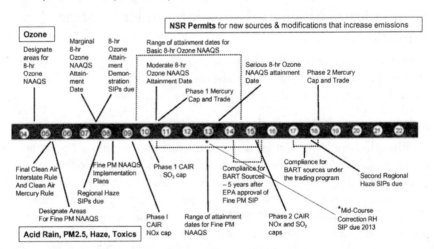

Note: The timeline was developed in May 2005 and reflects EPA assumptions about rulemakings that had not been completed at that time. EPA's rulemakings are conducted through the usual notice-and-comment process, and the conclusions may vary from these assumptions.
Source: Environmental Protection Agency.

Greenhouse Gas Emissions

Existing statutes are not well suited to tackling problems that were not considered when the original laws were written. In the context of climate change, the unique characteristics of GHGs and the ubiquity of GHG emission sources present significant challenges for economically efficient regulatory design under the existing Clean Air Act or other statutes. Unlike most traditional air pollutants, GHG emissions become well mixed throughout the global atmosphere, so a unit of GHG emissions has the same effect on environmental quality regardless of where it comes from, and, once emitted, GHGs can remain in the atmosphere for decades to centuries. Therefore, while policies can control the flow of GHG emissions, the ultimate concern is the stock—the cumulative concentration of GHGs in the atmosphere. These characteristics suggest that GHGs are particularly well suited to market-oriented policies that do not dictate the exact location and timing of emission reductions as opposed to the command and control type of regulation under the CAA that is used for some other pollutants.

There are examples of CAA regulations in which market-oriented approaches have been used for groups of mobile or stationary sources, such as in the Acid Rain Control Program, and even some cases in which multi-sector trading programs have been established. However, economists have demonstrated that taking a more integrated approach to control GHGs, such as through a common cap or price on emissions across sectors, would allow the market to identify a combination of methods to reduce the cost of achieving a given emission reduction. For example, expanding the coverage of such a market-oriented policy to include the industrial, electricity, and transportation sectors has been found to substantially decrease the cost of achieving a given emission reduction compared to one that is limited to the electricity and transportation sectors. However, if a policymaker's goal is to transform technology in a single area to the point where developing countries would voluntarily adopt the new low-carbon technology, then the advantage of a sector-specific approach is that it may help to ensure that technology investment remains within that sector.

It is unclear whether it would be legally possible to implement an economy-wide system for GHGs under the CAA. However, any economy-wide program under one provision of the CAA would likely trigger additional source-specific or sector-based requirements as a result of other CAA provisions, thus resulting in multiple programs affecting a particular sector, source category, or GHG. With multiple market-oriented policies focused on the same problem, the overall emissions reductions may not be achieved in the least costly way because there would not be a common price of pollution across all activities that directly result in GHG emissions. Without such a common price, full trading opportunities to reduce control costs will not be realized. In addition, emissions leakage across sectors and countries can occur when the cost of reducing one ton of emissions differs across them. When faced with a high cost of complying with new environmental regulations, a firm may move its operations to a jurisdiction with less stringent (and less costly) emissions controls. Current requirements under the CAA do not consider the actions (or inaction) of other countries or allow for consideration of unequal treatment of emissions across different types of emitters.

The Clean Air Act is also not designed to implement any carbon-pricing policy so that it operates in an efficient and transparent manner. For example, economists suggest that it would be economically efficient to employ a broad-based emissions tax, using the proceeds to decrease distortionary taxes. A well designed cap-and-trade system can have much in common with a well designed tax, but policy considerations should weigh heavily on how emissions allowances would be distributed under such a program. The economic literature broadly finds that there are significant efficiency advantages to auctioning emissions allowances, particularly if the revenues are used for reducing existing distortionary taxes. Also, cost-containment provisions in a cap-and-trade program, such as a safety valve allowance price, help to prevent caps from resulting in allowance prices that are higher than the social cost of the emissions. However, the CAA does not authorize the EPA to impose taxes or to administer a broad cap-and-trade program with auctioning and cost-containment provisions, making the Act ill suited to address the unique challenges posed by GHG emissions.

The globalized nature of GHG emissions is also likely to create difficulties in other statutes, such as the Endangered Species Act (ESA) and the National Environmental Policy Act (NEPA), which were designed to address local or regional concerns. For example, the ESA requires consultation between Federal agencies when a Federal action is likely to cause effects that pose a threat to a listed species. However, because the effects of GHG emissions have global repercussions, any causal connection between the effects of any particular action and the loss of a listed animal or its habitat is not discernible, or at least not significant or proximate enough to warrant such consultation. Similarly, the types of environmental impacts included in NEPA analyses are local or regional in nature and do not fit into the complexities related to global climate change effects.

Given the difficulties in applying existing statutes to the unique problems presented by GHGs, policymakers should seek new approaches for enacting comprehensive and market-oriented solutions. The scientific debate over the specific GHG concentrations needed to affect global temperatures and the probability of catastrophic damages will continue for some time, and the policy debate over tough questions such as to how to value future emissions reductions is far from settled. In the face of such uncertainty and discussion of numerous other policy design issues, flexibility and transparency will be vital to the success of any policy designed to address global climate change.

Global Action on Climate Change

Finally, perhaps the most significant challenge in tackling climate change is developing broad-based global action to make meaningful progress in reducing GHG emissions.

As shown in Chart 3-5, U.S. greenhouse gas intensity (as measured by GHG emissions per unit of GDP) has been improving over time. In 2002, the President set a goal of reducing U.S. GHG intensity by 18 percent by 2012, and the Nation is on track to meet and exceed this target. Between 2002 and 2007, both energy-related CO_2 emissions per unit of GDP and total GHG emissions per unit of GDP declined by about 10 percent. In the spring of 2008, the President also set a new goal to stop U.S. growth in total GHG emissions by 2025. Despite U.S. action toward meeting these or future domestic GHG reduction targets, it is important to understand that U.S. action alone will not reverse global emission growth or stabilize global atmospheric GHG concentrations. Many assert that it is the responsibility of developed countries to reduce GHG emissions, since they have a longer historical record of emissions and therefore are responsible for most of the existing atmospheric concentrations. This formulation does not account for the reduction in the

Chart 3-5 **Greenhouse Gas Intensity of U.S. Economy, 1990–2007**
The greenhouse gas intensity of the U.S. economy has improved dramatically over time

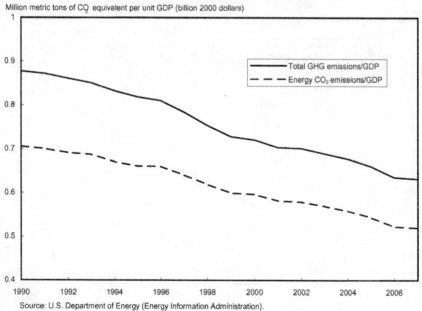

Million metric tons of CO_2 equivalent per unit GDP (billion 2000 dollars)

Source: U.S. Department of Energy (Energy Information Administration).

natural absorption of CO_2 (for example, in forests) due to land-use change that has occurred throughout the world. More important, actions by developed countries alone will not stabilize atmospheric concentrations given the recent and projected emissions growth in large rapidly developing economies.

Chart 3-6 provides one example of why it is important for all countries, particularly major economies involved in negotiations, to limit GHG emissions. The chart shows the future path of global CO_2 concentrations if the United States takes action to reduce GHG emissions under various cap-and-trade bills recently debated in Congress. One of the main reasons why future global concentrations do not decrease substantially compared to the reference case (which is a business-as-usual case that includes current international efforts to address climate change) is that major emerging economies represent a large and growing share of global GHG emissions. In addition, international emissions leakage may reduce global mitigation if only a handful of countries take action. Just as sector-based regulation of GHG emissions under the CAA raises worry about potential leakage of emissions across source categories, there are concerns about potential shifts in GHG emissions to countries where GHGs face no regulations. Energy-intensive industries in which domestic firms would face significantly higher costs due to regulation may move operations to unregulated foreign markets where costs are lower. International sectoral agreements in energy-intensive industries can help alleviate some of these competitiveness concerns.

Chart 3-6 **Global CO₂ Concentrations**
Carbon emissions are projected to rise over the next several decades.

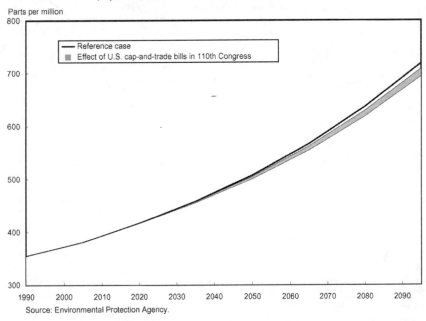

Parts per million

Source: Environmental Protection Agency.

It is clear from the projections above, as well as other recent analyses of climate mitigation scenarios, that climate change requires a global solution, with participation by all major economies. The Administration has recently taken several steps to encourage wider international action to address GHGs, including promoting consensus toward commitments in developing countries. In 2007, the Administration launched the Major Economies Meeting (MEM) process, involving those of the world's major economies that use the most energy and emit the most GHGs, to help promote international action to slow, stop, and eventually reverse the growth of GHGs. This process is intended to support the United Nations Framework Convention on Climate Change (UNFCCC) negotiations by elaborating on areas of shared understanding among the major GHG emitters. At the July 2008 MEM meeting in Japan, leaders issued a Leaders Declaration that emphasizes "ambitious, realistic, and achievable" steps toward achieving these goals and agreement to take near-term actions. Leaders agreed to continue to work together to promote the success of the negotiations under the UNFCCC.

In addition to achieving commitments by all major economies, accelerating the deployment of clean energy technology in emerging economies is critical to mitigating climate change. To this end, the United States has taken several steps to form international partnerships to support national climate change efforts. In 2007, the Administration led efforts to produce an international agreement to accelerate the phase-out of the hydrochlorofluorocarbon (HCFC) refrigerants—a potent GHG—under the Montreal Protocol on Substances that Deplete the Ozone Layer. Under this agreement, both developed and developing countries explicitly agreed to accept binding and enforceable commitments that have climate change benefits. In 2008, the President launched the Clean Technology Fund to help bridge the gap between current technology and cleaner, more efficient ways of fueling the world's growth. The President has asked Congress for an initial U.S. commitment of $2 billion, and many other nations have pledge support. Altogether, the United States, the United Kingdom, Japan, France, Germany, Sweden, Australia, and Spain have pledged over $5 billion to the Fund, which will be housed at and overseen by the World Bank.

To be eligible for funding, a project must be consistent with the recipient country's national low-carbon growth strategy and must help move the relevant industry or sector toward a clean-energy path. Competition is intended to be technology-neutral, with projects competing for financing based on lifetime GHG reductions compared to the baseline technology and relative to the Fund's investment. The recipient country would contribute public and/or private capital to meet the project's baseline costs. The Clean Technology Fund would help finance the cost difference between the clean energy technology and the standard baseline, higher-emissions technology.

In partnership with the European Union, the United States also proposed the Environmental Goods and Services Agreement in the World Trade Organization (WTO) to eliminate tariff and non-tariff barriers to environmental technologies and services. This proposal included an agreement in the WTO to eliminate tariffs worldwide on 43 climate-friendly technologies identified by the World Bank. It also included a higher level of commitment from developed and most advanced developing countries to eliminate trade barriers across a broader range of goods and services. Global trade in the environmental goods covered by the proposal totaled approximately $613 billion in 2006, and global exports of these goods have grown annually by an average of 15 percent since 2000. The World Bank suggests that by removing trade barriers on key technologies, trade could increase by an additional 7 to 14 percent annually.

Other international partnerships to pursue development and diffusion of clean energy include the 21-member Global Nuclear Energy Partnership (GNEP) and the 7-country Asia-Pacific Partnership on Clean Development and Climate (APP). These are primarily sectoral efforts to support national climate change efforts. The GNEP, announced by the President in 2006, focuses on promoting technology breakthroughs to support the long-term expansion of clean, safe, proliferation-resistant nuclear power here and abroad. As mentioned earlier, safer ways to deal with storage of nuclear waste are crucial to this effort. The APP has a somewhat broader mission. It aims to promote coordination among different sectors to create new investment opportunities, build local capacity, and remove barriers to the introduction of a wide range of cleaner, more efficient technologies.

Conclusion

Energy policy will continue to be one of the major challenges facing the United States for many years to come. As the Federal Government moves toward a more integrated approach in confronting energy security, climate change, and other environmental challenges, we will need to ensure that we consider the economic efficiency of future laws and regulations. In addition to advancing clean and renewable energy technologies, a key challenge going forward will be leading all countries to work cooperatively to achieve global climate goals with meaningful participation by all major economies.

CHAPTER 4

The Benefits of Open Trade and Investment Policies

An open economy is characterized by receptiveness to foreign ideas, technology, products, services, and investment. The United States has one of the most open economies in the world, ranking very high in common measures of openness to trade and investment. As a large and diverse economy, the United States engages in more trade and investment than any other country in dollar terms, and it also has, on average, very low barriers to cross-border flows of goods, services, and capital.

In the long run, open economic policies generate many benefits. Trade and investment linkages with other countries increase competition in domestic industries; enhance the purchasing power of consumers; provide exposure to new products, services, and ideas from abroad; and give domestic firms wider markets in which to sell goods and services. In the short run, the interdependence among open economies generally provides benefits—open economies may rely on foreign borrowing or foreign demand for domestically produced exports to cushion an economic downturn—but may also create visible costs that obscure these benefits, as when foreign investment shifts abruptly out of certain sectors or when foreign demand for domestic exports falls. Nevertheless, any potential negative effects from our openness to trade and investment do not outweigh the enormous gains society has realized over decades from this openness.

This chapter begins with a discussion of key facts about trade and investment in the United States, followed by a discussion of the benefits of free trade and open investment, and the policies that the United States has taken to enhance both. These policies include an increased number of free trade agreements (FTAs) and the strong commitment of the United States to maintain openness to foreign direct investment (FDI) while still addressing legitimate national security concerns. The chapter continues with a discussion of international development assistance, and concludes with a review of issues that could affect future U.S. trade policy. The key points of this chapter are:

- Openness to trade and investment has boosted U.S. economic growth. Openness can also reduce the impact of shocks and increase the resilience of the U.S. economy.
- The number of U.S. FTAs has increased greatly during this Administration, and these agreements have contributed to the growth in U.S. exports.

- Portfolio and direct investment into the United States reached historic levels over the past decade, in part due to the depth, diversity, and openness of U.S. financial markets and the competitiveness of U.S. firms.
- The United States has maintained an open investment policy, facilitating FDI flows between the United States and the world while addressing legitimate national security concerns.
- U.S. development and trade initiatives, as well as U.S. engagement in multilateral institutions such as the World Trade Organization and the World Bank have helped increase growth and foster political and economic stability in developing countries throughout the world.
- Continued commitment to open economic policies throughout the world will help ensure continued economic gains for the United States and the rest of the world.

Trade and Investment in the United States

Trade in goods and services has played an increased role in the U.S. economy over the past decade. As seen in Table 4-1, in the first half of 2008, the United States exported goods and services equivalent to 13.0 percent of Gross Domestic Product (GDP), and imported goods and services equal to 18.1 percent of GDP. These figures are the highest on record, considerably above figures from 2000, when exports were equal to 10.9 percent, and imports 14.8 percent, of GDP. The *current account,* which measures the net value of the flow of current international transactions, is chiefly composed of the difference between exports and imports. The U.S. current account deficit widened over this period from 4.1 percent of GDP in the first quarter of 2000 to a peak of 6.6 percent of GDP in the final quarter of 2005. The current account deficit then narrowed to 4.8 percent of GDP at the end of 2007 before expanding slightly over the first half of 2008.

TABLE 4-1.—*U.S. Trade and Investment*

	2007 value (billion dollars)	Share of U.S. GDP (percent)		
		2000	2007	2008 Q1–Q2
Current account balance, (-) = deficit	**–731**	**–4.3**	**–5.3**	**–5.0**
Exports of goods and services	1,646	10.9	11.9	13.0
Imports of goods and services	2,346	14.8	17.0	18.1
Other	–31	–0.4	–0.2	0.0
Net capital inflows into the U.S.	**768**	**4.9**	**5.6**	**4.7**
Net inflows for foreign investments in the U.S.	2,058	10.6	14.9	6.8
Net outflows for U.S. investments abroad	1,290	5.7	9.3	2.1

Source: Department of Commerce (Bureau of Economic Analysis).

As a matter of accounting, the current account deficit is mirrored by net inflows of capital into the United States, which have provided the financing that has allowed us to purchase more in imports than we sell in exports. From Table 4-1, we can see that net capital inflows into the United States were equal to 4.7 percent of GDP in the first half of 2008, a figure that approximately matches the current account deficit, with a discrepancy caused by measurement errors, omissions, and the exclusion of certain types of capital flows for which only partial data are available. The increase in net capital inflows looks modest compared with the huge increase in capital inflows to and outflows from the United States from 2000 to 2007, although the data for 2008 imply a sharp decline to levels lower than those of 2000 as a percentage of GDP.

Openness to Trade and Investment Has Substantially Contributed to U.S. Growth

Many studies have shown that greater openness to trade and investment is associated with faster growth in the long run. There are many ways to measure openness, including by looking at both the extent of trade and investment and the size of barriers to these flows. By either measure, countries that increased openness have grown faster and have had greater increases in living standards than countries that have remained less open. Research has not yet conclusively determined the incremental gain in income that a country receives from a specific increase in trade because the exact change can depend on particular policies and circumstances.

In the current U.S. downturn that began at the end of 2007, trade has improved the resiliency of the U.S. economy. Strong global demand for U.S. goods and services in 2007 and the first half of 2008 boosted U.S. GDP growth in this period. As the trade deficit declined, the improvement in net exports (exports minus imports) became a sizeable contributor to U.S. growth in this period. Chart 4-1 shows real GDP growth and the contribution of net exports to that growth since 2001. Net exports have accounted for over half of real GDP growth in the past 2 years. Some of the recent U.S. strength in net exports has likely been driven by the depreciation of the dollar. The value of the dollar declined fairly steadily from its peak in 2002 to the summer of 2008, when it reached a level last seen in the mid-1990s. The depreciated dollar contributed to the increase in exports and the decline in real imports. In the second half of 2008, however, the value of the dollar increased, in part reflecting increased international demand for U.S. Treasury bonds in a time of global turmoil and rapidly deteriorating global growth.

The deteriorating performance of foreign economies in the second half of 2008 has recently reduced demand for U.S. exports. In the most recent U.S. data through October, both imports and exports have begun to decline, as they did during the global slowdown of 2001–02. The decline in exports will likely reduce the contribution of trade to GDP growth in the short term, and net exports may provide no boost to growth in the fourth quarter of 2008. Trade may still hold up better than other components of GDP, however, as consumption and investment are expected to decline enough to make overall GDP growth negative in the short term (see the discussion of the near-term macroeconomic environment in Chapter 1).

Strong global demand for goods drove up prices of a broad range of commodities through the middle of 2008, but global weakness in the second half of the year has reversed most of these gains. This is good news for users, both consumers and producers, but raises some concerns for the exporters that had benefited from the higher prices. However, the broad-based decline in prices of oil, food, and agricultural commodities has considerably eased earlier fears of inflation.

The Benefits of Free Trade

Free trade contributes to economic prosperity in many ways. One of the greatest benefits of trade is that international differences in prices allow countries to utilize their *comparative advantage,* because trade gives a country access to goods and services at relatively low prices, while simultaneously

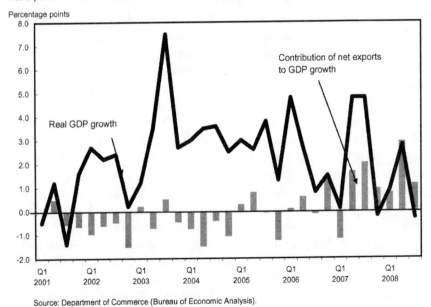

Chart 4-1 **Contribution of Net Exports to Real U.S. GDP Growth**
Net exports have accounted for more than half of U.S. growth in the last two years.

Source: Department of Commerce (Bureau of Economic Analysis).

allowing domestic producers to find profitable export markets in which to sell goods that can be produced at lower prices at home than abroad. Trade allows a nation to achieve higher overall consumption of goods and services than would be possible if no trade occurred. Trade also benefits consumers by increasing the number and variety of goods available domestically.

Trade raises the productivity of domestic firms in multiple ways: (1) Trade shifts production toward goods in which the country has a comparative advantage, so that over time, capital and labor will become concentrated in relatively more productive sectors, raising national income; (2) trade connects domestic producers to new technology and a greater variety of inputs, and it exposes them to more competition; and (3) firms that gain access to new markets can increase average productivity as unit costs fall, thus benefiting from what economists call *economies of scale* in production. Because trade allows the most productive firms and sectors to increase their share of U.S. production, trade makes possible increases in productivity, profitability, and wages that raise national standards of living.

Firms engaged in export trade provide important benefits to the economy. Exporting firms are a large engine of growth and employment in the U.S. economy. In 2006, 20 percent of manufacturing jobs were generated directly or indirectly by exports. Not only do exporters play a major role in job creation, but on average, productivity per worker is up to one-quarter higher in exporting firms than in nonexporters, and exporters pay each worker 13–18 percent more. Some of this exceptional performance occurs because exporters tend to concentrate in productive industries, but exporters also have higher productivity and higher wages than nonexporting firms in the *same* sector.

Among exporting firms, multinational enterprises, which own and control business operations in more than one county, account for an important share of U.S. trade and productivity growth. In the United States, U.S.-owned multinationals account for over one-half of total exports, and over 90 percent of U.S. exports to manufacturing affiliates were inputs for further processing. The extent of trade in intermediate inputs is an indication that trade is part of an increasingly complex chain, and companies have substantially improved productivity through the development of these global supply chains. Research shows that multinationals in the United States, both U.S.-owned and U.S. affiliates of foreign companies, were responsible for more than half of the increase in U.S. nonfarm labor productivity between 1977 and 2000.

Trade, while broadly beneficial, does not reward all people equally, and changes in trade can negatively affect some workers. In some cases, workers can receive lower wages when trade liberalization reduces the price of goods and services that they produce, and workers can lose jobs when imports reduce domestic production or jobs are relocated overseas. Over time, however, increased trade has made the United States more productive and has contributed to large increases in the U.S. standard of living. Estimates of the gains to the United States from the postwar increase in global trade and the reduction in global trade barriers range up to $1 trillion dollars per year, or about $10,000 per household. In other cases, the use of global supply chains has led to the displacement of some U.S. workers, but as noted above, multinational companies generate considerable benefits for U.S. workers, generating high-wage jobs, substantial employment, and considerable improvements to U.S. productivity.

Although some jobs are lost due to trade, there are many other reasons for job loss in the United States, such as technological change and domestic competition. The United States has several programs to help workers adjust to displacements caused by trade. Chief among these programs is Trade Adjustment Assistance (see Box 8-2 in Chapter 8), which provides benefits and training to workers whose jobs are affected by trade and promotes their rapid reemployment.

Free Trade Agreements

Trade policy is an important determinant of a country's openness to trade, and hence of its growth. In the past 8 years, U.S. policy has supported engagement in global free trade, which has been most evident in the increase in the number of U.S. free trade agreements (FTAs). FTAs are agreements that eliminate tariffs on substantially all trade between two or more countries; U.S. FTAs also reduce other barriers, such as restrictions on services trade and investment. Before 2001, the United States had implemented FTAs with three countries. To date, the United States has concluded FTAs with 20 countries, including 16 in force, one approved by Congress but not yet in force, and three concluded but not yet approved by Congress. The United States has concluded FTAs with trading partners on five continents and with three of our top 10 trading partners. In addition, the United States is currently negotiating FTAs with Malaysia and the members of the Trans-Pacific Strategic Economic Partnership. Chart 4-2 illustrates the progress of U.S. FTAs since 2000, from negotiation to the President's signature to enactment by Congress to being fully in force.

FTAs can dramatically increase trade. U.S. exports to countries whose FTAs came into force during this Administration increased 61 percent from 2000 to 2007, while U.S. imports from these countries increased 26 percent. Recent research shows that, on average worldwide, FTAs increase trade among member countries by about a third after 5 years and more than double trade after 15 years. Because many U.S. FTAs have been in force for less than 5 years, the experience of other countries suggests that these FTAs may continue to expand trade for another decade.

Increased duty-free trade has substantially reduced costs to U.S. importers and exporters and also lowered prices for U.S. consumers. In 2007, 41 percent

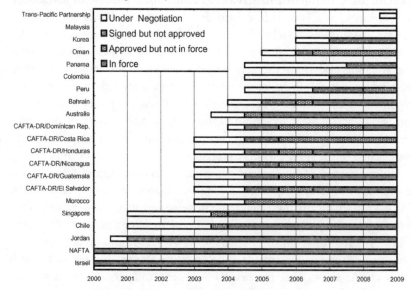

Chart 4-2 **U.S. FTA Progress, 2000-2009**
The number of FTAs at all stages in the process has increased since 2000.

Note: U.S. FTAs with Costa Rica and Oman entered into force on January 1, 2009.
Source: Office of the United States Trade Representative.

of U.S. exports went to FTA partners, and over 98 percent of U.S. products were eligible to enter these foreign markets duty free. In the same year, 31 percent of U.S. imports came from FTA partners, and 95 percent of these imports entered the United States duty free. The reduction in tariffs and quantitative limits, such as quotas, on goods trade in FTAs provides important benefits. Countries gain over time when they liberalize their own market, because capital and labor relocate to sectors in which they will be used more efficiently. Countries also gain immediately when FTA partners liberalize, because this liberalization lowers trade costs and improves the competitive position of exporters.

The size of initial foreign trade barriers is an important determinant of potential export gains from FTAs. One reason that U.S. exports to recent FTA partners increased more than imports from them did, is that in most cases, prior to these agreements, foreign tariffs were higher than U.S. tariffs. Many of these countries apply relatively high tariffs to imports from non-FTA partners, so U.S. FTAs considerably reduced costs to U.S. exporters and improved their competitive position. In contrast, goods from these countries were often already eligible to enter the United States duty free. Several FTA partners also had prior preferential access to the U.S. market under programs such as the Andean Trade Preferences Act and the Generalized System of Preferences, which are discussed in the development assistance section below.

U.S. FTAs also contain many beneficial nontariff provisions; particularly important are investment and services liberalization. Because of investment provisions in U.S. FTAs, U.S. companies that operate abroad benefit from more transparent and less burdensome regulation and greater certainty for investors. Developing countries can benefit from an improved legal framework at home and from the stability of permanent preferential access to U.S. markets, which can make the countries more attractive to international investment in all sectors. Liberalization of foreign services markets can improve access to the telecommunications, financial services, professional services, and other sectors. This access can generate large trade and welfare gains because of the high barriers to services trade in many countries.

Reducing barriers to investment and services can have large effects on trade and even greater effects on economic welfare than tariff liberalization does. FTAs have dramatically increased trade in some sectors with preexisting low, or even zero, tariff rates, demonstrating the positive effects of nontariff liberalizations. International data on barriers to services trade and investment flows are less precise than data on goods trade, so estimates vary, but recent research on U.S. FTAs shows that increased investment and reductions in services barriers can each provide more than twice the gains in purchasing power than can tariff liberalizations alone.

Quantifying the gains from FTAs is difficult because of the many uncertainties involved in estimating the effects that these agreements have on trade flows and on the behavior of producers and consumers, and because data limitations make some benefits currently unquantifiable. One series of reports that has focused on only the gains from tariff liberalizations under all U.S. FTAs finds that U.S. consumers gain about $22 billion in increased purchasing power annually. Other studies, though necessarily more speculative, have also included the gains from greater economies of scale, more product variety, long-run gains from capital accumulation, and reduced services barriers. These studies suggest that cumulatively, U.S. FTAs, both those in force and those pending, could increase U.S. purchasing power by about $150 billion, equivalent to about $1,300 per U.S. household, annually.

Reductions in Tariffs

The United States has one of the lowest average tariff rates in the world. U.S. average tariff rates have been steadily decreasing as duty-free imports from FTA partners have increased in the past decade. The trade-weighted average tariff rate, which gives each of over 11,000 tariff rates a weight equal to the value of U.S. imports in that sector, has been below 2 percent since 1999, and has now fallen below 1.4 percent. Trade-weighted averages can be misleading, however. Because high tariffs reduce trade, sectors with high tariffs are counted less when weighting by trade. The restrictiveness of U.S.

tariffs is better measured by calculating a single, "uniform" tariff that would produce the same volume of trade (or the same purchasing power for U.S. consumers) if applied to all sectors. Recent estimates of such a uniform tariff have been near 5 to 6 percent for the United States. This higher value captures a number of relatively high U.S. tariffs, particularly in agriculture, that are not well represented by the average rate.

The U.S. "uniform" tariff rate of 5 to 6 percent is lower than comparable estimates of tariff protection in major U.S. trading partners, both developing and developed. As in the United States, agricultural tariffs are a major source of other countries' high rates of protection. Because high agricultural protection is a global concern, efforts to reduce it are best negotiated in multilateral institutions such as the World Trade Organization (WTO), which is currently negotiating the Doha Round of trade liberalizations (initiated in Doha, Qatar). The United States and numerous other countries have proposed ambitious reductions in both agricultural tariffs and trade-distorting agricultural subsidies (see Box 4-1) that are critical to a successful market-opening outcome of the Doha Round.

Box 4-1: Farm Subsidies

Government payments to the farm sector have been part of U.S. farm policy since the 1930s, with the goal of increasing the standard of living of American farmers. Although they benefit some farmers, government payments can induce economically wasteful overproduction by encouraging production of higher-cost goods that would be unprofitable without subsidies. Thus, subsidies can generate costs to taxpayers that exceed the benefits received by U.S. producers and consumers. Due to the rise of large commercial farms, subsidies have also become increasingly directed toward high-income farmers. In 2006, farm households with an income over $100,000 received the majority of government payments (compared with the median U.S. household income of approximately $48,000). In addition to monetary costs, farm subsidies can also raise other concerns. Some subsidies require that land be reserved for specific crops, potentially limiting the variety of foodstuffs in local communities, and subsidy-induced production may raise fertilizer use, which contributes to environmentally damaging runoff.

Despite the fact that farm income in the United States is forecast to reach record levels in 2008, taxpayers will provide a projected $13 billion in payments to U.S. farmers this year. In real terms, direct government payments have come down by over half since 2000, when they were the highest ever, even exceeding payments during the farm debt crisis

continued on the next page

Box 4-1 — continued

of the 1980s. This decline was driven primarily by higher market prices for agricultural commodities, rather than by policy initiatives to reduce support. For example, government payments under several programs that provide support when commodity prices drop below a threshold level have declined over 80 percent since 2005, while farm bills, such as the Food, Conservation, and Energy Act of 2008, continue most existing support programs.

Agricultural subsidies are widespread in developed countries, although they represent a lower share of gross farm receipts in the United States than in the EU and in many other countries, including Japan, Korea, and Canada. Because subsidies can impose greater costs than benefits, reducing subsidies would increase incomes and economic welfare; indeed, research suggests eliminating agricultural subsidies in developed countries would increase U.S. welfare by several billion dollars per year. In developing countries, reducing subsidies would raise agricultural prices and improve the lives of producers, although it could also raise the cost of some food for consumers. Given the prevalence of agricultural support, multilateral agreements are the single most effective way to address this issue. The Doha Round of the WTO trade talks has included negotiations on limiting subsidies with the greatest potential to stimulate overproduction and distort trade. In July 2008, as part of the Doha talks, the U.S. Trade Representative announced that the United States was prepared to limit this subset of subsidies to $15 billion annually, down from the $22 billion limit offered in 2005. In the United States, these subsidies have exceeded the proposed new $15 billion limit in seven of the last 10 years.

The Benefits of Open Investment

The ability to either export excess savings in return for foreign assets or to borrow savings and invest more than is saved within the country can allow nations both to achieve higher income growth than would otherwise be possible and to cushion temporary shocks to the economy. Over time, the United States has benefited in both ways. For example, foreign demand for secure investments has lowered borrowing costs for the U.S. Government. There have also been benefits from accumulating assets overseas: U.S. businesses and investors have been able to make use of their foreign asset holdings to diversify, reduce risk, and raise overall returns on investments.

Economic growth has likely been supported by openness to foreign investment in a variety of ways, including an increase in the amount of capital available for investment; greater transfer of technology; increased employment; and greater access to global capital, goods, and services by domestic firms. Although still a matter of debate among economists, foreign direct investment is generally considered to convey all of these benefits in a particularly straightforward fashion. According to the latest data available from the Commerce Department, in 2006, U.S. affiliates of foreign companies accounted for 6.1 percent of U.S. nonbank private sector production, provided more than 5.3 million jobs to American workers (4.6 percent of the U.S. workforce), spent $34.3 billion on research and development (14 percent of U.S. expenditure on R&D), and accounted for 19 percent of U.S. exports.

The benefits that a country receives are related to the volume and composition of its investment flows. The net flow of investment across borders is equal to the gap between the value of goods and services that a nation exports and the value of the goods and services it imports. This is also equal to the difference between a nation's savings and its domestic investment. Nations that save more than they invest domestically invest these extra savings in the rest of the world, and in the process purchase foreign assets, including bonds, equities, and FDI. Nations whose domestic investment exceeds their savings receive investments from abroad and, in doing so, sell assets to foreign residents.

The composition of investment flows is in part determined by the willingness of the investor to accept greater risk in exchange for a potentially higher return. Chart 4-3a provides a breakdown of types of foreign assets accumulated by U.S. investors (including the government), and Chart 4-3b shows the types of U.S. assets accumulated by foreign investors. Relative to foreign investors in the United States, U.S. private investors have been relatively risk-tolerant in their holdings of foreign assets, particularly in holdings of private *portfolio* stocks and FDI. Portfolio stocks constituted 30 percent of total private foreign investment by U.S. investors in 2007, whereas they constituted 17 percent for foreign investors in the United States. Likewise, U.S. investors allocated 19 percent of their foreign holdings to FDI, whereas private foreign investors only allocated 14 percent of their U.S. investments to FDI. In keeping with their lower risk appetite, foreign private investors held twice the share of bonds, including U.S. Treasury bonds, in their U.S. asset holdings (24 percent of private investment) than U.S. investors held in their foreign asset holdings (9 percent of private investment). There was also a pronounced difference in official government holdings. Foreign governments and official institutions held 17 percent of all U.S. assets owned by foreigners, whereas the U.S. Government held only 2 percent of the total foreign assets in U.S. residents' possession. The majority of foreign official holdings of U.S. assets in 2007 were U.S. Treasury bonds and bonds issued by government-sponsored enterprises (GSEs) such as Fannie Mae and Freddie Mac.

Chart 4-3a **U.S. Holdings of Foreign Assets, 2007 (US$ bil)**
U.S. investors abroad are relatively risk-tolerant.

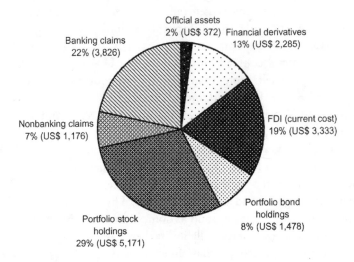

Source: Department of Commerce (Bureau of Economic Analysis).

Chart 4-3b **Foreign Holdings of U.S. Assets, 2007 (US$ bil)**
Foreign investors in the United States are relatively risk-averse.

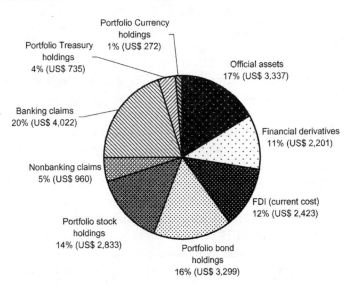

Source: Department of Commerce (Bureau of Economic Analysis).

U.S. Investment and Investment Policy

Since the early 1980s, the United States has received more capital from foreign investors than U.S. residents invested abroad. Table 4-2 provides capital flow data for the years 2000 through 2007, the latest available data. There are many aspects about the United States that have proved attractive to foreign investors, including the size, diversity, liquidity, and depth of U.S. financial markets. According to one estimate, U.S. financial markets accounted for approximately one-third of the world supply of financial assets in 2006 (the latest year for which data are available). The U.S. share of the world supply of securities available to investors may even be much higher, given that in many countries the fraction of a company's shares available on the market may be much lower due to the large controlling stake in the company held by the government, a financial institution, or a family. In addition, U.S. markets offer strong minority shareholder rights and other property rights, a large domestic market, opportunities to invest in technological innovation, and demographic trends that result in a younger and faster-growing population than in most other advanced nations.

Much attention has been given to the large purchases of U.S. assets by foreign governments (primarily central banks and sovereign wealth funds; see Box 4-2). Although official flows (primarily foreign exchange reserves invested in the United States) are important, private flows are much larger. In 2000, for example, total foreign capital inflows into the United States were $1,038 billion of which private capital flows were $995 billion, or 96 percent of the total. Since then the share of *private* flows has not fallen below 68 percent, and it stood at 80 percent in 2007, the last year for which data are available. FDI and other investment flows are likely to be affected, even if only in the short to medium term, by the current financial crisis. This is the subject of Box 4-3.

TABLE 4-2.—*Capital Flows into and out of the United States*
(billions of U.S. dollars)

	2000	2001	2002	2003	2004	2005	2006	2007
Foreign Capital Inflow.................	$1,038	$783	$795	$858	$1,533	$1,247	$2,061	$2,058
Of Which: Private Flows................	995	755	679	580	1,135	988	1,573	1,647
U.S. Capital Outflow..........................	561	383	295	325	1,001	547	1,252	1,290
Net Capital Inflow into the U.S.........	417	385	461	523	625	729	788	731

Note: The net capital inflow figures are equal to those reported as the current account. This series differs from a straight subtraction of outflows from inflows due to omissions of certain types of financial transactions and statistical discrepancies.
Source: Department of Commerce (Bureau of Economic Analysis).

Box 4-2: Sovereign Wealth Funds

A *sovereign wealth fund* (SWF) is a state-owned investment fund. While there is no widely recognized definition of a SWF, typical hallmarks include that it holds foreign financial assets; makes some long- or medium-term investments that are riskier than the safe, liquid assets that make up official foreign currency reserves held for balance of payments or monetary policy purposes; and has few or no defined obligations, such as paying pension benefits or other specific liabilities. Nations may create SWFs for many purposes, including to earn higher returns on foreign currency holdings in excess of desired reserve assets, stabilize fiscal revenues, save wealth across generations, or fund development projects. SWFs are typically funded through commodity exports such as oil, gas, or diamonds, or through transfer of official foreign reserves accumulated as a result of large trade surpluses. Examples of some large SWFs include the United Arab Emirates' Abu Dhabi Investment Authority, Norway's Norges Bank Investment Management, the Government of Singapore Investment Corporation, and the China Investment Corporation.

Sovereign wealth funds have existed at least since the 1950s, but the amount of money estimated to be in such funds has increased dramatically in the past 10 to 15 years. One recent study estimates that SWFs currently manage $3.6 trillion in assets, and that total could rise to $10 trillion by 2015, although recent decreases in commodity prices will lower this projection. In 2006–2007, the amount of assets held by SWFs was large compared to the amounts held by private equity ($0.8 trillion) and hedge funds ($1.9 trillion), but was dwarfed by the assets held by insurance companies, mutual funds, and pension funds (on the order of $20 trillion each).

Sovereign wealth funds have the potential to promote global financial stability by acting as long-term, stable investors that provide significant capital to the system. They are not typically highly leveraged and would therefore not be under pressure to sell off assets for the purpose of meeting debt obligations. At the same time, the performance incentives that SWFs face remain opaque, and like all large, concentrated investors, SWFs could cause market volatility by abruptly shifting their asset allocations to avoid losses. The extent to which SWFs act as a stabilizing force in financial markets is an open empirical question that may be difficult to answer due to the lack of transparency of many SWFs.

Foreign investment, including investment by SWFs, provides capital to U.S. businesses, improves productivity, and creates jobs. The United States is currently the largest recipient of SWF investment. Investment

continued on the next page

Box 4-2 — continued

from SWFs has helped to shore up financial institutions during the credit crisis: sovereign wealth funds invested an estimated $92 billion in global financial institutions from January 2007 to July 2008.

The increasing size of SWFs in global financial markets has prompted some concern, however. For recipient countries, ownership of sensitive assets by foreign governments may pose national security concerns. High-profile investments by SWFs may also provoke a protectionist backlash against foreign investment. In April 2008, the Organization for Economic Co-operation and Development (OECD) published investment policy principles for countries that receive SWF investment, endorsing long-standing OECD principles against protectionist investment barriers and for nondiscriminatory treatment of investors. The principles stress that when additional investment restrictions are required to address legitimate national security concerns, then investment safeguards by recipient countries should be transparent and predictable, proportional to clearly identified national security risks, and supportive of accountability.

Countries that own SWFs have also raised concerns about the governance and accountability of these funds, and recognize that it is in their interest to ensure that their money is invested well. In October 2008, a group of 23 countries with SWFs published the Generally Accepted Principles and Practices, known as the "Santiago Principles," for sovereign wealth funds. The voluntary principles stress that SWFs should be transparent and accountable and should make investment decisions based on commercial principles. Adherence to these principles not only will help ensure that SWFs are well managed, but will have the additional benefit of reassuring recipient countries that SWF investments are financially stable and are economically and financially motivated.

Box 4-3: The Effect of the Current Economic Slowdown on Foreign Investment into the United States.

The large capital inflows into the United States over the past decade have led to many benefits described in this chapter. It is too early to say definitively how the financial crisis will affect these inflows. There are two aspects to this issue. First, there is the question of whether the supply of credit that net-saver nations provide to the rest of the world will be reduced. This credit has primarily flowed from Asian economies

continued on the next page

Box 4-3 — continued

(including Japan's), whose combined current account surplus (a measure of capital outflows) was $608 billion higher in 2007 than it was in 1997, and Middle East economies, whose combined current account surplus was $253 billion higher in 2007 than in 1997. To the extent that the recent slowdown in global economic activity reduces demand for Asian exports and petroleum products (as well as other commodities), the net savings available from these nations may fall if savings rates do not rise sharply. Moreover, foreign countries' savings are also likely to decline if governments decide to engage in higher spending to boost their flagging economies, thereby lowering the amount of government saving. Such spending would reduce the gap between national saving and domestic investment and reduce the supply of credit to the rest of the world, raising world interest rates.

The second question is whether the cost of foreign savings to the United States will rise. This depends on U.S. demand for foreign savings and the relative desirability of U.S. assets for foreign investors. The rising U.S. demand for foreign savings over the past decade is evident in Table 4-2. To add further evidence, the current account *deficit* of the United States (equal to net capital inflows) was $591 billion higher in 2007 than in 1997, and the United States received net investment from the rest of the world equal to 1.3 percent of world GDP in 2007, compared with average net foreign investment in the United States equal to 0.7 percent of world GDP from 1994 to 2001. Although predictions vary, U.S. imports and exports are both anticipated to fall sharply, likely leading to continued high levels of net capital inflows, and therefore high demand for foreign savings. If other nations that have relied on net capital inflows also maintain their same level of demand for foreign savings as well, unchanged demand in the United States for a potentially shrinking supply of global savings would tend to raise the cost of obtaining these inflows.

Yet the cost of foreign savings has not increased for the United States, and this primarily reflects an increase in the relative desirability of U.S. Treasury bonds for global investors. The net inflow of foreign savings into U.S. Treasuries has permitted the U.S. Government to borrow at a relatively low cost, and this has so far helped cushion the impact of the crisis on the U.S. economy. The relative desirability of U.S. Government bonds reflects a seismic decrease in global investors' appetite for risk. This has generated enormous demand for low risk assets such as U.S. Treasuries. If global investors' appetite for risk returns, demand for Treasuries will likely fall and whether the cost of foreign savings will rise for the United States will depend on the relative attractiveness of U.S. investments compared to opportunities abroad.

Foreign Direct Investment into the United States

For statistical purposes, the United States defines foreign direct investment (FDI) as the acquisition of at least 10 percent of an existing U.S. business, or the establishment of a new business, by a foreign person. The business acquired or formed as a result of the FDI is known as a U.S. affiliate of the foreign *parent*. Outlays for new FDI into the United States rose in 2006 and 2007, and the rate of increase of spending for new FDI greatly exceeded the rate of increase of U.S. merger and acquisition activity. Of total new FDI outlays into the United States of $277 billion in 2007, $255 billion (92 percent) was for the acquisition of existing U.S. firms, while $22 billion (8 percent) was for the establishment of entirely new businesses, according to preliminary data. In 2006, the three countries with the greatest production (or *value added*) by U.S. affiliates as a share of total U.S. affiliate production were the United Kingdom (19.6 percent), Japan (12.3 percent), and Germany (11.0 percent). The three biggest industry recipients of FDI new investment outlays in 2007 were manufacturing (49 percent), finance and insurance (9 percent), and real estate and rental and leasing (7 percent).

U.S. affiliates of foreign businesses are a large force in the U.S. economy, and their importance has increased in certain ways. Over the past 20 years, U.S. affiliates have increased their contribution to U.S. production from 3.8 percent of U.S. private sector production in 1988 to 6.1 percent of production by 2006 (the latest year available). The employment share of U.S. affiliates reached 4.6 percent in 2006. In 2007, newly acquired or established U.S. affiliates employed 487,600 people (including 147,500 in manufacturing and 143,600 in retail).

Although U.S. affiliates of foreign businesses are distinguished by relatively high wages and productivity, these attributes may reflect the nature of the industries to which FDI is attracted rather than any special attribute of foreign ownership itself. However, the ability to sell a business to foreign investors interested in acquiring new technology creates an incentive for entrepreneurs to innovate by increasing the potential rewards. There are other benefits as well. Studies that investigate the unique benefits of FDI, as opposed to other forms of foreign financing, typically claim that FDI can introduce new technologies to domestic industries and increase the nation's growth rate as these new technologies are adopted and spread throughout the economy.

Efforts to measure *technological spillovers* have often come to conflicting conclusions about the extent of these benefits. Many studies indicate that the benefits of FDI for the host country depend heavily on context. One recent study, for example, finds results that are sensitive to the level of worker education in the region where the investment is being made. Its findings indicate that FDI stimulates economic growth most for U.S. States where worker education exceeds certain threshold levels.

U.S. affiliates may be most productive if they are located near other firms with similar technical and knowledge requirements, or near a large number of workers with specialized skills and suppliers with specialized inputs. A recent study that finds that U.S. affiliates tend to cluster in specific areas (often with other U.S. affiliates with parents from the same country). For example, Connecticut and South Carolina tied for the largest U.S. affiliate share of private industry employment at 7.1 percent. Most of the U.S. affiliates in Connecticut were controlled by Dutch businesses, whereas the U.S. affiliates in South Carolina were heavily associated with German businesses.

Foreign Investment Policy

The perception that openness to foreign investment must be traded off against security is misguided. Foreign investment gives investors in other countries an economic stake in the prosperity of the United States, creating an incentive to support policies that are good for U.S. growth and stability. Nonetheless, foreign acquisition of assets or businesses may create a risk to national security if production of key resources could be disrupted or if sensitive information or technologies may be disclosed. The Exon-Florio provision of the Defense Production Act of 1950, which became law in 1988, provides for the President or the President's designee to review certain foreign investments in the United States. If a transaction threatens to impair national security, the President is authorized to prohibit the transaction.

In October 2007, the Foreign Investment and National Security Act of 2007 (FINSA) became effective, amending Exon-Florio in various ways, including by codifying the structure, role, process, and responsibilities of the interagency Committee on Foreign Investment in the United States (CFIUS), which has been designated by the President to undertake Exon-Florio reviews since 1988. Although FINSA expands government oversight of some foreign acquisitions, it also increases the transparency and predictability of the CFIUS process. With the publication of final regulations in November 2008, FINSA is now fully implemented.

Development Assistance Initiatives

The United States benefits from increased trade as other economies grow and become more open, but the main benefits of development assistance programs include improving the lives of disadvantaged populations, increasing economic and political stability abroad, and fostering closer ties to the United States. The United States has many long-standing economic assistance commitments, including those funded through the United States Agency for International Development (USAID), the Departments of State and Defense, and funding for multilateral development institutions such as the World Bank. Under this Administration, the United States has initiated and expanded specific economic assistance programs in developing economies, particularly those that practice good governance; make trade a prominent feature of their development plans; and demonstrate a commitment to taking ownership of the reforms, planning, and logistics required for the success of development programs and projects. Economic assistance programs, including trade capacity building (TCB) programs, are provided primarily by the Millennium Challenge Corporation (MCC) and USAID, and investment promotion programs are provided by the Overseas Private Investment Corporation (OPIC). The United States offers developing countries, particularly the least developed, preferential access to the U.S. market through several preferential trade programs. The United States also has health and education initiatives such as the President's Emergency Plan for AIDS Relief (PEPFAR).

To put these programs in context, U.S. spending on four of these initiatives from fiscal year 2000 to 2007 is shown in Chart 4-4. MCC has had a steady increase in funding since its inception in 2004. Spending on "Other TCB" in Chart 4-4 does not include TCB funds that are already included in spending by MCC and OPIC; overall, TCB funding rose to $2.3 billion in 2008. The highest spending from 2004 through 2006 was on PEPFAR, reaching $4 billion in 2007. The MCC, TCB, and OPIC, in addition to trade preference

Chart 4-4 **U.S. Obligations on Select Development Assistance Initiatives, 2000-2007**
Spending on innovative new development initiatives such as PEPFAR and the MCC has increased significantly.

Billions of U.S. dollars

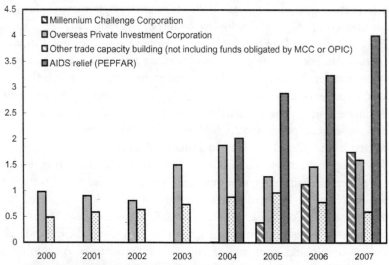

Sources: U.S. Agency for International Development, President's Emergency Plan for AIDS Relief, Millennium Challenge Corporation, and Overseas Private Investment Corporation.

programs, are each discussed below, while PEPFAR is described in the section on health programs in Chapter 7.

Millennium Challenge Corporation

In 2002, the President announced the creation of the Millennium Challenge Account (MCA), a new bilateral initiative aimed at reducing poverty through investment programs, or *compacts*, of up to five years with countries that practice good governance, provide economic freedoms, and invest in their people's health and education. The Millennium Challenge Corporation (MCC) was set up to administer the MCA, and the importance of the MCC's focus on reducing poverty through economic growth is supported by research showing that economic growth is an important precursor for poverty reduction. In recognition of this relationship, before approving projects, MCC gathers evidence that the problems to be addressed by potential MCC-funded projects are indeed critical constraints to a country's growth. The strong commitment by MCC to near-universal application of cost–benefit analysis and rigorous, state-of-the-art project evaluation will allow the development community to better understand and learn important lessons about the effectiveness of various types of aid projects. Without making advances in knowledge about which projects are effective, U.S. efforts to improve the lives of targeted populations may not ultimately succeed. Given that most of MCC's compacts are currently in progress, it is too early to evaluate whether MCC has met its objectives.

Trade Capacity Building

An important goal of U.S. trade policy is to create opportunities for individuals and companies in developing countries. Trade capacity building (TCB), also called Aid for Trade, helps developing countries build capacity so that they can take advantage of global markets and implement trade rules. Top priorities for this aid are to develop infrastructure, strengthen financial markets, improve customs operations, develop sound business environments, and facilitate trade. The United States is the largest single-country donor of TCB assistance, spending $2.3 billion in the 2008 fiscal year, and it has committed to provide $2.7 billion in annual spending by 2010.

A key component of TCB is improving key physical infrastructure needs—such as transportation, ports, telecommunications, electricity, and water—in developing regions. In recent years, the United States has supported road building in rural Colombia, pipeline rehabilitation in Georgia, and the construction of a new international airport in Ecuador. TCB funds also strengthen developing countries' financial infrastructure. A number of programs are aimed at improving the productivity and business practices in micro-, small-, and medium-sized businesses, and at improving lending to these businesses.

Trade facilitation is another important part of TCB. Trade facilitation funds are used chiefly to modernize customs practices, promote exports from developing countries, and provide business support and training to help firms participate in global markets. Improvements in these areas are often key to generating new trade and investment flows in these countries. For example, trade may increase because improved customs practices reduce costs and shorten delivery times. The United States has supported projects to improve the flow of goods at the Kenya-Uganda border and along the route from coastal Namibia to South Africa. Investment may increase because trade facilitation addresses areas of chief concern to many international investors; a 2007 survey reported that customs and ports improvements are the highest priority for international investors in some emerging markets.

Recent U.S. trade agreements, such as the Dominican Republic-Central America-United States Free Trade Agreement, include a formal Committee on TCB to help trading partners implement the agreement and to smooth the transition to new trading regimes. The United States also promotes TCB more broadly. For example, the United States supports efforts by the WTO and the OECD to expand worldwide funding for Aid for Trade. This aid helps developing countries, particularly least-developed countries, enhance trade-related skills and improve infrastructure needed to expand trade and benefit from trade agreements. Along these lines, the Africa Global Competitiveness Initiative, announced by the President in 2005 to build on the African Growth and Opportunity Act, provides technical assistance to bolster the trade competitiveness of African countries. This initiative has been credited with supporting $35 million in exports by African Growth and Opportunity Act beneficiaries in 2007. The United States also supports the Integrated Framework that coordinates efforts by six multilateral organizations (including the International Monetary Fund, the World Bank, the WTO, and other organizations) to reduce poverty in developing countries by better integrating trade into national development strategies.

Investment Promotion Programs

The United States also facilitates investment in emerging and developing countries by U.S. companies through the Overseas Private Investment Corporation. According to the corporation's 2007 annual report, it has supported over $177 billion in U.S. investment abroad through its pioneering use of U.S. Government-backed political risk insurance, direct loans, guaranties, and equity funds. These investments, which help provide crucial opportunities to households and firms in developing economics, also contribute to increased foreign asset holdings of U.S. residents.

In addition, *bilateral investment treaties* foster market-oriented investment policies in partner countries, and support international standards for investment protection. In February 2008, the Administration signed a bilateral investment treaty with Rwanda. When implemented, it will bring the number of U.S. bilateral investment treaties in force to 41. The U.S. Government is pursuing investment treaties with key emerging markets, as demonstrated by the 2008 announcements of treaty negotiations with China, India, and Vietnam.

Trade Preference Programs

Four U.S. preference programs are among the central elements of U.S. trade policy to promote growth and stability in developing countries. These programs provide preferential duty-free access for thousands of products that would otherwise be subject to duty upon entry to the United States. The U.S. Generalized System of Preferences, for example, provides duty-free access to the U.S. market for over 3,400 products from 132 beneficiary developing countries, and provides even broader duty-free access for products from 44 least developed countries. In addition to the Generalized System of Preferences, U.S. preferential trade programs include the African Growth and Opportunity Act, the Caribbean Basin Initiative, and the Andean Trade Preference Act. These programs have been successful in increasing and diversifying developing countries' exports, which better integrates these countries into the global trading system and expands choices for U.S. manufacturers and consumers. These programs have also improved economic stability, promoted internationally recognized labor rights, and provided adequate and effective means to secure and enforce property rights, including intellectual property rights. Researchers have cautioned that preference programs can have negative consequences if preferences divert limited resources in developing countries to sectors that would not otherwise be competitive. Research on specific U.S. programs, however, suggests that in general these programs have increased exports and improved welfare.

These programs have generated many successes. The Generalized System of Preferences has a large and geographically diverse impact. For example, for 15 beneficiary countries, more than one-third of their exports to the United States received preferential duty-free access under the program in 2007. Under the Caribbean Basin Initiative and the associated Haiti Hope Act, Haiti—the poorest country in the Western Hemisphere—increased apparel exports to the United States by 75 percent between 2000 and 2007. These benefits helped to preserve an important sector of the Haitian economy. The African Growth and Opportunity Act has also been successful in increasing trade. For January to October 2008, exports from the original African beneficiary countries to the United States increased over 250 percent compared to the same period in 2001, and exports that entered the United States duty free under the program exceeded $50 billion, up almost 700 percent. U.S. exports to sub-Saharan Africa more than doubled in the same period, totaling over $15 billion in 2008 through October.

Trade Policy Going Forward

Notwithstanding the rapid increase in U.S. regional and bilateral trade and investment agreements, the multilateral trading system remains at the heart of U.S. trade policy. The rules-based multilateral system of the WTO is the essential foundation of an increasingly integrated global economy, and the WTO remains the single best forum to generate progress on many global trade and investment issues. Such issues include reducing trade-distorting support and protection for agricultural sectors maintained by many countries, both developing and developed; and liberalizing trade barriers and burdensome restrictions on FDI in services sectors in developing countries.

The United States must continue to lead international efforts to address these and similar issues in order to expand the benefits of open markets and economic integration. In particular, the WTO Doha Round remains a top U.S. trade policy objective, with the goal of concluding an agreement that creates new trade flows in agricultural, industrial, and services markets that will expand global economic growth, development, and opportunity. The United States and many other countries remain committed to reaching a successful final agreement that achieves an ambitious market-opening outcome for both developed and developing countries.

In the history of global trade liberalization, there has not been smooth and uniform progress toward ever lower barriers. There have been long periods of inactivity or, worse, periods of rising protectionism. Previous periods of economic hardship have often coincided with an increase in protectionism and economic isolationism; for example, the use of nontariff barriers such as quotas rose in the 1970s and 1980s. In the current troubled economic environment, an increase in protectionism at home or abroad could further slow global economic progress. Limiting trade would jeopardize the strongest engine of growth of the past 2 years in the U.S. economy. In the short term, the United States must provide global leadership to oppose any resurgence of protectionism, while continuing to recognize and support the extensive benefits that an open trade and investment environment conveys.

In the longer term, the forces of greater global economic integration appear strong. During this Administration, as the United States implemented FTAs with 13 countries, more than 100 other countries put more than 75 other FTAs into force. Other nations will press forward and so must the United

States to avoid becoming economically disadvantaged in foreign markets. The United States should continue to pursue free trade agreements and, in particular, put into force those that have already been negotiated. The growth in bilateral agreements further emphasizes the importance of multi-lateral initiatives such as the WTO Doha Round, which can magnify gains by simultaneously reducing barriers in many countries, ensure that the benefits of market access are shared more widely among nations, and lead to trans-parent and less complex global trading rules.

Conclusion

The United States' commitment to openness in trade and investment and promotion of open markets abroad has led to a greater diversity in consumer choices, more exposure to new technologies and ideas, and higher levels of investment and economic growth than would otherwise have been possible. Openness to trade and investment has contributed to higher U.S. standards of living and has allowed the United States some structural flexibility to cushion economic shocks. On balance, strong links to other economies are likely to increase the resilience of the U.S. economy in the short and long term, even taking into account the potential for negative shocks, such as a decline in demand for U.S. exports. Short-run hardships will surely occur, and it may take some time for current weaknesses to be resolved, but the U.S. commitment to openness provides substantial benefits in both the short and long run.

With regard to trade, the U.S. commitment to openness has been most evident in the increased number of U.S. free trade agreements. These agreements have improved the competitiveness and performance of U.S. producers abroad and have provided substantial savings for U.S. producers and consumers at home. In investment, the United States has benefited from inflows of capital from abroad. Although it is unclear how future flows will be affected by the current crisis, U.S. investors have historically earned high returns on their investments abroad. The recent reform of the Committee on Foreign Investment in the United States represents a careful effort to remain open to foreign investors while safeguarding national security.

U.S. development assistance has supported openness in developing and emerging economies through investment in infrastructure, trade capacity building, trade preference programs, and investment promotion. U.S. efforts to relieve poverty and promote economic growth and stability have helped numerous developing countries. In addition, the United States' continued promotion of trade with developing countries will improve their access to, and ability to benefit from, global markets.

CHAPTER 5

Tax Policy

Economists agree that taxes affect people's incentives and behavior. For example, allowing tax deductions for educational expenses makes it cheaper to go to college, which may encourage more people to go to college. Taxes can also discourage people from engaging in certain activities. Taxes on cigarettes, for example, make them more expensive to purchase, which may discourage people from buying them. Similarly, taxes on *dividends* (periodic distributions of a firm's profits to stockholders) and *capital gains* (the growth in value of an asset, such as corporate stock) decrease the return people receive from investing their money, which might cause them to invest less. When a higher tax rate is imposed on an activity, people have less incentive to engage in that activity. To encourage people to work and invest more, the tax rates on labor and investment income should be reduced. Over the past 8 years, several policy changes have resulted in lower tax rates for both individuals and businesses.

Individual income tax rates for all income levels are lower now than they were in 2001. Also, specific incentives have been established to reduce the adverse tax consequences of certain desirable activities, from running a small business to buying an alternative-fuel vehicle. Lower tax rates have increased the benefit to these activities; in particular, lower tax rates on dividends and capital gains helped business investment expand, thereby increasing the amount of capital per worker which improves worker productivity. Tax relief has contributed to the solid economic growth and job creation that prevailed over most of the past several years.

However, important challenges remain. Foremost among these is the fact that most of these tax reductions are scheduled to expire at the end of 2010. Allowing them to expire would constitute one of the largest tax increases in history and could have serious consequences for the U.S. economy. Another challenge is to further reduce business tax burdens and thereby encourage business investment in the United States. The United States should continue to attract such investment in today's global economy in order to develop better jobs for U.S. workers and to continue improving our standard of living.

Of course, individuals and businesses would prefer not to be taxed at all. Yet governments perform many functions desired by citizens—such as building roads and bridges, maintaining law and order, and providing for the national defense—and impose taxes to raise revenue for these activities. While this chapter focuses on the economic effects of taxes, it should be noted that this is only one side of the Government's budget; a complete analysis of fiscal policy should consider the economic effects of both the revenue and spending sides of the budget.

The key points of this chapter are:

- Taxes alter individual and business incentives and have the potential to distort their behavior. This Administration consistently fought to reduce tax burdens on individuals and businesses; tax rates are now much lower than they were just 8 years ago.
- Tax reductions over the past 8 years have improved incentives to work, save, and invest.
- Globally, nations compete for businesses and the associated jobs; the United States may need to reduce tax rates on businesses to remain competitive in today's world.
- Future goals should include permanently extending the tax relief of the past 8 years and reforming the Alternative Minimum Tax (AMT).

Individual Income Tax Reform

Governments impose taxes to obtain the revenue needed to perform their duties. The transfer of resources from individuals to the government does not directly impose a burden on the overall economy because the ability to purchase goods and services shifts from the individual to the government— there is no net loss for the economy as a whole. However, taxes can impose a considerable burden on the economy for other reasons. Most significantly, taxes interfere with the efficient allocation of resources by altering the rewards from working, saving, and investing.

Resources are allocated efficiently when individuals and firms allocate them to the activities for which they are best suited, thus achieving the highest possible output for the economy. Without taxes, individuals and firms can allocate resources in the most efficient manner possible. With taxes, people receive lower benefits from taxed activities and adjust their behavior accordingly. (In some cases, such as when people engage in an activity that produces negative consequences for others, imposing a tax can improve economic efficiency; for example, high taxes on cigarettes can reduce the damage caused by secondhand smoke.)

High tax rates on labor income can induce people to reduce the time they spend working. This is particularly true for people with flexible work weeks and in households with a second worker. High tax rates on dividends and capital gains discourage people from investing and reduce the funds available in financial markets. In turn, this reduces business investment, which reduces the amount of capital available in the economy. Less capital means less machinery and equipment for each worker to use, making workers less productive and leading to reductions in wages. The net result of these tax-caused changes is an inefficient allocation of resources: output is lower than it would have been in the absence of taxes. Economic research indicates that the total economic burden imposed on the economy for each dollar of income tax revenue collected actually exceeds 1 dollar, but estimates of the exact burden vary widely.

A second problem arises when people engage in activities to avoid paying taxes. The possibilities here include both legal activities, such as using complicated tax shelters to prevent income from being taxed, and illegal activities, such as not filing a tax return. While the great majority of people pay the taxes they owe, the latest Internal Revenue Service (IRS) estimate suggests that the gap between the amount of tax people owed and the amount actually paid was approximately $290 billion in 2001, or 13.7 percent of all taxes owed. One consequence of people failing to pay their fair share of taxes is that a higher tax rate must be imposed on those who do comply with tax laws in order to collect the desired amount of revenue.

Lowering Tax Rates Stimulates Economic Growth

Taxing earned income reduces incentives to work because it reduces the return from work. Similarly, taxing capital income (such as interest, dividends, and capital gains) reduces the return from saving and investing and therefore reduces the incentive to save and invest. The changes in incentives, along with any associated behavioral changes that result from changes in tax rates, are what economists mean when they assert that taxes "distort" the normal operation of labor and capital markets. When taxes are imposed on choices people make, distortions tend to occur and markets operate at less than peak efficiency. Because different types of taxes create different types and sizes of distortions, one goal of tax policy should be to choose tax rates that minimize the distortions and the accompanying inefficiencies whenever possible.

Key determinants of the effect a tax system has on the economy are the *average tax rate*—the fraction of income paid in taxes—and the *marginal tax rate*—the amount of tax owed on an additional (that is, marginal) dollar of income. A high average tax rate tends to discourage people from engaging in an activity at all. For example, a high average tax rate on labor income can reduce the total after-tax return so much that it discourages people from working at all. In contrast, a high marginal tax rate on labor income reduces an individual's after-tax return from *increased* work effort and from investing in additional education. The example in Box 5-1 examines this particular issue in more detail. Because education levels positively affect productivity, economic growth will generally be higher when people acquire more education.

By reducing both average and marginal tax rates on labor and capital income at almost every income level, the tax policies of the past 8 years reduced the distortionary effects of these taxes and thereby improved the efficiency of the labor and capital markets and of the U.S. economy as a whole.

Box 5-1: Encouraging Human Capital Investment

High marginal tax rates can discourage people from pursuing additional education and improving their skills to qualify for a higher-paying job. To see this, consider a high school teacher who is choosing between continuing to work for about $50,000 per year (the median salary for high school teachers in 2007), and getting additional education so he can become a school principal and earn $80,000 per year (the median salary for elementary and secondary education administrators in 2007). Although there may be other factors, suppose this worker's main concern is his after-tax income.

Consider the impact of two different tax regimes: In the first regime, assume the high school teacher would owe $5,000 per year in income tax and the principal would owe $12,500 per year in income tax. The difference, $7,500, is the additional tax he would owe if he were to acquire the skills needed to be a principal. Comparing this amount to the expected increase in income ($30,000), we see that the marginal tax rate imposed on the additional income is 25 percent ($7,500/$30,000). In the second regime, assume an alternate tax system in which the high school teacher owes $3,000 per year in tax and the principal owes $15,000 per year in tax. Under this new system, the tax impact of acquiring additional skills is $12,000. Comparing this to the expected increase in income (still $30,000) reveals that the marginal tax rate imposed on the additional income is 40 percent ($12,000/$30,000).

The larger marginal tax rate in the second regime means the worker experiences a smaller increase in after-tax income; thus, his incentive to acquire the skills necessary for the higher-paying job is smaller in this regime and may cause him not to pursue additional education.

As an aside, notice that if the worker chooses to stay a high school teacher, he pays more in income tax in the first regime ($5,000) than he would in the second ($3,000). Part of the reason the first regime has a lower marginal tax rate for additional education is that there is a higher average tax rate on lower-earning individuals than in the second regime.

Increased Work Incentives

A labor income tax decreases the incentive workers have to supply labor to the market by reducing their take-home pay. Workers may choose to work fewer hours, and some may even choose not to work at all. These behavioral changes reduce the efficiency of the labor market and of the economy as a whole. The tax relief of 2001 reduced tax rates on labor income and thereby reduced the distortions and efficiency losses created by taxing wages.

Economists have found that different people can be affected differently by taxes. Some people exhibit very little change in labor supply as tax rates vary, while others may enter or exit the workforce entirely. Consider a married couple in which one person works at a full-time job; call this person the primary breadwinner for the family and assume he makes $50,000 per year and works a fixed 40-hour week. The other person has the option of working at an hourly job and can earn up to $10,000 per year, depending on how many hours she works; call this person the secondary earner. When there is a change in tax rates, the breadwinner will probably continue to work the same amount of time because of the importance of his income to the family and his fixed work hours. However, the work decisions for the secondary earner are not as clear. Because married couples are taxed on their combined income, any income earned by the secondary earner will be taxed at the marginal tax rate facing the couple. Because an income tax lowers the reward for working outside the home, it makes other activities (such as leisure or raising a family) look relatively more attractive compared to work. An increase in the marginal tax rate facing the couple could reduce the return the secondary earner receives from working by enough to cause her to choose not to work at all. Alternatively, if a worker wants to earn a specific amount of income, higher tax rates could cause her to increase work time.

In practice, economists find the labor supply of married men to be relatively stable regardless of changes in tax rates. Research shows, however, the labor supply of married women to be quite sensitive to changes in tax rates, although this sensitivity has declined over the last few decades as labor force participation by women aged 25–54 increased from about 50 percent in 1970 to over 75 percent in 2008.

The tax relief of the past 8 years reduced marginal tax rates at almost every income level, reduced the distortions inherent in taxing earned income, and thereby increased the rewards from working and encouraged more people to work. In addition, tax relief that reduced marriage penalties improved the incentives for secondary earners to participate in the labor force.

Increased Saving and Investment Incentives

When individuals receive income, they can either spend it for current consumption or save it to finance future consumption. Financial intermediaries, such as banks and insurance companies, pool individual savings to finance capital investments. For example, a bank may combine the savings deposits of many individuals to make a loan to a small business owner. The business owner plans to make a profit so she can pay interest on her loan, which the bank uses to pay interest to the depositors. Similarly, when people purchase stock in a company, the company can use the funds to invest in new machinery and equipment. These new assets generate income for the company that gets returned to the investor in the form of dividends or capital gains. These investments increase the amount of machinery and equipment used by each worker, raising the productivity of workers; this helps to increase workers' wages and, ultimately, increases the average standard of living for Americans.

An important tax policy issue is the double taxation of income earned from saving and investing. Taxing this income discourages individual saving and investment, which reduces the funds available to finance new businesses and for existing businesses to expand. Currently, corporations first pay tax on their profit, then the after-tax profit is either distributed to shareholders as dividends or reinvested in the company by retaining it and allowing shareholders to benefit via capital gains (that is, increased equity); either way, the shareholder then pays taxes on the income he or she earns. As a result, income from new capital investment by corporations, financed by individual equity investment, is taxed twice—once by a tax on the corporation's profit, and again by a tax on the dividends and capital gains earned by the individual investor. This double taxation of corporate income generates an effective tax rate on equity investment that is greater than either the statutory corporate tax rate or the individual income tax rate. Ultimately, such taxes lower the capital-to-labor ratio, suppress wages, and harm long-run economic growth. Box 5-2 gives an example of how double taxation can slow economic growth.

The tax reductions of the past 8 years increased individual incentives to save and invest. In 2001, the top marginal income tax rate was reduced from 39.6 percent to 35 percent, thus reducing the tax on flow-through businesses (businesses whose profits are not taxed directly; instead, any profit they earn "flows through" the business to the owners, who then pay individual income tax on it). Before 2003, capital gains were taxed at a maximum of 20 percent, and dividends were taxed as ordinary income (at a maximum rate of 38.6 percent in 2002). As part of the Jobs and Growth Tax Relief Reconciliation Act of 2003 (JGTRRA), the maximum tax rate for long-term capital gains and dividends was reduced to 15 percent. (The next section elaborates on the significance of reducing tax rates on dividend income.)

Box 5-2: Double Taxation Slows Economic Growth

From an individual perspective, the act of saving reduces consumption today so more can be consumed in the future. Similarly, when firms invest they reduce present production so they can be more productive and profitable in the future. Taxing capital income lowers the return to saving and investment, which encourages current consumption and discourages future consumption. For example, suppose a corporation is considering selling additional stock to finance the construction of a new plant. The corporation expects that the *net return* on this investment (the return after subtracting depreciation) will be 10 percent. Suppose further that individuals will purchase the shares if they receive a return of at least 6 percent. The investment is socially beneficial because it generates a higher return (10 percent) than the savers providing the funds require (6 percent).

When the new plant begins operating, the income it generates for the firm is subject to the corporate income tax; currently, the corporate income tax has a top marginal rate of 35 percent. Similarly, individuals investing in the firm owe tax on the income they receive from their investments; currently, the top marginal rate on dividends and long-term capital gains is 15 percent.

Now consider an individual who invests $1,000 in the company's new stock. The new plant generates $100 of net income on this investment. The firm owes 35 percent in tax, leaving $65 of after-tax profit for the firm. Suppose the firm immediately returns all of this money to the investor as a dividend. The investor owes 15 percent in tax, leaving about $55 for her to use. That is, after applying the two taxes, the investor receives a return of only 5.5 percent on her initial investment. Because this is less than her required return of 6 percent she will choose not to invest in this company's stock and the new plant would not be built. In summary, taxing both corporate income and individual capital income can produce an effective tax rate high enough to alter saving and investment decisions enough to cause socially beneficial projects to go unfunded.

Dividend Tax Relief

A major Administration accomplishment was reducing the tax rate applied to corporate dividends. JGTRRA reclassified dividends so they are taxed at the same rate as long-term capital gains, currently a maximum of 15 percent. As Chart 5-1 shows, the change appears to have been effective in expanding dividend payments: since 2003, real dividend income has grown at an average of 11.1 percent per year, while from 1983 until 2003, real dividend income grew at an average of only 5.8 percent per year. (The 2004 spike in the chart reflects a special one-time dividend paid by Microsoft Corporation.)

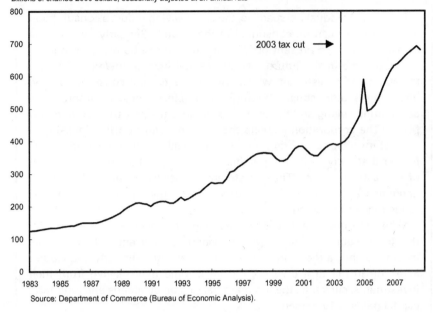

Chart 5-1 Real Personal Dividend Income
Dividend payments have increased since the 2003 tax cut.

Billions of chained 2000 dollars, seasonally adjusted at an annual rate

Source: Department of Commerce (Bureau of Economic Analysis).

Reducing tax rates on corporate dividend payments directly reduces the double taxation of corporate income. It also reduces the incentive corporations have to use debt, rather than equity, to finance purchases of new capital. The fact that corporations can deduct interest payments from taxable income, but cannot deduct dividend payments, makes it cheaper for firms to borrow (rather than issue stock) to finance additional spending. Excessive borrowing increases the chances of insolvency because the higher a firm's debt payments, the greater the chance the firm's income will be insufficient to cover these payments. Insofar as insolvency triggers bankruptcy, this subjects equity holders and employees to additional costs and uncertainty.

Changing the tax treatment of dividends also reduced the tax bias against paying dividends compared to retaining earnings. Paying dividends returns funds to stockholders, who can decide for themselves how to use them, rather than having to leave the funds invested in a particular company. Also, paying dividends is a way firms can provide tangible evidence of their profitability. Clear signals about how profitable different firms are help investors identify the most efficient allocation of their resources. When the tax code penalizes dividends relative to capital gains and penalizes equity financing relative to debt financing, corporate financing decisions will be inefficient.

The Macroeconomic Benefits of Lower Tax Rates

Over the past 8 years, tax relief has reduced distortions to labor supply, saving, investment, and corporate governance. Making the tax relief permanent can substantially improve economic efficiency and increase economic activity. The Treasury Department estimates, for example, that if the tax relief of 2001 and 2003 were made permanent and were paid for by reductions in future government spending, economic output would increase by 0.7 percent in the long run. The benefits would be smaller or even negative, however, if the extension of the tax relief results in additional government borrowing or future tax increases rather than spending reductions. The Treasury Department estimates, for example, that if the tax relief were made permanent but the lost revenues were made up with other tax increases, economic output would decline by 0.9 percent over the long run. The concern about long-term financing for the tax relief is particularly important because of the likelihood of rising spending pressures in the future, as discussed in Chapter 6.

A Record of Tax Reform

One of the Administration's major tax policy objectives has been to change tax laws so they better encourage activities that are beneficial to the economy as a whole, such as work effort, saving and investing, education, and the creation of new jobs. With regard to individual income taxes, the Administration took steps each year to reduce the burden imposed on the American taxpayer. Here are some of the highlights of the actions taken:

- The Economic Growth and Tax Relief Reconciliation Act of 2001 was the most significant tax reduction since 1981. It created a new low 10 percent tax bracket and phased in reductions of the other existing marginal tax rates. It reduced marriage penalties by increasing the standard deduction and the lowest tax bracket threshold for married taxpayers, increased the child tax credit, and made many other tax preferences more generous. It also began phasing out the estate tax.
- The Jobs and Growth Tax Relief Reconciliation Act of 2003 accelerated the phasing-in of many of the tax reductions enacted in 2001. It also reduced capital gains tax rates and applied the capital gains tax rates to dividends.
- The Working Families Tax Relief Act of 2004 and American Jobs Creation Act of 2004 further accelerated the tax reductions previously enacted, including increasing the child tax credit to $1,000. These laws further reduced marriage penalties by making the standard deduction for joint returns twice the single standard deduction, and expanding the

10 and 15 percent tax brackets for joint returns to twice the size of the corresponding brackets for single returns.

- The Pension Protection Act of 2006 made permanent a number of pension-related provisions of previous tax bills, such as higher dollar amounts for IRA contributions, higher dollar limits on defined contribution plans, and catch-up contributions for older workers.
- The Tax Increase Prevention Act (TIPA) of 2007 and the Emergency Economic Stabilization Act of 2008 each extended AMT relief. TIPA also increased the number of personal credits that could be used to reduce AMT liability.

Each of the above measures was intended to promote long-term growth and improve economic efficiency. Another significant measure was the Economic Stimulus Act of 2008, which returned approximately $100 billion to consumers via tax rebates—up to $600 per taxpayer ($1,200 for couples filing jointly) and $300 for each dependent. Rebates were phased out for taxpayers with over $75,000 in income (over $150,000 for couples filing jointly). On the business tax side, the Economic Stimulus Act increased the dollar value of new equipment that could be deducted in 2008 and provided an expanded depreciation allowance of 50 percent on certain business property put into service in 2008. The primary purpose of these actions was to provide short-term, counter-cyclical stimulus to the economy by encouraging short-run growth in consumer spending and business investment. Tax rebates were chosen as the best way to provide this short-term stimulus because of the speed with which they put money into the hands of people most likely to spend it. Similarly, the business tax incentives were designed to encourage firms to accelerate purchases of capital equipment, making such purchases in 2008 rather than waiting until 2009 or later. Compared to the paths consumption and investment would have otherwise followed, the rebates appear to have boosted real personal consumption expenditures in the second quarter of 2008 and the accelerated depreciation was expected to boost business investment throughout 2008.

In total, the tax relief enjoyed by taxpayers from 2001 to 2008 saved Americans nearly $1.7 trillion in taxes. Chart 5-2 illustrates how those benefits were distributed over these years. The value for 2008 includes over $100 billion from the Economic Stimulus Act of 2008. Aside from stimulus, the amount of tax relief granted to individuals declines after 2008 because of the expiration of temporary changes to the AMT (discussed in detail later in this chapter) and declines significantly in 2011 because most of the tax reductions are scheduled to expire at the end of 2010.

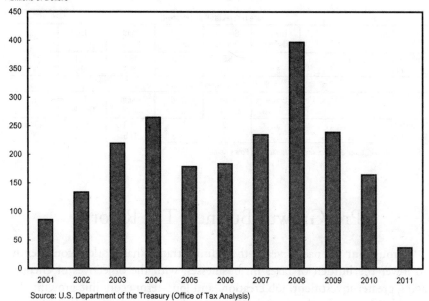

Source: U.S. Department of the Treasury (Office of Tax Analysis)

Lower Tax Burdens

As a result of the tax relief of the past 8 years, the average Federal individual income tax rate declined to 20.4 percent in 2008. Without tax relief, the average Federal tax rate would have been 24.2 percent. The top half of Table 5-1 shows the rates taxpayers at different income levels face in 2008 as a result of the tax relief of the past 8 years and the tax rates they would have faced if it were not for this tax relief. Notice that taxpayers at all income levels experienced a reduction in their average Federal tax rate for 2008. For example, among people in the lowest income quintile, the average Federal income tax rate would have been 5.2 percent without tax relief, but with tax relief it was only 1.1 percent; while for people in the highest income quintile, the average Federal income tax rate would have been 29 percent without tax relief, and with tax relief it was only 25.4 percent.

The distribution of the burden of Federal individual income taxes is shown in the bottom half of Table 5-1. Without tax relief, the lowest quintile would have borne 0.8 percent of the Federal tax burden in 2008. With tax relief, the lowest quintile bore only 0.2 percent of all Federal taxes. The highest income quintile was the only group to see its share of Federal taxes increase in 2008, from 66.3 percent of Federal taxes before tax relief to 68.9 percent after tax relief.

TABLE 5-1.—*Estimated 2008 Effects of Individual Income Tax Relief from the Past 8 Years*

	Average Federal Tax Rates (percent)					
	Lowest Quintile	Second Quintile	Third Quintile	Fourth Quintile	Top Quintile	All
With Tax Cuts..................................	1.1	8.3	15.0	18.1	25.4	20.4
Without Tax Cuts.............................	5.2	13.0	18.9	21.9	29.0	24.2
	Share of Federal Taxes (percent)					
	Lowest Quintile	Second Quintile	Third Quintile	Fourth Quintile	Top Quintile	All
With Tax Cuts..................................	0.2	3.3	10.2	17.3	68.9	100.0
Without Tax Cuts.............................	0.8	4.4	10.8	17.6	66.3	100.0

Source: Urban Institute and Brookings Institution Tax Policy Center.

Pro-Growth Business Tax Reform

Throughout the past 8 years, the Administration has worked consistently to lower the burden of taxes on businesses, with the objectives of encouraging greater investment, job creation, and long-term economic growth. To accomplish these goals, the Administration has pursued two primary strategies: first, addressing enduring aspects of the tax system that diminish returns on investment for both individuals and businesses; and second, providing new tax incentives for businesses to stimulate greater investment.

Reducing the Double Taxation of Corporate Income

As indicated earlier, one aspect of the current tax system that diminishes returns on investment is the practice of double taxation of corporate income, which reduces the return to saving and investing. The Administration's 2003 tax relief reduced the magnitude of double taxation by reducing the tax rate on both dividends and capital gains. In addition, there have been amendments to the legal structure of corporations that have helped reduce corporate tax burdens.

To understand these changes, it is first helpful to understand the basic framework of corporate taxation. The tax treatment of business income varies depending on the organizational structure of the firm. There are two basic classifications of corporations for purposes of taxation and regulation: (1) *C corporations*, the traditional large, stock-issuing corporations; and (2) *flow-through* businesses, which include S corporations, partnerships, and sole proprietorships. For tax purposes, the main difference between these two groups is that flow-through businesses are exempt from the corporate profits tax that is imposed on C corporations. In flow-through businesses, profits are distributed to owners and shareholders (flowing "through" the company directly to their owners), who then pay income taxes on their gains. (There are restrictions on both size and financial activities that prevent most firms from qualifying to be S corporations.) This arrangement allows flow-through business owners to avoid the double taxation of corporate profits and to face lower effective tax rates than do shareholders of C corporations. One goal of tax relief has been to "level the playing field" by reducing the difference between the tax rates applied to income generated by S corporations and C corporations.

Two types of changes helped to reduce the burden of corporate taxes. First, regulatory changes in 2004 and 2007 relaxed some of the restrictions that limit which firms can be S corporations. In addition to increasing the maximum allowable number of shareholders, new rules were enacted to make it easier for a firm to elect to become, and to remain, an S corporation. Second, each year from 2002 to 2005, and again in 2008, allowances for depreciation deductions were extended or expanded. As described below, these changes allow firms to take a greater deduction from income when new capital equipment is purchased, which effectively decreases the tax burden on income generated by that equipment.

Accelerating Depreciation Allowances

A consistent goal of the Administration has been to provide tax incentives for businesses to invest in new facilities and equipment. One way this goal was promoted was by accelerating business depreciation allowances. When physical assets (such as machinery and equipment that can be used over and over when producing goods and services) are used by businesses, their value declines (depreciates) over time due to the wear and tear they experience. With this in mind, businesses are allowed to deduct from their taxable income the dollar amount of the depreciation of their assets. The more quickly a firm is able to deduct, through depreciation, the cost of new investment, the more attractive new investment becomes. Because different types of assets have different useful lives and therefore depreciate at different rates, the IRS established the Modified Accelerated Cost Recovery System, which specifies the rates at which different types of assets can be depreciated.

Accelerating depreciation rates improves investment incentives for firms. As part of a temporary stimulus program, the Administration succeeded in expanding businesses' first-year depreciation allowance on qualified property by an additional 30 percent of its adjusted basis in 2002, to encourage greater business investment in new machinery and equipment in that year. In 2003, to provide additional short-term stimulus, the first-year depreciation allowance was expanded further, to 50 percent of the adjusted basis for qualified property. This expanded depreciation allowance expired in 2004, but was reintroduced—at 50 percent of the adjusted basis—as part of the Economic Stimulus Act of 2008.

Increasing Small Business Expensing

In addition to accelerating business depreciation rates, the Administration has supported pro-growth business tax policies by increasing the amount of "expensing" small businesses can do for their use of depreciable property. Distinct from the traditional concept of "business expensing," which refers to a business's ability to deduct expenses incurred that are not associated with acquiring or improving assets, Section 179 of the U.S. Internal Revenue Code allows individuals and small businesses to deduct the cost of property used to generate income, rather than having to capitalize the benefits through the depreciation schedule discussed above. The Administration expanded the capability of businesses to expense the cost of property under Section 179; in 2003, the maximum dollar amount that could be expensed under Section 179 was increased to $100,000. In 2007 the limit was again increased, to $125,000, and indexed for inflation for 2008 through 2010. Then, as part of the Economic Stimulus Act of 2008, the limit was increased to $250,000 for 2008.

Tax Credits for Research and Development

Finally, a number of tax credits have been extended to businesses to encourage the types of research and development investment that have benefits for the public. Economists use the term "public goods" to describe things that could easily be used by more and more people with little or no additional production cost. From a social perspective, private companies generally make insufficient investments in public goods, such as scientific research to develop new technologies for health care or to expand utilization of renewable energy resources. This "underinvestment" occurs because companies pursue investment projects based on the potential value to themselves and generally do not consider the full benefit to society that could result from the investment.

For example, suppose a company was considering investing in research to develop a vaccine against diabetes. Once developed, the company would sell the drug at a price set high enough to recover its research costs and to generate some profit. Ultimately, the company would evaluate the merits of the investment based on the profit it expected to receive from selling the vaccine relative to the profit it could earn on other possible investments. Unfortunately, the price the firm would need to charge could exceed what some people who would benefit from the drug can afford to pay. As a result, some people who could benefit from the vaccine will not get it, and the company will underestimate the full value of this research investment. That is, the research will have a public value that is greater than its private value to the company. Put another way, for goods with large social benefits, private markets tend to offer smaller returns than are needed to result in efficient levels of investment.

Tax credits can be used to "fill the gap," by providing the company with an additional incentive that will encourage it to undertake this publicly beneficial investment. In the area of alternative energy, the Administration successfully extended existing research and development tax credits and expanded upon them in 2005 and 2006, providing an additional 20 percent credit for qualified energy research and increasing the percentage of research and development expenses that qualify for the credit. In 2005 and 2006, private industry research and development grew notably. Annual research and development spending by private industry grew by only 2.9 percent per year over the 20 years from 1985 through 2004. Subsequently, private industry research and development grew at an average rate of 5.1 percent per year in 2005 and 2006.

International Competitiveness

Today's global economy enjoys more economic interconnectedness than ever before. Efficiency improvements in information, communication, and transportation technologies have increased the ability of international firms to compete with U.S. firms in domestic and international markets. Associated improvements in the international mobility of capital mean that modern companies have a high degree of international flexibility regarding the location of new facilities. Thus, companies that want to open new facilities can compare investment opportunities across the globe to find locations with the highest after-tax return. As a result, a country's corporate tax policy, including its statutory tax rates, can have a significant impact on both job creation and the competitiveness of businesses within that country. There is ample evidence that companies include tax considerations when determining where to locate new facilities, a fact that has led to a sense of competition between countries as they try to attract companies by reducing their respective corporate tax rates.

To illustrate the trend toward lower corporate tax rates, Chart 5-3 shows the statutory corporate tax rate for the United States and the average (weighted by gross domestic product (GDP)) statutory corporate tax rate for non-U.S. members of the Organization for Economic Co-operation and Development (OECD) since 1981. (State and local rates are combined with the Federal statutory rates where appropriate.) During the early 1980s, the United States had a statutory corporate tax rate of nearly 50 percent, which was higher than the OECD average. Significant tax reform in 1986 reduced the United States's combined (Federal and State) rate to about 39 percent, a level it has roughly maintained since then. While this change reduced the U.S. tax rate to well below that of most other OECD countries in the late

1980s, other countries soon began reducing their corporate tax rates as well. By 2008, the non-U.S. OECD average corporate tax rate had fallen to about 30 percent, and the non-U.S. median corporate tax rate stood at 27.5 percent. Table 5-2 gives statutory tax rates for most OECD countries; the United States currently has the second highest statutory corporate tax rate of any industrialized country, less than 1 percentage point below Japan's.

That said, the United States offers companies a more generous depreciation allowance than do most other countries—only Italy and Greece offer greater allowances (see Table 5-2). When considered together, the high statutory tax rate in the United States is somewhat mitigated by its generous depreciation allowance. However, as shown in the last column of Table 5-2, the United States still has the fourth highest effective marginal tax rate on equity-financed projects, which can dampen the competitiveness of U.S. businesses and can dissuade firms from locating new facilities—and the associated jobs—here in the United States.

Future Challenges

The tax policy changes of the past 8 years have considerably reduced the burden on taxpayers and improved the efficiency of U.S. income tax laws. However, there is more work to be done. In addition to making these changes a permanent part of the tax code, the AMT needs to be reformed or even eliminated, and the tax code should be greatly simplified because complying with its incredible complexity consumes resources that could be put to better use elsewhere.

Making Tax Relief Permanent

Failing to extend the tax relief enacted over the past 8 years would amount to one of the largest tax increases in history. Individuals at all income levels, from low-income Earned Income Tax Credit recipients to high-income taxpayers, would be negatively affected. The total increase would average nearly 1.9 percent of GDP per year over the next 10 years and would increase the tax burden on the economy to well above the average over the past 40 years of 18.3 percent of GDP.

Taxing business income reduces the incentive people have to invest in businesses. Tax relief has encouraged greater business investment over the last several years. Going back to the high tax rates of the 1990s could reduce business investment, which could in turn reduce workers' wages and economic growth. In an international context, higher corporate tax rates would make locating new businesses in the United States less attractive, and would further depress jobs and growth.

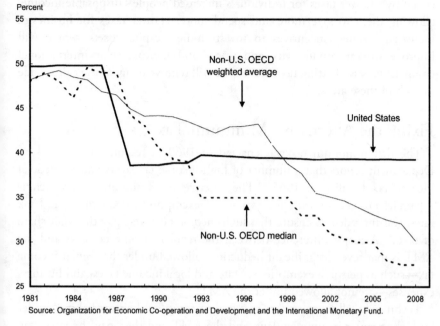

Chart 5-3 Combined (Federal and State) Corporate Income Tax Rate

U.S. corporate tax rates are now well above those of most other developed countries.

Percent

Source: Organization for Economic Co-operation and Development and the International Monetary Fund.

TABLE 5-2.—*Statutory Corporate Income Tax Rates, Depreciation Allowances, and Effective Marginal Tax Rates for Selected OECD Countries, 2005*

Country	Statutory Corporate Income Tax Rate (percent)	Discounted Value of Depreciation Allowance— Equipment (equity)	Effective Marginal Tax Rate Equipment (equity; percent)
Japan	40	73	28
United States	39	79	24
Germany	38	71	29
Italy	37	82	19
Canada	36	73	25
Spain	35	78	21
Belgium	34	75	22
France	34	77	20
Switzerland	34	78	20
Greece	32	87	12
Netherlands	32	73	21
Australia	30	66	24
United Kingdom	30	73	20
Norway	28	67	22
Portugal	28	79	15
Sweden	28	78	16
Finland	26	73	17
Austria	25	66	20
Ireland	13	66	10
Average (unweighted)	31	75	20
G-7 Average (unweighted)	36	76	24

Source: Institute for Fiscal Studies, Corporate Tax Database.

These lower tax rates have had many positive consequences for the economy. Lower taxes for individuals increased people's disposable income, allowing them to save more and spend more. Lower taxes for businesses increased business incentives to invest in new capital assets, which will improve worker productivity and wages and increase their international competitiveness. Letting tax relief expire will remove many of the gains made in each of these areas.

Fixing the Alternative Minimum Tax

The first minimum tax was enacted in 1969 in response to a Treasury Department report that a number of high-income taxpayers had no Federal income tax liability in 1966. The Alternative Minimum Tax, which is a parallel tax system with its own set of exemptions, deductions, and tax rates, was intended to ensure that high-income taxpayers pay their fair share of taxes. A major difference between the regular income tax laws and the AMT is that several significant deductions allowed under the regular income tax—such as personal exemptions, State and local income taxes, and business expenses—are not allowed under the AMT.

Technically, all taxpayers are required to compute their tax liability under both the regular income tax laws and the AMT and then pay the larger tax amount. Having to compute one's tax liability twice increases both compliance costs and the complexity of the tax code. In practice, the large income exemption available under the AMT means low-income taxpayers hardly ever owe more under the AMT. For many years, middle-income taxpayers were similarly unaffected by the AMT. However, the major problem with the AMT is that, unlike the regular tax exemptions and bracket thresholds, the AMT values are not indexed for inflation. This means that, as people's incomes naturally rise, even if only with inflation, an increasing number of middle-income taxpayers find themselves having a greater tax liability under the AMT than they do under the regular tax code. To counteract this problem, the exemption has been permanently increased several times, most recently in 1993, to $45,000 for joint returns and to $33,750 for singles. Above the exemption amount, the AMT tax rate is 26 percent on the first $175,000 of taxable income and 28 percent thereafter. (Adjusting for inflation, the $45,000 exemption in 1993 is worth more than $66,000 in 2008 dollars.)

In its first year of operation, the minimum tax affected only 19,000 taxpayers and raised about $122 million, meaning this tax caused these taxpayers to owe $122 million more in tax than they owed under the regular tax laws. In 2007, the AMT affected over 4 million taxpayers and raised roughly $26 billion in revenue (about 1 percent of all Federal revenue). Under current law, these numbers are projected to increase to over 29 million taxpayers and over $100 billion in revenue in 2009.

Chart 5-4 shows the number of taxpayers who are forecast to be affected by the AMT under different future policies. Under current law—with the AMT parameters returning to their 1993 levels after 2008 and tax relief expiring at the end of 2010—the number of AMT-affected taxpayers will rise sharply in 2009, ultimately reaching nearly 44 million taxpayers in 2018. In 2008, Congress enacted an AMT "patch," which adjusted the AMT parameters for 1 year to $69,950 for joint returns and $46,200 for singles (Congress has enacted short-term changes to the AMT parameters several times since 2001). If this patch is permanently extended and tax relief is allowed to expire at the end of 2010, the number of AMT-affected taxpayers would rise to 8 million in 2018. Alternately, if tax relief is extended (the "policy baseline" lines in Chart 5-4) the number of AMT-affected taxpayers will grow to 56 million in 2018 if the AMT parameters are allowed to return to their 1993 levels or to 21 million taxpayers if the AMT patch is permanently extended.

Taxpayers with many dependents or significant business deductions and those in high-tax States are more likely to be subject to the AMT. Three reductions to taxable income allowed under regular tax laws but not under the AMT are personal exemptions, miscellaneous business deductions, and State and local taxes. Taxpayers claiming more dependents may be accustomed to

Chart 5-4 **Number of Taxpayers Subject to the Alternative Minimum Tax**
The number of taxpayers affected by the AMT in the future depends on whether the AMT parameters are adjusted for inflation and on whether tax relief is allowed to expire after 2010 (current law) or is extended (policy baseline).

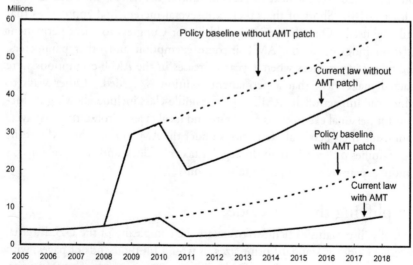

Note: Permanent patch at 2007 exemption levels.
Source: U.S. Department of the Treasury (Office of Tax Analysis).

seeing a large reduction in taxable income because of the personal exemption allowed for each dependent, but no corresponding reduction is available under the AMT. Similarly, miscellaneous business deductions, allowable under the regular tax laws when they exceed 2 percent of adjusted gross income (AGI), are not deductible under the AMT. Taxpayers in a State with relatively high income taxes or relatively high property taxes receive a relatively large deduction under the regular tax laws but receive no relief for this expense under the AMT. The result of these items not being deductible under the AMT is that people with these deductions are more likely to be subject to the AMT than are people without these deductions. Among otherwise similar people, taxpayers with these deductions generally still pay less in Federal income tax than do people without these deductions, but the existence of the AMT reduces the tax benefit these deductions provide and means these people will have the extra work of filling out the additional form(s) required for the AMT.

Prior to 1998, most personal credits (such as the education tax credits and the child and dependent care credit) could not be used to reduce tax liability owed under the AMT. In fact, even if a taxpayer did not owe additional tax under the AMT, he or she would be prohibited from using the full amount of a credit if it would reduce his or her tax liability below the level determined under the AMT. This reduction in credit usefulness was yet another way people could be "hit" by the AMT.

AMT Reform Ideas

The most obvious way to deal with the AMT would be to abolish it entirely, although this would require the Federal Government to forgo over $1.7 trillion in revenue over the next 10 years (assuming tax relief is extended through at least 2018). Short of that, there are several incremental approaches that could be used. One alternative would be for Congress to enact permanent inflation indexing of the AMT income exemption and other parameters. The recent experiences when 1-year increases in the AMT exemptions were enacted make clear that a permanent solution is needed. Other ways to reduce the impact of the AMT on the middle class include allowing deductions for personal exemptions and State and local taxes. Prohibiting taxpayers from using their personal exemptions under the AMT means the AMT treats large families differently than the regular tax code does, and effectively makes it more expensive for people to raise a family.

Simplifying the Tax Code

Finally, it remains difficult to overstate the complexity of the U.S. Internal Revenue Code: at standard print sizes, it would fill thousands of pages, with more added nearly every year. Deductions, exemptions, phase-outs, credits, and the AMT add complexity to the tax code that makes it challenging for ordinary people to determine their tax liability. See Box 5-3 for a fuller discussion of these issues.

Box 5-3: Tax Code Complexity

The U.S. individual income tax system is extremely difficult to understand and, as a result, imposes a substantial burden on taxpayers in the form of time and money spent complying with its various rules. There are dozens of tax credits and deductions, many of which target specific social goals. As the number of credits and deductions has grown over the years, the number of overlapping provisions has also increased, which often creates complicated interactions among provisions. Further, eligibility can vary across similar tax preferences due to idiosyncratic definitions and complicated phase-out provisions intended to limit tax benefits to lower-income taxpayers. For example:

- The tax code currently contains a dozen special tax preferences relating to educational expenses. Three commonly utilized preferences—the Hope credit, the Lifetime Learning credit, and the tuition deduction—help families meet the costs of post-secondary education, but each provision varies in terms of eligibility and benefits. Also, the use of one tax provision may affect a student's ability to use one of the other provisions and can even affect a student's eligibility for subsidized student loans or Pell Grants.

- Phase-out provisions reduce the benefit of certain tax preferences (such as personal exemptions and the tuition deduction) for high-income taxpayers. Similarly, the maximum allowable amount of itemized deductions can be reduced for taxpayers with an AGI above $159,950 (in 2008). These provisions require additional calculations for taxpayers and also effectively increase their marginal tax rate. In 2008, an estimated 13 percent of taxpayers who itemized deductions will have their allowable itemized deductions reduced.

- When the parents of a qualifying child file separate tax returns, the tax code contains a number of special rules to determine which parent can claim the child as a dependent. These rules depend on the marital status and adjusted gross income of the parents as well as on the amount of time the child lives with each parent.

- To prevent parents from shifting investment income to their children, the unearned income of dependent filers is taxed at the parents' marginal tax rate. However, to limit this provision to higher-income families, this applies only to a child's unearned income in excess of a certain limit ($1,800 in 2008).

- As discussed in the text, the AMT, which requires taxpayers to calculate their tax liability a second time using a different set of tax rules and rates, affects a growing number of taxpayers.

Complying with these complex laws costs taxpayers time and money. It takes time to read and understand the laws, to collect the relevant data and keep records, and to fill in the forms themselves (or to have someone else do it). In fact, the tax laws are so complex that an entire industry of lawyers and accountants exists to help people comply with the laws and even to find ways to avoid paying the taxes they owe. The resources used in this industry are unavailable for use to produce other goods and services. In effect, other than for tax-related purposes, there are no consumable goods or services produced by these resources—one could argue that the economy is wasting these resources. Several studies have examined the social cost of the complexity of our tax code. A Government summary of these studies concludes that the annual cost of complying with the tax laws averages at least 1 percent of GDP (about $140 billion in 2008) and may be even higher. Tax reform that substantially simplified the tax code would free up these resources for more beneficial uses.

Conclusion

Taxes distort incentives to work, save, and invest. By lowering individual income tax rates at all income levels over the past 8 years, the Administration has substantially reduced these distortions and increased incentives to work, save, and invest. Lower Federal tax rates on capital gains and dividend income, along with the temporary increases in depreciation allowances, increased business incentives to purchase new capital equipment and reduced the double taxation of corporate income. Each of these changes improves the efficiency of the tax structure, enhances economic growth, and improves our standard of living over the long run. However, most of these tax reductions are scheduled to expire at the end of 2010, which would eliminate many of the gains made over the past 8 years. Allowing these tax reductions to expire will increase taxes for all income groups, with the lower- and middle-income groups experiencing the largest percentage increases.

Despite the improvements of the past 8 years, there remains much to be done to make the tax code as efficient as possible. In the international arena, the relatively low U.S. corporate tax rates of the late 1980s were left unchanged while most other developed countries dramatically reduced rates. As a result, U.S. corporate tax rates are now among the highest in the developed world. This handicap is partly offset by other tax provisions, such as generous depreciation allowances. But the resulting tax burden still places U.S. companies at a competitive disadvantage relative to companies in lower-tax jurisdictions, and it reduces our ability to attract capital in an environment where capital is highly mobile across international borders. In addition, two long-standing problems needing attention are the Alternative Minimum Tax and the complexity of the U.S. income tax laws. Without its annual "patch," the AMT would affect more than 20 million more taxpayers each year.

CHAPTER 6

The Long-Run Challenges of Entitlement Spending

Federal spending on entitlement programs is expected to increase dramatically in the coming decades, particularly for Social Security, Medicare, and Medicaid. Taken together, these programs currently constitute 45 percent of Federal non-interest spending; assuming there are no major changes to these programs, this share is projected to rise dramatically in coming decades. An aging population and rising health care spending per person are major reasons for these projected increases. The primary objective of this chapter is to highlight the budgetary challenges facing each of the three major entitlement programs and to outline possible strategies for addressing these challenges.

The key points of this chapter are:

- Federal entitlement spending is on an unsustainable path. Spending on the three major entitlement programs—Social Security, Medicare, and Medicaid—is projected to increase much faster than tax revenues or than the overall economy over the coming decades. Paying all scheduled benefits would eventually require substantial reductions in other Government spending, or major tax increases, or both.

- The aging population is a major cause of the expected increase, especially for Social Security, representing a permanent, as opposed to temporary, shift in the entitlement landscape. Currently, one out of six adults is age 65 or older; by 2020, one out of five adults will be 65 or older; and, by 2030, one out of four adults will be age 65 or older.

- The pay-as-you-go financing structure of Social Security, coupled with the aging population, creates a sizeable structural imbalance that will cause current and future generations of workers to bear increasing costs, or receive smaller benefits than now scheduled, or both.

- Over the past 30 years, real per capita health care spending has grown considerably faster than real gross domestic product (GDP) per capita. Real growth in Medicare spending is being driven by increasing enrollment, greater utilization of more expensive high-technology medical treatments, and expansion of the goods and services covered by the program.

- Long-term care expenditures for low-income elderly and disabled persons represent a large and growing share of total Medicaid spending. The demand for long-term care is expected to grow in the United States as a result of the aging population. In turn, this will place even greater financial strain on Federal and State budgets.

Background Facts About Entitlement Programs

Social Security, Medicare, and Medicaid are key components of the U.S. social safety net. This section briefly reviews the evolution and current structure of each program.

Social Security

The Social Security system protects people from income loss due to life events such as retirement, a period of disability, or the death of a household wage earner. This system was introduced in 1935, when it is estimated that over half of the elderly lacked the income needed to care for themselves. In 2007, approximately 50 million beneficiaries received $585 billion in benefit payments. Approximately $486 billion of these benefits was paid to over 40 million retirees and survivors, and $99 billion was paid to 8.9 million disabled workers and their families. Nearly 90 percent of all individuals aged 65 and over received some benefit from Social Security in 2006 (the most recent year for which these data are available). Social Security benefits provided about 58 percent of all income received by individuals age 65 and older and for 32 percent of recipients, Social Security benefits provided over 90 percent of their entire income.

Social Security is largely a pay-as-you-go program, meaning that current benefits are financed primarily with a payroll tax on wages earned by current workers. Employers and employees each pay 6.2 percent of wages—although economists generally believe the employer's portion is passed on to workers in the form of lower wages—up to a maximum amount of taxable wages. This maximum, called the contribution and benefit base, increases each year as average wages increase; it was $102,000 in 2008, increasing to $106,800 in 2009. Self-employed individuals pay the entire 12.4 percent.

As a result of legislation enacted in 1983, Social Security began collecting more revenue than was needed to pay benefits each year, thereby requiring current workers to partially prefund future retirement benefits. The annual surpluses have been placed in the Social Security Trust Fund, which is invested in special U.S. Treasury bonds, used only for this purpose. In 2007, Social Security ran a surplus of $190 billion, which brought the balance in the Trust Fund to over $2.2 trillion. Because the value of the assets accumulated in the Trust Fund is exactly offset by the liability of the general fund to repay the special Treasury bonds, the Social Security Trust Fund has zero *net* value for the Government.

The Social Security benefit a worker receives in retirement is based on the average wage he or she earns when working and paying the Social Security payroll tax. Workers who earned higher wages get larger benefits, but the portion of preretirement income replaced by Social Security declines as preretirement wage income rises. An individual must have worked and paid Social Security taxes for 40 quarters (10 years of employment) to be eligible for retirement benefits. Individuals become eligible for a reduced benefit at age 62, while those who work past full retirement age can receive a larger benefit for each year worked up to age 70. Once a retiree's initial benefit has been determined, it increases each year with annual cost-of-living adjustments that are based on the inflation rate for the previous year.

More than one in six recipients of Social Security benefits receive their benefits through the Disability Insurance program. This program provides monthly benefits to workers and their families for workers who are unable to work for a year or more. The Social Security Administration has guidelines about the conditions that must be met before an individual can receive this benefit.

Medicare

Beginning in the 1930s and for several subsequent decades, policymakers considered legislation that would create a larger role for Government in the provision of health insurance for Americans, particularly for those who faced financial barriers to medical care. Before Medicare was created in 1965, almost 50 percent of older adults lacked health insurance. Originally, only people age 65 and older were eligible for Medicare. In 1972, eligibility was expanded to include those receiving Social Security Disability Insurance payments for 2 consecutive years and those with end-stage renal disease who meet specific eligibility requirements. Today, nearly 45 million individuals are enrolled in Medicare, including approximately 38 million elderly and 7 million disabled beneficiaries.

Medicare has four parts:

- Part A, also known as Hospital Insurance, provides coverage for inpatient hospital services, some home health care, hospice, and up to 100 days in a skilled nursing facility after a qualifying inpatient stay. Individuals who have worked at least 40 quarters in qualified employment are automatically enrolled in Part A upon reaching age 65. Individuals who lack 40 quarters of employment can buy into Part A when they reach 65 years of age by paying a monthly premium (plus a late penalty if enrolling after the initial eligibility period); in 2009, the maximum monthly premium is $443.
- Part B provides coverage for outpatient services, including outpatient provider visits, emergency room services, and certain preventive screening measures. Enrollment in Part B is optional (there is a penalty for enrolling after the initial eligibility period) and requires a premium contribution, which is higher for individuals who make more than $85,000 per year, based on their most recent Federal income tax return.

- Part C, also called Medicare Advantage, uses private health plans to provide Part A and B and, in most cases, Part D benefits. Medicare Advantage plans often include benefits not covered by traditional Medicare. The Medicare Prescription Drug, Improvement, and Modernization Act of 2003 changed how the Government reimburses health plans for the coverage they provide to enrollees. This resulted in an increase in the number of private plan choices available to beneficiaries in every county in America. Enrollment growth has been steady, most likely due to improved access to Medicare Advantage plans and more generous benefits. Current enrollment is nearly 10 million beneficiaries, representing over 20 percent of all Medicare beneficiaries.
- Part D, also created by the 2003 legislation, is an optional, outpatient prescription drug benefit. This benefit is administered by private health insurance plan sponsors that contract with the Federal Government. In 2008, 32 million Medicare beneficiaries were enrolled in stand-alone prescription drug plans, Medicare Advantage prescription drug plans, or employer/union plans receiving the Retiree Drug Subsidy.

Medicare is financed primarily through a combination of payroll taxes, general revenues, and premiums paid by beneficiaries. Part A is financed primarily by a dedicated payroll tax of 2.9 percent, which is split evenly between employees and employers. If total non-interest revenues exceed Medicare Part A spending for a particular year, the difference is placed into the Hospital Insurance Trust Fund. If non-interest revenues are lower than spending, money is withdrawn from the Hospital Insurance Trust Fund. At the end of 2007, the Hospital Insurance Trust Fund had a balance of $326 billion; however, under the Medicare Trustees' intermediate estimates, this balance is expected to begin declining in 2008.

Medicare Part B is financed by general revenues and beneficiary premiums, the latter of which are set to equal approximately 25 percent of total expected spending. Part D is also financed through beneficiary premiums and general revenues, as well as State payments for low-income beneficiaries who are also enrolled in Medicaid. Medicare Advantage (Part C) is not separately financed; rather, it is simply a vehicle for providing Part A, Part B, and typically Part D benefits. Projections by the Medicare Trustees indicate that in 2010, approximately 45 percent of non-interest income will come from payroll taxes, 39 percent from general revenues, 12 percent from beneficiary premiums, and the remainder from miscellaneous sources.

Medicaid

Medicaid provides medical assistance to low-income individuals, including children and parents in working families, children and adults with severe disabilities, and low-income Medicare beneficiaries, who are known as "dual eligibles" because of their eligibility for both programs. The Federal and State Governments share responsibility for administering and funding Medicaid. For States to receive Federal funding, their Medicaid plans must cover specific populations, including children under the age of 6 and pregnant women whose family income is below 133 percent of the poverty level; school-age children (ages 6 to 18) with family income below 100 percent of the poverty level; parents with income below States' July 1996 welfare eligibility levels; and certain other low-income and disabled persons. In addition, with approval from the Centers for Medicare and Medicaid Services, States have the flexibility to expand Medicaid eligibility to other groups of individuals, including those whose incomes exceed the mandatory thresholds indicated above.

Medicaid programs cover a broad set of health care services, including inpatient and outpatient services, dental care, family planning, mental health, substance abuse treatment, home health care, and long-term care services. In 2007, Medicaid monthly enrollment averaged approximately 48.1 million people, including 23.5 million children.

Medicaid is jointly financed by the Federal Government and the States. The Federal Government's share of each State's Medicaid spending is based on the Federal Medical Assistance Percentage (FMAP), which is calculated using a formula that incorporates data on average per capita income for each State and for the United States as a whole for the most recent 3 years. The FMAP formula is designed to provide a larger Federal share of spending for States with lower per capita income relative to the national average, with Federal shares ranging from a minimum of 50 percent to a maximum of 83 percent. Overall, Federal Government expenditures on Medicaid account for approximately 57 percent of total annual Medicaid spending. Unlike Medicare, the Medicaid program does not have any dedicated revenue sources; rather, Federal expenditures come from the general fund of the Federal Government.

As part of the Balanced Budget Act of 1997, the State Children's Health Insurance Program (SCHIP) was created to provide health insurance to uninsured children under age 19 who live in low-income families that are not eligible for Medicaid. In 2007, more than 7 million children enrolled in SCHIP. States have significant flexibility in terms of their program design. In particular, they can implement SCHIP by expanding their existing Medicaid programs, creating separate programs, or using a combination of the two approaches. States that implement SCHIP as a Medicaid expansion must provide all of the benefits offered through their Medicaid programs, while States that choose to have separate SCHIP programs must provide benefits that meet specific Federal standards. Like Medicaid, the SCHIP program is financed jointly by the Federal Government and the States, although the Federal matching rate for SCHIP is higher than the rate used for Medicaid, and ranges from 65 percent to 83 percent of total spending.

Unlike Medicaid, SCHIP is not actually an entitlement program, but is instead a matching grant program that has a fixed limit on Federal spending, both nationally and State by State.

Major Entitlement Spending Over Time

Federal Government expenditures for Social Security, Medicare, and Medicaid have grown from 3.8 percent of GDP in 1970 to roughly 8.4 percent of GDP in 2008. (For comparison, Federal revenue generated from all sources averaged 18.3 percent of GDP over the last several decades.) Estimates of expected future growth in entitlement spending consistently predict sharply rising expenditures in coming decades, although such projections depend on specific assumptions made for a variety of economic and demographic variables. The Office of Management and Budget (OMB) projects that in the absence of reforms, by 2020, spending on these three programs will exceed 10 percent of GDP; by 2040, it will reach 14.9 percent of GDP, and by 2080, it will reach 18.9 percent of GDP. It is important to note, however, that there is considerable uncertainty among long-run forecasts. For example, under its Alternative Fiscal Scenario, the Congressional Budget Office (CBO) projects that Federal spending will rise much faster, reaching 11.2 percent of GDP by 2020, 16.8 percent of GDP by 2040, and exceeding 25 percent of GDP by 2080. The primary difference between the OMB and CBO projections (and other projections) is in their forecasts of future health care expenditures; in contrast, their forecasts of Social Security growth are very similar. Chart 6-1 uses the OMB projections to contrast the projected growth in these programs with other Federal spending, which fell in the 1990s with declines in defense spending, rose with increased Homeland Security spending over the past few years, and is assumed to decline in the coming decades, primarily due to declines in defense and other discretionary spending. Two trends can be discerned from Chart 6-1. One trend is the growth in Social Security spending expected over the next two decades. In 2008, Social Security spending constituted approximately 4.3 percent of GDP. CBO estimates this share will grow to 6.1 percent of GDP by 2030, with OMB estimating growth to 5.9 percent of GDP by 2030. After 2030, the share of GDP spent on Social Security remains relatively constant under both forecasts. Population aging is the main cause of this growth, a factor that also affects Medicare costs.

The second trend shown in Chart 6-1 is that after the period of Social Security's rapid cost growth, health care expenditure growth will cause Medicare and Medicaid spending to grow far more over the long term. In 2008, Medicare and Medicaid respectively constituted 2.7 percent and 1.4 percent of GDP. CBO projects that, absent reforms, in 2030 these

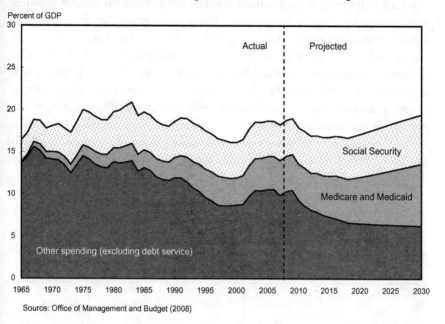

Chart 6-1 **Expenditures as a Percent of GDP**
Social Security, Medicare, and Medicaid will all grow as a share of GDP over the next generation.

Percent of GDP

Actual | Projected

Social Security

Medicare and Medicaid

Other spending (excluding debt service)

1965 1970 1975 1980 1985 1990 1995 2000 2005 2010 2015 2020 2025 2030

Source: Office of Management and Budget (2008)

shares will rise to 5.9 percent of GDP for Medicare and 2.5 percent of GDP for Medicaid. In comparison, OMB predicts that, absent reforms, in 2030 Medicare spending will be 5.0 percent of GDP and Medicaid spending will be 2.4 percent of GDP. By 2060, CBO projects spending for these programs will grow to 11.2 and 3.3 percent of GDP, respectively, while OMB projects spending will grow to 7.7 and 3.2 percent of GDP, respectively. Note that the major difference between the two forecasts lies in their estimates of the growth in health care expenditures per beneficiary.

Even under the more optimistic OMB projections, expected growth in entitlement spending will place a significant burden on the Federal budget and will require policymakers to make hard choices about the financing and benefit structures of these entitlement programs, as well as other Federal spending.

Social Security

During the program's first four decades, spending for Social Security benefits steadily increased relative to the size of the economy, reaching about 4 percent of GDP in the mid-1970s. This initial growth was driven largely by repeated program expansions that broadened coverage to include benefits for spouses and dependent children of retirees (1939), survivors of deceased workers (1939), the self-employed (1950), and disabled individuals (1956). Since then, annual spending for Social Security benefits has generally fluctuated between 4.1 percent and 4.5 percent of GDP.

As shown in Table 6-1, the number of Social Security beneficiaries is expected to more than double from 2000 to 2050, while the total population will increase by roughly 50 percent. The relative growth of the number of elderly individuals means that a larger share of the adult (age 18 and over) population will be drawing Social Security benefits in the years ahead. The demands imposed on the Social Security program by the baby boomers will diminish by the middle of the 21st century, but the expectation of a relatively constant fertility rate in combination with increasing lifespans means the portion of the adult population drawing Social Security benefits will remain high by historical standards. Box 6-1 describes some of the ways in which the Social Security program influences the saving behavior and labor supply decisions of individuals.

TABLE 6-1.—*Old-Age, Survivors, and Disability Insurance (OASDI) Benefits and Beneficiaries, 1950–2050*

Year	Benefits Paid (billions of dollars)	Percent of GDP	Beneficiaries (thousands of people)	Percent of Adult Population
1950	1.5	0.5	2,930	2.8
1975	68.7	4.2	31,123	20.9
2000	418.2	4.3	45,162	21.5
2025	1,814.1	5.7	77,138	28.3
2050	5,989.4	6.1	95,640	28.3

Source: Congressional Budget Office, Department of Commerce (Bureau of the Census and Bureau of Economic Analysis), and Social Security Administration.

Box 6-1: Undesirable Consequences of Social Security

The specific taxation and benefit structure of Social Security produces some undesirable consequences that may discourage participants from working and saving. Reduced work and saving levels reduce national output (GDP) and gradually reduce the U.S. standard of living over time from what it could have been. Efforts to reform Social Security should address each of these disincentives.

There are at least three ways Social Security discourages work and saving. First, the system imposes high effective tax rates on secondary earners. The benefit available to a married couple is either the sum of the benefits they are each individually eligible for or up to 150 percent of the higher earner's benefit, whichever is larger. This structure means the lower earner in a couple receives very little return on his or her Social

continued on the next page

Box 6-1 — continued

Security tax contributions and, if the low earner's wage is low enough, may not realize any benefit from his or her tax contributions. This reduces the reward for the second member of a married couple to work outside the home and can contribute to a decision not to participate in the labor force at all. As an extreme example, this can also cause the Social Security taxes paid by a low-income two-earner couple to subsidize the benefits received by a high-income one-earner couple.

Second, the program encourages early retirement. The existence of an Early Eligibility Age encourages workers to retire earlier than they may have done in the absence of Social Security. In fact, while the decision of when to retire probably depends on many factors, the mere existence of a sure income source in retirement, via Social Security benefits, could encourage people to retire earlier. The average age of retirement has been declining steadily, from over 67 in the early 1950s to under 63 in the early 2000s. When workers retire early, they pay less tax into Social Security and draw benefits for a longer period of time. This provision thus places additional stresses on Social Security finances and reduces the total amount of labor supplied to the economy.

Few people work past normal retirement age, perhaps because, in terms of one's Social Security benefit, the return to working past normal retirement age is modest at best. While a person who delays taking Social Security benefits receives a larger monthly benefit, they receive this benefit for a shorter period of time. The actuarial present value of the deferred payments is almost identical to the value of the payments that could be taken at normal retirement age. When one considers the additional taxes a person pays on labor income earned after normal retirement age, the return to working after this age may even be negative. This provides little incentive for people to work past their normal retirement age.

Third, Social Security discourages private saving. Social Security is a system that effectively forces people to save for their retirement—a portion of their wage is taken away and, in return, they expect income during retirement. From the perspective of an individual planning for his or her retirement, it makes little difference whether this income comes from a government program or from his or her own investments. However, when individuals do their own saving, the money is used by the financial markets to expand the economy. With a pay-as-you-go Social Security system, the taxes collected today are used to pay benefits for current retirees, and no actual saving occurs in terms of money going into financial markets. This means that a pay-as-you-go Social Security system actually reduces economy-wide saving, which reduces economic growth from what it could have been.

Medicare and Medicaid

Public spending on health care has increased as a share of total U.S. personal health care expenditures over the past several decades, as shown in Chart 6-2. In 1960, only 21 percent of personal health care spending was paid for by Federal and State Governments. With the introduction of Medicare and Medicaid in 1965, and SCHIP in 1997, public spending as a share of total health care spending has more than doubled to 45 percent. In contrast, the share of personal health care spending that is paid out of pocket by individuals has fallen dramatically from 55 percent in 1960 to just 15 percent of total spending in 2006.

Medicare expenditures, which include benefit payments and administrative expenses, were $432 billion, or approximately $10,500 per enrollee, in 2007. Between 1980 and 2006, real Medicare spending, that is, spending adjusted for the effects of inflation, grew at an average annual rate of 6.4 percent. This rate is higher than the 3.1 percent average annual growth rate for real GDP during that period. From 2008 to 2017, the Medicare Trustees' intermediate projections, which take into account currently legislated reductions in physician payment rates, suggest real Medicare spending will grow at an average rate of 6.0 percent per year. This rate exceeds projected average real economic growth of 2.8 percent per year over the same period.

Chart 6-2 **Changes in Source of Funds for Personal Health Care Expenditures**
The share of health care expenditures paid out of pocket by individuals has declined, while the shares paid by the Government and private insurers have increased.

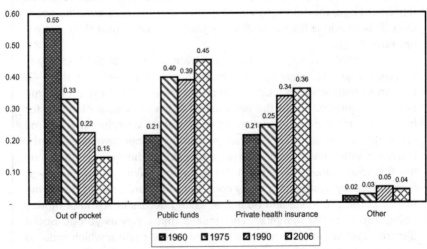

Source: National Health Expenditures Data, Department of Health and Human Services (Centers for Medicare and Medicaid Services).

Government spending on Medicaid and SCHIP includes benefit payments, administrative expenses, and payments for the Vaccines for Children Program. Collectively, the Federal Government and States spent $352 billion on Medicaid and an additional $10 billion on SCHIP in 2008. Of this total, Federal spending was approximately $190 billion for Medicaid and $7 billion for SCHIP. The amount spent on different Medicaid enrollee groups varies considerably. While the elderly and disabled represent the smallest groups in terms of numbers of enrollees (28.1 percent), they account for over 67 percent of spending, as depicted in Chart 6-3. (See Box 6-2 for a discussion of Medicaid and long-term care expenditures.) In contrast, children are much less expensive to cover. In 2007, almost half of total Medicaid enrollees were children, and yet they generated less than 20 percent of total spending.

Between 1997 and 2007, real Federal Medicaid spending grew at an average of 3.5 percent per year. This growth reflects a number of factors, including increased enrollment from outreach efforts and eligibility expansions, increased use of high-technology services (such as advanced diagnostic imaging and prescription drugs), and greater reliance on Medicaid to cover long-term care expenses. Medicaid spending is expected to continue growing faster in real terms than the overall economy throughout the coming decade.

Chart 6-3 Medicaid Enrollees and Expenditures by Enrollment Group, 2007
The elderly and disabled comprise 28.1% of Medicaid enrollees and 67.1% of Medicaid expenditures.

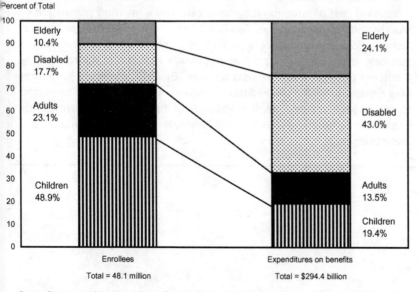

Source: Department of Health and Human Services (Centers for Medicare and Medicaid Services) 2008 Actuarial Report on the Financial Outlook for Medicaid.

Box 6-2: Long-Term Care and Medicaid

Today, about 10 million Americans receive long-term care services. Long-term care refers to medical care and support required by someone with a chronic illness or disability over an extended period of time. Typical long-term care services range from providing assistance with eating, bathing, and dressing, to managing medications and preparing food. Most people who require long-term care are 65 years of age or older. This demographic cohort is projected to grow dramatically over the next several decades, greatly increasing demand for long-term care services.

Current estimates suggest the average cost of nursing home care is $68,000 per year, an amount high enough to strain most families' finances. Private long-term care insurance represents one way individuals can obtain financial protection from these costs. Yet most people do not purchase long-term care insurance.

In 2005, Medicaid expenditures for long-term care services were $101 billion, representing 49 percent of the Nation's spending on long-term care. Under Federal law, State Medicaid programs must cover nursing home care and home health care, and may opt to cover some personal care services as well for qualified individuals. In contrast, Medicare covers only some home health care and limited recuperative care in skilled nursing facilities following a qualified inpatient hospitalization. In 2005, Medicare's share of total U.S. long-term care spending was approximately 20 percent.

Medicaid expenditures have grown rapidly in recent years with the increasing cost of covering long-term care and a growing population of elderly and disabled people. Medicaid expenditures on long-term care, including skilled nursing care as well as home- and community-based services, are expected to grow at an average real rate of approximately 6 percent per year over the next decade. By 2017, Medicaid long-term care expenditures for the Federal Government and States are projected to reach $228 billion. In the absence of fundamental reforms, this enormous entitlement burden will severely strain both Federal and State budgets.

Factors That Drive Expenditure Growth Over Time

Growth in expenditures for Social Security is expected to accelerate as the baby-boom generation retires, after which it is expected to level off. In contrast, expenditures for Medicare and Medicaid are expected to continue rising faster than GDP. This section examines the main factors that drive these expected increases in expenditures.

Demographic Shifts

The changing demographics of the United States population is an important factor in the growth of entitlement spending. With slowing birth rates and increasing life expectancy, the U.S. population is aging. For example, in 1950, less than 12 percent of the adult population was 65 or older; in 2008 this group constituted nearly 17 percent of the adult population. Demographers estimate that this trend will continue and that by 2030, twenty-five percent of the adult population—72 million people—will be at least 65 years of age.

This demographic shift means there are fewer workers paying taxes into the Social Security system for each retired person. To illustrate, in 1950, there were 16 workers paying taxes into the Social Security system for each Social Security beneficiary, meaning the effective tax burden on each worker was only one-sixteenth of the average amount paid to each beneficiary. In 2007, there were 3.3 workers per beneficiary. The number of workers per beneficiary is expected to fall further, to 2.6 workers per beneficiary in 2020 and to 2.1 workers per beneficiary in 2035. As the number of workers per beneficiary falls, the effective individual burden of taxes for both Social Security and Medicare Part A increases. For example, for Social Security, the payroll tax rate has been raised more than 20 times and the maximum annual amount of taxable income has been increased statutorily 11 times since the program's inception. This maximum is now (since 1981) adjusted annually to reflect average wage growth.

It is important to note that the demographic shift is not a temporary phenomenon brought on simply by the aging of the baby-boom generation. That is, assuming stable fertility rates and immigration patterns, one should not expect to return to a world with 16 workers—or even 5—contributing to each Social Security recipient's benefit after the baby-boom generation stops collecting Social Security benefits. Chart 6-4 shows that in the very near future, as the baby boomers retire en masse, the share of the adult population that is eligible for Social Security and Medicare will begin shifting from a recent average of about 16 percent to over 25 percent, where it will stay for the foreseeable future.

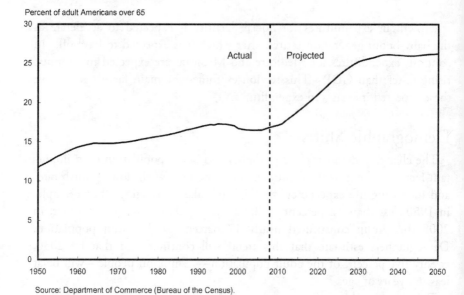

Chart 6-4 **The Population Age 65 or Older as a Percentage of the Total Adult Population**
The share of the U.S. adult population age 65 or older will increase from about 16 percent to over 25 percent over the next two decades.

Percent of adult Americans over 65

Source: Department of Commerce (Bureau of the Census).

A clear implication of this trend is that there will be fewer workers to pay taxes to support each Social Security and Medicare recipient.

Increased Health Care Spending per Beneficiary

Advances in medicine over the past few decades have created new methods for diagnosing illness and disease, as well as new therapies for preventing and treating medical conditions. While these advances have contributed to improvements in quality of life and longer life expectancy, they also have contributed to greater utilization of complex, expensive treatments and higher spending per person. This phenomenon is not restricted to Medicare and Medicaid enrollees, but instead reflects broader health spending patterns among individuals in the United States.

Although health insurance, including Medicare and Medicaid, provides important financial protections, one consequence of comprehensive coverage and a third-party payment system is that individuals have little incentive to consider providers' costs when making decisions about the medical care they receive. This moral hazard effect can lead people to demand more medical care than they would without insurance because their out-of-pocket cost at the point of use constitutes only a small portion of the total cost of the service.

Among Medicare enrollees, moral hazard problems are exacerbated by the widespread use of supplemental insurance, including retiree coverage, private

Medigap plans, and Medicaid (for dual eligibles). In effect, the combination of Medicare and supplemental insurance means enrollees pay only a very small portion or none of the total cost of care, and as a result, price is removed as a factor in determining how much medical care enrollees consume.

The Bottom Line

The permanent demographic shift and growth in per-person health care spending suggest that there are two distinct aspects of these programs that must be addressed. One aspect is program solvency: that is, how will the Government finance the benefits scheduled to be paid over the near term to current and future beneficiaries? Given the permanent nature of the demographic shift and the likelihood that future health care expenditures will grow, it will be impossible for the Government to continue these entitlement programs indefinitely as they currently exist. Thus, the second aspect that must be addressed is the long-term sustainability of the programs.

The Financial Future of Social Security

The demographic transition to an older population that is already underway in the United States will place increasing stress on the financing of Social Security in the years ahead. This section examines the issues inherent in ensuring that benefits can be paid in the near term (solvency) and the issues that must be addressed to ensure long-term sustainability of this important program.

Addressing Future Solvency

Projections by the Social Security Administration (SSA) indicate that payroll tax revenues will exceed expenses through 2016, then, beginning in 2017, it will be necessary to draw on Social Security Trust Fund assets to pay all scheduled benefits. This would require making increasing amounts of general revenue available from 2017–2041 to pay full scheduled benefits, after which time the trust fund would be exhausted. Payroll tax revenues are projected to be sufficient to pay 78 percent of scheduled benefits in 2041 and beyond.

As Social Security costs continue to rise faster than revenues, increasing pressure will be placed on the general fund of the Federal Government. By purchasing Treasury bonds with its annual surpluses, the Social Security Trust Fund has been effectively lending money to the general fund of the Federal Government. As Social Security's annual surpluses decline, beginning after 2009, less money will be available to the Treasury Department from this channel and the Government will increasingly be forced to find other revenue sources or reduce spending. The problems for the Federal budget intensify in 2017, when Social Security will first need money *from* the general fund to pay scheduled benefits. During the 2020s, Social Security will require larger and larger transfers from the general fund as it redeems the Treasury bonds that have accumulated in the trust fund, putting greater and greater pressure on the Federal budget.

Most proposed solutions to the solvency issue involve some form of revenue increases, or benefit reductions, or both. Social Security revenues could be increased either by raising the payroll tax rate or increasing the maximum amount of taxable earnings. However, as discussed in the preceding chapter, imposing taxes distorts markets—higher taxes would decrease economic efficiency by worsening the adverse labor incentives discussed in Box 6-1.

There are a variety of ways Social Security benefits could be reduced, such as further delaying the normal retirement age, or reducing scheduled benefits, particularly for higher-income workers. To help address the solvency issue, the President embraced the concept of progressive price indexing for new retirees. Progressive price indexing would reduce the growth in initial benefits for new retirees, particularly for high-income workers, and thus would reduce projected program costs in the decades ahead, while retaining currently scheduled benefits for very low income workers.

Workers with higher preretirement earnings are eligible for a larger initial benefit, but the marginal increase in the initial benefit decreases as a worker's preretirement income gets higher and higher. Progressive price indexing would further reduce the rate at which benefits grow with preretirement income, which would slow the year-by-year growth of initial benefits for high- and middle-income retirees. This proposal would ensure that retirees of the future will receive real benefits that are at least as high as those of today's retirees who are at comparable positions on the wage spectrum. Benefits for all recipients would still increase annually via cost-of-living adjustments to maintain the purchasing power of the benefits. Note that the current benefit formula would be preserved for individuals with low preretirement income. Estimates suggest that progressive price indexing would cover about 70 percent of the gap between income and outlays over the long term. Benefits paid under the Disability Insurance program would not be affected by this proposal.

Funding Future Benefits

The current Social Security system was designed in an era in which average life expectancy was less than 65 years and few women participated in the labor force. Today, average life expectancy is 78 years and about 60 percent of all women participate in the labor force. The demographic and labor market changes that have occurred in the last 70 years or so render the pay-as-you-go system of the 1930s inappropriate for the 21st century.

A central feature of the Administration's 2005 proposals for Social Security reform, the Personal Retirement Account (PRA), was designed to pre-fund a portion of future benefit obligations. Participation in PRAs would be entirely voluntary. Workers could choose to have up to 4 percentage points of their current Social Security taxes go into their own, individual account. The Federal Government would administer these accounts, making contributions and withdrawals as appropriate for each worker's wages and individual choices.

Each worker could choose to have the funds in their account invested in any of a set of prescreened, broadly diversified investment funds, similar to those currently available to Government employees in their retirement savings plan. Recent stock market declines raise concerns about the desirability of investing even a portion of Social Security assets in the stock market. However, market declines, like market increases, are a normal part of stock market behavior and do not negate the desirability of owning stocks as part of a long-term investment strategy. From 1926 to 2000, even with several periods of significant market decline, stocks generated an average annual return of 10.7 percent.

Nevertheless, there is currently much concern about the risks of investing Social Security assets in the stock market. One way to mitigate these risks could occur automatically; as workers near retirement age, their PRA investments could be moved to lower-risk, life-cycle funds, which ensure the safety of the worker's retirement benefits by progressively shifting more of the worker's investment from growth funds to secure bonds as the worker nears retirement age.

A PRA-based system offers a partially self-funded retirement benefit while retaining the social safety net aspects of the current system. A primary advantage of this system would be significantly reduced intergenerational transfers from future workers entering the system. This system would give workers a partial alternative to the current, pay-as-you-go, Social Security system that, as discussed above, will require reducing benefits when the Social Security Trust Fund is exhausted or force workers to bear ever-increasing tax burdens as the population continues to age.

PRAs could be phased in to ensure that current retirees and workers nearing retirement would receive the full Social Security benefits they are expecting. PRAs would offer those who want it individual ownership and management of retirement assets and could be transferable to family members if the worker were to die prematurely. Finally, PRAs would reduce the disincentives the current system generates regarding labor supply and saving decisions. (Box 6-1 describes the disincentives present in the current system.) For example, PRAs reduce possible adverse labor supply effects for secondary earners by giving them explicit rights to a portion of their Social Security assets.

The Financial Future of Medicare and Medicaid

Medicare and Medicaid are currently responsible for purchasing health care services for over 80 million individuals in the United States annually—a number that is expected to exceed 100 million by 2017. This section takes a closer look at the future budgetary impact of these programs and identifies possible strategies for promoting long-term sustainability of Medicare and Medicaid.

Recall that Medicare is financed predominately by payroll taxes, general revenues, and beneficiary premiums. Under current projections in the 2008 Medicare Trustees Report, the Medicare Hospital Insurance Trust Fund for Part A is projected to be exhausted in 2019. The projected 75-year deficit for the Medicare Hospital Insurance Trust Fund is 3.54 percent of taxable payroll. That is, the Medicare Hospital Insurance payroll tax would have to immediately increase from a total of 2.90 percent to 6.44 percent to cover all projected spending for Part A over the next 75 years. Thus, one option for keeping Part A solvent would be to more than double the Medicare payroll tax rate. For Medicare Parts B and D, as well as Medicaid, general revenues are the largest source of financing. This suggests that, in the absence of significant reforms to slow spending growth, spending on other government programs will have to be dramatically reduced, budget deficits will grow larger, or income taxes will have to increase.

Real spending growth for Medicare and Medicaid is on a much steeper trajectory than projected growth for the economy as a whole. The long-term sustainability of these programs is in question unless policymakers implement a comprehensive set of reforms to slow both the overall growth in health care spending as well as the Federal Government's liabilities. Although key stakeholders have not yet discovered a silver bullet for slowing overall spending growth, insurers and providers are pursuing a variety of approaches in an attempt to improve the efficiency of resource allocation and to slow the growth of costs.

Some of these efforts focus on greater use of high-value health care services by individuals, including preventive care (certain types of screening for diseases), wellness initiatives (flu shots or smoking cessation advice), and disease management for those with chronic conditions. Other efforts target provider behavior, including adopting health information technology that may reduce medical errors and duplication of services, and participating in quality-measurement activities and public reporting. In value-based purchasing, insurers design payment systems that are tied more directly to the quality and efficiency of care that is delivered by providers. One example includes pay-for-performance programs, whereby providers may receive financial rewards if the quality of care they provide achieves certain outcomes (such as a physician making sure that all of his diabetic patients receive HbA1c tests during the year) or if a provider shows improvement over time in the quality of care he or she provides. Of course, many of these initiatives are fairly recent and as a result, the empirical evidence is not yet available to establish what impact these particular initiatives might have for slowing overall cost growth.

A second strategy directly targets Federal spending growth vis-à-vis structural changes to the designs of the Medicare and Medicaid programs. Several types of reform proposals are specifically aimed to reduce Federal spending by altering the current structure of Medicare benefits. Increasing the age of eligibility for Medicare, raising premiums, and modifying the benefit design are three examples. Similar to the changes that were made to Social Security in 1983, the age at which individuals become eligible for Medicare could gradually increase. However, unlike Social Security, the savings generated from delaying eligibility may not be substantial, since younger Medicare beneficiaries have much lower average costs relative to older beneficiaries.

Beneficiary premiums are an important source of income for Medicare Parts B and D. Raising beneficiary premiums is one option for reducing Federal spending, although raising premiums for all beneficiaries may impose a significant financial burden on lower-income beneficiaries who are not also eligible for Medicaid. One suggested proposal calls for the broader use of income-related premiums, whereby higher-income beneficiaries would pay more for their coverage. Income-related premiums are already being used for Part B; however, as of 2007 the threshold was set so high that it affected less than 3 percent of the Medicare population. Using more stringent thresholds and adopting income-related premiums for Medicare Part D are two possible strategies for reducing the implicit subsidy that Medicare provides to higher-income beneficiaries.

Modifying the benefit design offers another approach to limiting Federal spending. Benefit design features, such as deductibles and coinsurance, are typically used to address moral hazard concerns. While increasing deductibles and coinsurance can reduce beneficiaries' incentives to overuse care and reduce spending, it may lead some beneficiaries to delay or forgo needed care due to cost. A related issue is the widespread use of supplemental Medicare insurance, which typically reimburses beneficiaries for deductibles and coinsurance amounts when they seek care. With this additional coverage, the price of medical care is effectively removed as a factor from decision making. Some economists have suggested that private supplemental Medicare insurance should be limited or eliminated altogether. Since greater utilization of high-technology treatments is a major driver of health care spending growth, an additional strategy is to base coverage decisions about new medical treatments on their comparative effectiveness and cost effectiveness relative to existing therapies. Certainly, this may raise concerns by patients and providers regarding the role of government in determining which medical treatments are prescribed.

In addition to strategies that alter the existing program structure, others have suggested more fundamental changes to promote long-run sustainability. For example, some have suggested moving completely to a market-based approach in which Medicare beneficiaries receive risk-adjusted and income-adjusted vouchers that could be applied toward the cost of private health plans. Such a reform could build upon the strengths of the current Medicare Advantage program and potentially strengthen competition in the market for health insurance. Moreover, a voucher system would provide greater certainty in terms of the Federal Government's future liabilities.

Medicare provider payment systems are complex and generally create poor incentives for limiting spending growth. Fee-for-service payment systems reward providers for how much they do rather than for the value that they provide to Medicare patients. Furthermore, administrative pricing may or may not necessarily reflect what would be observed in a competitive market, due to inflation and technological advances in medicine. Competitive bidding has been proposed as one alternative method for setting prices. Specifically, competitive bidding requires providers to submit bids that reflect costs plus a normal rate of profit. Providers with the lowest cost can be identified. Over time, this type of system can enable providers to more easily adjust prices to reflect changes in production costs resulting from changes in input prices (such as the wages of nurses) or technology (such as MRI or CT scanners).

For Medicaid, one of the most pressing issues is the anticipated growth in long-term care. While some people require the level of care provided by nursing homes, many eligible Medicaid beneficiaries would actually prefer less expensive community-based care. Transitioning away from primarily institutional care and toward a more community-based long-term care system is one potential cost-saving measure; however, it is not clear to what extent overall demand for services will rise when access to this option improves. Encouraging the purchase of private long-term care insurance through tax credits or Qualified State Long-Term Care Partnerships, which protect some assets of those with long-term care insurance while still allowing them to qualify for Medicaid, may both reduce the spending burden on Medicaid and protect many seniors from poverty. Additionally, better coordination of care between Medicare, which is often responsible for financing initial nursing home stays through its post-acute care coverage, and Medicaid, which often assumes responsibility for nursing home patients after their Medicare benefits end, could also help reduce costs.

Conclusion

There are no painless solutions to the budgetary challenges arising from long-term projected growth in Social Security, Medicare, and Medicaid. While there is no specific year when one can be sure a crisis is imminent, it is clear that these problems will only grow larger the longer policymakers delay in developing and implementing reform strategies. The environments in which Social Security, Medicare, and Medicaid were created no longer exist, and the Legislative and Executive branches of the Federal and State Governments need to take up the budgetary challenges entitlement programs present and ensure that these programs are adapted to their new realities.

CHAPTER 7

Balancing Private and Public Roles in Health Care

Health care is one of the largest and fastest growing sectors of the U.S. economy, employing millions of individuals in hospitals, physician offices, home health agencies, long-term care facilities, insurance, and pharmaceutical and medical device companies. Today, Americans are living longer as a result of public health improvements and advances in medical treatment. While modern health care provides substantial benefits, there are growing concerns about its rising cost. In 2008, the United States is projected to spend approximately $2.4 trillion, or almost $8,000 per person, on health care, and forecasts indicate that spending will continue to grow at a rate faster than the gross domestic product (GDP). Recognizing that rising costs pose a threat to Americans' access to health insurance and medical care, the Administration has pursued several initiatives to encourage the efficient provision of health care through private markets and to improve access to affordable health care for individuals in the United States.

This chapter begins with a brief overview of U.S. performance with respect to the population's health status and spending on health care. This is followed by a discussion of key efforts by the Administration to address issues of health care quality, cost, and access. The key points of this chapter are:

- Health care spending is expected to grow rapidly over the next several decades, a trend that is driven by the increased use of high-technology medical procedures, comprehensive health insurance that decreases consumer incentives to shop for cost-effective care, rising rates of chronic disease, and the aging of the population in the United States.
- Markets for health care services can function more efficiently when payers, providers, and consumers have more complete information as well as incentives to use medical care that is clinically effective and of high value.
- Health insurance improves individuals' well-being by providing financial protection against uncertain medical costs and by improving access to care. Market-based approaches and innovative benefit designs can enable people to select coverage that best fits their preferences and to more actively participate in their own health care decision making.
- The Federal Government has an important role in investing in public health infrastructure, particularly with respect to improving the availability of community-based health care for the underserved, preparing for possible public health crises, supporting health-related research and development, and promoting global health improvement.

The Health of the U.S. Population

Health can be defined as a state of complete physical, mental, and social well-being. Individuals who are healthy are more productive and happier. Genetic factors; the environment; lifestyle behaviors such as smoking, eating healthy foods, and exercise; and medical care consumption are all factors that have been shown to affect an individual's health.

There are several different ways to measure health outcomes for a population. One consistent and reliable measure is life expectancy, defined as the average number of years of life remaining to a person at a particular age. Chart 7-1 shows how U.S. life expectancy at birth has changed over the past century. In the early part of the 20th century, life expectancy averaged 51 years until an influenza pandemic in 1918 resulted in a significant drop, to 39 years. Following that crisis, there have been steady increases in life expectancy over time. This positive trend can be explained by several factors, most notably, public health improvements such as cleaner water, improved sanitation, and vaccinations, as well as medical innovation.

A second way to measure population health is by examining disease prevalence. Rising rates of age-adjusted chronic diseases, which are conditions

Chart 7-1 **Life Expectancy at Birth**

Life expectancy at birth has increased over time.

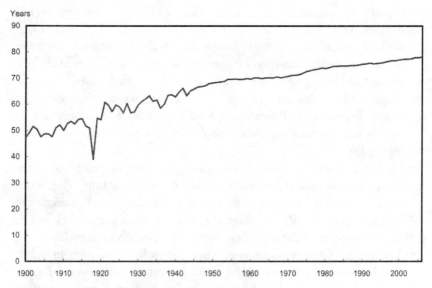

Note: Data from before 1929 are only from states that recorded death statistics.
Source: Centers for Disease Control.

expected to last at least 1 year, are particularly concerning to the medical, public health, and health policy communities. Heart disease and diabetes are two examples of chronic diseases that afflict millions of Americans each year. Heart disease, which affects 7.3 percent of adults 20 years of age and older, has been the leading cause of death for the past 90 years, as well as a major cause of disability. Diabetes affects 7.8 percent of the population, or roughly 23.6 million children and adults, and has numerous costly complications, including kidney damage, eye problems, nerve damage, foot problems, and depression.

In 2005, approximately 60 percent of people 18 years of age and older in the United States had at least one chronic condition, and older adults were considerably more likely to have multiple chronic conditions (Chart 7-2). Managing many chronic diseases can be quite costly. More than 50 percent of total medical care expenditures generated by the adult U.S. population (excluding expenditures for dental care and medical equipment and services) is for the treatment of chronic conditions. However, with medical management and lifestyle changes, people can remain productive and lower their risk of disability from these conditions.

Chart 7-2 **Distribution of Adults by Age Group According to Number of Chronic Conditions, 2005**
Chronic conditions are more prevalent among older people.

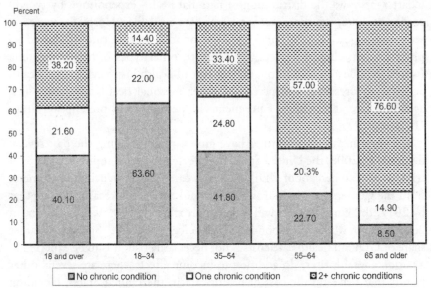

Source: Center for Financing, Access, and Cost Trends, AHRQ, Medical Expenditure Panel Survey, Statistical Brief #203: Health Care Expenses for Adults with Chronic Conditions, 2005.

The good news is that many chronic diseases are preventable. Healthy lifestyle decisions, such as being a nonsmoker, eating nutritious foods, and getting regular physical activity, can significantly lower the likelihood of developing a wide variety of serious medical conditions. In the United States, the rate of smoking has fallen during the past several decades, a trend partially explained by better information about the associated health risks, as well as public policies that deter smoking behavior. However, a major health concern remains in that about 20 percent of adults still report being current smokers. Another major public health concern is the rapid rise in obesity rates among adults and children. Currently, more than 72 million people ages 20 and older are obese, which is defined as having a body mass index (a measure using information on a person's weight and height to indicate body fat) greater than or equal to 30. Obesity is a known risk factor for several costly medical conditions, including heart disease, diabetes, stroke, and some forms of cancer. Continued efforts to promote healthy eating and regular physical activity are critical for reversing this rising trend.

U.S. Health Care Spending

Health-related goods and services include hospital care, physician and clinical services, nursing home care, prescription drugs, and more. Over time, there have been large spending increases across all of these major categories. Chart 7-3 shows the distribution of national health expenditures by type of service in 2006, the most recent year of data available. Hospital care represents the largest segment, at 31 percent of total expenditures, followed by physician and clinical services (21 percent), other types of health spending (which include administration, the net cost of health insurance, public health activity, and research (16 percent)), other personal health care costs such as dental care and medical equipment (13 percent), and prescription drugs (10 percent).

U.S. health care expenditures have grown rapidly during the past several decades. In 2008, the United States is projected to spend approximately $2.4 trillion, or 16.6 percent of GDP, on health care. Based on actuarial estimates from the Centers for Medicare and Medicaid Services, forecasts indicate that by 2017, the United States will spend approximately $10,592 per person (in 2008 dollars), which corresponds to 19.5 percent of GDP. Spending a larger share of GDP on health care costs is not necessarily bad; it is to be expected as a nation's wealth rises. In addition to income effects, there are several other factors that drive up the cost of health care in the United States, including population aging, increases in input prices that are greater than inflation, technological advances, and third-party payment.

Approximately 50% of national health care expenditures are for hospital care and physician services.

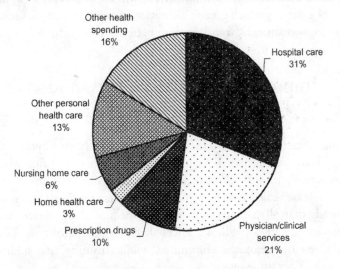

Note: "Other personal health care" includes dental and other professional health services and durable and non-durable medical equipment. "Other health spending" includes administration and net cost of private health insurance, public health activity, research, and structures and equipment.
Source: Centers for Medicare and Medicaid Services, Office of the Actuary, National Health Statistics Group.

Researchers who have investigated the catalysts of health care spending growth suggest that third-party payment and advances in medical technology can account for a significant proportion of the long-term, historical spending trends. Although health insurance provides valuable financial protection, benefit designs that have low out-of-pocket costs at the point of use (such as doctor or hospital visits) greatly inhibit consumers' incentives to search for the lowest-priced providers or to engage providers in discussion about alternative treatment options and their respective costs. Health insurance that has low out-of-pocket cost-sharing can also create distorted incentives regarding the development and diffusion of new medical technologies. Of course, many advances in medicine have been instrumental in helping Americans live longer and healthier lives. For example, providers now have more advanced technologies to diagnose specific problems (such as MRI or CT scanners), treat existing ailments (such as using minimally invasive surgical procedures), and prevent the onset and spread of new diseases or illnesses (such as use of vaccinations or screening procedures). However, when providers and consumers lack strong incentives to control spending, one potential result is that new, more expensive technologies may be prescribed and received, even if they are only slightly more effective than existing therapies. As the amount of financial resources allocated to health care rises, it is important to consider the role that incentives play in determining the quantity and types of medical care that consumers receive. Additionally, it will be important to continue evaluating the extent to which greater utilization of medical services, including high-technology treatments, translates into better health outcomes.

Improving the Effectiveness and Efficiency of Health Care

The terms "effectiveness" and "efficiency" are frequently used in the context of discussions about improving health system performance. But what do these terms actually mean? *Effective care* includes services that are of proven clinical value. It is medical care for which the benefits to patients far outweigh the risks, such that all patients with specific medical needs should receive it. *Efficient care* includes medical services that maximize quality and health outcomes, given the resources committed, while ensuring that additional investments yield net value over time.

In the United States, there is clear empirical evidence that many patients do not receive the highest quality of care possible. That is, patients do not receive care that fully complies with current clinical guidelines. In one well-respected study, researchers found that only 54 percent of acute care and 56 percent of chronic care provided by physicians conformed to clinical recommendations in the medical literature. Receiving better quality care, particularly for those with chronic conditions, has the potential to reduce the adverse impacts of existing illnesses and prolong life.

There are large differences in the levels of effective care provided in the United States, a result that reflects differences both in provider practice styles and in patient preferences. Researchers associated with the Dartmouth Atlas of Health Care have reported extensive geographic variation in medical care spending and in the use of medical care across a wide range of services such as preventive screenings, diabetes management, joint replacement surgeries, and end-of-life care. Differences across regions of the United States cannot be fully explained by differences in illness rates or well-informed patient preferences. In fact, this research finds that higher rates of utilization reported across the United States do not appear to be correlated with better health outcomes, and that nearly 30 percent of Medicare's costs could be saved without adverse health consequences if spending in high- and medium-cost areas of the country was reduced to levels in low-cost areas. The Administration has strongly advocated, in its policies, using information and better incentives to improve the effectiveness and the efficiency of health care delivery, including hospital care, physician services, and long-term care.

Health Information Technology

There is optimism among policymakers about the ability of health information technology (IT) to generate significant production efficiencies in the delivery of health care. This is because health IT permits the management of medical information and the secure exchange of information among consumers, providers, and payers. Using IT in health care may help reduce medical errors, provide physicians with information on best practices for diagnosis and treatment, improve care coordination, and reduce duplication of services. The most comprehensive form of health IT is an electronic health record, which is a longitudinal record of patient information that typically includes the patient's demographic characteristics, past medical history, medication use, vital signs, laboratory data, and radiology reports.

One goal of the Administration is for most Americans to have an electronic health record by 2014. While providers have expressed interest in the potential benefits of IT for workflow improvement, adoption has been somewhat slower than anticipated. Results from a survey conducted by the Office of the National Coordinator for Health IT indicate that 14 percent of outpatient doctors currently use an electronic health record, and a study sponsored by the American Hospital Association finds that 68 percent of hospitals have or are in the process of implementing an electronic health record. Key barriers to adoption of health IT include lack of a business case to support adoption; privacy and security concerns; technical issues that make exchanging information difficult; and organizational culture issues, including providers' resistance to changing business processes.

In response to these concerns, the Administration formed the American Health Information Community, a Federal advisory body that includes experts from the public and private sectors, to make recommendations to the Secretary of Health and Human Services about how to accelerate the development and adoption of health IT. Over the past few years, this advisory body has also provided recommendations on how to make records digital and available for providers to share easily, as well as how to assure the privacy and security of those records.

Comparative Effectiveness

For many types of medical conditions, a patient may have a choice between at least two diagnostic methods and/or treatments that have different benefits and risks. Selecting the most appropriate course of care relies on having current information about the effectiveness of each option, given a patient's characteristics. Comparative effectiveness research studies are rigorous evaluations that compare the performance of various diagnostic and treatment options for specific medical conditions and sets of patients. By using comparative effectiveness research findings, providers can help patients select the most clinically appropriate course of treatment. Advocates of comparative effectiveness research also suggest that widespread use of research findings may help to reduce some of the geographic variation in utilization and spending that exists in the United States.

The number of comparative effectiveness studies has increased in recent decades, and provides the potential to improve the quality of care delivered to patients. A recent Federally-sponsored comparative effectiveness initiative is the Agency for Healthcare Research and Quality's Effective Health Care Program. Created as part of the Medicare Prescription Drug, Improvement, and Modernization Act of 2003, this program funds the creation of new research, synthesizes current research on the benefits and risks of alternative medical interventions, and translates these findings into useful formats that can be easily accessed by health care providers and patients.

Price and Quality Information Transparency

When individuals shop for many goods or services, often they can access information on prices and quality using readily available sources. With this information, they can compare alternatives and then select the one of highest value. Unfortunately, the same information is not readily available for health-related goods and services. Having information on prices and provider quality may be important as people consider which physicians or hospitals to select for care and what impact this might have on their out-of-pocket costs (such as copayments or coinsurance) and their potential health outcomes.

To illustrate, suppose a couple learns that they are expecting their first child and that their physician has admitting privileges at the two hospitals in their community. Wanting to make an informed decision about which hospital they should use for the birth, this couple would benefit from being able to look on their insurer's web site to find information about the price that each hospital charges for different types of deliveries. With this information, they could assess how much it will likely cost them out of pocket for a normal delivery, given their insurance coverage. Additionally, the couple would be able to find information on each hospital's web site about the quality of its maternity services, including the volume of deliveries during the past year, the proportion of deliveries that were performed by Cesarean section, and whether there is a neonatal intensive care unit at the facility.

One challenge in health care is that there are actually two types of prices: list prices and transaction prices. List prices, which are also called charges, are well-documented and are found in all standardized information that hospitals and physicians submit when seeking payment for services. However, list prices are often not relevant because most payers, whether private insurers, Medicare, or Medicaid, pay much less than the list price. The payment that is actually made by the insurer to the provider is called a *transaction price*. Unfortunately, this information is more difficult to access because it is insurer-specific and providers may be sensitive about having negotiated rates available in the public domain.

In the past 20 years there have been tremendous advances in the development of objective measures of clinical quality for chronic diseases, acute care, preventive care, and long-term care. Improvements in health care quality measurement as well as better information systems are making it easier to evaluate provider performance and generate information that is relevant and timely for providers and individuals. Increasing the transparency of information about health care quality can motivate providers to improve the care that they deliver, and it can help consumers to make more informed decisions regarding their provider choices. A key priority for the Administration has been public reporting of price and quality information. In addition to advocating for greater transparency across the entire health care system, the Federal Government and the Centers for Medicare and Medicaid Services, in particular, have developed Hospital Compare, Nursing Home Compare, and the Medicare Prescription Drug Plan Finder, which are comprehensive, web-based resources providing quality and pricing information.

Pay-for-Performance

Pay-for-performance refers to purchasing practices aimed at improving the value of health care services that are provided to patients, where value depends on both quality and cost. Private insurers, as well as Medicare and Medicaid, are using pay-for-performance programs that provide doctors and hospitals with financial incentives to meet certain performance measures for quality and efficiency or to show quality improvement. Researchers in the private and public sectors are conducting numerous evaluations of pay-for-performance programs to assess whether these programs affect provider behavior and improve the quality of care that patients receive.

One such evaluation includes the Premier Hospital Quality Incentive Demonstration Project, which started in 2003. In this Medicare demonstration, hospitals receive bonus payments based on their performance on five medical conditions, including acute myocardial infarction (heart attack), coronary artery bypass graft, pneumonia, heart failure, and hip/knee replacement. Improvements in quality of care during the first 3 years of the demonstration have saved the lives of an estimated 2,500 acute myocardial infarction patients, based on an analysis of mortality rates at participating hospitals. Additionally, more than 1.1 million patients treated in the five clinical areas at participating hospitals have received approximately 300,000 additional services or recommendations that align with evidence-based clinical quality measures, such as smoking cessation advice, discharge instructions, and pneumococcal vaccination.

Using Market-Based Approaches to Improve Access to Health Insurance

The financial burden of health care costs can be extensive, particularly for those who have a serious health episode, such as cancer or a trauma-related injury. In the United States, about 80 percent of medical care expenditures each year are generated by about 20 percent of the population. Health insurance provides individuals with financial protection against costs associated with medical treatment, giving them access to needed and valuable care that otherwise might not be affordable. This section provides an overview of current health insurance coverage patterns and discusses key Administration initiatives to promote market-based approaches and new types of insurance benefit designs to provide individuals with greater flexibility as they choose coverage that best meets their needs.

Private Health Insurance

The private market for health insurance is really two markets—one for employer groups and another for individuals. Currently, 165 million Americans under 65 years of age obtain their coverage through an employer source, either as a worker or a dependent of a worker, and approximately 17 million non-elderly individuals purchase coverage in the individual market.

In the United States, employer provision of health insurance is voluntary, and while 99 percent of large firms (those with 200 or more workers) offer coverage to their workers as a benefit, a smaller percentage of small firms do. In 2008, 62 percent of small firms (those with 3–199 workers) offered their workers health insurance, down from 68 percent in 2000. Two main factors cause small firms to be less likely to offer health insurance as a fringe benefit relative to large firms. First, small firms may have difficulty pooling risk effectively. Very small groups, in particular, may be less able to absorb the financial shock of a high-cost, low-probability medical problem by one or more of their employees, which may result in higher premiums for a specific amount of coverage, as well as larger rate increases over time. Second, there are human resources costs for firms when they shop for insurance, coordinate enrollment with employees, and integrate employee contributions toward the premium with payroll. If the per-worker administrative costs of insurance are higher for small firms, they may be less likely to offer coverage.

For individuals who are not offered health insurance through an employer, the individual market is an alternative way to acquire coverage. Many who purchase insurance in this market use it as a bridge between jobs that provide employer-sponsored insurance or between employer-sponsored coverage and

Medicare. For others, including the self-employed, coverage purchased in the individual market may need to serve their needs over the long term.

There are several different types of health insurance plans available in the private market, including health maintenance organizations, preferred provider organizations, and point-of-service plans. In addition to traditional managed care plans, a new generation of insurance benefit designs, called *consumer-directed health plans*, is emerging. Consumer-directed health plans typically have three basic features: a high deductible, which is the dollar amount that has to be paid before an insurer covers any medical expenses; an associated account that can be funded with pre-tax dollars and can be used to pay for out-of-pocket medical expenses; and tools to help enrollees make decisions about their medical care treatment options. The two most prevalent forms of consumer-directed health plans are Health Reimbursement Arrangements, which are offered by employers, and Health Savings Accounts, which are offered in both the employer group and individual markets. See Box 7-1 for information about Health Savings Accounts.

Box 7-1: Health Savings Accounts: Innovation in Benefit Design

Health Savings Accounts (HSAs) were signed into law by the President in 2003 as part of the Medicare Prescription Drug, Improvement, and Modernization Act. HSAs are tax-advantaged savings accounts to which individuals can contribute funds that they can then use to pay for qualified medical expenses. HSAs are used in conjunction with High-Deductible Health Plans that meet specific criteria. In particular, these plans must have a minimum deductible of $1,150 for single coverage and $2,300 for family coverage in 2009, an annual out-of-pocket limit of no more than $5,800 for individuals and $11,600 for families in 2009, and catastrophic coverage in case an individual or family exceeds the out-of-pocket limit as a result of a serious medical episode. Health plans that meet these criteria are referred to as HSA-compatible or HSA-eligible plans.

HSAs are available in both the employer group and individual markets. When offered in an employer setting, both an employer and employee can contribute money to the account, up to specific limits ($3,000 for individuals and $5,950 for families in 2009). Also, employees whose health plans meet the deductible and out-of-pocket limit criteria described above can open an HSA on their own if their employer does not open an account for them. Unused balances may be rolled over from year to year and accumulate interest, thus allowing individuals to build up savings that can be used to cover future medical expenses. Additionally, HSAs are portable, which means that individuals are able to

continued on the next page

Box 7-1 — continued

keep any unspent funds in the account when they change employment or exit the labor force.

Enrollment in HSA-compatible health plans has been growing steadily each year. In 2006, over 6.8 million employees and dependents were enrolled in High-Deductible Health Plans, and over 30 percent of these enrollees were in small firms. As of January 2008, approximately 1.5 million consumers had purchased HSA-compatible plans in the individual market. HSAs in combination with a High-Deductible Health Plan are playing an increasingly important role in the individual market, providing an option that is more affordable, on average, than other traditional types of health plans.

HSAs and High-Deductible Health Plans are designed to encourage more consumer control over health care decision making, but concerns have arisen about the impact that these plans may have on policy-holders' care-seeking behavior. In particular, some believe that the deductible may lead individuals to forgo or delay getting care such as preventive screenings (for example, mammograms). To mitigate this concern, most insurers now provide some coverage before the insured person meets his or her deductible. Research that analyzes the impact of HSAs and High-Deductible Health Plans on medical care utilization and expenditures is mixed. In coming years, as these plans gain market share, research may help to clarify the full effect of this type of benefit design on care-seeking behavior and costs.

The employer group and individual markets for health insurance have unique advantages and disadvantages. Employer groups are generally able to pool risk, as individuals within an employer group initially come together for a purpose other than buying health insurance and because larger numbers of covered people makes it easier to predict the average expenditure of the group. Effective risk pooling is often more challenging in the individual market, given the potential for adverse selection, whereby individuals who expect high health care costs are more likely to buy coverage, while those who expect to have low costs may be less likely to do so. If insurers are not able to fully identify the risk of individuals seeking coverage and premiums are set according to the average risk in the population, then there will be insufficient funds to cover the claims that are generated. In most States, health insurers use medical underwriting to assess individuals' risk for generating medical expenditures based on their demographics, health status, and past utilization.

Another important distinction between the employer group and individual markets is the tax treatment of premiums. For employer-sponsored insurance, premiums that are paid by employers are exempt from the Federal income tax, State income taxes in 43 States, and Social Security and Medicare taxes. In addition, many employees can pay their share of the insurance premium with pre-tax dollars if their firm offers a "Section 125" plan. The amount of forgone revenue associated with excluding tax on premiums is often referred to as the "tax subsidy" for employer-sponsored health insurance. The tax exclusion encourages employers to provide a larger share of workers' total compensation in the form of health insurance benefits, leading employers to offer generous coverage with low levels of coinsurance and deductibles. In turn, these low levels of cost-sharing can encourage moral hazard, whereby individuals use more medical care than they would if they were responsible for the full price of that care.

For self-employed workers and their families, there is a partial tax subsidy of health insurance, which allows them to deduct health insurance for themselves and their families from the Federal income tax (up to the net profit of their business) but not from the self-employment tax (equivalent to the combined tax that they would pay for Social Security and Medicare). For those who neither are self-employed nor have an offer of employer group insurance, medical care expenses, including the premiums for coverage purchased in the individual market, are tax deductible only when these expenses exceed 7.5 percent of adjusted gross income.

As discussed before, not all workers have access to employer-sponsored insurance; those who do may have limited choices, particularly if they are employed at a small firm. While the individual market provides an alternative way to acquire health insurance, for many it is not perceived to be as attractive as employer-sponsored insurance. One way to move toward balancing the attractiveness of the employer group and individual markets is to alter the current tax treatment of premiums. Removing the tax exclusion for employer premiums has the potential to eliminate many of the inefficiencies and equity issues associated with the current system; it would also increase Federal Government income tax revenues by up to $168 billion in FY 2009.

The President has proposed replacing the current tax exclusion with a flat $15,000 standard deduction for health insurance for families or $7,500 for individuals. The amount of the standard deduction would be independent of the actual amount spent on a health insurance policy, which would need to meet a set of minimum requirements for catastrophic coverage. Thus, individuals and families would still be able to take the full amount of the deduction from income and payroll taxes, even if their health insurance premium cost less than that amount. Although individuals with small tax liabilities would not stand to gain as much from a tax deduction as individuals with higher tax liabilities, this approach would make health insurance more affordable, particularly for those who do not have access to employer-sponsored coverage.

Public Insurance

Several programs funded by the Federal Government exist to provide health care to specific populations. These programs include the Federal Employees Health Benefits Program (FEHBP), TRICARE, the Veterans Health Administration (VHA), the Indian Health Service (IHS), Medicaid, the State Children's Health Insurance Program (SCHIP), and Medicare. The FEHBP and TRICARE are health insurance programs for Federal employees and active duty personnel, respectively. The Federal Government also provides medical care to veterans through the Veterans Health Administration. Run by the Department of Veterans Affairs, the VHA provided services to 5.5 million patients in 2007, up from 3.8 million in 2000. The Indian Health Service provides health care to members of Federally-recognized tribes and their descendants. This too is a public health care system in the sense that the Federal Government operates the IHS hospitals and employs the program's health care providers. In 2007, the IHS provided services to 1.5 million American Indians and Alaska Natives.

Established in 1965, Medicaid provides medical assistance for certain children, families, and elderly and disabled individuals with low incomes and low resources. Medicaid is administered by the States and is jointly funded by the Federal Government and States. In 2007, there were approximately 48 million Medicaid enrollees. Another public insurance program is the State Children's Health Insurance Program (SCHIP), which was created in 1997. SCHIP enables States to provide health insurance coverage for low-income children who do not qualify for Medicaid. SCHIP is also administered by the States and jointly funded by the Federal Government and the States. States receive an enhanced Federal matching rate for SCHIP that is higher than their Medicaid matching rate but capped at a fixed level. During fiscal year 2007, more than seven million children were enrolled in SCHIP.

Medicare, also begun in 1965, provides health insurance to nearly all individuals aged 65 and older, as well as some younger individuals with permanent disabilities or those who have been diagnosed with end-stage renal disease. Today, there are approximately 44.6 million Medicare beneficiaries. As discussed in Chapter 6, Medicare consists of four parts: Part A provides coverage for inpatient hospital services, some home health care, and up to 100 days in a skilled nursing facility. Part B provides coverage for outpatient services, including outpatient provider visits and certain preventive screening measures. Part C, also known as Medicare Advantage, provides beneficiaries with the option of enrolling in one of several types of private health plans rather than traditional, fee-for-service Medicare. Finally, Part D provides coverage for outpatient prescription drugs.

Revitalizing and strengthening Medicare Advantage has been a key priority for the Administration. As an alternative to traditional Medicare, beneficiaries may enroll in one of several types of private health plans, including health maintenance organizations (HMOs), preferred provider organizations (PPOs), and private fee-for-service (PFFS) plans. For the past 3 years, 100 percent of Medicare beneficiaries have had at least one Medicare Advantage plan available in their local geographic market, up from 75 percent in 2004. Currently, nearly 10 million people, or over 20 percent of all Medicare beneficiaries, are enrolled in Medicare Advantage plans.

Many beneficiaries are attracted to Medicare Advantage plans because these plans typically cover services that are not covered under traditional Medicare, such as dental care, certain preventive services, and care management for those with chronic conditions. Additionally, Medicare Advantage enrollees may have lower out-of-pocket costs. For 2008, Medicare Advantage plans offered an average of approximately $1,100 in additional annual value to enrollees in terms of cost savings and added benefits. Of course, it is important to acknowledge that beneficiaries who enroll in Medicare Advantage plans must comply with the particular policies of those plans when using services. In some cases, this may include using only providers in the plan's network.

One of the most significant changes in Medicare during this Administration was the creation of Part D, a voluntary program in which beneficiaries are able to purchase prescription drug coverage from private health plans that contract with Medicare. On average, beneficiaries pay 25.5 percent of the cost for standard drug coverage, while the Federal Government subsidizes the remaining 74.5 percent. Each year, beneficiaries can choose a drug benefit plan from a large number of diverse plan offerings. This variety ensures that beneficiaries are able to select the insurance policy that best meets their preferences.

Before Part D was created, beneficiaries could obtain drug coverage by using an employer retiree plan, if they had one; purchasing a private Medigap plan; enrolling in a Medicare managed care plan; or using Medicaid coverage if they were dually eligible. Chart 7-4 illustrates the change in prescription drug coverage among beneficiaries between 2004 and 2006, the year that Part D was fully implemented. In 2004, 24 percent of Medicare beneficiaries lacked prescription drug coverage. By 2006, many of these Medicare beneficiaries obtained prescription drug coverage by choosing a stand-alone drug plan or a Medicare Advantage (MA) plan.

Part D has had important effects on beneficiaries' out-of-pocket spending and their adherence to the medication protocols they have been prescribed. Recent analyses from the Health and Retirement Study data found that the introduction of Part D has been associated with a median decrease of

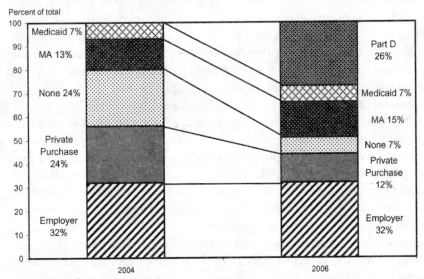

Chart 7-4 **Prescription Drug Coverage for Medicare Beneficiaries in 2004 and 2006**
The implementation of Medicare Part D resulted in significant changes for how Medicare beneficiaries obtain coverage for prescription drugs.

Note: Due to rounding, percentages may not add to 100.
Source: The University of Michigan Health and Retirement Study.

$30 per month in out-of-pocket spending among the newly insured population, compared to median baseline spending of $100 per month. When prescription drugs are not affordable, individuals may not adhere to their prescribed regimes. They may skip doses, reduce doses, or let prescriptions go unfilled. Recent work finds a small but significant overall decrease in cost-related medication non-adherence following the implementation of Part D. Both the revitalization of Medicare Advantage and the creation of Medicare Part D represent important steps for ensuring that beneficiaries have affordable choices for their health insurance.

The Uninsured

An important issue facing policymakers today is that a large number of individuals lack health insurance in the United States. In addition to providing important financial protection, health insurance can help people obtain timely access to medical care. Research has shown that having health insurance is positively related to having a usual source of medical care, receiving preventive services, and getting recommended tests or prescriptions. Based on U.S. Census data, the current number of individuals who lacked insurance during the calendar year is estimated to be 45.7 million people, or roughly 15.3 percent of the population. It is important to note that some people in Federal survey-based counts of the uninsured actually may have access to public insurance, but do not wish to report their program enrollment due to the possible stigma, or have not yet enrolled despite their eligibility. Also, others in Federal survey-based counts of the uninsured may have access to private insurance but have chosen not to purchase it.

The uninsured are diverse in terms of their employment and demographic characteristics. Individuals in households that have a full-time, full-year worker make up about 62 percent of the non-elderly uninsured population. Even with strong ties to the labor force, many people may not be offered employer-sponsored coverage. Even if such coverage is available to them, many people may choose not to buy insurance because it is not affordable or they do not place much value on having insurance. Individuals who lack insurance also tend to be younger.

In 2007, roughly 58 percent of the uninsured were under the age of 35. Finally, the uninsured are more likely to be from lower-income households, although a significant proportion of the uninsured population is made up of people in higher-income households. As shown in Table 7-1, among households earning less than $50,000 per year, more than 20 percent of those households are uninsured. This contrasts with the highest household income category, where only 7.8 percent of individuals lack insurance.

Going forward, it is important that as the Federal Government continues to work on increasing the number of Americans who have health insurance, it uses approaches that effectively target those who are the greatest risk for being uninsured.

TABLE 7-1.—*Uninsurance Rates by Household Income Category*

Household Income	Population	Number of Uninsured	Percentage of Population That is Uninsured
Less than $25,0000	55,267,000	13,539,000	24.5%
$25,000–$49,999	68,915,000	14,515,000	21.1%
$50,000–$74,999	58,355,000	8,488,000	14.5%
Greater than $75,000	116,568,000	9,115,000	7.8%

Source: Income, Poverty, and Health Insurance Coverage in the United States, 2007, U.S. Census.
Note: Due to rounding, percentages do not add to 100.

Investing in Public Health

The Federal Government plays an important role in identifying and addressing public health issues. This Administration has pursued several public health investment areas, including building a stronger safety net for the medically underserved, preparing for disease outbreaks and bioterrorism threats, supporting health-related research, and taking a leadership role in global health-improvement activities focused on HIV/AIDS and malaria.

Strengthening Community-Based Health Care

The Health Center Program is a Federal grant program that offers funding to local communities for providing family-oriented primary and preventive health care services. Health centers serve as an important safety net for people who need medical care but are underserved, including those without health insurance. Health centers provided care to more than 16 million individuals in 2006, and they are located in all 50 States and the District of Columbia. In 2002, the President made a commitment to create 1,200 new or expanded sites—a goal that was attained in 2007. Additionally, Federal funding for health centers has increased to $2 billion annually.

Preparing for Public Health Emergencies

The Federal Government plays an important role in ensuring a timely and appropriate response in the event of a public health emergency, such as an influenza pandemic or a bioterrorism threat. These types of situations could potentially lead to high levels of illness, social disruption, and economic loss, and therefore it is important for the Federal Government to invest resources in developing strategies to prepare for them. Working in collaboration with the States, the Federal Government has provided funding, advice, and other assistance to State and local planning efforts.

Supporting Research

Health-related research is multidisciplinary. It includes biomedical and epidemiological work that can reduce a population's mortality and morbidity risks from disease; economic analyses that investigate consumer and provider decision making; and health services research that examines issues such as medical care utilization, quality, and access to services. Americans rate health research as a high national priority. For fiscal year 2009, Federal funding for the National Institutes of Health is $29.5 billion. These resources will be used predominantly for supporting more than 38,000 research grant awards. It is beneficial to have a balance between investments that support biomedical research and those that address critical issues pertaining to the delivery and financing of health care, particularly given the substantial amount of resources that are going to be required to meet the medical care needs of the population in future decades.

Promoting Global Health Improvement

Many nations across the world are developing strategies to deal with consequences from the broad transmission of serious diseases, including HIV/AIDS, malaria, and tuberculosis, among others. In less developed parts of the world, people who contract these diseases face a much higher risk of mortality than do people in more developed parts of the world. There is also a significant economic impact from disease. In addition to the direct costs of medical treatment, high rates of serious disease within a population can hinder economic development. For example, HIV/AIDS may lead to large-scale losses in work productivity as the disease progresses and leaves those who are infected and their caregivers unable to work. Studies suggest that the high rate of HIV/AIDS has reduced the average national growth rates in African countries by 2 to 4 percent per year. Over the long term, high levels of disease also may inhibit educational investment, as shorter life expectancy diminishes incentives for human capital investment.

In 2003, the United States took a leadership role in supporting HIV/AIDS treatment, care, and prevention programs around the world, including in 15 countries that together have half of the world's HIV infections: Botswana, Côte d'Ivoire, Ethiopia, Guyana, Haiti, Kenya, Mozambique, Namibia, Nigeria, Rwanda, South Africa, Tanzania, Uganda, Vietnam, and Zambia. Known as the President's Emergency Plan for AIDS Relief (PEPFAR), this program has supported more than 57 million HIV counseling and testing sessions and has supported care for more than 10.1 million people infected or affected by HIV/AIDS, including more than 4 million orphans and vulnerable children worldwide. Additionally, through September 30, 2008, PEPFAR supported antiretroviral treatment for approximately 2.1 million people and prevention of mother-to-child transmission interventions during more than 16 million pregnancies. In 2008, Congress extended this program for an additional 5 years and significantly increased its authorized funding level.

A second global health initiative pursued by the Administration has been prevention and treatment of malaria. Each year, more than 1 million people die of malaria, most of them young children in Sub-Saharan Africa. It also causes serious morbidity, as those who are infected tend to lose, on average, 6 weeks from school or work due to the illness. Spending related to the disease can account for as much as 40 percent of public health expenditures, as well as high levels of household out-of-pocket expenditures. Beyond imposing high medical costs and lower incomes due to absenteeism, malaria is likely to impose indirect costs through broader macroeconomic channels, including underdeveloped tourism industries and lower levels of foreign direct investment.

In June 2005, the President's Malaria Initiative was announced. This initiative represents a public–private partnership among the U.S. Government, nongovernmental organizations, corporations, foundations, and faith-based service organizations, with the goal of reducing the mortality rate from malaria in 15 African countries by 50 percent. In 2007, the initiative's second year, 25 million people in Sub-Saharan Africa are estimated to have benefited from the program. More than 6 million long-lasting, insecticide-treated mosquito nets have been purchased, with two-thirds of those nets distributed.

Conclusion

The U.S. health care system is at a critical juncture. While advances in medical technology help millions of Americans lead longer and healthier lives, the rising cost of health care is both threatening the ability of Americans to access care that is affordable and is increasing the strain on Federal and State budgets. There are several opportunities to increase the value of health care and improve health insurance coverage. This Administration has pursued policies to improve the efficiency of health care markets through increased consumer involvement, improved choices, information transparency, and incentives to providers for delivering high-quality, efficient care.

This Administration has also pursued policies to improve the health insurance options of Americans. With the Medicare Prescription Drug, Improvement, and Modernization Act of 2003, Medicare was expanded to provide beneficiaries with improved access to affordable prescription drugs. Additionally, this legislation created Health Savings Accounts, which, in combination with High Deductible Health Plans, give individuals the incentive to become more active decision makers regarding their health care and health investments. Finally, this Administration has held to its commitment to make important investments in public health, including the expansion of Health Centers, collaboration with States and local governments to prepare for potential crises or threats, support of health-related research and development, and promotion of global health-improvement initiatives.

CHAPTER 8

Education and Labor

Long-term economic growth requires a productive workforce with the skills necessary to compete in a global labor market. The Administration's commitment to boosting the high productivity of American workers is evident in successful education and training policies. These include initiatives to increase primary and secondary school accountability, to ensure broader access to higher education, and to train workers so that they may take advantage of new high-paying job opportunities.

Real disposable income grew steadily during the Administration, and earnings per hour outpaced inflation despite large increases in energy prices and a growing portion of employee compensation being paid in non-wage benefits. Real median household income did fall slightly during the Administration, but this decline began prior to the Administration taking office. The Administration included several years of strong growth in real median household income from 2004 to 2007. The strongest pension reform measures in over three decades were also enacted. These offered important protections to workers who depend on their firm's pension plans for their retirement incomes.

Challenges lie ahead, however, and the most successful initiatives of the Administration must be bolstered. A continued commitment to better quality in kindergarten through twelfth-grade (K–12) education and broader access to higher education will help produce the additional workers the United States needs to meet the increasing worldwide demand for highly skilled labor.

In addition to these challenges, some related issues will need to be addressed, and education and labor policy will be important elements. First, the high level of income inequality in the United States calls for educating and training a greater number of workers, as better and more widely dispersed skills will be a force in reducing income inequality in the United States. Furthermore, the United States also needs comprehensive reform of its immigration policies. The principles of this Administration's immigration plan, which include a number of education and labor initiatives, will likely be the starting point for future discussions.

The key points of this chapter are:

- Education benefits individuals through higher earnings, and benefits society as a whole. Administration initiatives to improve K–12 education, most notably the No Child Left Behind Act, are demonstrating clear, measurable results.

- Access to higher education was maintained through an expanded Pell Grant program and proactive efforts that helped protect Federally subsidized student loans from recent credit issues faced elsewhere in the economy.
- Despite a small decline in real median household income, which had begun prior to the Administration taking office, hourly earnings of workers outpaced inflation, and real per capita disposable income rose substantially during the past 8 years. Median household income increased steadily after the recovery began in earnest in 2004. Also, pension reforms were enacted to help protect retirement income.
- Income inequality and immigration reform must still be addressed. Strong support for education and a focus on workers' skills can help close income gaps. Reform of immigration policies must provide border security while allowing the economic benefits that immigrant labor provides to the economy.

Economic Benefits of Education

Education is an investment. As with other investments, people compare benefits and costs when deciding whether to invest. The benefits of a quality education are widespread, with greater earnings being enjoyed by people and families who invest in education. Also, there are additional, non-pecuniary benefits of education that are enjoyed by both individuals and society at large. Education is also a key component of worker productivity and long-term economic growth.

For most people, a strong motivation to obtain additional years of schooling is the labor market return they expect to receive. Indeed, according to Chart 8-1, adults with a bachelor's or an advanced degree earn considerably more than adults with a high school degree. Likewise, those with a high school degree earn more than those who failed to complete high school. The gap between the earnings of those with a college education and those with a high school education, however, has grown since the 1970s. Currently, the average recipient of a college degree earns well over twice the amount earned by the average adult without a degree. Although any one individual's benefit from a college degree will differ due to ability, choice of major, and other factors, the expected return for investments in education undoubtedly motivate people to attend college.

Chart 8-1 does not take into account other individual benefits of education, most notably improved health. A substantial number of recent studies have

Chart 8-1 **Average Adult Real Earnings by Educational Attainment**
Earnings increase substantially with education, and the return has grown over time.

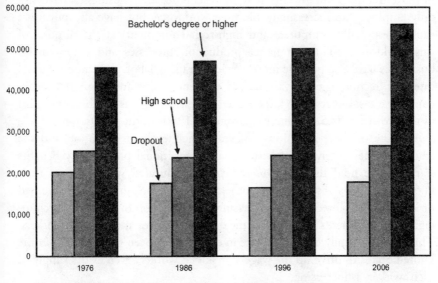

Income per year (constant 2000 dollars)

Source: Department of Commerce (Bureau of the Census, Current Population Survey).

shown that a direct link exists between educational attainment and health, even after holding income constant. One reason for this link may be the fact that people with greater educational attainment make better choices that impact their health positively, such as getting more exercise or not smoking. Education might also improve one's ability to navigate a complex health care system. Although the health returns to education are difficult to price in monetary terms, people surely value their health.

In addition to an individual's benefit from more education (greater earnings and better health), society benefits from a better-educated population. Education has been shown to foster civic-mindedness. For example, education makes it more likely someone will vote or support free speech. It also improves social skills and reduces crime. These effects of education positively affect fellow citizens as well as the individuals obtaining the education.

Finally, education is a key component of economic growth. Chart 8-2 illustrates the sustained productivity growth the United States has enjoyed throughout the past half century. It sets an index of output per hour of work for all non-farm workers to 100 in 1952 and displays the index over 5-year increments through 2007. The chart indicates that productivity has grown more than 200 percent over the past half century. Chart 8-2 also plots indexes of educational attainment (measured as the share of adults with a bachelor's degree) and capital services (for example, machinery and equipment) per hour. Both educational attainment and capital intensity, which measures the extent to which capital is used with labor, show strong upward trends. This means that in recent decades, businesses have not only employed an increasingly educated workforce, but have also put more capital (especially computers and high-tech equipment) at the disposal of this workforce. Through better production processes and management, businesses have also become more efficient in using labor. Education, capital intensity, technological advances, and efficiency gains are all interrelated in complex ways, but research has credited education with as much as one-third of the growth of U.S. productivity from the 1950s to the 1990s.

As more of the population achieves higher levels of education and the education they receive is of better quality, additional productivity benefits start to take hold through *spillover effects*. Educated workers share their knowledge and skills with each other, thereby increasing their combined productivity. Moreover, an increasingly skilled workforce fosters technological advancements that increase the demand for even more skilled workers. This technologically driven increase in demand has been great enough in the United States to drive up the wages for skilled workers even as the supply of such workers is increasing.

Chart 8-2 **Growth in Educational Attainment, Capital Intensity, and Labor Productivity over Time**
Education and the use of capital per hour of work have grown, spurring productivity growth.

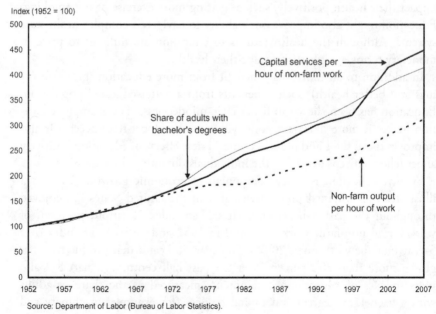

Index (1952 = 100)

Source: Department of Labor (Bureau of Labor Statistics).

There are also benefits to moving the entire population up to a basic level of competence because the labor market continues to demand increasing skills of its participants in virtually all tasks. Thus, the focus of the current Administration on improving K–12 instruction of every student in the United States is well placed.

Primary and Secondary Education

A strong commitment to education begins with ensuring that every child has access to quality primary and secondary schools. The No Child Left Behind Act (NCLB), which is intended to accomplish this goal, has been the centerpiece of the Administration's education policy. The NCLB Act was signed into law in January 2002 and has since reshaped the Federal role in the provision of K–12 education in the United States. It holds schools accountable for the performance of students, provides parents with more information and more choices, gives States and localities more flexibility in using Federal funds to meet the needs of children they serve, and promotes proven education methods. Among its many provisions, two innovative approaches to improve the quality of education stand out: holding schools accountable for making adequate yearly progress toward NCLB goals, and facilitating school choice options and supplemental education services for students in schools that are failing to meet standards.

Under the adequate yearly progress provisions of NCLB, each State is charged with developing its own guidelines for determining whether schools make sufficient progress each year toward the NCLB goal that all students be proficient in math and reading by 2014. If a school receives NCLB funds due to its low-income status and fails to meet its State's standards for adequate yearly progress for consecutive years, that school is identified as needing improvement and faces an escalating set of interventions. Students can transfer to another school in the same district. In addition, low-income students in the schools are offered supplemental education services (such as tutoring services or other academic help), which are paid for out of Federal funds. School districts have the obligation to notify parents of these options and to provide a list of approved supplemental education service providers in their area. A school that continually fails to make adequate yearly progress is subject to takeover or restructuring by the State.

Early Signs of NCLB Success

The success of NCLB will take years to determine, as current cohorts of students complete high school and move on to college or the workforce, but early indications are encouraging. The top panel of Table 8-1 summarizes recent trends in standardized math test scores for fourth graders as reported by the National Assessment of Educational Progress, which periodically tests fourth and eighth graders across the country. Researchers suggest that math test scores are a good way to judge achievement because they predict future labor market success well. The scores of students who were in fourth grade in 2005 and 2007 (no test was given in 2006) provide the most information because most if not all of their schooling to that point was during the time of the NCLB. These scores are from national standardized tests, and each State sets it own definition of proficiency, so the table is more indicative of general changes in student performance over time rather than actual progress toward a specific State's proficiency standard.

Table 8-1 shows that early in this decade, less than 10 percent of low-income students and less than 25 percent of all students were proficient in math (with low-income defined as being eligible for government-sponsored free lunch programs). Over 50 percent of low-income students were below even basic levels at that time. By 2007, however, 82 percent of students had reached the basic level, and the number of students achieving proficiency had increased from 24 percent in 2000 to 39 percent in 2007. For low-income students, the percent proficient has nearly tripled, from 8 percent in 2000 to 22 percent in 2007. This is encouraging evidence, but we must use caution in attributing these increased test scores to NCLB directly. For example, there were increases in math and reading scores from 2000 though 2003, and this may reflect some upward trending of scores before NCLB took effect in 2002. This pre-NCLB trend could be reflective of an accountability movement that was taking shape across the country, which culminated in Federal

TABLE 8-1.—*Proficiency Levels of Fourth Graders*

Math Achievement					
	1996	2000	2003	2005	2007
Percent Proficient or Above					
Among All Students..	21%	24%	32%	36%	39%
Among Students Eligible for Federal Lunch Programs............	8%	8%	15%	19%	22%
Percent at Basic Level or Above					
Among All Students..	63%	65%	77%	80%	82%
Among Students Eligible for Federal Lunch Programs............	40%	43%	62%	67%	70%
Reading Achievement					
	1998	2000	2003	2005	2007
Percent Proficient or Above					
Among All Students..	29%	29%	31%	31%	33%
Among Students Eligible for Federal Lunch Programs............	13%	13%	15%	16%	17%
Percent at Basic Level or Above					
Among All Students..	60%	59%	63%	64%	67%
Among Students Eligible for Federal Lunch Programs............	39%	38%	45%	46%	50%

Source: U.S. Department of Education (National Center for Educational Statistics)

law through NCLB. The continuing upward trend after NCLB was enacted is noteworthy, however, and under NCLB, test scores clearly are higher than they were before NCLB.

Although not shown, math test scores for eighth graders have improved as well, but the gains are slightly more modest. This is perhaps because the eighth graders have not had the benefit of NCLB for their entire school careers. More time will need to pass to appropriately evaluate results for eighth graders.

NCLB Challenges

Although the success in math that is illustrated in Table 8-1 is encouraging, the reading scores in the bottom panel of Table 8-1 have not increased as much as math scores. Math scores are better predictors of future labor market success, but the slower pace of improvement in reading scores should not be dismissed. The Administration's Reading First Program was enacted as part of the NCLB Act in 2002. This Department of Education program supports State educational agencies and local school districts that submit a plan to implement a scientifically based instructional reading program. Each submitted plan must demonstrate that students will be able to read by the end of third grade. The amount of support is based on the proportion of children in low-income households in each State. The program has demonstrated success in improving reading comprehension. For example, 44 State educational agencies reported improvements, and 31 of them reported an increase of at least 5 percentage points. Unfortunately, funding for this program was substantially reduced in fiscal year (FY) 2008.

Low test scores in poorer households are improving, according to Table 8-1, and achievement gaps are narrowing. Continuing to narrow the achievement gaps by raising test scores of low-income students remains an ongoing challenge that will require that attention be paid to some unique problems facing schools in high-poverty areas. For example, there is a high rate of teacher turnover in schools that serve low-income students. The most recent data available show a turnover rate in public schools in high-poverty areas that is 50 percent higher than in low-poverty areas.

Two components of the NCLB program that may help address the needs of low-income students are NCLB's supplemental education service and school choice options for students in failing schools. These programs are currently underutilized, alarmingly so in some districts. Parental outreach could be improved by providing more timely and better information about students' eligibility for these programs, and new Department of Education regulations specifying early notification requirements may help. In addition, ways to make school choice options more convenient for parents should be explored, because many parents are currently reluctant to enroll their children in alternative schools largely because of the perceived inconvenience of doing so. School choice options are limited, however, for many districts where there are no schools to which a student can reasonably transfer.

Finally, high school graduation is valuable for future labor market success (Chart 8-1) and is the most likely path to college enrollment. An accurate method of calculating graduation rates that is uniform across States is necessary to improve high school accountability. Requiring school officials to have written confirmation that a student transferred out, immigrated to another country, or is deceased before removing the student from their graduation cohort will improve the accuracy of graduation rate calculations. Written confirmation will ensure that students who have dropped out of school are not counted as transfers; consequently, schools will be held accountable for dropouts and others who do not graduate from high school with a regular diploma. The final NCLB regulations require States to use the methodology adopted by the National Governors Association. This "4-year adjusted cohort graduation rate" uses the number of students who graduate in 4 years with a regular high school diploma divided by the number of students who entered high school 4 years earlier (adjusting for transfers in and out). The use of the 4-year adjusted cohort graduation rate is an improvement over previous systems not only because it is a uniform method of calculating graduation rates, which will allow for more meaningful cross-State comparisons, but also because this particular method will give parents and educators a more accurate picture of high school completion in their communities. This will improve the understanding of the scope and characteristics of the population of students who do not earn regular high school diplomas or take longer to graduate. Educators will be able to use this information to help local education agencies meet their State graduation rate goals and thus make adequate yearly progress.

Currently, high school dropout rates hover around 10 percent and have fallen since the inception of NCLB, from 10.5 percent in 2002 to 9.3 percent in 2006. High school dropout rates among certain population groups, however, remain remarkably high. For example, Hispanic students dropped out of school at a rate of 22.1 percent in 2006. Although this has decreased from 25.7 percent in 2002, it is still over twice the national average. Dropout rates in the southern United States (11.7 percent) far exceed those in the Midwest (6.1 percent) and Northeast (6.5 percent).

Because teachers are on the front line of the NCLB mission, future Administrations will need to do more to keep our best teachers in the classroom, particularly those who have been successful in reaching low-income students. The Administration supported tax deductions for the out-of-pocket expenses teachers incur while providing instruction, as well as loan forgiveness programs for teachers in low-income schools. While both of these programs are likely to provide some financial incentives, the need to find new ways to help keep good teachers in classrooms still remains a challenge for improving K–12 education. The President's Teacher Incentive Fund has supported several pay-for-performance models around the country to help reward and retain outstanding teachers.

Higher Education

The U.S. higher education system is the best in the world. World rankings are dominated by American institutions, and the United States has long been the destination of many of the world's best students, teachers, and researchers. The American Competitiveness Initiative embodies the Administration's strong commitment to maintain the United States's standing as a leading producer of scientific knowledge, and it would increase the funding capabilities of grant organizations and expand the math and science curricula at primary and secondary schools. While keeping American universities competitive should remain a priority, maintaining student access to these institutions is perhaps even more important.

After several decades of growth, the share of high school graduates immediately transitioning to either a 2- or 4-year college has hovered around two-thirds since 1996. Although college enrollment is more likely among high school graduates from high-income families, about half of the students who graduated from high school in the poorest fifth of families have immediately enrolled in college since 2000.

Enrollment does not necessarily mean that a student receives a college degree. According to Chart 8-1, completing a 4-year degree is associated with the highest earnings. Thus, Chart 8-3 shows an unfortunate trend. Since 1996, there has been a large and steady gap between the number of students completing a bachelor's degree and the number of students enrolling in college 4 years before. Because it is true that many students take longer than 4 years to graduate from college, the gap depicted in Chart 8-3 does not capture everyone who will drop out. Nevertheless, the relative steady space between the two trends does show that college completion rates are low. This finding is backed up by more exact information on the number of enrollees who ultimately complete college (regardless of the number of years it takes), which indicates that the completion rate is only slightly above 50 percent. Furthermore, among 25- to 29-year-olds, the proportion of all college attendees with no bachelor's degree has remained at about 50 percent over the past decade. There are two things that can be done to help increase completion rates: continue with the Administration's efforts to improve K–12 education so that students are better prepared for college, and maintain access to grant aid to defray the increasing costs of education.

Chart 8-3 Enrollees and Degrees Conferred

The number of college graduates continues to rise, but the number of enrollees far exceed the number of degrees conferred.

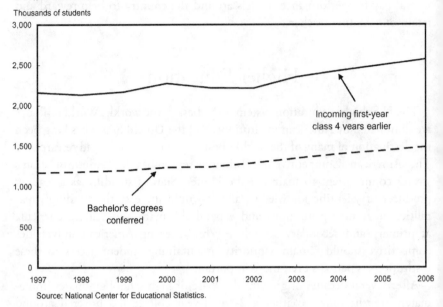

Thousands of students

Source: National Center for Educational Statistics.

College Preparedness

One reason for low college completion rates may be that many students are ill-prepared for the rigors of college education. One recent study suggests that nearly half of public high school graduates attending college in 2005 felt that there were notable gaps in their high school preparation. Moreover, college professors reported that about 42 percent of public high school graduates are not prepared for college-level classes.

There are reasons to be optimistic, however, because of the improved scores for fourth and, to some extent, eighth graders. In addition, the American Competitiveness Initiative contains a sound plan to devote significant resources to improving college preparedness through investments in math and science education. Congress also recently enacted the Adjunct Teacher Corps, a program proposed by the President that encourages well-qualified math and science professionals to serve as adjunct middle or high school teachers. There is more work to do at the high school level, however, and encouraging good teachers to remain in classrooms would likely improve college preparedness.

Funding Higher Education

The real cost of education (tuition and fees less aid and tax benefits) has increased substantially during this decade. In response to the rising costs, the Administration substantially expanded the Pell Grant program. Under this Administration, the total value of Pell Grants more than doubled from $8 billion in the 2000–2001 school year to $16.3 billion in the 2008–2009 school year. During 2008–2009, the maximum award available was $4,731, which exceeds the annual tuition and fees of attending a public 2-year institution and covers over 70 percent of the average tuition and fees of a public 4-year college. Pell Grant aid, however, is targeted to families with the greatest financial need, so the reality is that even large expansions in grant programs cannot keep up with increasing college costs for many families whose incomes are too high to qualify for Pell Grants. For millions of students, Federal Stafford loans provide essential assistance to help cover costs.

Stafford loans come in two forms. *Subsidized loans* defer payments until after students complete college, and the Government pays the interest while the students are in school. *Unsubsidized loans* allow deferred payments, but interest accrues while students are in school. Schools can sign up for Stafford loans to be handled by the Department of Education through the Federal Direct Loan Program or through private lenders that offer students loans through the Federal Family Education Loan Program. Because students represent a greater credit risk (they tend to be younger and have lower incomes), private lenders rely on the Government's guarantee against borrowers defaulting on loan payments. The Administration took action this year, as discussed in Box 8-1, to ensure continued access to the Federal student loan program in the face of credit markets disruptions.

Box 8-1: The Ensuring Continued Access to Student Loans Act of 2008

Largely unnoticed in the turmoil of the financial markets in 2008 was the fact that the Administration was proactive in avoiding a crisis in the student loan market. Many student lenders finance their lending by repackaging student loans and reselling them to investors in the secondary market. However, in early 2008, the disruption in credit markets made it increasingly difficult for lenders to resell loans. As a result, many of these lenders warned that they might not take part in the Federal student loan program for the 2008–2009 school year.

continued on the next page

Box 8-1 — continued

The Administration stepped in with an innovative program that was embraced by both parties in Congress.

On May 7, 2008, the President signed into law HR 5715, the Ensuring Continued Access to Student Loans Act of 2008. One of the critical provisions of this law granted the Secretary of Education the authority to purchase Federal Family Education Loan (FFEL) Program loans. Under this authority, the Department of Education created two programs: one in which it offers lenders the option to sell fully disbursed FFEL loans and another in which it purchases a participation interest in 2008–2009 FFEL loans. The programs were designed to retain lenders who might otherwise not have participated in the FFEL program; the ability to sell loans to the Department assured lenders that even if they had difficulty reselling the loans in the secondary market, they would not be stuck with the loans. The programs have also ensured that lenders originated new loans to students because lenders who sold their loans to the Department then had the funds necessary to originate new loans.

The intervention has helped the Federal student loan program function effectively so far this academic year despite the condition of financial markets. A projected 8.5 million students are attending college partly because they were able to finance their studies through the FFEL program. Recognizing that the financial crisis may impact the student loan program for the 2009–2010 year, Congress recently extended the authority for the Department of Education to purchase loans for another year. The Department has announced that it will replicate the current programs for the 2009–2010 school year. This will help ensure that students who are investing in their future through education will have access to Federal student loans despite current conditions in credit markets.

Labor Issues: Income Trends, Worker Flexibility, and Pension Reform

Real hourly earnings grew during the Administration, and real per capita disposable income (which includes income from labor and non-labor sources) rose substantially. The Administration also worked to promote retraining so that workers could fill jobs in demand. Finally, pension reform enacted in 2006 will help protect retirement incomes.

Recent Trends in Real Incomes

A common belief is that the incomes of working American families have not kept pace with inflation in recent years. Adjusting for inflation, it is indeed true that the annual median household income (measured in 2007 dollars) was $408 less in 2007 than it was at its peak in 1999, two years before this Administration took office. Although this is a decline in real terms, it tells an incomplete story of what happened during the Administration. Real median household income fell through 2004, but this represented a trend that began before the Presidency. Real median income strongly rebounded beginning in 2004 and reached near-peak levels by 2007.

Annual median household income, as reported by the Census Bureau, also includes both labor income and non-labor income. Thus, changes in median household income can be driven not only by changes in labor income but also by changes in income from investments and government transfer payments, such as Social Security or unemployment benefits. Turning to more specific measures of labor income, workers fared well during the Administration. Chart 8-4 plots an index of real hourly earnings for private non-farm production or non-supervisory workers from 1988–2007 (with real earnings in 1988 set to 100). The chart shows that real hourly earnings fell slightly through the early 1990s. After that, however, there was a long period of strong growth starting in the mid 1990s and continuing into the early part of this decade. Although it is true that real earnings are still less than their historic highs in the 1970s, 2007 marked their highest point since 1979.

Chart 8-4 reveals one other important point about recent trends in labor income. Workers are increasingly getting less of their pay in terms of cash wages and more in terms of benefits. Real total compensation per hour for private non-farm workers is plotted using the Employer Cost Index, which includes wages, salaries, and employer costs for employee benefits. Again, the index is set to 100 in 1988. Real total employee compensation grew considerably faster throughout the last 20 years than real hourly earnings. In 2007, total employee compensation in real terms reached its highest point on record. The growth appears most pronounced during the first half of this decade. This rise in total compensation likely stems from the growth in the costs of employer-provided health and retirement benefits, which far outpaced the growth in cash wages (and inflation) during the Administration. The increase in the dollar value of compensation received in the form of non-wage benefits has reduced the real wage increases that workers would have otherwise received.

Finally, the real household income decline noted at the start of this section, as well as the changes in worker wages, masks one other important factor. These are pretax measures and therefore are imperfect gauges of what people and households are able to spend, save, and invest. One measure that looks at after-tax income tells a much different story. Specifically, real per capita disposable income, another important measure of income derived from the Bureau of Economic Analysis's National Income and Product Accounts, reflects after-tax income and is more reflective of purchasing power. From 2000 to 2007, there was a steady increase in per capita real disposable income that averaged 1.68 percent per year, compared with 2.12 percent annual growth in real disposable income over the 8 years from 1992 to 2000. Given the rise in energy prices during the current Administration, however, as well as the fact that there was an economic downturn over its first several years, the growth in real disposable income is noteworthy. Like real median household income, however, real per capita disposable income reflects both labor and non-labor income.

Although 2008 and 2009 will undeniably be difficult for many workers and their families as unemployment rises, data from 2000–2007 show that most measures of real income (that is, labor income, total compensation, and per capita disposable income) grew during the Administration.

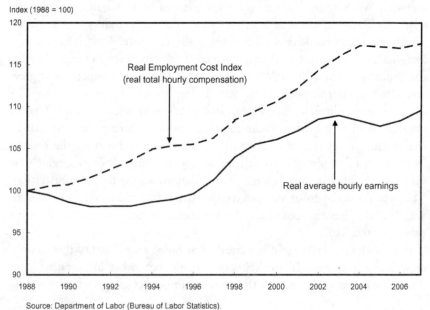

Chart 8-4 **Real Hourly Earnings and Real Total Compensation Costs over Time**
Real hourly employment costs (total compensation) have grown faster than real hourly earnings.

Source: Department of Labor (Bureau of Labor Statistics).

Worker Flexibility and Training

The U.S. labor market is part of a dynamic worldwide market with constantly changing demands brought about by technological change and international trade. The U.S. labor market, however, is well structured to meet these challenges. The United States has a long history of limiting the amount of government intervention between workers and firms, thus allowing for flexibility in the American workforce. Specifically, businesses in the United States are less limited than businesses in other developed countries in their ability to discharge a worker, thereby making them more willing to hire workers, knowing that they can more easily fire an unproductive employee. In times of growth, job openings are plentiful and workers are willing to search for the job that best matches them. The flexible employment relationship in the United States is evidenced by the relatively high rate of job mobility. Although it must be recognized that workers do build up specific skills from remaining at a firm and that not all job separations are advantageous, a growing economy still requires that workers be flexible and change jobs to find the correct match for their skills.

Among countries in the Organization for Economic Co-operation and Development (OECD), the United States has by far the most mobile workforce. Since January 2001, about 1 in 30 workers separated from their job in an average month (or about 4.39 million jobs were vacated). During these months, an average of 4.54 million workers were hired each month, suggesting that the economy was both creating new jobs and that workers were quickly filling positions that opened. The majority of job separations during these years were also created by workers voluntarily quitting, suggesting that many workers left jobs for new opportunities. Although these numbers have become more volatile in the latter half of 2008, with layoffs making up a higher percentage of job separations, during times of growth the rate of job openings in the United States is a testament to the relative flexibility of the U.S. labor market.

Workers in the United States have also shown more willingness to move to where jobs are located. According to the OECD, in each year from 2000 to 2005, over 3 percent of the U.S. working-age population moved across State lines. In comparison, only 1 percent of the working-age population in the EU-15 (the 15 European Union members before the 2004 expansion) moved between the 72 recognized European regional subdivisions. Moreover, less than 0.25 percent moved between EU-15 countries annually over this period. Obviously language barriers preclude some EU-15 mobility, but the greater geographic mobility in the United States also compares favorably to Australia and Canada. In short, the willingness of workers in the United States to move is an important part of the structure of the labor force and a reason for its flexibility.

Another key to meeting the growing demand for new and changing skills in the labor force will be the continued willingness of American workers to get the education and training needed to fill the new jobs that are created in the economy. A commitment to education, particularly in more technical fields, will prove to be important in the coming decades. The Administration's job training initiatives, including the Community-Based Job Training Grants and the High Growth Job Training Initiative, have helped prepare workers for jobs in high-demand industries. The Administration also proposed Career Advancement Accounts that put funds directly in the hands of people to pay for expenses related to education and training and put strict limits on administrative overhead in order to increase resources available for job training. Finally, international trade has also created many new opportunities for American workers, and Box 8-2 describes programs aimed to help workers take advantage of these opportunities.

Retiree Income

As life expectancies increase, American workers will likely spend an increasing amount of time in retirement. The Federal Government provides substantial retirement assistance through the Medicare and Social Security programs, but the challenges faced by these entitlement programs are substantial and are discussed in Chapter 6. Private savings and individual pensions provided by employers continue to be essential.

Box 8-2: Trade Adjustment Assistance

International trade brings substantial benefits to the U.S. economy. Not only are American consumers able to take advantage of a greater number of goods at lower prices, but workers in industries whose products and services are in high demand internationally benefit as well. In 2006, for example, an estimated 13 million U.S. jobs were supported by exports. The wages of manufacturing workers in plants that export are 9 percent higher than the wages of workers in non-exporting plants, and the wage premium in service-oriented firms that export is 13 percent over non-exporting firms. Furthermore, exports accounted for approximately 30 percent of economic growth in 2006.

Although the benefits of trade are enormous, workers in industries that must compete with imports can be adversely affected. Because of this, Trade Adjustment Assistance (TAA) exists to provide benefits to workers who are potentially adversely affected by trade. Though

continued on the next page

Box 8-2 — continued

the TAA has been in operation since 1974, it was changed substantially when it was reauthorized in the Trade Act of 2002. The Act consolidated the TAA and the North American Free Trade Agreement (NAFTA) TAA programs, expanded the eligibility to cover workers affected by shifts in production to certain other countries and to workers secondarily affected upstream or downstream from TAA-certified firms, expanded the training opportunities available, provided a health coverage tax credit, and promoted earlier intervention to allow more rapid enrollment, training, and reemployment of eligible workers. In FY 2007, firms covered by TAA certifications employed nearly 147,000 workers. Of these, over 49,000 eligible workers entered TAA training.

Of the eligible workers who took up benefits in the program in fiscal year 2007, 68 percent received some form of training, 59 percent received specific occupational training, and 13 percent received remedial training. The TAA program has also become successful over time in finding new employment for workers. While in 2001 only 63 percent of workers who exited the program were successfully reemployed, with a wage replacement rate of 87 percent, by 2006, 72 percent of workers exiting the program were reemployed, with a wage replacement rate of 89 percent.

In discussions of TAA reauthorization during 2007, debate developed in Congress over potential ways to expand the TAA program. The Administration supported reforms to the TAA to improve the delivery of services, to offer greater flexibility, and to enhance training for eligible workers. Several legislators and policymakers, however, suggested a number of expansions to TAA benefits, most notably: (a) allowing service workers, in addition to manufacturing workers, to receive benefits; (b) allowing workers who produce service-related goods to receive benefits; (c) allowing entire sectors to be eligible for coverage under TAA benefits; and (d) increasing the amount of funding for benefits and training. The fiscal and economic costs of such an expansion were uncertain, and some estimates indicated they would be substantial (the Congressional Budget Office estimated an additional $8.6 billion over the 2008–2017 period). Beyond the fiscal cost, however, there were additional concerns regarding economic efficiency. Extending TAA benefits to substantially more workers could lead to economic losses by creating longer-term, higher unemployment in the covered industries. Furthermore, service workers experience minimal wage loss during displacement when compared with manufacturing workers, indicating that expanding benefits to them may not be justified. Finally, there were worries that expansion would open the door for further, unwarranted expansions of TAA benefits.

Employer-provided pensions come in one of two types: defined benefit plans or defined contribution plans. *Defined benefit pension plans* specify an amount to be paid upon retirement, normally calculated using a formula based on an employee's years of service with the company and his or her earnings history. *Defined contribution pension plans* consist of an individual employee account into which the employer and/or employee contribute, usually at a fixed percentage of the employee's salary. Upon retirement, individuals have access to the balance in the account. Historically, defined benefit plans have been dominant, but over the past several decades, defined contribution plans have become more popular.

The first Federal protections of worker pensions were set by the Employee Retirement Income Security Act (ERISA) of 1974, which, among other things, established the fiduciary responsibilities of plan managers. It also established the Pension Benefit Guaranty Corporation, which protects the defined benefit plans (up to a statutory limit) of private sector workers against the possibility that an employer will fail to pay the promised benefits. The Pension Benefit Guaranty Corporation is funded primarily through premiums established by law paid by the sponsors of defined benefit plans.

There have been many changes in pension provision since ERISA was passed in 1974, including the increased prevalence of defined contribution plans and heightened concerns regarding underfunded private plans. The Pension Protection Act of 2006 accomplished several important goals. First, with regard to defined benefit plans, greater premiums were imposed on companies with underfunded plans. Moreover, caps on the amount employers could put into plans were raised to allow employers to build a cushion during good economic times.

The Pension Protection Act also addressed the growing use of defined contribution plans by including provisions that give workers more information and control over the investment of their account balances. It also provided incentives for employers to automatically enroll new employees in defined contribution plans, which likely will increase plan participation. Furthermore, after observing the potential for notable shortfalls in pension plan funding, the act also improved the process employed to value plan assets and liabilities. By utilizing fair-market valuations, the pension reform was able to limit the use of valuation-smoothing practices that often made it difficult to detect gaps in pension funding, thus helping to prevent funding shortfalls. The various reforms in the Pension Protection Act followed an initiative led by the President in his 2005 pension reform proposal. These reforms will make retirement incomes of millions of Americans more secure.

Looking Ahead

As we look toward the future, there are a number of education and labor issues that will likely receive attention. First, the distribution of income in the United States is more skewed toward the wealthy than in other developed countries. The lower level of intergenerational economic mobility in the United States, compared with other countries, suggests this is a concern that will persist. Second, a need for comprehensive immigration reform exists and will necessarily require education and labor policies to be balanced with border security. The Administration has been a strong supporter of such reform, and the ideas generated by the Administration will likely shape discussions in the years ahead.

Income Inequality

In addition to arguments centered in theories of social justice, high income inequality may create more tangible problems. Some argue that inequality leads to a breakdown in social cohesion, which lowers a population's aggregate health (even holding income constant). Violent crime also increases as gaps between the poor and wealthy widen. Apart from that, high inequality threatens to squander the abilities and talents of a larger number of children in poorer families if upward economic mobility is also low. This is the case in the United States, where intergenerational mobility is relatively low and income inequality is high.

The most common method for measuring income inequality is the Gini coefficient, which is a value that ranges from zero (perfect equality, or everyone has an equal amounts of income) to one (perfect inequality, or all income is held by one family). The U.S. Gini coefficient is currently 0.45, according to the most recent cross-country comparison measures from the Central Intelligence Agency (or 0.46, according to the most recent Census Bureau estimates, which measures U.S. inequality). This level of inequality exceeds that of most other developed countries, with many European nations having Gini coefficients below 0.30. In fact, the U.S. level of inequality exceeds that in some lesser developed countries such as Indonesia (0.36) and is comparable to Kenya (0.45). Only a few countries noticeably exceed the United States in terms of inequality (for example, Brazil (0.57) and South Africa (0.65)). In short, the level of inequality in the United States is unusually high given our level of development and wealth.

In addition to the Gini coefficient of the United States being high by international standards, it has steadily risen over the past several decades. Many researchers have tried to explain the reasons for the high and growing level of income inequality in the United States. Although some have attributed the greater inequality to institutional factors such as the declining real value of the minimum wage and lower rates of unionization, institutional explanations fail to match some of the more recent trends in inequality that look beyond the Gini coefficient. Specifically, an analysis of the wage distribution of workers suggests that the gap between mid-level earners and low-wage workers has remained relatively steady over the past decade despite a declining real value of the minimum wage. Instead, the gap between the highest earners and mid-level earners has increased over the past decade.

This most recent analysis of trends argues that technological change since the 1990s, particularly in the area of information technology, has benefited workers who possess skills for which these advances are complementary. These include highly skilled workers who are in jobs where technology is used in combination with interpersonal skills, such as in management or professional positions. These jobs are not as easily automated or outsourced as the tasks performed by middle-educated white collar or production workers. Those with less education but wages in the middle of the distribution have seen the difference between their wages and the wages of the highest earners widen.

One way to bring more of the workforce into the group of highly skilled workers whose jobs are not easily automated or outsourced is to provide a greater emphasis on education, particularly in math and science. Recent successes in raising math test scores and expanding the Pell Grant program are important steps. A continuing focus on increasing educational attainment for children across the income distribution is critical. Increased access to quality education will create more productive workers and greater wages for an increasing share of the population, thereby closing income gaps.

Immigration Reform

The United States is a nation of immigrants and has long depended on the contributions of the foreign-born to its economy. A sound immigration policy must continue to foster the economic benefits of immigrants by recognizing that foreign-born labor complements the existing strengths of the U.S. workforce. Such an immigration policy should also promote fluency in English, which not only enhances the earnings potential of immigrants but also can help improve productivity. Furthermore, the flow of immigration must also be regulated and restricted to legal channels.

Residents of foreign countries will immigrate when the benefits of migration outweigh the costs. The benefits typically are the earnings differentials between the United States and their home country. Because of this, the United States usually attracts immigrants of all skill levels. The highly skilled are attracted to the greater earnings they receive in the United States given their skill level. Immigrants with fewer skills are attracted to the better wages and potential opportunities for their families.

The United States benefits from both types of immigration. The scientific establishment and high-technology industries have long benefited from workers with superior skills who immigrate to the United States and boost productivity. Immigrants with fewer skills perform jobs that complement existing labor in this country.

Education and labor policies have their roles in a comprehensive approach to immigration policy in the United States. While many immigrants are highly skilled, the average educational attainment of immigrants lags behind the native-born. Promoting English fluency is important because it increases labor market opportunities for immigrants, boosts their productivity, facilitates higher earnings, and promotes greater assimilation. To enhance the potential contribution of immigrants and to improve their well-being, it is also important to continue this Administration's sound education policies. NCLB, Reading First, and policies that increase access to higher education are all targeted toward students that need the most assistance, and the U.S. immigrant population stands to gain much from these programs. The U.S. economy will benefit in turn.

The issues the United States confronts with regard to its immigration policy are complex, and the Administration introduced comprehensive immigration reform as part of its domestic policy agenda in 2004. This proposal addressed many issues, including devoting more manpower to border security and increasing worksite enforcement of immigration laws. To ensure that the United States has an immigrant workforce that complements the existing U.S. workforce and meets economic needs, the Administration called for a flexible temporary guest worker program. To improve the productivity of immigrants, enhance their contributions to U.S. labor markets, and improve their welfare, assimilation proposals that promoted English and cultural literacy were advanced. The sweeping reforms of this proposal, however, failed to gain the necessary Congressional support. The need for these immigration reforms endures, and the Administration's plan remains one that is sound in terms of both securing borders and promoting economic progress.

Conclusion

The Administration has been committed to ensuring that the U.S. labor force remains productive for decades to come. Significant progress has been made in the U.S. educational system to help current and future students meet the ever-increasing and changing demand for skills in the more global, competitive labor market. K–12 education has improved, test scores are rising, and students in underperforming schools now have more education options. Also, access to the U.S. higher education system has improved through expansions of the Pell Grant program and reforms enacted in the student loan program. Despite these successes, there are challenges that remain. Income inequality in the United States is high and suggests that a continued emphasis on education is necessary to raise the incomes of those in the lower half of the income distribution. Also, education and labor policy will need to be part of comprehensive immigration reform in the United States. This reform must reduce illegal immigration while continuing to allow the U.S. economy to benefit from legal immigrants.

CHAPTER 9

Economic Regulation

The United States relies on the private sector to organize most economic activity. Through price signals and competition, markets allocate scarce resources to their highest-value uses, encourage businesses to avoid waste, and create incentives to invest in new technologies. Government plays a vital role in a market system by guaranteeing property rights and enforcing contracts, meaning that businesses and individuals can invest and trade with confidence that their agreements will be honored and free from fraud. A private enterprise system supported by consistent enforcement of laws protecting property and contracts has been at the heart of the American economy's tremendous prosperity and growth.

Although free markets produce the most efficient outcome in most cases, there are markets in which government intervention can increase economic efficiency. A *market failure* is an instance in which unregulated markets yield an outcome that is inefficient from society's point of view. As discussed in Chapter 2, regulation is important in financial markets because of imperfect information; for example, investors often have far less information about the firms they invest in than the managers who control those firms. Chapter 3 discusses the role of regulation when production of a good creates a *negative externality*, such as environmental harm, that does not represent a cost from the producer's perspective but imposes a cost on society. Regulation can mitigate the costs of negative externalities by ensuring that consumers and producers bear the full cost of their activities. Regulation can also reduce harm from *natural monopoly*, which occurs when a single seller can produce a good or service more cheaply than a competitive industry. In the presence of natural monopoly, an unregulated market will yield output levels that are too low and prices that are too high from society's perspective. In cases like these, where there is a specific market failure that can be effectively addressed by the government, regulation may be able to improve economic outcomes.

When unregulated markets produce inefficiencies, however, government is not always effective in eliminating or reducing the inefficiencies. There are several reasons that government is often inefficient in carrying out regulation. First, competitive market prices, which efficiently coordinate decisions in competitive markets, are unavailable where market failures have caused inefficiencies. The lack of reliable price information makes it difficult for government to design effective regulation. Second, government does not face market incentives to keep costs low and to use resources in the most efficient way possible. Third, government decision making reflects the results of a political process in which decision makers may be motivated by narrow interests rather than the broader goals of society. Market participants may spend resources on attempts to influence the political process, when other uses of resources would produce greater public benefit. These factors mean that government intervention can have significant costs, which must be weighed against the potential benefits of addressing market failures.

One way government can mitigate these problems is by designing regulations that take advantage of markets or market mechanisms whenever possible. "Command and control" regulation, which replaces decentralized market choices with centralized decision making by government officials, exacerbates the three problems identified above. Regulation that relies on market mechanisms, however, can take advantage of individuals' information about costs and benefits, give individuals the incentive to make socially efficient decisions, and reduce the ways that narrow interests can influence policy choices.

This chapter reviews several areas in which markets have been affected by government policy in the past 8 years. The Administration has pursued market-oriented policies that favor individual choice over government decision making and has supported new rules when needed to address identified market failures. The Administration has also considered the effectiveness of the overall regulatory structure for financial markets in particular, a summary of which is provided in Chapter 2. The key points of this chapter are:

- Regulation is appropriate when, and only when, there is an important market failure that can be effectively addressed by the government. For example, the Administration has taken steps to reduce restrictive regulation of broadband markets, preserving an environment conducive to innovation and new investment. Conversely, the Administration supported new rules for financial reporting when it became clear that existing laws did not adequately reduce information asymmetries between investors and management.

- When the government intervenes to address market failures, it should attempt to take advantage of market-based incentives whenever possible. The Administration has helped ensure that scarce spectrum licenses are allocated more efficiently by increasing the amount of bandwidth allocated through auctions rather than through arbitrary allotments. In transportation, the Administration has supported market-based approaches to financing infrastructure such as roads and the air traffic control system.

- The Administration has endeavored to ensure that, when the government does intervene in markets, it does so in a way that supports the operation of competitive markets. When the market for terrorism insurance was disrupted following the attacks of 9/11, the Administration supported a temporary program of Federal support for terrorism insurance, and the Administration has insisted that subsidies be phased out as private insurers adapt and return to the market. By supporting tort reform, the Administration has helped reduce the scope for class action lawsuits that create costs that outweigh their social benefits.

Telecommunications and Broadband

Digital technologies and the Internet are rapidly changing the market for telecommunications. Much of our system for regulating telecommunications, however, is designed to address local monopolies in telephone service. Regulation that was well suited to markets based on prior technologies should be revisited as markets change. Particularly when innovation is transforming an industry, outdated regulations can hamper investment and prevent new products and services from developing in the way that best serves consumers.

Governments regulate local telephone service because it has long been considered a natural monopoly. It is expensive to build and maintain a network of lines to homes and businesses, but once the lines are in place, the extra cost of providing each call is small. This means new entrants would find it very hard to challenge an incumbent phone company. A potential competitor would need to invest large amounts to duplicate an incumbent phone company's network of lines, and resulting competition would make it hard for either firm to charge rates high enough to pay for the investment. To prevent incumbent phone companies from charging monopoly prices, government regulates rates for local phone service. In addition, the Federal Government attempts to encourage competition in local service by requiring incumbent phone companies to make their lines available to competitors and by regulating the price for access to their lines.

New Technologies Permit Greater Competition in Telecommunications

New technologies are changing the telecommunications market. A new market has developed in *broadband* Internet connections that can transmit data at high speeds. Broadband data can be delivered along the same physical lines that carry telephone signals, but can also be delivered via cable, via fiber optic connections, wirelessly via "third-generation" networks or satellites, or via newer technologies such as broadband over power lines. Because digital signals can be delivered in a variety of ways, the broadband market is more open to competition than the traditional phone system, which required copper wires connected to every home.

Unlike local phone service, for which Americans traditionally had only one provider available, the large majority of Americans can now choose among competing broadband providers. As of June 2007, 99 percent of U.S. ZIP codes had access to two or more high-speed Internet service providers, and more than three-quarters of ZIP codes were served by five or more providers. The price of broadband service has fallen in real terms even as the average broadband connection has become more advanced. Chart 9-1 shows that the total number of subscribers has grown dramatically, with an increasing variety of technologies used.

These same digital technologies, combined with large investments in wireless telephone networks, mean that consumers have new choices for local telephone service, a market situation that undermines the traditional arguments for regulation in local telephone markets. Between 2002 and 2006, the number of households that use a wireline for their primary phone connection fell from 102 million to under 90 million, and the number of "wireless-only" households increased from 2 million to 19 million. That new competitors are challenging the longstanding monopoly position of local telephone providers raises questions about the best approach to regulating local telephone service going forward.

Chart 9-1 **High-Speed Internet Lines in the United States by Type of Connection, 1999–2007**
Broadband connections have grown rapidly.

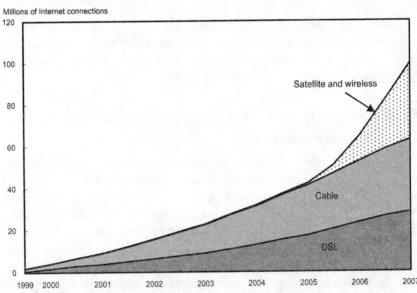

Note: Fiber and powerline connections are a small fraction of connections and have been omitted.
Source: Federal Communications Commission.

Telecommunications Regulation in an Evolving Market

The Administration's approach to broadband regulation has recognized that a dynamic and competitive broadband market should not be governed by rules designed for monopoly telephone services. That does not mean that no rules are appropriate. Broadband companies should disclose the policies they use in managing their networks; if consumers know what they are getting, competitive pressures will offer the most effective means of providing consumers with low prices and high-quality service. However, prescriptive regulation of a growing, dynamic market carries two risks. First, because the market continues to evolve, a regulation aimed at temporary or hypothetical problems may cause permanent harm by preventing new and innovative ways of delivering service. Second, regulations that make it harder for broadband providers to price or manage their networks effectively may lower the incentives to invest in new capacity, ultimately harming consumers.

Following the principles outlined in the previous paragraph, the Administration has supported policies that avoid unwarranted regulation of the broadband market and encourage private sector investments in the market. In a series of decisions, the Federal Communications Commission (FCC) determined that broadband service providers would not be regulated as a local phone service; in particular, they are not required to make their high-speed lines available to competitors at a regulated price. While government-mandated access can facilitate competition between a large incumbent provider and potential competitors, applying it to an emerging industry that features competing technologies would have risked undermining incentives to invest in new capacity. In fact, the private sector has invested more each year in building broadband networks, in real terms, than the Federal Government invested annually in the Interstate Highway System in the 1950s. These investments in turn have meant more options for consumers, and ultimately more competition in the broadband market.

There is certainly a role for telecommunications regulations that target specific failures in the telecommunications market. For example, 911 services provide external benefits by making it more likely that emergencies are promptly reported to emergency services. The Administration supported the FCC's efforts to ensure that 911 services are available for subscribers of Voice over Internet Protocol telephone providers. When there is a role for regulation, the rules should facilitate competition and consumer choice whenever possible. In implementing the "Do Not Call" list, for example, the Federal Trade Commission did not dictate a market outcome but created a way for people to decide whether they wanted to receive certain telemarketing calls (see Box 9-1).

Box 9-1: The Do Not Call List

Telemarketing can be an effective way to inform people about products and services, but it generates a negative externality by wasting the time of those who are not interested in the product being sold. Although the harm from each call may be small, many consumers have found the aggregate externality to be quite large. The policy behind the Do Not Call list is to permit consumers to decide for themselves whether the benefits of telemarketing calls outweigh the costs. Individuals who do not want to receive calls simply add their phone numbers to a central registry, and telemarketers must delete any numbers listed in the registry from those they plan to call. The program has proved quite popular: as of 2007, according to one survey, 72 percent of Americans had registered on the list, and 77 percent of those say that it made a large difference in the number of telemarketing calls that they receive (another 14 percent report a small reduction in calls). Another survey, conducted less than a year after the Do Not Call list was implemented, found that people who registered for the list saw a reduction in telemarketing calls from an average of 30 calls per month to an average of 6 per month.

Spectrum Policy

Since the 1920s, the U.S. Government has required a license of anyone who transmits radio signals on most frequencies. Radio communication works by transmitting a signal on a specific frequency of the electromagnetic spectrum. Mandatory licensing prevents *interference*: when multiple signals are broadcast on the same frequency, it is difficult to receive any of those signals clearly. Interference is an example of an externality, because when one person decides to broadcast a signal, he or she does not take into account the harm this causes to people who are attempting to send or receive other signals on the same frequency.

While licensing addresses the externality problem, it puts the government in the position of allocating a scarce and valuable resource. Given spectrum's value, it is important to allocate it efficiently. Radio waves can be used in many different ways: for two-way communication, to broadcast radio or television programs, and for radar, among other uses. The more spectrum is set aside for broadcast television stations, for example, the less spectrum is available for wireless phones. The challenge of spectrum licensing is to ensure that spectrum is divided among competing uses in the way that creates the greatest benefits to society.

Ordinarily, markets allocate scarce resources using prices, ensuring that resources are dedicated to their highest-value uses. For many decades, however, the U.S. Government awarded spectrum licenses through an administrative process, deciding both how spectrum would be used and who would be allowed to use it. Prospective users submitted applications to the FCC, and the FCC attempted to identify the applicant who would offer the greatest public benefit.

The optimal allocation of spectrum, however, depends on information not easily available to government, from technical information about how much spectrum is needed to effectively carry out different activities and how that is likely to change in the future, to questions about the value to consumers of the various services that require spectrum. Administrative assignment of licenses also gives firms no incentive to find ways to use spectrum more efficiently, because they cannot change their method of transmission and cannot sell or lease unused capacity to others who would use spectrum in a different way.

The United States began using a more market-oriented approach to allocating spectrum rights in 1994 with the first auctions of radio spectrum for use in wireless phones. In the auctions, the FCC announces the portion of the spectrum for which licenses will be made available, and all interested parties are invited to submit bids. By 2008, the FCC had held more than 70 auctions that raised tens of billions of dollars for the Federal Government. More important than the revenue, however, is that auctions ensure that spectrum will go to those who are able to use it in the most efficient way. When one company outbids others, it generally means that the winner believes it can produce more value using that spectrum, by using it more effectively or in a more innovative way than its competitors. Instead of a government evaluation of which applicant is best able to use spectrum to serve the public, the bidding process allocates licenses based on what companies reveal about the benefits they can actually produce.

The Administration has worked to increase the role of auctions in allocating spectrum. Most spectrum remains under licenses granted long ago; as of 2001, less than 7 percent of the most valuable spectrum was available for allocation through market mechanisms. One obstacle to reallocating spectrum is that incumbent license holders have a strong incentive to retain spectrum they use, even if others might be able to use it more efficiently. One way the Administration has tried to overcome this obstacle is by making it easier for incumbents to transfer their spectrum to others. In October 2003, the FCC established new procedures for holders of existing licenses to more easily sublicense their spectrum to third parties, helping to foster secondary spectrum markets. More broadly, the Administration has supported policies under which incumbents are compensated as part of a process that reduces the total amount of spectrum they use. Two major spectrum auctions using this general approach since 2001 have freed up significant bands of spectrum, nearly doubling the amount of spectrum allocated through auctions for wireless use.

In early 2008, the FCC held an auction to allocate spectrum that will be vacated when the United States makes the transition to digital television broadcasting, pursuant to the Digital Television Transition and Public Safety Act of 2005. Digital signals allow broadcasters to transmit television programming more efficiently, so that the spectrum that was used to broadcast a single analog television channel is now able to carry multiple digital channels. One result of the transition is that spectrum that was previously used for channels 52 to 69 (between 698 and 806 megahertz (MHz)) will become vacant. Television stations using other frequencies will be able to transmit using digital signals. Much of the newly vacated spectrum was auctioned for wireless communications use.

In December 2004, the President signed the Commercial Spectrum Enhancement Act, which created a mechanism for transferring spectrum from government use into the private sector. Government users of these frequencies were given the opportunity to switch to other parts of the spectrum, with the transition costs (including new equipment) paid for using a portion of the auction proceeds. Under the Act, the reallocation of spectrum was not to take place unless the auction raised sufficient funds to compensate the affected agencies. In fact, auction revenues were several times what the agencies had reported was necessary to compensate them for the switch. The large difference between the market value of spectrum and the costs of the transition demonstrate the large efficiency gains available from reallocation of spectrum. Together with the transition to digital television, the Commercial Spectrum Enhancement Act has freed up 152 MHz of spectrum to be auctioned for wireless communications use, and all but 10 MHz had been auctioned by 2008. This represents an increase of 80 percent over spectrum available for mobile telephones at the beginning of this Administration.

The President's Spectrum Policy Initiative for the 21st Century, which was announced in 2003, requires a studied look at the current spectrum management policies and practices in the United States. As part of this program, the Commerce Department's National Telecommunications and Information Administration has worked to establish or expand incentives for promoting efficient spectrum use by the private sector as well as Federal agencies, using market-based approaches wherever appropriate. Areas of particular interest have included revising the traditional "command and control" management of Federal spectrum, developing user fees that reflect market worth, and creating property rights that would permit spectrum trading.

Tort Reform

Even when businesses are not regulated directly by the government, they face the possibility of being sued under the tort system. "Tort" refers to the body of law that permits individuals to sue others, seeking compensation when they have been accidentally or deliberately injured. Many tort suits arise from harms involving strangers, such as automobile accidents, but an important class of torts arises when buyers of a good or service sue the seller in response to harm related to the purchase of the good or service.

Tort law can be a response to the market failure of imperfect information. Buyers often cannot tell ahead of time whether a product is safe or a service provider is qualified. By providing buyers with redress when a product or service they buy causes harm, tort law can encourage sellers to exercise appropriate care and to make sure buyers are getting what they expect when they enter into a transaction.

Like more direct forms of government regulation, tort law establishes rules that firms must follow to avoid being penalized. Tort law can increase sellers' incentives to provide safe, high-quality products and services. It also compensates victims of some accidents, providing a form of insurance when an accident is caused by another's negligence. However, the tort system is an expensive form of regulation, and tort law can be abused in ways that make its costs to society greater than its benefits. One study found that out of each dollar of costs in the tort system, only 46 cents goes to compensating plaintiffs for their losses. This makes the tort system much more expensive to administer than other systems that compensate victims for unexpected losses, such as worker's compensation.

Total tort costs represent a significant part of U.S. economic activity. Tort costs in 2007 totaled $252 billion, or 1.83 percent of gross domestic product (GDP), including damages paid to compensate plaintiffs, costs of defense, and administrative costs. As shown in Chart 9-2, more than half of tort costs come from lawsuits against businesses (including doctors) as compared with personal lawsuits such as automobile accidents.

The Administration has worked to reduce the scope of lawsuits in areas where costs often outweigh benefits. A type of lawsuit that may be especially susceptible to abuse is the class action suit, in which a single suit is filed on behalf of a large number of plaintiffs with the claim that everyone in the class has been harmed by the defendant. Class actions can be efficient in some cases in which a large number of people have suffered a similar type of harm, because they eliminate the redundancy of multiple courts exploring similar sets of facts, and because absent a class action, each individual may have little incentive to bear the costs of a lawsuit. A potential problem with class action lawsuits, however, is that plaintiffs' lawyers may have incentives that are not

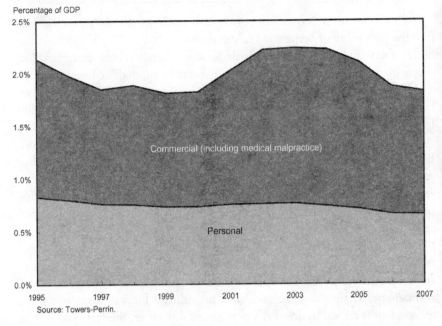

Chart 9-2 **U.S. Tort Costs, 1995-2007**
Tort costs as a percentage of GDP have moderated in recent years.

Percentage of GDP

Commercial (including medical malpractice)

Personal

Source: Towers-Perrin.

aligned with those of their clients. Because individual plaintiffs may not have a large stake in the outcome, they may not effectively monitor their attorneys, and plaintiffs' attorneys may negotiate a settlement with the defendant that works well for the attorneys but does not represent meaningful redress for the people actually harmed.

In 2005, the President signed the Class Action Fairness Act, which contained provisions aimed at reducing the number of abusive class action lawsuits. An important set of reforms addressed "coupon settlements," one arrangement that may often serve the interests of defendants and plaintiffs' lawyers at the expense of plaintiffs themselves. In a coupon settlement, members of the affected class receive coupons that can be redeemed for discounts on the defendant's product, but attorneys receive what may be a very large cash payment based on the nominal value of the coupons. For example, in one case, plaintiffs alleged that a video rental company had failed to disclose its late-fee policy. Members of the class received coupons worth $1 off a future rental, while the plaintiffs' attorneys received a fee of $9.25 million. Experts estimated that at most 20 percent of the coupons would be redeemed. Moreover, it is plausible that the coupons were more effective as a marketing effort by the defendant than as a deterrent to poor disclosure policies. The Act reduced possible abuse of settlements through a number of reforms, including instructing courts to scrutinize settlement agreements more carefully and a requirement that attorney fees be based on the value of coupons actually redeemed, rather than coupons issued.

The Act also took steps to curtail "forum shopping"—that is, efforts by plaintiffs to choose a jurisdiction that they expect will be friendly to their case. Lawsuits are generally tried in a jurisdiction that has some connection to the parties, but because class actions often include a large number of plaintiffs nationwide, attorneys had the opportunity to initiate a lawsuit in a location where they felt either the court or the local jury pool would be most favorable to their case. The Class Action Fairness Act addresses this issue by making it easier for defendants to have their case heard in Federal court, reducing opportunities for plaintiffs to shop around for a jurisdiction in which they are likely to have an advantage.

Corporate Governance Reform

For small businesses, a firm's owner is likely to be its manager. But large corporations may be owned by thousands of shareholders at once, and such a large, dispersed group must delegate management to a smaller group of people. This separation of ownership and control makes it possible to maintain central control over a firm's operations while raising the large amounts of capital needed for many corporate investments. But it also introduces the problem of ensuring that managers make decisions that are in the best interests of the shareholders. Corporate governance refers to the systems through which shareholders are able to control the choices of those who manage the firm on their behalf.

Regulation of corporate governance arises from the fact that managers know more about the corporation's situation than the shareholders on whose behalf they are making decisions. Most shareholders would like the corporation's managers to make decisions that maximize profits. To encourage this, corporate boards attempt to design incentives that reward managers when their actions increase profits. For these incentive systems to work, however, they must be based on accurate financial reports that are generated in a transparent way.

A corporation will be better off if it can ensure accurate financial reporting, because if investors doubt the information they receive, they will be less willing to invest. But it is difficult for shareholders to observe the mechanisms that a corporation uses to improve accuracy and to prevent management from making misleading reports. Furthermore, shareholders are a large, dispersed group, so that an individual shareholder will not receive the full benefit of costly efforts to monitor management. In the face of these challenges to private monitoring of financial reporting, the U.S. Government attempts to ensure the accuracy of financial reporting through the securities laws enforced by the Securities and Exchange Commission (SEC).

Beginning in the late 1990s, an increase in earnings restatements and some large accounting scandals at major companies led to concerns that corporations had been misleading investors about the extent of their profits. In March of 2002, the President proposed a plan to improve corporate governance, centered on three principles: accuracy and accessibility of information, management accountability, and auditor independence. Congress later passed the Sarbanes-Oxley Act of 2002, which incorporated these three principles by introducing a number of changes to U.S. securities laws. Some of the key reforms are described in the following paragraphs.

To promote greater accuracy and accessibility of information, Sarbanes-Oxley requires corporations to disclose more information about internal control structures and the members of their audit committees. It also significantly increases the penalties for criminal fraud, increasing the maximum term for securities fraud to 25 years in prison and permitting terms of up to 20 years for destroying documents.

To promote greater management accountability, Sarbanes-Oxley requires chief executive officers and chief financial officers to certify the accuracy and completeness of financial reports that they file with the SEC and makes it a criminal offense to knowingly certify a false report. In addition, executives must forfeit any bonuses or other incentive compensation to which they would have been entitled during the year after a false report is issued.

To increase auditor independence, the Act creates the Public Company Accounting Oversight Board, which oversees the firms that audit corporations' financial reports. The Board conducts regular reviews of accounting firms' activities, and if it discovers problems it can impose sanctions and can bar a firm from providing audit services to corporations listed on U.S. securities exchanges. In addition, the Act creates new requirements to ensure that accounting firms are more independent of a corporation's management. Accounting firms are no longer permitted to sell certain non-audit services to their corporate audit clients, and a company's accountants must be chosen by a committee of directors who have no ties to management.

Since passage of the Sarbanes-Oxley Act, many have expressed concern about the cost of compliance with its requirements. There is evidence that some firms, especially smaller firms and foreign firms, have chosen to cease or to avoid trading on U.S. public markets because of the expense of complying with Sarbanes-Oxley, although there is no definitive evidence on how large this effect has been. While some increase in costs is the inevitable result of stricter reporting standards, it is important to ensure that the increased costs are justified by greater accuracy and transparency. Many of the specifics of Sarbanes-Oxley depend on rules and standards under the control of the SEC and the Public Company Accounting Oversight Board. As regulators and corporations become more familiar with the implementation of the Act, and as reporting companies adapt their practices and regulators adjust rules to eliminate inefficient requirements, the costs should fall.

Insurance Against Terrorism and Natural Disasters

When disasters occur, such as the terrorist attacks of September 11, 2001, or hurricanes such as Katrina in 2005 or Ike in 2008, the government plays an important role in providing emergency relief and helping communities to recover. At the same time, insurance coverage is vital in helping individuals and businesses recover from catastrophic events. Most insurance is provided by the private sector, regulated to make sure that insurers are able to repay claims if they come due. But disaster relief acts as a form of public sector insurance, and this means that the market for insurance against catastrophic events is inevitably affected by government policy. To preserve private insurers' important role in mitigating disasters, government disaster relief should help the Nation recover from major losses without discouraging the operation of private insurance markets.

Insurance markets give individuals and businesses a way to reduce risk. For example, anyone who owns a building faces a small risk of losing property in a fire. Rather than accepting a small probability of suffering a large financial loss, insurance allows one to substantially reduce this risk by paying a regular fee, called a *premium*, in exchange for compensation for some or all of the losses sustained in the case of a fire. Because only a small fraction of the population will suffer a fire in any given period, the premiums from the overall pool of insured people provide funds to pay for the damage suffered by those few who do suffer fires.

Insurance markets work most effectively if premiums are tailored to risks that are observable or can be controlled by the insured customer. If individuals with different risk profiles are grouped together and charged the same premium, then those who in fact have low risks are being charged premiums that are greater than the expected value of their losses and may choose to go without insurance. Differences in premiums can also lead individuals to make more efficient choices about what risks to take and how best to mitigate risks—for example, if driving a safer car means paying lower insurance premiums, people will have an incentive to choose safer vehicles. Similarly, it may be more expensive to live in some coastal areas because a high risk of storm damage leads to higher insurance premiums. This means that when home buyers decide whether to live in those areas, they will take into account the extra cost associated with potential storm losses.

For risks such as house fires or automobile accidents, the fraction of the population that will suffer losses each year is relatively stable. This means that insurers can feel reasonably confident about what level of premiums will be sufficient to cover the year's losses. Losses from major catastrophes are much more difficult to predict—for example, flood losses in 2005 related to Hurricane Katrina were many times larger than the annual flood losses from preceding years. This creates the risk that total losses in a year will be greater than the funds available to the insurer to pay claims. Insurance companies address this risk by purchasing *reinsurance* for large losses: in exchange for premiums, reinsurers agree to bear a fraction of insurer's losses if those losses exceed a certain amount. Because reinsurers typically diversify their risks internationally, they are in a position to pay claims arising from catastrophic losses in a single country.

The 9/11 attacks seriously disrupted the market for terrorism insurance. Prior to the 9/11 attacks, the risk of terrorist attacks was covered by most commercial insurance policies. In the months following the attacks, however, insurers were forced to reassess the likelihood of potential terrorist attacks and the capital reserves they would require, and many insurers began excluding terrorism risk from commercial insurance policies. Congress passed the Terrorism Risk Insurance Act (TRIA) to address this disruption in the market and to help reassure businesses that they could obtain insurance against the commercial risks associated with the threat of terrorism. Under TRIA, the U.S. Government provides reinsurance for terrorism losses: in the event of a claim for terrorism-related losses, an insurer would pay the claim to the insured party and then be compensated by the Government for a large share of the losses above certain limits. Insurers do not pay premiums up front for this reinsurance. Instead, TRIA specifies that assessments from insurers would be made after the fact.

TRIA was intended to address a sharp temporary disruption in insurance markets, not to be a long-term subsidy to insurers that provide terrorism coverage. Providing insurance at subsidized rates reduces the efficiency of the insurance market. First, it undermines the incentive effects of premiums that reflect expected losses as discussed above. This can encourage people to undertake risks that they would otherwise not be willing to bear and discourages people from taking actions that would mitigate risk. Second, government-provided reinsurance undermines the private market for reinsurance, discouraging innovation and efficient pricing of risk.

Because of these problems with government-subsidized insurance, the Administration has insisted that TRIA should be a temporary program and that subsidies should be reduced as markets adjust to the post-9/11 environment. The subsidies provided by TRIA have gradually been reduced. The insurer's deductible was initially 7 percent of the insurance company's previous year's premiums, and this fraction had been increased to 20 percent by 2007. In addition, the Federal share of insured losses has been reduced from 90 percent to 85 percent, and as of 2007, Federal payments will not be made unless insured losses from a terrorist event exceed $100 million. The program is scheduled to expire in December of 2014.

The market in terrorism insurance has grown since 2002, even as subsidies for terrorism insurance have been reduced. As shown in Chart 9-3, the fraction of policyholders purchasing terrorism insurance increased from 27 percent in 2003 to 59 percent in 2007, even as deductibles for the Federal reinsurance program were increasing. As the private market develops to accommodate the post-9/11 environment, government assistance should be eliminated to allow the market to operate efficiently.

Chart 9-3 **Terrorism Risk Insurance (TRI) Deductibles and Take-up Rates 2003–2007**
TRI take-up has increased as deductibles have risen and Federal payout shares have fallen.

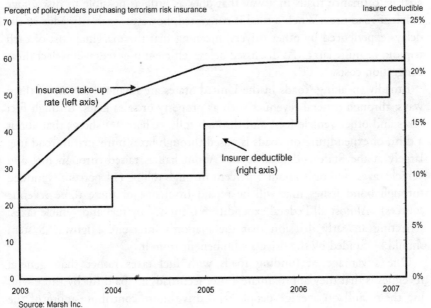

Source: Marsh Inc.

Roads

The Nation's roads are built and maintained primarily by State and local governments; the Federal Government's role has been to help fund these activities. Like some other infrastructure projects, roads are often natural monopolies: once a road is constructed, it is usually less expensive to accommodate extra traffic on that road than to construct a competing road. But rather than organizing roads under a regulated, private sector monopolist, the government generally owns and operates the roads itself—at least in part because of the expense that would be involved in limiting access to roads to paying drivers and collecting revenue from road users.

When government provides a service itself to an identifiable subset of society, it is often most efficient to pay for the service through user fees that reflect the *marginal cost* of providing it—that is, the extra cost created by each user. This approach, when practical, both ensures that the service will be used when its value is greater than its costs and provides information about whether and when capacity should be expanded. User fees that reflect marginal costs will lead drivers to make efficient decisions, choosing to drive when the benefits they receive are greater than the costs their trip generates.

On an uncongested road, the marginal congestion imposed by each driver is very small, and fees that reflect marginal cost may often be insufficient to pay the fixed costs of building and operating the road. In this case, the goal is to finance roads in a way that does as little as possible to discourage efficient road use. When a road is congested, however, each trip adds to the delays experienced by other drivers, meaning that the marginal cost of each trip can be quite large. As discussed below, efficient user fees will reflect these congestion costs.

Broadly speaking, roads in the United States are financed in one of three ways: through general revenues such as property or sales taxes, through fuel taxes and other vehicle fees, and through tolls. Chart 9-4 shows that about a third of expenditure on roads is raised through taxes unrelated to road use, largely at the State and local level. About half is raised through fuel and vehicle taxes, and only about 5 percent through tolling (11 percent is funded through bond issues that will be repaid from one of these three revenue sources). Almost all Federal expenditure is funded by fuel and vehicle taxes, reflecting an early decision that the Nation's Interstate Highway System should be funded by the drivers who benefit from it.

One advantage of funding roads with fuel taxes rather than general revenues is that they approximate a user fee: roads are paid for by those who use them, and on average people who drive more contribute more of the cost of providing the roads. However, fuel taxes do not do a good job of capturing the marginal cost of using the road. One of the most important

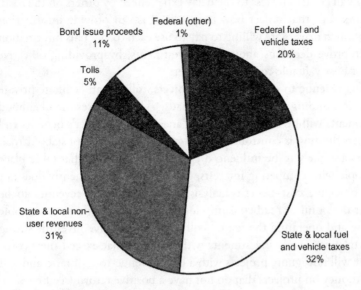

Chart 9-4 **Highway Expenditures by Revenue Source, 2006**
Fuel and vehicle taxes represent just over half of highway revenue.

Federal (other)
1%

Bond issue proceeds
11%

Federal fuel and
vehicle taxes
20%

Tolls
5%

State & local non-
user revenues
31%

State & local fuel
and vehicle taxes
32%

Source: Department of Transportation (Federal Highway Administration).

costs associated with road use is congestion: when a driver uses a congested road, she or he increases the delays experienced by everyone else. The increased delay is a negative externality, because each driver does not take into account these costs when deciding when, where, and whether to drive. The fuel tax fails to account for this negative externality, because drivers pay the same amount whether driving on an urban highway at rush hour or on an empty rural road. Many economists point out that fuel taxes can be effective in addressing some negative externalities directly related to fuel use, such as environmental degradation and petroleum dependence. But this does not imply that fuel taxes are the best way to finance roads. In fact, as vehicles become more fuel efficient, they will produce less revenue for each mile driven, so that the same amount of driving will contribute less and less highway revenue.

The Administration has supported exploring ways to begin moving away from fuel taxes toward forms of direct pricing, such as tolls, that would be more effective at matching what drivers pay to the costs they impose. Not only are tolls independent of a vehicle's fuel efficiency, but they also have the flexibility to address congestion externalities because they can be adjusted according to time and place, so that drivers pay more to travel on busy routes or during busy times. Such tolls encourage drivers to drive at times and places where they will contribute less to the delay experienced by others on the road. Furthermore, tolls that reflect how busy a road is can provide information about how much drivers are willing to pay to use each road. This information can help improve decisions about new investments, by providing objective measures of how valuable roads are to drivers.

By linking revenue to particular road projects, tolling can facilitate private investment in building and maintaining roads. This increases the likelihood that investments will be based on a careful analysis of a project's benefits and costs. When funding is controlled by the government, decisions about road investments are likely to be influenced by a political process that takes place among people with competing interests, and the process frequently does not reflect an objective cost–benefit analysis. Tolling permits revenues to be collected at the point of road consumption and directed to those responsible for building and operating the road. Toll revenues can give investors strong incentives to pursue only investments with revenues that exceed their costs, so that they will not ignore projects with a large revenue-to-cost ratio and will not spend money on projects that do not have a positive return (see Box 9-2). However, private infrastructure investments may not give weight to public benefits of an investment that are not reflected in the project's revenues, such as increased safety or reduced pollution. For projects for which such benefits are substantial, it is important to have a public partner that can contribute funding that reflects the public benefits of the project.

To encourage development of more efficient forms of highway finance, the Department of Transportation has entered into Urban Partnership Agreements with several metropolitan areas that will undertake programs that include congestion pricing or variable toll demonstration projects. Calling for broader reform to highway finance, the Secretary of Transportation proposed a plan in 2008 to reform Federal highway policy by initiating a movement away from the fuel-tax-based approach to funding highway investment to methods that link fees more closely to use of the road system, such as congestion pricing. The Secretary also proposed expanding support for private sector participation in road projects, including removing current Federal statutory and regulatory barriers to tolling on Federally supported highways.

Box 9-2: The Role of Incentives in Road Investments

When private sector road operators rely on user fees for their revenue, the potential for profit gives them incentives to invest in projects that improve service to the public. Examples of such investment can be seen on the Indiana Toll Road, which provides a key route between Chicago and Ohio. In 2006, the State agreed to turn over operations on the road to the Indiana Toll Road Concession Company under a 75-year lease. Within the first year, the company installed electronic tolling facilities, easing congestion and saving commuters valuable time. The company also spent $250 million to add lanes to highly trafficked areas of the road. Because the company's profits depend on the toll revenues it generates, the operators have an incentive to improve road conditions when the cost of doing so is less than the extra revenue it gains from improving service to drivers.

While some State and local governments use cost–benefit analyses to guide their infrastructure investment decisions, many others fail to make the investments that offer the greatest net benefits. Traffic signal optimization is one area in which municipal governments have frequently failed to invest resources despite very high expected returns. Over time, pedestrian and vehicle traffic patterns change substantially as cities grow and residential and commercial areas develop. Retiming traffic signals to optimize traffic flow can reduce vehicle stops, which in turn reduces delays, fuel use, and vehicle emissions. Transportation engineers recommend retiming signals every 3 to 5 years, but a recent survey showed that only 60 percent of State and local traffic agencies retime their signals at least every 5 years.

Signal optimization is relatively inexpensive, and recent projects have seen benefits in time and fuel savings exceed their cost by more than 40 to 1. Cities like Nashville, Austin, and Portland, Oregon, have invested in signal optimization plans and seen improvements in traffic delay and air quality, but State and local agencies often fail to allocate resources to signal optimization programs. Many retime their signals infrequently or conduct traffic assessments only in response to citizen complaints. Local governments will better serve drivers if they follow the private sector's lead and base their investment decisions more heavily on cost–benefit analysis.

Aviation

Like roads, airports and air traffic control services are often provided by the public sector. As with fees to finance roads, it would be economically efficient to set aviation fees where a competitive market would set them, at marginal cost. In fact, aviation fees bear little relationship to marginal costs. Airport landing fees are generally based on aircraft weight, and air traffic control operations are funded largely by a ticket tax of 7.5 percent on each airline ticket. Air traffic control operations are also funded by fuel taxes and additional fees.

This approach to financing means that fees do not reflect marginal costs in at least two important respects. The cost of air traffic control services depends on the number of planes, not on the size of those planes or the number of passengers each carries. Similarly, each flight at a congested airport contributes approximately the same amount to congestion, regardless of the plane's size. Because fees are roughly proportional to the size of each plane and the value of tickets sold, an airline that flies a single plane with 200 passengers might pay roughly the same fees as an airline that flies 10 planes with 20 passengers each. The second airline, however, generates approximately 10 times as much congestion and requires about 10 times as much air traffic controller time.

The result is that airlines do not take into account the external cost they impose when they schedule a flight using a crowded airport. Airlines schedule frequent flights with small aircraft rather than fewer flights with larger aircraft. Overcrowded airports mean delayed flights, and delays have been increasing in recent years, with congestion at the Nation's busiest airports a significant contributing factor. Delays were especially severe in New York City airports in the summer of 2007; for example, at John F. Kennedy International Airport (JFK), only 56 percent of flights arrived on time during the summer months.

One method the government can use to address overcrowding is to place caps on the number of flights permitted to land at an airport, in order to limit those flights to the capacity the airport can accept. When the Federal Aviation Administration (FAA) establishes a cap at an airport, each airline is assigned "slots" permitting its aircraft to land or take off at particular times. Delays are thereby reduced by excluding other airlines from the airport. In the past, slots have been assigned through a negotiated process, and this approach was used in 2008 at JFK and Newark Liberty International airports after severe delays in the summer of 2007.

A problem with this approach is that the government must decide whose planes can and cannot land at the airport. The need to obtain slots from the government acts as a barrier to new entry at the airport, so that passengers are denied the benefits of competition. Even if the FAA makes wise decisions about which airlines should initially receive slots when a cap is imposed at an airport, this allocation will become inefficient over time. But the FAA will find it difficult to further reallocate the slots regardless of how inefficient a given distribution of slots becomes: given their scarcity, slots are very valuable, so an incumbent authorized to use the slot will go to great lengths to maintain its allocation.

Recognizing the inefficiency that results when the government decides which airlines have access to an airport, the Administration has sought to use market-based mechanisms to allocate scarce airport capacity. One approach is to allow airports to charge landing fees in a way that reflects the greater demand to operate at certain times of the day. The Department of Transportation published guidance in 2008 clarifying that airports have the authority to charge congestion-based prices that would help encourage planes to use the airport when it is less busy, as long as the total charges imposed do not exceed the eligible costs of operating the airport. Under such an approach, airlines—and ultimately passengers—would decide whether it was worth paying a premium to schedule a flight at the most popular time.

Another approach with a similar result is to auction slots so that each slot is used by the airline that values it most highly. As with congestion-based landing fees, an auction would drive up the price of slots at the busiest times, but it would be less expensive to schedule a flight when the airport is less crowded. Auctions would permit new entry by airlines if they believed they could serve consumers more efficiently. In New York City, the Administration issued rules that would implement this approach for a limited number of slots. Apart from efficiently allocating the slots within the cap, an auction would reveal the market value of the other slots held by the airlines. This could help encourage airlines to trade slots among themselves if they discover that particular slots would be worth more in the hands of a different airline.

Conclusion

Government can play an important role in addressing the market failures associated with natural monopoly, externalities, and imperfect information. However, it would be naive to assume that government can eliminate all inefficiency in a market. Government lacks the information and incentives that make competitive markets work efficiently. Before intervening in a market, policymakers should first examine whether the inefficiencies of government involvement are outweighed by the inefficiencies of an unregulated market.

Regulation will be most efficient if it takes advantage of market mechanisms where possible. The Administration has taken an approach to regulation that supports competitive markets and attempts to take advantage of private sector incentives rather than working against them. There are many opportunities to further improve the efficiency of regulations, and this chapter has laid out a number of areas where such improvements are possible.

Appendix A
REPORT TO THE PRESIDENT ON THE ACTIVITIES OF THE COUNCIL OF ECONOMIC ADVISERS DURING 2008

LETTER OF TRANSMITTAL

COUNCIL OF ECONOMIC ADVISERS
Washington, D.C., December 31, 2008

MR. PRESIDENT:

The Council of Economic Advisers submits this report on its activities during calendar year 2008 in accordance with the requirements of the Congress, as set forth in section 10(d) of the Employment Act of 1946 as amended by the Full Employment and Balanced Growth Act of 1978.

Sincerely,

Edward P. Lazear, *Chairman*
Donald B. Marron, *Member*

Council Members and Their Dates of Service

Name	Position	Oath of office date	Separation date
Edwin G. Nourse	Chairman	August 9, 1946	November 1, 1949
Leon H. Keyserling	Vice Chairman	August 9, 1946	
	Acting Chairman	November 2, 1949	
	Chairman	May 10, 1950	January 20, 1953
John D. Clark	Member	August 9, 1946	
	Vice Chairman	May 10, 1950	February 11, 1953
Roy Blough	Member	June 29, 1950	August 20, 1952
Robert C. Turner	Member	September 8, 1952	January 20, 1953
Arthur F. Burns	Chairman	March 19, 1953	December 1, 1956
Neil H. Jacoby	Member	September 15, 1953	February 9, 1955
Walter W. Stewart	Member	December 2, 1953	April 29, 1955
Raymond J. Saulnier	Member	April 4, 1955	
	Chairman	December 3, 1956	January 20, 1961
Joseph S. Davis	Member	May 2, 1955	October 31, 1958
Paul W. McCracken	Member	December 3, 1956	January 31, 1959
Karl Brandt	Member	November 1, 1958	January 20, 1961
Henry C. Wallich	Member	May 7, 1959	January 20, 1961
Walter W. Heller	Chairman	January 29, 1961	November 15, 1964
James Tobin	Member	January 29, 1961	July 31, 1962
Kermit Gordon	Member	January 29, 1961	December 27, 1962
Gardner Ackley	Member	August 3, 1962	
	Chairman	November 16, 1964	February 15, 1968
John P. Lewis	Member	May 17, 1963	August 31, 1964
Otto Eckstein	Member	September 2, 1964	February 1, 1966
Arthur M. Okun	Member	November 16, 1964	
	Chairman	February 15, 1968	January 20, 1969
James S. Duesenberry	Member	February 2, 1966	June 30, 1968
Merton J. Peck	Member	February 15, 1968	January 20, 1969
Warren L. Smith	Member	July 1, 1968	January 20, 1969
Paul W. McCracken	Chairman	February 4, 1969	December 31, 1971
Hendrik S. Houthakker	Member	February 4, 1969	July 15, 1971
Herbert Stein	Member	February 4, 1969	
	Chairman	January 1, 1972	August 31, 1974
Ezra Solomon	Member	September 9, 1971	March 26, 1973
Marina v.N. Whitman	Member	March 13, 1972	August 15, 1973
Gary L. Seevers	Member	July 23, 1973	April 15, 1975
William J. Fellner	Member	October 31, 1973	February 25, 1975
Alan Greenspan	Chairman	September 4, 1974	January 20, 1977
Paul W. MacAvoy	Member	June 13, 1975	November 15, 1976
Burton G. Malkiel	Member	July 22, 1975	January 20, 1977
Charles L. Schultze	Chairman	January 22, 1977	January 20, 1981

Council Members and Their Dates of Service

Name	Position	Oath of office date	Separation date
William D. Nordhaus	Member	March 18, 1977	February 4, 1979
Lyle E. Gramley	Member	March 18, 1977	May 27, 1980
George C. Eads	Member	June 6, 1979	January 20, 1981
Stephen M. Goldfeld	Member	August 20, 1980	January 20, 1981
Murray L. Weidenbaum	Chairman	February 27, 1981	August 25, 1982
William A. Niskanen	Member	June 12, 1981	March 30, 1985
Jerry L. Jordan	Member	July 14, 1981	July 31, 1982
Martin Feldstein	Chairman	October 14, 1982	July 10, 1984
William Poole	Member	December 10, 1982	January 20, 1985
Beryl W. Sprinkel	Chairman	April 18, 1985	January 20, 1989
Thomas Gale Moore	Member	July 1, 1985	May 1, 1989
Michael L. Mussa	Member	August 18, 1986	September 19, 1988
Michael J. Boskin	Chairman	February 2, 1989	January 12, 1993
John B. Taylor	Member	June 9, 1989	August 2, 1991
Richard L. Schmalensee	Member	October 3, 1989	June 21, 1991
David F. Bradford	Member	November 13, 1991	January 20, 1993
Paul Wonnacott	Member	November 13, 1991	January 20, 1993
Laura D'Andrea Tyson	Chair	February 5, 1993	April 22, 1995
Alan S. Blinder	Member	July 27, 1993	June 26, 1994
Joseph E. Stiglitz	Member	July 27, 1993	
	Chairman	June 28, 1995	February 10, 1997
Martin N. Baily	Member	June 30, 1995	August 30, 1996
Alicia H. Munnell	Member	January 29, 1996	August 1, 1997
Janet L. Yellen	Chair	February 18, 1997	August 3, 1999
Jeffrey A. Frankel	Member	April 23, 1997	March 2, 1999
Rebecca M. Blank	Member	October 22, 1998	July 9, 1999
Martin N. Baily	Chairman	August 12, 1999	January 19, 2001
Robert Z. Lawrence	Member	August 12, 1999	January 12, 2001
Kathryn L. Shaw	Member	May 31, 2000	January 19, 2001
R. Glenn Hubbard	Chairman	May 11, 2001	February 28, 2003
Mark B. McClellan	Member	July 25, 2001	November 13, 2002
Randall S. Kroszner	Member	November 30, 2001	July 1, 2003
N. Gregory Mankiw	Chairman	May 29, 2003	February 18, 2005
Kristin J. Forbes	Member	November 21, 2003	June 3, 2005
Harvey S. Rosen	Member	November 21, 2003	
	Chairman	February 23, 2005	June 10, 2005
Ben S. Bernanke	Chairman	June 21, 2005	January 31, 2006
Katherine Baicker	Member	November 18, 2005	July 11, 2007
Matthew J. Slaughter	Member	November 18, 2005	March 1, 2007
Edward P. Lazear	Chairman	February 27, 2006	
Donald B. Marron	Member	July 17, 2008	

Report to the President on the Activities of the Council of Economic Advisers During 2008

The Council of Economic Advisers was established by the Employment Act of 1946 to provide the President with objective economic analysis and advice on the development and implementation of a wide range of domestic and international economic policy issues.

The Chairman of the Council

Edward P. Lazear continued to chair the Council during 2008. Dr. Lazear is on a leave of absence from the Stanford Graduate School of Business where he is the Jack Steele Parker Professor of Human Resources Management and Economics. He also served as the Morris Arnold Cox Senior Fellow at the Hoover Institution.

Dr. Lazear is responsible for communicating the Council's views on economic matters directly to the President through personal discussions and written reports. He represents the Council at daily White House senior staff meetings, a variety of inter-agency meetings, Cabinet meetings, and other formal and informal meetings with the President. He also travels within the United States and overseas to present the Administration's views on the economy. Dr. Lazear is the Council's chief public spokesperson. He directs the work of the Council and exercises ultimate responsibility for the work of the professional staff.

The Members of the Council

Donald B. Marron was confirmed by the Senate as a Member of the Council of Economic Advisers on June 27, 2008, was appointed by the President on June 30, and was sworn in on July 17. While awaiting confirmation, Dr. Marron had served as Senior Economic Adviser to the Council. Dr. Marron previously served as Deputy Director of the Congressional Budget Office, including more than a year as its Acting Director. His earlier government service included serving as Chief Economist at the Council and as Executive Director and Chief Economist of the Congressional Joint Economic Committee. At the Council Dr. Marron's responsibilities include work on financial markets, housing, and a variety of macroeconomic and microeconomic policy issues.

Macroeconomic Policies

As is its tradition, the Council devoted much time during 2008 to assisting the President in formulating economic policy objectives and designing programs to implement them. In this regard the Chairman kept the President informed, on a continuing basis, of important macroeconomic developments and other major policy issues through regular macroeconomic briefings. The Council prepares for the President, the Vice President, and the White House senior staff regular memoranda that report key economic data and analyze current economic events and financial market developments. Council staff also regularly provides assistance with economic data and analysis to other offices within the Executive Office of the President.

The Council, the Department of the Treasury, and the Office of Management and Budget—the Administration's economic "troika"—are responsible for producing the economic forecasts that underlie the Administration's budget proposals. The Council, under the leadership of the Chairman and the Chief Economist, initiates the forecasting process twice each year. In preparing these forecasts, the Council consults with a variety of outside sources, including leading private sector forecasters.

In 2008, the Council took part in discussions on a range of macroeconomic issues. The Council contributed significantly to discussions on the macroeconomic impact of this year's housing and credit market disruptions, and provided analysis and support for the Administration's economic growth package and various policies to promote financial stability.

The Council works closely with the Department of the Treasury, the Federal Reserve, and other government agencies in providing analyses to the Administration on these topics of concern. It also works closely with the National Economic Council, the Domestic Policy Council, the Office of Management and Budget, and other offices within the Executive Office of the President in assessing the economy and economic policy proposals.

International Economic Policies

The Council was involved in a range of international trade and finance issues, with a particular focus on the determinants of the international financial crisis and related global economic slowdown. The Council was an active participant in discussions at the global, regional, and bilateral levels. Council members regularly met with economists and policy officials of foreign countries, finance ministers, other government officials, and members of the private sector to discuss prevailing issues relating to the global economy.

In response to high commodity prices in 2007 and the first half of 2008, the Council provided analysis on the causes and impact of rising crop prices on the United States and on developing economies. The Council also examined the effects of global biofuels policies including the U.S. ethanol mandate.

On the international trade front, the Council provided empirical analysis of pending free trade agreements including the Colombia, Panama, and South Korea free trade agreements. The Council was also a participant in the U.S. Trade Policy Review, conducted by the World Trade Organization.

The Council also prepared in-depth analyses for the President's international itinerary, including travel to Africa, as well as the annual Asia Pacific Economic Cooperation (APEC) summit in Peru.

In the area of investment and security, the Council took part in discussions on the implementation of the Foreign Investment and National Security Act of 2007 (FINSA), which clarified and improved the operations of the Committee on Foreign Investment in the United States (CFIUS), including participating in the drafting and publication of new regulations governing CFIUS under FINSA. The Council also participated in discussions of individual cases before CFIUS.

The Council is a leading participant in the Organization for Economic Cooperation and Development (OECD), the principal forum for economic cooperation among the high-income industrial economies. Senior Council members participated in the OECD's Economic Policy Committee (EPC) meetings, the Economic Development Review Committee, as well as the Working Party meetings on macroeconomic policy and coordination.

Microeconomic Policies

A wide variety of microeconomic issues received Council attention during 2008. The Council actively participated in the Cabinet-level National Economic Council and Domestic Policy Council meetings, dealing with issues including health care, labor, energy policy, legal reform, the environment, homeland security, education, pensions, transportation, and technology among others.

The Council was active in the examination of health care policy related to Medicare spending growth and reform, Health Savings Accounts, health information technology adoption, tobacco regulation, and the promotion of price and quality information transparency. The Council was also heavily involved in the policy process for the two 2008 State of the Union healthcare proposals: the Standard Deduction for Health Insurance and the Affordable Choices Initiative.

The Council was also active in energy and environmental policy discussions, where it analyzed energy markets, alternatives to fossil fuels, energy efficiency issues, and environmental regulatory reform. This included issues such as oil price volatility, the Renewable Fuels Standard, fuel economy standards, the Strategic Petroleum Reserve, global climate change, air quality, and the international trade of energy.

The Council examined transportation policies relating to airports, infra-structure and congestion pricing. The Council also played a role in the analysis of policy for telecommunications, broadband, spectrum allocation and patent reform.

The Council participated in discussions related to catastrophic risk insur-ance relating to natural disasters and attacks. The Council also participated in ongoing policy discussions relating to the government's role in terrorism risk insurance.

The Council was involved with a number of issues within the scope of education and labor policy. The Council assisted the Department of Education with analysis of plans to ensure the viability of Federal student loan programs and also continued to participate in discussions on regulatory changes to No Child Left Behind. In the realm of labor policy, the Council was involved with policy discussions and analysis concerning proposed regu-latory changes in Trade Adjustment Assistance and Immigration, as well as an extension of Unemployment Insurance.

The Council was active in tax policy discussions relating to fiscal stimulus and individual income tax, business tax credits, and corporate taxation issues. Many additional tax policy discussions were held in connection with other microeconomic discussions including labor, insurance, pensions, and health care.

The Staff of the Council of Economic Advisers

The professional staff of the Council consists of the Chief of Staff, the Chief Economist, the Director of Macroeconomic Forecasting, and the Director of the Statistical Office, nine senior economists, and seven junior staff including staff economists, analysts and research assistants. The professional staff and their areas of concentration at the end of 2008 were:

Chief of Staff
Pierce E. Scranton

Chief Economist
Jane E. Ihrig

Director of Macroeconomic Forecasting Steven N. Braun	*Director Statistical Office* Adrienne T. Pilot

Senior Economists

Jean M. Abraham .... Health
Scott J. Adams .... Labor, Immigration, Education, Welfare
Benjamin Dennis .... International Trade
Erik Durbin .... Legal, Transportation, Regulation
Wendy M. Edelberg .... Macroeconomics, Labor, Small Business
Elizabeth A. Kopits .... Agriculture, Environment, Natural Resources
Michael S. Piwowar .... Public Finance, Technology
William M. Powers .... International Finance
Robert P. Rebelein .... Tax, Budget

Staff Economist

Kristopher J. Dawsey .... Macroeconomics
Joshua K. Goldman .... Microeconomics and Regulation
Elizabeth M. Schultz .... International Finance and US Finance/Banking
Brian T. Waters .... Public Finance and Macroeconomics

Research Assistants

Sharon E. Boyd .... Labor, Immigration, Education and Welfare
Michael B. Love .... Labor and Education
Aditi P. Sen .... International Trade and Investment

Statistical Office

The Statistical Office administers and updates the Council's statistical information. Duties include preparing material for and overseeing publication of the monthly *Economic Indicators* and the statistical appendix to the *Economic Report of the President*. Staff verifies statistical content in Presidential memoranda and produces background materials for economic analysis. The Office also serves as the Council's liaison to the statistical community.

Brian A. Amorosi .... Program Analyst
Dagmara A. Mocala .... Program Analyst

Administrative Office

The Administrative Office provides general support for the Council's activities. This includes financial management, ethics, human resource management, travel, operations of facilities, security, information technology, and telecommunications management support.

Rosemary M. Rogers .... Administrative Officer
Archana A. Snyder .... Financial Officer
Doris T. Searles .... Information Management Specialist

Office of the Chairman

Alice H. Williams .... Executive Assistant to the Chairman
Sandra F. Daigle .... Executive Assistant to the Chairman
and Assistant to the Chief of Staff
Lisa D. Branch .... Executive Assistant to the Member
and Assistant to the Chief Economist
Mary E. Jones .... Executive Assistant to the Member

Staff Support

Sharon K. Thomas .... Administrative Support Assistant

Jane Tufts, Bruce Kaplan, and Anna Paganelli provided editorial assistance in the preparation of the 2009 Economic Report of the President.

Student Interns during the year were: William J. Allen; Carl B. Blau; Andrew V. Carfang; Stacy L. Carlson; Gordon N. Cook; Lauri J. Feldman; Matthew D. Kaczmarek; John V. Komkov; Jacob N. Mohs; Jacob A. Procuniar; Kevin L. Richards; Joanne C. Rodrigues; Alex D. Rosner; Tejas A. Sathian; and Sonia Sohaili.

Departures

The Council's senior economists, in most cases, are on leave of absence from academic institutions, government agencies, or private research institutions. Their tenure with the Council is usually limited to 1 or 2 years. The senior economists who resigned during the year were: Scott L. Baier (Clemson University); Charles W. Griffiths (Environmental Protection Agency); Daniel E. Polsky (University of Pennsylvania); Korok Ray (University of Chicago); Dan T. Rosenbaum (University of North Carolina); Howard Shatz (Rand Corporation); Sita N. Slavov (Occidental College); and John J. Stevens (Federal Reserve Board).

The economists are supported by a team of junior staff made up of staff economists, analysts, and research assistants who generally work with the Council for 1 or 2 years before returning to school or other endeavors. The staff economist who resigned during 2008 was: Elizabeth J. Akers. Those who served as research assistants at the Council and resigned during 2008 were: Mark W. Clements and Chen Zhao.

Public Information

The Council's annual *Economic Report of the President* is an important vehicle for presenting the Administration's domestic and international economic policies. It is available for purchase through the Government Printing Office, and is viewable on the Internet at *www.gpoaccess.gov/eop*. The Council also publishes the monthly *Economic Indicators*, which is available on-line at *www.gpoaccess.gov/indicators*. The Council's home page is located at *www.whitehouse.gov/cea*.

Appendix B
STATISTICAL TABLES RELATING TO INCOME, EMPLOYMENT, AND PRODUCTION

CONTENTS

General Notes

Detail in these tables may not add to totals because of rounding.

Because of the formula used for calculating real gross domestic product (GDP), the chained (2000) dollar estimates for the detailed components do not add to the chained-dollar value of GDP or to any intermediate aggregate. The Department of Commerce (Bureau of Economic Analysis) no longer publishes chained-dollar estimates prior to 1990, except for selected series.

Unless otherwise noted, all dollar figures are in current dollars.

Symbols used:
> p Preliminary.
> ... Not available (also, not applicable).

Data in these tables reflect revisions made by the source agencies through December 5, 2008. In particular, tables containing national income and product accounts (NIPA) estimates reflect revisions released by the Department of Commerce in July 2008.

TABLE B-1.—*Gross domestic product, 1959–2008*

[Billions of dollars, except as noted; quarterly data at seasonally adjusted annual rates]

Year or quarter	Gross domestic product	Personal consumption expenditures				Gross private domestic investment							Change in private inventories
		Total	Durable goods	Non-durable goods	Services	Total	Fixed investment						
							Total	Nonresidential				Residential	
								Total	Total	Structures	Equipment and software		
1959	506.6	317.6	42.7	148.5	126.5	78.5	74.6	46.5	18.1	28.4	28.1	
1960	526.4	331.7	43.3	152.8	135.6	78.9	75.7	49.4	19.6	29.8	26.3	
1961	544.7	342.1	41.8	156.6	143.8	78.2	75.2	48.8	19.7	29.1	26.4	
1962	585.6	363.3	46.9	162.8	153.6	88.1	82.0	53.1	20.8	32.3	29.0	
1963	617.7	382.7	51.6	168.2	162.9	93.8	88.1	56.0	21.2	34.8	32.1	
1964	663.6	411.4	56.7	178.6	176.1	102.1	97.2	63.0	23.7	39.2	34.3	
1965	719.1	443.8	63.3	191.5	189.0	118.2	109.0	74.8	28.3	46.5	34.2	
1966	787.8	480.9	68.3	208.7	203.8	131.3	117.7	85.4	31.3	54.0	32.3	
1967	832.6	507.8	70.4	217.1	220.3	128.6	118.7	86.4	31.5	54.9	32.4	
1968	910.0	558.0	80.8	235.7	241.6	141.2	132.1	93.4	33.6	59.9	38.7	
1969	984.6	605.2	85.9	253.1	266.1	156.4	147.3	104.7	37.7	67.0	42.6	
1970	1,038.5	648.5	85.0	272.0	291.5	152.4	150.4	109.0	40.3	68.7	41.4	
1971	1,127.1	701.9	96.9	285.5	319.5	178.2	169.9	114.1	42.7	71.5	55.8	
1972	1,238.3	770.6	110.4	308.0	352.2	207.6	198.5	128.8	47.2	81.7	69.7	
1973	1,382.7	852.4	123.5	343.1	385.8	244.5	228.6	153.3	55.0	98.3	75.3	
1974	1,500.0	933.4	122.3	384.5	426.6	249.4	235.4	169.5	61.2	108.2	66.0	
1975	1,638.3	1,034.4	133.5	420.7	480.2	230.2	236.5	173.7	61.4	112.4	62.7	
1976	1,825.3	1,151.9	158.9	458.3	534.7	292.0	274.8	192.4	65.9	126.4	82.5	
1977	2,030.9	1,278.6	181.2	497.1	600.2	361.3	339.0	228.7	74.6	154.1	110.3	
1978	2,294.7	1,428.5	201.7	550.2	676.6	438.0	412.2	280.6	93.6	187.0	131.6	
1979	2,563.3	1,592.2	214.4	624.5	753.3	492.9	474.9	333.9	117.7	216.2	141.0	
1980	2,789.5	1,757.1	214.2	696.1	846.9	479.3	485.6	362.4	136.2	226.2	123.2	
1981	3,128.4	1,941.1	231.3	758.9	950.8	572.4	542.6	420.0	167.3	252.7	122.6	
1982	3,255.0	2,077.3	240.2	787.6	1,049.4	517.2	532.1	426.5	177.6	248.9	105.7	
1983	3,536.7	2,290.6	280.8	831.2	1,178.6	564.3	570.1	417.2	154.3	262.9	152.9	
1984	3,933.2	2,503.3	326.5	884.6	1,292.2	735.6	670.2	489.6	177.4	312.2	180.6	
1985	4,220.3	2,720.3	363.5	928.7	1,428.1	736.2	714.4	526.2	194.5	331.7	188.2	
1986	4,462.8	2,899.7	403.0	958.4	1,538.3	746.5	739.9	519.8	176.5	343.3	220.1	
1987	4,739.5	3,100.2	421.7	1,015.3	1,663.3	785.0	757.8	524.1	174.2	349.9	233.7	
1988	5,103.8	3,353.6	453.6	1,083.5	1,816.5	821.6	803.1	563.8	182.8	381.0	239.3	
1989	5,484.4	3,598.5	471.8	1,166.7	1,960.0	874.9	847.3	607.7	193.7	414.0	239.5	
1990	5,803.1	3,839.9	474.2	1,249.9	2,115.9	861.0	846.4	622.4	202.9	419.5	224.0	
1991	5,995.9	3,986.1	453.9	1,284.8	2,247.4	802.9	803.3	598.2	183.6	414.6	205.1	
1992	6,337.7	4,235.3	483.6	1,330.5	2,421.2	864.8	848.5	612.1	172.6	439.6	236.3	
1993	6,657.4	4,477.9	526.7	1,379.4	2,571.8	953.4	932.5	666.6	177.2	489.4	266.0	
1994	7,072.2	4,743.3	582.2	1,437.2	2,723.9	1,097.1	1,033.3	731.4	186.8	544.6	301.9	
1995	7,397.7	4,975.8	611.6	1,485.1	2,879.1	1,144.0	1,112.9	810.0	207.3	602.8	302.8	
1996	7,816.9	5,256.8	652.6	1,555.5	3,048.7	1,240.3	1,209.5	875.4	224.6	650.8	334.1	
1997	8,304.3	5,547.4	692.7	1,619.0	3,235.8	1,389.8	1,317.8	968.7	250.3	718.3	349.1	
1998	8,747.0	5,879.5	750.2	1,683.6	3,445.7	1,509.1	1,438.4	1,052.6	275.2	777.3	385.8	
1999	9,268.4	6,282.5	817.6	1,804.8	3,660.0	1,625.7	1,558.8	1,133.9	282.2	851.7	424.9	
2000	9,817.0	6,739.4	863.3	1,947.2	3,928.8	1,735.5	1,679.0	1,232.1	313.2	918.9	446.9	
2001	10,128.0	7,055.0	883.7	2,017.1	4,154.3	1,614.3	1,646.1	1,176.8	322.6	854.2	469.3	
2002	10,469.6	7,350.7	923.9	2,079.6	4,347.2	1,582.1	1,570.2	1,066.3	279.2	787.1	503.9	
2003	10,960.8	7,703.6	942.7	2,190.2	4,570.8	1,664.1	1,649.8	1,077.4	277.2	800.2	572.4	
2004	11,685.9	8,195.9	983.9	2,343.7	4,868.3	1,888.6	1,830.0	1,154.5	298.2	856.3	675.5	
2005	12,421.9	8,694.1	1,020.8	2,514.1	5,159.2	2,086.1	2,042.8	1,273.1	337.6	935.5	769.6	
2006	13,178.4	9,207.2	1,052.1	2,685.2	5,469.9	2,220.4	2,171.1	1,414.1	410.4	1,003.7	757.0	
2007	13,807.5	9,710.2	1,082.8	2,833.0	5,794.4	2,130.4	2,134.0	1,503.8	480.3	1,023.5	630.2	
2005: I	12,155.4	8,480.9	1,006.6	2,432.4	5,041.9	2,046.0	1,963.3	1,233.6	326.9	906.7	729.7	
II	12,297.5	8,610.8	1,033.3	2,469.9	5,107.6	2,039.7	2,020.3	1,261.0	333.8	927.2	759.3	
III	12,538.2	8,791.1	1,038.7	2,554.8	5,197.6	2,084.2	2,073.2	1,286.1	337.3	948.8	787.1	
IV	12,696.4	8,893.7	1,004.4	2,599.4	5,289.9	2,174.6	2,114.3	1,311.8	352.4	959.3	802.5	
2006: I	12,959.6	9,026.3	1,046.5	2,629.3	5,350.5	2,236.7	2,183.6	1,375.5	377.4	998.1	808.1	
II	13,134.1	9,161.9	1,049.1	2,681.5	5,431.3	2,253.7	2,187.9	1,408.3	406.0	1,002.3	779.6	
III	13,249.6	9,283.7	1,054.4	2,726.3	5,502.9	2,231.7	2,169.2	1,433.0	424.4	1,008.6	736.2	
IV	13,370.1	9,357.0	1,058.2	2,703.8	5,595.0	2,159.5	2,143.6	1,439.6	433.9	1,005.6	704.0	
2007: I	13,510.9	9,524.9	1,076.6	2,761.5	5,686.8	2,117.8	2,133.4	1,456.4	449.6	1,006.8	677.0	
II	13,737.5	9,657.5	1,085.3	2,817.7	5,754.4	2,147.2	2,148.1	1,493.7	469.8	1,023.9	654.4	
III	13,950.6	9,765.6	1,086.2	2,846.6	5,832.8	2,164.0	2,141.0	1,522.9	492.9	1,030.0	618.1	
IV	14,031.2	9,892.7	1,083.0	2,906.2	5,903.5	2,092.3	2,113.4	1,542.1	508.7	1,033.4	571.3	
2008: I	14,150.8	10,002.3	1,071.0	2,950.7	5,980.6	2,056.1	2,081.7	1,553.6	522.7	1,030.9	528.1	
II	14,294.5	10,138.0	1,059.3	3,026.2	6,052.5	2,000.9	2,077.0	1,571.9	549.8	1,022.1	505.0	
III p	14,420.5	10,169.5	1,015.1	3,046.5	6,107.9	2,013.6	2,062.1	1,582.7	568.9	1,013.9	479.4	

See next page for continuation of table.

[Billions of dollars, except as noted; quarterly data at seasonally adjusted annual rates]

Year or quarter	Net exports of goods and services			Government consumption expenditures and gross investment						Final sales of domestic product	Gross domestic purchases [1]	Addendum: Gross national product [2]	Percent change from preceding period	
	Net exports	Exports	Imports	Total	Federal			State and local					Gross domestic product	Gross domestic purchases [1]
					Total	National defense	Nondefense							
59	0.4	22.7	22.3	110.0	65.4	53.8	11.5	44.7	502.7	506.2	509.3	8.4	8.5
60	4.2	27.0	22.8	111.6	64.1	53.4	10.7	47.5	523.2	522.2	529.5	3.9	3.2
61	4.9	27.6	22.7	119.5	67.9	56.5	11.4	51.6	541.7	539.8	548.2	3.5	3.4
62	4.1	29.1	25.0	130.1	75.3	61.1	14.2	54.9	579.5	581.5	589.7	7.5	7.7
63	4.9	31.1	26.1	136.4	76.9	61.0	15.9	59.5	612.1	612.8	622.2	5.5	5.4
64	6.9	35.0	28.1	143.2	78.5	60.3	18.2	64.8	658.8	656.7	668.5	7.4	7.2
65	5.6	37.1	31.5	151.5	80.4	60.6	19.8	71.0	709.9	713.5	724.4	8.4	8.6
66	3.9	40.9	37.1	171.8	92.5	71.7	20.8	79.2	774.2	783.9	792.9	9.5	9.9
67	3.6	43.5	39.9	192.7	104.8	83.5	21.3	87.9	822.7	829.0	838.0	5.7	5.8
68	1.4	47.9	46.6	209.4	111.4	89.3	22.1	98.0	900.9	908.6	916.1	9.3	9.6
69	1.4	51.9	50.5	221.5	113.4	89.5	23.8	108.2	975.4	983.2	990.7	8.2	8.2
70	4.0	59.7	55.8	233.8	113.5	87.6	25.8	120.3	1,036.5	1,034.6	1,044.9	5.5	5.2
71	.6	63.0	62.3	246.5	113.7	84.6	29.1	132.8	1,118.9	1,126.5	1,134.7	8.5	8.9
72	-3.4	70.8	74.2	263.5	119.7	87.0	32.7	143.8	1,229.2	1,241.7	1,246.8	9.9	10.2
73	4.1	95.3	91.2	281.7	122.5	88.2	34.3	159.2	1,366.8	1,378.6	1,395.3	11.7	11.0
74	-.8	126.7	127.5	317.9	134.6	95.6	39.0	183.4	1,486.0	1,500.8	1,515.5	8.5	8.9
75	16.0	138.7	122.7	357.7	149.1	103.9	45.1	208.7	1,644.6	1,622.4	1,651.3	9.2	8.1
76	-1.6	149.5	151.1	383.0	159.7	111.1	48.6	223.3	1,808.2	1,826.9	1,842.1	11.4	12.6
77	-23.1	159.4	182.4	414.1	175.4	120.9	54.5	238.7	2,008.6	2,054.0	2,051.2	11.3	12.4
78	-25.4	186.9	212.3	453.6	190.9	130.5	60.4	262.6	2,268.9	2,320.1	2,316.3	13.0	13.0
79	-22.5	230.1	252.7	500.8	210.6	145.2	65.4	290.2	2,545.3	2,585.9	2,595.3	11.7	11.5
80	-13.1	280.8	293.8	566.2	243.8	168.0	75.8	322.4	2,795.8	2,802.6	2,823.7	8.8	8.4
81	-12.5	305.2	317.8	627.5	280.2	196.3	84.0	347.3	3,098.6	3,141.0	3,161.4	12.2	12.1
82	-20.0	283.2	303.2	680.5	310.8	225.9	84.9	369.7	3,269.9	3,275.0	3,291.5	4.0	4.3
83	-51.7	277.0	328.6	733.5	342.9	250.7	92.3	390.5	3,542.4	3,588.3	3,573.8	8.7	9.6
84	-102.7	302.4	405.1	797.0	374.4	281.6	92.8	422.6	3,867.8	4,035.9	3,969.5	11.2	12.5
85	-115.2	302.0	417.2	879.0	412.8	311.2	101.6	466.2	4,198.4	4,335.5	4,246.8	7.3	7.4
86	-132.7	320.5	453.3	949.3	438.6	330.9	107.8	510.7	4,456.3	4,595.6	4,480.6	5.7	6.0
87	-145.2	363.9	509.1	999.5	460.1	350.0	110.0	539.4	4,712.3	4,884.7	4,757.4	6.2	6.3
88	-110.4	444.1	554.5	1,039.0	462.3	354.9	107.4	576.7	5,085.3	5,214.2	5,127.4	7.7	6.7
89	-88.2	503.3	591.5	1,099.1	482.2	362.2	120.0	616.9	5,456.7	5,572.5	5,510.6	7.5	6.9
90	-78.0	552.4	630.3	1,180.2	508.3	374.0	134.3	671.9	5,788.5	5,881.1	5,837.9	5.8	5.5
91	-27.5	596.8	624.3	1,234.4	527.7	383.2	144.5	706.7	5,996.3	6,023.4	6,026.3	3.3	2.4
92	-33.2	635.3	668.6	1,271.0	533.9	376.9	157.0	737.1	6,321.4	6,371.0	6,367.4	5.7	5.8
93	-65.0	655.8	720.9	1,291.2	525.2	362.9	162.4	766.0	6,636.6	6,722.4	6,689.3	5.0	5.5
94	-93.6	720.9	814.5	1,325.5	519.1	353.7	165.5	806.3	7,008.4	7,165.8	7,098.4	6.2	6.6
95	-91.4	812.2	903.6	1,369.2	519.2	348.7	170.5	850.0	7,366.5	7,489.0	7,433.4	4.6	4.5
96	-96.2	868.6	964.8	1,416.0	527.4	354.6	172.8	888.6	7,786.1	7,913.1	7,851.9	5.7	5.7
97	-101.6	955.3	1,056.9	1,468.7	530.9	349.6	181.3	937.8	8,232.3	8,405.9	8,337.3	6.2	6.2
98	-159.9	955.9	1,115.9	1,518.3	530.4	345.7	184.7	987.9	8,676.2	8,906.9	8,768.3	5.3	6.0
99	-260.5	991.2	1,251.7	1,620.8	555.8	360.6	195.2	1,065.0	9,201.5	9,528.9	9,302.2	6.0	7.0
00	-379.5	1,096.3	1,475.8	1,721.6	578.8	370.3	208.5	1,142.8	9,760.5	10,196.4	9,855.9	5.9	7.0
01	-367.0	1,032.8	1,399.8	1,825.6	612.9	392.6	220.3	1,212.8	10,159.7	10,495.0	10,171.6	3.2	2.9
02	-424.4	1,005.9	1,430.3	1,961.1	679.7	437.1	242.5	1,281.5	10,457.7	10,894.0	10,500.2	3.4	3.8
03	-499.4	1,040.8	1,540.2	2,092.5	756.4	497.2	259.2	1,336.0	10,946.5	11,460.2	11,017.6	4.7	5.2
04	-615.4	1,182.4	1,797.8	2,216.8	825.6	550.7	274.9	1,391.2	11,627.3	12,301.3	11,762.1	6.6	7.3
05	-713.6	1,311.5	2,025.1	2,355.3	875.5	588.1	287.4	1,479.8	12,378.6	13,135.5	12,514.9	6.3	6.8
06	-757.3	1,480.8	2,238.1	2,508.1	932.2	624.1	308.0	1,575.9	13,129.0	13,935.7	13,256.6	6.1	6.1
07	-707.8	1,662.4	2,370.2	2,674.8	979.3	662.2	317.1	1,695.5	13,811.2	14,515.3	13,910.0	4.8	4.2
05: I	-670.7	1,266.8	1,937.5	2,299.2	861.0	576.1	284.9	1,438.2	12,072.7	12,826.1	12,258.0	7.1	6.3
II	-680.9	1,305.1	1,986.0	2,328.0	867.1	584.4	282.8	1,460.9	12,278.1	12,978.4	12,389.7	4.8	4.8
III	-725.1	1,314.5	2,039.6	2,388.0	894.2	606.3	288.0	1,493.8	12,527.2	13,263.3	12,641.2	8.1	9.1
IV	-777.7	1,359.6	2,137.4	2,405.9	879.5	585.4	294.1	1,526.4	12,636.1	13,474.1	12,770.6	5.1	6.5
06: I	-761.7	1,423.2	2,184.9	2,458.4	922.8	613.6	309.3	1,535.5	12,906.5	13,721.4	13,039.2	8.6	7.5
II	-777.2	1,462.8	2,240.0	2,495.7	928.5	623.1	305.4	1,567.2	13,068.3	13,911.3	13,219.4	5.5	5.7
III	-792.7	1,492.5	2,285.2	2,526.9	935.5	624.0	311.5	1,591.4	13,187.1	14,042.3	13,316.1	3.6	3.8
IV	-697.7	1,544.5	2,242.2	2,551.4	941.7	635.9	305.9	1,609.7	13,354.3	14,067.9	13,452.0	3.7	.7
07: I	-728.8	1,560.5	2,289.4	2,597.0	950.3	636.9	313.4	1,646.8	13,526.5	14,239.7	13,583.3	4.3	5.0
II	-723.1	1,614.4	2,337.5	2,655.9	974.6	656.8	317.8	1,681.3	13,738.4	14,460.6	13,797.2	6.9	6.4
III	-682.6	1,714.9	2,397.5	2,703.5	994.0	675.6	318.3	1,709.5	13,927.6	14,633.1	14,062.8	6.3	4.9
IV	-696.7	1,759.7	2,456.5	2,742.9	998.3	679.3	319.0	1,744.6	14,052.3	14,728.0	14,196.6	2.3	2.6
08: I	-705.7	1,820.8	2,526.5	2,798.1	1,026.5	699.9	326.6	1,771.6	14,176.4	14,856.6	14,289.0	3.5	3.5
II	-718.2	1,923.2	2,641.4	2,873.7	1,056.1	723.3	332.9	1,817.6	14,370.5	15,012.7	14,408.3	4.1	4.3
III p	-706.5	1,971.3	2,677.9	2,943.9	1,097.7	759.5	338.2	1,846.2	14,469.1	15,127.0	14,538.0	3.6	3.1

[1] Gross domestic product (GDP) less exports of goods and services plus imports of goods and services.
[2] GDP plus net income receipts from rest of the world.

Source: Department of Commerce (Bureau of Economic Analysis).

TABLE B–2.—Real gross domestic product, 1959–2008

[Billions of chained (2000) dollars, except as noted; quarterly data at seasonally adjusted annual rates]

Year or quarter	Gross domestic product	Personal consumption expenditures				Gross private domestic investment						
		Total	Durable goods	Non-durable goods	Services	Total	Fixed investment					Change in private inventories
							Total	Nonresidential			Residential	
								Total	Structures	Equipment and software		
1959	2,441.3	1,554.6	....	....	....	266.7	....	....	....	....	....	....
1960	2,501.8	1,597.4	....	....	....	266.6	....	....	....	....	....	....
1961	2,560.0	1,630.3	....	....	....	264.9	....	....	....	....	....	....
1962	2,715.2	1,711.1	....	....	....	298.4	....	....	....	....	....	....
1963	2,834.0	1,781.6	....	....	....	318.5	....	....	....	....	....	....
1964	2,998.6	1,888.4	....	....	....	344.7	....	....	....	....	....	....
1965	3,191.1	2,007.7	....	....	....	393.1	....	....	....	....	....	....
1966	3,399.1	2,121.8	....	....	....	427.7	....	....	....	....	....	....
1967	3,484.6	2,185.0	....	....	....	408.1	....	....	....	....	....	....
1968	3,652.7	2,310.5	....	....	....	431.9	....	....	....	....	....	....
1969	3,765.4	2,396.4	....	....	....	457.1	....	....	....	....	....	....
1970	3,771.9	2,451.9	....	....	....	427.1	....	....	....	....	....	....
1971	3,898.6	2,545.5	....	....	....	475.7	....	....	....	....	....	....
1972	4,105.0	2,701.3	....	....	....	532.1	....	....	....	....	....	....
1973	4,341.5	2,833.8	....	....	....	594.4	....	....	....	....	....	....
1974	4,319.6	2,812.3	....	....	....	550.6	....	....	....	....	....	....
1975	4,311.2	2,876.9	....	....	....	453.1	....	....	....	....	....	....
1976	4,540.9	3,035.5	....	....	....	544.7	....	....	....	....	....	....
1977	4,750.5	3,164.1	....	....	....	627.0	....	....	....	....	....	....
1978	5,015.0	3,303.1	....	....	....	702.6	....	....	....	....	....	....
1979	5,173.4	3,383.4	....	....	....	725.0	....	....	....	....	....	....
1980	5,161.7	3,374.1	....	....	....	645.3	....	....	....	....	....	....
1981	5,291.7	3,422.2	....	....	....	704.9	....	....	....	....	....	....
1982	5,189.3	3,470.3	....	....	....	606.0	....	....	....	....	....	....
1983	5,423.8	3,668.6	....	....	....	662.5	....	....	....	....	....	....
1984	5,813.6	3,863.3	....	....	....	857.7	....	....	....	....	....	....
1985	6,053.7	4,064.0	....	....	....	849.7	....	....	....	....	....	....
1986	6,263.6	4,228.9	....	....	....	843.9	....	....	....	....	....	....
1987	6,475.1	4,369.8	....	....	....	870.0	....	....	....	....	....	....
1988	6,742.7	4,546.9	....	....	....	890.5	....	....	....	....	....	....
1989	6,981.4	4,675.0	....	....	....	926.2	....	....	....	....	....	....
1990	7,112.5	4,770.3	453.5	1,484.0	2,851.7	895.1	886.6	595.1	275.2	355.0	298.9	15.4
1991	7,100.5	4,778.4	427.9	1,480.5	2,900.0	822.2	829.1	563.2	244.6	345.9	270.2	–.5
1992	7,336.6	4,934.8	453.0	1,510.1	3,000.8	889.0	878.3	581.3	229.9	371.1	307.6	16.5
1993	7,532.7	5,099.8	488.4	1,550.4	3,085.7	968.3	953.5	631.9	228.3	417.4	332.7	20.6
1994	7,835.5	5,290.7	529.4	1,603.9	3,176.6	1,099.6	1,042.3	689.9	232.3	467.2	364.8	63.6
1995	8,031.7	5,433.5	552.6	1,638.6	3,259.9	1,134.0	1,109.6	762.5	247.1	523.1	353.1	29.9
1996	8,328.9	5,619.4	595.9	1,680.4	3,356.0	1,234.3	1,209.2	833.6	261.1	578.7	381.3	28.7
1997	8,703.5	5,831.8	646.9	1,725.3	3,468.0	1,387.7	1,320.6	934.2	280.1	658.3	388.6	71.2
1998	9,066.9	6,125.8	720.3	1,794.4	3,615.0	1,524.1	1,455.0	1,037.8	294.5	745.6	418.3	72.6
1999	9,470.3	6,438.6	804.6	1,876.6	3,758.0	1,642.6	1,576.3	1,133.3	293.2	840.2	443.6	68.9
2000	9,817.0	6,739.4	863.3	1,947.2	3,928.8	1,735.5	1,679.0	1,232.1	313.2	918.9	446.9	56.5
2001	9,890.7	6,910.4	900.7	1,986.7	4,023.2	1,598.4	1,629.4	1,180.5	306.1	874.2	448.5	–31.7
2002	10,048.8	7,099.3	964.8	2,037.1	4,100.4	1,557.1	1,544.6	1,071.5	253.8	820.2	469.9	12.5
2003	10,301.0	7,295.3	1,020.6	2,103.0	4,178.8	1,613.1	1,596.9	1,081.8	243.5	843.1	509.4	14.3
2004	10,675.8	7,561.4	1,084.8	2,177.6	4,311.0	1,770.2	1,712.8	1,144.3	246.7	905.1	560.2	–54.3
2005	10,989.5	7,791.7	1,185.1	2,252.7	4,420.9	1,873.5	1,829.8	1,226.2	249.8	989.6	595.4	38.9
2006	11,294.8	8,029.0	1,185.1	2,335.3	4,529.9	1,912.5	1,865.5	1,318.2	270.3	1,061.0	552.9	42.3
2007	11,523.9	8,252.8	1,242.4	2,392.6	4,646.2	1,809.7	1,808.5	1,382.9	304.6	1,078.9	453.8	–2.5
2005: I	10,875.8	7,697.5	1,111.6	2,220.7	4,379.3	1,869.1	1,790.5	1,200.4	253.1	956.6	582.1	74.6
II	10,946.1	7,766.4	1,143.7	2,243.7	4,398.2	1,844.8	1,823.5	1,219.0	252.3	977.9	595.8	16.7
III	11,050.0	7,838.1	1,158.9	2,260.1	4,439.4	1,862.8	1,847.2	1,237.1	246.2	1,006.5	601.7	11.0
IV	11,086.1	7,864.9	1,123.3	2,286.3	4,466.9	1,917.3	1,858.0	1,248.2	247.4	1,017.4	602.0	53.5
2006: I	11,217.3	7,947.4	1,173.1	2,310.8	4,484.7	1,946.3	1,895.2	1,295.2	256.5	1,056.6	596.5	45.9
II	11,291.7	8,002.1	1,178.3	2,328.7	4,515.7	1,944.3	1,883.1	1,315.4	268.3	1,061.2	570.1	56.9
III	11,314.1	8,046.3	1,188.4	2,342.0	4,537.6	1,917.8	1,860.0	1,332.7	277.4	1,066.4	536.7	53.3
IV	11,356.4	8,119.9	1,200.7	2,359.8	4,581.5	1,841.6	1,823.7	1,329.3	279.1	1,059.9	508.4	13.1
2007: I	11,357.8	8,197.2	1,227.3	2,380.1	4,616.1	1,795.9	1,807.8	1,340.4	286.6	1,060.0	486.4	–15.0
II	11,491.4	8,237.3	1,242.3	2,391.5	4,632.7	1,822.9	1,821.3	1,373.8	298.9	1,077.9	471.7	–2.8
III	11,625.7	8,278.5	1,249.4	2,398.6	4,659.8	1,838.7	1,817.0	1,402.9	313.2	1,087.5	445.3	16.0
IV	11,620.7	8,298.2	1,250.6	2,400.2	4,676.1	1,781.3	1,788.2	1,414.7	319.7	1,090.1	411.6	–8.1
2008: I	11,646.0	8,316.1	1,237.0	2,397.9	4,704.3	1,754.7	1,762.4	1,423.1	326.4	1,088.6	383.0	–10.2
II	11,727.4	8,341.3	1,228.3	2,420.7	4,712.1	1,702.0	1,754.9	1,431.8	340.5	1,074.7	369.6	–50.6
III p	11,712.3	8,262.1	1,178.8	2,377.8	4,712.2	1,703.9	1,730.0	1,426.5	346.0	1,059.2	352.1	–29.1

See next page for continuation of table.

TABLE B–2.—*Real gross domestic product, 1959–2008*—Continued

[Billions of chained (2000) dollars, except as noted; quarterly data at seasonally adjusted annual rates]

Year or quarter	Net exports of goods and services			Government consumption expenditures and gross investment					Final sales of domestic product	Gross domestic purchases [1]	Adden- dum: Gross national product [2]	Percent change from preceding period	
	Net exports	Exports	Imports	Total	Federal			State and local				Gross domestic product	Gross domestic purchases [1]
					Total	National defense	Non- defense						
59	....	77.2	101.9	714.3	....	....	....	....	2,442.7	2,485.9	2,457.4	7.1	7.1
60	....	90.6	103.3	715.4	....	....	....	....	2,506.8	2,529.6	2,519.4	2.5	1.8
61	....	91.1	102.6	751.3	....	....	....	....	2,566.8	2,587.6	2,579.3	2.3	2.3
62	....	95.7	114.3	797.6	....	....	....	....	2,708.5	2,751.4	2,736.9	6.1	6.3
63	....	102.5	117.3	818.1	....	....	....	....	2,830.3	2,866.0	2,857.2	4.4	4.2
64	....	114.6	123.6	836.1	....	....	....	....	2,999.9	3,023.2	3,023.6	5.8	5.5
65	....	117.8	136.7	861.3	....	....	....	....	3,173.8	3,228.6	3,217.3	6.4	6.8
66	....	126.0	157.1	937.1	....	....	....	....	3,364.8	3,450.3	3,423.7	6.5	6.9
67	....	128.9	168.5	1,008.9	....	....	....	....	3,467.6	3,545.1	3,510.1	2.5	2.7
68	....	139.0	193.6	1,040.5	....	....	....	....	3,640.3	3,727.5	3,680.0	4.8	5.1
69	....	145.7	204.6	1,038.0	....	....	....	....	3,753.7	3,844.1	3,792.0	3.1	3.1
70	....	161.4	213.4	1,012.9	....	....	....	....	3,787.7	3,837.4	3,798.2	.2	-.2
71	....	164.1	224.7	990.8	....	....	....	....	3,893.4	3,974.2	3,927.8	3.4	3.6
72	....	176.5	250.0	983.5	....	....	....	....	4,098.6	4,192.8	4,136.2	5.3	5.5
73	....	209.7	261.6	980.0	....	....	....	....	4,315.9	4,399.1	4,383.6	5.8	4.9
74	....	226.3	255.7	1,004.7	....	....	....	....	4,305.5	4,343.8	4,367.5	-.5	-1.3
75	....	224.9	227.3	1,027.4	....	....	....	....	4,352.5	4,297.0	4,348.4	-.2	-1.1
76	....	234.7	271.7	1,031.9	....	....	....	....	4,523.3	4,575.0	4,585.3	5.3	6.5
77	....	240.3	301.4	1,043.3	....	....	....	....	4,721.6	4,818.5	4,800.3	4.6	5.3
78	....	265.7	327.6	1,074.0	....	....	....	....	4,981.6	5,081.5	5,064.4	5.6	5.5
79	....	292.0	333.0	1,094.1	....	....	....	....	5,161.2	5,206.8	5,240.1	3.2	2.5
80	....	323.5	310.9	1,115.4	....	....	....	....	5,196.7	5,108.9	5,227.6	-.2	-1.9
81	....	327.4	319.1	1,125.6	....	....	....	....	5,265.1	5,244.7	5,349.7	2.5	2.7
82	....	302.4	315.0	1,145.4	....	....	....	....	5,233.4	5,175.1	5,249.7	-1.9	-1.3
83	....	294.6	354.8	1,187.3	....	....	....	....	5,454.0	5,477.6	5,482.5	4.5	5.8
84	....	318.7	441.1	1,227.0	....	....	....	....	5,739.2	5,951.6	5,869.3	7.2	8.7
85	....	328.3	469.8	1,312.5	....	....	....	....	6,042.1	6,215.8	6,093.4	4.1	4.4
86	....	353.7	510.0	1,392.5	....	....	....	....	6,271.8	6,443.6	6,290.6	3.5	3.7
87	....	391.8	540.2	1,426.7	....	....	....	....	6,457.2	6,644.1	6,500.9	3.4	3.1
88	....	454.6	561.4	1,445.1	....	....	....	....	6,734.5	6,857.9	6,775.2	4.1	3.2
89	....	506.8	586.0	1,482.5	....	....	....	....	6,962.2	7,060.8	7,015.4	3.5	3.0
90	-54.7	552.5	607.1	1,530.0	659.1	479.4	178.6	868.4	7,108.5	7,161.6	7,155.2	1.9	1.4
91	-14.6	589.1	603.7	1,547.2	658.0	474.2	182.8	886.8	7,115.0	7,101.2	7,136.8	-.2	-.8
92	-15.9	629.7	645.6	1,555.3	646.6	450.7	195.4	906.5	7,331.1	7,338.9	7,371.8	3.3	3.3
93	-52.1	650.0	702.1	1,541.1	619.6	425.3	194.1	919.5	7,522.3	7,577.2	7,568.6	2.7	3.2
94	-79.4	706.5	785.9	1,541.3	596.4	404.6	191.7	943.3	7,777.8	7,911.3	7,864.2	4.0	4.4
95	-71.0	778.2	849.1	1,549.7	580.3	389.2	191.0	968.3	8,010.2	8,098.4	8,069.8	2.5	2.4
96	-79.6	843.4	923.0	1,564.9	573.5	383.8	189.6	990.5	8,306.5	8,405.7	8,365.3	3.7	3.8
97	-104.6	943.7	1,048.3	1,594.0	567.6	373.0	194.5	1,025.9	8,636.6	8,807.6	8,737.5	4.5	4.8
98	-203.7	966.5	1,170.3	1,624.4	561.2	365.3	195.9	1,063.0	8,997.6	9,272.5	9,088.7	4.2	5.3
99	-296.2	1,008.2	1,304.4	1,686.9	573.7	372.2	201.5	1,113.2	9,404.0	9,767.7	9,504.7	4.5	5.3
00	-379.5	1,096.3	1,475.8	1,721.6	578.8	370.3	208.5	1,142.8	9,760.5	10,196.4	9,855.9	3.7	4.4
01	-399.1	1,036.7	1,435.8	1,780.3	601.4	384.9	216.5	1,179.0	9,920.9	10,290.1	9,933.6	.8	.9
02	-471.3	1,013.3	1,484.6	1,858.8	643.4	413.2	230.2	1,215.4	10,036.5	10,517.7	10,079.0	1.6	2.2
03	-518.9	1,026.1	1,545.0	1,904.8	687.1	449.0	238.0	1,217.8	10,285.1	10,815.5	10,355.3	2.5	2.8
04	-593.8	1,126.1	1,719.9	1,931.8	715.9	475.0	240.7	1,215.8	10,619.8	11,261.4	10,746.0	3.6	4.1
05	-616.6	1,205.3	1,821.9	1,939.0	724.5	482.2	242.0	1,214.3	10,947.3	11,597.8	11,072.1	2.9	3.0
06	-615.7	1,314.8	1,930.5	1,971.2	741.0	490.0	250.8	1,230.2	11,249.3	11,904.1	11,362.3	2.8	2.6
07	-546.5	1,425.9	1,972.4	2,012.1	752.9	502.1	250.4	1,259.0	11,523.4	12,066.8	11,609.8	2.0	1.4
05: I	-623.7	1,177.9	1,801.7	1,929.6	718.0	476.3	241.5	1,211.4	10,799.3	11,490.6	10,968.4	3.0	2.5
II	-601.3	1,203.1	1,804.4	1,934.0	720.1	481.0	238.8	1,213.8	10,925.9	11,539.4	11,028.4	2.6	1.7
III	-603.6	1,204.3	1,807.9	1,950.4	736.8	495.1	241.4	1,213.6	11,035.5	11,645.4	11,140.7	3.8	3.7
IV	-637.8	1,235.7	1,873.6	1,941.9	723.2	476.5	246.5	1,218.5	11,028.4	11,716.2	11,151.2	1.3	2.5
06: I	-636.0	1,284.3	1,920.2	1,960.5	740.6	486.7	253.8	1,219.9	11,167.6	11,846.2	11,286.5	4.8	4.5
II	-619.4	1,301.4	1,920.9	1,966.6	737.7	489.0	248.5	1,228.8	11,232.1	11,904.4	11,365.1	2.7	2.0
III	-623.0	1,312.6	1,935.7	1,974.9	741.1	487.9	253.1	1,233.7	11,257.8	11,930.6	11,370.8	.8	.9
IV	-584.3	1,361.1	1,945.3	1,982.7	744.4	496.3	247.8	1,238.2	11,339.7	11,935.6	11,426.5	1.5	.2
07: I	-618.6	1,363.2	1,981.8	1,987.1	737.5	488.8	248.6	1,249.3	11,370.5	11,970.9	11,419.1	.1	1.2
II	-571.2	1,392.2	1,963.4	2,006.4	749.6	498.8	250.5	1,256.6	11,490.5	12,058.2	11,541.7	4.8	2.9
III	-511.8	1,466.2	1,978.0	2,025.3	762.7	511.0	251.2	1,262.6	11,605.0	12,135.1	11,719.9	4.8	2.6
IV	-484.5	1,482.1	1,966.5	2,029.4	761.7	509.9	251.5	1,267.5	11,628.0	12,103.2	11,758.3	-.2	-1.0
08: I	-462.0	1,500.6	1,962.6	2,039.1	772.6	518.9	253.2	1,266.7	11,653.7	12,105.8	11,760.9	.9	.1
II	-381.3	1,544.7	1,926.0	2,058.9	785.0	528.1	256.3	1,274.4	11,778.8	12,102.6	11,822.2	2.8	-.1
III p	-352.3	1,557.8	1,910.2	2,085.9	810.4	550.5	259.1	1,276.9	11,737.9	12,057.1	11,809.6	-.5	-1.5

[1] Gross domestic product (GDP) less exports of goods and services plus imports of goods and services.
[2] GDP plus net income receipts from rest of the world.

Source: Department of Commerce (Bureau of Economic Analysis).

TABLE B–3.—*Quantity and price indexes for gross domestic product, and percent changes, 1959–2008*

[Quarterly data are seasonally adjusted]

Year or quarter	Index numbers, 2000=100					Percent change from preceding period [1]				
	Gross domestic product (GDP)			Personal consumption expenditures (PCE)		Gross domestic product (GDP)			Personal consumption expenditures (PCE)	
	Real GDP (chain-type quantity index)	GDP chain-type price index	GDP implicit price deflator	PCE chain-type price index	PCE less food and energy price index	Real GDP (chain-type quantity index)	GDP chain-type price index	GDP implicit price deflator	PCE chain-type price index	PCE less food and energy price index
1959	24.868	20.754	20.751	20.432	21.031	7.1	1.2	1.2	1.6	2.2
1960	25.484	21.044	21.041	20.767	21.382	2.5	1.4	1.4	1.6	1.7
1961	26.077	21.281	21.278	20.985	21.640	2.3	1.1	1.1	1.0	1.2
1962	27.658	21.572	21.569	21.232	21.911	6.1	1.4	1.4	1.2	1.3
1963	28.868	21.801	21.798	21.479	22.175	4.4	1.1	1.1	1.2	1.2
1964	30.545	22.134	22.131	21.786	22.497	5.8	1.5	1.5	1.4	1.5
1965	32.506	22.538	22.535	22.103	22.771	6.4	1.8	1.8	1.5	1.2
1966	34.625	23.180	23.176	22.662	23.246	6.5	2.8	2.8	2.5	2.1
1967	35.496	23.897	23.893	23.237	23.915	2.5	3.1	3.1	2.5	2.9
1968	37.208	24.916	24.913	24.151	24.931	4.8	4.3	4.3	3.9	4.2
1969	38.356	26.153	26.149	25.255	26.089	3.1	5.0	5.0	4.6	4.6
1970	38.422	27.534	27.534	26.448	27.270	.2	5.3	5.3	4.7	4.5
1971	39.713	28.916	28.911	27.574	28.538	3.4	5.0	5.0	4.3	4.6
1972	41.815	30.171	30.166	28.528	29.462	5.3	4.3	4.3	3.5	3.2
1973	44.224	31.854	31.849	30.081	30.533	5.8	5.6	5.6	5.4	3.6
1974	44.001	34.721	34.725	33.191	32.825	−.5	9.0	9.0	10.3	7.5
1975	43.916	38.007	38.002	35.955	35.543	−.2	9.5	9.4	8.3	8.3
1976	46.256	40.202	40.196	37.948	37.716	5.3	5.8	5.8	5.5	6.1
1977	48.391	42.758	42.752	40.410	40.112	4.6	6.4	6.4	6.5	6.4
1978	51.085	45.762	45.757	43.248	42.756	5.6	7.0	7.0	7.0	6.6
1979	52.699	49.553	49.548	47.059	45.735	3.2	8.3	8.3	8.8	7.0
1980	52.579	54.062	54.043	52.078	49.869	−.2	9.1	9.1	10.7	9.0
1981	53.904	59.128	59.119	56.720	54.215	2.5	9.4	9.4	8.9	8.7
1982	52.860	62.738	62.726	59.859	57.776	−1.9	6.1	6.1	5.5	6.6
1983	55.249	65.214	65.207	62.436	60.823	4.5	3.9	4.0	4.3	5.3
1984	59.220	67.664	67.655	64.795	63.352	7.2	3.8	3.8	3.8	4.2
1985	61.666	69.724	69.713	66.936	65.778	4.1	3.0	3.0	3.3	3.8
1986	63.804	71.269	71.250	68.569	68.244	3.5	2.2	2.2	2.4	3.7
1987	65.958	73.204	73.196	70.947	70.772	3.4	2.7	2.7	3.5	3.7
1988	68.684	75.706	75.694	73.755	73.838	4.1	3.4	3.4	4.0	4.3
1989	71.116	78.569	78.556	76.972	76.884	3.5	3.8	3.8	4.4	4.1
1990	72.451	81.614	81.590	80.498	80.156	1.9	3.9	3.9	4.6	4.3
1991	72.329	84.457	84.444	83.419	83.292	−.2	3.5	3.5	3.6	3.9
1992	74.734	86.402	86.385	85.824	86.130	3.3	2.3	2.3	2.9	3.4
1993	76.731	88.390	88.381	87.804	88.332	2.7	2.3	2.3	2.3	2.6
1994	79.816	90.265	90.259	89.654	90.372	4.0	2.1	2.1	2.1	2.3
1995	81.814	92.115	92.106	91.577	92.388	2.5	2.0	2.0	2.1	2.2
1996	84.842	93.859	93.852	93.547	94.124	3.7	1.9	1.9	2.2	1.9
1997	88.658	95.415	95.414	95.124	95.644	4.5	1.7	1.7	1.7	1.6
1998	92.359	96.475	96.472	95.978	96.895	4.2	1.1	1.1	.9	1.3
1999	96.469	97.868	97.868	97.575	98.343	4.5	1.4	1.4	1.7	1.5
2000	100.000	100.000	100.000	100.000	100.000	3.7	2.2	2.2	2.5	1.7
2001	100.751	102.402	102.399	102.094	101.904	.8	2.4	2.4	2.1	1.9
2002	102.362	104.193	104.187	103.542	103.705	1.6	1.7	1.7	1.4	1.8
2003	104.931	106.409	106.404	105.597	105.175	2.5	2.1	2.1	2.0	1.4
2004	108.748	109.462	109.462	108.392	107.338	3.6	2.9	2.9	2.6	2.1
2005	111.944	113.039	113.034	111.581	109.644	2.9	3.3	3.3	2.9	2.1
2006	115.054	116.676	116.676	114.675	112.129	2.8	3.2	3.2	2.8	2.3
2007	117.388	119.819	119.816	117.659	114.548	2.0	2.7	2.7	2.6	2.2
2005: I	110.786	111.778	111.765	110.187	108.838	3.0	4.0	4.0	2.5	2.5
II	111.502	112.357	112.346	110.881	109.405	2.6	2.1	2.1	2.5	2.1
III	112.560	113.487	113.468	112.168	109.838	3.8	4.1	4.1	4.7	1.6
IV	112.928	114.536	114.525	113.089	110.495	1.3	3.7	3.8	3.3	2.4
2006: I	114.264	115.536	115.533	113.581	111.076	4.8	3.5	3.6	1.8	2.1
II	115.022	116.317	116.317	114.499	111.887	2.7	2.7	2.7	3.3	3.0
III	115.250	117.109	117.107	115.381	112.531	.8	2.8	2.7	3.1	2.3
IV	115.681	117.742	117.732	115.239	113.022	1.5	2.2	2.2	−.5	1.8
2007: I	115.696	118.935	118.956	116.202	113.682	.1	4.1	4.2	3.4	2.4
II	117.056	119.531	119.547	117.246	114.201	4.8	2.0	2.0	3.6	1.8
III	118.425	119.984	119.997	117.969	114.797	4.8	1.5	1.5	2.5	2.1
IV	118.374	120.826	120.743	119.221	115.512	−.2	2.8	2.5	4.3	2.5
2008: I	118.631	121.613	121.508	120.283	116.158	.9	2.6	2.6	3.6	2.3
II	119.460	121.951	121.890	121.544	116.782	2.8	1.1	1.3	4.3	2.2
III *p*	119.307	123.205	123.122	123.091	117.540	−.5	4.2	4.1	5.2	2.6

[1] Quarterly percent changes are at annual rates.

Source: Department of Commerce (Bureau of Economic Analysis).

TABLE B–4.—*Percent changes in real gross domestic product, 1959–2008*

[Percent change from preceding period; quarterly data at seasonally adjusted annual rates]

Year or quarter	Gross domestic product	Personal consumption expenditures				Gross private domestic investment				Exports and imports of goods and services		Government consumption expenditures and gross investment		
						Nonresidential fixed			Residential fixed					
		Total	Durable goods	Non-durable goods	Services	Total	Structures	Equipment and software		Exports	Imports	Total	Federal	State and local
59	7.1	5.6	12.1	4.1	5.3	8.0	2.4	11.9	25.4	10.3	10.5	3.4	3.1	3.8
60	2.5	2.8	2.0	1.5	4.5	5.7	7.9	4.2	-7.1	17.4	1.3	.2	-2.7	4.4
61	2.3	2.1	-3.8	1.8	4.2	-.6	1.4	-1.9	.3	.5	-.7	5.0	4.2	6.2
62	6.1	5.0	11.7	3.1	5.0	8.7	4.5	11.6	9.6	5.1	11.3	6.2	8.5	3.1
63	4.4	4.1	9.7	2.1	4.6	5.6	1.1	8.4	11.8	7.1	2.7	2.6	.1	6.0
64	5.8	6.0	9.3	4.9	6.1	11.9	10.4	12.8	5.8	11.8	5.3	2.2	-1.3	6.8
65	6.4	6.3	12.7	5.3	5.3	17.4	15.9	18.3	-2.9	2.8	10.6	3.0	.0	6.7
66	6.5	5.7	8.4	5.5	5.0	12.5	6.8	16.0	-8.9	6.9	14.9	8.8	11.0	6.3
67	2.5	3.0	1.6	1.6	4.9	-1.4	-2.5	-.7	-3.1	2.3	7.3	7.7	9.9	5.0
68	4.8	5.7	11.0	4.6	5.2	4.5	1.5	6.2	13.6	7.9	14.9	3.1	.8	5.9
69	3.1	3.7	3.5	2.7	4.8	7.6	5.4	8.8	3.0	4.8	5.7	-.2	-3.4	3.4
70	.2	2.3	-3.2	2.4	4.0	-.5	.3	-1.0	-6.0	10.7	4.3	-2.4	-7.4	2.8
71	3.4	3.8	10.0	1.8	3.9	.0	-1.6	1.0	27.4	1.7	5.3	-2.2	-7.7	3.1
72	5.3	6.1	12.7	4.4	5.7	9.2	3.1	12.9	17.8	7.5	11.3	-.7	-4.1	2.2
73	5.8	4.9	10.3	3.3	4.7	14.6	8.2	18.3	-.6	18.9	4.6	-.4	-4.2	2.8
74	-.5	-.8	-6.9	-2.0	2.3	.8	-2.1	2.6	-20.6	7.9	-2.3	2.5	.9	3.8
75	-.2	2.3	.0	1.5	3.7	-9.9	-10.5	-9.5	-13.0	-.6	-11.1	2.3	.3	3.7
76	5.3	5.5	12.8	4.9	4.4	4.9	2.4	6.2	23.6	4.4	19.5	.4	.0	.7
77	4.6	4.2	9.3	2.4	4.3	11.3	4.1	15.1	21.5	2.4	10.9	1.1	2.1	.4
78	5.6	4.4	5.3	3.7	4.7	15.0	14.4	15.2	6.3	10.5	8.7	2.9	2.5	3.3
79	3.2	2.4	-.3	2.7	3.1	10.1	12.7	8.7	-3.7	9.9	1.7	1.9	2.4	1.5
80	-.2	-.3	-7.8	-.2	1.8	-.3	5.8	-3.6	-21.2	10.8	-6.6	2.0	4.7	-.1
81	2.5	1.4	1.2	1.2	1.7	5.7	8.0	4.3	-8.0	1.2	2.6	.9	4.8	-2.0
82	-1.9	1.4	-.1	1.0	2.1	-3.8	-1.7	-5.2	-18.2	-7.6	-1.3	1.8	3.9	.1
83	4.5	5.7	14.6	3.3	5.5	-1.3	-10.8	5.4	41.4	-2.6	12.6	3.7	6.6	1.2
84	7.2	5.3	14.6	4.0	4.1	17.7	14.0	19.8	14.8	8.2	24.3	3.3	3.1	3.6
85	4.1	5.2	10.1	2.7	5.6	6.6	7.1	6.4	1.6	3.0	6.5	7.0	7.8	6.2
86	3.5	4.1	9.7	3.6	2.9	-2.9	-11.0	1.9	12.3	7.7	8.6	6.1	5.7	6.4
87	3.4	3.3	1.7	2.4	4.3	-.1	-2.9	1.4	2.0	10.8	5.9	2.5	3.6	1.5
88	4.1	4.1	6.0	3.3	4.0	5.2	.6	7.5	-1.0	16.0	3.9	1.3	-1.6	3.7
89	3.5	2.8	2.2	2.8	3.0	5.6	2.0	7.3	-3.0	11.5	4.4	2.6	1.5	3.4
90	1.9	2.0	-.3	1.6	2.9	.5	1.5	.0	-8.6	9.0	3.6	3.2	2.0	4.1
91	-.2	.2	-5.6	-.2	1.7	-5.4	-11.1	-2.6	-9.6	6.6	-.6	1.1	-.2	2.1
92	3.3	3.3	5.9	2.0	3.5	3.2	-6.0	7.3	13.8	6.9	7.0	.5	-1.7	2.2
93	2.7	3.3	7.8	2.7	2.8	8.7	-.7	12.5	8.2	3.2	8.8	-.9	-4.2	1.4
94	4.0	3.7	8.4	3.5	2.9	9.2	1.8	11.9	9.6	8.7	11.9	.0	-3.7	2.6
95	2.5	2.7	4.4	2.2	2.6	10.5	6.4	12.0	-3.2	10.1	8.0	.5	-2.7	2.6
96	3.7	3.4	7.8	2.6	2.9	9.3	5.6	10.6	8.0	8.4	8.7	1.0	-1.2	2.3
97	4.5	3.8	8.6	2.7	3.3	12.1	7.3	13.8	1.9	11.9	13.6	1.9	-1.0	3.6
98	4.2	5.0	11.3	4.0	4.2	11.1	5.1	13.3	7.6	2.4	11.6	1.9	-1.1	3.6
99	4.5	5.1	11.7	4.6	4.0	9.2	-.4	12.7	6.0	4.3	11.5	3.9	2.2	4.7
00	3.7	4.7	7.3	3.8	4.5	8.7	6.8	9.4	.8	8.7	13.1	2.1	.9	2.7
01	.8	2.5	4.3	2.0	2.4	-4.2	-2.3	-4.9	.4	-5.4	-2.7	3.4	3.9	3.2
02	1.6	2.7	7.1	2.5	1.9	-9.2	-17.1	-6.2	4.8	-2.3	3.4	4.4	7.0	3.1
03	2.5	2.8	5.8	3.2	1.9	1.0	-4.1	2.8	8.4	1.3	4.1	2.5	6.8	.2
04	3.6	3.6	6.3	3.5	3.2	5.8	1.3	7.4	10.0	9.7	11.3	1.4	4.2	-.2
05	2.9	3.0	4.6	3.4	2.6	7.2	1.3	9.3	6.3	7.0	5.9	.4	1.2	-.1
06	2.8	3.0	4.5	3.7	2.5	7.5	8.2	7.2	-7.1	9.1	6.0	1.7	2.3	1.3
07	2.0	2.8	4.8	2.5	2.6	4.9	12.7	1.7	-17.9	8.4	2.2	2.1	1.6	2.3
05: I	3.0	1.7	.6	2.4	1.7	3.7	7.5	2.3	8.1	8.1	3.2	-.2	1.1	-1.0
II	2.6	3.6	12.1	4.2	1.7	6.3	-1.3	9.2	9.7	8.8	.6	.9	1.1	.8
III	3.8	3.7	5.4	3.0	3.8	6.1	-9.2	12.2	4.0	.4	.8	3.4	9.7	-.1
IV	1.3	1.4	-11.7	4.7	2.5	3.7	1.9	4.4	.2	10.9	15.3	-1.7	-7.2	1.6
06: I	4.8	4.3	18.9	4.4	1.6	15.9	15.6	16.3	-3.6	16.7	10.3	3.9	10.0	.5
II	2.7	2.8	1.8	3.1	2.8	6.4	19.7	1.7	-16.6	5.5	.1	1.2	-1.5	2.9
III	.8	2.2	3.5	2.3	2.0	5.3	14.3	2.0	-21.4	3.5	3.1	1.7	1.9	1.6
IV	1.5	3.7	4.2	3.1	3.9	-1.0	2.5	-2.4	-19.5	15.6	2.0	1.6	1.8	1.5
07: I	.1	3.9	9.2	3.5	3.1	3.4	11.2	.0	-16.2	.6	7.7	.9	-3.6	3.6
II	4.8	2.0	5.0	1.9	1.4	10.3	18.3	6.9	-11.5	8.8	-3.7	3.9	6.7	2.4
III	4.8	2.0	2.3	1.2	2.4	8.7	20.5	3.6	-20.6	23.0	3.0	3.8	7.2	1.9
IV	-.2	1.0	.4	.3	1.4	3.4	8.5	1.0	-27.0	4.4	-2.3	.8	-.5	1.6
08: I	.9	.9	-4.3	-.4	2.4	2.4	8.6	-.6	-25.1	5.1	-8	1.9	5.8	-.3
II	2.8	1.2	-2.8	3.9	.7	2.5	18.5	-5.0	-13.3	12.3	-7.3	3.9	6.6	2.5
III p	-.5	-3.7	-15.2	-6.9	.0	-1.5	6.6	-5.7	-17.6	3.4	-3.2	5.4	13.6	.8

Note.—Percent changes based on unrounded data.

Source: Department of Commerce (Bureau of Economic Analysis).

TABLE B–5.—*Contributions to percent change in real gross domestic product, 1959–2008*

[Percentage points, except as noted; quarterly data at seasonally adjusted annual rates]

Year or quarter	Gross domestic product (percent change)	Personal consumption expenditures				Gross private domestic investment						Change in private inventories
		Total	Durable goods	Non-durable goods	Services	Total	Fixed investment Total	Nonresidential Total	Structures	Equipment and software	Residential	
1959	7.1	3.55	0.97	1.25	1.33	2.80	1.94	0.73	0.09	0.64	1.21	
1960	2.5	1.73	.17	.44	1.12	.00	.13	.52	.28	.24	−.39	
1961	2.3	1.30	−.31	.53	1.08	−.10	−.04	−.06	.05	−.11	.01	
1962	6.1	3.11	.89	.90	1.31	1.81	1.24	.78	.16	.61	.46	
1963	4.4	2.56	.77	.59	1.20	1.00	1.08	.50	.04	.46	.58	
1964	5.8	3.71	.77	1.33	1.61	1.25	1.37	1.07	.36	.71	.30	
1965	6.4	3.91	1.07	1.43	1.42	2.16	1.50	1.65	.57	1.07	−.15	
1966	6.5	3.50	.73	1.46	1.31	.87	.87	1.29	.27	1.02	−.43	
1967	2.5	1.81	.13	.42	1.26	−.76	−.28	−.15	−.10	−.05	−.13	
1968	4.8	3.50	.93	1.19	1.38	.90	1.00	.46	.06	.41	.53	
1969	3.1	2.27	.31	.69	1.28	.90	.90	.78	.20	.58	.13	
1970	.2	1.42	−.28	.61	1.08	−1.04	−.31	−.06	.01	−.07	−.26	
1971	3.4	2.38	.81	.47	1.09	1.67	1.10	.00	−.06	.07	1.10	
1972	5.3	3.80	1.07	1.11	1.61	1.87	1.81	.92	.12	.81	.89	
1973	5.8	3.05	.90	.82	1.33	1.96	1.46	1.50	.31	1.19	−.04	
1974	−.5	−.47	−.61	−.51	.65	−1.04	−1.30	.09	−.09	.18	−1.13	
1975	−.2	1.42	.00	.37	1.05	−2.98	−1.71	−1.14	−.43	−.70	−.57	−1.2
1976	5.3	3.48	1.04	1.24	1.19	2.84	1.42	.52	.09	.43	.90	1.4
1977	4.6	2.68	.80	.60	1.27	2.43	2.18	1.19	.15	1.04	.99	
1978	5.6	2.76	.47	.91	1.38	2.16	2.04	1.69	.54	1.15	.35	
1979	3.2	1.52	−.03	.65	.90	1.02	1.23	1.23	.52	.71	−.21	
1980	−.2	−.17	−.65	−.04	.52	−2.12	−1.21	−.04	.27	−.30	−1.17	
1981	2.5	.90	.09	.29	.51	1.59	.39	.74	.40	.34	−.35	
1982	−1.9	.87	.00	.23	.65	−2.55	−1.22	−.51	−.09	−.42	−.71	
1983	4.5	3.65	1.07	.80	1.79	1.45	1.17	−.16	−.57	.41	1.33	
1984	7.2	3.44	1.15	.93	1.36	4.63	2.68	2.05	.60	1.44	.64	
1985	4.1	3.31	.83	.61	1.87	−.17	.89	.82	.32	.50	.07	
1986	3.5	2.62	.83	.78	1.01	−.12	.20	−.36	−.50	.15	.55	
1987	3.4	2.17	.16	.52	1.50	.51	.09	−.01	−.11	.10	.10	
1988	4.1	2.66	.53	.70	1.43	.39	.52	.57	.02	.55	−.05	
1989	3.5	1.86	.19	.59	1.07	.64	.47	.61	.07	.54	−.14	
1990	1.9	1.34	−.02	.33	1.03	−.53	−.32	.05	.05	.00	−.37	
1991	−.2	.11	−.46	−.05	.62	−1.20	−.94	−.57	−.39	−.18	−.37	
1992	3.3	2.18	.44	.43	1.31	1.07	.79	.32	−.18	.50	.47	
1993	2.7	2.23	.59	.56	1.09	1.21	1.14	.83	−.02	.85	.31	
1994	4.0	2.52	.66	.71	1.14	1.93	1.30	.91	.05	.87	.39	
1995	2.5	1.81	.36	.44	1.01	.48	.94	1.08	.17	.91	−.14	
1996	3.7	2.31	.64	.51	1.15	1.35	1.34	1.01	.16	.85	.33	
1997	4.5	2.54	.70	.53	1.31	1.95	1.42	1.33	.21	1.12	.08	
1998	4.2	3.36	.93	.78	1.66	1.63	1.60	1.28	.16	1.12	.32	
1999	4.5	3.44	.99	.89	1.56	1.33	1.36	1.09	−.01	1.11	.27	
2000	3.7	3.17	.63	.74	1.80	.99	1.09	1.06	.21	.85	.03	
2001	.8	1.74	.37	.40	.97	−1.39	−.50	−.52	−.07	−.44	.02	
2002	1.6	1.90	.61	.50	.79	−.41	−.84	−1.06	−.55	−.51	.22	
2003	2.5	1.94	.50	.64	.80	.54	.51	.10	−.11	.21	.41	
2004	3.6	2.56	.53	.71	1.32	1.48	1.10	.56	.03	.53	.53	
2005	2.9	2.13	.38	.69	1.06	.95	1.08	.71	.03	.67	.37	
2006	2.8	2.13	.36	.74	1.02	.35	.32	.77	.23	.54	−.45	
2007	2.0	1.95	.38	.50	1.07	−.90	−.50	.52	.40	.13	−1.02	
2005: I	3.0	1.25	.04	.49	.72	1.48	.85	.37	.19	.18	.48	
II	2.6	2.50	.95	.83	.72	−.86	1.21	.64	−.04	.68	.57	−2.0
III	3.8	2.59	.44	.59	1.55	.69	.88	.64	−.26	.90	.25	
IV	1.3	.94	−1.02	.93	1.02	1.98	.41	.40	.05	.35	.01	1.5
2006: I	4.8	2.86	1.37	.85	.64	1.15	1.39	1.62	.42	1.20	−.23	
II	2.7	1.88	.14	.62	1.12	−.02	−.40	.71	.54	.16	−1.11	
III	.8	1.52	.27	.46	.79	−.92	−.81	.59	.42	.17	−1.40	
IV	1.5	2.55	.33	.62	1.61	−2.68	−1.27	−.09	.08	−.18	−1.18	−1.4
2007: I	.1	2.71	.71	.71	1.29	−1.63	−.57	.33	.35	−.02	−.91	−1.0
II	4.8	1.42	.40	.40	.62	.94	.47	1.07	.57	.50	−.60	
III	4.8	1.44	.19	.25	1.00	.54	−.15	.91	.65	.26	−1.06	
IV	−.2	.67	.03	.05	.59	−1.93	−.97	.36	.29	.07	−1.33	
2008: I	.9	.61	−.33	−.08	1.02	−.89	−.86	.26	.30	−.04	−1.12	
II	2.8	.87	−.21	.80	.28	−1.74	−.25	.27	.64	−.37	−.52	−1.5
III ᵖ	−.5	−2.69	−1.19	−1.51	.00	.06	−.82	−.16	.25	−.41	−.66	

See next page for continuation of table.

[Percentage points, except as noted; quarterly data at seasonally adjusted annual rates]

| Year or quarter | Net exports of goods and services | | | | | | | Government consumption expenditures and gross investment | | | | |
| | Net exports | Exports | | | Imports | | | Total | Federal | | | State and local |
		Total	Goods	Services	Total	Goods	Services		Total	National defense	Non-defense	
59	0.00	0.45	−0.02	0.48	−0.45	−0.48	0.03	0.76	0.42	−0.23	0.65	0.34
60	.72	.78	.76	.02	−.06	.05	−.11	.03	−.35	−.17	−.18	.39
61	.06	.03	.02	.01	.03	.00	.02	1.07	.51	.45	.06	.56
62	−.21	.25	.17	.08	−.47	−.40	−.07	1.36	1.07	.63	.44	.29
63	.24	.35	.29	.06	−.12	−.12	.00	.58	.01	−.25	.26	.57
64	.36	.59	.52	.07	−.23	−.19	−.04	.49	−.17	−.40	.23	.65
65	−.30	.15	.02	.13	−.45	−.41	−.04	.65	.00	−.19	.19	.66
66	−.29	.36	.27	.09	−.65	−.49	−.16	1.87	1.24	1.21	.03	.63
67	−.22	.12	.02	.10	−.34	−.17	−.16	1.68	1.17	1.19	−.02	.51
68	−.30	.41	.30	.10	−.70	−.68	−.03	.73	.10	.16	−.06	.63
69	−.04	.25	.20	.05	−.29	−.20	−.09	−.06	−.42	−.49	.06	.37
70	.34	.56	.44	.12	−.22	−.15	−.07	−.55	−.86	−.83	−.03	.31
71	−.19	.10	−.02	.11	−.29	−.33	.04	−.50	−.85	−.97	.12	.36
72	−.21	.42	.43	−.01	−.63	−.57	−.06	−.16	−.42	−.61	.18	.26
73	.82	1.12	1.01	.11	−.29	−.34	.05	−.08	−.41	−.39	−.02	.33
74	.75	.58	.46	.12	.18	.17	.00	.52	.08	−.05	.13	.44
75	.89	−.05	−.16	.10	.94	.87	.07	.48	.03	−.06	.09	.45
76	−1.08	.37	.31	.05	−1.45	−1.35	−.10	.10	.00	−.02	.03	.09
77	−.72	.20	.08	.11	−.92	−.84	−.07	.23	.19	.07	.12	.04
78	.05	.82	.68	.15	−.78	−.67	−.11	.60	.22	.05	.16	.38
79	.66	.82	.77	.06	−.16	−.14	−.02	.37	.20	.17	.03	.17
80	1.68	.97	.86	.11	.71	.67	.04	.38	.39	.25	.14	−.01
81	−.15	.12	−.09	.21	−.27	−.18	−.09	.19	.42	.38	.04	−.23
82	−.60	−.73	−.67	−.06	.12	.20	−.08	.35	.35	.48	−.13	.01
83	−1.35	−.22	−.19	−.03	−1.13	−1.00	−.13	.77	.63	.50	.13	.13
84	−1.58	.63	.46	.17	−2.21	−1.83	−.39	.70	.30	.35	−.05	.40
85	−.42	.23	.20	.02	−.65	−.52	−.13	1.41	.74	.60	.14	.67
86	−.30	.54	.26	.28	−.84	−.82	−.02	1.27	.55	.47	.08	.71
87	.17	.78	.56	.21	−.61	−.39	−.22	.52	.36	.35	.01	.17
88	.82	1.24	1.04	.20	−.42	−.36	−.07	.27	−.15	−.03	−.12	.42
89	.52	.99	.75	.24	−.47	−.38	−.10	.52	.14	−.03	.17	.39
90	.43	.81	.56	.26	−.39	−.26	−.13	.64	.18	.00	.18	.46
91	.69	.63	.46	.16	.06	.01	.05	.23	−.02	−.07	.06	.24
92	−.04	.68	.52	.16	−.72	−.77	.05	.11	−.15	−.32	.17	.26
93	−.59	.32	.23	.09	−.91	−.85	−.06	−.18	−.35	−.33	−.02	.17
94	−.43	.85	.67	.18	−1.29	−1.18	−.11	.00	−.30	−.27	−.03	.30
95	.11	1.04	.85	.19	−.93	−.87	−.06	.10	−.20	−.19	−.01	.30
96	−.14	.91	.68	.22	−1.05	−.94	−.11	.18	−.08	−.07	−.02	.26
97	−.34	1.30	1.11	.19	−1.64	−1.45	−.19	.34	−.07	−.13	.06	.41
98	−1.16	.27	.18	.09	−1.43	−1.20	−.23	.34	−.07	−.09	.02	.41
99	−.99	.47	.29	.18	−1.46	−1.31	−.15	.67	.14	.08	.06	.54
00	−.86	.93	.84	.09	−1.79	−1.55	−.25	.36	.05	−.02	.07	.31
01	−.20	−.60	−.48	−.12	.40	.39	.01	.60	.23	.15	.08	.37
02	−.69	−.23	−.28	.06	−.46	−.41	−.05	.80	.43	.29	.14	.37
03	−.44	.12	.12	.00	−.56	−.56	.00	.47	.44	.37	.08	.02
04	−.68	.93	.60	.33	−1.61	−1.33	−.27	.27	.29	.27	.03	−.02
05	−.21	.71	.54	.17	−.93	−.89	−.04	.07	.09	.07	.01	−.01
06	−.02	.96	.73	.23	−.98	−.82	−.16	.32	.16	.08	.08	.16
07	.58	.95	.59	.36	−.37	−.25	−.12	.40	.11	.12	.00	.28
05: I	.28	.80	.49	.31	−.52	−.67	.15	−.04	.08	.14	−.07	−.12
II	.79	.89	.98	−.09	−.10	−.10	.00	.17	.08	.18	−.11	.10
III	−.07	.04	−.06	.10	−.11	−.14	.03	.65	.66	.56	.10	−.01
IV	−1.26	1.09	.91	.18	−2.35	−2.18	−.17	−.34	−.53	−.73	.20	.19
06: I	.09	1.70	1.27	.42	−1.61	−1.18	−.43	.72	.66	.39	.27	.06
II	.59	.58	.49	.09	.01	−.04	.05	.23	−.11	.09	−.20	.34
III	−.12	.39	.28	.11	−.51	−.51	.01	.32	.13	−.04	.17	.19
IV	1.33	1.66	.78	.87	−.33	.13	−.46	.30	.12	.32	−.20	.18
07: I	−1.20	.06	.15	−.09	−1.25	−1.14	−.11	.17	−.26	−.29	.03	.43
II	1.66	1.01	.55	.46	.65	.59	.06	.77	.47	.40	.07	.30
III	2.03	2.54	1.66	.88	−.51	−.34	−.17	.75	.51	.48	.03	.24
IV	.94	.53	.43	.10	.40	.38	.02	.16	−.04	−.04	.01	.19
08: I	.77	.63	.39	.24	.14	.29	−.15	.38	.41	.34	.06	−.03
II	2.93	1.54	1.39	.15	1.39	1.14	.25	.78	.47	.36	.11	.31
III p	1.07	.46	.36	.10	.61	.70	−.09	1.06	.96	.85	.10	.10

Source: Department of Commerce (Bureau of Economic Analysis).

TABLE B–6.—*Chain-type quantity indexes for gross domestic product, 1959–2008*

[Index numbers, 2000=100; quarterly data seasonally adjusted]

Year or quarter	Gross domestic product	Personal consumption expenditures				Gross private domestic investment					
		Total	Durable goods	Non-durable goods	Services	Total	Fixed investment				
							Total	Nonresidential			Residential
								Total	Structures	Equipment and software	
1959	24.868	23.067	10.822	33.491	20.794	15.367	15.736	10.760	36.530	6.065	37.8
1960	25.484	23.702	11.041	33.994	21.720	15.362	15.870	11.371	39.433	6.322	35.1
1961	26.077	24.191	10.622	34.621	22.626	15.261	15.820	11.299	39.966	6.200	35.2
1962	27.658	25.389	11.865	35.710	23.747	17.197	17.248	12.284	41.775	6.917	38.6
1963	28.868	26.436	13.017	36.463	24.830	18.351	18.584	12.966	42.239	7.500	43.1
1964	30.545	28.020	14.222	38.248	26.345	19.863	20.378	14.504	46.626	8.457	45.6
1965	32.506	29.791	16.025	40.277	27.749	22.650	22.459	17.031	54.058	10.007	44.3
1966	34.625	31.484	17.377	42.487	29.129	24.644	23.745	19.160	57.751	11.609	40.3
1967	35.496	32.422	17.648	43.157	30.552	23.517	23.306	18.900	56.284	11.532	39.0
1968	37.208	34.284	19.594	45.126	32.148	24.887	24.935	19.746	57.102	12.250	44.4
1969	38.356	35.558	20.289	46.326	33.691	26.338	26.486	21.246	60.189	13.334	45.7
1970	38.422	36.381	19.631	47.436	35.038	24.608	25.931	21.134	60.364	13.201	42.9
1971	39.713	37.770	21.593	48.294	36.400	27.413	27.894	21.135	59.370	13.332	54.7
1972	41.815	40.082	24.336	50.422	38.469	30.658	31.246	23.072	61.201	15.052	64.5
1973	44.224	42.048	26.849	52.068	40.274	34.249	34.101	26.429	66.200	17.812	64.1
1974	44.001	41.729	25.001	51.020	41.216	31.729	31.971	26.653	64.785	18.268	50.8
1975	43.916	42.688	24.996	51.771	42.743	26.111	28.541	24.022	57.984	16.529	44.2
1976	46.256	45.041	28.187	54.301	44.475	31.387	31.356	25.200	59.390	17.562	54.6
1977	48.391	46.950	30.809	55.609	46.392	36.130	35.863	28.045	61.841	20.208	66.4
1978	51.085	49.012	32.435	57.687	48.558	40.486	40.205	32.243	70.769	23.284	70.6
1979	52.699	50.204	32.325	59.226	50.044	41.776	42.473	35.489	79.731	25.318	68.0
1980	52.579	50.065	29.788	59.137	50.921	37.182	39.708	35.388	84.350	24.407	53.6
1981	53.904	50.779	30.149	59.839	51.773	40.615	40.591	37.398	91.074	25.445	49.3
1982	52.860	51.493	30.128	60.409	52.865	34.918	37.737	35.981	89.528	24.122	40.3
1983	55.249	54.436	34.535	62.417	55.760	38.172	40.491	35.518	79.865	25.420	57.0
1984	59.220	57.325	39.577	64.898	58.026	49.420	47.331	41.788	91.016	30.462	65.5
1985	61.666	60.303	43.577	66.665	61.303	48.963	49.823	44.561	97.502	32.397	66.6
1986	63.804	62.749	47.785	69.060	63.111	48.629	50.403	43.287	86.817	33.011	74.7
1987	65.958	64.840	48.616	70.715	65.843	50.130	50.682	43.259	84.340	33.463	76.2
1988	68.684	67.468	51.549	73.016	68.506	51.309	52.352	45.520	84.885	35.987	75.4
1989	71.116	69.369	52.686	75.044	70.555	53.369	53.928	48.063	86.583	38.624	73.2
1990	72.451	70.782	52.532	76.209	72.583	51.574	52.803	48.302	87.867	38.636	66.8
1991	72.329	70.903	49.564	76.033	73.812	47.378	49.379	45.712	78.091	37.643	60.4
1992	74.734	73.224	52.470	77.553	76.379	51.223	52.312	47.179	73.423	40.387	68.8
1993	76.731	75.672	56.577	79.619	78.540	55.795	56.788	51.287	72.891	45.428	74.4
1994	79.816	78.504	61.321	82.369	80.854	63.358	62.079	55.999	74.180	50.846	81.6
1995	81.814	80.623	64.011	84.152	82.973	65.340	66.090	61.885	78.903	56.930	79.0
1996	84.842	83.382	69.025	86.300	85.420	71.123	72.018	67.661	83.354	62.981	85.3
1997	88.658	86.533	74.935	88.605	88.270	79.961	78.657	75.820	89.432	71.641	86.9
1998	92.359	90.896	83.432	92.154	92.011	87.821	86.657	84.232	94.019	81.137	93.5
1999	96.469	95.537	93.192	96.374	95.652	94.647	93.884	91.980	93.619	91.437	99.2
2000	100.000	100.000	100.000	100.000	100.000	100.000	100.000	100.000	100.000	100.000	100.0
2001	100.751	102.537	104.327	102.027	102.403	92.130	97.047	95.817	97.737	95.136	100.3
2002	102.362	105.340	111.752	104.614	104.366	89.724	91.997	86.969	81.029	89.265	105.1
2003	104.931	108.249	118.214	108.002	106.363	92.949	95.110	87.804	77.735	91.747	113.9
2004	108.748	112.197	125.652	111.833	109.726	102.003	102.012	92.873	78.760	98.505	125.3
2005	111.944	115.615	131.397	115.687	112.525	107.953	108.984	99.520	79.747	107.695	133.2
2006	115.054	119.135	137.274	119.930	115.298	110.200	111.109	106.967	86.318	115.467	123.7
2007	117.388	122.456	143.908	122.872	118.259	104.278	107.717	112.244	97.264	117.412	101.5
2005: I	110.786	114.217	128.761	114.043	111.465	107.702	106.643	97.429	80.813	104.100	130.2
II	111.502	115.239	132.478	115.225	111.946	106.298	108.608	98.935	80.545	106.425	133.3
III	112.560	116.303	134.236	116.068	112.995	107.337	110.022	100.407	78.627	109.536	134.6
IV	112.928	116.701	130.112	117.412	113.696	110.477	110.661	101.311	79.001	110.717	134.7
2006: I	114.264	117.925	135.877	118.670	114.149	112.150	112.880	105.125	81.910	114.985	133.4
II	115.022	118.737	136.485	119.590	114.938	112.032	112.156	106.766	85.668	115.484	127.5
III	115.250	119.393	137.652	120.275	115.495	110.504	110.779	108.164	88.574	116.049	120.1
IV	115.681	120.485	139.081	121.187	116.612	106.115	108.621	107.893	89.121	115.349	113.7
2007: I	115.696	121.631	142.162	122.232	117.494	103.483	107.674	108.794	91.526	115.360	108.8
II	117.056	122.226	143.894	122.815	117.916	105.040	108.475	111.502	95.447	117.302	105.5
III	118.425	122.838	144.720	123.182	118.605	105.950	108.218	113.863	100.005	118.348	99.6
IV	118.374	123.130	144.856	123.261	119.020	102.639	106.503	114.819	102.076	118.636	92.1
2008: I	118.631	123.395	143.284	123.147	119.739	101.110	104.969	115.504	104.206	118.470	85.6
II	119.460	123.770	142.273	124.317	119.937	98.071	104.522	116.212	108.716	116.961	82.6
III *p*	119.307	122.595	136.538	122.113	119.940	98.179	103.036	115.783	110.474	115.272	78.7

See next page for continuation of table.

[Index numbers, 2000=100; quarterly data seasonally adjusted]

Year or quarter	Exports of goods and services			Imports of goods and services			Government consumption expenditures and gross investment				
								Federal			State and local
	Total	Goods	Services	Total	Goods	Services	Total	Total	National defense	Non-defense	
59	7.043	6.198	9.641	6.908	5.403	15.462	41.489	68.666	89.447	33.305	26.999
60	8.266	7.651	9.797	7.000	5.314	16.669	41.553	66.779	87.977	30.672	28.182
61	8.309	7.689	9.857	6.953	5.307	16.385	43.639	69.564	91.851	31.599	29.918
62	8.729	8.031	10.535	7.742	6.092	17.150	46.329	75.492	97.412	38.144	30.839
63	9.353	8.662	11.070	7.951	6.339	17.137	47.522	75.540	95.085	42.217	32.696
64	10.454	9.849	11.733	8.374	6.757	17.579	48.563	74.530	91.304	45.880	34.913
65	10.747	9.901	12.926	9.265	7.714	18.096	50.028	74.508	89.403	48.995	37.252
66	11.492	10.589	13.814	10.642	8.930	20.395	54.430	82.737	102.205	49.501	39.590
67	11.757	10.638	14.905	11.417	9.400	22.887	58.604	90.960	115.571	49.059	41.589
68	12.681	11.481	16.049	13.118	11.342	23.298	60.436	91.681	117.416	47.912	44.048
69	13.294	12.082	16.646	13.866	11.963	24.767	60.290	88.525	111.604	49.186	45.534
70	14.723	13.460	18.128	14.457	12.432	26.059	58.833	81.997	101.477	48.674	46.797
71	14.973	13.408	19.527	15.229	13.474	25.317	57.553	75.686	89.980	50.961	48.232
72	16.096	14.849	19.404	16.943	15.307	26.390	57.128	72.574	82.921	54.551	49.291
73	19.131	18.259	20.775	17.729	16.388	25.500	56.926	69.519	78.322	54.213	50.694
74	20.643	19.709	22.396	17.327	15.932	25.472	58.360	70.134	77.714	57.023	52.603
75	20.512	19.252	23.773	15.402	13.924	24.367	59.675	70.360	76.977	58.965	54.536
76	21.408	20.165	24.476	18.413	17.073	26.049	59.940	70.388	76.706	59.523	54.937
77	21.923	20.429	26.055	20.426	19.153	27.347	60.598	71.880	77.597	62.089	55.137
78	24.234	22.712	28.234	22.196	20.871	29.297	62.383	73.681	78.259	65.947	56.938
79	26.637	25.396	29.103	22.565	21.229	29.700	63.549	75.465	80.648	66.640	57.775
80	29.506	28.422	30.919	21.066	19.653	29.037	64.790	79.043	84.160	70.373	57.736
81	29.868	28.114	34.211	21.620	20.058	30.711	65.381	82.818	89.486	71.310	56.577
82	27.586	25.573	33.263	21.348	19.554	32.346	66.530	86.018	96.244	67.888	56.607
83	26.875	24.838	32.710	24.041	22.210	34.958	68.964	91.726	103.158	71.398	57.268
84	29.068	26.801	35.627	29.893	27.584	43.724	71.273	94.550	108.186	70.035	59.322
85	29.951	27.790	36.051	31.833	29.310	47.050	76.240	101.957	117.355	74.169	63.003
86	32.259	29.217	41.325	34.561	32.314	47.638	80.885	107.754	124.871	76.764	67.064
87	35.742	32.456	45.502	36.602	33.812	53.205	82.873	111.674	130.779	76.984	68.041
88	41.469	38.572	49.616	38.039	35.181	55.010	83.940	109.898	130.161	73.037	70.582
89	46.233	43.172	54.723	39.706	36.686	57.678	86.110	111.594	129.518	79.075	72.994
90	50.394	46.810	60.480	41.139	37.770	61.430	88.869	113.873	129.472	85.651	75.991
91	53.736	50.042	64.082	40.905	37.741	59.849	89.872	113.679	128.050	87.700	77.600
92	57.439	53.785	67.590	43.748	41.263	58.321	90.342	111.713	121.708	93.749	79.318
93	59.291	55.534	69.726	47.576	45.423	60.026	89.513	107.056	114.860	93.087	80.459
94	64.447	60.937	74.097	53.256	51.466	63.421	89.525	103.050	109.259	91.957	82.543
95	70.982	68.070	78.793	57.539	56.104	65.492	90.015	100.254	105.093	91.613	84.728
96	76.930	74.086	84.483	62.544	61.337	69.094	90.896	99.091	103.648	90.955	86.668
97	86.082	84.717	89.509	71.037	70.172	75.600	92.588	98.066	100.733	93.320	89.770
98	88.164	86.614	92.077	79.299	78.364	84.222	94.354	96.970	98.650	93.985	93.014
99	91.969	89.907	97.207	88.391	88.078	90.038	97.987	99.122	100.515	96.646	97.409
00	100.000	100.000	100.000	100.000	100.000	100.000	100.000	100.000	100.000	100.000	100.000
01	94.565	93.871	96.302	97.291	96.833	99.706	103.412	103.908	103.936	103.859	103.162
02	92.430	90.143	98.104	100.601	100.377	101.824	107.969	111.169	111.578	110.441	106.354
03	93.599	91.771	98.148	104.693	105.294	101.857	110.644	118.712	121.239	114.181	106.557
04	102.723	100.011	109.451	116.546	117.173	113.589	112.210	123.693	128.282	115.441	106.384
05	109.942	107.698	115.535	123.455	125.164	115.216	112.626	125.181	130.227	116.104	106.256
06	119.937	118.407	123.826	130.815	132.613	122.153	114.497	128.019	132.315	120.318	107.642
07	130.068	127.335	136.868	133.654	134.921	127.581	116.871	130.078	135.596	120.127	110.167
05: I	107.447	104.279	115.288	122.083	123.580	114.891	112.079	124.058	128.624	115.848	106.001
II	109.747	107.860	114.468	122.271	123.807	114.888	112.337	124.408	129.887	114.535	106.214
III	109.853	107.632	115.385	122.509	124.154	114.586	113.291	127.310	133.707	115.770	106.189
IV	112.721	111.023	117.001	126.955	129.114	116.499	112.797	124.950	128.689	116.262	106.621
06: I	117.147	115.734	120.750	130.118	131.940	121.337	113.877	127.952	131.428	121.759	106.746
II	118.712	117.614	121.557	130.161	132.115	120.740	114.228	127.459	132.053	119.209	107.520
III	119.734	118.658	122.526	131.164	133.338	120.663	114.714	128.048	131.759	121.429	107.954
IV	124.153	121.621	130.470	131.818	133.057	125.872	115.167	128.616	134.019	118.877	108.348
07: I	124.343	122.251	129.591	134.289	135.772	127.166	115.421	127.426	131.986	119.235	109.314
II	126.992	124.300	133.690	133.041	134.401	126.515	116.541	129.507	134.701	120.154	109.957
III	133.747	130.571	141.620	134.033	135.197	128.460	117.642	131.772	138.002	120.506	110.484
IV	135.189	132.219	142.570	133.254	134.315	128.185	117.879	131.610	137.694	120.614	110.914
08: I	136.880	133.690	144.792	132.991	133.654	129.913	118.443	133.488	140.125	121.469	110.844
II	140.908	138.826	146.131	130.509	131.212	127.217	119.594	135.628	142.621	122.949	111.517
III p	142.100	140.150	147.004	129.436	129.740	128.226	121.163	140.023	148.649	124.299	111.734

Source: Department of Commerce (Bureau of Economic Analysis).

TABLE B–7.—*Chain-type price indexes for gross domestic product, 1959–2008*

[Index numbers, 2000=100, except as noted; quarterly data seasonally adjusted]

Year or quarter	Gross domestic product	Personal consumption expenditures				Gross private domestic investment					
		Total	Durable goods	Non-durable goods	Services	Total	Fixed investment				
							Total	Nonresidential			Residential
								Total	Structures	Equipment and software	
1959	20.754	20.432	45.662	22.765	15.485	29.474	28.262	35.114	15.923	50.882	16.630
1960	21.044	20.767	45.444	23.089	15.887	29.619	28.414	35.275	15.904	51.305	16.743
1961	21.281	20.985	45.551	23.227	16.173	29.538	28.325	35.076	15.810	51.025	16.769
1962	21.572	21.232	45.755	23.412	16.466	29.558	28.346	35.087	15.941	50.774	16.799
1963	21.801	21.479	45.915	23.683	16.701	29.467	28.267	35.088	16.085	50.495	16.663
1964	22.134	21.786	46.142	23.986	17.016	29.634	28.440	35.268	16.316	50.474	16.796
1965	22.538	22.103	45.721	24.423	17.334	30.107	28.926	35.672	16.791	50.520	17.272
1966	23.180	22.662	45.517	25.232	17.810	30.726	29.536	36.206	17.398	50.654	17.899
1967	23.897	23.237	46.228	25.830	18.349	31.538	30.364	37.129	17.943	51.776	18.521
1968	24.916	24.151	47.749	26.820	19.128	32.714	31.582	38.431	18.835	53.167	19.504
1969	26.153	25.255	49.067	28.062	20.106	34.264	33.140	40.018	20.074	54.645	20.853
1970	27.538	26.448	50.148	29.446	21.175	35.713	34.565	41.908	21.390	56.657	21.526
1971	28.916	27.574	51.975	30.359	22.340	37.493	36.306	43.880	23.040	58.340	22.775
1972	30.171	28.528	52.531	31.373	23.304	39.062	37.865	45.367	24.704	59.044	24.158
1973	31.854	30.081	53.301	33.838	24.381	41.172	39.958	47.115	26.619	60.047	26.297
1974	34.721	33.191	56.676	38.702	26.345	45.263	43.890	51.658	30.295	64.474	29.011
1975	38.007	35.955	61.844	41.735	28.595	50.847	49.384	58.763	33.911	74.001	31.706
1976	40.202	37.948	65.278	43.346	30.603	53.654	52.244	62.018	35.571	78.355	33.743
1977	42.758	40.410	68.129	45.911	32.933	57.677	56.342	66.258	38.651	83.011	37.147
1978	45.762	43.248	72.038	48.985	35.464	62.381	61.101	70.695	42.382	87.391	41.696
1979	49.553	47.059	76.830	54.148	38.316	68.027	66.642	76.440	47.313	92.932	46.374
1980	54.062	52.078	83.277	60.449	42.332	74.424	72.887	83.198	51.740	100.868	51.394
1981	59.128	56.720	88.879	65.130	46.746	81.278	79.670	91.245	58.880	108.077	55.587
1982	62.738	59.859	92.358	66.955	50.528	85.455	84.047	96.295	63.566	112.293	58.564
1983	65.214	62.436	94.181	68.386	53.799	85.237	83.912	95.432	61.939	112.530	59.908
1984	67.664	64.795	95.550	70.004	56.680	85.845	84.399	95.195	62.468	111.547	61.630
1985	69.724	66.936	96.620	71.543	59.295	86.720	85.457	95.936	63.940	111.413	63.219
1986	71.269	68.569	97.685	71.273	62.040	88.599	87.501	97.566	65.168	113.178	65.868
1987	73.204	70.947	100.465	73.731	64.299	90.289	89.118	98.435	66.199	113.796	68.561
1988	75.706	73.755	101.921	76.206	67.493	92.354	91.431	100.625	69.016	115.216	70.928
1989	78.569	76.972	103.717	79.842	70.708	94.559	93.641	102.731	71.707	116.657	73.211
1990	81.614	80.498	104.561	84.226	74.197	96.379	95.542	104.695	74.015	118.168	74.930
1991	84.457	83.419	106.080	86.779	77.497	97.749	96.960	106.314	75.355	119.854	75.912
1992	86.402	85.824	106.756	88.105	80.684	97.395	96.670	105.411	75.330	118.444	76.836
1993	88.390	87.804	107.840	88.973	83.345	98.521	97.805	105.487	77.602	117.243	79.941
1994	90.265	89.654	109.978	89.605	85.748	99.813	99.133	106.008	80.388	116.572	82.754
1995	92.115	91.577	110.672	90.629	88.320	100.941	100.292	106.239	83.879	115.224	85.769
1996	93.859	93.547	109.507	92.567	90.844	100.520	100.028	105.011	86.045	112.451	87.610
1997	95.415	95.124	107.068	93.835	93.305	100.157	99.785	103.696	89.381	109.120	89.843
1998	96.475	95.978	104.152	93.821	95.319	99.035	98.861	101.421	93.474	104.259	92.239
1999	97.868	97.575	101.626	96.173	97.393	98.972	98.888	100.057	96.257	101.366	95.780
2000	100.000	100.000	100.000	100.000	100.000	100.000	100.000	100.000	100.000	100.000	100.000
2001	102.402	102.094	98.114	101.531	103.257	101.013	101.023	99.683	105.403	97.708	104.633
2002	104.193	103.542	95.766	102.089	106.018	101.640	101.660	99.513	110.030	95.956	107.240
2003	106.409	105.597	92.366	104.145	109.379	103.191	103.313	99.591	113.872	94.912	112.372
2004	109.462	108.392	90.696	107.626	112.929	106.686	106.845	100.896	120.912	94.600	120.587
2005	113.039	111.581	89.984	111.606	116.700	111.381	111.638	103.829	135.177	94.534	129.268
2006	116.676	114.675	88.772	114.984	120.752	116.102	116.380	107.277	151.822	94.594	136.897
2007	119.819	117.659	87.154	118.407	124.712	117.735	117.995	108.739	157.662	94.870	138.884
2005: I	111.778	110.187	90.547	109.554	115.140	109.513	109.683	102.778	129.122	94.777	125.407
II	112.357	110.881	90.343	110.100	116.139	110.603	110.816	103.459	132.274	94.800	127.492
III	113.487	112.168	89.629	113.057	117.088	111.961	112.249	103.972	136.911	94.260	130.852
IV	114.536	113.089	89.417	113.712	118.433	113.446	113.803	105.107	142.400	94.299	133.320
2006: I	115.536	113.581	89.208	113.794	119.313	114.891	115.208	106.217	147.181	94.471	135.418
II	116.317	114.499	89.027	115.155	120.285	115.877	116.172	107.070	151.404	94.457	136.670
III	117.109	115.381	88.726	116.412	121.279	116.348	116.610	107.530	153.108	94.578	137.089
IV	117.742	115.239	88.126	114.578	122.130	117.293	117.528	108.291	155.595	94.870	138.412
2007: I	118.935	116.202	87.717	116.025	123.200	117.756	118.008	108.654	156.912	94.976	139.181
II	119.531	117.246	87.365	117.830	124.218	117.659	117.945	108.730	157.195	94.992	138.733
III	119.984	117.969	86.938	118.682	125.179	117.566	117.836	108.558	157.402	94.712	138.820
IV	120.826	119.221	86.598	121.092	126.253	117.960	118.189	109.015	159.138	94.798	138.802
2008: I	121.613	120.283	86.581	123.059	127.133	117.815	118.117	109.177	160.182	94.700	137.900
II	121.951	121.544	86.237	125.021	128.450	117.926	118.353	109.788	161.496	95.101	136.687
III ᵖ	123.205	123.091	86.110	128.131	129.624	118.687	119.202	110.955	164.432	95.720	136.164

See next page for continuation of table.

TABLE B–7.—*Chain-type price indexes for gross domestic product, 1959–2008*—Continued

[Index numbers, 2000=100, except as noted; quarterly data seasonally adjusted]

Year or quarter	Exports and imports of goods and services		Government consumption expenditures and gross investment					Final sales of domestic product	Gross domestic purchases [1]		Percent change [2]		
	Exports	Imports	Total	Federal			State and local		Total	Less food and energy	Gross domestic product	Gross domestic purchases [1]	
				Total	National defense	Non-defense						Total	Less food and energy
1959	29.433	21.901	15.404	16.450	16.257	16.591	14.475	20.581	20.365	....	1.2	1.2	....
1960	29.846	22.110	15.597	16.590	16.383	16.798	14.738	20.872	20.646	....	1.4	1.4	....
1961	30.300	22.110	15.909	16.871	16.619	17.296	15.093	21.108	20.865	....	1.1	1.1	....
1962	30.375	21.849	16.314	17.228	16.940	17.808	15.564	21.398	21.139	....	1.4	1.3	....
1963	30.307	22.273	16.669	17.597	17.320	18.116	15.911	21.629	21.385	....	1.1	1.2	....
1964	30.556	22.743	17.132	18.191	17.822	19.036	16.234	21.963	21.725	....	1.5	1.6	....
1965	31.529	23.059	17.588	18.658	18.314	19.408	16.685	22.368	22.102	....	1.8	1.7	....
1966	32.481	23.596	18.330	19.330	18.950	20.190	17.507	23.010	22.724	....	2.8	2.8	....
1967	33.725	23.688	19.099	19.913	19.518	20.815	18.488	23.729	23.389	....	3.1	2.9	....
1968	34.461	24.048	20.128	20.995	20.539	22.116	19.475	24.752	24.380	....	4.3	4.2	....
1969	35.627	24.675	21.341	22.130	21.664	23.251	20.780	25.988	25.580	....	5.0	4.9	....
1970	36.993	26.135	23.079	23.915	23.321	25.478	22.488	27.369	26.964	....	5.3	5.4	....
1971	38.358	27.739	24.875	25.957	25.387	27.400	24.087	28.741	28.351	....	5.0	5.1	....
1972	40.146	29.682	26.788	28.495	28.319	28.780	25.524	29.994	29.619	....	4.3	4.5	....
1973	45.425	34.841	28.743	30.449	30.396	30.394	27.477	31.673	31.343	....	5.6	5.8	....
1974	55.965	49.847	31.646	33.162	33.217	32.819	30.500	34.517	34.546	....	9.0	10.2	....
1975	61.682	53.997	34.824	36.615	36.460	36.746	33.481	37.789	37.761	....	9.5	9.3	....
1976	63.707	55.622	37.118	39.217	39.117	39.209	35.563	39.987	39.938	....	5.8	5.8	....
1977	66.302	60.523	39.694	42.180	42.079	42.152	37.872	42.546	42.634	....	6.4	6.8	....
1978	70.342	64.798	42.235	44.785	45.035	43.983	40.359	45.551	45.663	....	7.0	7.1	....
1979	78.808	75.879	45.775	48.231	48.628	47.099	43.944	49.322	49.669	....	8.3	8.8	....
1980	86.801	94.513	50.761	53.299	53.908	51.683	48.858	53.806	54.876	....	9.1	10.5	....
1981	93.217	99.594	55.752	58.476	59.229	56.516	53.709	58.859	59.896	....	9.4	9.1	....
1982	93.645	96.235	59.414	62.446	63.392	60.020	57.140	62.489	63.296	62.221	6.1	5.7	....
1983	94.015	92.629	61.778	64.612	65.617	62.038	59.666	64.958	65.515	64.685	3.9	3.5	4.0
1984	94.887	91.829	64.955	68.426	70.290	63.577	62.336	67.399	67.822	67.106	3.8	3.5	3.7
1985	91.983	88.813	66.970	69.974	71.621	65.740	64.739	69.494	69.760	69.232	3.0	2.9	3.2
1986	90.639	88.871	68.175	70.352	71.554	67.395	66.624	71.060	71.338	71.474	2.2	2.3	3.2
1987	92.874	94.251	70.056	71.200	72.281	68.616	69.361	72.985	73.527	73.716	2.7	3.1	3.1
1988	97.687	98.774	71.899	72.704	73.631	70.609	71.485	75.519	76.043	76.429	3.4	3.4	3.7
1989	99.310	100.944	74.139	74.677	75.528	72.826	73.940	78.383	78.934	79.151	3.8	3.8	3.6
1990	99.982	103.826	77.139	77.142	78.010	75.260	77.357	81.440	82.144	82.109	3.9	4.1	3.7
1991	101.313	103.420	79.787	80.232	80.821	79.100	79.681	84.286	84.836	84.942	3.5	3.3	3.5
1992	100.892	103.552	81.719	82.602	83.628	80.411	81.300	86.237	86.828	87.169	2.3	2.3	2.6
1993	100.898	102.671	83.789	84.788	85.313	83.728	83.294	88.226	88.730	89.211	2.3	2.2	2.3
1994	102.033	103.634	86.002	87.061	87.412	86.375	85.472	90.108	90.583	91.213	2.1	2.1	2.2
1995	104.376	106.412	88.358	89.503	89.598	89.351	87.778	91.965	92.483	93.176	2.0	2.1	2.2
1996	102.988	104.529	90.491	91.982	92.379	91.216	89.709	93.736	94.145	94.616	1.9	1.8	1.5
1997	101.232	100.816	92.139	93.533	93.716	93.192	91.414	95.320	95.440	95.865	1.7	1.4	1.3
1998	98.905	95.353	93.469	94.511	94.643	94.268	92.934	96.428	96.060	96.797	1.1	.6	1.0
1999	98.313	95.960	96.079	96.884	96.886	96.880	95.667	97.847	97.556	98.165	1.4	1.6	1.4
2000	100.000	100.000	100.000	100.000	100.000	100.000	100.000	100.000	100.000	100.000	2.2	2.5	1.9
2001	99.624	97.497	102.544	101.907	102.002	101.739	102.868	102.406	101.994	101.882	2.4	2.0	1.9
2002	99.273	96.341	105.507	105.631	105.792	105.345	105.435	104.197	103.583	103.796	1.7	1.6	1.9
2003	101.429	99.685	109.849	110.094	110.751	108.898	109.712	106.430	105.966	105.749	2.1	2.3	1.9
2004	104.997	104.526	114.754	115.322	115.932	114.218	114.431	109.487	109.235	108.587	2.9	3.1	2.7
2005	108.814	111.154	121.470	120.834	121.944	118.744	121.862	113.074	113.263	111.955	3.3	3.7	3.1
2006	112.618	115.932	127.239	125.806	127.381	122.803	128.109	116.710	117.066	115.371	3.2	3.4	3.1
2007	116.586	120.168	132.941	130.076	131.874	126.636	134.671	119.853	120.294	118.194	2.7	2.8	2.4
2005: I	107.557	107.582	119.162	119.921	120.965	117.965	118.722	111.801	111.638	110.775	4.0	3.7	3.9
II	108.489	110.096	120.378	120.433	121.503	118.423	120.355	112.385	112.484	111.514	2.1	3.1	2.7
III	109.169	112.840	122.443	121.364	122.454	119.313	123.099	113.526	113.913	112.326	4.1	5.2	2.9
IV	110.042	114.098	123.897	121.618	122.854	119.273	125.273	114.585	115.016	113.204	3.7	3.9	3.2
2006: I	110.834	113.796	125.399	124.614	126.069	121.844	125.880	115.576	115.832	114.150	3.5	2.9	3.4
II	112.418	116.619	126.911	125.866	127.426	122.891	127.548	116.353	116.859	115.065	2.7	3.6	3.2
III	113.722	118.055	127.955	126.233	127.897	123.054	128.999	117.141	117.700	115.778	2.8	2.9	2.5
IV	113.499	115.258	128.690	126.513	128.131	123.423	130.008	117.769	117.873	116.492	2.2	.6	2.5
2007: I	114.520	115.514	130.705	128.856	130.326	126.067	131.828	118.967	118.931	117.339	4.1	3.6	2.9
II	116.011	119.050	132.386	130.037	131.701	126.869	133.806	119.569	119.908	117.872	2.0	3.3	1.8
III	117.018	121.200	133.497	130.342	132.232	126.711	135.400	120.020	120.571	118.437	1.5	2.2	1.9
IV	118.794	124.907	135.174	131.070	133.237	126.886	137.649	120.856	121.766	119.129	2.8	4.0	2.4
2008: I	121.397	128.722	137.237	132.879	134.905	128.986	139.866	121.653	122.821	119.770	2.6	3.5	2.2
II	124.560	137.136	139.588	134.553	136.967	129.868	142.632	122.008	124.103	120.421	1.1	4.2	2.2
III *p*	126.608	140.181	141.147	135.460	138.004	130.503	144.597	123.274	125.541	121.318	4.2	4.7	3.0

[1] Gross domestic product (GDP) less exports of goods and services plus imports of goods and services.
[2] Quarterly percent changes are at annual rates.

Source: Department of Commerce (Bureau of Economic Analysis).

TABLE B–8.—*Gross domestic product by major type of product, 1959–2008*

[Billions of dollars; quarterly data at seasonally adjusted annual rates]

Year or quarter	Gross domestic product	Final sales of domestic product	Change in private inventories	Goods							Services [2]	Structures
				Total		*	Durable goods		Nondurable goods			
				Total	Final sales	Change in private inventories	Final sales	Change in private inventories [1]	Final sales	Change in private inventories [1]		
1959	506.6	502.7	3.9	237.6	233.6	3.9	86.3	2.9	147.3	1.1	206.5	62.
1960	526.4	523.2	3.2	246.6	243.4	3.2	90.2	1.7	153.2	1.6	217.9	61.
1961	544.7	541.7	3.0	250.1	247.2	3.0	90.2	-.1	157.0	3.0	231.0	63.
1962	585.6	579.5	6.1	268.1	262.0	6.1	99.4	3.4	162.6	2.7	249.7	67.
1963	617.7	612.1	5.6	280.1	274.5	5.6	106.0	2.6	168.5	3.0	265.0	72.
1964	663.6	658.8	4.8	300.9	296.0	4.8	116.4	3.8	179.7	1.0	284.3	78.
1965	719.1	709.9	9.2	329.4	320.2	9.2	128.4	6.2	191.8	3.0	305.0	84.
1966	787.8	774.2	13.6	364.5	350.9	13.6	142.0	10.0	208.9	3.6	335.3	88.
1967	832.6	822.7	9.9	373.9	364.0	9.9	146.4	4.8	217.6	5.0	369.1	89.
1968	910.0	900.9	9.1	402.6	393.6	9.1	158.7	4.5	234.8	4.5	407.4	100.
1969	984.6	975.4	9.2	432.0	422.8	9.2	171.1	6.0	251.7	3.2	444.4	108.
1970	1,038.5	1,036.5	2.0	446.9	444.9	2.0	173.6	-2	271.3	2.2	481.9	109.
1971	1,127.1	1,118.9	8.3	472.9	464.7	8.3	181.1	2.9	283.6	5.3	525.8	128.
1972	1,238.3	1,229.2	9.1	516.6	507.5	9.1	202.4	6.4	305.1	2.7	574.8	146.
1973	1,382.7	1,366.8	15.9	597.1	581.2	15.9	236.6	13.0	344.6	2.9	622.7	162.
1974	1,500.0	1,486.0	14.0	643.3	629.3	14.0	254.5	10.9	374.8	3.1	691.0	165.
1975	1,638.3	1,644.6	-6.3	691.4	697.7	-6.3	284.5	-7.5	413.2	1.2	780.2	166.
1976	1,825.3	1,808.2	17.1	777.5	760.4	17.1	321.2	10.8	439.2	6.3	856.6	191.
1977	2,030.9	2,008.6	22.3	851.5	829.1	22.3	363.8	9.5	465.3	12.8	952.7	226.
1978	2,294.7	2,268.9	25.8	961.0	935.2	25.8	413.2	18.2	522.0	7.6	1,059.7	273.
1979	2,563.3	2,545.3	18.0	1,078.1	1,060.1	18.0	472.0	12.8	588.1	5.2	1,171.9	313.
1980	2,789.5	2,795.8	-6.3	1,145.7	1,152.0	-6.3	500.1	-2.3	651.9	-4.0	1,322.5	321.
1981	3,128.4	3,098.6	29.8	1,288.2	1,258.3	29.8	542.2	7.3	716.1	22.5	1,487.7	352.
1982	3,255.0	3,269.9	-14.9	1,277.3	1,292.2	-14.9	539.7	-16.0	752.5	1.1	1,633.2	344.
1983	3,536.7	3,542.4	-5.8	1,365.0	1,370.8	-5.8	578.1	2.5	792.7	-8.2	1,802.9	368.
1984	3,933.2	3,867.8	65.4	1,549.6	1,484.2	65.4	650.2	41.4	834.0	24.0	1,957.8	425.
1985	4,220.3	4,198.4	21.8	1,607.4	1,585.6	21.8	711.0	4.4	874.6	17.4	2,154.1	458.
1986	4,462.8	4,456.3	6.6	1,657.0	1,650.5	6.6	739.9	-1.9	910.6	8.4	2,325.7	480.
1987	4,739.5	4,712.3	27.1	1,751.3	1,724.2	27.1	764.9	22.9	959.3	4.2	2,490.5	497.
1988	5,103.8	5,085.3	18.5	1,903.4	1,884.9	18.5	841.8	22.7	1,043.1	-4.3	2,685.3	515.
1989	5,484.4	5,456.7	27.7	2,066.6	2,038.9	27.7	917.1	20.0	1,121.9	7.7	2,888.7	529.
1990	5,803.1	5,788.5	14.5	2,155.8	2,141.3	14.5	950.2	7.7	1,191.1	6.8	3,113.7	533.
1991	5,995.9	5,996.3	-.4	2,184.7	2,185.1	-.4	944.1	-13.6	1,241.0	13.2	3,311.3	499.
1992	6,337.7	6,321.4	16.3	2,282.3	2,266.0	16.3	986.1	-3.0	1,279.8	19.3	3,532.7	522.
1993	6,657.4	6,636.6	20.8	2,387.8	2,367.0	20.8	1,047.9	17.1	1,319.1	3.7	3,711.7	557.
1994	7,072.2	7,008.4	63.8	2,563.8	2,500.0	63.8	1,125.0	35.7	1,375.0	28.1	3,901.2	607.
1995	7,397.7	7,366.5	31.1	2,661.1	2,630.0	31.1	1,202.2	33.6	1,427.8	-2.4	4,098.4	638.
1996	7,816.9	7,786.1	30.8	2,807.0	2,776.3	30.8	1,298.0	19.1	1,478.3	11.7	4,312.7	697.
1997	8,304.3	8,232.3	72.0	3,007.7	2,935.7	72.0	1,409.1	39.9	1,526.6	32.1	4,548.4	748.
1998	8,747.0	8,676.2	70.8	3,143.4	3,072.6	70.8	1,487.8	42.8	1,584.8	28.0	4,789.8	813.
1999	9,268.4	9,201.5	66.9	3,311.3	3,244.4	66.9	1,576.5	40.0	1,667.9	26.9	5,081.8	875.
2000	9,817.0	9,760.5	56.5	3,449.3	3,392.8	56.5	1,653.3	36.1	1,739.5	20.4	5,425.6	942.
2001	10,128.0	10,159.7	-31.7	3,412.6	3,444.3	-31.7	1,630.3	-41.8	1,814.0	10.0	5,725.6	989.
2002	10,469.6	10,457.7	11.9	3,442.4	3,430.5	11.9	1,559.9	15.1	1,870.7	-3.2	6,031.4	995.
2003	10,960.8	10,946.5	14.3	3,524.2	3,509.9	14.3	1,574.1	11.1	1,935.8	3.2	6,367.4	1,069.
2004	11,685.9	11,627.3	58.6	3,707.1	3,648.5	58.6	1,615.7	35.2	2,032.8	23.4	6,778.1	1,200.
2005	12,421.9	12,378.6	43.3	3,873.5	3,830.2	43.3	1,718.7	33.5	2,111.4	9.8	7,200.0	1,348.
2006	13,178.4	13,129.0	49.3	4,109.4	4,060.1	49.3	1,816.0	20.3	2,244.1	29.0	7,644.6	1,424.
2007	13,807.5	13,811.2	-3.6	4,272.7	4,276.4	-3.6	1,895.6	-10.2	2,380.8	6.5	8,134.5	1,400.
2005: I	12,155.4	12,072.7	82.6	3,823.2	3,740.5	82.6	1,664.0	53.4	2,076.5	29.2	7,043.2	1,289.
II	12,297.5	12,278.1	19.4	3,844.7	3,825.3	19.4	1,722.1	8.3	2,103.3	11.1	7,121.6	1,331.
III	12,538.2	12,527.2	11.0	3,905.0	3,894.0	11.0	1,754.9	16.9	2,139.1	-5.9	7,265.5	1,367.
IV	12,696.4	12,636.1	60.3	3,921.1	3,860.8	60.3	1,734.0	55.5	2,126.8	4.8	7,369.8	1,405.
2006: I	12,959.6	12,906.5	53.1	4,045.7	3,992.6	53.1	1,804.4	17.1	2,188.2	36.0	7,483.2	1,430.
II	13,134.1	13,068.3	65.9	4,103.9	4,038.0	65.9	1,809.0	32.4	2,229.0	33.5	7,588.4	1,441.
III	13,249.6	13,187.1	62.5	4,135.6	4,073.0	62.5	1,814.4	41.0	2,258.6	21.6	7,693.5	1,420.
IV	13,370.1	13,354.3	15.8	4,152.5	4,136.6	15.8	1,836.0	-9.1	2,300.6	24.9	7,813.5	1,404.
2007: I	13,510.9	13,526.5	-15.6	4,165.3	4,180.9	-15.6	1,847.2	-5.9	2,333.7	-9.7	7,941.6	1,404.
II	13,737.5	13,738.4	-.9	4,260.2	4,261.0	-.9	1,890.5	-29.4	2,370.5	28.6	8,067.1	1,410.
III	13,950.6	13,927.6	23.0	4,336.2	4,313.1	23.0	1,908.8	.8	2,404.4	22.2	8,208.8	1,405.
IV	14,031.2	14,052.3	-21.1	4,329.4	4,350.5	-21.1	1,935.8	-6.1	2,414.6	-14.9	8,320.7	1,381.
2008: I	14,150.8	14,176.4	-25.6	4,343.9	4,369.5	-25.6	1,935.9	-7.2	2,433.6	-18.4	8,460.2	1,346.
II	14,294.5	14,370.5	-76.0	4,337.1	4,413.1	-76.0	1,924.9	-43.9	2,488.2	-32.1	8,597.0	1,360.
III p	14,420.5	14,469.1	-48.6	4,340.6	4,389.2	-48.6	1,907.2	14.5	2,481.9	-63.1	8,718.8	1,361.

[1] Estimates for durable and nondurable goods for 1996 and earlier periods are based on the Standard Industrial Classification (SIC); later estimates are based on the North American Industry Classification System (NAICS).

[2] Includes government consumption expenditures, which are for services (such as education and national defense) produced by government. In current dollars, these services are valued at their cost of production.

Source: Department of Commerce (Bureau of Economic Analysis).

TABLE B–9.—*Real gross domestic product by major type of product, 1959–2008*

[Billions of chained (2000) dollars; quarterly data at seasonally adjusted annual rates]

Year or quarter	Gross domestic product	Final sales of domestic product	Change in private inventories	Goods							Services [2]	Structures
				Total			Durable goods		Nondurable goods			
				Total	Final sales	Change in private inventories	Final sales	Change in private inventories [1]	Final sales	Change in private inventories [1]		
1959	2,441.3	2,442.7	12.3	700.7							1,391.1	392.8
1960	2,501.8	2,506.8	10.4	721.1							1,433.0	389.1
1961	2,560.0	2,566.8	9.4	726.7							1,489.4	399.9
1962	2,715.2	2,708.5	19.5	773.8							1,574.3	422.8
1963	2,834.0	2,830.3	18.0	803.4							1,642.4	451.3
1964	2,998.6	2,999.9	15.4	856.4							1,720.1	481.7
1965	3,191.1	3,173.8	29.3	927.3							1,803.6	505.8
1966	3,399.1	3,364.8	42.1	1,005.2							1,916.7	506.4
1967	3,484.6	3,467.6	30.3	1,006.4							2,034.8	499.0
1968	3,652.7	3,640.3	27.4	1,047.9							2,140.4	529.7
1969	3,765.4	3,753.7	27.0	1,082.2							2,212.2	536.5
1970	3,771.9	3,787.7	5.0	1,076.3							2,255.4	513.4
1971	3,898.6	3,893.4	22.3	1,105.7							2,313.6	561.0
1972	4,105.0	4,098.6	23.1	1,180.5							2,393.7	602.7
1973	4,341.5	4,315.9	35.0	1,299.5							2,461.3	615.6
1974	4,319.6	4,305.5	25.9	1,288.1							2,522.8	551.8
1975	4,311.2	4,352.5	–11.3	1,263.7							2,612.1	501.7
1976	4,540.9	4,522.3	30.7	1,359.8							2,676.9	548.7
1977	4,750.5	4,721.6	38.5	1,423.2							2,770.5	600.6
1978	5,015.0	4,981.6	41.1	1,515.6							2,874.9	658.3
1979	5,173.4	5,161.2	25.1	1,577.9							2,943.3	677.0
1980	5,161.7	5,196.7	–8.0	1,567.1							3,004.2	627.8
1981	5,291.7	5,265.1	34.9	1,634.5							3,062.5	619.2
1982	5,189.3	5,233.4	–17.5	1,559.7							3,120.0	566.1
1983	5,423.8	5,454.0	–6.4	1,625.4							3,251.0	607.1
1984	5,813.6	5,739.2	71.3	1,810.9							3,341.1	689.2
1985	6,053.7	6,042.1	23.7	1,851.3							3,520.8	725.1
1986	6,263.6	6,271.8	8.3	1,906.0							3,671.0	735.9
1987	6,475.1	6,457.2	30.3	1,984.9							3,797.3	739.2
1988	6,742.7	6,734.5	20.3	2,108.9							3,930.9	737.9
1989	6,981.4	6,962.2	28.3	2,223.3							4,049.5	732.8
1990	7,112.5	7,108.5	15.4	2,252.7	2,244.3	15.4	872.8	7.2	1,402.1	3.5	4,170.0	718.3
1991	7,100.5	7,115.0	–.5	2,221.5	2,228.9	–.5	852.7	–13.6	1,410.3	6.1	4,251.2	662.8
1992	7,336.6	7,331.1	16.5	2,307.8	2,297.7	16.5	894.7	–3.0	1,434.3	8.7	4,373.7	688.3
1993	7,532.7	7,522.3	20.6	2,394.8	2,380.3	20.6	949.8	16.4	1,457.7	1.5	4,457.5	709.3
1994	7,835.5	7,777.8	63.6	2,550.6	2,493.9	63.6	1,016.4	33.4	1,501.4	12.6	4,558.3	746.0
1995	8,031.7	8,010.2	29.9	2,639.0	2,614.9	29.9	1,096.9	31.0	1,536.9	–1.2	4,654.7	753.5
1996	8,328.9	8,306.5	28.7	2,772.4	2,747.4	28.7	1,193.8	17.8	1,566.5	4.5	4,765.6	803.1
1997	8,703.5	8,636.6	71.2	2,971.3	2,904.6	71.2	1,317.4	38.5	1,593.4	32.4	4,901.1	835.7
1998	9,066.9	8,997.6	72.6	3,132.7	3,063.7	72.6	1,431.8	42.4	1,634.2	29.8	5,057.5	879.1
1999	9,470.3	9,404.0	68.9	3,312.6	3,246.4	68.9	1,554.3	40.4	1,692.6	28.1	5,245.1	913.0
2000	9,817.0	9,760.5	56.5	3,449.3	3,392.8	56.5	1,653.3	36.1	1,739.5	20.4	5,425.6	942.1
2001	9,890.7	9,920.9	–31.7	3,390.9	3,421.9	–31.7	1,655.6	–42.4	1,766.1	10.3	5,553.2	945.6
2002	10,048.8	10,036.5	12.5	3,432.5	3,419.7	12.5	1,610.8	15.5	1,806.3	–2.8	5,693.4	922.1
2003	10,301.0	10,285.1	14.3	3,538.3	3,521.7	14.3	1,669.4	11.2	1,850.5	3.3	5,810.8	952.3
2004	10,675.8	10,619.8	54.3	3,705.4	3,645.6	54.3	1,744.7	34.1	1,900.9	20.8	5,972.7	1,001.4
2005	10,989.5	10,947.3	38.9	3,864.9	3,820.2	38.9	1,862.9	31.7	1,962.1	8.5	6,101.4	1,033.7
2006	11,294.8	11,249.3	42.3	4,074.4	4,026.1	42.3	1,979.1	18.3	2,054.5	23.8	6,243.4	1,011.0
2007	11,523.9	11,523.4	–2.5	4,201.9	4,206.5	–2.5	2,095.8	–8.7	2,123.3	5.3	6,415.6	960.0
2005: I	10,875.8	10,799.3	74.6	3,801.7	3,719.0	74.6	1,797.6	50.6	1,923.8	25.1	6,057.1	1,024.0
II	10,946.1	10,925.9	16.7	3,845.9	3,826.1	16.7	1,862.1	8.0	1,968.3	8.7	6,072.5	1,036.8
III	11,050.0	11,035.5	11.0	3,896.5	3,882.6	11.0	1,906.5	16.3	1,982.8	–4.2	6,131.0	1,035.3
IV	11,086.1	11,028.4	53.5	3,915.8	3,853.2	53.5	1,885.2	52.0	1,973.7	4.5	6,145.1	1,038.6
2006: I	11,217.3	11,167.6	45.9	4,020.2	3,967.0	45.9	1,959.9	15.7	2,016.0	29.6	6,185.1	1,036.6
II	11,291.7	11,232.1	56.9	4,077.8	4,013.1	56.9	1,968.5	29.3	2,051.4	27.9	6,219.7	1,026.6
III	11,314.1	11,257.8	53.3	4,093.2	4,032.5	53.3	1,980.0	36.5	2,059.7	17.8	6,254.9	1,003.2
IV	11,356.4	11,339.7	13.1	4,106.3	4,091.8	13.1	2,007.9	–8.2	2,090.9	20.0	6,313.9	977.5
2007: I	11,357.8	11,370.5	–15.0	4,080.6	4,100.3	–15.0	2,024.6	–5.0	2,084.7	–9.9	6,347.3	967.9
II	11,491.4	11,490.5	–2.8	4,181.7	4,185.7	–2.8	2,081.3	–25.7	2,116.2	20.0	6,389.7	969.9
III	11,625.7	11,605.0	16.0	4,272.6	4,253.2	16.0	2,119.8	.9	2,146.3	14.2	6,452.0	962.7
IV	11,620.7	11,628.0	–8.1	4,272.9	4,286.7	–8.1	2,157.5	–5.2	2,146.3	–3.2	6,473.6	939.5
2008: I	11,646.0	11,653.7	–10.2	4,282.9	4,297.4	–10.2	2,162.2	–6.1	2,152.2	–4.3	6,517.6	914.7
II	11,727.4	11,778.8	–50.6	4,334.3	4,401.6	–50.6	2,169.7	–36.1	2,240.2	–16.9	6,545.3	922.2
III [p]	11,712.3	11,737.9	–29.1	4,295.4	4,331.1	–29.1	2,143.8	12.2	2,197.2	–36.3	6,570.8	913.6

[1] Estimates for durable and nondurable goods for 1996 and earlier periods are based on the Standard Industrial Classification (SIC); later estimates are based on the North American Industry Classification System (NAICS).

[2] Includes government consumption expenditures, which are for services (such as education and national defense) produced by government. In current dollars, these services are valued at their cost of production.

Source: Department of Commerce (Bureau of Economic Analysis).

[Billions of dollars; quarterly data at seasonally adjusted annual rates]

Year or quarter	Gross domestic product	Business [1] Total	Business Nonfarm [1]	Business Farm	Households and institutions Total	Households	Nonprofit institutions serving households [2]	General government [3] Total	Federal	State and local	Addendum: Gross housing value added
1959	506.6	408.2	390.9	17.3	40.1	29.8	10.3	58.3	31.9	26.5	36
1960	526.4	420.4	402.3	18.2	43.9	32.3	11.7	62.0	33.1	28.9	39
1961	544.7	432.0	413.7	18.3	46.7	34.3	12.4	66.0	34.4	31.6	42
1962	585.6	464.5	446.1	18.4	50.4	36.7	13.6	70.7	36.5	34.2	46
1963	617.7	488.7	470.2	18.5	53.6	38.8	14.8	75.5	38.4	37.1	48
1964	663.6	525.6	508.2	17.3	56.9	40.8	16.1	81.1	40.7	40.4	51
1965	719.1	571.4	551.5	19.9	61.0	43.3	17.7	86.7	42.4	44.2	54
1966	787.8	625.1	604.3	20.8	65.8	45.9	19.9	96.9	47.3	49.6	58
1967	832.6	654.5	634.4	20.1	70.9	48.8	22.1	107.2	51.7	55.5	62
1968	910.0	714.5	694.0	20.5	76.5	51.6	25.0	119.0	56.4	62.5	65
1969	984.6	770.3	747.5	22.8	84.3	55.6	28.7	130.0	60.0	70.0	71
1970	1,038.5	803.6	779.9	23.7	91.4	59.4	32.0	143.6	64.1	79.5	76
1971	1,127.1	869.9	844.5	25.4	100.9	65.1	35.7	156.4	67.8	88.6	83
1972	1,238.3	959.0	929.4	29.7	109.9	70.3	39.5	169.4	71.6	97.9	91
1973	1,382.7	1,079.4	1,032.7	46.8	120.0	76.0	44.0	183.3	74.0	109.3	98
1974	1,500.0	1,166.9	1,122.6	44.2	131.7	82.5	49.2	201.4	79.6	121.8	106
1975	1,638.3	1,268.5	1,222.8	45.6	145.4	90.3	55.1	224.5	87.3	137.1	117
1976	1,825.3	1,423.7	1,380.7	43.0	158.1	98.1	60.0	243.5	93.8	149.7	126
1977	2,030.9	1,593.5	1,549.9	43.5	172.8	107.3	65.6	264.6	102.1	162.6	140
1978	2,294.7	1,813.4	1,762.7	50.7	193.8	120.4	73.4	287.5	109.7	177.8	155
1979	2,563.3	2,032.9	1,972.8	60.1	217.4	135.0	82.5	313.0	117.6	195.4	172
1980	2,789.5	2,191.1	2,139.7	51.4	249.9	155.5	94.4	348.6	131.3	217.3	199
1981	3,128.4	2,459.4	2,394.5	65.0	283.7	176.8	106.9	385.3	147.4	237.9	228
1982	3,255.0	2,520.7	2,460.3	60.4	315.3	195.7	119.6	419.0	161.3	257.7	255
1983	3,536.7	2,747.2	2,702.3	44.9	344.0	211.7	132.4	445.4	171.3	274.1	277
1984	3,933.2	3,071.8	3,007.7	64.2	376.2	230.2	146.0	485.2	192.1	293.1	301
1985	4,220.3	3,290.8	3,227.4	63.4	406.0	249.6	156.4	523.5	205.1	318.4	332
1986	4,462.8	3,468.8	3,409.4	59.4	438.0	267.4	170.6	556.1	212.6	343.5	359
1987	4,739.5	3,669.9	3,608.4	61.6	478.4	287.6	190.8	591.2	223.4	367.8	385
1988	5,103.8	3,948.6	3,887.2	61.3	525.1	312.8	212.4	630.1	234.9	395.2	415
1989	5,484.4	4,243.2	4,169.7	73.6	569.6	337.0	232.6	671.5	246.6	424.9	443
1990	5,803.1	4,462.6	4,386.0	76.6	618.9	362.9	256.0	721.6	258.9	462.6	478
1991	5,995.9	4,569.3	4,499.5	69.9	660.7	383.4	277.3	765.9	275.0	490.9	508
1992	6,337.7	4,840.4	4,761.7	78.7	697.9	397.2	300.7	799.4	282.1	517.3	531
1993	6,657.4	5,096.2	5,025.6	70.6	732.0	413.7	318.3	829.3	286.3	543.0	549
1994	7,072.2	5,444.0	5,362.4	81.6	771.3	439.5	331.7	857.0	286.2	570.7	582
1995	7,397.7	5,700.6	5,632.0	68.5	815.5	463.3	352.1	881.6	284.7	596.9	613
1996	7,816.9	6,056.7	5,966.0	90.7	852.2	484.7	367.5	908.0	288.6	619.3	638
1997	8,304.3	6,471.9	6,383.8	88.1	895.8	509.6	386.2	936.7	290.9	645.8	667
1998	8,747.0	6,827.1	6,748.2	78.9	949.7	538.0	411.7	970.3	293.1	677.2	700
1999	9,268.4	7,243.4	7,174.7	68.8	1,012.3	576.4	435.9	1,012.7	300.9	711.8	747
2000	9,817.0	7,666.7	7,595.1	71.5	1,080.7	615.6	465.1	1,069.6	315.4	754.2	794
2001	10,128.0	7,841.2	7,768.0	73.1	1,160.4	662.0	498.4	1,126.4	325.7	800.8	849
2002	10,469.6	8,040.5	7,969.7	70.8	1,227.3	687.7	539.6	1,201.8	352.9	848.9	876
2003	10,960.8	8,411.5	8,323.2	88.3	1,269.2	699.9	569.3	1,280.1	383.9	896.2	878
2004	11,685.9	8,987.5	8,872.8	114.7	1,350.0	744.9	605.1	1,348.4	412.6	935.8	929
2005	12,421.9	9,591.8	9,487.7	104.1	1,405.2	772.3	632.9	1,424.9	438.2	986.6	963
2006	13,178.4	10,183.8	10,092.6	91.1	1,497.3	834.5	662.8	1,497.3	460.1	1,037.2	1,038
2007	13,807.5	10,642.3	10,505.1	137.3	1,582.0	882.1	699.9	1,583.2	484.2	1,099.0	1,106
2005: I	12,155.4	9,368.0	9,262.0	106.0	1,383.7	762.0	621.7	1,403.7	437.3	966.4	951
II	12,297.5	9,488.0	9,379.4	108.7	1,395.5	765.8	629.6	1,414.0	436.2	977.8	956
III	12,538.2	9,695.4	9,589.6	105.7	1,409.0	771.5	637.5	1,433.8	438.9	995.0	962
IV	12,696.4	9,815.9	9,719.7	96.1	1,432.6	789.9	642.7	1,448.0	440.5	1,007.4	984
2006: I	12,959.6	10,024.1	9,937.4	86.7	1,464.6	812.0	652.6	1,470.9	455.3	1,015.6	1,009
II	13,134.1	10,160.3	10,080.0	80.3	1,489.7	830.3	659.4	1,484.1	458.8	1,025.3	1,031
III	13,249.6	10,229.7	10,139.6	90.1	1,513.2	849.3	663.9	1,506.8	461.7	1,045.1	1,055
IV	13,370.1	10,321.0	10,213.5	107.4	1,521.7	846.4	675.2	1,527.5	464.8	1,062.7	1,057
2007: I	13,510.9	10,405.2	10,277.1	128.1	1,549.7	863.7	686.0	1,556.0	479.0	1,077.1	1,080
II	13,737.5	10,594.7	10,460.4	134.3	1,570.1	876.4	693.8	1,572.7	482.8	1,089.9	1,099
III	13,950.6	10,767.0	10,623.7	143.2	1,590.8	887.4	703.3	1,592.8	486.2	1,106.6	1,114
IV	14,031.2	10,802.5	10,659.1	143.4	1,617.4	900.9	716.5	1,611.3	488.9	1,122.4	1,132
2008: I	14,150.8	10,874.7	10,739.2	135.5	1,638.1	908.1	730.0	1,638.0	502.4	1,135.6	1,142
II	14,294.5	10,969.5	10,838.2	131.3	1,664.0	924.5	739.5	1,661.0	511.1	1,149.9	1,164
III *p*	14,420.5	11,042.4	10,918.2	124.2	1,692.1	940.6	751.5	1,686.0	520.7	1,165.3	1,186

[1] Gross domestic business value added equals gross domestic product excluding gross value added of households and institutions and of general government. Nonfarm value added equals gross domestic business value added excluding gross farm value added.
[2] Equals compensation of employees of nonprofit institutions, the rental value of nonresidential fixed assets owned and used by nonprofit institutions serving households, and rental income of persons for tenant-occupied housing owned by nonprofit institutions.
[3] Equals compensation of general government employees plus general government consumption of fixed capital.

Source: Department of Commerce (Bureau of Economic Analysis).

TABLE B–11.—*Real gross value added by sector, 1959–2008*

[Billions of chained (2000) dollars; quarterly data at seasonally adjusted annual rates]

| Year or quarter | Gross domestic product | Business[1] | | | Households and institutions | | | General government[3] | | | Addendum: Gross housing value added |
		Total	Nonfarm[1]	Farm	Total	Households	Nonprofit institutions serving households[2]	Total	Federal	State and local	
1959	2,441.3	1,716.0	1,684.1	21.2	261.7	161.6	97.8	514.5	279.4	236.7	195.0
1960	2,501.8	1,748.8	1,713.5	22.4	279.6	171.4	106.6	532.2	284.6	249.3	207.3
1961	2,560.0	1,782.8	1,747.8	22.6	291.5	179.6	109.6	550.9	290.5	262.1	219.2
1962	2,715.2	1,897.7	1,867.0	22.1	307.7	189.8	115.4	572.5	302.5	271.8	232.8
1963	2,834.0	1,985.4	1,954.3	22.8	320.4	197.7	120.0	589.5	305.2	285.9	244.3
1964	2,998.6	2,111.7	2,086.0	22.1	333.7	205.7	125.4	609.7	308.2	303.1	255.4
1965	3,191.1	2,260.6	2,233.5	23.5	350.2	215.2	132.6	630.3	310.4	321.5	268.9
1966	3,399.1	2,413.6	2,393.2	22.7	366.3	224.0	140.2	669.7	330.7	340.6	281.0
1967	3,484.6	2,459.5	2,434.1	24.5	381.6	233.1	146.5	705.2	352.2	354.9	294.0
1968	3,652.7	2,581.7	2,561.5	23.6	400.4	239.3	161.0	732.7	358.1	376.2	304.6
1969	3,765.4	2,660.3	2,639.1	24.5	417.8	249.1	168.8	751.3	359.0	393.4	318.7
1970	3,771.9	2,659.3	2,636.0	25.1	425.0	254.7	170.0	754.1	343.6	410.8	328.9
1971	3,898.6	2,761.5	2,736.2	26.4	443.0	266.5	176.1	755.3	327.8	427.5	343.8
1972	4,105.0	2,939.8	2,918.4	26.4	460.7	277.7	182.4	753.8	311.8	442.3	360.1
1973	4,341.5	3,145.0	3,131.5	26.2	476.3	287.5	188.2	757.2	300.1	457.8	373.0
1974	4,319.6	3,101.3	3,089.1	25.6	493.9	299.9	193.1	772.6	299.2	474.4	390.7
1975	4,311.2	3,071.2	3,037.5	30.5	513.7	308.0	205.2	785.1	297.5	488.9	402.7
1976	4,540.9	3,272.9	3,249.1	29.1	521.5	313.3	207.5	791.8	297.9	495.3	408.3
1977	4,750.5	3,456.2	3,431.1	30.7	528.3	316.2	211.6	800.1	298.8	502.9	418.3
1978	5,015.0	3,673.3	3,656.8	29.6	552.4	335.1	216.3	815.5	302.5	514.6	436.8
1979	5,173.4	3,796.7	3,774.2	32.2	576.7	350.4	225.3	824.2	302.3	523.7	453.9
1980	5,161.7	3,756.1	3,736.1	31.1	606.9	372.9	232.8	836.0	307.0	530.8	481.9
1981	5,291.7	3,859.5	3,814.7	41.0	626.5	384.7	240.5	840.6	311.7	530.6	501.0
1982	5,189.3	3,743.1	3,691.9	43.1	647.2	391.8	254.4	849.2	316.8	534.0	514.7
1983	5,423.8	3,944.3	3,932.8	26.9	665.9	399.4	265.7	854.6	324.2	531.8	526.2
1984	5,813.6	4,286.3	4,254.3	37.2	687.8	413.3	273.6	865.2	331.5	535.0	543.0
1985	6,053.7	4,484.5	4,434.2	46.7	700.1	423.2	275.9	890.0	341.0	550.3	564.4
1986	6,263.6	4,652.0	4,606.2	44.9	718.5	428.7	289.1	911.9	347.0	566.3	574.9
1987	6,475.1	4,815.5	4,769.8	45.5	745.7	440.3	304.8	931.8	356.1	577.2	588.8
1988	6,742.7	5,023.0	4,987.7	40.9	780.6	457.1	323.1	956.0	360.5	596.9	606.2
1989	6,981.4	5,206.6	5,162.3	46.4	812.3	471.5	340.6	978.8	364.9	615.3	620.3
1990	7,112.5	5,287.0	5,237.9	49.3	841.2	483.2	357.9	1,003.9	371.6	633.6	635.7
1991	7,100.5	5,245.4	5,194.7	50.0	865.3	497.8	367.5	1,014.3	373.8	641.7	657.2
1992	7,336.6	5,456.5	5,395.2	57.5	882.6	502.6	379.9	1,017.7	366.0	652.6	666.2
1993	7,532.7	5,625.9	5,576.0	50.6	904.8	507.9	396.9	1,019.8	358.9	661.6	669.9
1994	7,835.5	5,905.3	5,841.4	60.9	923.1	524.7	398.4	1,019.9	347.2	673.1	690.8
1995	8,031.7	6,076.8	6,030.2	49.6	945.1	534.3	410.8	1,020.6	334.1	686.5	705.7
1996	8,328.9	6,356.0	6,300.4	56.1	957.8	540.8	417.0	1,022.1	325.0	697.2	712.1
1997	8,703.5	6,693.8	6,627.2	64.4	983.5	554.0	429.5	1,030.0	318.8	711.2	726.5
1998	9,066.9	7,017.1	6,955.3	61.6	1,010.4	563.8	446.9	1,041.0	315.2	725.8	735.5
1999	9,470.3	7,376.8	7,314.2	62.9	1,042.3	590.7	451.6	1,051.4	312.7	738.7	767.2
2000	9,817.0	7,666.7	7,595.1	71.5	1,080.7	615.6	465.1	1,069.6	315.4	754.2	794.3
2001	9,890.7	7,691.0	7,625.7	65.6	1,110.0	634.8	475.1	1,089.3	317.0	772.3	815.1
2002	10,048.8	7,806.9	7,736.9	70.1	1,130.9	634.2	496.6	1,110.4	323.3	787.1	809.0
2003	10,301.0	8,050.3	7,974.3	76.0	1,129.1	629.4	499.6	1,123.9	331.9	791.9	789.9
2004	10,675.8	8,387.0	8,304.3	82.1	1,165.6	661.9	504.1	1,129.4	335.2	794.1	825.6
2005	10,989.5	8,680.9	8,589.9	89.6	1,181.8	673.7	508.7	1,137.8	337.4	800.2	840.0
2006	11,294.8	8,945.6	8,860.8	83.4	1,219.3	708.5	512.6	1,144.4	337.0	807.4	881.4
2007	11,523.9	9,128.2	9,034.5	91.5	1,251.7	729.9	523.9	1,159.5	339.5	820.1	913.7
2005: I	10,875.8	8,574.6	8,486.5	86.9	1,174.2	668.0	506.7	1,136.2	337.8	798.2	833.8
II	10,946.1	8,642.0	8,541.1	92.4	1,177.7	670.1	508.2	1,136.8	336.9	799.7	836.1
III	11,050.0	8,743.0	8,648.4	93.1	1,181.6	671.9	510.2	1,137.8	336.7	801.0	837.7
IV	11,086.1	8,764.1	8,676.6	86.1	1,193.7	684.9	509.8	1,140.3	338.1	802.1	852.6
2006: I	11,217.3	8,885.1	8,802.9	80.9	1,207.4	698.6	510.3	1,138.9	335.4	803.5	868.5
II	11,291.7	8,948.5	8,865.6	81.5	1,217.6	707.3	512.1	1,140.7	335.5	805.2	878.8
III	11,314.1	8,955.8	8,871.6	82.9	1,225.1	714.2	512.9	1,147.2	338.5	808.7	888.0
IV	11,356.4	8,993.1	8,903.1	88.6	1,227.0	714.0	514.9	1,150.6	338.6	812.0	890.3
2007: I	11,357.8	8,977.4	8,884.0	91.2	1,239.8	723.9	518.1	1,153.5	337.9	815.7	903.6
II	11,491.4	9,101.5	9,010.0	89.8	1,249.2	728.8	522.5	1,155.9	337.5	818.6	912.0
III	11,625.7	9,224.0	9,130.4	91.6	1,257.1	732.8	526.4	1,161.9	340.7	821.3	918.4
IV	11,620.7	9,209.7	9,113.6	93.5	1,260.6	733.9	528.7	1,166.5	341.9	824.7	920.7
2008: I	11,646.0	9,225.2	9,134.3	89.6	1,263.3	731.6	533.3	1,172.9	345.0	827.9	918.5
II	11,727.4	9,285.5	9,198.2	87.1	1,277.1	740.6	538.2	1,180.0	348.7	831.2	930.7
III p	11,712.3	9,244.6	9,154.9	88.9	1,290.9	750.5	542.4	1,188.5	354.5	833.8	943.1

[1] Gross domestic business value added equals gross domestic product excluding gross value added of households and institutions and of general government. Nonfarm value added equals gross domestic business value added excluding gross farm value added.

[2] Equals compensation of employees of nonprofit institutions, the rental value of nonresidential fixed assets owned and used by nonprofit institutions serving households, and rental income of persons for tenant-occupied housing owned by nonprofit institutions.

[3] Equals compensation of general government employees plus general government consumption of fixed capital.

Source: Department of Commerce (Bureau of Economic Analysis).

TABLE B–12.—*Gross domestic product (GDP) by industry, value added, in current dollars and as a percentage of GDP, 1977–2007*

[Billions of dollars; except as noted]

Year	Gross domestic product	Private industries									
		Total private industries	Agriculture, forestry, fishing, and hunting	Mining	Construction	Manufacturing			Utilities	Wholesale trade	Retail trade
						Total manufacturing	Durable goods	Non-durable goods			
						Value added					
1977	2,030.9	1,739.4	51.3	43.4	94.2	438.6	265.0	173.6	45.9	134.9	158
1978	2,294.7	1,977.0	59.8	49.5	111.5	489.9	303.4	186.5	50.4	153.4	177
1979	2,563.3	2,217.7	70.6	58.4	127.0	543.8	331.1	212.7	51.9	175.8	193
1980	2,789.5	2,405.8	62.0	91.3	130.3	556.6	333.9	222.7	60.0	188.7	200
1981	3,128.4	2,702.5	75.4	122.9	131.8	616.5	370.4	246.1	70.7	208.3	221
1982	3,255.0	2,792.6	71.3	120.0	128.8	603.2	353.4	249.8	81.7	207.9	229
1983	3,536.7	3,043.5	57.1	103.1	139.8	653.1	379.3	273.8	91.6	222.9	261
1984	3,933.2	3,395.1	77.1	107.2	164.4	724.0	443.5	280.5	102.3	249.4	293
1985	4,220.3	3,637.0	77.1	105.4	184.6	740.3	449.2	291.1	109.2	268.3	318
1986	4,462.8	3,842.9	74.2	68.9	207.7	766.0	459.3	306.7	114.4	278.5	336
1987	4,739.5	4,080.4	79.8	71.5	218.2	811.3	483.8	327.5	123.0	285.3	349
1988	5,103.8	4,399.1	80.2	71.4	232.7	876.9	519.0	357.9	122.8	318.1	366
1989	5,484.4	4,732.3	92.8	76.0	244.8	927.3	543.2	384.1	135.9	337.4	389
1990	5,803.1	4,997.8	96.7	84.9	248.5	947.4	542.7	404.7	142.9	347.7	398
1991	5,995.9	5,138.7	89.2	76.0	230.2	957.5	540.9	416.6	152.5	360.5	405
1992	6,337.7	5,440.4	99.6	71.3	232.5	996.7	562.8	433.8	157.4	378.9	430
1993	6,657.4	5,729.3	93.1	72.1	248.3	1,039.9	593.1	446.8	165.3	401.2	458
1994	7,072.2	6,110.5	105.6	73.6	274.4	1,118.8	647.7	471.1	174.6	442.7	493
1995	7,397.6	6,407.2	93.1	74.1	287.0	1,177.3	677.2	500.0	181.5	457.0	514
1996	7,816.9	6,795.2	113.8	87.5	311.7	1,209.4	706.5	502.9	183.3	489.1	543
1997	8,304.3	7,247.5	110.7	92.6	337.6	1,279.8	755.5	524.3	179.6	521.2	574
1998	8,747.0	7,652.5	102.4	74.8	374.4	1,343.9	806.9	537.0	180.8	542.9	598
1999	9,268.4	8,127.2	93.8	85.4	406.6	1,373.1	820.4	552.7	185.4	577.7	635
2000	9,817.0	8,614.3	98.0	121.3	435.9	1,426.2	865.3	560.9	189.3	591.7	662
2001	10,128.0	8,869.7	97.9	118.7	469.5	1,341.3	778.9	562.5	202.3	607.1	691
2002	10,469.6	9,131.2	95.4	106.5	482.3	1,352.6	774.8	577.9	207.3	615.4	719
2003	10,960.8	9,542.3	114.4	143.3	496.2	1,359.3	771.8	587.5	220.0	637.0	751
2004	11,685.9	10,194.3	142.2	171.3	539.2	1,427.9	807.5	620.4	240.3	686.7	776
2005	12,433.9	10,861.5	128.8	225.7	607.9	1,483.9	840.9	643.0	249.5	723.7	812
2006	13,194.7	11,556.0	125.4	262.4	630.0	1,549.7	882.8	666.9	273.4	762.2	848
2007	13,841.3	12,103.8	161.4	275.8	562.6	1,615.8	926.7	689.1	295.9	799.1	886
	Percent					Industry value added as a percentage of GDP (percent)					
1977	100.0	85.6	2.5	2.1	4.6	21.6	13.1	8.5	2.3	6.6	7
1978	100.0	86.2	2.6	2.2	4.9	21.3	13.2	8.1	2.2	6.7	7
1979	100.0	86.5	2.8	2.3	5.0	21.2	12.9	8.3	2.0	6.9	7
1980	100.0	86.2	2.2	3.3	4.7	20.0	12.0	8.0	2.2	6.8	7
1981	100.0	86.4	2.4	3.9	4.2	19.7	11.8	7.9	2.3	6.7	7
1982	100.0	85.8	2.2	3.7	4.0	18.5	10.9	7.7	2.5	6.4	7
1983	100.0	86.1	1.6	2.9	4.0	18.5	10.7	7.7	2.6	6.3	7
1984	100.0	86.3	2.0	2.7	4.2	18.4	11.3	7.1	2.6	6.3	7
1985	100.0	86.2	1.8	2.5	4.4	17.5	10.6	6.9	2.6	6.4	7
1986	100.0	86.1	1.7	1.5	4.7	17.2	10.3	6.9	2.6	6.2	7
1987	100.0	86.1	1.7	1.5	4.6	17.1	10.2	6.9	2.6	6.0	7
1988	100.0	86.2	1.6	1.4	4.6	17.2	10.2	7.0	2.4	6.2	7
1989	100.0	86.3	1.7	1.4	4.5	16.9	9.9	7.0	2.5	6.2	7
1990	100.0	86.1	1.7	1.5	4.3	16.3	9.4	7.0	2.5	6.0	6
1991	100.0	85.7	1.5	1.3	3.8	16.0	9.0	6.9	2.5	6.0	6
1992	100.0	85.8	1.6	1.1	3.7	15.7	8.9	6.8	2.5	6.0	6
1993	100.0	86.1	1.4	1.1	3.7	15.6	8.9	6.7	2.5	6.0	7
1994	100.0	86.4	1.5	1.0	3.9	15.8	9.2	6.7	2.5	6.3	7
1995	100.0	86.6	1.3	1.0	3.9	15.9	9.2	6.8	2.5	6.2	7
1996	100.0	86.9	1.5	1.1	4.0	15.5	9.0	6.4	2.3	6.3	7
1997	100.0	87.3	1.3	1.1	4.1	15.4	9.1	6.3	2.2	6.3	6
1998	100.0	87.5	1.2	.9	4.3	15.4	9.2	6.1	2.1	6.2	6
1999	100.0	87.7	1.0	.9	4.4	14.8	8.9	6.0	2.0	6.2	6
2000	100.0	87.7	1.0	1.2	4.4	14.5	8.8	5.7	1.9	6.0	6
2001	100.0	87.6	1.0	1.2	4.6	13.2	7.7	5.6	2.0	6.0	6
2002	100.0	87.2	.9	1.0	4.6	12.9	7.4	5.5	2.0	5.9	6
2003	100.0	87.1	1.0	1.3	4.5	12.4	7.0	5.4	2.0	5.8	6
2004	100.0	87.2	1.2	1.5	4.6	12.2	6.9	5.3	2.1	5.9	6
2005	100.0	87.4	1.0	1.8	4.9	11.9	6.8	5.2	2.0	5.8	6
2006	100.0	87.6	1.0	2.0	4.8	11.7	6.7	5.1	2.1	5.8	6
2007	100.0	87.4	1.2	2.0	4.1	11.7	6.7	5.0	2.1	5.8	6

[1] Consists of agriculture, forestry, fishing, and hunting; mining; construction; and manufacturing.

[2] Consists of utilities; wholesale trade; retail trade; transportation and warehousing; information; finance, insurance, real estate, rental, and leasing; professional and business services; educational services, health care, and social assistance; arts, entertainment, recreation, accommodation, and food service; and other services, except government.

Note.—Industry detail data for 2005 and 2006, released in January 2008, and data for 2007, released in April 2008, do not incorporate revised statistics of the national income and product accounts that were released in July 2008. The sum of value added for all industries differs slightly from GDP in these earlier data because value added for manufacturing included source data that were not included in GDP as reported in the national income and product accounts (NIPAs).

See next page for continuation of table.

TABLE B–12.—*Gross domestic product (GDP) by industry, value added, in current dollars and as a percentage of GDP, 1977–2007*—Continued

[Billions of dollars; except as noted]

| Year | Private industries—continued | | | | | | | Government | Private goods-producing industries [1] | Private services-producing industries [2] |
	Transportation and warehousing	Information	Finance, insurance, real estate, rental, and leasing	Professional and business services	Educational services, health care, and social assistance	Arts, entertainment, recreation, accommodation, and food services	Other services, except government			
					Value added					
1977	76.2	71.1	304.0	122.7	93.8	58.8	46.1	291.5	627.5	1,111.9
1978	86.7	81.4	347.4	141.9	106.4	67.9	53.2	317.7	710.6	1,266.4
1979	96.6	90.3	390.3	164.0	120.5	77.1	58.2	345.7	799.7	1,417.9
1980	102.3	99.0	442.4	186.3	139.7	83.5	62.6	383.7	840.2	1,565.6
1981	109.9	112.7	498.4	213.2	159.9	93.5	68.5	425.9	946.6	1,755.9
1982	105.9	123.6	539.9	230.9	177.9	100.9	70.7	462.4	923.3	1,869.3
1983	117.8	140.0	604.6	262.5	198.3	112.0	79.2	493.1	953.1	2,090.5
1984	131.4	147.1	670.2	303.8	214.1	121.2	89.3	538.1	1,072.7	2,322.3
1985	136.3	162.9	729.7	340.8	231.3	134.3	98.0	583.3	1,107.4	2,529.5
1986	145.6	173.1	795.1	378.8	252.0	144.9	107.2	620.0	1,116.7	2,726.1
1987	151.1	185.0	840.3	414.1	286.5	152.1	112.3	659.1	1,180.8	2,899.5
1988	161.1	194.0	910.1	466.3	309.1	165.9	124.4	704.7	1,261.3	3,137.8
1989	164.1	210.4	975.4	518.0	347.0	180.2	133.9	752.0	1,341.0	3,391.4
1990	169.4	225.1	1,042.1	569.8	386.7	195.2	142.6	805.3	1,377.4	3,620.4
1991	178.2	235.2	1,103.6	579.3	424.8	202.2	144.2	857.2	1,352.8	3,785.9
1992	186.6	250.9	1,177.4	626.7	463.5	216.2	153.0	897.3	1,400.0	4,040.5
1993	201.0	272.6	1,241.5	659.1	488.0	225.5	163.7	928.1	1,453.4	4,275.9
1994	218.0	294.0	1,297.8	698.4	511.1	235.0	173.2	961.8	1,572.4	4,538.0
1995	226.3	307.6	1,380.0	743.1	533.3	248.3	180.9	990.4	1,631.4	4,775.8
1996	235.2	335.7	1,470.7	810.1	552.5	264.4	188.1	1,021.6	1,722.4	5,072.8
1997	253.7	347.8	1,593.3	896.5	573.1	289.8	197.4	1,056.8	1,820.8	5,426.8
1998	273.7	381.6	1,684.6	976.2	601.5	306.0	211.1	1,094.5	1,895.4	5,757.1
1999	287.4	439.3	1,798.4	1,064.5	634.5	327.8	217.8	1,141.2	1,958.9	6,168.3
2000	301.6	458.3	1,931.0	1,140.8	678.4	350.1	229.1	1,202.7	2,081.5	6,532.8
2001	296.9	476.9	2,059.2	1,165.9	739.3	361.5	241.5	1,258.3	2,027.5	6,842.2
2002	304.6	483.0	2,141.9	1,189.0	799.6	381.5	252.5	1,338.4	2,036.9	7,094.3
2003	316.6	489.1	2,244.6	1,248.9	857.3	398.9	265.3	1,418.4	2,113.3	7,429.1
2004	344.6	530.6	2,378.8	1,338.2	916.3	427.5	273.9	1,491.6	2,280.6	7,913.7
2005	358.5	570.5	2,549.0	1,453.2	961.5	448.4	288.1	1,568.7	2,446.2	8,415.2
2006	385.4	598.8	2,756.6	1,560.9	1,022.3	479.8	301.1	1,649.4	2,567.5	8,988.5
2007	403.5	645.3	2,860.7	1,684.2	1,090.7	505.7	316.6	1,741.0	2,615.5	9,488.2
				Industry value added as a percentage of GDP (percent)						
1977	3.8	3.5	15.0	6.0	4.6	2.9	2.3	14.4	30.9	54.7
1978	3.8	3.5	15.1	6.2	4.6	3.0	2.3	13.8	31.0	55.2
1979	3.8	3.5	15.2	6.4	4.7	3.0	2.3	13.5	31.2	55.3
1980	3.7	3.5	15.9	6.7	5.0	3.0	2.2	13.8	30.1	56.1
1981	3.5	3.6	15.9	6.8	5.1	3.0	2.2	13.6	30.3	56.1
1982	3.3	3.8	16.6	7.1	5.5	3.1	2.2	14.2	28.4	57.4
1983	3.3	4.0	17.1	7.4	5.6	3.2	2.2	13.9	26.9	59.1
1984	3.3	3.7	17.0	7.7	5.4	3.1	2.3	13.7	27.3	59.0
1985	3.2	3.9	17.3	8.1	5.5	3.2	2.3	13.8	26.2	59.9
1986	3.3	3.9	17.8	8.5	5.6	3.2	2.4	13.9	25.0	61.1
1987	3.2	3.9	17.7	8.7	6.0	3.2	2.4	13.9	24.9	61.2
1988	3.2	3.8	17.8	9.1	6.1	3.3	2.4	13.8	24.7	61.5
1989	3.0	3.8	17.8	9.4	6.3	3.3	2.4	13.7	24.5	61.8
1990	2.9	3.9	18.0	9.8	6.7	3.4	2.5	13.9	23.7	62.4
1991	3.0	3.9	18.4	9.7	7.1	3.4	2.4	14.3	22.6	63.1
1992	2.9	4.0	18.6	9.9	7.3	3.4	2.4	14.2	22.1	63.8
1993	3.0	4.1	18.6	9.9	7.3	3.4	2.5	13.9	21.8	64.2
1994	3.1	4.2	18.4	9.9	7.2	3.3	2.4	13.6	22.2	64.2
1995	3.1	4.2	18.7	10.0	7.2	3.4	2.4	13.4	22.1	64.6
1996	3.0	4.3	18.8	10.4	7.1	3.4	2.4	13.1	22.0	64.9
1997	3.1	4.2	19.2	10.8	6.9	3.5	2.4	12.7	21.9	65.3
1998	3.1	4.4	19.3	11.2	6.9	3.5	2.4	12.5	21.7	65.8
1999	3.1	4.7	19.4	11.5	6.8	3.5	2.3	12.3	21.1	66.6
2000	3.1	4.7	19.7	11.6	6.9	3.6	2.3	12.3	21.2	66.5
2001	2.9	4.7	20.3	11.5	7.3	3.6	2.4	12.4	20.0	67.6
2002	2.9	4.6	20.5	11.4	7.6	3.6	2.4	12.8	19.5	67.8
2003	2.9	4.5	20.5	11.4	7.8	3.6	2.4	12.9	19.3	67.8
2004	2.9	4.5	20.4	11.5	7.8	3.7	2.3	12.8	19.5	67.7
2005	2.9	4.6	20.5	11.7	7.7	3.6	2.3	12.6	19.7	67.7
2006	2.9	4.5	20.9	11.8	7.7	3.6	2.3	12.5	19.5	68.1
2007	2.9	4.7	20.7	12.2	7.9	3.7	2.3	12.6	18.9	68.5

Note (cont'd).—Value added is the contribution of each private industry and of government to GDP. Value added is equal to an industry's gross output minus its intermediate inputs. Current-dollar value added is calculated as the sum of distributions by an industry to its labor and capital, which are derived from the components of gross domestic income.

Value added industry data shown in Tables B–12 and B–13 are based on the 1997 North American Industry Classification System (NAICS). GDP by industry data based on the Standard Industrial Classification (SIC) are available from the Department of Commerce, Bureau of Economic Analysis.

Source: Department of Commerce (Bureau of Economic Analysis).

TABLE B–13.—*Real gross domestic product by industry, value added, and percent changes,*
1977–2007

Year	Gross domestic product	Private industries									
		Total private industries	Agriculture, forestry, fishing, and hunting	Mining	Construction	Manufacturing			Utilities	Wholesale trade	Retail trade
						Total manufacturing	Durable goods	Non-durable goods			
	Chain-type quantity indexes for value added (2000=100)										
1977	48.391	46.088	46.430	86.262	74.057	46.745	37.736	64.010	59.909	33.611	38.41
1978	51.085	48.802	45.057	88.929	78.442	49.157	40.159	66.062	59.583	37.065	40.65
1979	52.699	50.606	48.573	79.749	81.174	50.843	40.808	70.282	54.661	39.888	40.70
1980	52.579	50.321	47.543	89.978	74.626	48.190	38.476	67.152	51.968	39.782	38.90
1981	53.904	51.720	59.731	90.260	67.939	50.480	39.563	72.303	51.733	42.074	40.03
1982	52.860	50.422	62.961	86.329	59.460	46.795	35.645	69.864	50.698	42.096	39.95
1983	55.249	52.785	43.338	81.175	62.805	50.455	37.953	76.660	52.706	43.770	44.12
1984	59.220	56.789	57.105	88.849	72.200	55.084	44.042	76.466	57.341	47.143	48.26
1985	61.666	59.383	69.555	93.077	79.043	56.582	45.187	78.688	60.940	49.523	51.23
1986	63.804	61.137	68.605	87.529	81.818	56.516	45.550	77.515	64.406	54.486	54.18
1987	65.958	63.367	71.483	91.661	82.448	60.746	48.859	83.572	72.315	53.070	52.13
1988	68.684	66.299	64.678	99.992	85.435	64.212	52.843	85.425	70.613	56.444	56.54
1989	71.116	68.710	71.099	97.072	87.646	65.033	53.696	86.109	79.002	58.603	58.83
1990	72.451	69.905	74.689	96.157	86.543	64.299	52.963	85.419	84.447	57.318	59.79
1991	72.329	69.779	75.398	97.638	79.137	63.412	51.496	85.835	85.285	59.387	59.48
1992	74.734	72.363	83.114	95.694	80.026	65.508	52.742	89.669	85.362	65.037	62.96
1993	76.731	74.291	72.838	97.020	82.010	68.255	55.173	92.943	85.814	67.135	65.35
1994	79.816	77.765	84.616	105.327	86.586	73.496	60.173	98.369	89.518	71.346	69.80
1995	81.814	79.722	73.099	105.681	86.312	76.819	65.218	97.783	93.835	70.800	72.97
1996	84.842	83.179	80.041	98.850	90.694	79.682	69.120	98.443	95.405	77.261	79.40
1997	88.658	87.362	88.315	102.463	93.267	84.518	75.335	100.438	91.161	85.648	86.03
1998	92.359	91.662	86.287	101.682	97.087	90.181	84.355	99.762	90.481	95.431	90.39
1999	96.469	96.183	89.163	104.300	99.411	94.104	89.627	101.298	94.672	100.412	95.68
2000	100.000	100.000	100.000	100.000	100.000	100.000	100.000	100.000	100.000	100.000	100.000
2001	100.751	100.908	93.661	94.715	100.163	94.436	94.031	95.034	95.081	107.003	106.97
2002	102.362	102.354	98.767	88.719	98.201	97.066	95.663	99.056	99.144	108.059	109.29
2003	104.931	105.068	106.173	87.922	96.189	98.168	98.169	98.265	105.990	110.380	113.55
2004	108.748	109.198	113.287	88.770	96.430	103.653	103.873	103.468	112.076	112.614	116.53
2005	112.086	112.910	118.862	86.639	99.028	104.681	108.970	99.416	109.578	114.637	123.65
2006	115.304	116.819	119.941	91.943	93.070	107.738	115.551	98.377	107.085	116.594	129.82
2007	117.825	119.290	121.607	91.983	81.790	110.199	121.193	97.311	112.787	117.687	136.21
	Percent change from year earlier										
1977	4.6	5.0	4.1	7.6	1.3	7.8	8.1	7.3	-0.5	5.1	4.
1978	5.6	5.9	-3.0	3.1	5.9	5.2	6.4	3.2	-.5	10.3	5.
1979	3.2	3.7	7.8	-10.3	3.5	3.4	1.6	6.4	-8.3	7.6	
1980	-.2	-.6	-2.1	12.8	-8.1	-5.2	-5.7	-4.5	-4.9	-.3	-4.
1981	2.5	2.8	25.6	.3	-9.0	4.8	2.8	7.7	-.5	5.8	2.
1982	-1.9	-2.5	5.4	-4.4	-12.5	-7.3	-9.9	-3.4	-2.0	.1	-
1983	4.5	4.7	-31.2	-6.0	5.6	7.8	6.5	9.7	4.0	4.0	10.
1984	7.2	7.6	31.8	9.5	15.0	9.2	16.0	-.3	8.8	7.7	9.
1985	4.1	4.6	21.8	4.8	9.5	2.7	2.6	2.9	6.3	5.0	6.
1986	3.5	3.0	-1.4	-6.0	3.5	-.1	.8	-1.5	5.7	10.0	5.
1987	3.4	3.6	4.2	4.7	.8	7.5	7.3	7.8	12.3	-2.6	-3.
1988	4.1	4.6	-9.5	9.1	3.6	5.7	8.2	2.2	-2.4	6.4	8.
1989	3.5	3.6	9.9	-2.9	2.6	1.3	1.6	.8	11.9	3.8	4.
1990	1.9	1.7	5.0	-.9	-1.3	-1.1	-1.4	-.8	6.9	-2.2	1.
1991	-.2	-.2	.9	1.5	-8.6	-1.4	-2.8	.5	1.0	3.6	-
1992	3.3	3.7	10.2	-2.0	1.1	3.3	2.4	4.5	.1	9.5	5.
1993	2.7	2.7	-12.4	1.4	2.5	4.2	4.6	3.7	.5	3.2	3.
1994	4.0	4.7	16.2	8.6	5.6	7.7	9.1	5.8	4.3	6.3	6.
1995	2.5	2.5	-13.6	.3	-.3	4.5	8.4	-.6	4.8	-.8	4.
1996	3.7	4.3	9.5	-6.5	5.1	3.7	6.0	.7	1.7	9.1	8.
1997	4.5	5.0	10.3	3.7	2.8	6.1	9.0	2.0	-4.4	10.9	8.
1998	4.2	4.9	-2.3	-.8	4.1	6.7	12.0	-.7	-.7	11.4	5.
1999	4.5	4.9	3.3	2.6	2.4	4.4	6.2	1.5	4.6	5.2	5.
2000	3.7	4.0	12.2	-4.1	.6	6.3	11.6	-1.3	5.6	-.4	4.
2001	.8	.9	-6.3	-5.3	.2	-5.6	-6.0	-5.0	-4.9	7.0	7.
2002	1.6	1.4	5.5	-6.3	-2.0	2.8	1.7	4.2	4.3	1.0	2
2003	2.5	2.7	7.5	-.9	-2.0	1.1	2.6	-.8	6.9	2.1	3
2004	3.6	3.9	6.7	1.0	.3	5.6	5.8	5.3	5.7	2.0	2
2005	3.1	3.4	4.9	-2.4	2.7	1.0	4.9	-3.9	-2.2	1.8	6.
2006	2.9	3.5	.9	6.1	-6.0	2.9	6.0	-1.0	-2.3	1.7	5.
2007	2.2	2.1	1.4	.0	-12.1	2.3	4.9	-1.1	5.3	.9	4

[1] Consists of agriculture, forestry, fishing, and hunting; mining; construction; and manufacturing.

[2] Consists of utilities; wholesale trade; retail trade; transportation and warehousing; information; finance, insurance, real estate, rental, and leasing; professional and business services; educational services, health care, and social assistance; arts, entertainment, recreation, accommodation, and food services and other services, except government.

See next page for continuation of table.

	Private industries—continued								Private goods-producing industries [1]	Private services-producing industries [2]
Year	Transportation and warehousing	Information	Finance, insurance, real estate, rental, and leasing	Professional and business services	Educational services, health care, and social assistance	Arts, entertainment, recreation, accommodation, and food services	Other services, except government	Government			

	Chain-type quantity indexes for value added (2000=100)										
1977	43.462	28.460	47.363	34.086	57.878	48.641	71.231	74.973		52.269	43.258
1978	45.697	31.532	50.358	36.884	60.672	52.049	75.107	76.694		54.587	46.163
1979	48.252	34.231	52.965	39.387	63.234	53.512	75.703	77.721		56.085	48.120
1980	47.232	36.394	55.414	40.529	66.887	52.407	74.411	79.023		53.880	48.764
1981	46.178	38.257	56.573	41.554	68.455	54.193	72.329	79.328		55.783	49.923
1982	43.855	38.155	56.986	41.345	68.856	55.695	69.103	79.456		52.029	49.794
1983	49.486	41.017	58.734	44.142	71.153	59.784	72.470	80.178		53.361	52.637
1984	52.121	40.717	61.282	48.913	72.366	62.194	77.498	81.038		59.454	55.727
1985	52.715	42.039	62.812	52.748	73.629	66.167	80.936	83.172		62.569	58.104
1986	53.021	42.672	63.965	56.860	75.166	69.642	82.885	85.105		62.534	60.576
1987	55.690	45.764	65.941	60.050	80.273	68.742	84.221	86.753		66.173	62.256
1988	57.990	47.649	68.652	64.420	80.570	71.515	89.044	88.812		69.104	65.186
1989	59.507	51.150	70.359	68.787	84.002	73.872	92.188	90.984		70.366	68.033
1990	62.281	53.420	71.877	72.073	87.047	76.063	94.369	93.215		69.858	69.877
1991	65.060	54.441	73.051	69.786	89.285	74.232	91.258	93.658		68.214	70.319
1992	68.758	57.568	74.863	72.008	91.728	77.250	92.502	94.134		70.330	73.074
1993	71.988	61.445	76.931	73.224	92.199	78.787	95.195	94.055		72.128	75.047
1994	77.827	65.223	78.506	75.430	92.413	80.604	98.624	94.407		77.818	77.745
1995	80.473	67.996	80.732	77.382	93.503	83.542	99.714	94.250		79.572	79.773
1996	84.585	72.714	82.893	82.053	94.144	86.796	99.072	94.768		82.596	83.377
1997	88.373	74.559	86.786	87.432	94.809	90.310	99.291	95.864		87.229	87.407
1998	91.454	82.252	90.201	91.976	95.603	93.446	101.871	96.923		91.878	91.591
1999	95.301	95.467	94.994	96.898	97.304	96.836	100.236	98.009		95.402	96.434
2000	100.000	100.000	100.000	100.000	100.000	100.000	100.000	100.000		100.000	100.000
2001	97.354	104.034	103.858	99.346	103.186	99.292	98.337	100.794		95.654	102.584
2002	99.531	106.263	104.800	99.192	107.527	101.022	98.667	102.467		96.853	104.107
2003	101.534	109.430	107.288	103.554	112.257	104.138	100.615	103.776		97.402	107.496
2004	110.780	122.221	110.433	107.750	115.949	108.114	100.770	104.252		101.328	111.692
2005	115.372	136.236	115.771	112.083	118.053	109.534	100.185	104.977		102.678	116.164
2006	121.419	146.005	122.523	116.324	122.229	112.916	99.877	105.447		103.543	121.078
2007	125.222	159.112	123.974	121.666	126.448	115.044	102.003	106.674		101.992	124.896

	Percent change from year earlier										
1977	4.1	7.5	1.4	8.6	6.4	6.8	0.3	0.9		6.4	4.1
1978	5.1	10.8	6.3	8.2	4.8	7.0	5.4	2.3		4.4	6.7
1979	5.6	8.6	5.2	6.8	4.2	2.8	.8	1.3		2.7	4.2
1980	−2.1	6.3	4.6	2.9	5.8	−2.1	−1.7	1.7		−3.9	1.3
1981	−2.2	5.1	2.1	2.5	2.3	3.4	−2.8	.4		3.5	2.4
1982	−5.0	−.3	.7	−.5	.6	2.8	−4.5	.2		−6.7	−.3
1983	12.8	7.5	3.1	6.8	3.3	7.3	4.9	.9		2.6	5.7
1984	5.3	−.7	4.3	10.8	1.7	4.0	6.9	1.1		11.4	5.9
1985	1.1	3.2	2.5	7.8	1.7	6.4	4.4	2.6		5.2	4.3
1986	.6	1.5	1.8	7.8	2.1	5.3	2.4	2.3		−1.	4.3
1987	5.0	7.2	3.1	5.6	6.8	−1.3	1.6	1.9		5.8	2.8
1988	4.1	4.1	4.1	7.3	.4	4.0	5.7	2.4		4.4	4.7
1989	2.6	7.3	2.5	6.8	4.3	3.3	3.5	2.4		1.8	4.4
1990	4.7	4.4	2.2	4.8	3.6	3.0	2.4	2.5		−.7	2.7
1991	4.5	1.9	1.6	−3.2	2.6	−2.4	−3.3	.5		−2.4	.6
1992	5.7	5.7	2.5	3.2	2.7	4.1	1.4	.5		3.1	3.9
1993	4.7	6.7	2.8	1.7	.5	2.0	2.9	−.1		2.6	2.7
1994	8.1	6.1	2.0	3.0	.2	2.3	3.6	.4		7.9	3.6
1995	3.4	4.3	2.8	2.6	1.2	3.6	1.1	−.2		2.3	2.6
1996	5.1	6.9	2.7	6.0	.7	3.9	−.6	.5		3.8	4.5
1997	4.5	2.5	4.7	6.6	.7	4.0	.2	1.2		5.6	4.8
1998	3.5	10.3	3.9	5.2	.8	3.5	2.6	1.1		5.3	4.8
1999	4.2	16.1	5.3	5.4	1.8	3.6	−1.6	1.1		3.8	5.3
2000	4.9	4.7	5.3	3.2	2.8	3.3	−.2	2.0		4.8	3.7
2001	−2.6	4.0	3.9	−.7	3.2	−.7	−1.7	.8		−4.3	2.6
2002	2.2	2.1	.9	−.2	4.2	1.7	.3	1.7		1.3	1.5
2003	2.0	3.0	2.4	4.4	4.4	3.1	2.0	1.3		.6	3.3
2004	9.1	11.7	2.9	4.1	3.3	3.8	.2	.5		4.0	3.9
2005	4.1	11.5	4.8	4.0	1.8	1.3	−.6	.7		1.3	4.0
2006	5.2	7.2	5.8	3.8	3.5	3.1	−.3	.4		.8	4.2
2007	3.1	9.0	1.2	4.6	3.5	1.9	2.1	1.2		−1.5	3.2

Note.—Data are based on the 1997 North American Industry Classification System (NAICS).
See Note, Table B–12.

Source: Department of Commerce (Bureau of Economic Analysis).

TABLE B–14.—*Gross value added of nonfinancial corporate business, 1959–2008*

[Billions of dollars; quarterly data at seasonally adjusted annual rates]

Year or quarter	Gross value added of nonfinancial corporate business[1]	Consumption of fixed capital	Net value added									Addenda		
			Total	Compensation of employees	Taxes on production and imports less subsidies	Net operating surplus						Profits before tax	Inventory valuation adjustment	Capital consumption adjustment
						Total	Net interest and miscellaneous payments	Business current transfer payments	Corporate profits with inventory valuation and capital consumption adjustments					
									Total	Taxes on corporate rate income	Profits after tax[2]			
1959	266.0	21.1	244.9	170.8	24.4	49.7	2.9	1.3	45.5	20.7	24.8	43.4	−0.3	2.3
1960	276.4	22.6	253.8	180.4	26.6	46.8	3.2	1.4	42.2	19.1	23.1	40.1	−.2	2.3
1961	283.7	23.2	260.5	184.5	27.6	48.4	3.7	1.5	43.2	19.4	23.8	39.9	.3	3.0
1962	309.8	23.9	285.9	199.3	29.9	56.8	4.3	1.7	50.8	20.6	30.2	44.6	.0	6.1
1963	329.9	25.2	304.7	210.1	31.7	62.9	4.7	1.7	56.5	22.8	33.8	49.7	.1	6.9
1964	356.1	26.4	329.7	225.7	33.9	70.2	5.2	2.0	63.0	23.9	39.2	55.9	−.5	7.2
1965	391.2	28.4	362.8	245.4	36.0	81.4	5.8	2.2	73.3	27.1	46.2	66.1	−1.2	8.4
1966	429.0	31.5	397.4	272.9	37.0	87.6	7.0	2.7	77.9	29.5	48.4	71.4	−2.1	8.5
1967	451.2	34.3	416.8	291.1	39.3	86.4	8.4	2.8	75.2	27.8	47.3	67.6	−1.6	9.1
1968	497.8	37.6	460.2	321.9	45.5	92.8	9.7	3.1	80.0	33.5	46.5	74.0	−3.7	9.2
1969	540.5	42.4	498.1	357.1	50.2	90.8	12.7	3.2	74.9	33.3	41.6	71.2	−5.9	9.6
1970	558.3	46.8	511.5	376.5	54.2	80.7	16.6	3.3	60.9	27.3	33.6	58.5	−6.6	8.5
1971	603.0	50.7	552.4	399.4	59.5	93.4	17.6	3.7	72.1	30.0	42.1	67.4	−4.6	9.3
1972	669.5	56.4	613.2	443.9	63.7	105.6	18.6	4.0	83.0	33.8	49.2	79.2	−6.6	10.5
1973	750.8	62.7	688.1	502.2	70.1	115.8	21.8	4.7	89.4	40.4	49.0	99.4	−19.6	9.5
1974	809.8	74.1	735.7	552.2	74.4	109.1	27.5	4.1	77.5	42.8	34.7	110.1	−38.2	5.6
1975	876.7	87.9	788.7	575.5	80.2	133.1	28.4	5.0	99.6	41.9	57.7	110.7	−10.5	−.5
1976	989.7	97.0	892.7	651.4	86.7	154.7	26.0	7.0	121.7	53.5	68.2	138.2	−14.1	−2.4
1977	1,119.4	110.5	1,008.8	735.3	94.6	178.9	28.5	9.0	141.4	60.6	80.9	159.4	−15.7	−2.2
1978	1,272.9	127.8	1,145.1	845.3	102.7	197.0	33.4	9.5	154.1	67.6	86.6	183.7	−23.7	−5.9
1979	1,415.9	147.3	1,268.6	959.9	108.8	200.0	41.8	9.5	148.8	70.6	78.1	197.0	−40.1	−8.1
1980	1,537.1	168.2	1,368.9	1,049.8	121.5	197.6	54.2	10.2	133.2	68.2	65.0	184.0	−42.1	−8.7
1981	1,746.0	191.5	1,554.5	1,161.5	146.7	246.4	67.2	11.4	167.7	66.0	101.7	185.0	−24.6	7.4
1982	1,806.2	211.2	1,594.9	1,203.9	152.9	238.1	77.4	8.8	151.9	48.8	103.1	139.9	−7.5	19.5
1983	1,933.0	217.6	1,715.4	1,266.9	168.0	280.5	77.0	10.5	192.9	61.7	131.2	163.3	−7.4	37.1
1984	2,167.5	230.7	1,936.8	1,406.1	185.0	345.7	86.0	11.7	248.0	75.9	172.0	197.6	−4.0	54.3
1985	2,302.0	247.4	2,054.6	1,504.2	196.6	353.8	91.5	16.1	246.3	71.1	175.2	173.4	.0	72.8
1986	2,387.5	255.3	2,132.2	1,583.1	204.6	344.5	95.1	27.3	222.1	76.2	145.9	149.7	7.1	65.3
1987	2,557.1	266.5	2,290.6	1,687.8	216.8	386.0	96.4	29.9	259.7	94.2	165.5	209.8	−16.2	66.2
1988	2,771.6	281.6	2,490.0	1,812.8	233.8	443.4	109.8	27.4	306.2	104.0	202.3	260.4	−22.2	68.0
1989	2,912.3	301.6	2,610.7	1,914.7	248.2	447.9	142.0	23.0	282.9	101.2	181.7	238.7	−16.3	60.8
1990	3,041.5	319.2	2,722.3	2,012.9	263.5	445.8	146.2	25.4	274.3	98.5	175.8	239.0	−12.9	48.2
1991	3,099.7	341.4	2,758.3	2,048.4	285.7	424.2	135.9	26.7	261.5	88.6	172.9	222.4	4.9	34.2
1992	3,236.0	353.6	2,882.3	2,154.1	302.5	425.7	111.3	25.2	289.2	94.4	194.8	258.2	−2.8	33.8
1993	3,397.8	363.4	3,034.4	2,244.8	318.8	470.8	102.0	29.6	339.2	108.0	231.2	303.3	−4.0	39.9
1994	3,669.5	391.5	3,278.0	2,381.5	349.6	546.9	101.0	30.0	415.9	132.9	283.1	380.1	−12.4	48.2
1995	3,879.5	415.0	3,464.5	2,509.8	356.9	597.8	115.2	30.2	452.5	141.0	311.4	419.3	−18.3	51.5
1996	4,109.5	436.5	3,673.0	2,630.8	369.1	673.1	111.9	38.0	523.2	153.1	370.1	458.5	3.1	61.6
1997	4,401.8	467.1	3,934.7	2,812.9	385.5	736.3	124.0	39.0	573.4	161.9	411.5	494.2	14.1	65.1
1998	4,655.0	493.3	4,161.7	3,045.6	398.7	717.4	143.8	35.2	538.3	158.6	379.7	449.4	20.2	68.8
1999	4,950.8	523.8	4,427.0	3,267.7	416.6	742.7	160.2	45.0	537.6	171.2	366.3	457.9	1.0	78.2
2000	5,272.2	567.8	4,704.3	3,544.4	443.4	716.5	191.7	48.4	476.4	170.2	306.2	423.9	−14.1	66.6
2001	5,293.5	646.8	4,646.7	3,595.9	439.1	611.8	204.0	50.6	357.2	111.7	245.5	310.6	11.3	35.2
2002	5,371.7	643.6	4,728.2	3,611.9	465.5	650.8	167.4	54.0	429.4	97.0	332.3	336.3	−2.2	95.3
2003	5,558.4	657.5	4,900.9	3,703.2	488.5	709.2	152.6	64.4	492.1	135.7	356.4	425.4	−13.6	80.1
2004	5,956.4	687.4	5,269.0	3,865.2	523.9	879.9	138.9	59.3	681.6	191.0	490.7	662.4	−43.1	62.4
2005	6,396.1	743.9	5,652.2	4,075.6	563.2	1,013.5	153.6	58.5	801.4	274.5	526.9	955.9	−37.8	−116.7
2006	6,863.4	775.2	6,088.3	4,316.8	591.1	1,180.3	169.6	71.8	939.0	309.3	629.7	1,127.4	−39.5	−149.0
2007	7,075.1	822.3	6,252.8	4,525.3	611.9	1,115.5	179.4	68.1	868.1	321.1	547.0	1,091.7	−51.2	−172.5
2005: I	6,210.3	702.0	5,508.4	3,991.9	548.9	967.5	145.2	72.1	750.2	256.9	493.3	896.5	−45.4	−100.1
II	6,358.1	714.4	5,643.7	4,038.9	560.6	1,044.3	150.7	73.9	819.7	268.0	551.7	941.5	−18.0	−103.8
III	6,418.9	810.4	5,608.5	4,115.4	568.6	924.4	156.9	20.5	747.0	267.6	479.4	921.1	−39.1	−134.9
IV	6,597.3	749.0	5,848.3	4,156.1	574.5	1,117.7	161.6	67.4	888.7	305.6	583.1	1,064.5	−48.7	−127.7
2006: I	6,771.2	755.7	6,015.5	4,264.7	582.7	1,168.1	165.1	73.0	930.0	302.6	627.4	1,093.3	−35.0	−128.3
II	6,817.5	769.3	6,048.3	4,282.3	589.5	1,176.4	169.4	72.0	935.0	312.3	622.7	1,137.3	−58.5	−143.9
III	6,931.7	781.9	6,149.7	4,318.3	593.6	1,237.8	169.8	71.3	996.7	323.3	673.4	1,196.1	−42.7	−156.2
IV	6,933.3	793.7	6,139.6	4,401.9	598.7	1,139.0	174.1	70.7	894.2	299.1	595.1	1,083.0	−21.8	−166.9
2007: I	6,999.6	804.6	6,195.0	4,464.1	604.1	1,126.9	174.6	68.8	883.6	319.8	563.8	1,086.8	−44.2	−159.0
II	7,066.7	816.0	6,250.7	4,497.4	609.9	1,143.5	178.9	68.0	896.6	330.9	565.7	1,119.2	−55.3	−167.4
III	7,098.6	828.1	6,270.6	4,537.2	614.2	1,119.1	178.8	67.7	872.6	318.9	553.7	1,080.4	−31.0	−176.3
IV	7,135.5	840.7	6,294.8	4,602.7	619.5	1,072.6	185.4	67.7	819.5	314.7	504.7	1,080.6	−74.1	−187.0
2008: I	7,119.3	852.6	6,266.7	4,623.0	617.9	1,025.8	180.5	57.9	787.4	279.8	507.6	939.6	−109.4	−42.1
II	7,153.1	868.5	6,284.6	4,630.8	625.6	1,028.2	186.7	58.2	783.2	294.0	489.2	993.3	−154.0	−56.5
III p	7,255.3	910.0	6,345.3	4,652.6	627.6	1,065.1	181.4	52.6	831.1	296.3	534.8	1,004.1	−92.4	−80.5

[1] Estimates for nonfinancial corporate business for 2000 and earlier periods are based on the Standard Industrial Classification (SIC); later estimates are based on the North American Industry Classification System (NAICS).
[2] With inventory valuation and capital consumption adjustments.

Source: Department of Commerce (Bureau of Economic Analysis).

TABLE B–15.—*Gross value added and price, costs, and profits of nonfinancial corporate business, 1959–2008*

[Quarterly data at seasonally adjusted annual rates]

Year or quarter	Gross value added of nonfinancial corporate business (billions of dollars) [1] — Current dollars	Chained (2000) dollars	Total	Compensation of employees (unit labor cost)	Unit nonlabor cost — Total	Consumption of fixed capital	Taxes on production and imports [3]	Net interest and miscellaneous payments	Corporate profits with inventory valuation and capital consumption adjustments [4] — Total	Taxes on corporate income	Profits after tax [5]
59	266.0	980.4	0.271	0.174	0.051	0.022	0.026	0.003	0.046	0.021	0.025
60	276.4	1,012.0	.273	.178	.053	.022	.028	.003	.042	.019	.023
61	283.7	1,033.6	.274	.179	.054	.022	.028	.004	.042	.019	.023
62	309.8	1,120.7	.276	.178	.053	.021	.028	.004	.045	.018	.027
63	329.9	1,186.7	.278	.177	.053	.021	.028	.004	.048	.019	.028
64	356.1	1,270.3	.280	.178	.053	.021	.028	.004	.050	.019	.031
65	391.2	1,375.1	.284	.178	.053	.021	.028	.004	.053	.020	.034
66	429.0	1,472.6	.291	.185	.053	.021	.027	.005	.053	.020	.033
67	451.2	1,508.9	.299	.193	.057	.023	.028	.006	.050	.018	.031
68	497.8	1,604.8	.310	.201	.059	.023	.030	.006	.050	.021	.029
69	540.5	1,667.6	.324	.214	.065	.025	.032	.008	.045	.020	.025
70	558.3	1,649.9	.338	.228	.073	.028	.035	.010	.037	.017	.020
71	603.0	1,716.6	.351	.233	.077	.030	.037	.010	.042	.017	.025
72	669.5	1,846.4	.363	.240	.078	.031	.037	.010	.045	.018	.027
73	750.8	1,957.7	.384	.257	.081	.032	.038	.011	.046	.021	.025
74	809.8	1,925.4	.421	.287	.093	.038	.041	.014	.040	.022	.018
75	876.7	1,898.8	.462	.303	.106	.046	.045	.015	.052	.022	.030
76	989.7	2,050.0	.483	.318	.106	.047	.046	.013	.059	.026	.033
77	1,119.4	2,200.0	.509	.334	.110	.050	.047	.013	.064	.028	.037
78	1,272.9	2,344.1	.543	.361	.117	.055	.048	.014	.066	.029	.037
79	1,415.9	2,418.7	.585	.397	.127	.061	.049	.017	.062	.029	.032
80	1,537.1	2,394.6	.642	.438	.148	.070	.055	.023	.056	.028	.027
81	1,746.0	2,491.5	.701	.466	.167	.077	.063	.027	.067	.026	.041
82	1,806.2	2,430.6	.743	.495	.186	.087	.067	.032	.062	.020	.042
83	1,933.0	2,545.1	.759	.498	.185	.085	.070	.030	.076	.024	.052
84	2,167.5	2,772.8	.782	.507	.185	.083	.071	.031	.089	.027	.062
85	2,302.0	2,896.3	.795	.519	.190	.085	.073	.032	.085	.025	.060
86	2,387.5	2,963.3	.806	.534	.196	.086	.078	.032	.075	.026	.049
87	2,557.1	3,119.6	.820	.541	.195	.085	.079	.031	.083	.030	.053
88	2,771.6	3,300.7	.840	.549	.197	.085	.079	.033	.093	.031	.061
89	2,912.3	3,361.8	.866	.570	.213	.090	.081	.042	.084	.030	.054
90	3,041.5	3,404.0	.894	.591	.222	.094	.085	.043	.081	.029	.052
91	3,099.7	3,376.2	.918	.607	.234	.101	.093	.040	.077	.026	.051
92	3,236.0	3,479.5	.930	.619	.228	.102	.094	.032	.083	.027	.056
93	3,397.8	3,575.5	.950	.628	.228	.102	.097	.029	.095	.030	.065
94	3,669.5	3,797.9	.966	.627	.230	.103	.100	.027	.110	.035	.075
95	3,879.5	3,977.4	.975	.631	.230	.104	.097	.029	.114	.035	.078
96	4,109.5	4,196.4	.979	.627	.228	.104	.097	.027	.125	.036	.088
97	4,401.8	4,469.3	.985	.629	.228	.105	.095	.028	.128	.036	.092
98	4,655.0	4,725.4	.985	.645	.226	.104	.092	.030	.114	.034	.080
99	4,950.8	5,011.0	.988	.652	.229	.105	.092	.032	.107	.034	.073
00	5,272.2	5,272.2	1.000	.672	.237	.108	.093	.036	.090	.032	.058
01	5,293.5	5,224.5	1.013	.688	.257	.124	.094	.039	.068	.021	.047
02	5,371.7	5,269.7	1.019	.685	.253	.122	.099	.032	.081	.018	.063
03	5,558.4	5,387.5	1.032	.687	.253	.122	.103	.028	.091	.025	.066
04	5,956.4	5,662.1	1.052	.683	.249	.121	.103	.025	.120	.034	.087
05	6,396.1	5,907.8	1.083	.690	.257	.126	.105	.026	.136	.046	.089
06	6,863.4	6,167.8	1.113	.700	.260	.126	.107	.027	.152	.050	.102
07	7,075.1	6,264.5	1.129	.722	.269	.131	.109	.029	.139	.051	.087
05: I	6,210.3	5,789.5	1.073	.690	.253	.121	.107	.025	.130	.044	.085
II	6,358.1	5,911.1	1.076	.683	.254	.121	.107	.026	.139	.045	.093
III	6,418.9	5,903.2	1.087	.697	.264	.137	.100	.027	.127	.045	.081
IV	6,597.3	6,027.3	1.095	.690	.258	.124	.107	.027	.147	.051	.097
06: I	6,771.2	6,129.6	1.105	.696	.257	.123	.107	.027	.152	.049	.102
II	6,817.5	6,141.6	1.110	.697	.261	.125	.108	.028	.152	.051	.101
III	6,931.7	6,212.5	1.116	.695	.260	.126	.107	.027	.160	.052	.108
IV	6,933.3	6,187.3	1.121	.711	.264	.128	.108	.028	.145	.048	.096
07: I	6,999.6	6,188.0	1.131	.721	.267	.130	.109	.028	.143	.052	.091
II	7,066.7	6,253.1	1.130	.719	.267	.130	.108	.029	.143	.053	.090
III	7,098.6	6,293.3	1.128	.721	.268	.132	.108	.028	.139	.051	.088
IV	7,135.5	6,323.5	1.128	.728	.271	.133	.109	.029	.130	.050	.080
08: I	7,119.3	6,302.0	1.130	.734	.271	.135	.107	.029	.125	.044	.081
II	7,153.1	6,394.4	1.119	.724	.272	.136	.107	.029	.122	.046	.076
III p	7,255.3	6,422.3	1.130	.724	.276	.142	.106	.028	.129	.046	.083

[1] Estimates for nonfinancial corporate business for 2000 and earlier periods are based on the Standard Industrial Classification (SIC); later estimates are used on the North American Industry Classification System (NAICS).
[2] The implicit price deflator for gross value added of nonfinancial corporate business divided by 100.
[3] Less subsidies plus business current transfer payments.
[4] Unit profits from current production.
[5] With inventory valuation and capital consumption adjustments.

Source: Department of Commerce (Bureau of Economic Analysis).

TABLE B–16.—*Personal consumption expenditures, 1959–2008*

[Billions of dollars; quarterly data at seasonally adjusted annual rates]

Year or quarter	Personal consumption expenditures	Durable goods			Nondurable goods					Services					
		Total[1]	Motor vehicles and parts	Furniture and household equipment	Total[1]	Food	Clothing and shoes	Gasoline and oil	Fuel oil and coal	Total[1]	Housing[2]	Household operation		Transportation	Medical care
												Total[1]	Electricity and gas		
1959	317.6	42.7	18.9	18.1	148.5	80.6	26.4	11.3	4.0	126.5	45.0	18.7	7.6	10.6	16.
1960	331.7	43.3	19.7	18.0	152.8	82.3	27.0	12.0	3.8	135.6	48.2	20.3	8.3	11.2	17.
1961	342.1	41.8	17.8	18.3	156.6	84.0	27.6	12.0	3.8	143.8	51.2	21.2	8.8	11.6	19.
1962	363.3	46.9	21.5	19.3	162.8	86.1	29.0	12.6	3.8	153.6	54.7	22.4	9.4	12.3	21.
1963	382.7	51.6	24.4	20.7	168.2	88.2	29.8	13.0	4.0	162.9	58.0	23.6	9.9	12.9	23.
1964	411.4	56.7	26.0	23.2	178.6	93.5	32.4	13.6	4.1	176.1	61.4	25.0	10.4	13.8	26.
1965	443.8	63.3	29.9	25.1	191.5	100.7	34.1	14.8	4.4	189.0	65.4	26.5	10.9	14.7	28.
1966	480.9	68.3	30.3	28.2	208.7	109.3	37.4	16.0	4.7	203.8	69.5	28.1	11.5	15.9	31.
1967	507.8	70.4	30.0	30.0	217.1	112.4	39.2	17.1	4.8	220.3	74.1	30.0	12.2	17.4	34.
1968	558.0	80.8	36.1	32.9	235.7	122.2	43.2	18.6	4.7	241.6	79.8	32.3	13.0	19.3	40.
1969	605.2	85.9	38.4	34.7	253.1	131.5	46.5	20.5	4.6	266.1	86.9	35.0	14.1	21.6	45.
1970	648.5	85.0	35.5	35.7	272.0	143.8	47.8	21.9	4.4	291.5	94.1	37.8	15.3	24.0	51.
1971	701.9	96.9	44.5	37.8	285.5	149.7	51.7	23.2	4.6	319.5	102.8	41.1	16.9	26.8	58.
1972	770.6	110.4	51.1	42.4	308.0	161.4	56.4	24.4	5.1	352.2	112.6	45.4	18.8	29.6	65.
1973	852.4	123.5	56.1	47.9	343.1	179.6	62.5	28.1	6.3	385.8	123.3	49.9	20.4	31.6	73.
1974	933.4	122.3	49.5	51.5	384.5	201.8	66.0	36.1	7.8	426.6	134.8	55.8	24.0	34.1	82.
1975	1,034.4	133.5	54.8	54.5	420.7	223.2	70.8	39.7	8.4	480.2	147.7	64.0	29.2	37.9	95.
1976	1,151.9	158.9	71.3	60.2	458.3	242.5	76.6	43.0	10.1	534.7	162.2	72.5	33.2	42.5	109.
1977	1,278.6	181.2	83.5	67.2	497.1	262.6	84.1	46.9	11.1	600.2	180.2	81.8	38.5	48.7	125.
1978	1,428.5	201.7	93.1	74.3	550.2	289.6	94.3	50.1	11.5	676.6	202.4	91.2	43.0	53.4	143.
1979	1,592.2	214.4	93.5	82.7	624.5	324.7	101.2	66.2	14.4	753.3	227.3	100.3	47.8	59.9	161.
1980	1,757.1	214.2	87.0	86.7	696.1	356.0	107.3	86.7	15.4	846.9	256.2	113.7	57.5	65.2	184.
1981	1,941.1	231.3	95.8	92.1	758.9	383.5	117.2	97.9	15.8	950.8	289.7	126.8	64.8	70.3	216.
1982	2,077.3	240.2	102.9	93.4	787.6	403.4	120.5	94.1	14.5	1,049.4	315.2	142.5	74.2	72.9	243.
1983	2,290.6	280.8	126.5	106.6	831.2	423.8	130.9	93.1	13.6	1,178.6	341.0	157.0	82.4	81.1	274.
1984	2,503.3	326.5	152.1	119.0	884.6	447.4	142.5	94.6	13.9	1,292.2	374.5	169.4	86.5	93.2	303.
1985	2,720.3	363.5	175.9	128.5	928.7	467.6	152.1	97.2	13.6	1,428.1	412.7	181.8	90.8	104.5	331.
1986	2,899.7	403.0	194.1	143.0	958.4	492.0	163.1	80.1	11.3	1,538.3	448.4	187.7	89.2	111.1	357.
1987	3,100.2	421.7	195.0	153.4	1,015.3	515.2	174.4	85.4	11.2	1,663.3	483.7	195.4	90.9	120.9	392.
1988	3,353.6	453.6	209.4	163.7	1,083.5	553.5	185.5	88.3	11.7	1,816.5	521.5	207.3	96.3	133.4	442.
1989	3,598.5	471.8	215.3	171.6	1,166.7	591.6	198.9	98.6	11.9	1,960.0	557.4	221.1	101.0	142.0	492.
1990	3,839.9	474.2	212.8	171.6	1,249.9	636.8	204.1	111.2	12.9	2,115.9	597.9	227.3	101.0	147.7	556.
1991	3,986.1	453.9	193.5	171.7	1,284.8	657.5	208.7	108.5	12.4	2,247.4	631.1	238.6	107.4	145.3	608.
1992	4,235.3	483.6	213.0	178.7	1,330.5	669.3	221.9	112.4	12.2	2,421.2	658.5	250.7	108.9	157.7	672.
1993	4,477.9	526.7	234.0	193.4	1,379.4	691.9	229.9	114.1	12.4	2,571.8	683.9	269.9	118.2	172.7	715.
1994	4,743.3	582.2	260.5	213.4	1,437.2	720.6	238.1	116.2	12.8	2,723.9	726.1	286.2	120.7	190.6	752.
1995	4,975.8	611.6	266.7	228.6	1,485.1	740.9	241.7	120.2	13.1	2,879.1	764.4	298.7	122.2	207.7	797.
1996	5,256.8	652.6	284.9	242.9	1,555.5	768.7	250.2	130.4	14.3	3,048.7	800.1	318.5	129.4	226.5	833.
1997	5,547.4	692.7	305.1	256.2	1,619.0	796.2	258.1	134.4	13.3	3,235.8	842.6	337.0	131.3	245.7	873.
1998	5,879.5	750.2	336.1	273.1	1,683.6	829.8	270.9	122.4	11.5	3,445.7	894.6	350.5	128.9	259.5	921.
1999	6,282.5	817.6	370.8	293.9	1,804.8	873.1	286.3	137.9	11.9	3,660.0	948.4	364.8	130.6	276.4	961.
2000	6,739.4	863.3	386.5	312.9	1,947.2	925.2	297.7	175.7	15.8	3,928.8	1,006.5	390.1	143.3	291.3	1,026.
2001	7,055.0	883.7	407.9	312.1	2,017.1	967.9	297.7	171.6	15.4	4,154.3	1,073.7	409.0	156.7	292.8	1,113.
2002	7,350.7	923.9	429.3	323.1	2,079.6	1,001.9	303.5	164.5	14.2	4,347.2	1,123.1	407.7	152.5	288.4	1,206.
2003	7,703.6	942.7	431.7	331.5	2,190.2	1,046.0	310.9	192.7	16.9	4,570.8	1,161.8	429.4	167.3	297.3	1,300.
2004	8,195.9	983.9	436.8	355.7	2,343.7	1,113.1	325.0	231.4	18.3	4,868.3	1,226.8	449.0	175.4	308.2	1,395.
2005	8,694.1	1,020.8	443.1	377.3	2,514.1	1,181.2	341.5	283.6	21.0	5,159.2	1,298.7	479.7	198.3	324.3	1,491.
2006	9,207.2	1,052.1	434.0	403.5	2,685.2	1,257.4	360.2	313.8	22.4	5,469.9	1,388.7	502.4	209.6	341.2	1,575.
2007	9,710.2	1,082.8	440.4	415.3	2,833.0	1,329.1	374.0	340.6	26.3	5,794.4	1,460.9	525.7	218.8	357.0	1,681.
2005: I	8,480.9	1,006.6	442.0	367.9	2,432.4	1,153.2	335.0	249.0	20.2	5,041.9	1,270.3	462.5	184.2	317.5	1,454.
II	8,610.8	1,033.3	458.5	374.3	2,469.9	1,171.7	341.4	254.4	20.3	5,107.6	1,288.7	469.8	189.7	322.5	1,477.
III	8,791.1	1,038.7	460.0	379.1	2,554.8	1,190.4	339.8	314.1	21.7	5,197.6	1,307.5	483.0	200.9	326.7	1,503.
IV	8,893.7	1,004.4	412.0	387.8	2,599.4	1,209.7	349.8	316.9	21.9	5,289.9	1,328.4	503.3	218.4	330.5	1,529.
2006: I	9,026.3	1,046.5	431.5	401.4	2,629.3	1,233.2	354.4	305.3	20.1	5,350.5	1,351.8	495.5	208.0	334.8	1,548.
II	9,161.9	1,049.1	433.9	402.0	2,681.5	1,252.2	357.9	320.2	23.1	5,431.3	1,377.9	499.7	209.0	340.2	1,566.
III	9,283.7	1,054.4	436.6	403.7	2,726.3	1,265.4	362.5	338.4	23.8	5,502.9	1,401.8	506.1	211.6	343.0	1,583.
IV	9,357.0	1,058.2	434.0	406.7	2,703.8	1,278.8	366.1	291.2	22.8	5,595.0	1,423.5	508.4	209.7	347.0	1,605.
2007: I	9,524.9	1,076.6	442.0	413.7	2,761.5	1,297.7	374.6	307.1	25.4	5,686.8	1,440.1	517.5	216.8	350.6	1,649.
II	9,657.5	1,085.3	444.0	415.2	2,817.7	1,321.2	372.9	336.9	25.8	5,754.4	1,453.8	524.0	219.0	354.2	1,663.
III	9,765.6	1,086.2	437.9	417.2	2,846.6	1,337.9	375.4	341.6	25.5	5,832.8	1,466.9	526.9	218.3	360.4	1,690.
IV	9,892.7	1,083.0	437.8	415.3	2,906.2	1,359.8	373.2	376.7	28.6	5,903.5	1,482.7	534.3	221.1	362.9	1,721.9
2008: I	10,002.3	1,071.0	424.7	415.1	2,950.7	1,380.5	375.5	393.4	30.2	5,980.6	1,495.1	541.7	228.1	368.8	1,746.6
II	10,138.0	1,059.3	400.6	423.0	3,026.2	1,416.3	382.4	409.5	32.3	6,052.5	1,508.8	554.5	236.3	372.9	1,769.
III p	10,169.5	1,015.1	370.9	410.5	3,046.5	1,416.9	374.1	437.2	30.8	6,107.9	1,520.9	558.6	234.9	377.2	1,793.

[1] Includes other items not shown separately.
[2] Includes imputed rental value of owner-occupied housing.

Source: Department of Commerce (Bureau of Economic Analysis).

TABLE B–17.—Real personal consumption expenditures, 1990–2008

[Billions of chained (2000) dollars; quarterly data at seasonally adjusted annual rates]

Year or quarter	Personal consumption expenditures	Durable goods			Nondurable goods					Services					
		Total¹	Motor vehicles and parts	Furniture and household equipment	Total¹	Food	Clothing and shoes	Gasoline and oil	Fuel oil and coal	Total¹	Housing²	Household operation		Transportation	Medical care
												Total¹	Electricity and gas		
....	4,770.3	453.5	256.1	119.9	1,484.0	784.4	188.2	141.8	16.7	2,851.7	802.2	266.4	117.4	195.7	797.6
....	4,778.4	427.9	226.6	121.1	1,480.5	783.3	188.8	140.3	16.6	2,900.0	820.1	269.9	121.1	186.3	824.5
....	4,934.8	453.0	244.9	127.8	1,510.1	787.9	199.2	146.0	17.0	3,000.8	832.7	277.4	120.4	194.2	863.6
....	5,099.8	488.4	259.2	141.1	1,550.4	802.2	207.4	149.7	17.4	3,085.7	841.8	291.1	126.8	202.5	877.2
....	5,290.7	529.4	276.2	156.8	1,603.9	821.8	218.5	151.7	18.2	3,176.6	869.3	303.3	128.8	218.4	887.1
....	5,433.5	552.6	272.3	173.3	1,638.6	827.1	227.4	154.5	18.7	3,259.9	887.5	312.9	130.2	231.8	906.4
....	5,619.4	595.9	285.4	193.4	1,680.4	834.7	238.7	157.9	18.4	3,356.0	901.1	327.3	134.7	247.5	922.5
....	5,831.8	646.9	304.7	216.3	1,725.3	845.2	246.0	162.8	16.9	3,468.0	922.5	340.4	133.7	263.2	942.8
....	6,125.8	720.3	339.0	244.7	1,794.4	865.6	263.1	170.3	16.0	3,615.0	948.8	357.1	136.7	272.0	970.7
....	6,438.6	804.6	372.4	280.7	1,876.6	893.6	282.7	176.3	16.4	3,758.0	978.6	371.9	138.1	283.4	989.0
....	6,739.4	863.3	386.5	312.9	1,947.2	925.2	297.7	175.7	15.8	3,928.8	1,006.5	390.1	143.3	291.3	1,026.8
....	6,910.4	900.7	405.8	331.8	1,986.7	940.2	303.7	178.3	15.2	4,023.2	1,033.7	391.0	140.9	288.0	1,075.2
....	7,099.3	964.8	429.0	364.3	2,037.1	954.6	318.3	181.9	15.5	4,100.4	1,042.1	393.2	144.9	280.2	1,136.6
....	7,295.3	1,020.6	442.1	397.8	2,103.0	977.7	334.2	183.2	15.4	4,178.8	1,051.9	398.8	147.5	280.6	1,180.8
....	7,561.4	1,084.8	450.8	445.1	2,177.6	1,009.4	350.7	186.7	14.6	4,311.0	1,083.8	408.5	149.1	284.6	1,216.5
....	7,791.7	1,134.4	449.9	490.9	2,252.7	1,047.7	372.3	187.4	13.2	4,420.9	1,118.4	415.2	152.8	287.9	1,257.3
....	8,029.0	1,185.1	437.9	550.2	2,335.3	1,090.1	394.4	184.2	12.4	4,529.9	1,154.6	413.5	148.3	293.7	1,290.2
....	8,252.8	1,242.4	446.7	594.0	2,392.6	1,110.5	412.9	184.5	13.7	4,646.2	1,171.7	421.2	151.1	299.2	1,327.8
5: I	7,697.5	1,111.6	447.9	470.7	2,220.7	1,033.0	362.4	184.8	14.1	4,379.3	1,103.6	412.9	151.6	287.0	1,241.2
II	7,766.4	1,143.7	464.3	482.0	2,243.7	1,040.9	371.5	187.7	13.3	4,398.2	1,113.2	413.3	151.6	287.7	1,250.9
III	7,838.1	1,158.9	469.0	497.0	2,260.1	1,053.3	371.6	188.6	13.0	4,439.4	1,123.7	417.5	154.5	288.3	1,263.4
IV	7,864.9	1,123.3	418.1	514.0	2,286.3	1,063.7	383.7	188.6	12.3	4,466.9	1,133.1	417.2	153.5	288.6	1,273.8
6: I	7,947.4	1,173.1	435.4	537.9	2,310.8	1,077.8	390.2	186.3	11.5	4,484.7	1,143.2	406.6	144.2	290.8	1,283.7
II	8,002.1	1,178.3	437.3	544.6	2,328.7	1,090.3	391.0	183.2	12.6	4,515.7	1,151.7	413.6	148.8	293.2	1,287.9
III	8,046.3	1,188.4	439.4	553.8	2,342.0	1,093.3	396.1	183.6	12.7	4,537.6	1,158.8	416.5	150.1	294.0	1,289.8
IV	8,119.9	1,200.7	439.6	564.5	2,359.8	1,099.1	400.4	183.8	13.0	4,581.5	1,164.7	417.3	149.8	296.9	1,299.2
7: I	8,197.2	1,227.3	449.5	580.3	2,380.1	1,102.5	409.4	185.1	14.3	4,616.1	1,168.0	419.3	151.5	297.7	1,316.0
II	8,237.3	1,242.3	451.3	588.3	2,391.5	1,110.1	412.2	184.3	13.8	4,632.7	1,170.4	419.8	150.6	298.8	1,319.4
III	8,278.5	1,249.4	443.5	600.8	2,398.6	1,110.9	416.6	184.7	13.3	4,659.8	1,172.5	421.5	151.0	300.5	1,331.4
IV	8,298.2	1,250.6	442.6	606.6	2,400.2	1,118.7	413.2	183.8	13.4	4,676.1	1,175.9	424.0	151.2	299.9	1,344.5
8: I	8,316.1	1,237.0	430.2	609.3	2,397.9	1,122.4	416.3	181.4	12.8	4,704.3	1,177.3	425.9	154.0	301.2	1,360.8
II	8,341.3	1,228.3	407.2	629.6	2,420.7	1,133.6	427.2	179.1	11.9	4,712.1	1,182.3	421.3	149.6	298.9	1,370.3
III p ...	8,262.1	1,178.8	377.1	615.1	2,377.8	1,111.2	411.9	175.1	11.1	4,712.2	1,184.5	414.5	143.0	297.5	1,379.2

¹ Includes other items not shown separately.
² Includes imputed rental value of owner-occupied housing.

Note.—See Table B–2 for data for total personal consumption expenditures for 1959–89.

Source: Department of Commerce (Bureau of Economic Analysis).

TABLE B–18.—*Private fixed investment by type, 1959–2008*

[Billions of dollars; quarterly data at seasonally adjusted annual rates]

Year or quarter	Private fixed investment	Nonresidential										Residential		
		Total nonresidential	Structures	Equipment and software								Total residential [1]	Structures	
				Total	Information processing equipment and software				Industrial equipment	Transportation equipment	Other equipment		Total [1]	Single family
					Total	Computers and peripheral equipment	Software	Other						
1959	74.6	46.5	18.1	28.4	4.0	0.0	0.0	4.0	8.5	8.3	7.6	28.1	27.5	16.
1960	75.7	49.4	19.6	29.8	4.9	.2	.1	4.6	9.4	8.5	7.1	26.3	25.8	14.
1961	75.2	48.8	19.7	29.1	5.3	.3	.2	4.8	8.8	8.0	7.0	26.4	25.9	14.
1962	82.0	53.1	20.8	32.3	5.7	.3	.2	5.1	9.3	9.8	7.5	29.0	28.4	15.
1963	88.1	56.0	21.2	34.8	6.5	.7	.4	5.4	10.0	9.4	8.8	32.1	31.5	16.
1964	97.2	63.0	23.7	39.2	7.4	.9	.5	5.9	11.4	10.6	9.9	34.3	33.6	17.
1965	109.0	74.8	28.3	46.5	8.5	1.2	.7	6.7	13.7	13.2	11.0	34.2	33.5	17.
1966	117.7	85.4	31.3	54.0	10.7	1.7	1.0	8.0	16.2	14.5	12.7	32.3	31.6	16.
1967	118.7	86.4	31.5	54.9	11.3	1.9	1.2	8.2	16.9	14.3	12.4	32.4	31.6	16.
1968	132.1	93.4	33.6	59.9	11.9	1.9	1.3	8.7	17.3	17.6	13.0	38.7	37.9	19.
1969	147.3	104.7	37.7	67.0	14.6	2.4	1.8	10.4	19.1	18.9	14.4	42.6	41.6	19.
1970	150.4	109.0	40.3	68.7	16.6	2.7	2.3	11.6	20.3	16.2	15.6	41.4	40.2	17.
1971	169.9	114.1	42.7	71.5	17.3	2.8	2.4	12.2	19.5	18.4	16.3	55.8	54.5	25.
1972	198.5	128.8	47.2	81.7	19.5	3.5	2.8	13.2	21.4	21.8	19.0	69.7	68.1	32.
1973	228.6	153.3	55.0	98.3	23.1	3.5	3.2	16.3	26.0	26.6	22.6	75.3	73.6	35.
1974	235.4	169.5	61.2	108.2	27.0	3.9	3.9	19.2	30.7	26.3	24.3	66.0	64.1	29.
1975	236.5	173.7	61.4	112.4	28.5	3.6	4.8	20.2	31.3	25.2	27.4	62.7	60.8	29.
1976	274.8	192.4	65.9	126.4	32.7	4.4	5.2	23.1	34.1	30.0	29.6	82.5	80.4	43.
1977	339.0	228.7	74.6	154.1	39.2	5.7	5.5	28.0	39.4	39.3	36.3	110.3	107.9	62.
1978	412.2	280.6	93.6	187.0	48.7	7.6	6.3	34.8	47.7	47.3	43.2	131.6	128.9	72.
1979	474.9	333.9	117.7	216.2	58.5	10.2	8.1	40.2	56.2	53.6	47.9	141.0	137.8	72.
1980	485.6	362.4	136.2	226.2	68.8	12.5	9.8	46.4	60.7	48.4	48.3	123.2	119.8	52.
1981	542.6	420.0	167.3	252.7	81.5	17.1	11.8	52.5	65.5	50.6	55.2	122.6	118.9	52.
1982	532.1	426.5	177.6	248.9	88.3	18.9	14.0	55.3	62.7	46.8	51.2	105.7	102.0	41.
1983	570.1	417.2	154.3	262.9	100.1	23.9	16.4	59.8	58.9	53.5	50.4	152.9	148.6	72.
1984	670.2	489.6	177.4	312.2	121.5	31.6	20.4	69.6	68.1	64.4	58.1	180.6	175.9	86.
1985	714.4	526.2	194.5	331.7	130.3	33.7	23.8	72.9	72.5	69.0	59.9	188.2	183.1	87.
1986	739.9	519.8	176.5	343.3	136.8	33.4	25.6	77.7	75.4	70.5	60.7	220.1	214.6	104.
1987	757.8	524.1	174.2	349.9	141.2	35.8	29.0	76.4	76.7	68.1	63.9	233.7	227.9	117.
1988	803.1	563.8	182.8	381.0	154.9	38.0	34.2	82.8	84.2	72.9	69.0	239.3	233.2	120.
1989	847.3	607.7	193.7	414.0	172.6	43.1	41.9	87.6	93.3	67.9	80.2	239.5	233.4	120.
1990	846.4	622.4	202.9	419.5	177.2	38.6	47.6	90.9	92.1	70.0	80.2	224.0	218.0	112.
1991	803.3	598.2	183.6	414.6	182.9	37.7	53.7	91.5	89.3	71.5	70.8	205.1	199.4	99.
1992	848.5	612.1	172.6	439.6	199.9	44.0	57.9	98.1	93.0	74.7	72.0	236.3	230.4	122.
1993	932.5	666.6	177.2	489.4	217.6	47.9	64.3	105.4	102.2	89.4	80.2	266.0	259.9	140.
1994	1,033.3	731.4	186.8	544.6	235.2	52.4	68.3	114.6	113.6	107.7	88.1	301.9	295.6	162.
1995	1,112.9	810.0	207.3	602.8	263.0	66.1	74.6	122.3	129.0	116.1	94.7	302.8	296.5	153.
1996	1,209.5	875.4	224.6	650.8	290.1	72.8	85.5	131.9	136.5	123.2	101.0	334.1	327.8	170.
1997	1,317.8	968.7	250.3	718.3	330.3	81.4	107.5	141.4	140.4	135.5	112.1	349.1	342.8	175.
1998	1,438.4	1,052.6	275.2	777.3	363.4	87.2	124.0	152.2	146.4	140.0	123.5	385.8	379.3	199.
1999	1,558.8	1,133.9	282.2	851.7	411.0	96.0	152.6	162.4	147.0	167.6	126.0	424.9	417.8	223.
2000	1,679.0	1,232.1	313.2	918.9	467.6	101.4	176.2	190.0	159.2	160.8	131.2	446.9	439.5	236.
2001	1,646.1	1,176.8	322.6	854.2	437.0	85.4	174.7	177.0	146.7	141.7	128.8	469.3	461.9	249.
2002	1,570.2	1,066.3	279.2	787.1	399.4	77.2	167.6	154.5	135.7	126.3	125.7	503.9	496.3	265.
2003	1,649.8	1,077.4	277.2	800.2	406.7	77.8	171.4	157.5	140.7	118.3	134.5	572.4	564.5	310.
2004	1,830.0	1,154.5	298.2	856.3	429.6	80.3	183.0	166.4	139.7	142.9	144.0	675.5	667.0	377.
2005	2,042.8	1,273.1	337.6	935.5	451.4	81.7	195.1	174.6	157.1	164.4	162.6	769.6	760.6	433.
2006	2,171.1	1,414.1	410.4	1,003.7	482.3	88.8	205.7	187.8	171.2	177.0	173.1	757.0	747.4	416.
2007	2,134.0	1,503.8	480.3	1,023.5	517.7	93.7	227.3	196.8	180.6	157.2	168.0	630.2	620.7	305.
2005: I	1,963.3	1,233.6	326.9	906.7	442.2	80.6	189.9	171.7	151.8	157.4	155.4	729.7	720.9	410.
II	2,020.3	1,261.0	333.8	927.2	448.0	81.1	195.0	171.9	152.2	164.2	162.7	759.3	750.3	424.
III	2,073.2	1,286.1	337.3	948.8	454.6	80.7	196.1	177.8	158.6	170.6	164.9	787.1	778.1	441.
IV	2,114.3	1,311.8	352.4	959.3	460.6	84.3	199.2	177.1	165.8	165.5	167.4	802.5	793.2	458.
2006: I	2,183.6	1,375.5	377.4	998.1	476.6	86.9	201.3	188.4	164.7	183.3	173.5	808.1	798.5	465.
II	2,187.9	1,408.3	406.0	1,002.3	487.7	89.1	203.6	186.0	174.2	174.8	174.6	779.6	770.0	435.
III	2,169.2	1,433.0	424.4	1,008.6	487.5	90.3	206.8	190.4	172.6	176.3	172.2	736.2	726.7	398.
IV	2,143.6	1,439.6	433.9	1,005.6	486.5	88.8	211.3	186.5	173.4	173.4	172.3	704.0	694.6	364.
2007: I	2,133.4	1,456.4	449.6	1,006.8	503.1	92.5	218.2	192.5	172.1	168.1	163.4	677.0	667.4	338.
II	2,148.1	1,493.7	469.8	1,023.9	514.1	92.8	225.8	195.5	185.1	157.8	166.9	654.4	644.8	323.
III	2,141.0	1,522.9	492.9	1,030.0	521.1	93.7	229.5	197.9	185.2	154.6	169.2	618.1	608.6	299.
IV	2,113.4	1,542.1	508.7	1,033.4	532.5	95.7	235.6	201.2	179.9	148.4	172.6	571.3	561.8	259.
2008: I	2,081.7	1,553.6	522.7	1,030.9	539.6	95.8	241.8	202.0	182.0	142.1	167.3	528.1	518.7	219.
II	2,077.0	1,571.9	549.8	1,022.1	550.9	96.8	244.6	209.5	183.2	121.4	166.5	505.0	495.6	197.
III p	2,062.1	1,582.7	568.9	1,013.9	549.5	90.3	246.2	213.0	182.3	105.2	176.8	479.4	470.2	176.

[1] Includes other items not shown separately.

Source: Department of Commerce (Bureau of Economic Analysis).

TABLE B–19.—*Real private fixed investment by type, 1990–2008*

[Billions of chained (2000) dollars; quarterly data at seasonally adjusted annual rates]

Year or quarter	Private fixed investment	Nonresidential										Residential		
		Total nonresidential	Structures	Equipment and software								Total residential [2]	Structures	
				Total	Information processing equipment and software				Industrial equipment	Transportation equipment	Other equipment		Total [2]	Single family
					Total	Computers and peripheral equipment [1]	Software	Other						
90	886.6	595.1	275.2	355.0	100.7	....	39.9	80.1	109.2	81.0	96.0	298.9	292.6	154.2
91	829.1	563.2	244.6	345.9	105.9	....	45.1	79.6	102.2	78.8	82.0	270.2	264.0	135.1
92	878.3	581.3	229.9	371.1	122.2	....	53.0	84.4	104.0	80.2	81.6	307.6	301.4	164.1
93	953.5	631.9	228.3	417.4	138.2	....	59.3	90.9	112.9	95.1	89.3	332.7	326.4	179.7
94	1,042.3	689.9	232.3	467.2	155.7	....	65.1	99.4	122.9	111.4	96.5	364.8	358.6	198.9
95	1,109.6	762.5	247.1	523.1	182.7	....	71.6	107.0	134.9	120.6	101.7	353.1	346.8	180.6
96	1,209.2	833.6	261.1	578.7	218.9	....	84.1	117.2	139.9	125.4	105.6	381.3	375.1	197.3
97	1,320.6	934.2	280.1	658.3	269.9	....	108.8	127.3	143.0	135.9	115.8	388.6	382.4	196.6
98	1,455.0	1,037.8	294.5	745.6	328.9	....	129.4	143.2	148.1	145.4	125.7	418.3	411.9	218.1
99	1,576.3	1,133.3	293.2	840.2	398.5	....	157.2	158.0	147.9	167.7	126.7	443.6	436.6	234.2
00	1,679.0	1,232.1	313.2	918.9	467.6	....	176.2	190.0	159.2	160.8	131.2	446.9	439.5	236.8
01	1,629.4	1,180.5	306.1	874.2	459.0	....	173.8	181.7	145.7	142.8	126.9	448.5	441.1	237.1
02	1,544.6	1,071.5	253.8	820.2	437.4	....	169.7	161.1	134.5	126.0	122.9	469.9	462.2	246.3
03	1,596.9	1,081.8	243.5	843.1	462.7	....	177.3	167.1	138.4	113.8	130.4	509.4	501.2	272.6
04	1,712.8	1,144.3	246.7	905.1	505.7	....	193.6	181.1	134.0	130.6	138.3	560.2	551.2	305.3
05	1,829.8	1,226.2	249.8	989.6	546.7	....	207.0	191.6	145.3	149.5	150.4	595.4	586.0	325.9
06	1,865.5	1,318.2	270.3	1,061.0	596.6	....	215.5	206.7	153.5	159.5	156.5	552.9	543.5	294.9
07	1,808.5	1,382.9	304.6	1,078.9	653.9	....	237.0	218.0	155.7	139.4	148.4	453.8	444.9	214.1
05: I	1,790.5	1,200.4	253.1	956.6	529.5	....	201.5	187.9	142.0	142.1	145.6	582.1	572.9	318.8
II	1,823.5	1,219.0	252.3	977.9	540.3	....	206.8	188.4	140.9	148.5	150.5	595.8	586.4	323.5
III	1,847.2	1,237.1	246.2	1,006.5	552.7	....	208.2	195.3	146.3	157.2	151.7	601.7	592.3	327.6
IV	1,858.0	1,248.2	247.4	1,017.4	564.3	....	211.4	194.9	152.0	150.3	153.7	602.0	592.4	333.7
06: I	1,895.2	1,295.2	256.5	1,056.6	586.2	....	212.5	207.6	149.9	165.3	158.2	596.5	586.8	333.1
II	1,883.1	1,315.4	268.3	1,061.2	590.9	....	213.2	205.1	157.2	157.9	158.7	570.1	560.6	308.7
III	1,860.0	1,332.7	277.4	1,066.4	603.9	....	215.8	209.4	153.8	159.7	155.2	536.7	527.4	282.7
IV	1,823.7	1,329.3	279.1	1,059.9	605.3	....	220.5	204.8	153.2	155.2	153.8	508.4	499.3	255.2
07: I	1,807.8	1,340.4	286.6	1,060.0	629.9	....	227.9	212.5	150.3	149.0	145.3	486.4	477.3	235.6
II	1,821.3	1,373.8	298.9	1,077.9	647.3	....	235.7	216.2	160.3	139.4	147.5	471.7	462.8	227.3
III	1,817.0	1,402.9	313.2	1,087.5	660.9	....	239.4	219.6	159.1	137.4	149.2	445.3	436.5	210.3
IV	1,788.2	1,414.7	319.7	1,090.1	677.6	....	245.1	223.5	153.1	131.9	151.5	411.6	403.0	182.9
08: I	1,762.4	1,423.1	326.4	1,088.6	689.6	....	251.0	223.6	153.4	127.0	146.5	383.0	374.6	156.7
II	1,754.9	1,431.8	340.5	1,074.7	702.9	....	252.3	230.6	152.0	108.6	145.3	369.6	361.1	142.9
III p	1,730.0	1,426.5	346.0	1,059.2	701.8	....	253.3	233.7	148.6	93.4	151.7	352.1	344.0	129.5

[1] For information on this component, see *Survey of Current Business* Table 5.3.6, Table 5.3.1 (for growth rates), Table 5.3.2 (for contributions), and Table 5.3.3 or quantity indexes).
[2] Includes other items not shown separately.

Source: Department of Commerce (Bureau of Economic Analysis).

TABLE B–20.—*Government consumption expenditures and gross investment by type, 1959–2008*

[Billions of dollars; quarterly data at seasonally adjusted annual rates]

Year or quarter	Total	Government consumption expenditures and gross investment												
		Federal									State and local			Gross investme
		Total	National defense				Nondefense				Total	Con-sumption expen-ditures	Struc-tures	Equip-ment and soft-ware
			Total	Con-sumption expen-ditures	Gross investment		Total	Con-sumption expen-ditures	Gross investment					
					Struc-tures	Equip-ment and soft-ware			Struc-tures	Equip-ment and soft-ware				
1959	110.0	65.4	53.8	40.1	2.5	11.2	11.5	9.8	1.5	0.2	44.7	30.7	12.8	
1960	111.6	64.1	53.4	41.0	2.2	10.1	10.7	8.7	1.7	.3	47.5	33.5	12.7	
1961	119.5	67.9	56.5	42.7	2.4	11.5	11.4	9.0	1.9	.6	51.6	36.6	13.8	
1962	130.1	75.3	61.1	46.6	2.0	12.5	14.2	11.3	2.1	.8	54.9	39.0	14.5	
1963	136.4	76.9	61.0	48.3	1.6	11.0	15.9	12.4	2.3	1.2	59.5	41.9	16.0	
1964	143.2	78.5	60.3	48.8	1.3	10.2	18.2	14.0	2.5	1.6	64.8	45.8	17.2	
1965	151.5	80.4	60.6	50.6	1.1	8.9	19.8	15.1	2.8	1.9	71.0	50.2	19.0	
1966	171.8	92.5	71.7	60.0	1.3	10.5	20.8	15.9	2.8	2.1	79.2	56.1	21.0	
1967	192.7	104.8	83.5	70.0	1.2	12.3	21.3	17.1	2.2	1.9	87.9	62.6	23.0	
1968	209.4	111.4	89.3	77.2	1.2	10.9	22.1	18.3	2.1	1.7	98.0	70.4	25.2	
1969	221.5	113.4	89.5	78.2	1.5	9.9	23.8	20.2	1.9	1.7	108.2	79.9	25.6	
1970	233.8	113.5	87.6	76.6	1.3	9.8	25.8	22.1	2.1	1.7	120.3	91.5	25.8	
1971	246.5	113.7	84.6	77.1	1.8	5.7	29.1	24.9	2.5	1.7	132.8	102.7	27.0	
1972	263.5	119.7	87.0	79.5	1.8	5.7	32.7	28.2	2.7	1.8	143.8	113.2	27.1	
1973	281.7	122.5	88.2	79.4	2.1	6.6	34.3	29.4	3.1	1.8	159.2	126.0	29.1	
1974	317.9	134.6	95.6	84.5	2.2	8.9	39.0	33.4	3.4	2.2	183.4	143.7	34.7	
1975	357.7	149.1	103.9	90.9	2.3	10.7	45.1	38.7	4.1	2.4	208.7	165.1	38.1	
1976	383.0	159.7	111.1	95.8	2.1	13.2	48.6	41.4	4.6	2.7	223.3	179.5	38.1	
1977	414.1	175.4	120.9	104.2	2.4	14.4	54.5	46.5	5.0	3.0	238.7	195.9	36.9	
1978	453.6	190.9	130.5	112.7	2.5	15.3	60.4	50.6	6.1	3.7	262.6	213.2	42.8	
1979	500.8	210.6	145.2	123.8	2.5	18.9	65.4	55.1	6.3	4.0	290.2	233.3	49.0	
1980	566.2	243.8	168.0	143.7	3.2	21.1	75.8	63.8	7.1	4.9	322.4	258.4	55.1	
1981	627.5	280.2	196.3	167.3	3.2	25.7	84.0	71.0	7.7	5.3	347.3	282.3	55.4	
1982	680.5	310.8	225.9	191.2	4.0	30.8	84.9	72.1	6.8	6.0	369.7	304.9	54.2	
1983	733.5	342.9	250.7	208.8	4.8	37.1	92.3	77.7	6.7	7.8	390.5	324.1	54.2	
1984	797.0	374.4	281.6	232.9	4.9	43.8	92.8	77.1	7.0	8.7	422.6	347.7	60.5	
1985	879.0	412.8	311.2	253.7	6.2	51.3	101.6	84.7	7.3	9.6	466.2	381.8	67.6	
1986	949.3	438.6	330.9	268.0	6.8	56.1	107.8	90.3	8.0	9.5	510.7	417.9	74.2	
1987	999.5	460.1	350.0	283.6	7.7	58.8	110.0	90.6	9.0	10.4	539.4	440.9	78.8	
1988	1,039.0	463.3	354.9	293.6	7.4	53.9	107.4	88.9	6.8	11.7	576.7	470.4	84.8	
1989	1,099.1	482.2	362.2	299.5	6.4	56.3	120.0	99.7	6.9	13.4	616.9	502.1	88.7	
1990	1,180.2	508.3	374.0	308.1	6.1	59.8	134.3	111.7	8.0	14.6	671.9	544.6	98.5	
1991	1,234.4	527.7	383.2	319.8	4.6	58.8	144.5	119.7	9.2	15.7	706.7	574.6	103.2	
1992	1,271.0	533.9	376.9	315.3	5.2	56.3	157.0	129.8	10.3	16.9	737.0	602.7	104.2	
1993	1,291.2	525.2	362.9	307.6	5.1	50.1	162.4	134.2	11.2	16.9	766.0	630.3	104.5	
1994	1,325.5	519.1	353.7	300.7	5.7	47.2	165.5	140.1	10.5	14.9	806.3	663.3	108.7	
1995	1,369.2	519.2	348.7	297.3	6.3	45.1	170.5	143.2	10.8	16.5	850.0	696.1	117.3	
1996	1,416.0	527.4	354.6	302.5	6.7	45.4	172.8	143.8	11.2	17.9	888.6	724.8	126.8	
1997	1,468.7	530.9	349.6	304.7	5.7	39.2	181.3	153.0	9.8	18.5	937.8	758.9	139.5	
1998	1,518.3	530.4	345.7	300.7	5.1	39.9	184.7	153.9	10.6	20.2	987.9	801.4	143.6	
1999	1,620.8	555.8	360.6	312.9	5.0	42.8	195.2	162.2	10.6	22.4	1,065.0	858.9	159.7	
2000	1,721.6	578.8	370.3	321.5	5.0	43.8	208.5	177.8	8.3	22.3	1,142.8	917.8	176.0	
2001	1,825.6	612.9	392.6	342.4	4.6	45.6	220.3	189.5	8.3	22.5	1,212.8	969.8	192.4	
2002	1,961.1	679.7	437.1	381.7	4.4	51.0	242.5	209.9	9.9	22.8	1,281.5	1,025.3	205.9	
2003	2,092.5	756.4	497.2	436.8	5.3	55.2	259.2	226.0	10.1	23.1	1,336.0	1,073.8	212.0	
2004	2,216.8	825.6	550.7	482.9	5.6	62.2	274.9	240.8	9.4	24.6	1,391.2	1,120.3	220.3	
2005	2,355.3	875.5	588.1	515.2	6.0	66.9	287.4	251.1	8.3	28.0	1,479.8	1,191.2	235.9	
2006	2,508.1	932.2	624.1	544.6	6.3	73.2	308.0	267.2	9.9	30.9	1,575.9	1,269.6	250.2	
2007	2,674.8	979.3	662.2	580.1	7.5	74.6	317.1	276.0	10.9	30.3	1,695.5	1,355.9	281.0	
2005: I	2,299.2	861.0	576.1	507.5	5.7	63.0	284.9	250.7	7.8	26.4	1,438.2	1,159.1	227.7	
II	2,328.0	867.1	584.4	512.1	5.5	66.8	282.8	248.2	7.3	27.2	1,460.9	1,174.1	234.3	
III	2,388.0	894.2	606.3	530.8	6.4	69.1	288.0	251.3	8.3	28.3	1,493.8	1,203.1	237.5	
IV	2,405.9	879.5	585.4	510.3	6.3	68.8	294.1	254.3	9.6	30.2	1,526.4	1,228.4	243.9	
2006: I	2,458.4	922.8	613.6	538.3	5.4	69.8	309.3	267.6	9.6	32.1	1,535.5	1,240.8	239.7	
II	2,495.7	928.5	623.1	543.6	5.3	74.3	305.4	265.6	9.5	30.3	1,567.2	1,260.2	251.1	
III	2,526.9	935.5	624.0	545.3	6.7	72.0	311.5	270.8	9.6	31.1	1,591.4	1,281.8	253.2	
IV	2,551.4	941.7	635.9	551.2	7.9	76.8	305.9	264.9	10.9	30.1	1,609.7	1,295.8	256.9	
2007: I	2,597.0	950.3	636.9	559.0	6.5	71.5	313.4	273.6	10.3	29.5	1,646.8	1,318.7	270.2	
II	2,655.9	974.6	656.8	574.8	6.6	75.4	317.8	276.4	10.6	30.8	1,681.3	1,344.4	278.4	
III	2,703.5	994.0	675.6	591.9	7.7	76.0	318.3	277.2	11.0	30.2	1,709.5	1,365.3	285.4	
IV	2,742.9	998.3	679.3	594.7	9.2	75.4	319.0	276.9	11.5	30.6	1,744.6	1,395.2	290.0	
2008: I	2,798.1	1,026.5	699.9	613.8	7.9	78.2	326.6	284.2	12.1	30.3	1,771.6	1,426.3	285.2	
II	2,873.7	1,056.1	723.3	629.0	8.9	85.4	332.9	289.2	12.0	31.7	1,817.6	1,462.7	294.1	
III p	2,943.9	1,097.7	759.5	659.6	10.6	89.3	338.2	294.5	12.3	31.4	1,846.2	1,486.1	299.1	

Source: Department of Commerce (Bureau of Economic Analysis).

TABLE B–21.—*Real government consumption expenditures and gross investment by type, 1990–2008*

[Billions of chained (2000) dollars; quarterly data at seasonally adjusted annual rates]

Year or quarter	Total	Government consumption expenditures and gross investment												
		Federal									State and local			
		Total	National defense				Nondefense				Total	Consumption expenditures	Gross investment	
			Total	Consumption expenditures	Gross investment		Total	Consumption expenditures	Gross investment				Structures	Equipment and software
					Structures	Equipment and software			Structures	Equipment and software				
1990	1,530.0	659.1	479.4	404.9	8.6	64.2	178.6	156.5	10.6	12.9	868.4	714.2	132.1	25.0
1991	1,547.2	658.0	474.2	404.4	6.4	61.8	182.8	158.4	11.8	13.7	886.8	729.0	136.5	24.8
1992	1,555.3	646.6	450.7	383.5	7.0	58.7	195.4	168.2	13.2	15.0	906.5	746.5	137.0	25.9
1993	1,541.1	619.6	425.3	367.2	6.4	51.1	194.1	166.0	14.1	15.0	919.5	761.4	133.9	26.8
1994	1,541.3	596.4	404.6	350.6	7.1	46.8	191.7	167.3	12.7	13.3	943.3	780.6	134.9	29.5
1995	1,549.7	580.3	389.2	338.1	7.4	43.7	191.0	164.7	12.6	14.7	968.3	798.4	139.5	31.7
1996	1,564.9	573.5	383.8	332.2	7.7	43.8	189.6	161.1	12.7	16.4	990.5	812.8	146.3	32.7
1997	1,594.0	567.6	373.0	328.1	6.4	38.9	194.5	166.6	10.9	17.5	1,025.9	834.9	155.8	36.1
1998	1,624.4	561.2	365.3	319.8	5.5	40.1	195.9	164.8	11.5	19.8	1,063.0	866.4	155.6	41.2
1999	1,686.9	573.7	372.2	324.6	5.2	42.5	201.5	168.1	11.1	22.3	1,113.2	900.3	167.0	45.9
2000	1,721.6	578.8	370.3	321.5	5.0	43.8	208.5	177.8	8.3	22.3	1,142.8	917.8	176.0	49.0
2001	1,780.3	601.4	384.9	334.1	4.4	46.4	216.5	185.8	8.0	22.7	1,179.0	941.2	186.0	51.7
2002	1,858.8	643.4	413.2	356.7	4.2	52.6	230.2	197.3	9.3	23.5	1,215.4	969.4	193.5	52.5
2003	1,904.8	687.1	449.0	387.5	4.8	56.9	238.0	204.5	9.3	24.2	1,217.8	969.8	194.7	53.4
2004	1,931.8	715.9	475.0	407.6	4.8	63.3	240.7	206.7	8.2	25.9	1,215.8	970.8	191.2	54.0
2005	1,939.0	724.5	482.2	411.6	4.7	67.2	242.0	206.7	6.6	29.5	1,214.3	971.9	186.9	56.2
2006	1,971.2	741.0	490.0	415.0	4.6	72.5	250.8	212.2	7.4	32.6	1,230.2	988.2	183.5	60.3
2007	2,012.1	752.9	502.1	425.8	5.2	72.9	250.4	211.7	7.7	32.3	1,259.0	1,008.0	190.1	63.1
2005: I	1,929.6	718.0	476.3	409.2	4.6	63.1	241.5	207.8	6.4	27.7	1,211.4	970.2	186.9	54.6
II	1,934.0	720.1	481.0	410.7	4.4	67.1	238.8	205.0	5.9	28.7	1,213.8	970.7	187.9	55.8
III	1,950.4	736.8	495.1	421.9	5.0	69.6	241.4	205.8	6.6	29.9	1,215.4	969.4	185.5	56.6
IV	1,941.9	723.2	476.5	404.4	4.9	69.1	246.5	208.4	7.5	31.9	1,218.5	974.6	187.0	57.9
2006: I	1,960.5	740.6	486.7	414.5	4.1	69.7	253.8	214.2	7.4	33.8	1,219.9	980.4	182.0	59.1
II	1,966.6	737.7	489.0	414.0	3.9	73.6	248.5	210.7	7.2	31.9	1,228.8	984.6	185.7	60.0
III	1,974.9	741.1	487.9	414.1	4.9	70.8	253.1	214.5	7.2	32.8	1,233.7	990.8	184.0	60.8
IV	1,982.7	744.4	496.3	417.6	5.7	75.7	247.8	209.2	8.0	31.9	1,238.2	996.8	182.3	61.3
2007: I	1,987.1	737.5	488.8	415.6	4.6	70.3	248.6	210.9	7.4	31.3	1,249.3	1,001.9	187.3	62.1
II	2,006.4	749.6	498.8	422.4	4.7	74.0	250.5	211.5	7.6	32.8	1,256.6	1,006.1	189.7	62.8
III	2,025.3	762.7	511.0	433.5	5.4	74.1	251.2	212.4	7.8	32.2	1,262.6	1,010.0	191.4	63.3
IV	2,029.4	761.7	509.9	431.9	6.4	73.3	251.5	212.0	8.0	32.7	1,267.5	1,013.9	191.8	64.0
2008: I	2,039.1	772.6	518.9	439.7	5.5	75.8	253.2	213.5	8.4	32.5	1,266.7	1,017.6	187.3	64.8
II	2,058.9	785.0	528.1	443.4	6.2	81.9	256.3	215.6	8.2	34.0	1,274.4	1,020.6	191.4	65.2
III p	2,085.9	810.4	550.5	461.5	7.3	85.1	259.1	218.4	8.3	33.7	1,276.9	1,023.3	191.2	65.1

Note.—See Table B–2 for data for total government consumption expenditures and gross investment for 1959–89.

Source: Department of Commerce (Bureau of Economic Analysis).

TABLE B–22.—*Private inventories and domestic final sales by industry, 1959–2008*

[Billions of dollars, except as noted; seasonally adjusted]

Quarter	Private inventories [1]								Final sales of domestic business [3]	Ratio of private inventories to final sales of domestic business	
	Total [2]	Farm	Mining, utilities, and construction [2]	Manufacturing	Wholesale trade	Retail trade	Other industries [2]	Non-farm [2]		Total	Non-farm
Fourth quarter:											
1959	132.9	42.1	....	47.7	16.5	20.5	6.1	90.8	31.6	4.20	2.
1960	136.2	42.7	....	48.7	16.9	21.9	6.1	93.5	32.7	4.17	2.
1961	139.6	44.3	....	50.1	17.3	21.3	6.6	95.2	34.3	4.07	2.
1962	147.2	46.7	....	53.2	18.0	22.7	6.6	100.5	36.0	4.09	2.
1963	149.7	44.2	....	55.1	19.5	23.9	7.1	105.5	38.3	3.91	2.
1964	154.3	42.1	....	58.6	20.8	25.2	7.7	112.2	41.2	3.75	2.
1965	169.3	47.1	....	63.4	22.5	28.0	8.3	122.2	45.3	3.73	2.
1966	185.7	47.4	....	73.0	25.8	30.6	8.9	138.3	47.8	3.88	2.
1967	194.9	45.8	....	79.9	28.1	30.9	10.1	149.1	50.3	3.87	2.
1968	208.2	48.9	....	85.1	29.3	34.2	10.6	159.3	55.4	3.76	2.
1969	227.7	53.1	....	92.6	32.5	37.5	12.0	174.6	59.1	3.85	2.
1970	236.0	52.7	....	95.5	36.4	38.5	12.9	183.3	62.4	3.78	2.
1971	253.9	59.5	....	96.6	39.4	44.7	13.7	194.4	68.0	3.73	2.
1972	283.9	74.0	....	102.1	43.1	49.8	14.8	209.9	76.3	3.72	2.
1973	352.2	102.8	....	121.5	51.7	58.4	17.7	249.4	84.3	4.18	2.
1974	406.3	88.2	....	162.6	66.9	63.9	24.7	318.1	90.4	4.49	3.
1975	409.3	90.3	....	162.2	66.5	64.4	25.9	319.0	101.7	4.02	3.
1976	440.1	85.8	....	178.7	74.1	73.0	28.5	354.2	111.9	3.93	3.
1977	482.4	91.0	....	193.2	84.0	80.9	33.3	391.4	124.8	3.86	3.
1978	571.4	119.7	....	219.8	99.0	94.1	38.8	451.7	144.7	3.95	3.
1979	668.2	135.6	....	261.8	119.5	104.7	46.6	532.6	160.1	4.17	3.
1980	739.8	141.1	....	293.4	139.4	111.7	54.1	598.7	175.0	4.23	3.
1981	779.2	127.5	....	313.1	148.8	123.2	66.6	651.7	187.7	4.15	3.
1982	774.1	131.5	....	304.6	147.9	123.2	66.8	642.6	195.8	3.95	3.
1983	797.6	132.5	....	308.9	153.4	137.6	65.2	665.1	216.8	3.68	3.
1984	869.3	131.8	....	344.5	169.1	157.0	66.9	737.6	234.8	3.70	3.
1985	876.1	125.9	....	333.3	175.9	171.4	69.5	750.2	250.7	3.49	2.
1986	858.0	112.9	....	320.6	182.0	176.2	66.3	745.1	265.7	3.23	2.
1987	924.2	119.8	....	339.6	195.8	199.1	69.9	804.4	279.3	3.31	2.
1988	999.2	130.2	....	372.4	213.9	213.2	69.5	869.1	305.6	3.27	2.
1989	1,044.4	129.6	....	390.5	222.8	231.4	70.1	914.7	324.4	3.22	2.
1990	1,082.3	133.4	....	404.5	236.8	236.6	71.0	948.9	337.6	3.21	2.
1991	1,057.2	123.2	....	384.1	239.2	240.2	70.5	934.0	347.6	3.04	2.
1992	1,082.4	132.9	....	377.6	248.3	249.4	74.3	949.5	372.7	2.90	2.
1993	1,115.8	132.1	....	380.1	258.6	268.6	76.5	983.7	393.6	2.83	2.
1994	1,194.3	134.3	....	404.3	281.5	293.6	80.6	1,060.0	416.8	2.87	2.
1995	1,257.0	130.9	....	424.5	303.7	312.2	85.6	1,126.1	439.2	2.86	2.
NAICS:											
1996	1,284.4	136.3	31.1	421.0	285.1	328.7	82.1	1,148.1	469.1	2.74	2.
1997	1,329.5	136.7	33.7	431.7	303.1	337.5	86.9	1,192.9	495.6	2.68	2.
1998	1,346.8	120.3	37.3	431.5	313.3	353.6	90.9	1,226.5	526.8	2.56	2.
1999	1,442.2	124.2	39.6	457.7	337.4	383.8	99.5	1,318.0	556.7	2.59	2.
2000	1,535.9	132.1	44.5	477.0	359.0	409.0	114.4	1,403.8	583.6	2.63	2.
2001	1,458.3	126.1	47.5	437.9	338.6	395.6	112.6	1,332.2	598.7	2.44	2.
2002	1,507.8	135.8	49.4	443.6	348.0	419.3	111.7	1,372.0	601.0	2.51	2.
2003	1,567.3	151.2	58.5	447.0	359.8	436.4	114.3	1,416.1	639.0	2.45	2.
2004	1,715.0	156.7	69.4	495.1	397.2	472.8	123.7	1,558.2	678.6	2.53	2.
2005: I	1,761.2	159.1	71.2	516.2	410.4	478.9	125.5	1,602.1	688.9	2.56	2.
II	1,765.5	156.0	75.9	515.5	414.4	476.8	126.9	1,609.5	702.6	2.51	2.
III	1,807.4	160.9	81.8	531.8	423.2	481.0	128.7	1,646.6	716.9	2.52	2.
IV	1,851.5	164.9	91.7	545.8	432.0	487.0	130.2	1,686.6	723.2	2.56	2.
2006: I	1,864.3	157.8	83.7	558.7	438.8	493.9	131.4	1,706.5	738.9	2.52	2.
II	1,913.5	157.6	83.0	581.4	455.2	501.5	134.9	1,755.9	747.7	2.56	2.
III	1,943.6	165.2	84.7	588.5	462.9	505.2	137.1	1,778.4	753.1	2.58	2.
IV	1,951.6	164.6	86.1	588.4	469.3	506.0	137.3	1,787.0	763.6	2.56	2.
2007: I	1,982.9	175.0	90.2	593.7	477.4	506.8	139.8	1,807.9	772.4	2.57	2.
II	2,009.3	175.5	93.5	603.4	483.9	510.4	142.6	1,833.8	784.8	2.56	2.
III	2,030.7	182.1	90.3	606.0	492.0	512.6	144.1	1,848.5	795.4	2.55	2.
IV	2,088.0	191.2	91.5	628.7	511.9	517.0	147.8	1,896.8	800.9	2.61	2.
2008: I	2,178.2	220.2	95.2	661.9	531.2	518.4	151.4	1,958.0	804.1	2.71	2.
II	2,264.4	235.1	103.5	697.2	552.3	522.4	153.9	2,029.3	813.7	2.78	2.
III p	2,230.6	220.5	98.9	679.8	547.4	527.4	156.6	2,010.1	814.9	2.74	2.

[1] Inventories at end of quarter. Quarter-to-quarter change calculated from this table is not the current-dollar change in private inventories component of gross domestic product (GDP). The former is the difference between two inventory stocks, each valued at its respective end-of-quarter prices. The latter is the change in the physical volume of inventories valued at average prices of the quarter. In addition, changes calculated from this table are at quarterly rates, whereas change in private inventories is stated at annual rates.

[2] Inventories of construction, mining, and utilities establishments are included in other industries through 1995.

[3] Quarterly totals at monthly rates. Final sales of domestic business equals final sales of domestic product less gross output of general government, gross value added of nonprofit institutions, compensation paid to domestic workers, and space rent for owner-occupied housing. Includes a small amount of final sa by farm and by government enterprises.

Note.—The industry classification of inventories is on an establishment basis. Estimates through 1995 are based on the Standard Industrial Classification (SIC). Beginning with 1996, estimates are based on the North American Industry Classification System (NAICS).

Source: Department of Commerce (Bureau of Economic Analysis).

Table B–23.—*Real private inventories and domestic final sales by industry, 1959–2008*

[Billions of chained (2000) dollars, except as noted; seasonally adjusted]

Quarter	Private inventories [1]								Final sales of domestic business [3]	Ratio of private inventories to final sales of domestic business	
	Total [2]	Farm	Mining, utilities, and construction [2]	Manufacturing	Wholesale trade	Retail trade	Other industries [2]	Non-farm [2]		Total	Non-farm
quarter:											
1959	428.1	106.9		143.5	57.6	63.9	29.8	298.7	131.3	3.26	2.27
1960	438.5	108.3		145.4	59.1	68.2	30.8	307.5	134.3	3.27	2.29
1961	448.0	110.4		149.8	60.7	66.9	33.9	314.4	140.1	3.20	2.24
1962	467.4	111.8		159.8	63.4	71.5	33.8	332.7	145.4	3.21	2.29
1963	485.4	112.9		165.9	68.4	75.3	36.2	349.7	153.9	3.15	2.27
1964	500.8	109.8		175.1	72.5	79.3	38.4	369.4	163.2	3.07	2.26
1965	530.1	111.8		187.4	77.4	87.1	40.1	396.8	177.2	2.99	2.24
1966	572.2	110.7		212.5	87.7	94.1	41.1	442.0	180.9	3.16	2.44
1967	602.5	112.8		229.3	94.7	94.1	46.0	470.4	185.3	3.25	2.54
1968	629.9	116.1		239.8	98.0	101.9	47.3	494.1	195.1	3.23	2.53
1969	656.9	116.1		250.9	105.1	108.9	49.7	521.9	198.9	3.30	2.62
1970	661.9	114.2		250.9	113.0	109.0	50.3	529.7	201.3	3.29	2.63
1971	684.2	117.5		247.9	119.1	123.6	52.1	548.3	211.5	3.24	2.59
1972	707.3	117.9		254.6	124.6	133.1	54.7	572.5	228.8	3.09	2.50
1973	742.2	119.3		273.5	128.1	143.7	57.5	609.1	236.9	3.13	2.57
1974	768.1	115.7		294.1	139.7	141.6	61.3	644.2	228.2	3.37	2.82
1975	756.8	120.4		286.7	133.7	134.6	62.9	625.0	238.7	3.17	2.62
1976	787.5	119.1		300.4	142.7	144.9	63.6	659.0	250.5	3.14	2.63
1977	826.0	125.0		308.8	154.1	153.2	68.4	691.1	263.6	3.13	2.62
1978	867.1	126.7		322.9	166.9	163.3	72.5	732.0	283.2	3.06	2.58
1979	892.2	130.2		335.3	175.0	163.3	72.4	753.5	289.8	3.08	2.60
1980	884.3	124.3		335.7	180.0	158.7	71.2	753.5	289.6	3.05	2.60
1981	919.2	132.5		340.2	185.1	167.5	79.2	779.0	287.2	3.20	2.71
1982	901.7	138.6		325.0	183.0	163.7	76.8	754.4	286.1	3.15	2.64
1983	895.3	124.4		324.5	182.7	177.0	75.9	764.6	307.6	2.91	2.49
1984	966.6	129.6		352.8	198.5	198.6	77.0	831.2	324.6	2.98	2.56
1985	990.3	135.3		346.6	204.9	214.0	81.4	848.7	339.4	2.92	2.50
1986	998.5	133.5		342.9	213.2	217.4	84.4	858.8	352.2	2.84	2.44
1987	1,028.8	126.1		351.1	220.6	238.5	86.6	896.5	362.6	2.84	2.47
1988	1,049.1	115.4		367.6	229.7	246.1	85.2	929.2	381.6	2.75	2.43
1989	1,077.4	115.4		381.4	233.6	260.5	81.4	958.0	392.5	2.75	2.44
1990	1,092.8	120.9		390.0	242.0	258.9	78.3	971.2	394.0	2.77	2.46
1991	1,092.3	119.4		383.5	246.4	259.5	81.4	972.2	394.6	2.77	2.46
1992	1,108.7	125.1		378.9	254.8	264.1	83.9	982.5	415.7	2.67	2.36
1993	1,129.4	119.1		382.4	261.0	279.4	86.9	1,010.2	429.8	2.63	2.35
1994	1,193.0	130.3		394.1	276.7	299.9	91.1	1,062.2	447.2	2.67	2.38
1995	1,222.8	119.6		407.8	289.9	312.0	93.3	1,103.5	464.2	2.63	2.38
:S:											
1996	1,251.6	126.4	33.6	409.9	273.3	325.9	82.7	1,125.2	488.5	2.56	2.30
1997	1,322.7	129.3	36.1	430.7	298.3	340.6	88.1	1,193.7	509.2	2.60	2.34
1998	1,395.3	130.7	43.3	449.3	320.9	357.9	94.0	1,264.9	538.0	2.59	2.35
1999	1,464.2	127.8	42.7	466.3	340.6	385.5	101.3	1,336.4	563.4	2.60	2.37
2000	1,520.7	126.4	41.1	474.2	358.2	407.1	113.7	1,394.3	581.0	2.62	2.40
2001	1,488.9	126.5	51.7	452.8	347.5	396.3	113.9	1,362.4	583.6	2.55	2.33
2002	1,501.4	124.0	48.1	447.0	348.8	420.6	112.5	1,377.6	582.5	2.58	2.37
2003	1,515.7	124.4	53.4	437.5	349.6	436.4	113.9	1,391.6	609.7	2.49	2.28
2004	1,570.0	130.3	53.9	440.1	367.6	458.6	119.5	1,439.8	630.9	2.49	2.28
: I	1,588.6	129.3	54.6	449.4	374.4	460.9	119.9	1,459.6	635.1	2.50	2.30
II	1,592.8	129.2	56.4	450.4	378.2	457.6	120.4	1,464.0	645.4	2.47	2.27
III	1,595.5	130.3	56.4	451.7	378.8	457.2	120.1	1,465.5	652.5	2.45	2.25
IV	1,608.9	130.5	56.2	455.3	383.5	462.2	120.7	1,478.8	652.4	2.47	2.27
: I	1,620.4	130.7	55.7	458.9	386.5	466.9	121.5	1,490.2	661.8	2.45	2.25
II	1,634.6	129.3	57.8	463.0	391.4	469.5	123.0	1,506.0	666.4	2.45	2.26
III	1,647.9	127.9	59.2	466.2	398.3	471.5	124.1	1,521.0	667.2	2.47	2.28
IV	1,651.2	127.3	60.8	467.1	398.4	472.1	124.5	1,525.1	673.5	2.45	2.26
: I	1,647.5	126.3	61.8	465.3	398.0	469.0	125.8	1,522.4	675.1	2.44	2.26
II	1,646.7	126.3	62.0	463.4	398.3	469.1	126.6	1,521.8	683.8	2.41	2.23
III	1,650.7	125.6	61.4	462.8	401.9	471.5	127.0	1,526.6	691.6	2.39	2.21
IV	1,648.7	128.3	60.2	463.6	401.5	466.4	127.5	1,521.4	693.1	2.38	2.20
: I	1,646.2	129.8	57.8	467.0	400.3	461.8	127.6	1,516.9	693.4	2.37	2.19
II	1,633.6	130.4	55.8	460.5	400.5	457.8	126.8	1,503.2	702.8	2.32	2.14
III *p*	1,626.3	130.3	53.9	454.1	402.2	459.0	126.5	1,495.8	696.1	2.34	2.15

[1] Inventories at end of quarter. Quarter-to-quarter changes calculated from this table are at quarterly rates, whereas the change in private inventories component of gross domestic product (GDP) is stated at annual rates.
Inventories of construction, mining, and utilities establishments are included in other industries through 1995.
[2] Quarterly totals at monthly rates. Final sales of domestic business equals final sales of domestic product less gross output of general government, gross value added of nonprofit institutions, compensation paid to domestic workers, and space rent for owner-occupied housing. Includes a small amount of final sales by farm and by government enterprises.
[3]

Note.—The industry classification of inventories is on an establishment basis. Estimates through 1995 are based on the Standard Industrial Classification (SIC). Beginning with 1996, estimates are based on the North American Industry Classification System (NAICS).
See *Survey of Current Business*, Tables 5.7.6A and 5.7.6B, for detailed information on calculation of the chained (2000) dollar inventory series.
Source: Department of Commerce (Bureau of Economic Analysis).

TABLE B–24.—*Foreign transactions in the national income and product accounts, 1959–2008*

[Billions of dollars; quarterly data at seasonally adjusted annual rates]

Year or quarter	Current receipts from rest of the world					Current payments to rest of the world									Balance on current account NIPA[2]
	Total	Exports of goods and services			Income receipts[1]	Total	Imports of goods and services			Income payments	Current taxes and transfer payments to rest of the world (net)				
		Total	Goods[1]	Services[1]			Total	Goods[1]	Services[1]		Total	From persons (net)	From government (net)	From business (net)	
1959	27.0	22.7	16.5	6.3	4.3	28.2	22.3	15.3	7.0	1.5	4.3	0.5	3.8	0.1	—
1960	31.9	27.0	20.5	6.6	4.9	28.7	22.8	15.2	7.6	1.8	4.1	.5	3.5	.1	.1
1961	32.9	27.6	20.9	6.7	5.3	28.6	22.7	15.1	7.6	1.8	4.2	.5	3.6	.1	.1
1962	35.0	29.1	21.7	7.4	5.9	31.1	25.0	16.9	8.1	1.8	4.3	.5	3.6	.1	.1
1963	37.6	31.1	23.3	7.7	6.5	32.6	26.1	17.7	8.4	2.1	4.4	.7	3.6	.1	.1
1964	42.3	35.0	26.7	8.3	7.2	34.7	28.1	19.4	8.7	2.3	4.3	.7	3.4	.2	.2
1965	45.0	37.1	27.8	9.4	7.9	38.8	31.5	22.2	9.3	2.6	4.7	.8	3.7	.2	.2
1966	49.0	40.9	30.7	10.2	8.1	45.1	37.1	26.3	10.7	3.0	5.0	.8	4.0	.2	.2
1967	52.1	43.5	32.2	11.3	8.7	48.6	39.9	27.8	12.2	3.3	5.4	1.0	4.1	.2	.2
1968	58.0	47.9	35.3	12.6	10.1	56.3	46.6	33.9	12.6	4.0	5.7	1.0	4.4	.3	.3
1969	63.7	51.9	38.3	13.7	11.8	61.9	50.5	36.8	13.7	5.7	5.8	1.1	4.4	.3	.3
1970	72.5	59.7	44.5	15.2	12.8	68.5	55.8	40.9	14.9	6.4	6.3	1.3	4.7	.4	.4
1971	77.0	63.0	45.6	17.4	14.0	76.4	62.3	46.6	15.8	6.4	7.6	1.3	5.9	.4	.4
1972	87.1	70.8	51.8	19.0	16.3	90.7	74.2	56.9	17.3	7.7	8.8	1.4	7.0	.5	—
1973	118.8	95.3	73.9	21.3	23.5	109.5	91.2	71.8	19.3	10.9	7.4	1.5	5.2	.7	.7
1974	156.5	126.7	101.0	25.7	29.8	149.8	127.5	104.5	22.9	14.3	8.1	1.3	5.8	1.0	1.0
1975	166.7	138.7	109.6	29.1	28.0	145.4	122.7	99.0	23.7	15.0	7.6	1.3	5.6	.7	2
1976	181.9	149.5	117.8	31.7	32.4	173.0	151.1	124.6	26.5	15.5	6.3	1.3	3.9	1.1	
1977	196.6	159.4	123.7	35.7	37.2	205.6	182.4	152.6	29.8	16.9	6.2	1.3	3.5	1.4	—
1978	233.1	186.9	145.4	41.5	46.3	243.6	212.3	177.4	34.8	24.7	6.7	1.5	3.8	1.4	-1
1979	298.5	230.1	184.0	46.1	68.3	297.0	252.7	212.8	39.9	36.4	8.0	1.6	4.3	2.0	
1980	359.9	280.8	225.8	55.0	79.1	348.5	293.8	248.6	45.3	44.9	9.8	1.8	5.5	2.4	1
1981	397.3	305.2	239.1	66.1	92.0	390.9	317.8	267.8	49.9	59.1	14.1	5.5	5.4	3.2	
1982	384.2	283.2	215.0	68.2	101.0	384.4	303.2	250.5	52.6	64.5	16.7	6.6	6.7	3.4	
1983	378.9	277.0	207.3	69.7	101.9	410.9	328.6	272.7	56.0	64.8	17.5	6.9	7.2	3.4	-3
1984	424.2	302.4	225.6	76.7	121.9	511.2	405.1	336.3	68.8	85.6	20.5	7.8	9.2	3.5	-8
1985	414.5	302.0	222.2	79.8	112.4	525.3	417.2	343.3	73.9	85.9	22.2	8.2	11.1	2.9	-11
1986	431.9	320.5	226.0	94.5	111.4	571.2	453.3	370.0	83.3	93.6	24.3	9.0	12.2	3.2	-13
1987	487.1	363.9	257.5	106.4	123.2	637.9	509.1	414.8	94.3	105.3	23.5	9.9	10.3	3.4	-15
1988	596.2	444.1	325.8	118.3	152.1	708.4	554.5	452.1	102.4	128.5	25.5	10.6	10.4	4.5	-11
1989	681.0	503.3	369.4	134.0	177.7	769.3	591.5	484.8	106.7	151.5	26.4	11.4	10.4	4.6	-8
1990	741.5	552.4	396.6	155.7	189.1	811.5	630.3	508.1	122.3	154.3	26.9	12.0	10.0	4.8	-7
1991	765.7	596.8	423.5	173.3	168.9	752.3	624.3	500.7	123.6	138.5	-10.6	13.0	-28.6	5.0	1
1992	788.0	635.3	448.0	187.4	152.7	824.9	668.6	544.9	123.6	123.0	33.4	12.3	17.1	3.9	-9
1993	812.1	655.8	459.9	195.9	156.2	882.5	720.9	592.8	128.1	124.3	37.3	14.2	17.8	5.4	-7
1994	907.3	720.9	510.1	210.8	186.4	1,012.5	814.5	676.8	137.7	160.2	37.8	15.4	15.8	6.6	-10
1995	1,046.1	812.2	583.3	228.9	233.9	1,137.1	903.6	757.4	146.1	198.1	35.4	16.2	10.1	9.1	-9
1996	1,117.3	868.6	618.3	250.2	248.7	1,217.6	964.8	807.4	157.4	213.7	39.1	18.0	14.1	7.1	-10
1997	1,242.0	955.3	687.7	267.6	286.7	1,352.2	1,056.9	885.3	171.5	253.7	41.6	21.0	10.9	9.7	-11
1998	1,243.1	955.9	680.9	275.1	287.1	1,430.5	1,115.9	929.0	186.9	265.8	48.8	24.6	11.2	12.9	-18
1999	1,312.1	991.2	697.2	294.0	320.8	1,585.9	1,251.7	1,045.5	206.3	287.0	47.2	28.3	11.6	7.3	-27
2000	1,478.9	1,096.3	784.3	311.9	382.7	1,875.6	1,475.8	1,243.5	232.3	343.7	56.1	31.5	13.5	11.2	-39
2001	1,355.2	1,032.8	731.2	301.6	322.4	1,725.6	1,399.8	1,167.9	231.9	278.8	47.0	33.0	9.5	4.5	-37
2002	1,311.6	1,005.9	697.6	308.4	305.7	1,769.9	1,430.3	1,189.3	241.0	275.0	64.5	40.0	14.3	10.3	-45
2003	1,377.6	1,040.8	724.4	316.4	336.8	1,889.8	1,540.2	1,283.9	256.2	280.0	69.7	40.2	17.6	11.9	-51
2004	1,619.9	1,182.4	818.3	364.1	437.5	2,244.0	1,797.8	1,499.5	298.3	361.3	84.9	43.1	19.2	22.6	-62
2005	1,885.0	1,311.5	908.4	403.1	573.5	2,595.9	2,025.1	1,705.3	319.8	480.5	90.3	47.9	26.5	15.9	-71
2006	2,206.1	1,480.8	1,032.1	448.7	725.4	2,977.7	2,238.1	1,882.7	355.4	647.1	92.5	51.1	19.6	21.8	-77
2007	2,524.1	1,662.4	1,149.2	513.2	861.7	3,242.7	2,370.2	1,985.2	385.1	759.3	113.2	56.3	25.9	31.0	-71
2005: I	1,802.8	1,266.8	871.8	394.9	536.0	2,485.9	1,937.5	1,626.5	311.0	433.4	115.1	48.5	31.8	34.8	-68
II	1,856.9	1,305.1	908.6	396.5	551.8	2,545.9	1,986.0	1,669.0	317.0	459.6	100.4	47.7	18.8	33.9	-68
III	1,897.4	1,314.5	909.6	404.9	582.9	2,556.3	2,039.6	1,717.5	322.1	479.9	36.9	47.1	22.7	-32.9	-65
IV	1,982.9	1,359.6	943.5	416.1	623.3	2,795.3	2,137.4	1,808.2	329.2	549.1	108.8	48.2	32.9	27.8	-81
2006: I	2,085.1	1,423.2	990.9	432.4	661.9	2,853.9	2,184.9	1,838.7	346.3	582.4	86.6	46.7	17.7	22.2	-76
II	2,182.9	1,462.8	1,022.3	440.5	720.0	2,971.8	2,240.0	1,887.2	352.8	634.8	97.0	52.0	23.8	21.1	-78
III	2,238.4	1,492.5	1,044.5	448.0	745.9	3,064.0	2,285.2	1,929.8	355.4	679.4	99.4	52.2	25.1	22.1	-82
IV	2,318.2	1,544.5	1,070.7	473.8	773.7	3,021.3	2,242.2	1,875.1	367.2	691.8	87.2	53.8	11.8	21.6	-70
2007: I	2,348.8	1,560.5	1,085.0	475.5	788.2	3,126.4	2,289.4	1,917.4	372.0	715.8	121.2	55.7	36.4	29.1	-77
II	2,467.3	1,614.4	1,116.8	497.6	852.8	3,231.0	2,337.5	1,957.1	380.5	793.2	100.3	56.0	16.3	27.9	-76
III	2,613.4	1,714.9	1,181.2	533.8	898.5	3,295.4	2,397.5	2,005.4	392.1	786.3	111.7	56.3	22.1	33.2	-68
IV	2,667.1	1,759.7	1,213.7	546.0	907.4	3,318.1	2,456.5	2,060.9	395.6	742.0	119.6	57.3	28.6	33.8	-65
2008: I	2,664.0	1,820.8	1,256.9	563.9	843.2	3,357.0	2,526.5	2,118.0	408.5	705.1	125.4	57.9	32.4	35.1	-69
II	2,746.0	1,923.2	1,343.7	579.5	822.8	3,468.6	2,641.4	2,225.5	415.9	708.9	118.2	62.7	21.5	34.0	-72
III p	2,777.2	1,971.3	1,375.3	596.0	805.8	3,483.3	2,677.9	2,252.6	425.2	688.4	117.0	62.1	21.3	33.6	-70

[1] Certain goods, primarily military equipment purchased and sold by the Federal Government, are included in services. Beginning with 1986, repairs and alterations of equipment were reclassified from goods to services.
[2] National income and product accounts (NIPA).

Source: Department of Commerce (Bureau of Economic Analysis).

TABLE B–25.—*Real exports and imports of goods and services, 1990–2008*

[Billions of chained (2000) dollars; quarterly data at seasonally adjusted annual rates]

or quarter	Exports of goods and services					Imports of goods and services				
	Total	Goods [1]			Services [1]	Total	Goods [1]			Services [1]
		Total	Durable goods	Non-durable goods			Total	Durable goods	Non-durable goods	
....	552.5	367.2	226.3	145.1	188.7	607.1	469.7	264.7	218.4	142.7
....	589.1	392.5	243.1	153.7	199.9	603.7	469.3	266.1	215.9	139.0
....	629.7	421.9	262.5	163.6	210.8	645.6	513.1	294.0	231.9	135.5
....	650.0	435.6	276.1	162.4	217.5	702.1	564.8	328.8	248.0	139.4
....	706.5	478.0	309.6	170.1	231.1	785.9	640.0	383.1	266.0	147.3
....	778.2	533.9	353.6	181.1	245.8	849.1	697.6	427.1	277.0	152.1
....	843.4	581.1	394.9	186.7	263.5	923.0	762.7	472.8	295.2	160.5
....	943.7	664.5	466.2	198.7	279.2	1,048.3	872.6	550.3	326.4	175.6
....	966.5	679.4	481.2	198.5	287.2	1,170.3	974.4	621.8	355.7	195.6
....	1,008.2	705.2	503.6	201.7	303.2	1,304.4	1,095.2	711.7	384.3	209.1
....	1,096.3	784.3	569.2	215.1	311.9	1,475.8	1,243.5	820.7	422.8	232.3
....	1,036.7	736.3	522.2	214.2	300.4	1,435.8	1,204.1	769.4	435.1	231.6
....	1,013.3	707.0	491.2	216.1	306.0	1,484.6	1,248.2	801.0	447.4	236.5
....	1,026.1	719.8	499.8	220.3	306.2	1,545.0	1,309.3	835.3	474.2	236.6
....	1,126.1	784.4	558.6	227.1	341.4	1,719.9	1,457.0	954.4	505.2	263.9
....	1,205.3	844.7	612.6	234.9	360.4	1,821.9	1,556.4	1,035.8	526.3	267.6
....	1,314.8	928.7	683.0	250.2	386.3	1,930.5	1,649.0	1,127.8	535.4	283.7
....	1,425.9	998.7	741.2	263.6	426.9	1,972.4	1,677.7	1,152.7	541.0	296.4
I	1,177.9	817.9	583.2	236.0	359.6	1,801.7	1,536.7	1,006.4	532.6	266.9
II	1,203.1	846.0	606.1	241.6	357.1	1,804.4	1,539.5	1,025.7	519.6	266.9
III	1,204.3	844.2	615.4	231.9	359.9	1,807.9	1,543.8	1,039.4	512.9	266.2
IV	1,235.7	870.8	645.7	230.0	365.0	1,873.6	1,605.5	1,071.8	540.0	270.6
I	1,284.3	907.8	667.8	244.3	376.7	1,920.2	1,640.6	1,111.9	540.0	281.9
II	1,301.4	922.5	676.4	250.2	379.2	1,920.9	1,642.8	1,124.9	532.5	280.5
III	1,312.6	930.7	683.5	251.5	382.2	1,935.7	1,658.0	1,134.4	538.0	280.3
IV	1,361.1	953.9	704.3	254.7	407.0	1,945.3	1,654.5	1,140.0	531.0	292.4
I	1,363.2	958.9	708.9	255.2	404.2	1,981.8	1,688.3	1,147.6	553.2	295.4
II	1,392.2	974.9	720.9	259.3	417.0	1,963.4	1,671.2	1,144.6	541.4	293.9
III	1,466.2	1,024.1	759.6	270.6	441.8	1,978.0	1,681.1	1,165.8	534.8	298.4
IV	1,482.1	1,037.0	775.5	269.2	444.7	1,966.5	1,670.2	1,153.0	534.6	297.8
I	1,500.6	1,048.6	771.2	281.6	451.7	1,962.6	1,662.0	1,134.3	539.9	301.8
II	1,544.7	1,088.9	798.8	293.9	455.8	1,926.0	1,631.6	1,144.6	512.6	295.5
III *p*	1,557.8	1,099.3	808.1	295.6	458.6	1,910.2	1,613.3	1,124.1	510.9	297.9

[1] Certain goods, primarily military equipment purchased and sold by the Federal Government, are included in services. Beginning with 1986, repairs and ctions of equipment were reclassified from goods to services.

te.—See Table B–2 for data for total exports of goods and services and total imports of goods and services for 1959–89.

urce: Department of Commerce (Bureau of Economic Analysis).

TABLE B–26.—*Relation of gross domestic product, gross national product, net national product, an national income, 1959–2008*

[Billions of dollars; quarterly data at seasonally adjusted annual rates]

Year or quarter	Gross domestic product	Plus: Income receipts from rest of the world	Less: Income payments to rest of the world	Equals: Gross national product	Less: Consumption of fixed capital			Equals: Net national product	Less: Statistical discrepancy	Equals National income
					Total	Private	Government			
1959	506.6	4.3	1.5	509.3	53.0	38.6	14.5	456.3	0.5	45
1960	526.4	4.9	1.8	529.5	55.6	40.5	15.0	473.9	−.9	47
1961	544.7	5.3	1.8	548.2	57.2	41.6	15.6	491.0	−.6	49
1962	585.6	5.9	1.8	589.7	59.3	42.8	16.5	530.5	.4	53
1963	617.7	6.5	2.1	622.2	62.4	44.9	17.5	559.8	−.8	56
1964	663.6	7.2	2.3	668.5	65.0	46.9	18.1	603.5	.8	6C
1965	719.1	7.9	2.6	724.4	69.4	50.5	18.9	655.0	1.6	65
1966	787.8	8.1	3.0	792.9	75.6	55.5	20.1	717.3	6.3	71
1967	832.6	8.7	3.3	838.0	81.5	59.9	21.6	756.5	4.6	75
1968	910.0	10.1	4.0	916.1	88.4	65.2	23.1	827.7	4.6	82
1969	984.6	11.8	5.7	990.7	97.9	73.1	24.8	892.8	3.2	88
1970	1,038.5	12.8	6.4	1,044.9	106.7	80.0	26.7	938.2	7.3	93
1971	1,127.1	14.0	6.4	1,134.7	115.0	86.7	28.3	1,019.7	11.6	1,00
1972	1,238.3	16.3	7.7	1,246.8	126.5	97.1	29.5	1,120.3	9.1	1,11
1973	1,382.7	23.5	10.9	1,395.3	139.3	107.9	31.4	1,256.0	8.6	1,24
1974	1,500.0	29.8	14.3	1,515.5	162.5	126.6	35.9	1,353.0	10.9	1,34
1975	1,638.3	28.0	15.0	1,651.3	187.7	147.8	40.0	1,463.6	17.7	1,44
1976	1,825.3	32.4	15.5	1,842.1	205.2	162.5	42.6	1,637.0	25.1	1,61
1977	2,030.9	37.2	16.9	2,051.2	230.0	184.3	45.7	1,821.2	22.3	1,79
1978	2,294.7	46.3	24.7	2,316.3	262.3	212.8	49.5	2,054.0	26.6	2,02
1979	2,563.3	68.3	36.4	2,595.3	300.1	245.7	54.5	2,295.1	46.0	2,24
1980	2,789.5	79.1	44.9	2,823.7	343.0	281.1	61.8	2,480.7	41.4	2,43
1981	3,128.4	92.0	59.1	3,161.4	388.1	317.9	70.1	2,773.3	30.9	2,74
1982	3,255.0	101.0	64.5	3,291.5	426.9	349.8	77.1	2,864.6	.3	2,86
1983	3,536.7	101.9	64.8	3,573.8	443.8	362.1	81.7	3,130.0	45.7	3,08
1984	3,933.2	121.9	85.6	3,969.5	472.6	385.6	87.0	3,496.9	14.6	3,48
1985	4,220.3	112.4	85.9	4,246.8	506.7	414.0	92.7	3,740.1	16.7	3,72
1986	4,462.8	111.4	93.6	4,480.6	531.3	431.8	99.5	3,949.3	47.0	3,90
1987	4,739.5	123.2	105.3	4,757.4	561.9	455.3	106.7	4,195.4	21.7	4,17
1988	5,103.8	152.1	128.5	5,127.4	597.6	483.5	114.1	4,529.8	−19.5	4,54
1989	5,484.4	177.7	151.5	5,510.6	644.3	522.1	122.2	4,866.3	39.7	4,82
1990	5,803.1	189.1	154.3	5,837.9	682.5	551.6	130.9	5,155.4	66.2	5,08
1991	5,995.9	168.9	138.5	6,026.3	725.9	586.9	139.1	5,300.4	72.5	5,22
1992	6,337.7	152.7	123.0	6,367.4	751.9	607.3	144.6	5,615.5	102.7	5,51
1993	6,657.4	156.2	124.3	6,689.3	776.4	624.7	151.8	5,912.9	139.5	5,77
1994	7,072.2	186.4	160.2	7,098.4	833.7	675.1	158.6	6,264.7	142.5	6,12
1995	7,397.7	233.9	198.1	7,433.4	878.4	713.4	165.0	6,555.1	101.2	6,45
1996	7,816.9	248.7	213.7	7,851.9	918.1	748.8	169.3	6,933.8	93.7	6,84
1997	8,304.3	286.7	253.7	8,337.3	974.4	800.3	174.1	7,362.8	70.7	7,29
1998	8,747.0	287.1	265.8	8,768.3	1,030.2	851.2	179.0	7,738.2	−14.6	7,75
1999	9,268.4	320.8	287.0	9,302.2	1,101.3	914.3	187.0	8,200.9	−35.7	8,23
2000	9,817.0	382.7	343.7	9,855.9	1,187.8	990.8	197.0	8,668.1	−127.2	8,79
2001	10,128.0	322.4	278.8	10,171.6	1,281.5	1,075.5	206.0	8,890.2	−89.6	8,97
2002	10,469.6	305.7	275.0	10,500.2	1,292.0	1,080.3	211.6	9,208.3	−21.0	9,22
2003	10,960.8	336.8	280.0	11,017.6	1,336.5	1,118.3	218.2	9,681.1	48.8	9,63
2004	11,685.9	437.5	361.3	11,762.1	1,436.1	1,206.0	230.2	10,326.0	19.1	10,30
2005	12,421.9	573.5	480.5	12,514.9	1,612.0	1,359.7	252.3	10,902.9	−71.2	10,97
2006	13,178.4	725.4	647.1	13,256.6	1,623.9	1,356.0	268.0	11,632.7	−163.0	11,79
2007	13,807.5	861.7	759.3	13,910.0	1,720.5	1,431.1	289.4	12,189.5	−81.4	12,27
2005: I	12,155.4	536.0	433.4	12,258.0	1,467.2	1,225.3	241.9	10,790.8	−35.6	10,82
II	12,297.5	551.8	459.6	12,389.7	1,494.1	1,248.0	246.1	10,895.6	−63.3	10,95
III	12,538.2	582.9	479.9	12,641.2	1,907.0	1,641.1	265.9	10,734.3	−45.3	10,77
IV	12,696.4	623.3	549.1	12,770.6	1,579.8	1,324.4	255.4	11,190.8	−140.5	11,33
2006: I	12,959.6	661.9	582.4	13,039.2	1,582.7	1,323.1	259.5	11,456.5	−154.6	11,61
II	13,134.1	720.0	634.8	13,219.4	1,612.5	1,346.8	265.8	11,606.8	−131.7	11,73
III	13,249.6	745.9	679.4	13,316.1	1,638.3	1,367.8	270.5	11,677.7	−170.8	11,84
IV	13,370.1	773.7	691.8	13,452.0	1,662.2	1,386.2	275.9	11,789.8	−194.9	11,98
2007: I	13,510.9	788.2	715.8	13,583.3	1,684.3	1,402.1	282.2	11,899.0	−188.4	12,08
II	13,737.5	852.8	793.2	13,797.2	1,707.0	1,420.0	287.0	12,090.1	−143.4	12,23
III	13,950.6	898.5	786.3	14,062.8	1,731.9	1,440.1	291.8	12,330.8	−7.8	12,33
IV	14,031.2	907.4	742.0	14,196.6	1,758.6	1,462.3	296.3	12,438.0	13.9	12,42
2008: I	14,150.8	843.2	705.1	14,289.0	1,778.0	1,477.5	300.5	12,511.1	63.4	12,44
II	14,294.5	822.8	708.9	14,408.3	1,803.1	1,497.4	305.7	12,605.2	136.6	12,46
III ᵖ	14,420.5	805.8	688.4	14,538.0	1,899.7	1,587.4	312.2	12,638.3	160.5	12,47

Source: Department of Commerce (Bureau of Economic Analysis).

TABLE B–27.—*Relation of national income and personal income, 1959–2008*

[Billions of dollars; quarterly data at seasonally adjusted annual rates]

Year or quarter	National income	Less: Corporate profits with inventory valuation and capital consumption adjustments	Less: Taxes on production and imports less subsidies	Less: Contributions for government social insurance	Less: Net interest and miscellaneous payments on assets	Less: Business current transfer payments (net)	Less: Current surplus of government enterprises	Less: Wage accruals less disbursements	Plus: Personal income receipts on assets	Plus: Personal current transfer receipts	Equals: Personal income
1959	455.8	55.7	40.0	13.8	9.6	1.8	1.0	0.0	34.6	24.2	392.8
1960	474.9	53.8	43.4	16.4	10.6	1.9	.9	.0	37.9	25.7	411.5
1961	491.6	54.9	45.0	17.0	12.5	2.0	.8	.0	40.1	29.5	429.0
1962	530.1	63.3	48.2	19.1	14.2	2.2	.9	.0	44.1	30.4	456.7
1963	560.6	69.0	51.2	21.7	15.2	2.7	1.4	.0	47.9	32.2	479.6
1964	602.7	76.5	54.6	22.4	17.4	3.1	1.3	.0	53.8	33.5	514.6
1965	653.4	87.5	57.8	23.4	19.6	3.6	1.3	.0	59.4	36.2	555.7
1966	711.0	93.2	59.3	31.3	22.4	3.5	1.0	.0	64.1	39.6	603.9
1967	751.9	91.3	64.2	34.9	25.5	3.8	.9	.0	69.0	48.0	648.3
1968	823.2	98.8	72.3	38.7	27.1	4.3	1.2	.0	75.2	56.1	712.0
1969	889.7	95.4	79.4	44.1	32.7	4.9	1.0	.0	84.1	62.3	778.5
1970	930.9	83.6	86.7	46.4	39.1	4.5	.0	.0	93.5	74.7	838.8
1971	1,008.1	98.0	95.9	51.2	43.9	4.3	−.2	.6	101.0	88.1	903.5
1972	1,111.2	112.1	101.4	59.2	47.9	4.9	.5	.0	109.6	97.9	992.7
1973	1,247.4	125.5	112.1	75.5	55.2	6.0	−.4	−.1	124.7	112.6	1,110.7
1974	1,342.1	115.8	121.7	85.2	70.8	7.1	−.9	−.5	146.4	133.3	1,222.6
1975	1,445.9	134.8	131.0	89.3	81.6	9.4	−3.2	.1	162.2	170.0	1,335.0
1976	1,611.8	163.3	141.5	101.3	85.5	9.5	−1.8	.1	178.4	184.0	1,474.8
1977	1,798.9	192.4	152.8	113.1	101.1	8.4	−2.6	.1	205.3	194.2	1,633.2
1978	2,027.4	216.6	162.2	131.3	115.0	10.6	−1.9	.3	234.8	209.6	1,837.7
1979	2,249.1	223.2	171.9	152.7	138.9	13.0	−2.6	−.2	274.7	235.3	2,062.2
1980	2,439.3	201.1	190.9	166.2	181.8	14.4	−4.8	.0	338.7	279.5	2,307.9
1981	2,742.4	226.1	224.5	195.7	232.3	17.6	−4.9	.1	421.9	318.4	2,591.3
1982	2,864.3	209.7	226.4	208.9	271.1	20.1	−4.0	.0	488.4	354.8	2,775.3
1983	3,084.2	264.2	242.5	226.0	285.3	22.5	−3.1	−.4	529.6	383.7	2,960.7
1984	3,482.3	318.6	269.3	257.5	327.1	30.1	−1.9	.2	607.9	400.1	3,289.5
1985	3,723.4	330.3	287.3	281.4	341.3	34.8	.8	−.2	654.0	424.9	3,526.7
1986	3,902.3	319.5	298.9	303.4	366.8	36.6	1.3	.0	695.5	451.0	3,722.4
1987	4,173.7	368.8	317.7	323.1	366.4	33.8	1.2	.0	717.0	467.6	3,947.4
1988	4,549.4	432.6	345.5	361.5	385.3	34.0	2.5	.0	769.3	496.6	4,253.7
1989	4,826.6	426.6	372.1	385.2	432.1	39.2	4.9	.0	878.0	543.4	4,587.8
1990	5,089.1	437.8	398.7	410.1	442.2	39.4	1.6	.1	924.0	595.2	4,878.6
1991	5,227.9	451.2	430.2	430.2	418.2	39.9	5.7	−.1	932.0	666.4	5,051.0
1992	5,512.8	479.3	453.9	455.0	388.5	42.4	7.6	−15.8	910.9	749.4	5,362.0
1993	5,773.4	541.9	467.0	477.7	365.7	40.7	7.2	6.4	901.8	790.1	5,558.5
1994	6,122.3	600.3	513.5	508.2	366.4	43.3	8.6	17.6	950.8	827.3	5,842.5
1995	6,453.9	696.7	524.2	532.8	367.1	46.9	11.4	16.4	1,016.4	877.4	6,152.3
1996	6,840.1	786.2	546.8	555.2	376.2	53.1	12.7	3.6	1,089.2	925.0	6,520.6
1997	7,292.2	868.5	579.1	587.2	415.6	49.9	12.6	−2.9	1,181.7	951.2	6,915.1
1998	7,752.8	801.6	604.4	624.2	487.1	64.7	10.3	−.7	1,283.2	978.6	7,423.0
1999	8,236.7	851.3	629.8	661.4	495.4	67.4	10.1	5.2	1,264.2	1,022.1	7,802.4
2000	8,795.2	817.9	664.6	702.7	559.0	87.1	5.3	.0	1,387.0	1,084.0	8,429.7
2001	8,979.8	767.3	673.3	731.1	566.3	92.8	−1.4	.0	1,380.0	1,193.9	8,724.1
2002	9,229.3	886.3	724.4	750.0	520.9	84.3	.9	.0	1,333.2	1,286.2	8,881.9
2003	9,632.3	993.1	759.3	778.6	524.7	83.8	1.7	15.0	1,336.6	1,351.0	9,163.6
2004	10,306.8	1,231.2	819.2	828.8	491.2	83.0	−4.2	−15.0	1,432.1	1,422.5	9,727.2
2005	10,974.0	1,447.9	868.9	874.3	569.1	70.0	−13.4	5.0	1,596.9	1,520.7	10,269.8
2006	11,795.7	1,668.5	926.4	925.5	631.2	85.4	−8.6	1.3	1,824.8	1,603.0	10,993.9
2007	12,270.9	1,642.4	963.2	965.1	664.4	100.2	−7.9	−6.3	2,000.1	1,713.3	11,663.2
2005: I	10,826.3	1,438.2	850.0	859.6	537.0	97.4	−7.1	.0	1,513.6	1,479.7	10,044.5
II	10,958.9	1,472.4	865.5	866.9	554.8	97.9	−9.3	.0	1,564.7	1,508.8	10,184.4
III	10,779.5	1,342.6	876.8	881.1	583.9	8.5	−25.8	.0	1,616.9	1,559.6	10,289.1
IV	11,331.3	1,538.6	883.5	889.5	600.8	76.1	−11.4	20.0	1,692.3	1,534.7	10,561.0
2006: I	11,611.1	1,634.2	908.5	917.1	615.5	85.1	−7.8	−20.0	1,735.4	1,567.6	10,781.6
II	11,738.5	1,681.6	923.8	918.9	629.7	83.5	−8.3	.0	1,809.5	1,594.5	10,913.2
III	11,848.6	1,713.8	932.0	925.5	630.1	86.0	−9.1	.0	1,865.8	1,620.1	11,056.1
IV	11,984.7	1,644.5	941.5	940.4	649.3	86.8	−9.2	25.0	1,888.6	1,629.8	11,224.7
2007: I	12,087.4	1,617.8	955.2	959.8	645.8	98.3	−10.8	−25.0	1,930.9	1,695.7	11,473.0
II	12,233.6	1,672.5	956.4	959.1	660.8	97.4	−8.5	.0	1,982.5	1,699.2	11,577.5
III	12,338.6	1,668.3	965.7	966.0	663.0	102.2	−5.5	.0	2,030.9	1,720.6	11,730.4
IV	12,424.1	1,611.1	975.3	975.3	688.1	103.1	−6.7	.0	2,056.2	1,737.8	11,872.1
2008: I	12,447.6	1,593.5	975.1	992.2	662.3	103.2	−7.1	.0	2,054.1	1,778.1	11,960.5
II	12,468.6	1,533.3	988.5	995.4	683.4	102.1	−7.7	.0	2,052.3	1,926.3	12,152.2
III ᵖ	12,477.8	1,518.7	992.1	998.7	655.8	92.8	−8.0	.0	2,056.8	1,872.4	12,156.8

Source: Department of Commerce (Bureau of Economic Analysis).

TABLE B–28.—*National income by type of income, 1959–2008*

[Billions of dollars; quarterly data at seasonally adjusted annual rates]

Year or quarter	National income	Compensation of employees							Proprietors' income with inventory valuation and capital consumption adjustments			Rental income of persons with capital consumption adjustment
		Total	Wage and salary accruals			Supplements to wages and salaries			Total	Farm	Non-farm	
			Total	Government	Other	Total	Employer contributions for employee pension and insurance funds	Employer contributions for government social insurance				
1959	455.8	281.0	259.8	46.1	213.8	21.1	13.3	7.9	50.7	10.0	40.6	16.2
1960	474.9	296.4	272.9	49.2	223.7	23.6	14.3	9.3	50.8	10.5	40.3	17.1
1961	491.6	305.3	280.5	52.5	228.0	24.8	15.2	9.6	53.2	11.0	42.2	17.9
1962	530.1	327.1	299.4	56.3	243.0	27.8	16.6	11.2	55.4	11.0	44.4	18.8
1963	560.6	345.2	314.9	60.0	254.8	30.4	18.0	12.4	56.5	10.8	45.7	19.5
1964	602.7	370.7	337.8	64.9	272.9	32.9	20.3	12.6	59.4	9.6	49.8	19.6
1965	653.4	399.5	363.8	69.9	293.8	35.7	22.7	13.1	63.9	11.8	52.1	20.2
1966	711.0	442.7	400.3	78.4	321.9	42.3	25.5	16.8	68.2	12.8	55.4	20.8
1967	751.9	475.1	429.0	86.5	342.5	46.1	28.1	18.0	69.8	11.5	58.4	21.2
1968	823.2	524.3	472.0	96.7	375.3	52.3	32.4	20.0	74.3	11.5	62.8	20.9
1969	889.7	577.6	518.3	105.6	412.7	59.3	36.5	22.8	77.4	12.6	64.7	21.2
1970	930.9	617.2	551.6	117.2	434.3	65.7	41.8	23.8	78.4	12.7	65.7	21.4
1971	1,008.1	658.9	584.5	126.8	457.8	74.4	47.9	26.4	84.8	13.2	71.6	22.4
1972	1,111.2	725.1	638.8	137.9	500.9	86.4	55.2	31.2	95.9	16.8	79.1	23.4
1973	1,247.4	811.2	708.8	148.8	560.0	102.5	62.7	39.8	113.5	28.9	84.6	24.3
1974	1,342.1	890.2	772.3	160.5	611.8	118.0	73.3	44.7	113.1	23.2	89.9	24.3
1975	1,445.9	949.1	814.8	176.2	638.6	134.3	87.6	46.7	119.5	21.7	97.8	23.7
1976	1,611.8	1,059.3	899.7	188.9	710.8	159.6	105.2	54.4	132.2	17.0	115.2	22.3
1977	1,798.9	1,180.5	994.2	202.6	791.6	186.4	125.3	61.1	145.7	15.7	130.0	20.7
1978	2,027.4	1,336.1	1,121.2	220.0	901.2	214.9	143.4	71.5	166.6	19.6	147.1	22.1
1979	2,249.1	1,500.8	1,255.8	237.1	1,018.7	245.0	162.4	82.6	180.1	21.8	158.3	23.8
1980	2,439.3	1,651.8	1,377.6	261.5	1,116.2	274.2	185.2	88.9	174.1	11.3	162.8	30.0
1981	2,742.4	1,825.8	1,517.5	285.8	1,231.7	308.3	204.7	103.6	183.0	18.7	164.3	38.0
1982	2,864.3	1,925.8	1,593.7	307.5	1,286.2	332.1	222.4	109.8	176.3	13.1	163.3	38.8
1983	3,084.2	2,042.6	1,684.6	324.8	1,359.8	358.0	238.1	119.9	192.5	6.0	186.5	37.8
1984	3,482.3	2,255.6	1,855.1	348.1	1,507.0	400.5	261.5	139.0	243.3	20.6	222.7	40.2
1985	3,723.4	2,424.7	1,995.5	373.9	1,621.6	429.2	281.5	147.7	262.3	20.8	241.5	41.9
1986	3,902.3	2,570.1	2,114.8	397.0	1,717.9	455.3	297.5	157.9	275.7	22.6	253.1	33.5
1987	4,173.7	2,750.2	2,270.7	422.6	1,848.1	479.5	313.2	166.3	302.2	28.7	273.5	33.5
1988	4,549.4	2,967.2	2,452.9	451.3	2,001.6	514.2	329.6	184.6	341.6	26.8	314.7	40.6
1989	4,826.6	3,145.2	2,596.3	480.2	2,116.2	548.9	355.2	193.7	363.3	33.0	330.3	43.1
1990	5,089.1	3,338.2	2,754.0	517.7	2,236.3	584.2	377.8	206.5	380.6	31.9	348.7	50.7
1991	5,227.9	3,445.2	2,823.0	546.8	2,276.2	622.3	407.1	215.1	377.1	26.7	350.4	60.3
1992	5,512.8	3,635.4	2,964.5	569.2	2,395.3	670.9	442.5	228.4	427.6	34.5	393.0	78.0
1993	5,773.4	3,801.4	3,089.2	586.8	2,502.4	712.2	472.4	239.8	453.8	31.2	422.6	95.6
1994	6,122.3	3,997.2	3,249.8	606.2	2,643.5	747.5	493.3	254.1	473.3	33.9	439.4	119.7
1995	6,453.9	4,193.3	3,435.7	625.5	2,810.2	757.7	493.6	264.0	492.1	22.7	469.5	122.1
1996	6,840.1	4,390.5	3,623.2	644.4	2,978.8	767.3	492.5	274.9	543.2	37.3	505.9	131.5
1997	7,292.2	4,661.7	3,874.7	668.1	3,206.6	787.0	497.5	289.5	576.0	34.2	541.8	128.8
1998	7,752.8	5,019.4	4,182.7	697.3	3,485.5	836.7	529.7	307.0	627.8	29.4	598.4	137.5
1999	8,236.7	5,357.1	4,471.4	729.3	3,742.1	885.7	562.4	323.3	678.3	28.6	649.7	147.3
2000	8,795.2	5,782.7	4,829.2	774.7	4,054.5	953.4	609.9	343.5	728.4	22.7	705.7	150.3
2001	8,979.8	5,942.1	4,942.8	815.9	4,126.9	999.3	642.7	356.6	771.9	19.7	752.2	167.4
2002	9,229.3	6,091.2	4,980.9	865.9	4,115.0	1,110.3	745.1	365.2	768.4	10.6	757.8	152.9
2003	9,632.3	6,325.4	5,127.7	904.4	4,223.3	1,197.7	815.6	382.1	811.3	29.2	782.1	133.0
2004	10,306.8	6,656.4	5,379.5	943.1	4,436.4	1,276.9	868.5	408.3	911.6	37.3	874.3	118.4
2005	10,974.0	7,030.8	5,676.7	980.7	4,695.9	1,354.1	926.0	428.1	959.8	34.1	925.7	40.9
2006	11,795.7	7,433.8	6,028.5	1,023.0	5,005.5	1,405.3	956.8	448.5	1,014.7	16.2	998.6	44.3
2007	12,270.9	7,812.3	6,355.7	1,075.2	5,280.5	1,456.6	991.9	464.7	1,056.2	44.0	1,012.2	40.0
2005: I	10,826.3	6,884.4	5,553.1	970.6	4,582.5	1,331.4	909.8	421.6	936.3	33.2	903.0	90.1
II	10,958.9	6,957.4	5,611.5	974.0	4,637.5	1,346.0	921.4	424.5	948.1	38.3	909.8	72.2
III	10,779.5	7,090.2	5,725.6	984.8	4,740.8	1,364.7	933.4	431.3	960.4	37.1	923.3	−56.9
IV	11,331.3	7,191.0	5,816.5	993.6	4,822.9	1,374.5	939.5	434.9	994.5	27.7	966.7	58.0
2006: I	11,611.1	7,318.0	5,926.4	1,007.7	4,918.7	1,391.6	946.6	445.0	1,004.7	17.3	987.5	52.8
II	11,738.5	7,364.2	5,966.2	1,013.2	4,953.0	1,398.0	952.9	445.1	1,018.3	9.8	1,008.4	45.6
III	11,848.6	7,441.9	6,034.2	1,029.4	5,004.8	1,407.8	959.5	448.2	1,013.4	13.8	999.6	40.4
IV	11,984.7	7,611.1	6,187.2	1,041.9	5,145.3	1,423.9	968.1	455.8	1,022.4	23.7	998.7	38.2
2007: I	12,087.4	7,709.0	6,269.0	1,059.9	5,209.0	1,440.0	977.6	462.3	1,037.2	39.3	997.9	35.1
II	12,233.6	7,760.1	6,310.7	1,068.1	5,242.5	1,449.4	987.7	461.7	1,050.2	42.3	1,007.9	44.6
III	12,338.6	7,839.3	6,377.7	1,080.8	5,297.0	1,461.6	996.5	465.1	1,063.8	47.4	1,016.4	41.8
IV	12,424.1	7,941.0	6,465.5	1,092.1	5,373.4	1,475.5	1,005.9	469.6	1,073.8	47.1	1,026.7	38.6
2008: I	12,447.6	8,009.7	6,518.0	1,109.7	5,408.3	1,491.7	1,015.3	476.4	1,071.7	41.6	1,030.1	39.1
II	12,468.6	8,033.5	6,531.3	1,123.4	5,407.9	1,502.2	1,024.4	477.8	1,076.9	38.0	1,039.0	58.6
III ᵖ	12,477.8	8,082.7	6,572.3	1,138.0	5,434.2	1,510.4	1,031.2	479.2	1,080.6	32.4	1,048.2	63.1

See next page for continuation of table.

TABLE B–28.—*National income by type of income, 1959–2008*—Continued

[Billions of dollars; quarterly data at seasonally adjusted annual rates]

Year or quarter	Corporate profits with inventory valuation and capital consumption adjustments									Net interest and miscellaneous payments	Taxes on production and imports	Less: Subsidies	Business current transfer payments (net)	Current surplus of government enterprises
	Total	Profits with inventory valuation adjustment and without capital consumption adjustment							Capital consumption adjustment					
		Total	Profits					Inventory valuation adjustment						
			Profits before tax	Taxes on corporate income	Profits after tax									
					Total	Net dividends	Undistributed profits							
1959	55.7	53.5	53.8	23.7	30.0	12.6	17.5	-0.3	2.2	9.6	41.1	1.1	1.8	1.0
1960	53.8	51.5	51.6	22.8	28.8	13.4	15.5	-.2	2.3	10.6	44.6	1.1	1.9	.9
1961	54.9	51.8	51.6	22.9	28.7	13.9	14.8	.3	3.0	12.5	47.0	2.0	2.0	.8
1962	63.3	57.0	57.0	24.1	32.9	15.0	17.9	.0	6.2	14.2	50.4	2.3	2.2	.9
1963	69.0	62.1	62.1	26.4	35.7	16.2	19.5	.1	6.8	15.2	53.4	2.2	2.7	1.4
1964	76.5	68.6	69.1	28.2	40.9	18.2	22.7	-.5	7.9	17.4	57.3	2.7	3.1	1.3
1965	87.5	78.9	80.2	31.1	49.1	20.2	28.9	-1.2	8.6	19.6	60.8	3.0	3.6	1.3
1966	93.2	84.6	86.7	33.9	52.8	20.7	32.1	-2.1	8.6	22.4	63.3	3.9	3.5	1.0
1967	91.3	82.0	83.5	32.9	50.6	21.5	29.1	-1.6	9.3	25.5	68.0	3.8	3.8	.9
1968	98.8	88.8	92.4	39.6	52.8	23.5	29.3	-3.7	10.0	27.1	76.5	4.2	4.3	1.2
1969	95.4	85.5	91.4	40.0	51.4	24.2	27.2	-5.9	9.9	32.7	84.0	4.5	4.9	1.0
1970	83.6	74.4	81.0	34.8	46.2	24.3	21.9	-6.6	9.2	39.1	91.5	4.8	4.5	.0
1971	98.0	88.3	92.9	38.2	54.7	25.0	29.7	-4.6	9.7	43.9	100.6	4.7	4.3	-.2
1972	112.1	101.2	107.8	42.3	65.5	26.8	38.6	-6.6	10.9	47.9	108.1	6.6	4.9	.5
1973	125.5	115.3	134.8	50.0	84.9	29.9	55.0	-19.6	10.2	55.2	117.3	5.2	6.0	-.4
1974	115.8	109.5	147.8	52.8	95.0	33.2	61.8	-38.2	6.2	70.8	125.0	3.3	7.1	-.9
1975	134.8	135.0	145.5	51.6	93.9	33.0	60.9	-10.5	-.2	81.6	135.5	4.5	9.4	-3.2
1976	163.3	165.6	179.7	65.3	114.4	39.0	75.4	-14.1	-2.3	85.5	146.6	5.1	9.5	-1.8
1977	192.4	194.7	210.4	74.4	136.0	44.8	91.2	-15.7	-2.3	101.1	159.9	7.1	8.4	-2.6
1978	216.6	222.4	246.1	84.9	161.3	50.8	110.5	-23.7	-5.8	115.0	171.2	8.9	10.6	-1.9
1979	223.2	231.8	271.9	90.0	181.9	57.5	124.4	-40.1	-8.5	138.9	180.4	8.5	13.0	-2.6
1980	201.1	211.4	253.5	87.2	166.3	64.1	102.2	-42.1	-10.2	181.8	200.7	9.8	14.4	-4.8
1981	226.1	219.1	243.7	84.3	159.4	73.8	85.6	-24.6	7.0	232.3	236.0	11.5	17.6	-4.9
1982	209.7	191.0	198.5	66.5	132.0	77.7	54.3	-7.5	18.6	271.1	241.3	15.0	20.1	-4.0
1983	264.2	226.5	233.9	80.6	153.3	83.5	69.8	-7.4	37.8	285.3	263.7	21.2	22.5	-3.1
1984	318.6	264.6	268.6	97.5	171.1	90.8	80.3	-4.0	54.0	327.1	290.2	21.0	30.1	-1.9
1985	330.3	257.5	257.4	99.4	158.0	97.6	60.5	.0	72.9	341.3	308.5	21.3	34.8	.8
1986	319.5	253.0	246.0	109.7	136.3	106.2	30.1	7.1	66.5	366.8	323.7	24.8	36.6	1.3
1987	368.8	301.4	317.6	130.4	187.2	112.3	74.9	-16.2	67.5	366.4	347.9	30.2	33.8	1.2
1988	432.6	363.9	386.1	141.6	244.4	129.9	114.5	-22.2	68.7	385.3	374.9	29.4	34.0	2.5
1989	426.6	367.4	383.7	146.1	237.7	158.0	79.7	-16.3	59.2	432.1	399.3	27.2	39.2	4.9
1990	437.8	396.6	409.5	145.4	264.1	169.1	95.0	-12.9	41.2	442.2	425.5	26.8	39.4	1.6
1991	451.2	427.9	423.0	138.6	284.4	180.7	103.7	4.9	23.3	418.2	457.5	27.3	39.9	5.7
1992	479.3	458.3	461.1	148.7	312.4	187.9	124.5	-2.8	21.1	388.5	483.8	29.9	42.4	7.6
1993	541.9	513.1	517.1	171.0	346.1	202.8	143.3	-4.0	28.8	365.7	503.4	36.4	40.7	7.2
1994	600.3	564.6	577.1	193.7	383.3	234.7	148.6	-12.4	35.7	366.4	545.6	32.2	43.3	8.6
1995	696.7	656.0	674.3	218.7	455.6	254.2	201.4	-18.3	40.7	367.1	558.2	34.0	46.9	11.4
1996	786.2	736.1	733.0	231.7	501.4	297.6	203.8	3.1	50.1	376.2	581.1	34.3	53.1	12.7
1997	868.5	812.3	798.2	246.1	552.1	334.5	217.6	14.1	56.2	415.6	612.0	32.9	49.9	12.6
1998	801.6	738.5	718.3	248.3	470.0	351.6	118.3	20.2	63.1	487.1	639.8	35.4	64.7	10.3
1999	851.3	776.8	775.9	258.6	517.2	337.4	179.9	1.0	74.5	495.4	674.0	44.2	67.4	10.1
2000	817.9	759.3	773.4	265.2	508.2	377.9	130.3	-14.1	58.6	559.0	708.9	44.3	87.1	5.3
2001	767.3	719.2	707.9	204.1	503.8	370.9	132.9	11.3	48.1	566.3	728.6	55.3	92.8	-1.4
2002	886.3	766.2	768.4	192.6	575.8	399.2	176.6	-2.2	120.1	520.9	762.8	38.4	84.3	.9
2003	993.1	894.5	908.1	243.3	664.8	424.7	240.1	-13.6	98.7	524.7	807.2	47.9	83.8	1.7
2004	1,231.2	1,161.6	1,204.7	307.4	897.3	539.5	357.8	-43.1	69.7	491.2	863.8	44.6	83.0	-4.2
2005	1,447.9	1,582.8	1,620.6	413.7	1,206.9	577.4	629.5	-37.8	-134.8	569.1	928.2	59.3	70.0	-13.4
2006	1,668.5	1,834.2	1,873.7	468.9	1,404.8	702.1	702.7	-39.5	-165.7	631.2	976.2	49.7	85.4	-8.6
2007	1,642.4	1,835.1	1,886.3	450.4	1,435.9	788.7	647.3	-51.2	-192.7	664.4	1,015.5	52.3	100.2	-7.9
2005: I	1,438.2	1,555.3	1,600.7	407.2	1,193.5	553.0	640.6	-45.4	-117.2	537.0	904.5	54.5	97.4	-7.1
II	1,472.4	1,594.0	1,612.0	412.0	1,200.1	561.6	638.5	-18.0	-121.7	554.8	924.0	58.6	97.9	-9.3
III	1,342.6	1,497.1	1,536.3	386.4	1,149.9	581.4	568.4	-39.1	-154.5	583.9	937.4	60.7	8.5	-25.8
IV	1,538.6	1,684.6	1,733.3	449.2	1,284.1	613.4	670.6	-48.7	-146.0	600.8	946.8	63.3	76.1	-11.4
2006: I	1,634.2	1,778.7	1,813.8	453.8	1,359.9	652.8	707.1	-35.0	-144.5	615.5	962.7	54.2	85.1	-7.8
II	1,681.6	1,841.6	1,900.1	474.8	1,425.2	688.8	736.4	-58.5	-160.0	629.7	973.6	49.8	83.5	-8.3
III	1,713.8	1,887.2	1,929.9	487.2	1,442.6	720.9	721.7	-42.7	-173.4	630.1	980.1	48.2	86.0	-9.1
IV	1,644.5	1,829.3	1,851.4	459.8	1,391.4	745.8	645.6	-21.8	-184.8	649.3	988.3	46.8	86.8	-9.2
2007: I	1,617.8	1,794.7	1,838.9	448.5	1,390.4	761.5	629.0	-44.2	-176.9	645.8	1,002.7	47.5	98.3	-10.8
II	1,672.5	1,859.5	1,914.8	468.5	1,446.3	779.2	667.1	-55.3	-187.0	660.8	1,012.3	55.9	97.4	-8.5
III	1,668.3	1,866.1	1,897.1	451.1	1,446.1	797.6	648.5	-31.0	-197.8	663.0	1,019.2	53.5	102.2	-5.5
IV	1,611.1	1,820.2	1,894.3	433.5	1,460.9	816.4	644.5	-74.1	-209.2	688.1	1,027.7	52.3	103.1	-6.7
2008: I	1,593.5	1,641.5	1,750.9	402.9	1,348.0	832.5	515.5	-109.4	-48.0	662.3	1,025.8	50.6	103.2	-7.1
II	1,533.3	1,596.0	1,750.0	406.8	1,343.2	846.4	496.7	-154.0	-62.7	683.4	1,039.4	50.8	102.1	-7.7
III p	1,518.7	1,606.9	1,699.3	396.9	1,302.4	841.4	461.0	-92.4	-88.2	655.8	1,042.5	50.4	92.8	-8.0

Source: Department of Commerce (Bureau of Economic Analysis).

TABLE B–29.—*Sources of personal income, 1959–2008*

[Billions of dollars; quarterly data at seasonally adjusted annual rates]

Year or quarter	Personal income	Compensation of employees, received							Proprietors' income with inventory valuation and capital consumption adjustments			Rental income of persons with capital consumption adjustment
		Total	Wage and salary disbursements			Supplements to wages and salaries			Total	Farm	Nonfarm	
			Total	Private industries	Government	Total	Employer contributions for employee pension and insurance funds	Employer contributions for government social insurance				
1959	392.8	281.0	259.8	213.8	46.1	21.1	13.3	7.9	50.7	10.0	40.6	16.2
1960	411.5	296.4	272.9	223.7	49.2	23.6	14.3	9.3	50.8	10.5	40.3	17.1
1961	429.0	305.3	280.5	228.0	52.5	24.8	15.2	9.6	53.2	11.0	42.2	17.9
1962	456.7	327.1	299.4	243.0	56.3	27.8	16.6	11.2	55.4	11.0	44.4	18.8
1963	479.6	345.2	314.9	254.8	60.0	30.4	18.0	12.4	56.5	10.8	45.7	19.5
1964	514.6	370.7	337.8	272.9	64.9	32.9	20.3	12.6	59.4	9.6	49.8	19.6
1965	555.7	399.5	363.8	293.8	69.9	35.7	22.7	13.1	63.9	11.8	52.1	20.2
1966	603.9	442.7	400.3	321.9	78.4	42.3	25.5	16.8	68.2	12.8	55.4	20.8
1967	648.3	475.1	429.0	342.5	86.5	46.1	28.1	18.0	69.8	11.5	58.4	21.2
1968	712.0	524.3	472.0	375.3	96.7	52.3	32.4	20.0	74.3	11.5	62.8	20.9
1969	778.5	577.6	518.3	412.7	105.6	59.3	36.5	22.8	77.4	12.6	64.7	21.2
1970	838.8	617.2	551.6	434.3	117.2	65.7	41.8	23.8	78.4	12.7	65.7	21.4
1971	903.5	658.3	584.0	457.4	126.6	74.4	47.9	26.4	84.8	13.2	71.6	22.4
1972	992.7	725.1	638.8	501.2	137.6	86.4	55.2	31.2	95.9	16.8	79.1	23.4
1973	1,110.7	811.3	708.8	560.0	148.8	102.5	62.7	39.8	113.5	28.9	84.6	24.3
1974	1,222.6	890.7	772.8	611.8	161.0	118.0	73.3	44.7	113.1	23.2	89.9	24.3
1975	1,335.0	949.0	814.7	638.6	176.1	134.3	87.6	46.7	119.5	21.7	97.8	23.7
1976	1,474.8	1,059.2	899.6	710.8	188.8	159.6	105.2	54.4	132.2	17.0	115.2	22.3
1977	1,633.2	1,180.4	994.1	791.6	202.5	186.4	125.3	61.1	145.7	15.7	130.0	20.7
1978	1,837.7	1,335.8	1,120.9	901.2	219.7	214.9	143.4	71.5	166.6	19.6	147.1	22.1
1979	2,062.2	1,501.0	1,256.0	1,018.7	237.3	245.0	162.4	82.6	180.1	21.8	158.3	23.8
1980	2,307.9	1,651.8	1,377.7	1,116.2	261.5	274.2	185.2	88.9	174.1	11.3	162.8	30.0
1981	2,591.3	1,825.7	1,517.5	1,231.7	285.8	308.3	204.7	103.6	183.0	18.7	164.3	38.0
1982	2,775.3	1,925.9	1,593.7	1,286.2	307.5	332.1	222.4	109.8	176.3	13.1	163.3	38.8
1983	2,960.7	2,043.0	1,685.0	1,359.8	325.2	358.0	238.1	119.9	192.5	6.0	186.5	37.8
1984	3,289.5	2,255.4	1,854.9	1,507.0	347.9	400.5	261.5	139.0	243.3	20.6	222.7	40.2
1985	3,526.7	2,424.9	1,995.7	1,621.6	374.1	429.2	281.5	147.7	262.3	20.8	241.5	41.9
1986	3,722.4	2,570.1	2,114.8	1,717.9	397.0	455.3	297.5	157.9	275.7	22.6	253.1	33.5
1987	3,947.4	2,750.2	2,270.7	1,848.1	422.6	479.5	313.2	166.3	302.2	28.7	273.5	33.5
1988	4,253.7	2,967.2	2,452.9	2,001.6	451.3	514.2	329.6	184.6	341.6	26.8	314.7	40.6
1989	4,587.8	3,145.2	2,596.3	2,116.2	480.2	548.9	355.2	193.7	363.3	33.0	330.3	43.1
1990	4,878.6	3,338.2	2,754.0	2,236.3	517.7	584.2	377.8	206.5	380.6	31.9	348.7	50.7
1991	5,051.0	3,445.3	2,823.0	2,276.2	546.8	622.3	407.1	215.1	377.1	26.7	350.4	60.3
1992	5,362.0	3,651.2	2,980.3	2,411.1	569.2	670.9	442.5	228.4	427.6	34.5	393.0	78.0
1993	5,558.5	3,794.9	3,082.7	2,496.0	586.8	712.2	472.4	239.8	453.8	31.2	422.6	95.6
1994	5,842.5	3,979.6	3,232.1	2,625.9	606.2	747.5	493.3	254.1	473.3	33.9	439.4	119.7
1995	6,152.3	4,177.0	3,419.3	2,793.8	625.5	757.7	493.6	264.0	492.1	22.7	469.5	122.1
1996	6,520.6	4,386.9	3,619.6	2,975.2	644.4	767.3	492.5	274.9	543.2	37.3	505.9	131.5
1997	6,915.1	4,664.6	3,877.6	3,209.5	668.1	787.0	497.5	289.5	576.0	34.2	541.8	128.8
1998	7,423.0	5,020.1	4,183.4	3,486.2	697.3	836.7	529.7	307.0	627.8	29.4	598.4	137.5
1999	7,802.4	5,352.0	4,466.3	3,736.9	729.3	885.7	562.4	323.3	678.3	28.6	649.7	147.3
2000	8,429.7	5,782.7	4,829.2	4,054.5	774.7	953.4	609.9	343.5	728.4	22.7	705.7	150.3
2001	8,724.1	5,942.1	4,942.8	4,126.9	815.9	999.3	642.7	356.6	771.9	19.7	752.2	167.4
2002	8,881.9	6,091.2	4,980.9	4,115.0	865.9	1,110.3	745.1	365.2	768.4	10.6	757.8	152.9
2003	9,163.6	6,310.4	5,112.7	4,208.3	904.4	1,197.7	815.6	382.1	811.3	29.2	782.1	133.0
2004	9,727.2	6,671.4	5,394.5	4,451.4	943.1	1,276.9	868.5	408.3	911.6	37.3	874.3	118.4
2005	10,269.8	7,025.8	5,671.7	4,690.9	980.7	1,354.1	926.0	428.1	959.8	34.1	925.7	40.9
2006	10,993.9	7,432.6	6,027.2	5,004.2	1,023.0	1,405.3	956.8	448.5	1,014.7	16.2	998.6	44.3
2007	11,663.2	7,818.6	6,362.0	5,286.7	1,075.2	1,456.6	991.9	464.7	1,056.2	44.0	1,012.2	40.0
2005: I	10,044.5	6,884.4	5,553.1	4,582.5	970.6	1,331.4	909.8	421.6	936.3	33.2	903.0	90.1
II	10,184.4	6,957.4	5,611.5	4,637.5	974.0	1,346.0	921.4	424.5	948.1	38.3	909.8	72.2
III	10,289.1	7,090.2	5,725.6	4,740.8	984.8	1,364.7	933.4	431.3	960.4	37.1	923.3	−56.9
IV	10,561.0	7,171.0	5,796.5	4,802.9	993.6	1,374.5	939.5	434.9	994.5	27.7	966.7	58.0
2006: I	10,781.6	7,338.0	5,946.4	4,938.7	1,007.7	1,391.6	946.6	445.0	1,004.7	17.3	987.5	52.8
II	10,913.2	7,364.2	5,966.2	4,953.0	1,013.2	1,398.0	952.9	445.1	1,018.3	9.8	1,008.4	45.6
III	11,056.1	7,441.9	6,034.2	5,004.8	1,029.4	1,407.8	959.5	448.2	1,013.4	13.8	999.6	40.4
IV	11,224.7	7,586.1	6,162.2	5,120.3	1,041.9	1,423.9	968.1	455.8	1,022.4	23.7	998.7	38.2
2007: I	11,473.0	7,734.0	6,294.0	5,234.0	1,059.9	1,440.0	977.6	462.3	1,037.2	39.3	997.9	35.1
II	11,577.5	7,760.1	6,310.7	5,242.5	1,068.1	1,449.4	987.7	461.7	1,050.2	42.3	1,007.9	44.6
III	11,730.4	7,839.3	6,377.7	5,297.0	1,080.8	1,461.6	996.5	465.1	1,063.8	47.4	1,016.4	41.8
IV	11,872.1	7,941.0	6,465.5	5,373.4	1,092.1	1,475.5	1,005.9	469.6	1,073.8	47.1	1,026.7	38.6
2008: I	11,960.5	8,009.7	6,518.0	5,408.3	1,109.7	1,491.7	1,015.3	476.4	1,071.7	41.6	1,030.1	39.1
II	12,152.2	8,033.5	6,531.3	5,407.9	1,123.4	1,502.2	1,024.4	477.8	1,076.9	38.0	1,039.0	58.6
III ᵖ	12,156.8	8,082.7	6,572.3	5,434.2	1,138.0	1,510.4	1,031.2	479.2	1,080.6	32.4	1,048.2	63.1

See next page for continuation of table.

[Billions of dollars; quarterly data at seasonally adjusted annual rates]

Year or quarter	Personal income receipts on assets			Personal current transfer receipts								Less: Contributions for government social insurance
					Government social benefits to persons						Other current transfer receipts, from business (net)	
	Total	Personal interest income	Personal dividend income	Total	Total	Old-age, survivors, disability, and health insurance benefits	Government unemploy-ment insur-ance benefits	Veterans benefits	Family assis-tance [1]	Other		
1959	34.6	22.0	12.6	24.2	22.9	10.2	2.8	4.6	0.9	4.5	1.3	13.8
1960	37.9	24.5	13.4	25.7	24.4	11.1	3.0	4.6	1.0	4.7	1.3	16.4
1961	40.1	26.2	13.9	29.5	28.1	12.6	4.3	5.0	1.1	5.1	1.4	17.0
1962	44.1	29.1	15.0	30.4	28.8	14.3	3.1	4.7	1.3	5.5	1.5	19.1
1963	47.9	31.7	16.2	32.2	30.3	15.2	3.0	4.8	1.4	5.9	1.9	21.7
1964	53.8	35.6	18.2	33.5	31.3	16.0	2.7	4.7	1.5	6.4	2.2	22.4
1965	59.4	39.2	20.2	36.2	33.9	18.1	2.3	4.9	1.7	7.0	2.3	23.4
1966	64.1	43.4	20.7	39.6	37.5	20.8	1.9	4.9	1.9	8.1	2.1	31.3
1967	69.0	47.5	21.5	48.0	45.8	25.8	2.2	5.6	2.3	9.9	2.3	34.9
1968	75.2	51.6	23.5	56.1	53.3	30.5	2.1	5.9	2.8	11.9	2.8	38.7
1969	84.1	59.9	24.2	62.3	59.0	33.1	2.2	6.7	3.5	13.4	3.3	44.1
1970	93.5	69.2	24.3	74.7	71.7	38.6	4.0	7.7	4.8	16.6	2.9	46.4
1971	101.0	75.9	25.0	88.1	85.4	44.7	5.8	8.8	6.2	20.0	2.7	51.2
1972	109.6	82.8	26.8	97.9	94.8	49.8	5.7	9.7	6.9	22.7	3.1	59.2
1973	124.7	94.8	29.9	112.6	108.6	60.9	4.4	10.4	7.2	25.7	3.9	75.5
1974	146.4	113.2	33.2	133.3	128.6	70.3	6.8	11.8	8.0	31.7	4.7	85.2
1975	162.2	129.3	32.9	170.0	163.1	81.5	17.6	14.5	9.3	40.2	6.8	89.3
1976	178.4	139.5	39.0	184.0	177.3	93.3	15.8	14.4	10.1	43.7	6.7	101.3
1977	205.3	160.6	44.7	194.2	189.1	105.3	12.7	13.8	10.6	46.7	5.1	113.1
1978	234.8	184.0	50.7	209.6	203.2	116.9	9.1	13.9	10.8	52.5	6.5	131.3
1979	274.7	217.3	57.4	235.3	227.1	132.5	9.4	14.4	11.1	59.6	8.2	152.7
1980	338.7	274.7	64.0	279.5	270.8	154.8	15.7	15.0	12.5	72.8	8.6	166.2
1981	421.9	348.3	73.6	318.4	307.2	182.1	15.6	16.1	13.1	80.2	11.2	195.7
1982	488.4	410.8	77.6	354.8	342.4	204.6	25.1	16.4	12.9	83.4	12.4	208.9
1983	529.6	446.3	83.3	383.7	369.9	222.2	26.2	16.6	13.8	91.0	13.8	226.0
1984	607.9	517.2	90.6	400.1	380.4	237.8	15.9	16.4	14.5	95.9	19.7	257.5
1985	654.0	556.6	97.4	424.9	402.6	253.0	15.7	16.7	15.2	102.0	22.3	281.4
1986	695.5	589.5	106.0	451.0	428.0	268.9	16.3	16.7	16.1	109.9	22.9	303.4
1987	717.0	604.9	112.2	467.6	447.4	282.6	14.5	16.6	16.4	117.3	20.2	323.1
1988	769.3	639.5	129.7	496.6	476.0	300.2	13.2	16.9	16.9	128.8	20.6	361.5
1989	878.0	720.2	157.8	543.4	519.9	325.6	14.3	17.3	17.5	145.3	23.5	385.2
1990	924.0	755.2	168.8	595.2	573.1	351.8	18.0	17.8	19.2	166.2	22.2	410.1
1991	932.0	751.7	180.3	666.4	648.5	381.7	26.6	18.3	21.1	200.8	17.9	430.2
1992	910.9	723.4	187.4	749.4	729.8	414.4	38.9	19.3	22.2	234.9	19.6	455.0
1993	901.8	699.6	202.2	790.1	775.7	443.4	34.1	20.1	22.8	255.3	14.4	477.7
1994	950.8	716.8	234.0	827.3	812.2	475.4	23.5	20.1	23.2	270.0	15.1	508.2
1995	1,016.4	763.2	253.2	877.4	858.4	506.8	21.4	20.9	22.6	286.7	19.0	532.8
1996	1,089.2	793.0	296.2	925.0	902.1	537.7	22.0	21.7	20.3	300.4	22.9	555.2
1997	1,181.7	848.7	333.0	951.2	931.8	563.2	19.9	22.5	17.9	308.3	19.4	587.2
1998	1,283.2	933.2	349.9	978.6	952.6	575.1	19.5	23.4	17.4	317.3	26.0	624.2
1999	1,264.2	928.6	335.6	1,022.1	988.0	588.9	20.3	24.3	17.9	336.7	34.1	661.4
2000	1,387.0	1,011.0	376.1	1,084.0	1,041.6	620.8	20.3	25.1	18.4	357.0	42.4	702.7
2001	1,380.0	1,011.0	369.0	1,193.9	1,143.9	668.5	31.7	26.7	18.1	398.9	50.0	731.1
2002	1,333.2	936.1	397.2	1,286.2	1,248.9	707.5	53.2	29.6	17.7	440.9	37.3	750.0
2003	1,336.6	914.1	422.6	1,351.0	1,316.7	741.3	52.8	32.0	18.4	472.2	34.3	778.6
2004	1,432.1	895.1	537.0	1,422.5	1,396.1	788.0	36.0	34.5	18.4	519.2	26.4	828.8
2005	1,596.9	1,022.0	574.9	1,520.7	1,481.9	844.5	31.3	36.8	18.2	551.1	38.8	874.3
2006	1,824.8	1,125.4	699.4	1,603.0	1,578.1	938.9	29.9	39.2	18.3	551.7	24.9	925.5
2007	2,000.1	1,214.3	785.8	1,713.3	1,681.4	999.4	32.3	41.9	18.8	588.9	31.9	965.1
2005: I	1,513.6	963.0	550.6	1,479.7	1,453.4	827.6	31.8	36.6	18.2	539.1	26.4	859.6
II	1,564.7	1,005.6	559.1	1,508.8	1,480.8	841.8	31.2	36.7	18.2	552.9	28.1	866.9
III	1,616.9	1,038.0	578.9	1,559.6	1,490.6	849.7	30.7	36.9	18.2	555.0	69.0	881.1
IV	1,692.3	1,081.4	610.9	1,534.7	1,502.9	858.8	31.6	37.0	18.2	557.3	31.8	889.5
2006: I	1,735.4	1,085.3	650.2	1,567.6	1,543.0	914.0	29.7	38.8	18.2	542.3	24.6	917.1
II	1,809.5	1,123.4	686.1	1,594.5	1,570.7	934.9	29.6	39.2	18.2	548.8	23.8	918.9
III	1,865.8	1,147.6	718.2	1,620.1	1,595.4	947.4	30.1	39.3	18.3	560.2	24.7	925.5
IV	1,888.6	1,145.6	743.0	1,629.8	1,603.1	959.2	30.4	39.6	18.4	555.6	26.7	940.4
2007: I	1,930.9	1,172.2	758.7	1,695.7	1,665.3	981.9	31.3	41.0	18.6	592.6	30.4	959.8
II	1,982.5	1,206.1	776.5	1,699.2	1,667.5	997.5	31.2	41.9	18.7	578.2	31.7	959.1
III	2,030.9	1,236.2	794.7	1,720.6	1,680.0	1,008.8	32.5	42.1	18.9	585.7	32.5	966.0
IV	2,056.2	1,242.7	813.5	1,737.8	1,704.7	1,009.6	34.3	42.7	19.0	599.2	33.1	975.3
2008: I	2,054.1	1,224.6	829.5	1,778.1	1,745.8	1,032.4	38.2	44.6	19.2	611.5	32.2	992.2
II	2,052.3	1,208.7	843.6	1,926.3	1,893.9	1,050.0	41.4	44.9	19.3	738.4	32.4	995.4
III *p*	2,056.8	1,218.5	838.3	1,872.4	1,830.9	1,068.9	59.2	45.7	19.4	637.6	41.5	998.7

[1] Consists of aid to families with dependent children and, beginning in 1996, assistance programs operating under the Personal Responsibility and Work Opportunity Reconciliation Act of 1996.

Source: Department of Commerce (Bureau of Economic Analysis).

TABLE B–30.—*Disposition of personal income, 1959–2008*

[Billions of dollars, except as noted; quarterly data at seasonally adjusted annual rates]

Year or quarter	Personal income	Less: Personal current taxes	Equals: Disposable personal income	Less: Personal outlays				Equals: Personal saving	Percent of disposable personal income[2]		
				Total	Personal consumption expenditures	Personal interest payments[1]	Personal current transfer payments		Personal outlays		Personal saving
									Total	Personal consumption expenditures	
1959	392.8	42.3	350.5	323.9	317.6	5.5	0.8	26.7	92.4	90.6	7.6
1960	411.5	46.1	365.4	338.8	331.7	6.2	.8	26.7	92.7	90.8	7.3
1961	429.0	47.3	381.8	349.6	342.1	6.5	1.0	32.2	91.6	89.6	8.4
1962	456.7	51.6	405.1	371.3	363.3	7.0	1.1	33.8	91.7	89.7	8.3
1963	479.6	54.6	425.1	391.8	382.7	7.9	1.2	33.3	92.2	90.0	7.8
1964	514.6	52.1	462.5	421.7	411.4	8.9	1.3	40.8	91.2	89.0	8.8
1965	555.7	57.7	498.1	455.1	443.8	9.9	1.4	43.0	91.4	89.1	8.6
1966	603.9	66.4	537.5	493.1	480.9	10.7	1.6	44.4	91.7	89.5	8.3
1967	648.3	73.0	575.3	520.9	507.8	11.1	2.0	54.4	90.5	88.3	9.5
1968	712.0	87.0	625.0	572.2	558.0	12.2	2.0	52.8	91.6	89.3	8.4
1969	778.5	104.5	674.0	621.4	605.2	14.0	2.2	52.5	92.2	89.8	7.8
1970	838.8	103.1	735.7	666.2	648.5	15.2	2.6	69.5	90.6	88.1	9.4
1971	903.5	101.7	801.8	721.2	701.9	16.6	2.8	80.6	89.9	87.5	10.1
1972	992.7	123.6	869.1	791.9	770.6	18.1	3.1	77.2	91.1	88.7	8.9
1973	1,110.7	132.4	978.3	875.6	852.4	19.8	3.4	102.7	89.5	87.1	10.5
1974	1,222.6	151.0	1,071.6	958.0	933.4	21.2	3.4	113.6	89.4	87.1	10.6
1975	1,335.0	147.6	1,187.4	1,061.9	1,034.4	23.7	3.8	125.6	89.4	87.1	10.6
1976	1,474.8	172.3	1,302.5	1,180.2	1,151.9	23.9	4.4	122.3	90.6	88.4	9.4
1977	1,633.2	197.5	1,435.7	1,310.4	1,278.6	27.0	4.8	125.3	91.3	89.1	8.7
1978	1,837.7	229.4	1,608.3	1,465.8	1,428.5	31.9	5.4	142.5	91.1	88.8	8.9
1979	2,062.2	268.7	1,793.5	1,634.4	1,592.2	36.2	5.9	159.1	91.1	88.8	8.9
1980	2,307.9	298.9	2,009.0	1,807.5	1,757.1	43.6	6.8	201.4	90.0	87.5	10.0
1981	2,591.3	345.2	2,246.1	2,001.8	1,941.1	49.3	11.4	244.3	89.1	86.4	10.9
1982	2,775.3	354.1	2,421.2	2,150.4	2,077.3	59.5	13.6	270.8	88.8	85.8	11.2
1983	2,960.7	352.3	2,608.4	2,374.8	2,290.6	69.2	15.0	233.6	91.0	87.8	9.0
1984	3,289.5	377.4	2,912.0	2,597.3	2,503.3	77.0	16.9	314.8	89.2	86.0	10.8
1985	3,526.7	417.4	3,109.3	2,829.3	2,720.3	90.4	18.6	280.0	91.0	87.5	9.0
1986	3,722.4	437.3	3,285.1	3,016.7	2,899.7	96.1	20.9	268.4	91.8	88.3	8.2
1987	3,947.4	489.1	3,458.3	3,216.9	3,100.2	93.6	23.1	241.4	93.0	89.6	7.0
1988	4,253.7	505.0	3,748.7	3,475.8	3,353.6	96.8	25.4	272.9	92.7	89.5	7.3
1989	4,587.8	566.1	4,021.7	3,734.5	3,598.5	108.2	27.8	287.1	92.9	89.5	7.1
1990	4,878.6	592.8	4,285.8	3,986.4	3,839.9	116.1	30.4	299.4	93.0	89.6	7.0
1991	5,051.0	586.7	4,464.3	4,140.1	3,986.1	118.5	35.6	324.2	92.7	89.3	7.3
1992	5,362.0	610.6	4,751.4	4,385.4	4,235.3	111.8	38.3	366.0	92.3	89.1	7.7
1993	5,558.5	646.6	4,911.9	4,627.9	4,477.9	107.3	42.7	284.0	94.2	91.2	5.8
1994	5,842.5	690.7	5,151.8	4,902.4	4,743.3	112.8	46.3	249.5	95.2	92.1	4.8
1995	6,152.3	744.1	5,408.2	5,157.3	4,975.8	132.7	48.9	250.9	95.4	92.0	4.6
1996	6,520.6	832.1	5,688.5	5,460.0	5,256.8	150.3	52.9	228.4	96.0	92.4	4.0
1997	6,915.1	926.3	5,988.8	5,770.5	5,547.4	163.9	59.2	218.3	96.4	92.6	3.6
1998	7,423.0	1,027.0	6,395.9	6,119.1	5,879.5	174.5	65.2	276.8	95.7	91.9	4.3
1999	7,802.4	1,107.5	6,695.0	6,536.4	6,282.5	181.0	73.0	158.6	97.6	93.8	2.4
2000	8,429.7	1,235.7	7,194.0	7,025.6	6,739.4	204.7	81.5	168.5	97.7	93.7	2.3
2001	8,724.1	1,237.3	7,486.8	7,354.5	7,055.0	212.2	87.2	132.3	98.2	94.2	1.8
2002	8,881.9	1,051.8	7,830.1	7,645.3	7,350.7	196.4	98.2	184.7	97.6	93.9	2.4
2003	9,163.6	1,001.1	8,162.5	7,987.7	7,703.6	182.5	101.5	174.9	97.9	94.4	2.1
2004	9,727.2	1,046.3	8,680.9	8,499.2	8,195.9	191.3	112.1	181.7	97.9	94.4	2.1
2005	10,269.8	1,207.8	9,062.0	9,029.5	8,694.1	215.0	120.4	32.5	99.6	95.9	.4
2006	10,993.9	1,353.2	9,640.7	9,570.0	9,207.2	235.4	127.4	70.7	99.3	95.5	.7
2007	11,663.2	1,492.8	10,170.5	10,113.1	9,710.2	265.4	137.5	57.4	99.4	95.5	.6
2005: I	10,044.5	1,163.8	8,880.7	8,808.1	8,480.9	206.8	120.5	72.5	99.2	95.5	.8
II	10,184.4	1,192.7	8,991.7	8,945.9	8,610.8	215.3	119.9	45.8	99.5	95.8	.5
III	10,289.1	1,222.3	9,066.9	9,129.8	8,791.1	219.0	119.7	–62.9	100.7	97.0	–.7
IV	10,561.0	1,252.5	9,308.6	9,234.2	8,893.7	218.9	121.5	74.4	99.2	95.5	.8
2006: I	10,781.6	1,316.0	9,465.6	9,371.2	9,026.3	223.8	121.1	94.4	99.0	95.4	1.0
II	10,913.2	1,341.1	9,572.1	9,518.0	9,161.9	228.5	127.6	54.2	99.4	95.7	.6
III	11,056.1	1,356.2	9,699.9	9,651.8	9,283.7	239.1	129.0	48.1	99.5	95.7	.5
IV	11,224.7	1,399.6	9,825.1	9,739.0	9,357.0	250.1	131.9	86.1	99.1	95.2	.9
2007: I	11,473.0	1,459.5	10,013.5	9,904.2	9,524.9	244.0	135.3	109.3	98.9	95.1	1.1
II	11,577.5	1,489.4	10,088.0	10,056.9	9,657.5	262.6	136.9	31.1	99.7	95.7	.3
III	11,730.4	1,501.6	10,228.8	10,182.0	9,765.6	278.2	138.1	46.8	99.5	95.5	.5
IV	11,872.1	1,520.5	10,351.5	10,309.2	9,892.7	276.7	139.8	42.4	99.6	95.6	.4
2008: I	11,960.5	1,535.0	10,425.5	10,404.9	10,002.3	261.7	140.8	20.6	99.8	95.9	.2
II	12,152.2	1,346.1	10,806.0	10,538.2	10,138.0	253.8	146.4	267.9	97.5	93.8	2.5
III p	12,156.8	1,473.5	10,683.3	10,567.6	10,169.5	251.1	146.9	115.7	98.9	95.2	1.1

[1] Consists of nonmortgage interest paid by households.
[2] Percents based on data in millions of dollars.

Source: Department of Commerce (Bureau of Economic Analysis).

TABLE B–31.—*Total and per capita disposable personal income and personal consumption expenditures, and per capita gross domestic product, in current and real dollars, 1959–2008*

[Quarterly data at seasonally adjusted annual rates, except as noted]

Year or quarter	Disposable personal income Total (billions of dollars) Current dollars	Disposable personal income Total (billions of dollars) Chained (2000) dollars	Disposable personal income Per capita (dollars) Current dollars	Disposable personal income Per capita (dollars) Chained (2000) dollars	Personal consumption expenditures Total (billions of dollars) Current dollars	Personal consumption expenditures Total (billions of dollars) Chained (2000) dollars	Personal consumption expenditures Per capita (dollars) Current dollars	Personal consumption expenditures Per capita (dollars) Chained (2000) dollars	Gross domestic product per capita (dollars) Current dollars	Gross domestic product per capita (dollars) Chained (2000) dollars	Population (thousands) [1]
1959	350.5	1,715.5	1,979	9,685	317.6	1,554.6	1,793	8,776	2,860	13,782	177,130
1960	365.4	1,759.7	2,022	9,735	331.7	1,597.4	1,835	8,837	2,912	13,840	180,760
1961	381.8	1,819.2	2,078	9,901	342.1	1,630.3	1,862	8,873	2,965	13,932	183,742
1962	405.1	1,908.2	2,171	10,227	363.3	1,711.1	1,947	9,170	3,139	14,552	186,590
1963	425.1	1,979.1	2,246	10,455	382.7	1,781.6	2,022	9,412	3,263	14,971	189,300
1964	462.5	2,122.8	2,410	11,061	411.4	1,888.4	2,144	9,839	3,458	15,624	191,927
1965	498.1	2,253.3	2,563	11,594	443.8	2,007.7	2,283	10,331	3,700	16,420	194,347
1966	537.5	2,371.9	2,734	12,065	480.9	2,121.8	2,446	10,793	4,007	17,290	196,599
1967	575.3	2,475.9	2,895	12,457	507.8	2,185.0	2,555	10,994	4,189	17,533	198,752
1968	625.0	2,588.0	3,114	12,892	558.0	2,310.5	2,780	11,510	4,533	18,196	200,745
1969	674.0	2,668.7	3,324	13,163	605.2	2,396.4	2,985	11,820	4,857	18,573	202,736
1970	735.7	2,781.7	3,587	13,563	648.5	2,451.9	3,162	11,955	5,064	18,391	205,089
1971	801.8	2,907.9	3,860	14,001	701.9	2,545.5	3,379	12,256	5,427	18,771	207,692
1972	869.1	3,046.5	4,140	14,512	770.6	2,701.3	3,671	12,868	5,899	19,555	209,924
1973	978.3	3,252.3	4,616	15,345	852.4	2,833.8	4,022	13,371	6,524	20,484	211,939
1974	1,071.6	3,228.5	5,010	15,094	933.4	2,812.3	4,364	13,148	7,013	20,195	213,898
1975	1,187.4	3,302.6	5,498	15,291	1,034.4	2,876.9	4,789	13,320	7,586	19,961	215,981
1976	1,302.5	3,432.2	5,972	15,738	1,151.9	3,035.5	5,282	13,919	8,369	20,822	218,086
1977	1,435.7	3,552.9	6,517	16,128	1,278.6	3,164.1	5,804	14,364	9,219	21,565	220,289
1978	1,608.3	3,718.8	7,224	16,704	1,428.5	3,303.1	6,417	14,837	10,307	22,526	222,629
1979	1,793.5	3,811.2	7,967	16,931	1,592.2	3,383.4	7,073	15,030	11,387	22,982	225,106
1980	2,009.0	3,857.7	8,822	16,940	1,757.1	3,374.1	7,716	14,816	12,249	22,666	227,726
1981	2,246.1	3,960.0	9,765	17,217	1,941.1	3,422.2	8,439	14,879	13,601	23,007	230,008
1982	2,421.2	4,044.9	10,426	17,418	2,077.3	3,470.3	8,945	14,944	14,017	22,346	232,218
1983	2,608.4	4,177.7	11,131	17,828	2,290.6	3,668.6	9,775	15,656	15,092	23,146	234,333
1984	2,912.0	4,494.1	12,319	19,011	2,503.3	3,863.3	10,589	16,343	16,638	24,593	236,394
1985	3,109.3	4,645.2	13,037	19,476	2,720.3	4,064.0	11,406	17,040	17,695	25,382	238,506
1986	3,285.1	4,791.0	13,649	19,906	2,899.7	4,228.9	12,048	17,570	18,542	26,024	240,683
1987	3,458.3	4,874.5	14,241	20,072	3,100.2	4,369.8	12,766	17,994	19,517	26,664	242,843
1988	3,748.7	5,082.6	15,297	20,740	3,353.6	4,546.9	13,685	18,554	20,827	27,514	245,061
1989	4,021.7	5,224.8	16,257	21,120	3,598.5	4,675.0	14,546	18,898	22,169	28,221	247,387
1990	4,285.8	5,324.2	17,131	21,281	3,839.9	4,770.3	15,349	19,067	23,195	28,429	250,181
1991	4,464.3	5,351.7	17,609	21,109	3,986.1	4,778.4	15,722	18,848	23,650	28,007	253,530
1992	4,751.4	5,536.3	18,494	21,548	4,235.3	4,934.8	16,485	19,208	24,668	28,556	256,922
1993	4,911.9	5,594.2	18,872	21,493	4,477.9	5,099.8	17,204	19,593	25,578	28,940	260,282
1994	5,151.8	5,746.4	19,555	21,812	4,743.3	5,290.7	18,004	20,082	26,844	29,741	263,455
1995	5,408.2	5,905.7	20,287	22,153	4,975.8	5,433.5	18,665	20,382	27,749	30,128	266,588
1996	5,688.5	6,080.9	21,091	22,546	5,256.8	5,619.4	19,490	20,835	28,982	30,881	269,714
1997	5,988.8	6,295.8	21,940	23,065	5,547.4	5,831.8	20,323	21,365	30,424	31,886	272,958
1998	6,395.9	6,663.9	23,161	24,131	5,879.5	6,125.8	21,291	22,183	31,674	32,833	276,154
1999	6,695.0	6,861.3	23,968	24,564	6,282.5	6,438.6	22,491	23,050	33,181	33,904	279,328
2000	7,194.0	7,194.0	25,472	25,472	6,739.4	6,739.4	23,862	23,862	34,759	34,759	282,433
2001	7,486.8	7,333.3	26,235	25,697	7,055.0	6,910.4	24,722	24,215	35,490	34,659	285,372
2002	7,830.1	7,562.2	27,167	26,238	7,350.7	7,099.3	25,504	24,632	36,326	34,866	288,215
2003	8,162.5	7,729.9	28,053	26,566	7,703.6	7,295.3	26,476	25,073	37,671	35,403	290,964
2004	8,680.9	8,008.9	29,563	27,274	8,195.9	7,561.4	27,911	25,750	39,796	36,356	293,644
2005	9,062.0	8,121.4	30,576	27,403	8,694.1	7,791.7	29,335	26,290	41,913	37,080	296,373
2006	9,640.7	8,407.0	32,222	28,098	9,207.2	8,029.0	30,773	26,835	44,046	37,750	299,199
2007	10,170.5	8,644.0	33,667	28,614	9,710.2	8,252.8	32,144	27,319	45,707	38,148	302,087
2005: I	8,880.7	8,060.4	30,069	27,292	8,480.9	7,697.5	28,716	26,063	41,157	36,825	295,342
II	8,991.7	8,110.0	30,381	27,401	8,610.8	7,766.4	29,093	26,241	41,550	36,984	295,969
III	9,066.9	8,084.0	30,557	27,245	8,791.1	7,838.1	29,628	26,416	42,256	37,241	296,719
IV	9,308.6	8,231.8	31,293	27,673	8,893.7	7,864.9	29,899	26,440	42,682	37,269	297,462
2006: I	9,465.6	8,334.2	31,753	27,958	9,026.3	7,947.4	30,279	26,660	43,474	37,629	298,101
II	9,572.1	8,360.4	32,038	27,983	9,161.9	8,002.1	30,665	26,783	43,960	37,793	298,774
III	9,699.9	8,407.1	32,380	28,064	9,283.7	8,046.3	30,990	26,860	44,229	37,768	299,568
IV	9,825.1	8,526.2	32,712	28,387	9,357.0	8,119.9	31,154	27,035	44,515	37,810	300,351
2007: I	10,013.5	8,617.7	33,267	28,630	9,524.9	8,197.2	31,644	27,233	44,886	37,733	301,004
II	10,088.0	8,604.5	33,441	28,523	9,657.5	8,237.3	32,014	27,306	45,539	38,093	301,667
III	10,228.8	8,671.1	33,820	28,669	9,765.6	8,278.5	32,288	27,371	46,125	38,438	302,452
IV	10,351.5	8,683.1	34,138	28,636	9,892.7	8,298.2	32,625	27,366	46,273	38,324	303,225
2008: I	10,425.5	8,667.9	34,309	28,525	10,002.3	8,316.1	32,917	27,367	46,569	38,326	303,868
II	10,806.0	8,891.0	35,485	29,196	10,138.0	8,341.3	33,291	27,391	46,940	38,510	304,528
III p	10,683.3	8,679.5	34,991	28,428	10,169.5	8,262.1	33,309	27,061	47,232	38,362	305,313

[1] Population of the United States including Armed Forces overseas; includes Alaska and Hawaii beginning in 1960. Annual data are averages of quarterly data. Quarterly data are averages for the period.

Source: Department of Commerce (Bureau of Economic Analysis and Bureau of the Census).

TABLE B–32.—*Gross saving and investment, 1959–2008*

[Billions of dollars, except as noted; quarterly data at seasonally adjusted annual rates]

Year or quarter	Total gross saving	Gross saving — Net saving — Total net saving	Net private saving — Total	Net private saving — Personal saving	Net private saving — Undistributed corporate profits[1]	Net private saving — Wage accruals less disbursements	Net government saving — Total	Net government saving — Federal	Net government saving — State and local	Consumption of fixed capital — Total	Consumption of fixed capital — Private	Consumption of fixed capital — Government
1959	106.2	53.2	46.0	26.7	19.4	0.0	7.1	3.3	3.8	53.0	38.6	14.5
1960	111.3	55.8	44.3	26.7	17.6	.0	11.5	7.2	4.3	55.6	40.5	15.0
1961	114.3	57.1	50.2	32.2	18.1	.0	6.9	2.6	4.3	57.2	41.6	15.6
1962	124.9	65.7	57.9	33.8	24.1	.0	7.8	2.5	5.2	59.3	42.8	16.5
1963	133.2	70.8	59.7	33.3	26.4	.0	11.1	5.4	5.7	62.4	44.9	17.5
1964	143.4	78.4	71.0	40.8	30.1	.0	7.4	1.0	6.4	65.0	46.9	18.1
1965	158.5	89.1	79.2	43.0	36.2	.0	9.9	3.3	6.5	69.4	50.5	18.9
1966	168.7	93.1	83.1	44.4	38.7	.0	10.0	2.3	7.8	75.6	55.5	20.1
1967	170.5	89.0	91.4	54.4	36.9	.0	−2.4	−9.4	7.0	81.5	59.9	21.6
1968	182.0	93.6	88.4	52.8	35.6	.0	5.2	−2.3	7.5	88.4	65.2	23.1
1969	198.3	100.4	83.7	52.5	31.2	.0	16.7	8.7	8.0	97.9	73.1	24.8
1970	192.7	86.0	94.0	69.5	24.6	.0	−8.1	−15.2	7.1	106.7	80.0	26.7
1971	208.9	93.9	115.8	80.6	34.8	.4	−21.9	−28.4	6.5	115.0	86.7	28.3
1972	237.5	111.0	119.8	77.2	42.9	−.3	−8.8	−24.4	15.6	126.5	97.1	29.5
1973	292.0	152.7	148.3	102.7	45.6	.0	4.4	−11.3	15.7	139.3	107.9	31.4
1974	301.5	139.0	143.4	113.6	29.8	.0	−4.4	−13.8	9.3	162.5	126.6	35.9
1975	297.0	109.2	175.8	125.6	50.2	.0	−66.6	−69.0	2.5	187.7	147.8	40.0
1976	342.1	137.0	181.3	122.3	59.0	.0	−44.4	−51.7	7.4	205.2	162.5	42.6
1977	397.5	167.5	198.5	125.3	73.2	.0	−31.0	−44.1	13.1	230.0	184.3	45.7
1978	478.0	215.7	223.5	142.5	81.0	.0	−7.8	−26.5	18.7	262.3	212.8	49.5
1979	536.7	236.6	234.9	159.1	75.7	.0	1.7	−11.3	13.0	300.1	245.7	54.5
1980	549.4	206.5	251.3	201.4	49.9	.0	−44.8	−53.6	8.8	343.0	281.1	61.8
1981	654.7	266.6	312.3	244.3	68.0	.0	−45.7	−53.3	7.6	388.1	317.9	70.1
1982	629.1	202.2	336.2	270.8	65.4	.0	−134.1	−131.9	−2.2	426.9	349.8	77.1
1983	609.4	165.6	333.7	233.6	100.1	.0	−168.1	−173.0	4.9	443.8	362.1	81.7
1984	773.4	300.9	445.0	314.8	130.3	.0	−144.1	−168.1	23.9	472.6	385.6	87.0
1985	767.5	260.7	413.4	280.0	133.4	.0	−152.6	−175.0	22.3	506.7	414.0	92.7
1986	733.5	202.2	372.0	268.4	103.7	.0	−169.9	−190.8	21.0	531.3	431.8	99.5
1987	796.8	234.9	367.4	241.4	126.1	.0	−132.6	−145.0	12.4	561.9	455.3	106.7
1988	915.0	317.4	434.0	272.9	161.1	.0	−116.6	−134.5	17.9	597.6	483.5	114.1
1989	944.7	300.4	409.7	287.1	122.6	.0	−109.3	−130.1	20.8	644.3	522.1	122.2
1990	940.4	258.0	422.7	299.4	123.3	.0	−164.8	−172.0	7.2	682.5	551.6	130.9
1991	964.1	238.2	456.1	324.2	131.9	.0	−217.9	−213.7	−4.2	725.9	586.9	139.1
1992	948.2	196.3	493.0	366.0	142.7	−15.8	−296.7	−297.4	.7	751.9	607.3	144.6
1993	962.4	186.0	458.6	284.0	168.1	6.4	−272.6	−273.5	.9	776.4	624.7	151.8
1994	1,070.7	237.1	438.9	249.5	171.8	17.6	−201.9	−212.3	10.5	833.7	675.1	158.6
1995	1,184.5	306.2	491.1	250.9	223.8	16.4	−184.9	−197.0	12.0	878.4	713.4	165.0
1996	1,291.1	373.0	489.0	228.4	256.9	3.6	−116.0	−141.8	25.8	918.1	748.8	169.3
1997	1,461.1	486.6	503.3	218.3	287.9	−2.9	−16.7	−55.8	39.1	974.4	800.3	174.1
1998	1,598.7	568.6	477.8	276.8	201.7	−.7	90.8	38.8	52.0	1,030.2	851.2	179.0
1999	1,674.3	573.0	419.0	158.6	255.3	5.2	154.0	103.6	50.4	1,101.3	914.3	187.0
2000	1,770.5	582.7	343.3	168.5	174.8	.0	239.4	189.5	50.0	1,187.8	990.8	197.0
2001	1,657.6	376.1	324.6	132.3	192.3	.0	51.5	46.7	4.8	1,281.5	1,075.5	206.0
2002	1,489.1	197.1	479.2	184.7	294.5	.0	−282.1	−247.9	−34.2	1,292.0	1,080.3	211.6
2003	1,459.0	122.5	515.0	174.9	325.1	15.0	−392.5	−372.1	−20.4	1,336.5	1,118.3	218.2
2004	1,618.1	182.0	551.1	181.7	384.4	−15.0	−369.1	−370.6	1.5	1,436.1	1,206.0	230.2
2005	1,844.2	232.2	494.4	32.5	456.9	5.0	−262.2	−291.7	29.5	1,612.0	1,359.7	252.3
2006	2,038.5	414.5	569.5	70.7	497.5	1.3	−155.0	−201.1	46.2	1,623.9	1,356.0	268.0
2007	1,956.0	235.6	454.5	57.4	403.4	−6.3	−218.9	−229.3	10.4	1,720.5	1,431.1	289.4
2005: I	1,780.3	313.1	550.5	72.5	478.0	.0	−237.5	−278.7	41.2	1,467.2	1,225.3	241.9
II	1,807.5	313.4	544.6	45.8	498.8	.0	−231.2	−269.5	38.3	1,494.1	1,248.0	246.1
III	1,873.4	−33.6	311.9	−62.9	374.8	.0	−345.4	−364.7	19.3	1,907.0	1,641.1	265.9
IV	1,915.5	335.7	570.4	74.4	476.0	20.0	−234.7	−253.8	19.1	1,579.8	1,324.4	255.4
2006: I	2,034.2	451.6	601.9	94.4	527.5	−20.0	−150.4	−207.9	57.5	1,582.7	1,323.1	259.5
II	2,022.8	410.3	572.1	54.2	518.0	.0	−161.8	−225.0	63.1	1,612.5	1,346.8	265.8
III	2,005.9	367.6	553.8	48.1	505.6	.0	−186.2	−218.4	32.2	1,638.3	1,367.8	270.5
IV	2,090.9	428.7	550.1	86.1	439.0	25.0	−121.4	−153.2	31.8	1,662.2	1,386.2	275.9
2007: I	1,974.4	290.2	492.1	109.3	407.8	−25.0	−202.0	−225.2	23.2	1,684.3	1,402.1	282.2
II	1,987.3	280.3	455.9	31.1	424.8	.0	−175.7	−211.4	35.8	1,707.0	1,420.0	287.0
III	1,958.9	226.9	466.5	46.8	419.7	.0	−239.5	−244.3	4.7	1,731.9	1,440.1	291.8
IV	1,903.6	145.0	403.6	42.4	361.2	.0	−258.6	−236.3	−22.3	1,758.6	1,462.3	296.3
2008: I	1,773.6	−4.4	378.7	20.6	358.1	.0	−383.1	−330.7	−52.4	1,778.0	1,477.5	300.5
II	1,634.6	−168.5	547.9	267.9	280.0	.0	−716.4	−649.6	−66.9	1,803.1	1,497.4	305.7
III *p*	1,650.7	−248.9	396.1	115.7	280.4	.0	−645.0	−543.2	−101.8	1,899.7	1,587.4	312.2

[1] With inventory valuation and capital consumption adjustments.

See next page for continuation of table.

[Billions of dollars, except as noted; quarterly data at seasonally adjusted annual rates]

| Year or quarter | Gross domestic investment, capital account transactions, and net lending, NIPA [2] | | | | | | | Addenda: | | | | | | |
| | Gross domestic investment | | | Capital account transactions (net) [4] | Net lending or net borrowing (−), NIPA [2,5] | Statistical discrepancy | Gross private saving | Gross government saving | | | Net domestic investment | Gross saving as a percent of gross national income | Net saving as a percent of gross national income |
	Total	Total	Gross private domestic investment	Gross government investment [3]					Total	Federal	State and local			
959	106.7	107.8	78.5	29.3	....	−1.2	0.5	84.6	21.6	13.6	8.0	54.8	20.9	10.4
960	110.4	107.2	78.9	28.3	....	3.2	−.9	84.8	26.5	17.8	8.7	51.6	21.0	10.5
961	113.8	109.5	78.2	31.3	....	4.3	−.6	91.8	22.5	13.5	9.0	52.3	20.8	10.4
962	125.3	121.4	88.1	33.3	....	3.9	.4	100.7	24.3	14.0	10.3	62.2	21.2	11.1
963	132.4	127.4	93.8	33.6	....	5.0	−.8	104.6	28.6	17.5	11.1	65.0	21.4	11.4
964	144.2	136.7	102.1	34.6	....	7.5	.8	117.9	25.5	13.4	12.1	71.7	21.5	11.7
965	160.0	153.8	118.2	35.6	....	6.2	1.6	129.7	28.8	16.0	12.8	84.4	21.9	12.3
966	175.0	171.1	131.3	39.8	....	3.9	6.3	138.6	30.1	15.5	14.6	95.5	21.4	11.8
967	175.1	171.6	128.6	43.0	....	3.6	4.6	151.3	19.2	4.7	14.5	90.1	20.5	10.7
968	186.6	184.8	141.2	43.6	....	1.7	4.6	153.7	28.3	12.5	15.8	96.5	20.0	10.3
969	201.5	199.7	156.4	43.3	....	1.8	3.2	156.8	41.5	24.2	17.3	101.8	20.1	10.2
970	200.0	196.0	152.4	43.6	....	4.0	7.3	174.1	18.6	.9	17.7	89.3	18.6	8.3
971	220.5	219.9	178.2	41.8	....	.6	11.6	202.5	6.4	−11.9	18.3	104.9	18.6	8.4
972	246.6	250.2	207.6	42.6	....	−3.6	9.1	216.8	20.7	−7.7	28.5	123.7	19.2	9.0
973	300.7	291.3	244.5	46.8	....	9.3	8.6	256.3	35.8	5.8	30.0	152.1	21.1	11.0
974	312.3	305.7	249.4	56.3	....	6.6	10.9	270.0	31.5	4.5	27.0	143.2	20.0	9.2
975	314.7	293.3	230.2	63.1	....	21.4	17.7	323.6	−26.6	−49.3	22.7	105.6	18.2	6.7
976	367.2	358.4	292.0	66.4	....	8.9	25.1	343.8	−1.7	−30.3	28.6	153.2	18.8	7.5
977	419.8	428.8	361.3	67.5	....	−9.0	22.3	382.8	14.7	−21.0	35.7	198.8	19.6	8.3
978	504.6	515.0	438.0	77.1	....	−10.4	26.6	436.3	41.7	−1.5	43.2	252.7	20.9	9.4
979	582.8	581.4	492.9	88.5	....	1.4	46.0	480.5	56.2	15.7	40.5	281.2	21.1	9.3
980	590.9	579.5	479.3	100.3	....	11.4	41.4	532.4	17.0	−23.6	40.6	236.6	19.7	7.4
981	685.6	679.3	572.4	106.9	....	6.3	30.9	630.3	24.4	−19.4	43.9	291.2	20.9	8.5
982	629.4	629.5	517.2	112.3	−0.2	.0	.3	686.0	−56.9	−94.2	37.3	202.6	19.1	6.1
983	655.1	687.2	564.3	122.9	−.2	−31.8	45.7	695.8	−86.5	−132.3	45.8	243.4	17.3	4.7
984	788.0	875.0	735.6	139.4	−.2	−86.7	14.6	830.6	−57.2	−123.5	66.3	402.4	19.6	7.6
985	784.1	895.0	736.2	158.8	−.3	−110.5	16.7	827.3	−59.9	−126.9	67.0	388.3	18.1	6.2
986	780.5	919.7	746.5	173.2	−.3	−138.9	47.0	803.9	−70.4	−139.2	68.8	388.4	16.5	4.6
987	818.5	969.2	785.0	184.3	−.4	−150.4	21.7	822.7	−25.9	−89.8	63.9	407.3	16.8	5.0
988	895.5	1,007.7	821.6	186.1	−.5	−111.7	−19.5	917.5	−2.5	−75.2	72.7	410.1	17.8	6.2
989	984.3	1,072.6	874.9	197.7	−.3	−88.0	39.7	931.8	12.9	−66.7	79.6	428.4	17.3	5.5
990	1,006.7	1,076.7	861.0	215.7	6.6	−76.6	66.2	974.3	−33.8	−104.1	70.3	394.2	16.3	4.5
991	1,036.6	1,023.2	802.9	220.3	4.5	9.0	72.5	1,042.9	−78.8	−141.5	62.7	297.3	16.2	4.0
992	1,051.0	1,087.9	864.8	223.1	.6	−37.5	102.7	1,100.4	−152.1	−222.7	70.6	336.0	15.1	3.1
993	1,102.0	1,172.4	953.4	219.0	1.3	−71.7	139.5	1,083.3	−120.8	−195.5	74.7	395.9	14.7	2.8
994	1,213.2	1,318.4	1,097.1	221.4	1.7	−106.9	142.5	1,114.0	−43.2	−132.2	88.9	484.7	15.4	3.4
995	1,285.7	1,376.7	1,144.0	232.7	.9	−91.9	101.2	1,204.5	−19.9	−115.1	95.2	498.4	16.2	4.2
996	1,384.8	1,485.2	1,240.3	244.9	.7	−101.0	93.7	1,237.8	53.3	−59.7	113.0	567.1	16.6	4.8
997	1,531.7	1,641.9	1,389.8	252.2	1.0	−111.3	70.7	1,303.6	157.5	26.7	130.7	667.5	17.7	5.9
998	1,584.1	1,771.5	1,509.1	262.4	.7	−188.1	−14.6	1,328.9	269.8	121.6	148.2	741.3	18.2	6.5
999	1,638.5	1,912.4	1,625.7	286.8	4.8	−278.7	−35.7	1,333.3	341.0	188.5	152.5	811.2	17.9	6.1
2000	1,643.3	2,040.0	1,735.5	304.5	.8	−397.4	−127.2	1,334.1	436.4	276.6	159.8	852.1	17.7	5.8
2001	1,567.9	1,938.3	1,614.3	324.0	1.1	−371.5	−89.6	1,400.1	257.5	134.9	122.6	656.9	16.2	3.7
2002	1,468.1	1,926.4	1,582.1	344.3	1.4	−459.7	−21.0	1,559.6	−70.5	−159.1	88.6	634.4	14.2	1.9
2003	1,507.8	2,020.0	1,664.1	356.0	3.2	−515.5	48.8	1,633.3	−174.3	−281.7	107.4	683.5	13.3	1.1
2004	1,637.3	2,261.4	1,888.6	372.8	2.4	−626.5	19.1	1,757.0	−138.9	−276.6	137.7	825.3	13.8	1.5
2005	1,773.0	2,483.9	2,086.1	397.8	4.0	−714.9	−71.2	1,854.1	−9.9	−192.6	182.7	871.9	14.7	1.8
2006	1,875.5	2,647.0	2,220.4	426.7	3.9	−775.5	−163.0	1,925.5	113.0	−95.5	208.5	1,023.1	15.2	3.1
2007	1,874.6	2,593.2	2,130.4	462.8	1.8	−720.4	−81.4	1,885.6	70.4	−117.5	187.9	872.7	14.0	1.7
2005: I	1,744.7	2,427.9	2,046.0	381.9	10.4	−693.5	−35.6	1,775.8	4.4	−181.4	185.8	960.7	14.5	2.5
II	1,744.1	2,433.2	2,039.7	393.5	2.0	−691.1	−63.3	1,792.6	14.8	−171.3	186.1	939.1	14.5	2.5
III	1,828.1	2,487.0	2,084.2	402.9	1.9	−660.8	−45.3	1,953.0	−79.6	−264.9	185.3	580.1	14.8	−.3
IV	1,775.1	2,587.5	2,174.6	412.9	1.9	−814.2	−140.5	1,894.8	20.8	−152.8	173.5	1,007.6	14.8	2.6
2006: I	1,879.6	2,648.4	2,236.7	411.7	6.9	−775.6	−154.6	1,925.1	109.1	−104.9	214.1	1,065.7	15.4	3.4
II	1,891.2	2,680.1	2,253.7	426.3	4.0	−793.0	−131.7	1,918.9	103.9	−120.0	224.0	1,067.5	15.2	3.1
III	1,835.1	2,660.6	2,231.7	428.9	2.1	−827.7	−170.8	1,921.6	84.4	−111.7	196.1	1,022.3	14.9	2.7
IV	1,896.0	2,599.1	2,159.5	439.6	2.5	−705.6	−194.9	1,936.4	154.5	−45.4	199.9	936.9	15.3	3.1
2007: I	1,786.0	2,563.6	2,117.8	445.8	2.2	−779.8	−188.4	1,894.2	80.2	−115.4	195.6	879.3	14.3	2.1
II	1,843.9	2,607.6	2,147.2	460.4	.4	−764.2	−143.4	1,875.9	111.4	−100.4	211.8	900.6	14.3	2.0
III	1,951.1	2,633.1	2,164.0	469.1	2.5	−684.5	−7.8	1,906.6	52.3	−131.8	184.0	901.2	13.9	1.6
IV	1,917.4	2,568.4	2,092.3	476.1	2.3	−653.3	13.9	1,865.9	37.7	−122.4	160.1	809.8	13.4	1.0
2008: I	1,837.0	2,530.0	2,056.1	473.9	2.4	−695.4	63.4	1,856.2	−82.6	−215.8	133.1	752.0	12.5	.0
II	1,771.2	2,493.8	2,000.9	492.8	2.6	−725.2	136.6	2,045.3	−410.7	−532.7	122.0	690.7	11.5	−1.2
III p	1,811.3	2,517.4	2,013.6	503.8	....		160.5	1,983.5	−332.8	−423.9	91.2	617.7	11.5	−1.7

[2] National income and product accounts (NIPA).
[3] For details on government investment, see Table B–20.
[4] Consists of capital transfers and the acquisition and disposal of nonproduced nonfinancial assets.
[5] Prior to 1982, equals the balance on current account, NIPA (see Table B–24).

Source: Department of Commerce (Bureau of Economic Analysis).

TABLE B–33.—*Median money income (in 2007 dollars) and poverty status of families and people, by race, selected years, 1994–2007*

Year	Families[1] Number (millions)	Families[1] Median money income (in 2007 dollars)[2]	Below poverty level Total Number (millions)	Below poverty level Total Percent	Below poverty level Female householder Number (millions)	Below poverty level Female householder Percent	People below poverty level Number (millions)	People below poverty level Percent	Median money income (in 2007 dollars) of people 15 years old and over with income[2] Males All people	Males Year-round full-time workers	Females All people	Females Year-round full-time workers
ALL RACES												
1994	69.3	$53,653	8.1	11.6	4.2	34.6	38.1	14.5	$30,049	$43,734	$15,863	$32,186
1995	69.6	54,863	7.5	10.8	4.1	32.4	36.4	13.8	30,480	43,499	16,387	32,121
1996	70.2	55,663	7.7	11.0	4.2	32.6	36.5	13.7	31,363	44,133	16,863	32,812
1997	70.9	57,407	7.3	10.3	4.0	31.6	35.6	13.3	32,475	45,402	17,650	33,527
1998	71.6	59,372	7.2	10.0	3.8	29.9	34.5	12.7	33,654	46,052	18,331	34,115
1999[3]	73.2	60,764	6.8	9.3	3.6	27.8	32.8	11.9	33,963	46,602	19,044	34,054
2000[4]	73.8	61,083	6.4	8.7	3.3	25.4	31.6	11.3	34,126	46,826	19,340	35,065
2001	74.3	60,206	6.8	9.2	3.5	26.4	32.9	11.7	34,082	47,005	19,458	35,627
2002	75.6	59,563	7.2	9.6	3.6	26.5	34.6	12.1	33,698	46,686	19,376	35,694
2003	76.2	59,389	7.6	10.0	3.9	28.0	35.9	12.5	33,743	46,789	19,457	35,684
2004[5]	76.9	59,342	7.8	10.2	4.0	28.3	37.0	12.7	33,497	45,738	19,393	35,254
2005	77.4	59,683	7.7	9.9	4.0	28.7	37.0	12.6	33,217	44,807	19,729	35,321
2006	78.5	60,064	7.7	9.8	4.1	28.3	36.5	12.3	33,180	46,233	20,582	35,982
2007	77.9	61,355	7.6	9.8	4.1	28.3	37.3	12.5	33,196	46,224	20,922	36,167
WHITE												
1994	58.4	56,561	5.3	9.1	2.3	29.0	25.4	11.7	31,362	44,880	16,090	33,056
1995	58.9	57,612	5.0	8.5	2.2	26.6	24.4	11.2	32,281	45,276	16,638	32,779
1996	58.9	58,895	5.1	8.6	2.3	27.3	24.7	11.2	32,830	45,716	17,055	33,369
1997	59.5	60,222	5.0	8.4	2.3	27.7	24.4	11.0	33,638	46,523	17,765	34,095
1998	60.1	62,276	4.8	8.0	2.1	24.9	23.5	10.5	35,120	47,251	18,569	34,685
1999[3]	61.1	63,562	4.4	7.3	1.9	22.5	22.2	9.8	35,669	48,795	19,104	34,843
2000[4]	61.3	63,849	4.3	7.1	1.8	21.2	21.6	9.5	35,877	48,466	19,360	36,062
2001	61.6	63,321	4.6	7.4	1.9	22.4	22.7	9.9	35,416	47,771	19,502	36,129
Alone[6]												
2002	62.3	62,966	4.9	7.8	2.0	22.6	23.5	10.2	35,018	47,686	19,406	36,190
2003	62.6	62,871	5.1	8.1	2.2	24.0	24.3	10.5	34,646	47,509	19,641	36,292
2004[5]	63.1	62,264	5.3	8.4	2.3	24.7	25.3	10.8	34,407	46,757	19,428	35,929
2005	63.4	63,000	5.1	8.0	2.3	25.3	24.9	10.6	34,177	46,409	19,828	36,217
2006	64.1	63,018	5.1	8.0	2.4	25.1	24.4	10.3	34,803	47,236	20,652	36,533
2007	63.6	64,427	5.0	7.9	2.3	24.7	25.1	10.5	35,141	47,235	21,069	36,728
Alone or in combination[6]												
2002	63.0	62,754	5.0	7.9	2.1	22.6	24.1	10.3	34,940	47,618	19,368	36,176
2003	63.5	62,686	5.2	8.1	2.2	24.2	25.0	10.6	34,563	47,438	19,606	36,278
2004[5]	64.0	62,113	5.4	8.5	2.3	24.8	26.1	10.9	34,331	46,637	19,395	35,887
2005	64.3	62,795	5.2	8.1	2.4	25.5	25.6	10.7	34,096	46,244	19,775	36,142
2006	65.0	62,934	5.2	8.0	2.4	25.0	25.2	10.4	34,628	47,169	20,607	36,497
2007	64.4	64,234	5.2	8.0	2.4	24.8	25.9	10.6	35,031	47,168	21,011	36,694
BLACK												
1994	8.1	34,169	2.2	27.3	1.7	46.2	10.2	30.6	20,727	33,763	14,587	28,538
1995	8.1	35,084	2.1	26.4	1.7	45.1	9.9	29.3	21,623	33,500	14,808	28,476
1996	8.5	34,900	2.2	26.1	1.7	43.7	9.7	28.4	21,701	35,708	15,491	28,937
1997	8.4	36,841	2.0	23.6	1.6	39.8	9.1	26.5	23,309	34,645	16,807	29,322
1998	8.5	37,353	2.0	23.4	1.6	40.8	9.1	26.1	24,544	34,899	16,688	30,315
1999[3]	8.7	39,634	1.9	21.8	1.5	39.2	8.4	23.6	25,436	37,523	18,387	31,285
2000[4]	8.7	40,547	1.7	19.3	1.3	34.3	8.0	22.5	25,698	36,710	19,121	31,004
2001	8.8	39,348	1.8	20.7	1.4	35.2	8.1	22.7	25,140	37,384	19,069	31,969
Alone[6]												
2002	8.9	38,639	1.9	21.5	1.4	35.8	8.6	24.1	24,850	36,803	19,281	31,839
2003	8.9	38,746	2.0	22.3	1.5	36.9	8.8	24.4	24,786	37,687	18,693	31,140
2004[5]	8.9	38,582	2.0	22.8	1.5	37.6	9.0	24.7	24,907	34,819	19,055	31,992
2005	9.1	37,666	2.0	22.1	1.5	36.1	9.2	24.9	24,059	36,358	18,726	32,248
2006	9.3	39,355	2.0	21.6	1.5	36.6	9.0	24.3	25,775	36,483	19,645	31,814
2007	9.3	40,143	2.0	22.1	1.5	37.3	9.2	24.5	25,822	36,736	19,752	31,591
Alone or in combination[6]												
2002	9.1	38,764	2.0	21.4	1.5	35.7	8.9	23.9	24,790	36,842	19,214	31,929
2003	9.1	39,015	2.0	22.1	1.5	36.8	9.1	24.3	24,729	37,726	18,647	31,200
2004[5]	9.1	38,772	2.1	22.8	1.5	37.6	9.4	24.7	24,932	34,809	19,042	32,045
2005	9.3	37,804	2.1	22.0	1.5	36.2	9.5	24.7	24,013	36,264	18,687	32,251
2006	9.5	39,613	2.0	21.5	1.5	36.4	9.4	24.2	25,786	36,517	19,606	31,863
2007	9.5	40,222	2.1	22.0	1.6	37.2	9.7	24.4	25,792	36,780	19,712	31,672

[1] The term "family" refers to a group of two or more persons related by birth, marriage, or adoption and residing together. Every family must include a reference person.

[2] Current dollar median money income adjusted by consumer price index research series (CPI-U-RS).

[3] Reflects implementation of Census 2000–based population controls comparable with succeeding years.

[4] Reflects household sample expansion.

[5] For 2004, figures are revised to reflect a correction to the weights in the 2005 Annual Social and Economic Supplement.

[6] Data are for "white alone," for "white alone or in combination," for "black alone," and for "black alone or in combination." ("Black" is also "black or African American.") Beginning with data for 2002 the Current Population Survey allowed respondents to choose more than one race; for earlier years respondents could report only one race group.

Note.—Poverty thresholds are updated each year to reflect changes in the consumer price index (CPI-U).
For details see publication Series P–60 on the Current Population Survey and Annual Social and Economic Supplements.

Source: Department of Commerce (Bureau of the Census).

POPULATION, EMPLOYMENT, WAGES, AND PRODUCTIVITY
TABLE B–34.—*Population by age group, 1929–2008*
[Thousands of persons]

July 1	Total	Age (years)						
		Under 5	5–15	16–19	20–24	25–44	45–64	65 and over
1929	121,767	11,734	26,800	9,127	10,694	35,862	21,076	6,474
1933	125,579	10,612	26,897	9,302	11,152	37,319	22,933	7,363
1939	130,880	10,418	25,179	9,822	11,519	39,354	25,823	8,764
1940	132,122	10,579	24,811	9,895	11,690	39,868	26,249	9,031
1941	133,402	10,850	24,516	9,840	11,807	40,383	26,718	9,288
1942	134,860	11,301	24,231	9,730	11,955	40,861	27,196	9,584
1943	136,739	12,016	24,093	9,607	12,064	41,420	27,671	9,867
1944	138,397	12,524	23,949	9,561	12,062	42,016	28,138	10,147
1945	139,928	12,979	23,907	9,361	12,036	42,521	28,630	10,494
1946	141,389	13,244	24,103	9,119	12,004	43,027	29,064	10,828
1947	144,126	14,406	24,468	9,097	11,814	43,657	29,498	11,185
1948	146,631	14,919	25,209	8,952	11,794	44,288	29,931	11,538
1949	149,188	15,607	25,852	8,788	11,700	44,916	30,405	11,921
1950	152,271	16,410	26,721	8,542	11,680	45,672	30,849	12,397
1951	154,878	17,333	27,279	8,446	11,552	46,103	31,362	12,803
1952	157,553	17,312	28,894	8,414	11,350	46,495	31,884	13,203
1953	160,184	17,638	30,227	8,460	11,062	46,786	32,394	13,617
1954	163,026	18,057	31,480	8,637	10,832	47,001	32,942	14,076
1955	165,931	18,566	32,682	8,744	10,714	47,194	33,506	14,525
1956	168,903	19,003	33,994	8,916	10,616	47,379	34,057	14,938
1957	171,984	19,494	35,272	9,195	10,603	47,440	34,591	15,388
1958	174,882	19,887	36,445	9,543	10,756	47,337	35,109	15,806
1959	177,830	20,175	37,368	10,215	10,969	47,192	35,663	16,248
1960	180,671	20,341	38,494	10,683	11,134	47,140	36,203	16,675
1961	183,691	20,522	39,765	11,025	11,483	47,084	36,722	17,089
1962	186,538	20,469	41,205	11,180	11,959	47,013	37,255	17,457
1963	189,242	20,342	41,626	12,007	12,714	46,994	37,782	17,778
1964	191,889	20,165	42,297	12,736	13,269	46,958	38,338	18,127
1965	194,303	19,824	42,938	13,516	13,746	46,912	38,916	18,451
1966	196,560	19,208	43,702	14,311	14,050	47,001	39,534	18,755
1967	198,712	18,563	44,244	14,200	15,248	47,194	40,093	19,071
1968	200,706	17,913	44,622	14,452	15,786	47,721	40,846	19,365
1969	202,677	17,376	44,840	14,800	16,480	48,064	41,437	19,680
1970	205,052	17,166	44,816	15,289	17,202	48,473	41,999	20,107
1971	207,661	17,244	44,591	15,688	18,159	48,936	42,482	20,561
1972	209,896	17,101	44,203	16,039	18,153	50,482	42,898	21,020
1973	211,909	16,851	43,582	16,446	18,521	51,749	43,235	21,525
1974	213,854	16,487	42,989	16,769	18,975	53,051	43,522	22,061
1975	215,973	16,121	42,508	17,017	19,527	54,302	43,801	22,696
1976	218,035	15,617	42,099	17,194	19,986	55,852	44,008	23,278
1977	220,239	15,564	41,298	17,276	20,499	57,561	44,150	23,892
1978	222,585	15,735	40,428	17,288	20,946	59,400	44,286	24,502
1979	225,055	16,063	39,552	17,242	21,297	61,379	44,390	25,134
1980	227,726	16,451	38,838	17,167	21,590	63,470	44,504	25,707
1981	229,966	16,893	38,144	16,812	21,869	65,528	44,500	26,221
1982	232,188	17,228	37,784	16,332	21,902	67,692	44,462	26,787
1983	234,307	17,547	37,526	15,823	21,844	69,733	44,474	27,361
1984	236,348	17,695	37,461	15,295	21,737	71,735	44,547	27,878
1985	238,466	17,842	37,450	15,005	21,478	73,673	44,602	28,416
1986	240,651	17,963	37,404	15,024	20,942	75,651	44,660	29,008
1987	242,804	18,052	37,333	15,215	20,385	77,338	44,854	29,626
1988	245,021	18,195	37,593	15,198	19,846	78,595	45,471	30,124
1989	247,342	18,508	37,972	14,913	19,442	79,943	45,882	30,682
1990	250,132	18,856	38,632	14,466	19,323	81,291	46,316	31,247
1991	253,493	19,208	39,349	13,992	19,414	82,844	46,874	31,812
1992	256,894	19,528	40,161	13,781	19,314	83,201	48,553	32,356
1993	260,255	19,729	40,904	13,953	19,101	83,766	49,899	32,902
1994	263,436	19,777	41,689	14,228	18,758	84,334	51,318	33,331
1995	266,557	19,627	42,510	14,522	18,391	84,933	52,806	33,769
1996	269,667	19,408	43,172	15,057	17,965	85,527	54,396	34,143
1997	272,912	19,233	43,833	15,433	17,992	85,737	56,283	34,402
1998	276,115	19,145	44,332	15,856	18,250	85,663	58,249	34,619
1999	279,295	19,136	44,755	16,164	18,672	85,408	60,362	34,798
2000	282,407	19,187	45,156	16,215	19,190	85,163	62,419	35,078
2001	285,339	19,350	45,188	16,258	19,871	84,926	64,416	35,330
2002	288,189	19,537	45,148	16,316	20,399	84,641	66,560	35,588
2003	290,941	19,774	45,073	16,368	20,814	84,330	68,634	35,949
2004	293,609	20,060	44,923	16,518	21,020	84,123	70,668	36,297
2005	296,329	20,300	44,754	16,654	21,096	83,976	72,802	36,746
2006	299,157	20,452	44,581	16,969	21,135	83,966	74,802	37,253
2007	302,045	20,724	44,429	17,224	21,182	83,993	76,605	37,888
2008	304,906	20,996	44,378	17,363	21,294	84,031	78,075	38,770

Note.—Includes Armed Forces overseas beginning with 1940. Includes Alaska and Hawaii beginning with 1950.
All estimates are consistent with decennial census enumerations.

Source: Department of Commerce (Bureau of the Census).

TABLE B–35.—*Civilian population and labor force, 1929–2008*

[Monthly data seasonally adjusted, except as noted]

Year or month	Civilian noninstitutional population [1]	Civilian labor force					Not in labor force	Civilian labor force participation rate [2]	Civilian employment/ population ratio [3]	Unemployment rate, civilian workers [4]
		Total	Employment			Unemployment				
			Total	Agricultural	Non-agricultural					
	Thousands of persons 14 years of age and over								Percent	
1929	....	49,180	47,630	10,450	37,180	1,550	....	....	....	3.2
1933	....	51,590	38,760	10,090	28,670	12,830	....	....	....	24.9
1939	....	55,230	45,750	9,610	36,140	9,480	....	....	....	17.2
1940	99,840	55,640	47,520	9,540	37,980	8,120	44,200	55.7	47.6	14.6
1941	99,900	55,910	50,350	9,100	41,250	5,560	43,990	56.0	50.4	9.9
1942	98,640	56,410	53,750	9,250	44,500	2,660	42,230	57.2	54.5	4.7
1943	94,640	55,540	54,470	9,080	45,390	1,070	39,100	58.7	57.6	1.9
1944	93,220	54,630	53,960	8,950	45,010	670	38,590	58.6	57.9	1.2
1945	94,090	53,860	52,820	8,580	44,240	1,040	40,230	57.2	56.1	1.9
1946	103,070	57,520	55,250	8,320	46,930	2,270	45,550	55.8	53.6	3.9
1947	106,018	60,168	57,812	8,256	49,557	2,356	45,850	56.8	54.5	3.9
	Thousands of persons 16 years of age and over									
1947	101,827	59,350	57,038	7,890	49,148	2,311	42,477	58.3	56.0	3.9
1948	103,068	60,621	58,343	7,629	50,714	2,276	42,447	58.8	56.6	3.8
1949	103,994	61,286	57,651	7,658	49,993	3,637	42,708	58.9	55.4	5.9
1950	104,995	62,208	58,918	7,160	51,758	3,288	42,787	59.2	56.1	5.3
1951	104,621	62,017	59,961	6,726	53,235	2,055	42,604	59.2	57.3	3.3
1952	105,231	62,138	60,250	6,500	53,749	1,883	43,093	59.0	57.3	3.0
1953 [5]	107,056	63,015	61,179	6,260	54,919	1,834	44,041	58.9	57.1	2.9
1954	108,321	63,643	60,109	6,205	53,904	3,532	44,678	58.8	55.5	5.5
1955	109,683	65,023	62,170	6,450	55,722	2,852	44,660	59.3	56.7	4.4
1956	110,954	66,552	63,799	6,283	57,514	2,750	44,402	60.0	57.5	4.1
1957	112,265	66,929	64,071	5,947	58,123	2,859	45,336	59.6	57.1	4.3
1958	113,727	67,639	63,036	5,586	57,450	4,602	46,088	59.5	55.4	6.8
1959	115,329	68,369	64,630	5,565	59,065	3,740	46,960	59.3	56.0	5.5
1960 [5]	117,245	69,628	65,778	5,458	60,318	3,852	47,617	59.4	56.1	5.5
1961	118,771	70,459	65,746	5,200	60,546	4,714	48,312	59.3	55.4	6.7
1962 [5]	120,153	70,614	66,702	4,944	61,759	3,911	49,539	58.8	55.5	5.5
1963	122,416	71,833	67,762	4,687	63,076	4,070	50,583	58.7	55.4	5.7
1964	124,485	73,091	69,305	4,523	64,782	3,786	51,394	58.7	55.7	5.2
1965	126,513	74,455	71,088	4,361	66,726	3,366	52,058	58.9	56.2	4.5
1966	128,058	75,770	72,895	3,979	68,915	2,875	52,288	59.2	56.9	3.8
1967	129,874	77,347	74,372	3,844	70,527	2,975	52,527	59.6	57.3	3.8
1968	132,028	78,737	75,920	3,817	72,103	2,817	53,291	59.6	57.5	3.6
1969	134,335	80,734	77,902	3,606	74,296	2,832	53,602	60.1	58.0	3.5
1970	137,085	82,771	78,678	3,463	75,215	4,093	54,315	60.4	57.4	4.9
1971	140,216	84,382	79,367	3,394	75,972	5,016	55,834	60.2	56.6	5.9
1972 [5]	144,126	87,034	82,153	3,484	78,669	4,882	57,091	60.4	57.0	5.6
1973 [5]	147,096	89,429	85,064	3,470	81,594	4,365	57,667	60.8	57.8	4.9
1974	150,120	91,949	86,794	3,515	83,279	5,156	58,171	61.3	57.8	5.6
1975	153,153	93,775	85,846	3,408	82,438	7,929	59,377	61.2	56.1	8.5
1976	156,150	96,158	88,752	3,331	85,421	7,406	59,991	61.6	56.8	7.7
1977	159,033	99,009	92,017	3,283	88,734	6,991	60,025	62.3	57.9	7.1
1978 [5]	161,910	102,251	96,048	3,387	92,661	6,202	59,659	63.2	59.3	6.1
1979	164,863	104,962	98,824	3,347	95,477	6,137	59,900	63.7	59.9	5.8
1980	167,745	106,940	99,303	3,364	95,938	7,637	60,806	63.8	59.2	7.1
1981	170,130	108,670	100,397	3,368	97,030	8,273	61,460	63.9	59.0	7.6
1982	172,271	110,204	99,526	3,401	96,125	10,678	62,067	64.0	57.8	9.7
1983	174,215	111,550	100,834	3,383	97,450	10,717	62,665	64.0	57.9	9.6
1984	176,383	113,544	105,005	3,321	101,685	8,539	62,839	64.4	59.5	7.5
1985	178,206	115,461	107,150	3,179	103,971	8,312	62,744	64.8	60.1	7.2
1986 [5]	180,587	117,834	109,597	3,163	106,434	8,237	62,752	65.3	60.7	7.0
1987	182,753	119,865	112,440	3,208	109,232	7,425	62,888	65.6	61.5	6.2
1988	184,613	121,669	114,968	3,169	111,800	6,701	62,944	65.9	62.3	5.5
1989	186,393	123,869	117,342	3,199	114,142	6,528	62,523	66.5	63.0	5.3
1990 [5]	189,164	125,840	118,793	3,223	115,570	7,047	63,324	66.5	62.8	5.6
1991	190,925	126,346	117,718	3,269	114,449	8,628	64,578	66.2	61.7	6.8
1992	192,805	128,105	118,492	3,247	115,245	9,613	64,700	66.4	61.5	7.5
1993	194,838	129,200	120,259	3,115	117,144	8,940	65,638	66.3	61.7	6.9
1994 [5]	196,814	131,056	123,060	3,409	119,651	7,996	65,758	66.6	62.5	6.1
1995	198,584	132,304	124,900	3,440	121,460	7,404	66,280	66.6	62.9	5.6
1996	200,591	133,943	126,708	3,443	123,264	7,236	66,647	66.8	63.2	5.4
1997 [5]	203,133	136,297	129,558	3,399	126,159	6,739	66,837	67.1	63.8	4.9
1998 [5]	205,220	137,673	131,463	3,378	128,085	6,210	67,547	67.1	64.1	4.5
1999 [5]	207,753	139,368	133,488	3,281	130,207	5,880	68,385	67.1	64.3	4.2

[1] Not seasonally adjusted.
[2] Civilian labor force as percent of civilian noninstitutional population.
[3] Civilian employment as percent of civilian noninstitutional population.
[4] Unemployed as percent of civilian labor force.

See next page for continuation of table.

[Monthly data seasonally adjusted, except as noted]

Year or month	Civilian noninstitutional population [1]	Civilian labor force					Not in labor force	Civilian labor force participation rate [2]	Civilian employment/ population ratio [3]	Unemployment rate, civilian workers [4]
		Total	Employment			Unemployment				
			Total	Agricultural	Nonagricultural					
	Thousands of persons 16 years of age and over							Percent		
2000 [5,6]	212,577	142,583	136,891	2,464	134,427	5,692	69,994	67.1	64.4	4.0
2001	215,092	143,734	136,933	2,299	134,635	6,801	71,359	66.8	63.7	4.7
2002	217,570	144,863	136,485	2,311	134,174	8,378	72,707	66.6	62.7	5.8
2003 [5]	221,168	146,510	137,736	2,275	135,461	8,774	74,658	66.2	62.3	6.0
2004 [5]	223,357	147,401	139,252	2,232	137,020	8,149	75,956	66.0	62.3	5.5
2005 [5]	226,082	149,320	141,730	2,197	139,532	7,591	76,762	66.0	62.7	5.1
2006 [5]	228,815	151,428	144,427	2,206	142,221	7,001	77,387	66.2	63.1	4.6
2007 [5]	231,867	153,124	146,047	2,095	143,952	7,078	78,743	66.0	63.0	4.6
2005: Jan [5]	224,837	147,981	140,224	2,115	138,099	7,757	76,856	65.8	62.4	5.2
Feb	225,041	148,308	140,354	2,134	138,198	7,954	76,733	65.9	62.4	5.4
Mar	225,236	148,295	140,563	2,183	138,402	7,732	76,942	65.8	62.4	5.2
Apr	225,441	148,912	141,244	2,240	139,037	7,669	76,528	66.1	62.7	5.1
May	225,670	149,276	141,597	2,220	139,364	7,679	76,394	66.1	62.7	5.1
June	225,911	149,244	141,708	2,308	139,236	7,536	76,667	66.1	62.7	5.0
July	226,153	149,479	142,055	2,299	139,804	7,424	76,674	66.1	62.8	5.0
Aug	226,421	149,826	142,457	2,184	140,306	7,369	76,595	66.2	62.9	4.9
Sept	226,693	150,022	142,429	2,176	140,337	7,593	76,671	66.2	62.8	5.1
Oct	226,959	150,061	142,613	2,184	140,483	7,449	76,897	66.1	62.8	5.0
Nov	227,204	150,099	142,564	2,175	140,357	7,535	77,105	66.1	62.7	5.0
Dec	227,425	150,041	142,778	2,111	140,643	7,262	77,384	66.0	62.8	4.8
2006: Jan [5]	227,553	150,111	143,086	2,169	140,901	7,025	77,442	66.0	62.9	4.7
Feb	227,763	150,505	143,362	2,193	141,118	7,143	77,258	66.1	62.9	4.7
Mar	227,975	150,694	143,619	2,165	141,451	7,075	77,280	66.1	63.0	4.7
Apr	228,199	150,904	143,791	2,235	141,557	7,113	77,296	66.1	63.0	4.7
May	228,428	151,126	144,088	2,191	141,859	7,038	77,302	66.2	63.1	4.7
June	228,671	151,386	144,369	2,267	142,006	7,017	77,285	66.2	63.1	4.6
July	228,912	151,471	144,295	2,264	142,116	7,176	77,442	66.2	63.0	4.7
Aug	229,167	151,799	144,671	2,235	142,492	7,128	77,369	66.2	63.1	4.7
Sept	229,420	151,741	144,846	2,166	142,742	6,896	77,678	66.1	63.1	4.5
Oct	229,675	152,130	145,395	2,163	143,256	6,735	77,545	66.2	63.3	4.4
Nov	229,905	152,403	145,583	2,163	143,384	6,820	77,502	66.3	63.3	4.5
Dec	230,108	152,709	145,949	2,257	143,670	6,760	77,399	66.4	63.4	4.4
2007: Jan [5]	230,650	152,958	145,915	2,225	143,691	7,043	77,692	66.3	63.3	4.6
Feb	230,834	152,725	145,888	2,327	143,535	6,837	78,110	66.2	63.2	4.5
Mar	231,034	152,884	146,145	2,202	143,966	6,738	78,150	66.2	63.3	4.4
Apr	231,253	152,542	145,713	2,053	143,678	6,829	78,711	66.0	63.0	4.5
May	231,480	152,776	145,913	2,081	143,799	6,863	78,704	66.0	63.0	4.5
June	231,713	153,085	146,087	1,957	144,066	6,997	78,628	66.1	63.0	4.6
July	231,958	153,182	146,045	1,997	144,096	7,137	78,776	66.0	63.0	4.7
Aug	232,211	152,886	145,753	1,856	143,928	7,133	79,325	65.8	62.8	4.7
Sept	232,461	153,506	146,260	2,065	144,259	7,246	78,955	66.0	62.9	4.7
Oct	232,715	153,306	146,016	2,089	143,933	7,291	79,409	65.9	62.7	4.8
Nov	232,939	153,828	146,647	2,148	144,503	7,181	79,111	66.0	63.0	4.7
Dec	233,156	153,866	146,211	2,248	143,933	7,655	79,290	66.0	62.7	5.0
2008: Jan [5]	232,616	153,824	146,248	2,213	144,052	7,576	78,792	66.1	62.9	4.9
Feb	232,809	153,374	145,993	2,213	143,820	7,381	79,436	65.9	62.7	4.8
Mar	232,995	153,784	145,969	2,192	143,796	7,815	79,211	66.0	62.6	5.1
Apr	233,198	153,957	146,331	2,109	144,258	7,626	79,241	66.0	62.7	5.0
May	233,405	154,534	146,046	2,122	143,898	8,487	78,871	66.2	62.6	5.5
June	233,627	154,390	145,891	2,137	143,650	8,499	79,237	66.1	62.4	5.5
July	233,864	154,603	145,819	2,123	143,589	8,784	79,261	66.1	62.4	5.7
Aug	234,107	154,853	145,477	2,142	143,284	9,376	79,253	66.1	62.1	6.1
Sept	234,360	154,732	145,255	2,189	143,064	9,477	79,628	66.0	62.0	6.1
Oct	234,612	155,038	144,958	2,167	142,773	10,080	79,575	66.1	61.8	6.5
Nov	234,828	154,616	144,285	2,203	142,015	10,331	80,212	65.8	61.4	6.7

[5] Not strictly comparable with earlier data due to population adjustments or other changes. See *Employment and Earnings* or population control adjustments to the Current Population Survey (CPS) at http://www.bls.gov/cps/documentation.htm#concepts for details on breaks in series.

[6] Beginning in 2000, data for agricultural employment are for agricultural and related industries; data for this series and for nonagricultural employment are not strictly comparable with data for earlier years. Because of independent seasonal adjustment for these two series, monthly data will not add to total civilian employment.

Note.—Labor force data in Tables B–35 through B–44 are based on household interviews and relate to the calendar week including the 12th of the month. For definitions of terms, area samples used, historical comparability of the data, comparability with other series, etc., see *Employment and Earnings* or population control adjustments to the CPS at http://www.bls.gov/cps/documentation.htm#concepts.

Source: Department of Labor (Bureau of Labor Statistics).

TABLE B–36.—Civilian employment and unemployment by sex and age, 1960–2008

[Thousands of persons 16 years of age and over; monthly data seasonally adjusted]

Year or month	Civilian employment							Unemployment						
	Total	Males			Females			Total	Males			Females		
		Total	16–19 years	20 years and over	Total	16–19 years	20 years and over		Total	16–19 years	20 years and over	Total	16–19 years	20 years and over
1960	65,778	43,904	2,361	41,543	21,874	1,768	20,105	3,852	2,486	426	2,060	1,366	286	1,080
1961	65,746	43,656	2,315	41,342	22,090	1,793	20,296	4,714	2,997	479	2,518	1,717	349	1,368
1962	66,702	44,177	2,362	41,815	22,525	1,833	20,693	3,911	2,423	408	2,016	1,488	313	1,175
1963	67,762	44,657	2,406	42,251	23,105	1,849	21,257	4,070	2,472	501	1,971	1,598	383	1,216
1964	69,305	45,474	2,587	42,886	23,831	1,929	21,903	3,786	2,205	487	1,718	1,581	385	1,195
1965	71,088	46,340	2,918	43,422	24,748	2,118	22,630	3,366	1,914	479	1,435	1,452	395	1,056
1966	72,895	46,919	3,253	43,668	25,976	2,468	23,510	2,875	1,551	432	1,120	1,324	405	921
1967	74,372	47,479	3,186	44,294	26,893	2,496	24,397	2,975	1,508	448	1,060	1,468	391	1,078
1968	75,920	48,114	3,255	44,859	27,807	2,526	25,281	2,817	1,419	426	993	1,397	412	985
1969	77,902	48,818	3,430	45,388	29,084	2,687	26,397	2,832	1,403	440	963	1,429	413	1,015
1970	78,678	48,990	3,409	45,581	29,688	2,735	26,952	4,093	2,238	599	1,638	1,855	506	1,349
1971	79,367	49,390	3,478	45,912	29,976	2,730	27,246	5,016	2,789	693	2,097	2,227	568	1,658
1972	82,153	50,896	3,765	47,130	31,257	2,980	28,276	4,882	2,659	711	1,948	2,222	598	1,625
1973	85,064	52,349	4,039	48,310	32,715	3,231	29,484	4,365	2,275	653	1,624	2,089	583	1,507
1974	86,794	53,024	4,103	48,922	33,769	3,345	30,424	5,156	2,714	757	1,957	2,441	665	1,777
1975	85,846	51,857	3,839	48,018	33,989	3,263	30,726	7,929	4,442	966	3,476	3,486	802	2,684
1976	88,752	53,138	3,947	49,190	35,615	3,389	32,226	7,406	4,036	939	3,098	3,369	780	2,588
1977	92,017	54,728	4,174	50,555	37,289	3,514	33,775	6,991	3,667	874	2,794	3,324	789	2,535
1978	96,048	56,479	4,336	52,143	39,569	3,734	35,836	6,202	3,142	813	2,328	3,061	769	2,292
1979	98,824	57,607	4,300	53,308	41,217	3,783	37,434	6,137	3,120	811	2,308	3,018	743	2,276
1980	99,303	57,186	4,085	53,101	42,117	3,625	38,492	7,637	4,267	913	3,353	3,370	755	2,615
1981	100,397	57,397	3,815	53,582	43,000	3,411	39,590	8,273	4,577	962	3,615	3,696	800	2,895
1982	99,526	56,271	3,379	52,891	43,256	3,170	40,086	10,678	6,179	1,090	5,089	4,499	886	3,613
1983	100,834	56,787	3,300	53,487	44,047	3,043	41,004	10,717	6,260	1,003	5,257	4,457	825	3,632
1984	105,005	59,091	3,322	55,769	45,915	3,122	42,793	8,539	4,744	812	3,932	3,794	687	3,107
1985	107,150	59,891	3,328	56,562	47,259	3,105	44,154	8,312	4,521	806	3,715	3,791	661	3,129
1986	109,597	60,892	3,323	57,569	48,706	3,149	45,556	8,237	4,530	779	3,751	3,707	675	3,032
1987	112,440	62,107	3,381	58,726	50,334	3,260	47,074	7,425	4,101	732	3,369	3,324	616	2,709
1988	114,968	63,273	3,492	59,781	51,696	3,313	48,383	6,701	3,655	667	2,987	3,046	558	2,487
1989	117,342	64,315	3,477	60,837	53,027	3,282	49,745	6,528	3,525	658	2,867	3,003	536	2,467
1990	118,793	65,104	3,427	61,678	53,689	3,154	50,535	7,047	3,906	667	3,239	3,140	544	2,596
1991	117,718	64,223	3,044	61,178	53,496	2,862	50,634	8,628	4,946	751	4,195	3,683	608	3,074
1992	118,492	64,440	2,944	61,496	54,052	2,724	51,328	9,613	5,523	806	4,717	4,090	621	3,469
1993	120,259	65,349	2,994	62,355	54,910	2,811	52,099	8,940	5,055	768	4,287	3,885	597	3,288
1994	123,060	66,450	3,156	63,294	56,610	3,005	53,606	7,996	4,367	740	3,627	3,629	580	3,049
1995	124,900	67,377	3,292	64,085	57,523	3,127	54,396	7,404	3,983	744	3,239	3,421	602	2,819
1996	126,708	68,207	3,310	64,897	58,501	3,190	55,311	7,236	3,880	733	3,146	3,356	573	2,783
1997	129,558	69,685	3,401	66,284	59,873	3,260	56,613	6,739	3,577	694	2,882	3,162	577	2,585
1998	131,463	70,693	3,558	67,135	60,771	3,493	57,278	6,210	3,266	686	2,580	2,944	519	2,424
1999	133,488	71,446	3,685	67,761	62,042	3,487	58,555	5,880	3,066	633	2,433	2,814	529	2,285
2000	136,891	73,305	3,671	69,634	63,586	3,519	60,067	5,692	2,975	599	2,376	2,717	483	2,235
2001	136,933	73,196	3,420	69,776	63,737	3,320	60,417	6,801	3,690	650	3,040	3,111	512	2,599
2002	136,485	72,903	3,169	69,734	63,582	3,162	60,420	8,378	4,597	700	3,896	3,781	553	3,228
2003	137,736	73,332	2,917	70,415	64,404	3,002	61,402	8,774	4,906	697	4,209	3,868	554	3,314
2004	139,252	74,524	2,952	71,572	64,728	2,955	61,773	8,149	4,456	664	3,791	3,694	543	3,150
2005	141,730	75,973	2,923	73,050	65,757	3,055	62,702	7,591	4,059	667	3,392	3,531	519	3,013
2006	144,427	77,502	3,071	74,431	66,925	3,091	63,834	7,001	3,753	622	3,131	3,247	496	2,751
2007	146,047	78,254	2,917	75,337	67,792	2,994	64,799	7,078	3,882	623	3,259	3,196	478	2,718
2007: Jan	145,915	78,221	3,067	75,154	67,694	3,047	64,647	7,043	3,846	594	3,252	3,197	485	2,712
Feb	145,888	78,184	3,036	75,148	67,704	3,018	64,686	6,837	3,815	605	3,210	3,021	461	2,561
Mar	146,145	78,297	3,011	75,286	67,849	2,990	64,859	6,738	3,700	576	3,124	3,038	451	2,586
Apr	145,713	78,293	3,013	75,279	67,420	2,941	64,479	6,829	3,743	594	3,149	3,086	488	2,598
May	145,913	78,277	2,934	75,343	67,637	2,926	64,710	6,863	3,776	622	3,154	3,087	479	2,607
June	146,087	78,243	2,951	75,292	67,845	3,017	64,828	6,997	3,859	648	3,212	3,138	485	2,652
July	146,045	78,237	2,914	75,324	67,808	3,016	64,792	7,137	3,887	592	3,295	3,250	476	2,774
Aug	145,753	78,066	2,792	75,274	67,687	2,861	64,826	7,133	3,863	612	3,252	3,270	480	2,790
Sept	146,260	78,229	2,897	75,332	68,030	2,998	65,033	7,246	4,008	650	3,357	3,238	476	2,762
Oct	146,016	78,177	2,903	75,274	67,838	3,011	64,827	7,291	4,032	643	3,389	3,258	462	2,796
Nov	146,647	78,604	2,770	75,834	68,043	3,063	64,980	7,181	3,910	670	3,240	3,271	475	2,796
Dec	146,211	78,260	2,761	75,499	67,951	3,040	64,912	7,655	4,188	683	3,505	3,467	513	2,953
2008: Jan	146,248	78,157	2,731	75,427	68,091	2,993	65,098	7,576	4,197	760	3,437	3,378	494	2,884
Feb	145,993	78,113	2,751	75,362	67,880	2,929	64,950	7,381	4,019	633	3,386	3,361	496	2,865
Mar	145,969	77,948	2,751	75,197	68,021	2,966	65,055	7,815	4,236	595	3,641	3,579	475	3,104
Apr	146,331	78,038	2,890	75,148	68,293	3,033	65,260	7,626	4,218	590	3,628	3,408	492	2,916
May	146,046	77,954	2,953	75,001	68,092	2,954	65,138	8,487	4,648	771	3,877	3,839	587	3,252
June	145,891	77,794	2,795	74,998	68,097	2,859	65,238	8,499	4,734	695	4,038	3,765	557	3,208
July	145,819	77,823	2,729	75,094	67,996	2,829	65,167	8,784	5,066	833	4,234	3,718	583	3,135
Aug	145,477	77,632	2,766	74,866	67,845	2,798	65,047	9,376	5,176	724	4,452	4,201	576	3,625
Sept	145,255	77,396	2,764	74,631	67,860	2,787	65,072	9,477	5,549	737	4,813	3,928	576	3,352
Oct	144,958	77,108	2,667	74,441	67,850	2,759	65,090	10,080	5,875	865	5,010	4,205	539	3,666
Nov	144,285	76,672	2,534	74,138	67,613	2,678	64,935	10,331	5,983	805	5,178	4,348	534	3,814

Note.—See footnote 5 and Note, Table B–35.

Source: Department of Labor (Bureau of Labor Statistics).

TABLE B–37.—*Civilian employment by demographic characteristic, 1960–2008*

[Thousands of persons 16 years of age and over; monthly data seasonally adjusted]

Year or month	All civilian workers	White [1] Total	Males	Females	Both sexes 16–19	Black and other [1] Total	Males	Females	Both sexes 16–19	Black or African American [1] Total	Males	Females	Both sexes 16–19
1960	65,778	58,850	39,755	19,095	3,700	6,928	4,149	2,779	430				
1961	65,746	58,913	39,588	19,325	3,693	6,833	4,068	2,765	414				
1962	66,702	59,698	40,016	19,682	3,774	7,003	4,160	2,843	420				
1963	67,762	60,622	40,428	20,194	3,851	7,140	4,229	2,911	404				
1964	69,305	61,922	41,115	20,807	4,076	7,383	4,359	3,024	440				
1965	71,088	63,446	41,844	21,602	4,562	7,643	4,496	3,147	474				
1966	72,895	65,021	42,331	22,690	5,176	7,877	4,588	3,289	545				
1967	74,372	66,361	42,833	23,528	5,114	8,011	4,646	3,365	568				
1968	75,920	67,750	43,411	24,339	5,195	8,169	4,702	3,467	584				
1969	77,902	69,518	44,048	25,470	5,508	8,384	4,770	3,614	609				
1970	78,678	70,217	44,178	26,039	5,571	8,464	4,813	3,650	574				
1971	79,367	70,878	44,595	26,283	5,670	8,488	4,796	3,692	538				
1972	82,153	73,370	45,944	27,426	6,173	8,783	4,952	3,832	573	7,802	4,368	3,433	509
1973	85,064	75,708	47,085	28,623	6,623	9,356	5,265	4,092	647	8,128	4,527	3,601	570
1974	86,794	77,184	47,674	29,511	6,796	9,610	5,352	4,258	652	8,203	4,527	3,677	554
1975	85,846	76,411	46,697	29,714	6,487	9,435	5,161	4,275	615	7,894	4,275	3,618	507
1976	88,752	78,853	47,775	31,078	6,724	9,899	5,363	4,536	611	8,227	4,404	3,823	508
1977	92,017	81,700	49,150	32,550	7,068	10,317	5,579	4,739	619	8,540	4,565	3,975	508
1978	96,048	84,936	50,544	34,392	7,367	11,112	5,936	5,177	703	9,102	4,796	4,307	571
1979	98,824	87,259	51,452	35,807	7,356	11,565	6,156	5,409	727	9,359	4,923	4,436	579
1980	99,303	87,715	51,127	36,587	7,021	11,588	6,059	5,529	689	9,313	4,798	4,515	547
1981	100,397	88,709	51,315	37,394	6,588	11,688	6,083	5,606	637	9,355	4,794	4,561	505
1982	99,526	87,903	50,287	37,615	5,984	11,624	5,983	5,641	565	9,189	4,637	4,552	428
1983	100,834	88,893	50,621	38,272	5,799	11,941	6,166	5,775	543	9,375	4,753	4,622	416
1984	105,005	92,120	52,462	39,659	5,836	12,885	6,629	6,256	607	10,119	5,124	4,995	474
1985	107,150	93,736	53,046	40,690	5,768	13,414	6,845	6,569	666	10,501	5,270	5,231	532
1986	109,597	95,660	53,785	41,876	5,792	13,937	7,107	6,830	681	10,814	5,428	5,386	536
1987	112,440	97,789	54,647	43,142	5,898	14,652	7,459	7,192	742	11,309	5,661	5,648	587
1988	114,968	99,812	55,550	44,262	6,030	15,156	7,722	7,434	774	11,658	5,824	5,834	601
1989	117,342	101,584	56,352	45,232	5,946	15,757	7,963	7,795	813	11,953	5,928	6,025	625
1990	118,793	102,261	56,703	45,558	5,779	16,533	8,401	8,131	801	12,175	5,995	6,180	598
1991	117,718	101,182	55,797	45,385	5,216	16,536	8,426	8,110	690	12,074	5,961	6,113	494
1992	118,492	101,669	55,959	45,710	4,985	16,823	8,482	8,342	684	12,151	5,930	6,221	492
1993	120,259	103,045	56,656	46,390	5,113	17,214	8,693	8,521	691	12,382	6,047	6,334	494
1994	123,060	105,190	57,452	47,738	5,398	17,870	8,998	8,872	763	12,835	6,241	6,595	552
1995	124,900	106,490	58,146	48,344	5,593	18,409	9,231	9,179	826	13,279	6,422	6,857	586
1996	126,708	107,808	58,888	48,920	5,667	18,900	9,319	9,580	832	13,542	6,456	7,086	613
1997	129,558	109,856	59,998	49,859	5,807	19,701	9,687	10,014	853	13,969	6,607	7,362	631
1998	131,463	110,931	60,604	50,327	6,089	20,532	10,089	10,443	962	14,556	6,871	7,685	736
1999	133,488	112,235	61,139	51,096	6,204	21,253	10,307	10,945	968	15,056	7,027	8,029	691
2000	136,891	114,424	62,289	52,136	6,160					15,156	7,082	8,073	711
2001	136,933	114,430	62,212	52,218	5,817					15,006	6,938	8,068	637
2002	136,485	114,013	61,849	52,164	5,441					14,872	6,959	7,914	611
2003	137,736	114,235	61,866	52,369	5,064					14,739	6,820	7,919	516
2004	139,252	115,239	62,712	52,527	5,039					14,909	6,912	7,997	520
2005	141,730	116,949	63,763	53,186	5,105					15,313	7,155	8,158	536
2006	144,427	118,833	64,883	53,950	5,215					15,765	7,354	8,410	618
2007	146,047	119,792	65,289	54,503	4,990					16,051	7,500	8,551	566
2007: Jan	145,915	119,742	65,341	54,401	5,185					16,242	7,579	8,662	603
Feb	145,888	119,651	65,281	54,370	5,118					16,141	7,525	8,615	599
Mar	146,145	120,065	65,531	54,534	5,068					15,979	7,385	8,595	592
Apr	145,713	119,505	65,404	54,102	5,029					16,048	7,465	8,583	584
May	145,913	119,711	65,393	54,318	4,969					15,939	7,407	8,532	562
June	146,087	119,835	65,367	54,468	5,040					15,989	7,406	8,583	561
July	146,045	119,713	65,231	54,482	5,009					16,172	7,603	8,569	558
Aug	145,753	119,340	64,923	54,417	4,805					16,176	7,664	8,512	525
Sept	146,260	119,992	65,153	54,838	4,996					16,046	7,536	8,510	541
Oct	146,016	119,883	65,229	54,654	4,985					15,946	7,436	8,510	558
Nov	146,647	120,194	65,412	54,782	4,863					15,980	7,522	8,458	553
Dec	146,261	119,889	65,237	54,653	4,853					15,961	7,470	8,491	556
2008: Jan	146,248	119,858	65,181	54,677	4,791					16,090	7,548	8,542	564
Feb	145,993	119,534	65,057	54,477	4,785					16,169	7,573	8,596	560
Mar	145,969	119,574	65,041	54,533	4,848					16,116	7,459	8,657	525
Apr	146,331	119,667	64,981	54,686	4,978					16,234	7,522	8,711	582
May	146,046	119,661	65,042	54,618	4,993					16,029	7,437	8,591	558
June	145,891	119,518	64,857	54,661	4,789					16,085	7,491	8,593	525
July	145,819	119,542	65,001	54,541	4,664					16,040	7,423	8,617	545
Aug	145,477	119,222	64,775	54,447	4,658					16,074	7,530	8,543	609
Sept	145,255	119,180	64,548	54,631	4,632					15,714	7,323	8,391	573
Oct	144,958	118,893	64,303	54,590	4,577					15,810	7,326	8,483	546
Nov	144,285	118,338	64,037	54,301	4,461					15,718	7,192	8,526	468

[1] Beginning in 2003, persons who selected this race group only. Prior to 2003, persons who selected more than one race were included in the group they identified as the main race. Data for "black or African American" were for "black" prior to 2003. Data discontinued for "black and other" series. See *Employment and Earnings* or concepts and methodology of the Current Population Survey (CPS) at http://www.bls.gov/cps/documentation.htm#concepts for details.

Note.—Beginning with data for 2000, detail will not sum to total because data for all race groups are not shown here. See footnote 5 and Note, Table B–35.

Source: Department of Labor (Bureau of Labor Statistics).

TABLE B–38.—*Unemployment by demographic characteristic, 1960–2008*

[Thousands of persons 16 years of age and over; monthly data seasonally adjusted]

Year or month	All civilian workers	White [1]				Black and other [1]				Black or African American [1]			
		Total	Males	Females	Both sexes 16–19	Total	Males	Females	Both sexes 16–19	Total	Males	Females	Both sexes 16–19
1960	3,852	3,065	1,988	1,077	575	788	498	290	138	....	....	....	....
1961	4,714	3,743	2,398	1,345	669	971	599	372	159	....	....	....	....
1962	3,911	3,052	1,915	1,137	580	861	509	352	142				
1963	4,070	3,208	1,976	1,232	708	863	496	367	176				
1964	3,786	2,999	1,779	1,220	708	787	426	361	165				
1965	3,366	2,691	1,556	1,135	705	678	360	318	171				
1966	2,875	2,255	1,241	1,014	651	622	310	312	186				
1967	2,975	2,338	1,208	1,130	635	638	300	338	203				
1968	2,817	2,226	1,142	1,084	644	590	277	313	194				
1969	2,832	2,260	1,137	1,123	660	571	267	304	193				
1970	4,093	3,339	1,857	1,482	871	754	380	374	235	....	....	....	....
1971	5,016	4,085	2,309	1,777	1,011	930	481	450	249				
1972	4,882	3,906	2,173	1,733	1,021	977	486	491	288	906	448	458	279
1973	4,365	3,442	1,836	1,606	955	924	440	484	280	846	395	451	262
1974	5,156	4,097	2,169	1,927	1,104	1,058	544	514	318	965	494	470	297
1975	7,929	6,421	3,627	2,794	1,413	1,507	815	692	355	1,369	741	629	330
1976	7,406	5,914	3,258	2,656	1,364	1,492	779	713	355	1,334	698	637	330
1977	6,991	5,441	2,883	2,558	1,284	1,550	784	766	379	1,393	698	695	354
1978	6,202	4,698	2,411	2,287	1,189	1,505	731	774	394	1,330	641	690	360
1979	6,137	4,664	2,405	2,260	1,193	1,473	714	759	362	1,319	636	683	333
1980	7,637	5,884	3,345	2,540	1,291	1,752	922	830	377	1,553	815	738	343
1981	8,273	6,343	3,580	2,762	1,374	1,930	997	933	388	1,731	891	840	357
1982	10,678	8,241	4,846	3,395	1,534	2,437	1,334	1,104	443	2,142	1,167	975	396
1983	10,717	8,128	4,859	3,270	1,387	2,588	1,401	1,187	441	2,272	1,213	1,059	392
1984	8,539	6,372	3,600	2,772	1,116	2,167	1,144	1,022	384	1,914	1,003	911	353
1985	8,312	6,191	3,426	2,765	1,074	2,121	1,095	1,026	394	1,864	951	913	357
1986	8,237	6,140	3,433	2,708	1,070	2,097	1,097	999	383	1,840	946	894	347
1987	7,425	5,501	3,132	2,369	995	1,924	969	955	353	1,684	826	858	312
1988	6,701	4,944	2,766	2,177	910	1,757	888	869	316	1,547	771	776	288
1989	6,528	4,770	2,636	2,135	863	1,757	889	868	331	1,544	773	772	300
1990	7,047	5,186	2,935	2,251	903	1,860	971	889	308	1,565	806	758	268
1991	8,628	6,560	3,859	2,701	1,029	2,068	1,087	981	330	1,723	890	833	280
1992	9,613	7,169	4,209	2,959	1,037	2,444	1,314	1,130	390	2,011	1,067	944	324
1993	8,940	6,655	3,828	2,827	992	2,285	1,227	1,058	373	1,844	971	872	313
1994	7,996	5,892	3,275	2,617	960	2,104	1,092	1,011	360	1,666	848	818	300
1995	7,404	5,459	2,999	2,460	952	1,945	984	961	394	1,538	762	777	325
1996	7,236	5,300	2,896	2,404	939	1,936	984	952	367	1,592	808	784	310
1997	6,739	4,836	2,641	2,195	912	1,903	935	967	359	1,560	747	813	302
1998	6,210	4,484	2,431	2,053	876	1,726	835	891	329	1,426	671	756	281
1999	5,880	4,273	2,274	1,999	844	1,606	792	814	318	1,309	626	684	268
2000	5,692	4,121	2,177	1,944	795	....	....	....	....	1,241	620	621	230
2001	6,801	4,969	2,754	2,215	845					1,416	709	706	260
2002	8,378	6,137	3,459	2,678	925					1,693	835	858	260
2003	8,774	6,311	3,643	2,668	909					1,787	891	895	255
2004	8,149	5,847	3,282	2,565	890					1,729	860	868	241
2005	7,591	5,350	2,931	2,419	845					1,700	844	856	267
2006	7,001	5,002	2,730	2,271	794					1,549	774	775	253
2007	7,078	5,143	2,869	2,274	805					1,445	752	693	235
2007: Jan	7,043	5,154	2,871	2,284	791					1,415	727	688	246
Feb	6,837	4,986	2,832	2,154	772					1,394	733	661	241
Mar	6,738	4,787	2,638	2,149	776					1,439	790	648	194
Apr	6,829	4,928	2,731	2,197	773					1,435	793	642	258
May	6,863	4,928	2,741	2,187	801					1,466	778	688	242
June	6,997	5,083	2,839	2,244	834					1,467	775	692	252
July	7,137	5,232	2,921	2,311	800					1,421	711	710	206
Aug	7,133	5,256	2,935	2,322	806					1,347	660	687	238
Sept	7,246	5,324	3,048	2,275	834					1,437	718	719	220
Oct	7,291	5,268	2,959	2,309	810					1,483	776	708	215
Nov	7,181	5,235	2,908	2,327	840					1,473	756	717	234
Dec	7,655	5,571	3,042	2,529	815					1,577	829	748	295
2008: Jan	7,576	5,482	3,076	2,406	887					1,623	859	764	313
Feb	7,381	5,406	3,001	2,405	807					1,463	749	714	259
Mar	7,815	5,616	3,086	2,530	736					1,586	797	789	239
Apr	7,626	5,504	3,119	2,385	799					1,520	761	759	189
May	8,487	6,101	3,450	2,652	978					1,713	864	849	268
June	8,499	6,186	3,477	2,709	951					1,632	873	759	221
July	8,784	6,428	3,754	2,675	1,094					1,726	942	784	257
Aug	9,376	6,760	3,797	2,962	965					1,899	947	952	248
Sept	9,477	6,775	4,065	2,711	974					2,023	1,082	941	239
Oct	10,080	7,495	4,404	3,090	1,038					1,983	1,087	896	262
Nov	10,331	7,691	4,536	3,155	1,009					1,992	1,089	903	223

[1] See footnote 1 and Note, Table B–37.

Note.—See footnote 5 and Note, Table B–35.

Source: Department of Labor (Bureau of Labor Statistics).

TABLE B–39.—*Civilian labor force participation rate and employment/population ratio, 1960–2008*

[Percent[1]; monthly data seasonally adjusted]

Year or month	Labor force participation rate							Employment/population ratio						
	All civilian workers	Males	Females	Both sexes 16–19 years	White[2]	Black and other[2]	Black or African American[2]	All civilian workers	Males	Females	Both sexes 16–19 years	White[2]	Black and other[2]	Black or African American[2]
1960	59.4	83.3	37.7	47.5	58.8	64.5		56.1	78.9	35.5	40.5	55.9	57.9	
1961	59.3	82.9	38.1	46.9	58.8	64.1		55.4	77.6	35.4	39.1	55.3	56.2	
1962	58.8	82.0	37.9	46.1	58.3	63.2		55.5	77.7	35.6	39.4	55.4	56.3	
1963	58.7	81.4	38.3	45.2	58.2	63.0		55.4	77.1	35.8	37.4	55.3	56.2	
1964	58.7	81.0	38.7	44.5	58.2	63.1		55.7	77.3	36.3	37.3	55.5	57.0	
1965	58.9	80.7	39.3	45.7	58.4	62.9		56.2	77.5	37.1	38.9	56.0	57.8	
1966	59.2	80.4	40.3	48.2	58.7	63.0		56.9	77.9	38.3	42.1	56.8	58.4	
1967	59.6	80.4	41.1	48.4	59.2	62.8		57.3	78.0	39.0	42.2	57.2	58.2	
1968	59.6	80.1	41.6	48.3	59.3	62.2		57.5	77.8	39.6	42.2	57.4	58.0	
1969	60.1	79.8	42.7	49.4	59.9	62.1		58.0	77.6	40.7	43.4	58.0	58.1	
1970	60.4	79.7	43.3	49.9	60.2	61.8		57.4	76.2	40.8	42.3	57.5	56.8	
1971	60.2	79.1	43.4	49.7	60.1	60.9		56.6	74.9	40.4	41.3	56.8	54.9	
1972	60.4	78.9	43.9	51.9	60.4	60.2	59.9	57.0	75.0	41.0	43.5	57.4	54.1	53.7
1973	60.8	78.8	44.7	53.7	60.8	60.5	60.2	57.8	75.5	42.0	45.9	58.2	55.0	54.5
1974	61.3	78.7	45.7	54.8	61.4	60.3	59.8	57.8	74.9	42.6	46.0	58.3	54.3	53.5
1975	61.2	77.9	46.3	54.0	61.5	59.6	58.8	56.1	71.7	42.0	43.3	56.7	51.4	50.1
1976	61.6	77.5	47.3	54.5	61.8	59.8	59.0	56.8	72.0	43.2	44.2	57.5	52.0	50.8
1977	62.3	77.7	48.4	56.0	62.5	60.4	59.4	57.9	72.8	44.5	46.1	58.6	52.5	51.4
1978	63.2	77.9	50.0	57.8	63.3	62.2	61.5	59.3	73.8	46.4	48.3	60.0	54.7	53.6
1979	63.7	77.8	50.9	57.9	63.9	62.2	61.4	59.9	73.8	47.5	48.5	60.6	55.2	53.8
1980	63.8	77.4	51.5	56.7	64.1	61.7	61.0	59.2	72.0	47.7	46.6	60.0	53.6	52.3
1981	63.9	77.0	52.1	55.4	64.3	61.3	60.8	59.0	71.3	48.0	44.6	60.0	52.6	51.3
1982	64.0	76.6	52.6	54.1	64.3	61.6	61.0	57.8	69.0	47.7	41.5	58.8	50.9	49.4
1983	64.0	76.4	52.9	53.5	64.3	62.1	61.5	57.9	68.8	48.0	41.5	58.9	51.0	49.5
1984	64.4	76.4	53.6	53.9	64.6	62.6	62.2	59.5	70.7	49.5	43.7	60.5	53.6	52.3
1985	64.8	76.3	54.5	54.5	65.0	63.3	62.9	60.1	70.9	50.4	44.4	61.0	54.7	53.4
1986	65.3	76.3	55.3	54.7	65.5	63.7	63.3	60.7	71.0	51.4	44.6	61.5	55.4	54.1
1987	65.6	76.2	56.0	54.7	65.8	64.3	63.8	61.5	71.5	52.5	45.5	62.3	56.8	55.6
1988	65.9	76.2	56.6	55.3	66.2	64.0	63.8	62.3	72.0	53.4	46.8	63.1	57.4	56.3
1989	66.5	76.4	57.4	55.9	66.7	64.7	64.2	63.0	72.5	54.3	47.5	63.8	58.2	56.9
1990	66.5	76.4	57.5	53.7	66.9	64.4	64.0	62.8	72.0	54.3	45.3	63.7	57.9	56.7
1991	66.2	75.8	57.4	51.6	66.6	63.8	63.3	61.7	70.4	53.7	42.0	62.6	56.7	55.4
1992	66.4	75.8	57.8	51.3	66.8	64.6	63.9	61.5	69.8	53.8	41.0	62.4	56.4	54.9
1993	66.3	75.4	57.9	51.5	66.8	63.8	63.2	61.7	70.0	54.1	41.7	62.7	56.3	55.0
1994	66.6	75.1	58.8	52.7	67.1	63.9	63.4	62.5	70.4	55.3	43.4	63.5	57.2	56.1
1995	66.6	75.0	58.9	53.5	67.1	64.3	63.7	62.9	70.8	55.6	44.2	63.8	58.1	57.1
1996	66.8	74.9	59.3	52.3	67.2	64.6	64.1	63.2	70.9	56.0	43.5	64.1	58.6	57.4
1997	67.1	75.0	59.8	51.6	67.5	65.2	64.7	63.8	71.3	56.8	43.4	64.6	59.4	58.2
1998	67.1	74.9	59.8	52.8	67.3	66.0	65.6	64.1	71.6	57.1	45.1	64.7	60.9	59.7
1999	67.1	74.7	60.0	52.0	67.3		65.9	64.3	71.6	57.4	44.7	64.8	61.3	60.6
2000	67.1	74.8	59.9	52.0	67.3		65.8	64.4	71.9	57.5	45.2	64.9		60.9
2001	66.8	74.4	59.8	49.6	67.0		65.3	63.7	70.9	57.0	42.3	64.2		59.7
2002	66.6	74.1	59.6	47.4	66.8		64.8	62.7	69.7	56.3	39.6	63.4		58.1
2003	66.2	73.5	59.5	44.5	66.5		64.3	62.3	68.9	56.1	36.8	63.0		57.4
2004	66.0	73.3	59.2	43.9	66.3		63.8	62.3	69.2	56.0	36.4	63.1		57.2
2005	66.0	73.3	59.3	43.7	66.3		64.2	62.7	69.6	56.2	36.5	63.4		57.7
2006	66.2	73.5	59.4	43.7	66.5		64.1	63.1	70.1	56.6	36.9	63.8		58.4
2007	66.0	73.2	59.3	41.3	66.4		63.7	63.0	69.8	56.6	34.8	63.6		58.4
2007: Jan	66.3	73.6	59.5	42.6	66.6		64.7	63.3	70.1	56.8	36.2	63.9		59.5
Feb	66.2	73.5	59.3	42.1	66.4		64.2	63.2	70.0	56.8	35.8	63.8		59.1
Mar	66.2	73.4	59.4	41.5	66.5		63.7	63.3	70.1	56.9	35.4	64.0		58.4
Apr	66.0	73.3	59.0	41.5	66.2		63.8	63.0	70.0	56.5	35.1	63.6		58.6
May	66.0	73.3	59.2	41.0	66.2		63.5	63.0	69.9	56.6	34.5	63.7		58.1
June	66.1	73.2	59.3	41.8	66.4		63.6	63.0	69.8	56.7	35.2	63.7		58.2
July	66.0	73.2	59.3	41.2	66.3		64.0	63.0	69.7	56.6	34.9	63.6		58.8
Aug	65.8	72.9	59.4	39.7	66.1		63.6	62.8	69.5	56.5	33.2	63.3		58.7
Sept	66.0	73.1	59.4	41.2	66.4		63.4	62.9	69.5	56.7	34.6	63.6		58.2
Oct	65.9	73.0	59.2	41.2	66.3		63.1	62.7	69.4	56.5	34.7	63.5		57.7
Nov	66.0	73.2	59.3	40.9	66.4		63.1	63.0	69.7	56.6	34.2	63.6		57.8
Dec	66.0	73.1	59.4	41.0	66.3		63.3	62.7	69.3	56.5	34.0	63.4		57.6
2008: Jan	66.1	73.2	59.5	41.0	66.4		64.1	62.9	69.5	56.7	33.6	63.5		58.2
Feb	65.9	72.9	59.3	40.0	66.1		63.7	62.7	69.4	56.5	33.4	63.3		58.4
Mar	66.0	72.9	59.3	39.8	66.2		63.9	62.6	69.2	56.5	33.5	63.3		58.2
Apr	66.0	72.9	59.6	41.1	66.2		64.0	62.7	69.2	56.7	34.7	63.3		58.5
May	66.2	73.2	59.7	42.6	66.4		63.9	62.6	69.0	56.5	34.6	63.2		57.7
June	66.1	73.0	59.3	40.5	66.4		63.7	62.4	68.8	56.5	33.1	63.1		57.8
July	66.1	73.3	59.4	40.8	66.4		63.8	62.4	68.8	56.3	32.5	63.1		57.6
Aug	66.1	73.1	59.6	40.2	66.3		64.4	62.1	68.5	56.2	32.6	62.8		57.6
Sept	66.0	73.1	59.4	40.1	66.3		63.5	62.0	68.2	56.1	32.5	62.8		56.2
Oct	66.1	73.1	59.5	39.9	66.5		63.6	61.8	67.9	56.0	31.7	62.5		56.5
Nov	65.8	72.7	59.4	38.3	66.3		63.2	61.4	67.5	55.8	30.4	62.2		56.1

[1] Civilian labor force or civilian employment as percent of civilian noninstitutional population in group specified.
[2] See footnote 1, Table B–37.

Note.—Data relate to persons 16 years of age and over.
See footnote 5 and Note, Table B–35.

Source: Department of Labor (Bureau of Labor Statistics).

TABLE B–40.—*Civilian labor force participation rate by demographic characteristic, 1965–2008*

[Percent [1]; monthly data seasonally adjusted]

Year or month	All civilian workers	White [2] Total	White Males Total	White Males 16–19 years	White Males 20 years and over	White Females Total	White Females 16–19 years	White Females 20 years and over	Black and other or black or African American [2] Total	Males Total	Males 16–19 years	Males 20 years and over	Females Total	Females 16–19 years	Females 20 years and over
									Black and other [2]						
1965	58.9	58.4	80.8	54.1	83.9	38.1	39.2	38.0	62.9	79.6	51.3	83.7	48.6	29.5	51
1966	59.2	58.7	80.6	55.9	83.6	39.2	42.6	38.8	63.0	79.0	51.4	83.3	49.4	33.5	51
1967	59.6	59.2	80.6	56.3	83.5	40.1	42.5	39.8	62.8	78.5	51.1	82.9	49.5	35.2	51
1968	59.6	59.3	80.4	55.9	83.2	40.7	43.0	40.4	62.2	77.7	49.7	82.2	49.3	34.8	51
1969	60.1	59.9	80.2	56.8	83.0	41.8	44.6	41.5	62.1	76.9	49.6	81.4	49.8	34.6	52
1970	60.4	60.2	80.0	57.5	82.8	42.6	45.6	42.2	61.8	76.5	47.4	81.4	49.5	34.1	51
1971	60.2	60.1	79.6	57.9	82.3	42.6	45.4	42.3	60.9	74.9	44.7	80.0	49.2	31.2	51
1972	60.4	60.4	79.6	60.1	82.0	43.2	48.1	42.7	60.2	73.9	46.0	78.6	48.8	32.3	51
									Black or African American [2]						
1972	60.4	60.4	79.6	60.1	82.0	43.2	48.1	42.7	59.9	73.6	46.3	78.5	48.7	32.2	51
1973	60.8	60.8	79.4	62.0	81.6	44.1	50.1	43.5	60.2	73.4	45.7	78.4	49.3	34.2	51
1974	61.3	61.4	79.4	62.9	81.4	45.2	51.7	44.4	59.8	72.9	46.7	77.6	49.0	33.4	51
1975	61.2	61.5	78.7	61.9	80.7	45.9	51.5	45.3	58.8	70.9	42.6	76.0	48.8	34.2	51
1976	61.6	61.8	78.4	62.3	80.3	46.9	52.8	46.2	59.0	70.0	41.3	75.4	49.8	32.9	52
1977	62.3	62.5	78.5	64.0	80.2	48.0	54.5	47.3	59.8	70.6	43.2	75.6	50.8	32.9	53
1978	63.2	63.3	78.6	65.0	80.1	49.4	56.7	48.7	61.5	71.5	44.9	76.2	53.1	37.3	55
1979	63.7	63.9	78.6	64.8	80.1	50.5	57.4	49.8	61.4	71.3	43.6	76.3	53.1	36.8	55
1980	63.8	64.1	78.2	63.7	79.8	51.2	56.2	50.6	61.0	70.3	43.2	75.1	53.1	34.9	55
1981	63.9	64.3	77.9	62.4	79.5	51.9	55.4	51.5	60.8	70.0	41.6	74.5	53.5	34.0	56
1982	64.0	64.3	77.4	60.0	78.9	52.4	55.0	52.2	61.0	70.1	39.8	74.7	53.7	33.5	56
1983	64.0	64.3	77.1	59.4	78.9	52.7	54.5	52.5	61.5	70.6	39.9	75.2	54.2	33.0	56
1984	64.4	64.6	77.1	59.0	78.7	53.3	55.4	53.1	62.2	70.8	41.7	74.8	55.2	35.0	57
1985	64.8	65.0	77.0	59.7	78.5	54.1	55.2	54.0	62.9	70.8	44.6	74.4	56.5	37.9	58
1986	65.3	65.5	76.9	59.3	78.5	55.0	56.3	54.9	63.3	71.2	43.7	74.8	56.9	39.1	59
1987	65.6	65.8	76.8	59.0	78.4	55.7	56.5	55.6	63.8	71.1	43.6	74.7	58.0	39.6	60
1988	65.9	66.2	76.9	60.0	78.3	56.4	57.2	56.3	63.8	71.0	43.8	74.6	58.0	37.9	60
1989	66.5	66.7	77.1	61.0	78.5	57.2	57.1	57.2	64.2	71.0	44.6	74.4	58.7	40.4	60
1990	66.5	66.9	77.1	59.6	78.5	57.4	55.3	57.6	64.0	71.0	40.7	75.0	58.3	36.8	60
1991	66.2	66.6	76.5	57.3	78.0	57.4	54.1	57.6	63.3	70.4	37.3	74.6	57.5	33.5	60
1992	66.4	66.8	76.5	56.9	78.0	57.7	52.5	58.1	63.9	70.7	40.6	74.3	58.5	35.2	60
1993	66.3	66.8	76.2	56.6	77.7	58.0	53.5	58.3	63.2	69.6	39.5	73.2	57.9	34.6	60
1994	66.6	67.1	75.9	54.7	77.3	58.9	55.1	59.2	63.4	69.1	40.8	72.5	58.7	36.3	60
1995	66.6	67.1	75.7	58.5	77.1	59.0	55.5	59.2	63.7	69.0	40.1	72.5	59.5	39.8	61
1996	66.8	67.2	75.8	57.1	77.3	59.1	54.7	59.4	64.1	68.7	39.5	72.3	60.4	38.9	62
1997	67.1	67.5	75.9	56.1	77.5	59.5	54.1	59.9	64.7	68.3	37.4	72.2	61.7	39.9	64
1998	67.1	67.3	75.6	56.6	77.2	59.4	55.4	59.7	65.6	69.0	40.7	72.5	62.8	42.5	64
1999	67.1	67.3	75.6	56.4	77.2	59.6	54.5	59.9	65.8	68.7	38.6	72.4	63.5	38.8	66
2000	67.1	67.3	75.5	56.5	77.1	59.5	54.5	59.9	65.8	69.2	39.2	72.8	63.1	39.6	65
2001	66.8	67.0	75.1	53.7	76.9	59.4	52.4	59.9	65.3	68.4	37.9	72.1	62.8	37.3	65
2002	66.6	66.8	74.8	50.3	76.7	59.3	50.8	60.0	64.8	68.4	37.3	72.1	61.8	34.7	64
2003	66.2	66.5	74.2	47.5	76.3	59.2	47.9	59.9	64.3	67.3	31.1	71.5	61.9	33.7	64
2004	66.0	66.3	74.1	47.4	76.2	58.9	46.7	59.7	63.8	66.7	30.0	70.9	61.5	32.8	64
2005	66.0	66.3	74.1	46.2	76.2	58.9	47.6	59.7	64.2	67.3	32.6	71.3	61.6	32.2	64
2006	66.2	66.5	74.3	46.9	76.4	59.0	46.6	59.9	64.1	67.0	32.3	71.1	61.7	35.6	64
2007	66.0	66.4	74.0	44.3	76.3	59.0	44.6	60.1	63.7	66.8	29.4	71.2	61.1	31.2	64
2007: Jan	66.3	66.6	74.4	46.6	76.6	59.2	45.3	60.1	64.7	67.8	30.7	72.1	62.3	34.3	65
Feb	66.2	66.4	74.3	45.6	76.5	59.0	45.0	59.9	64.2	67.3	31.5	71.5	61.7	32.6	64
Mar	66.2	66.5	74.3	45.1	76.6	59.1	44.7	60.1	63.7	66.5	28.6	71.0	61.4	31.3	64
Apr	66.0	66.2	74.2	45.1	76.4	58.6	43.9	59.7	63.8	67.1	31.5	71.3	61.2	32.6	64
May	66.0	66.3	74.1	44.6	76.4	58.8	43.9	59.9	63.5	66.4	30.8	70.6	61.1	30.3	64
June	66.1	66.4	74.1	45.5	76.4	59.0	44.6	60.0	63.6	66.2	29.6	70.6	61.4	32.0	64
July	66.0	66.3	74.0	44.3	76.3	59.0	44.7	60.1	64.0	67.2	27.1	72.0	61.3	30.7	64
Aug	65.8	66.1	73.6	42.8	76.0	58.9	43.2	60.1	63.6	67.2	27.3	71.9	60.7	30.2	63
Sept	66.0	66.4	73.9	44.2	76.2	59.3	45.1	60.3	63.4	66.5	28.4	71.0	60.8	29.0	63
Oct	65.9	66.3	73.8	44.0	76.1	59.1	44.7	60.1	63.1	66.1	28.8	70.4	60.7	29.4	63
Nov	66.0	66.4	73.9	42.0	76.4	59.2	45.3	60.2	63.1	66.5	29.6	70.8	60.3	29.6	63
Dec	66.0	66.3	73.8	41.6	76.3	59.2	45.2	60.2	63.3	66.5	31.6	70.7	60.7	32.4	63
2008: Jan	66.1	66.4	73.9	41.9	76.4	59.2	45.2	60.2	64.1	67.7	37.4	71.3	61.1	28.7	64
Feb	65.9	66.1	73.7	41.9	76.1	58.9	43.8	60.0	63.7	66.9	28.6	71.5	61.1	32.9	63
Mar	66.0	66.2	73.7	41.8	76.2	59.1	43.7	60.2	63.9	66.3	25.3	71.2	61.9	31.9	64
Apr	66.0	66.2	73.6	43.8	75.9	59.1	44.6	60.1	64.0	66.4	25.7	71.3	62.0	32.0	6
May	66.2	66.4	74.0	46.5	76.1	59.2	44.8	60.3	63.9	66.5	29.8	70.8	61.7	31.9	6
June	66.1	66.4	73.7	44.0	76.1	59.3	43.8	60.4	63.7	66.9	27.8	71.5	61.1	28.0	6
July	66.1	66.4	74.1	44.5	76.4	59.1	43.5	60.2	63.8	66.8	29.2	71.3	61.3	30.7	6
Aug	66.1	66.4	73.9	43.2	76.2	59.2	42.7	60.4	64.4	67.6	31.1	71.9	61.8	32.7	6
Sept	66.0	66.3	73.8	42.9	76.2	59.1	42.7	60.3	63.5	66.9	30.3	71.2	60.7	30.2	6
Oct	66.1	66.5	73.9	42.9	76.3	59.4	42.8	60.6	63.6	66.8	32.7	70.9	60.9	27.6	6
Nov	65.8	66.3	73.7	42.2	76.1	59.2	41.3	60.4	63.2	65.7	24.9	70.5	61.2	26.4	6

[1] Civilian labor force as percent of civilian noninstitutional population in group specified.
[2] See footnote 1, Table B–37.

Note.—Data relate to persons 16 years of age and over.
See footnote 5 and Note, Table B–35.

Source: Department of Labor (Bureau of Labor Statistics).

TABLE B–41.—*Civilian employment/population ratio by demographic characteristic, 1965–2008*

[Percent [1]; monthly data seasonally adjusted]

Year or month	All civilian workers	White [2] Total	Males Total	Males 16–19 years	Males 20 years and over	Females Total	Females 16–19 years	Females 20 years and over	Black and other or black or African American [2] Total	Males Total	Males 16–19 years	Males 20 years and over	Females Total	Females 16–19 years	Females 20 years and over
									Black and other [2]						
965	56.2	56.0	77.9	47.1	81.5	36.2	33.7	36.5	57.8	73.7	39.4	78.7	44.1	20.2	47.3
966	56.9	56.8	78.3	50.1	81.7	37.5	37.5	37.5	58.4	74.0	40.5	79.2	45.1	23.1	48.2
967	57.3	57.2	78.4	50.2	81.7	38.3	37.7	38.3	58.2	73.8	38.8	79.4	45.0	24.8	47.9
968	57.5	57.4	78.3	50.3	81.6	38.9	37.8	39.1	58.0	73.3	38.7	78.9	45.2	24.7	48.2
969	58.0	58.0	78.2	51.1	81.4	40.1	39.5	40.1	58.1	72.8	39.0	78.4	45.9	25.1	48.9
970	57.4	57.5	76.8	49.6	80.1	40.3	39.5	40.4	56.8	70.9	35.5	76.8	44.9	22.4	48.2
971	56.6	56.8	75.7	49.2	79.0	39.9	38.6	40.1	54.9	68.1	31.8	74.2	43.9	20.2	47.3
972	57.0	57.4	76.0	51.5	79.0	40.7	41.3	40.6	54.1	67.3	32.4	73.2	43.3	19.9	46.7
									Black or African American [2]						
972	57.0	57.4	76.0	51.5	79.0	40.7	41.3	40.6	53.7	66.8	31.6	73.0	43.0	19.2	46.5
973	57.8	58.2	76.5	54.3	79.2	41.8	43.6	41.6	54.5	67.5	32.8	73.7	43.8	22.0	47.2
974	57.8	58.3	75.9	54.4	78.6	42.4	44.3	42.2	53.5	65.8	31.4	71.9	43.5	20.9	46.9
975	56.1	56.7	73.0	50.6	75.7	42.0	42.5	41.9	50.1	60.6	26.3	66.5	41.6	20.2	44.9
976	56.8	57.5	73.4	51.5	76.0	43.2	44.2	43.1	50.8	60.6	25.8	66.8	42.8	19.2	46.4
977	57.9	58.6	74.1	54.4	76.5	44.5	45.9	44.4	51.4	61.4	26.4	67.5	43.3	18.5	47.0
978	59.3	60.0	75.0	56.3	77.2	46.3	48.5	46.1	53.6	63.3	28.5	69.1	45.8	22.1	49.3
979	59.9	60.6	75.1	55.7	77.3	47.5	49.4	47.3	53.8	63.4	28.7	69.1	46.0	22.4	49.3
980	59.2	60.0	73.4	53.4	75.6	47.8	47.9	47.8	52.3	60.4	27.0	65.8	45.7	21.0	49.1
981	59.0	60.0	72.8	51.3	75.1	48.3	46.2	48.5	51.3	59.1	24.6	64.5	45.1	19.7	48.5
982	57.8	58.8	70.6	47.0	73.0	48.1	44.6	48.4	49.4	56.0	20.3	61.4	44.2	17.7	47.5
983	57.9	58.9	70.4	47.4	72.6	48.5	44.5	48.9	49.5	56.3	20.4	61.6	44.1	17.0	47.4
984	59.5	60.5	72.1	49.1	74.3	49.8	47.0	50.0	52.3	59.2	23.9	64.1	46.7	20.1	49.8
985	60.1	61.0	72.3	49.9	74.3	50.7	47.1	51.0	53.4	60.0	26.3	64.6	48.1	23.1	50.9
986	60.7	61.5	72.3	49.6	74.3	51.7	47.9	52.0	54.1	60.6	26.5	65.1	48.8	23.8	51.6
987	61.5	62.3	72.7	49.9	74.7	52.8	49.0	53.1	55.6	62.0	28.5	66.4	50.3	25.8	53.0
988	62.3	63.1	73.2	51.7	75.1	53.8	50.2	54.0	56.3	62.7	29.4	67.1	51.2	25.8	53.9
989	63.0	63.8	73.7	52.6	75.4	54.6	50.5	54.9	56.9	62.8	30.4	67.0	52.0	27.1	54.6
990	62.8	63.7	73.3	51.0	75.1	54.7	48.3	55.2	56.7	62.6	27.7	67.1	51.9	25.8	54.7
991	61.7	62.6	71.6	47.2	73.5	54.2	45.9	54.8	55.4	61.3	23.8	65.9	50.6	21.5	53.6
992	61.5	62.4	71.1	46.4	73.1	54.2	44.2	54.9	54.9	59.9	23.6	64.3	50.8	22.1	53.6
993	61.7	62.7	71.4	46.6	73.3	54.6	45.7	55.2	55.0	60.0	23.6	64.3	50.9	21.6	53.8
994	62.5	63.5	71.8	48.3	73.6	55.8	47.5	56.4	56.1	60.8	25.4	65.0	52.3	24.5	55.0
995	62.9	63.8	72.0	49.4	73.8	56.1	48.1	56.7	57.1	61.7	25.2	66.1	53.4	26.1	56.1
996	63.2	64.1	72.3	48.2	74.2	56.3	47.6	57.0	57.4	61.1	24.9	65.5	54.4	27.1	57.1
997	63.8	64.6	72.7	48.1	74.7	57.0	47.2	57.8	58.2	61.4	23.7	66.1	55.6	28.5	58.4
998	64.1	64.7	72.7	48.6	74.7	57.1	49.3	57.7	59.7	62.9	28.4	67.1	57.2	31.8	59.7
999	64.3	64.8	72.8	49.3	74.8	57.3	48.3	58.0	60.6	63.1	26.7	67.5	58.6	29.0	61.5
000	64.4	64.9	73.0	49.5	74.9	57.4	48.8	58.0	60.9	63.6	28.9	67.7	58.6	30.6	61.3
001	63.7	64.2	72.0	46.2	74.0	57.0	46.5	57.7	59.7	62.1	26.4	66.3	57.8	27.0	60.7
002	62.7	63.4	70.8	42.3	73.1	56.4	44.1	57.3	58.1	61.1	25.6	65.2	55.8	24.9	58.7
003	62.3	63.0	70.1	39.4	72.5	56.3	41.5	57.3	57.4	59.5	19.9	64.1	55.6	23.4	58.6
004	62.3	63.1	70.4	39.7	72.8	56.1	40.3	57.2	57.2	59.3	19.3	63.9	55.5	23.6	58.5
005	62.7	63.4	70.8	38.8	73.3	56.3	41.8	57.4	57.7	60.2	20.8	64.7	55.7	22.4	58.9
006	63.1	63.8	71.3	40.0	73.7	56.6	41.1	57.7	58.4	60.6	21.7	65.2	56.5	26.4	59.4
007	63.0	63.6	70.9	37.3	73.5	56.7	39.2	57.9	58.4	60.7	19.5	65.5	56.5	23.3	59.8
007: Jan	63.3	63.9	71.3	40.0	73.7	56.8	39.8	58.0	59.5	61.8	20.1	66.7	57.7	25.9	60.7
Feb	63.2	63.8	71.2	39.0	73.7	56.7	39.7	57.9	59.1	61.3	20.3	66.1	57.3	25.4	60.4
Mar	63.3	64.0	71.4	38.5	74.0	56.8	39.4	58.1	58.4	60.1	21.3	64.7	57.1	23.8	60.3
Apr	63.0	63.6	71.2	38.6	73.7	56.4	38.6	57.6	58.6	60.6	20.7	65.4	56.9	23.7	60.2
May	63.0	63.7	71.1	37.9	73.7	56.5	38.4	57.8	58.1	60.1	19.9	64.8	56.5	22.8	59.8
June	63.0	63.7	71.0	38.1	73.6	56.7	39.3	57.9	58.2	60.0	19.7	64.7	56.8	22.8	60.1
July	63.0	63.6	70.8	37.5	73.4	56.6	39.3	57.9	58.8	61.5	18.7	66.5	56.6	23.5	59.8
Aug	62.8	63.3	70.4	35.7	73.1	56.5	37.9	57.8	58.7	61.9	18.2	67.0	56.2	21.3	59.6
Sept	62.9	63.6	70.6	37.0	73.2	56.9	39.6	58.1	58.2	60.7	18.8	65.7	56.1	22.0	59.4
Oct	62.7	63.5	70.6	37.0	73.2	56.7	39.3	57.9	57.7	59.8	18.5	64.7	56.0	23.5	59.2
Nov	63.0	63.6	70.8	34.5	73.6	56.8	40.0	58.0	57.8	60.4	19.3	65.3	55.6	22.2	58.8
Dec	62.7	63.4	70.5	34.6	73.3	56.6	39.7	57.8	57.6	59.9	19.1	64.7	55.7	22.6	59.0
008: Jan	62.9	63.5	70.6	33.9	73.5	56.7	39.6	57.9	58.2	60.8	22.0	65.4	56.1	20.5	59.6
Feb	62.7	63.3	70.4	34.7	73.2	56.4	38.6	57.7	58.4	60.9	19.3	65.8	56.4	22.8	59.6
Mar	62.6	63.3	70.4	35.7	73.1	56.5	38.6	57.7	58.2	59.9	15.5	65.2	56.7	23.8	59.9
Apr	62.7	63.3	70.2	37.1	72.8	56.6	39.1	57.8	58.5	60.3	18.5	65.3	57.0	25.0	60.1
May	62.6	63.2	70.3	38.3	72.7	56.5	38.1	57.8	57.7	59.6	17.8	64.5	56.2	23.9	59.3
June	62.4	63.1	70.0	36.1	72.6	56.5	37.1	57.9	57.8	59.9	17.9	64.9	56.1	21.3	59.5
July	62.4	63.1	70.1	34.6	72.8	56.3	36.7	57.7	57.6	59.3	18.1	64.2	56.2	22.6	59.5
Aug	62.1	62.8	69.8	34.9	72.5	56.2	36.3	57.6	57.6	60.0	22.0	64.5	55.6	23.4	58.8
Sept	62.0	62.8	69.5	34.6	72.2	56.3	36.2	57.8	56.2	58.3	20.4	62.8	54.6	22.3	57.7
Oct	61.8	62.5	69.1	33.3	71.9	56.2	36.7	57.6	56.5	58.2	20.6	62.6	55.1	20.1	58.5
Nov	61.4	62.2	68.8	33.1	71.5	55.9	35.0	57.4	56.1	57.1	14.4	62.1	55.3	20.3	58.7

[1] Civilian employment as percent of civilian noninstitutional population in group specified.
[2] See footnote 1, Table B–37.

Note.—Data relate to persons 16 years of age and over.
See footnote 5 and Note, Table B–35.

Source: Department of Labor (Bureau of Labor Statistics).

TABLE B–42.—*Civilian unemployment rate, 1960–2008*

[Percent [1]; monthly data seasonally adjusted, except as noted]

Year or month	All civilian workers	Males Total	Males 16–19 years	Males 20 years and over	Females Total	Females 16–19 years	Females 20 years and over	Both sexes 16–19 years	White [2]	Black and other [2]	Black or African American [2]	Asian (NSA) [2,3]	Hispanic or Latino ethnicity [4]	Married men, spouse present	Women who maintain families (NSA)
1960	5.5	5.4	15.3	4.7	5.9	13.9	5.1	14.7	5.0	10.2				3.7	
1961	6.7	6.4	17.1	5.7	7.2	16.3	6.3	16.8	6.0	12.4				4.6	
1962	5.5	5.2	14.7	4.6	6.2	14.6	5.4	14.7	4.9	10.9				3.6	
1963	5.7	5.2	17.2	4.5	6.5	17.2	5.4	17.2	5.0	10.8				3.4	
1964	5.2	4.6	15.8	3.9	6.2	16.6	5.2	16.2	4.6	9.6				2.8	
1965	4.5	4.0	14.1	3.2	5.5	15.7	4.5	14.8	4.1	8.1				2.4	
1966	3.8	3.2	11.7	2.5	4.8	14.1	3.8	12.8	3.4	7.3				1.9	
1967	3.8	3.1	12.3	2.3	5.2	13.5	4.2	12.9	3.4	7.4				1.8	
1968	3.6	2.9	11.6	2.2	4.8	14.0	3.8	12.7	3.2	6.7				1.6	
1969	3.5	2.8	11.4	2.1	4.7	13.3	3.7	12.2	3.1	6.4				1.5	
1970	4.9	4.4	15.0	3.5	5.9	15.6	4.8	15.3	4.5	8.2				2.6	
1971	5.9	5.3	16.6	4.4	6.9	17.2	5.7	16.9	5.4	9.9				3.2	
1972	5.6	5.0	15.9	4.0	6.6	16.7	5.4	16.2	5.1	10.0	10.4			2.8	
1973	4.9	4.2	13.9	3.3	6.0	15.3	4.9	14.5	4.3	9.0	9.4		7.5	2.3	
1974	5.6	4.9	15.6	3.8	6.7	16.6	5.5	16.0	5.0	9.9	10.5		8.1	2.7	
1975	8.5	7.9	20.1	6.8	9.3	19.7	8.0	19.9	7.8	13.8	14.8		12.2	5.1	
1976	7.7	7.1	19.2	5.9	8.6	18.7	7.4	19.0	7.0	13.1	14.0		11.5	4.2	
1977	7.1	6.3	17.3	5.2	8.2	18.3	7.0	17.8	6.2	13.1	14.0		10.1	3.6	
1978	6.1	5.3	15.8	4.3	7.2	17.1	6.0	16.4	5.2	11.9	12.8		9.1	2.8	
1979	5.8	5.1	15.9	4.2	6.8	16.4	5.7	16.1	5.1	11.3	12.3		8.3	2.8	
1980	7.1	6.9	18.3	5.9	7.4	17.2	6.4	17.8	6.3	13.1	14.3		10.1	4.2	
1981	7.6	7.4	20.1	6.3	7.9	19.0	6.8	19.6	6.7	14.2	15.6		10.4	4.3	
1982	9.7	9.9	24.4	8.8	9.4	21.9	8.3	23.2	8.6	17.3	18.9		13.8	6.5	
1983	9.6	9.9	23.3	8.9	9.2	21.3	8.1	22.4	8.4	17.8	19.5		13.7	6.5	
1984	7.5	7.4	19.6	6.6	7.6	18.0	6.8	18.9	6.5	14.4	15.9		10.7	4.6	
1985	7.2	7.0	19.5	6.2	7.4	17.6	6.6	18.6	6.2	13.7	15.1		10.5	4.3	
1986	7.0	6.9	19.0	6.1	7.1	17.6	6.2	18.3	6.0	13.1	14.5		10.6	4.4	
1987	6.2	6.2	17.8	5.4	6.2	15.9	5.4	16.9	5.3	11.6	13.0		8.8	3.9	
1988	5.5	5.5	16.0	4.8	5.6	14.4	4.9	15.3	4.7	10.4	11.7		8.2	3.3	
1989	5.3	5.2	15.9	4.5	5.4	14.0	4.7	15.0	4.5	10.0	11.4		8.0	3.0	
1990	5.6	5.7	16.3	5.0	5.5	14.7	4.9	15.5	4.8	10.1	11.4		8.2	3.4	
1991	6.8	7.2	19.8	6.4	6.4	17.5	5.7	18.7	6.1	11.1	12.5		10.0	4.4	
1992	7.5	7.9	21.5	7.1	7.0	18.6	6.3	20.1	6.6	12.7	14.2		11.6	5.1	
1993	6.9	7.2	20.4	6.4	6.6	17.5	5.9	19.0	6.1	11.7	13.0		10.8	4.4	
1994	6.1	6.2	19.0	5.4	6.0	16.2	5.4	17.6	5.3	10.5	11.5		9.9	3.7	
1995	5.6	5.6	18.4	4.8	5.6	16.1	4.9	17.3	4.9	9.6	10.4		9.3	3.3	
1996	5.4	5.4	18.1	4.6	5.4	15.2	4.8	16.7	4.7	9.3	10.5		8.9	3.0	
1997	4.9	4.9	16.9	4.2	5.0	15.0	4.4	16.0	4.2	8.8	10.0		7.7	2.7	
1998	4.5	4.4	16.2	3.7	4.6	12.9	4.1	14.6	3.9	7.8	8.9		7.2	2.4	
1999	4.2	4.1	14.7	3.5	4.3	13.2	3.8	13.9	3.7	7.0	8.0		6.4	2.2	
2000	4.0	3.9	14.0	3.3	4.1	12.1	3.6	13.1	3.5		7.6	3.6	5.7	2.0	
2001	4.7	4.8	16.0	4.2	4.7	13.4	4.1	14.7	4.2		8.6	4.5	6.6	2.7	
2002	5.8	5.9	18.1	5.3	5.6	14.9	5.1	16.5	5.1		10.2	5.9	7.5	3.6	
2003	6.0	6.3	19.3	5.6	5.7	15.6	5.1	17.5	5.2		10.8	6.0	7.7	3.8	
2004	5.5	5.6	18.4	5.0	5.4	15.5	4.9	17.0	4.8		10.4	4.4	7.0	3.1	
2005	5.1	5.1	18.6	4.4	5.1	14.5	4.6	16.6	4.4		10.0	4.0	6.0	2.8	
2006	4.6	4.6	16.9	4.0	4.6	13.8	4.1	15.4	4.0		8.9	3.0	5.2	2.4	
2007	4.6	4.7	17.6	4.1	4.5	13.8	4.0	15.7	4.1		8.3	3.2	5.6	2.5	
2007: Jan	4.6	4.7	16.2	4.1	4.5	13.7	4.1	15.0	4.1		8.0	3.2	5.7	2.5	
Feb	4.5	4.7	16.6	4.1	4.3	13.2	3.8	15.0	4.0		8.0	2.7	5.2	2.6	
Mar	4.4	4.5	16.1	4.0	4.3	13.1	3.8	14.6	3.8		8.3	3.0	5.2	2.5	
Apr	4.5	4.6	16.5	4.0	4.4	14.2	3.9	15.4	4.0		8.2	3.3	5.5	2.5	
May	4.5	4.6	17.5	4.0	4.4	14.1	3.9	15.8	4.0		8.4	2.9	5.8	2.6	
June	4.6	4.7	18.0	4.1	4.4	13.9	3.9	16.0	4.1		8.4	3.1	5.7	2.4	
July	4.7	4.7	16.9	4.2	4.6	13.6	4.1	15.3	4.2		8.1	3.0	5.9	2.7	
Aug	4.7	4.7	18.0	4.1	4.6	14.4	4.1	16.2	4.2		7.7	3.4	5.5	2.5	
Sept	4.7	4.9	18.3	4.3	4.5	13.7	4.1	16.0	4.2		8.2	3.2	5.7	2.5	
Oct	4.8	4.9	18.1	4.3	4.6	13.3	4.1	15.7	4.2		8.5	3.7	5.6	2.6	
Nov	4.7	4.7	19.5	4.1	4.6	13.4	4.1	16.4	4.2		8.4	3.6	5.7	2.6	
Dec	5.0	5.1	19.8	4.4	4.9	14.4	4.4	17.1	4.4		9.0	3.7	6.3	2.7	
2008: Jan	4.9	5.1	21.8	4.4	4.7	14.2	4.2	18.0	4.4		9.2	3.2	6.3	2.7	
Feb	4.8	4.9	18.7	4.3	4.7	14.5	4.2	16.6	4.3		8.3	3.0	6.2	2.7	
Mar	5.1	5.2	17.8	4.6	5.0	13.8	4.6	15.8	4.5		9.0	3.6	6.9	2.8	
Apr	5.0	5.1	16.9	4.6	4.8	14.0	4.3	15.4	4.4		8.6	3.2	6.9	2.8	
May	5.5	5.6	20.7	4.9	5.3	16.6	4.8	18.7	4.9		9.7	3.8	6.9	2.9	
June	5.5	5.7	19.9	5.1	5.2	16.3	4.7	18.1	4.9		9.2	4.5	7.7	3.0	
July	5.7	6.1	23.4	5.3	5.2	17.1	4.6	20.3	5.1		9.7	4.0	7.4	3.2	
Aug	6.1	6.3	20.7	5.6	5.8	17.1	5.3	18.9	5.4		10.6	4.4	8.0	3.5	
Sept	6.1	6.7	21.0	6.1	5.5	17.1	4.9	19.1	5.4		11.4	3.8	7.8	3.8	
Oct	6.5	7.1	24.5	6.3	5.8	16.3	5.3	20.6	5.9		11.1	3.8	8.8	4.1	
Nov	6.7	7.2	24.1	6.5	6.0	16.6	5.5	20.4	6.1		11.2	4.8	8.6	4.1	

[1] Unemployed as percent of civilian labor force in group specified.
[2] See footnote 1, Table B–37.
[3] Not seasonally adjusted (NSA).
[4] Persons whose ethnicity is identified as Hispanic or Latino may be of any race.

Note.—Data relate to persons 16 years of age and over.
See footnote 5 and Note, Table B–35.

Source: Department of Labor (Bureau of Labor Statistics).

TABLE B–43.—*Civilian unemployment rate by demographic characteristic, 1965–2008*

[Percent [1]; monthly data seasonally adjusted]

Year or month	All civilian workers	White [2] Total	White Males Total	White Males 16–19 years	White Males 20 years and over	White Females Total	White Females 16–19 years	White Females 20 years and over	Black and other or black or African American [2] Total	Males Total	Males 16–19 years	Males 20 years and over	Females Total	Females 16–19 years	Females 20 years and over
									Black and other [2]						
1965	4.5	4.1	3.6	12.9	2.9	5.0	14.0	4.0	8.1	7.4	23.3	6.0	9.2	31.7	7.5
1966	3.8	3.4	2.8	10.5	2.2	4.3	12.1	3.3	7.3	6.3	21.3	4.9	8.7	31.3	6.6
1967	3.8	3.4	2.7	10.7	2.1	4.6	11.5	3.8	7.4	6.0	23.9	4.3	9.1	29.6	7.1
1968	3.6	3.2	2.6	10.1	2.0	4.3	12.1	3.4	6.7	5.6	22.1	3.9	8.3	28.7	6.3
1969	3.5	3.1	2.5	10.0	1.9	4.2	11.5	3.4	6.4	5.3	21.4	3.7	7.8	27.6	5.8
1970	4.9	4.5	4.0	13.7	3.2	5.4	13.4	4.4	8.2	7.3	25.0	5.6	9.3	34.5	6.9
1971	5.9	5.4	4.9	15.1	4.0	6.3	15.1	5.3	9.9	9.1	28.8	7.3	10.9	35.4	8.7
1972	5.6	5.1	4.5	14.2	3.6	5.9	14.2	4.9	10.0	8.9	29.7	6.9	11.4	38.4	8.8
									Black or African American [2]						
1972	5.6	5.1	4.5	14.2	3.6	5.9	14.2	4.9	10.4	9.3	31.7	7.0	11.8	40.5	9.0
1973	4.9	4.3	3.8	12.3	3.0	5.3	13.0	4.3	9.4	8.0	27.8	6.0	11.1	36.1	8.6
1974	5.6	5.0	4.4	13.5	3.5	6.1	14.5	5.1	10.5	9.8	33.1	7.4	11.3	37.4	8.8
1975	8.5	7.8	7.2	18.3	6.2	8.6	17.4	7.5	14.8	14.8	38.1	12.5	14.8	41.0	12.2
1976	7.7	7.0	6.4	17.3	5.4	7.9	16.4	6.8	14.0	13.7	37.5	11.4	14.3	41.6	11.7
1977	7.1	6.2	5.5	15.0	4.7	7.3	15.9	6.2	14.0	13.3	39.2	10.7	14.9	43.4	12.3
1978	6.1	5.2	4.6	13.5	3.7	6.2	14.4	5.2	12.8	11.8	36.7	9.3	13.8	40.8	11.2
1979	5.8	5.1	4.5	13.9	3.6	5.9	14.0	5.0	12.3	11.4	34.2	9.3	13.3	39.1	10.9
1980	7.1	6.3	6.1	16.2	5.3	6.5	14.8	5.6	14.3	14.5	37.5	12.4	14.0	39.8	11.9
1981	7.6	6.7	6.5	17.9	5.6	6.9	16.6	5.9	15.6	15.7	40.7	13.5	15.6	42.2	13.4
1982	9.7	8.6	8.8	21.7	7.8	8.3	19.0	7.3	18.9	20.1	48.9	17.8	17.6	47.1	15.4
1983	9.6	8.4	8.8	20.2	7.9	7.9	18.3	6.9	19.5	20.3	48.8	18.1	18.6	48.2	16.5
1984	7.5	6.5	6.4	16.8	5.7	6.5	15.2	5.8	15.9	16.4	42.7	14.3	15.4	42.6	13.5
1985	7.2	6.2	6.1	16.5	5.4	6.4	14.8	5.7	15.1	15.3	41.0	13.2	14.9	39.2	13.1
1986	7.0	6.0	6.0	16.3	5.3	6.1	14.9	5.4	14.5	14.8	39.3	12.9	14.2	39.2	12.4
1987	6.2	5.3	5.4	15.5	4.8	5.2	13.4	4.6	13.0	12.7	34.4	11.1	13.2	34.9	11.6
1988	5.5	4.7	4.7	13.9	4.1	4.7	12.3	4.1	11.7	11.7	32.7	10.1	11.7	32.0	10.4
1989	5.3	4.5	4.5	13.7	3.9	4.5	11.5	4.0	11.4	11.5	31.9	10.0	11.4	33.0	9.8
1990	5.6	4.8	4.9	14.3	4.3	4.7	12.6	4.1	11.4	11.9	31.9	10.4	10.9	29.9	9.7
1991	6.8	6.1	6.5	17.6	5.8	5.6	15.2	5.0	12.5	13.0	36.3	11.5	12.0	36.0	10.6
1992	7.5	6.6	7.0	18.5	6.4	6.1	15.8	5.5	14.2	15.2	42.0	13.5	13.2	37.2	11.8
1993	6.9	6.1	6.3	17.7	5.7	5.7	14.7	5.2	13.0	13.8	40.1	12.1	12.1	37.4	10.7
1994	6.1	5.3	5.4	16.3	4.8	5.2	13.8	4.6	11.5	12.0	37.6	10.3	11.0	32.6	9.8
1995	5.6	4.9	4.9	15.6	4.3	4.8	13.4	4.3	10.4	10.6	37.1	8.8	10.2	34.3	8.6
1996	5.4	4.7	4.7	15.5	4.1	4.7	12.9	4.1	10.5	11.1	36.9	9.4	10.0	30.3	8.7
1997	4.9	4.2	4.2	14.3	3.6	4.2	12.8	3.7	10.0	10.2	36.5	8.5	9.9	28.7	8.8
1998	4.5	3.9	3.9	14.1	3.2	3.9	10.9	3.4	8.9	8.9	30.1	7.4	9.0	25.3	7.9
1999	4.2	3.7	3.6	12.6	3.0	3.8	11.3	3.3	8.0	8.2	30.9	6.7	7.8	25.1	6.8
2000	4.0	3.5	3.4	12.3	2.8	3.6	10.4	3.1	7.6	8.0	26.2	6.9	7.1	22.8	6.2
2001	4.7	4.2	4.2	13.9	3.7	4.1	11.4	3.6	8.6	9.3	30.4	8.0	8.1	27.5	7.0
2002	5.8	5.1	5.3	15.9	4.7	4.9	13.1	4.4	10.2	10.7	31.3	9.5	9.8	28.3	8.8
2003	6.0	5.2	5.6	17.1	5.0	4.8	13.3	4.4	10.8	11.6	36.0	10.3	10.2	30.3	9.2
2004	5.5	4.8	5.0	16.3	4.4	4.7	13.6	4.2	10.4	11.1	35.6	9.9	9.8	28.2	8.9
2005	5.1	4.4	4.4	16.1	3.8	4.4	12.3	3.9	10.0	10.5	36.3	9.2	9.5	30.3	8.5
2006	4.6	4.0	4.0	14.6	3.5	4.0	11.7	3.6	8.9	9.5	32.7	8.3	8.4	25.9	7.5
2007	4.6	4.1	4.2	15.7	3.7	4.0	12.1	3.6	8.3	9.1	33.8	7.9	7.5	25.3	6.7
07: Jan	4.6	4.1	4.2	14.2	3.7	4.0	12.2	3.6	8.0	8.8	34.3	7.5	7.4	24.3	6.5
Feb	4.5	4.0	4.2	14.4	3.7	3.8	11.8	3.4	8.0	8.9	35.5	7.5	7.1	22.3	6.4
Mar	4.4	3.8	3.9	14.6	3.4	3.8	11.8	3.4	8.3	9.7	25.7	8.9	7.0	23.8	6.2
Apr	4.5	4.0	4.0	14.4	3.5	3.9	12.1	3.5	8.2	9.6	34.3	8.3	7.0	27.1	6.0
May	4.5	4.0	4.0	15.2	3.5	3.9	12.5	3.4	8.4	9.5	35.4	8.2	7.5	24.8	6.7
June	4.6	4.1	4.2	16.3	3.6	4.0	12.0	3.5	8.4	9.5	33.5	8.3	7.5	28.7	6.4
July	4.7	4.2	4.3	15.5	3.8	4.1	12.0	3.6	8.1	8.6	31.1	7.6	7.6	23.5	6.9
Aug	4.7	4.2	4.3	16.5	3.8	4.1	12.2	3.7	7.7	7.9	33.2	6.8	7.5	29.4	6.5
Sept	4.7	4.2	4.5	16.4	3.9	4.0	12.2	3.5	8.2	8.7	33.9	7.5	7.8	24.2	7.1
Oct	4.8	4.2	4.3	15.9	3.8	4.1	12.0	3.6	8.5	9.4	36.0	8.2	7.7	20.1	7.1
Nov	4.7	4.2	4.3	17.8	3.7	4.1	11.8	3.7	8.4	9.1	34.6	7.9	7.8	24.9	7.0
Dec	5.0	4.4	4.5	16.8	3.9	4.4	12.1	4.0	9.0	10.0	39.5	8.4	8.1	30.1	7.0
08: Jan	4.9	4.4	4.5	19.0	3.9	4.2	12.3	3.8	9.2	10.2	41.3	8.3	8.2	28.5	7.3
Feb	4.8	4.3	4.4	17.1	3.9	4.2	11.8	3.8	8.3	9.0	32.6	7.9	7.7	30.9	6.5
Mar	5.1	4.5	4.5	14.7	4.1	4.4	11.7	4.1	9.0	9.6	38.9	8.4	8.4	25.4	7.5
Apr	5.0	4.4	4.6	15.2	4.1	4.2	12.4	3.7	8.6	9.2	27.9	8.4	8.0	21.9	7.4
May	5.5	4.9	5.0	17.7	4.4	4.6	14.9	4.1	9.7	10.4	40.1	8.9	9.0	25.2	8.2
June	5.5	4.9	5.1	17.8	4.5	4.7	15.3	4.2	9.2	10.4	35.5	9.3	8.1	23.9	7.4
July	5.7	5.1	5.5	22.2	4.7	4.7	15.6	4.1	9.7	11.3	38.0	10.0	8.3	26.5	7.5
Aug	6.1	5.4	5.5	19.2	4.9	5.2	15.0	4.7	10.6	11.2	29.2	10.3	10.0	28.3	9.1
Sept	6.1	5.4	5.9	19.4	5.3	4.7	15.2	4.2	11.4	12.9	32.6	11.9	10.1	26.3	9.3
Oct	6.5	5.9	6.4	22.4	5.7	5.4	14.4	4.9	11.1	12.9	36.8	11.6	9.6	27.3	8.8
Nov	6.7	6.1	6.6	21.5	6.0	5.5	15.2	5.0	11.2	13.2	42.1	11.9	9.6	23.2	9.0

[1] Unemployed as percent of civilian labor force in group specified.
[2] See footnote 1, Table B–37.

Note.—Data relate to persons 16 years of age and over.
See footnote 5 and Note, Table B–35.

Source: Department of Labor (Bureau of Labor Statistics).

TABLE B–44.—*Unemployment by duration and reason, 1960–2008*

[Thousands of persons, except as noted; monthly data seasonally adjusted [1]]

Year or month	Un-employ-ment	Duration of unemployment						Reason for unemployment					
		Less than 5 weeks	5–14 weeks	15–26 weeks	27 weeks and over	Average (mean) duration (weeks)	Median duration (weeks)	Job losers [3]			Job leavers	Re-entrants	New entrants
								Total	On layoff	Other			
1960	3,852	1,719	1,176	503	454	12.8	....	....	....	....	....	....	....
1961	4,714	1,806	1,376	728	804	15.6	....	....	....	....	....	....	....
1962	3,911	1,663	1,134	534	585	14.7	....	....	....	....	....	....	....
1963	4,070	1,751	1,231	535	553	14.0	....	....	....	....	....	....	....
1964	3,786	1,697	1,117	491	482	13.3	....	....	....	....	....	....	....
1965	3,366	1,628	983	404	351	11.8	....	....	....	....	....	....	....
1966	2,875	1,573	779	287	239	10.4	....	....	....	....	....	....	....
1967 [2]	2,975	1,634	893	271	177	8.7	2.3	1,229	394	836	438	945	396
1968	2,817	1,594	810	256	156	8.4	4.5	1,070	334	736	431	909	407
1969	2,832	1,629	827	242	133	7.8	4.4	1,017	339	678	436	965	413
1970	4,093	2,139	1,290	428	235	8.6	4.9	1,811	675	1,137	550	1,228	504
1971	5,016	2,245	1,585	668	519	11.3	6.3	2,323	735	1,588	590	1,472	630
1972	4,882	2,242	1,472	601	566	12.0	6.2	2,108	582	1,526	641	1,456	677
1973	4,365	2,224	1,314	483	343	10.0	5.2	1,694	472	1,221	683	1,340	649
1974	5,156	2,604	1,597	574	381	9.8	5.2	2,242	746	1,495	768	1,463	681
1975	7,929	2,940	2,484	1,303	1,203	14.2	8.4	4,386	1,671	2,714	827	1,892	823
1976	7,406	2,844	2,196	1,018	1,348	15.8	8.2	3,679	1,050	2,628	903	1,928	895
1977	6,991	2,919	2,132	913	1,028	14.3	7.0	3,166	865	2,300	909	1,963	953
1978	6,202	2,865	1,923	766	648	11.9	5.9	2,585	712	1,873	874	1,857	885
1979	6,137	2,950	1,946	706	535	10.8	5.4	2,635	851	1,784	880	1,806	817
1980	7,637	3,295	2,470	1,052	820	11.9	6.5	3,947	1,488	2,459	891	1,927	872
1981	8,273	3,449	2,539	1,122	1,162	13.7	6.9	4,267	1,430	2,837	923	2,102	981
1982	10,678	3,883	3,311	1,708	1,776	15.6	8.7	6,268	2,127	4,141	840	2,384	1,185
1983	10,717	3,570	2,937	1,652	2,559	20.0	10.1	6,258	1,780	4,478	830	2,412	1,216
1984	8,539	3,350	2,451	1,104	1,634	18.2	7.9	4,421	1,171	3,250	823	2,184	1,110
1985	8,312	3,498	2,509	1,025	1,280	15.6	6.8	4,139	1,157	2,982	877	2,256	1,039
1986	8,237	3,448	2,557	1,045	1,187	15.0	6.9	4,033	1,090	2,943	1,015	2,160	1,029
1987	7,425	3,246	2,196	943	1,040	14.5	6.5	3,566	943	2,623	965	1,974	920
1988	6,701	3,084	2,007	801	809	13.5	5.9	3,092	851	2,241	983	1,809	816
1989	6,528	3,174	1,978	730	646	11.9	4.8	2,983	850	2,133	1,024	1,843	677
1990	7,047	3,265	2,257	822	703	12.0	5.3	3,387	1,028	2,359	1,041	1,930	688
1991	8,628	3,480	2,791	1,246	1,111	13.7	6.8	4,694	1,292	3,402	1,004	2,139	792
1992	9,613	3,376	2,830	1,453	1,954	17.7	8.7	5,389	1,260	4,129	1,002	2,285	937
1993	8,940	3,262	2,584	1,297	1,798	18.0	8.3	4,848	1,115	3,733	976	2,198	919
1994	7,996	2,728	2,408	1,237	1,623	18.8	9.2	3,815	977	2,838	791	2,786	604
1995	7,404	2,700	2,342	1,085	1,278	16.6	8.3	3,476	1,030	2,446	824	2,525	579
1996	7,236	2,633	2,287	1,053	1,262	16.7	8.3	3,370	1,021	2,349	774	2,512	580
1997	6,739	2,538	2,138	995	1,067	15.8	8.0	3,037	931	2,106	795	2,338	569
1998	6,210	2,622	1,950	763	875	14.5	6.7	2,822	866	1,957	734	2,132	520
1999	5,880	2,568	1,832	755	725	13.4	6.4	2,622	848	1,774	783	2,005	469
2000	5,692	2,558	1,815	669	649	12.6	5.9	2,517	852	1,664	780	1,961	433
2001	6,801	2,853	2,196	951	801	13.1	6.8	3,476	1,067	2,409	835	2,031	459
2002	8,378	2,893	2,580	1,369	1,535	16.6	9.1	4,607	1,124	3,483	866	2,368	537
2003	8,774	2,785	2,612	1,442	1,936	19.2	10.1	4,838	1,121	3,717	818	2,477	641
2004	8,149	2,696	2,382	1,293	1,779	19.6	9.8	4,197	998	3,199	858	2,408	686
2005	7,591	2,667	2,304	1,130	1,490	18.4	8.9	3,667	933	2,734	872	2,386	666
2006	7,001	2,614	2,121	1,031	1,235	16.8	8.3	3,321	921	2,400	827	2,237	617
2007	7,078	2,542	2,232	1,061	1,243	16.8	8.5	3,515	976	2,539	793	2,142	627
2007: Jan	7,043	2,596	2,298	995	1,138	16.5	8.2	3,399	1,017	2,382	791	2,195	61
Feb	6,837	2,567	2,181	935	1,216	16.6	8.2	3,449	1,016	2,433	810	2,029	58
Mar	6,738	2,338	2,156	976	1,207	17.2	8.6	3,240	865	2,375	755	2,143	60
Apr	6,829	2,442	2,147	1,066	1,193	17.0	8.6	3,316	1,019	2,297	749	2,169	59
May	6,863	2,467	2,187	1,099	1,137	16.6	8.3	3,375	997	2,379	768	2,149	55
June	6,997	2,505	2,140	1,136	1,159	16.8	8.3	3,418	862	2,555	810	2,125	62
July	7,137	2,496	2,220	1,091	1,311	17.3	8.9	3,629	983	2,646	823	2,082	60
Aug	7,133	2,610	2,201	1,124	1,252	16.9	8.6	3,632	981	2,652	794	2,076	60
Sept	7,246	2,537	2,330	1,112	1,280	16.6	8.9	3,622	963	2,660	839	2,103	7
Oct	7,291	2,508	2,454	1,052	1,315	17.0	8.7	3,731	1,064	2,668	790	2,160	66
Nov	7,181	2,633	2,157	1,014	1,384	17.2	8.7	3,609	979	2,630	783	2,160	66
Dec	7,655	2,793	2,330	1,182	1,338	16.6	8.4	3,857	975	2,882	798	2,343	69
2008: Jan	7,576	2,634	2,396	1,124	1,380	17.5	8.8	3,796	1,040	2,756	830	2,201	64
Feb	7,381	2,639	2,396	1,079	1,299	16.8	8.4	3,854	971	2,883	769	2,112	64
Mar	7,815	2,767	2,525	1,118	1,282	16.2	8.1	4,154	1,056	3,098	781	2,117	66
Apr	7,626	2,484	2,495	1,272	1,353	16.9	9.3	4,014	1,099	2,915	850	2,134	6
May	8,487	3,244	2,469	1,223	1,550	16.6	8.3	4,282	1,113	3,169	870	2,460	8
June	8,499	2,712	2,999	1,328	1,587	17.5	10.0	4,370	1,077	3,292	833	2,498	7
July	8,784	2,835	2,823	1,440	1,678	17.1	9.7	4,407	1,037	3,370	861	2,705	8
Aug	9,376	3,235	2,821	1,561	1,841	17.4	9.2	4,824	1,266	3,559	999	2,652	8
Sept	9,477	2,853	3,051	1,598	2,008	18.4	10.2	5,171	1,407	3,764	974	2,555	8
Oct	10,080	3,065	3,003	1,805	2,257	19.7	10.6	5,719	1,340	4,379	940	2,623	8
Nov	10,331	3,251	3,091	1,757	2,206	18.8	10.0	6,072	1,395	4,677	935	2,636	7

[1] Because of independent seasonal adjustment of the various series, detail will not sum to totals.
[2] For 1967, the sum of the unemployed categorized by reason for unemployment does not equal total unemployment.
[3] Beginning with January 1994, job losers and persons who completed temporary jobs.

Note.—Data relate to persons 16 years of age and over.
See footnote 5 and Note, Table B–35.

Source: Department of Labor (Bureau of Labor Statistics).

TABLE B–45.—Unemployment insurance programs, selected data, 1978–2008

[Thousands of persons, except as noted]

Year or month	All programs			State programs				Benefits paid	
	Covered employment [1,2]	Insured unemployment (weekly average) [3,4]	Total benefits paid (millions of dollars) [3,5]	Insured unemployment (weekly average) [4]	Initial claims (weekly average)	Exhaustions (weekly average) [6]	Insured unemployment as percent of covered employment	Total (millions of dollars) [5]	Average weekly check (dollars) [7]
	88,804	2,645	9,007	2,359	346	39	3.3	7,717	83.67
	92,062	2,592	9,401	2,434	388	39	2.9	8,613	89.67
	92,659	3,837	16,175	3,350	488	59	3.9	13,761	98.95
	93,300	3,410	15,287	3,047	460	57	3.5	13,262	106.70
	91,628	4,592	24,491	4,059	583	80	4.6	20,649	119.34
	91,898	3,774	20,968	3,395	438	80	3.9	18,549	123.59
	96,474	2,560	13,739	2,475	377	50	2.8	13,237	123.47
	99,186	2,699	15,217	2,617	397	49	2.9	14,707	128.11
	101,099	2,739	16,563	2,643	378	52	2.8	15,950	135.65
	103,936	2,369	14,684	2,300	328	46	2.4	14,211	140.39
	107,156	2,135	13,481	2,081	310	38	2.0	13,086	144.74
	109,929	2,205	14,569	2,158	330	37	2.1	14,205	151.43
	111,500	2,575	18,387	2,522	388	45	2.4	17,932	161.20
	109,606	3,406	26,327	3,342	447	67	3.2	25,479	169.56
	110,167	3,348	[8] 26,035	3,245	408	74	3.1	25,056	173.38
	112,146	2,845	[8] 22,629	2,751	341	62	2.6	21,661	179.41
	115,255	2,746	22,508	2,670	340	57	2.4	21,537	181.91
	118,068	2,639	21,991	2,572	357	51	2.3	21,226	187.04
	120,567	2,656	22,495	2,595	356	53	2.2	21,820	189.27
	121,044	2,370	20,324	2,323	323	48	1.9	19,735	192.84
	124,184	2,260	19,941	2,222	321	44	1.8	19,431	200.58
	127,042	2,223	21,024	2,188	298	44	1.7	20,563	212.10
	129,877	2,146	20,983	2,110	301	41	1.6	20,507	221.01
	129,636	3,012	32,228	2,974	404	54	2.3	31,680	238.07
	128,234	3,624	[9] 42,980	3,585	407	85	2.8	47,251	256.79
	127,796	3,573	[9] 42,413	3,531	404	85	2.8	43,159	261.67
	129,278	2,999	[9] 36,388	2,950	345	68	2.3	35,776	262.50
	131,572	2,709	32,073	2,661	328	55	2.0	31,238	266.62
	133,834	2,521	30,640	2,476	313	51	1.9	29,800	277.19
	135,366	2,613	33,004	2,572	324 **	51 **	1.9 **	32,241	287.73
Jan		3,163	3,591.5	2,482	314	56	1.9	3,509.8	287.20
Feb		3,104	3,122.7	2,523	324	51	1.9	3,056.3	290.49
Mar		2,741	3,052.2	2,500	313	48	1.9	2,987.0	290.62
Apr		2,833	2,890.7	2,524	320	58	1.9	2,828.3	288.90
May		2,240	2,602.8	2,504	307	52	1.9	2,544.6	288.94
June		2,281	2,297.7	2,529	318	48	1.9	2,248.3	284.23
July		2,705	2,771.3	2,550	309	55	1.9	2,711.8	279.60
Aug		2,272	2,543.1	2,579	324	47	2.0	2,483.9	281.22
Sept		2,346	2,222.2	2,553	319	48	1.9	2,166.4	286.52
Oct		2,260	2,589.2	2,573	329	51	1.9	2,520.5	289.42
Nov		2,277	2,427.4	2,620	339	46	2.0	2,365.1	290.02
Dec		3,075	3,081.2	2,696	344	54	2.0	3,010.7	294.17
Jan		3,275	3,872.7	2,718	337	57	2.0	3,795.6	297.86
Feb		3,260	3,555.6	2,776	346	53	2.1	3,490.1	300.02
Mar		3,557	3,778.6	2,910	374	60	2.2	3,713.4	299.60
Apr		3,040	3,563.6	3,012	365	65	2.3	3,503.0	298.80
May		2,669	2,991.8	3,096	369	58	2.3	2,942.1	297.40
June		3,110	3,145.8	3,126	389	62	2.3	3,094.0	293.66
July		3,008	[10] 3,470.7	3,233	406	66	2.4	3,413.6	290.97
Aug		3,181	[10] 3,203.1	3,429	440	66	2.6	3,146.6	290.65
Sept		3,163	[10] 3,493.6	3,581	475	69	2.7	3,430.0	294.78
Oct [p]		2,981	[10] 3,444.4	3,787	478	98	2.8	3,373.5	297.24

Monthly data are seasonally adjusted.

[1] Through 1996, includes persons under the following programs: State, Unemployment Compensation for Federal Employees (UCFE), Railroad Retirement (RRB), and Unemployment Compensation for Ex-Servicemembers (UCX). Beginning with 1997, covered employment data are under the State and UCFE programs only. Workers covered by State programs account for about 97 percent of wage and salary earners.

[2] Covered employment data beginning 2001 are based on the North American Industry Classification System (NAICS). Prior data are based on the Standard Industrial Classification (SIC).

[3] Includes State, UCFE, RRB, and UCX. Also includes Federal and State extended benefit programs. Does not include Federal Supplemental Benefits, Special Unemployment Assistance (SUA), Federal Supplemental Compensation, Emergency Unemployment Compensation, and Temporary Extended Unemployment Compensation (TEUC) programs.

[4] Covered workers who have completed at least one week of unemployment.

[5] Annual data are net amounts, and monthly data are gross amounts.

[6] Individuals receiving final payments in benefit year.

[7] For total unemployment only.

[8] Including Emergency Unemployment Compensation (EUC), total benefits paid would be approximately (in millions of dollars): 39,990 for 1992 and 34,876 for 1993.

[9] Including TEUC, total benefits paid (not including RRB program) would be approximately (in millions of dollars): 52,709 for 2002; 63,097 for 2003; and 2 for 2004.

[10] Including EUC 2008, total benefits paid (not including RRB program) would be approximately (in millions of dollars): 3,837.5 for July; 4,727.2 for August; 5 for September; and 4,697.0 for October.

Note.—Insured unemployment and initial claims programs include Puerto Rican sugar cane workers.

Source: Department of Labor (Employment and Training Administration).

[Thousands of persons; monthly data seasonally adjusted]

Year or month	Total	Goods-producing industries						Service-providing industries		
		Total	Natural resources and mining	Construction	Manufacturing			Total	Trade, transportation, and utilities [1]	
					Total	Durable goods	Nondurable goods		Total	Retail trade
1960	54,296	19,182	771	2,973	15,438	9,071	6,367	35,114	11,147	5,5
1961	54,105	18,647	728	2,908	15,011	8,711	6,300	35,458	11,040	5,5
1962	55,659	19,203	709	2,997	15,498	9,099	6,399	36,455	11,215	5,6
1963	56,764	19,385	694	3,060	15,631	9,226	6,405	37,379	11,367	5,7
1964	58,391	19,733	697	3,148	15,888	9,414	6,474	38,658	11,677	5,9
1965	60,874	20,595	694	3,284	16,617	9,973	6,644	40,279	12,139	6,2
1966	64,020	21,740	690	3,371	17,680	10,803	6,878	42,280	12,611	6,5
1967	65,931	21,882	679	3,305	17,897	10,952	6,945	44,049	12,950	6,7
1968	68,023	22,292	671	3,410	18,211	11,137	7,074	45,731	13,334	6,9
1969	70,512	22,893	683	3,637	18,573	11,396	7,177	47,619	13,853	7,2
1970	71,006	22,179	677	3,654	17,848	10,762	7,086	48,827	14,144	7,4
1971	71,335	21,602	658	3,770	17,174	10,229	6,944	49,734	14,318	7,6
1972	73,798	22,299	672	3,957	17,669	10,630	7,039	51,499	14,788	8,0
1973	76,912	23,450	693	4,167	18,589	11,414	7,176	53,462	15,349	8,3
1974	78,389	23,364	755	4,095	18,514	11,432	7,082	55,025	15,693	8,5
1975	77,069	21,318	802	3,608	16,909	10,266	6,643	55,751	15,606	8,6
1976	79,502	22,025	832	3,662	17,531	10,640	6,891	57,477	16,128	8,9
1977	82,593	22,972	865	3,940	18,167	11,132	7,035	59,620	16,765	9,3
1978	86,826	24,156	902	4,322	18,932	11,770	7,162	62,670	17,658	9,8
1979	89,932	24,997	1,008	4,562	19,426	12,220	7,206	64,935	18,303	10,1
1980	90,528	24,263	1,077	4,454	18,733	11,679	7,054	66,265	18,413	10,2
1981	91,289	24,118	1,180	4,304	18,634	11,611	7,023	67,172	18,604	10,3
1982	89,677	22,550	1,163	4,024	17,363	10,610	6,753	67,127	18,457	10,3
1983	90,280	22,110	997	4,065	17,048	10,326	6,722	68,171	18,668	10,6
1984	94,530	23,435	1,014	4,501	17,920	11,050	6,870	71,095	19,653	11,2
1985	97,511	23,585	974	4,793	17,819	11,034	6,784	73,926	20,379	11,7
1986	99,474	23,318	829	4,937	17,552	10,795	6,757	76,156	20,795	12,0
1987	102,088	23,470	771	5,090	17,609	10,767	6,842	78,618	21,302	12,4
1988	105,345	23,909	770	5,233	17,906	10,969	6,938	81,436	21,974	12,8
1989	108,014	24,045	750	5,309	17,985	11,004	6,981	83,969	22,510	13,1
1990	109,487	23,723	765	5,263	17,695	10,737	6,958	85,764	22,666	13,1
1991	108,375	22,588	739	4,780	17,068	10,220	6,848	85,787	22,281	12,8
1992	108,726	22,095	689	4,608	16,799	9,946	6,853	86,631	22,125	12,8
1993	110,844	22,219	666	4,779	16,774	9,901	6,872	88,625	22,378	13,0
1994	114,291	22,774	659	5,095	17,020	10,132	6,889	91,517	23,128	13,4
1995	117,298	23,156	641	5,274	17,241	10,373	6,868	94,142	23,834	13,8
1996	119,708	23,409	637	5,536	17,237	10,486	6,751	96,299	24,239	14,1
1997	122,776	23,886	654	5,813	17,419	10,705	6,714	98,890	24,700	14,3
1998	125,930	24,354	645	6,149	17,560	10,911	6,649	101,576	25,186	14,6
1999	128,993	24,465	598	6,545	17,322	10,831	6,491	104,528	25,771	14,9
2000	131,785	24,649	599	6,787	17,263	10,877	6,386	107,136	26,225	15,
2001	131,826	23,873	606	6,826	16,441	10,336	6,105	107,952	25,983	15,
2002	130,341	22,557	583	6,716	15,259	9,485	5,774	107,784	25,497	15,
2003	129,999	21,816	572	6,735	14,510	8,964	5,546	108,183	25,287	14,
2004	131,435	21,882	591	6,976	14,315	8,925	5,390	109,553	25,533	15,0
2005	133,703	22,190	628	7,336	14,226	8,956	5,271	111,513	25,959	15,
2006	136,086	22,531	684	7,691	14,155	8,981	5,174	113,556	26,276	15,
2007	137,623	22,221	723	7,614	13,884	8,816	5,068	115,402	26,608	15,
2007: Jan	137,108	22,447	706	7,726	14,015	8,897	5,118	114,661	26,493	15,
Feb	137,133	22,322	711	7,623	13,988	8,883	5,105	114,811	26,516	15,
Mar	137,310	22,362	715	7,694	13,953	8,863	5,090	114,948	26,584	15,
Apr	137,356	22,300	718	7,660	13,922	8,847	5,075	115,056	26,571	15,
May	137,518	22,272	719	7,643	13,910	8,832	5,078	115,246	26,593	15,
June	137,625	22,267	721	7,656	13,890	8,816	5,074	115,358	26,600	15,
July	137,682	22,242	726	7,632	13,884	8,817	5,067	115,440	26,617	15,
Aug	137,756	22,176	727	7,605	13,844	8,792	5,052	115,580	26,640	15,
Sept	137,837	22,138	727	7,589	13,822	8,778	5,044	115,699	26,649	15,
Oct	137,977	22,101	727	7,577	13,797	8,761	5,036	115,876	26,644	15,
Nov	138,037	22,049	735	7,520	13,794	8,763	5,031	115,988	26,693	15,
Dec	138,078	21,976	739	7,465	13,772	8,739	5,033	116,102	26,658	15,
2008: Jan	138,002	21,907	744	7,426	13,737	8,718	5,019	116,095	26,631	15,
Feb	137,919	21,816	744	7,382	13,690	8,685	5,005	116,103	26,579	15,
Mar	137,831	21,737	750	7,343	13,644	8,652	4,992	116,094	26,552	15,
Apr	137,764	21,628	752	7,284	13,592	8,607	4,985	116,136	26,496	15,
May	137,717	21,577	760	7,246	13,571	8,594	4,977	116,140	26,451	15,
June	137,617	21,491	768	7,196	13,527	8,564	4,963	116,126	26,431	15,
July	137,550	21,437	777	7,173	13,487	8,541	4,946	116,113	26,393	15,
Aug	137,423	21,367	788	7,153	13,426	8,482	4,944	116,056	26,346	15,
Sept	137,020	21,250	795	7,098	13,357	8,433	4,924	115,770	26,225	15,
Oct p	136,700	21,083	796	7,034	13,253	8,349	4,904	115,617	26,124	15,
Nov p	136,167	20,920	800	6,952	13,168	8,287	4,881	115,247	25,977	15,

[1] Includes wholesale trade, transportation and warehousing, and utilities, not shown separately.

Note.—Data in Tables B–46 and B–47 are based on reports from employing establishments and relate to full- and part-time wage and salary workers in nonagricultural establishments who received pay for any part of the pay period that includes the 12th of the month. Not comparable with labor force data (Tables B–35 through B–44), which include proprietors, self-employed persons, unpaid family workers, and private household workers; which count persons as employed when they are not at work because of industrial disputes, bad weather, etc., even if they are not paid for the time off; which are based on a

See next page for continuation of table.

[Thousands of persons; monthly data seasonally adjusted]

ear or month	Information	Financial activities	Profes-sional and business services	Education and health services	Leisure and hospitality	Other services	Government Total	Federal	State	Local
							Government			
....	1,728	2,532	3,694	2,937	3,460	1,152	8,464	2,381	1,536	4,547
....	1,693	2,590	3,744	3,030	3,468	1,188	8,706	2,391	1,607	4,708
....	1,723	2,656	3,885	3,172	3,557	1,243	9,004	2,455	1,669	4,881
....	1,735	2,731	3,990	3,288	3,639	1,288	9,341	2,473	1,747	5,121
....	1,766	2,811	4,137	3,438	3,772	1,346	9,711	2,463	1,856	5,392
....	1,824	2,878	4,306	3,587	3,951	1,404	10,191	2,495	1,996	5,700
....	1,908	2,961	4,517	3,770	4,127	1,475	10,910	2,690	2,141	6,080
....	1,955	3,087	4,720	3,986	4,269	1,558	11,525	2,852	2,302	6,371
....	1,991	3,234	4,918	4,191	4,453	1,638	11,972	2,871	2,442	6,660
....	2,048	3,404	5,156	4,428	4,670	1,731	12,330	2,893	2,533	6,904
....	2,041	3,532	5,267	4,577	4,789	1,789	12,687	2,865	2,664	7,158
....	2,009	3,651	5,328	4,675	4,914	1,827	13,012	2,828	2,747	7,437
....	2,056	3,784	5,523	4,863	5,121	1,900	13,465	2,815	2,859	7,790
....	2,135	3,920	5,774	5,092	5,341	1,990	13,862	2,794	2,923	8,146
....	2,160	4,023	5,974	5,322	5,471	2,078	14,303	2,858	3,039	8,407
....	2,061	4,047	6,034	5,497	5,544	2,144	14,820	2,882	3,179	8,758
....	2,111	4,155	6,287	5,756	5,794	2,244	15,001	2,863	3,273	8,865
....	2,185	4,348	6,587	6,052	6,065	2,359	15,258	2,859	3,377	9,023
....	2,287	4,599	6,972	6,427	6,411	2,505	15,812	2,893	3,474	9,446
....	2,375	4,843	7,312	6,767	6,631	2,637	16,068	2,894	3,541	9,633
....	2,361	5,025	7,544	7,072	6,721	2,755	16,375	3,000	3,610	9,765
....	2,382	5,163	7,782	7,357	6,840	2,865	16,180	2,922	3,640	9,619
....	2,317	5,209	7,848	7,515	6,874	2,924	15,982	2,884	3,640	9,458
....	2,253	5,334	8,039	7,766	7,078	3,021	16,011	2,915	3,662	9,434
....	2,398	5,553	8,464	8,193	7,489	3,186	16,159	2,943	3,734	9,482
....	2,437	5,815	8,871	8,657	7,869	3,366	16,533	3,014	3,832	9,687
....	2,445	6,128	9,211	9,061	8,156	3,523	16,838	3,044	3,893	9,901
....	2,507	6,385	9,608	9,515	8,446	3,699	17,156	3,089	3,967	10,100
....	2,585	6,500	10,090	10,063	8,778	3,907	17,540	3,124	4,076	10,339
....	2,622	6,562	10,555	10,616	9,062	4,116	17,927	3,136	4,182	10,609
....	2,688	6,614	10,848	10,984	9,288	4,261	18,415	3,196	4,305	10,914
....	2,677	6,558	10,714	11,506	9,256	4,249	18,545	3,110	4,355	11,081
....	2,641	6,540	10,970	11,891	9,437	4,240	18,787	3,111	4,408	11,267
....	2,668	6,709	11,495	12,303	9,732	4,350	18,989	3,063	4,488	11,438
....	2,738	6,867	12,174	12,807	10,100	4,428	19,275	3,018	4,576	11,682
....	2,843	6,827	12,844	13,289	10,501	4,572	19,432	2,949	4,635	11,849
....	2,940	6,969	13,462	13,683	10,777	4,690	19,539	2,877	4,606	12,056
....	3,084	7,178	14,335	14,087	11,018	4,825	19,664	2,806	4,582	12,276
....	3,218	7,462	15,147	14,446	11,232	4,976	19,909	2,772	4,612	12,525
....	3,419	7,648	15,957	14,798	11,543	5,087	20,307	2,769	4,709	12,829
....	3,630	7,687	16,666	15,109	11,862	5,168	20,790	2,865	4,786	13,139
....	3,629	7,808	16,476	15,645	12,036	5,258	21,118	2,764	4,905	13,449
....	3,395	7,847	15,976	16,199	11,986	5,372	21,513	2,766	5,029	13,718
....	3,188	7,977	15,987	16,588	12,173	5,401	21,583	2,761	5,002	13,820
....	3,118	8,031	16,394	16,953	12,493	5,409	21,621	2,730	4,982	13,909
....	3,061	8,153	16,954	17,372	12,816	5,395	21,804	2,732	5,032	14,041
....	3,038	8,328	17,566	17,826	13,110	5,438	21,974	2,732	5,075	14,167
....	3,029	8,308	17,962	18,327	13,474	5,491	22,203	2,727	5,125	14,351
Jan	3,028	8,349	17,848	18,072	13,306	5,462	22,103	2,728	5,105	14,270
Feb	3,036	8,347	17,873	18,111	13,331	5,470	22,127	2,729	5,114	14,284
Mar	3,030	8,333	17,875	18,153	13,351	5,479	22,143	2,729	5,114	14,300
Apr	3,034	8,315	17,903	18,211	13,375	5,486	22,161	2,729	5,117	14,315
May	3,037	8,322	17,938	18,247	13,428	5,495	22,186	2,727	5,119	14,340
June	3,033	8,317	17,935	18,314	13,461	5,496	22,202	2,720	5,126	14,356
July	3,027	8,331	17,958	18,360	13,476	5,501	22,170	2,726	5,123	14,321
Aug	3,024	8,312	17,979	18,422	13,494	5,497	22,212	2,724	5,123	14,365
Sept	3,031	8,294	18,000	18,451	13,552	5,495	22,227	2,721	5,138	14,368
Oct	3,027	8,283	18,070	18,490	13,604	5,496	22,262	2,722	5,138	14,402
Nov	3,022	8,260	18,079	18,522	13,628	5,506	22,278	2,728	5,131	14,419
Dec	3,018	8,252	18,131	18,568	13,635	5,507	22,333	2,735	5,153	14,445
Jan	3,014	8,244	18,101	18,617	13,644	5,508	22,336	2,717	5,159	14,460
Feb	3,016	8,231	18,073	18,665	13,660	5,517	22,362	2,725	5,158	14,479
Mar	3,013	8,231	18,014	18,709	13,676	5,522	22,377	2,726	5,157	14,494
Apr	3,007	8,229	18,031	18,757	13,690	5,525	22,401	2,734	5,170	14,497
May	3,002	8,226	17,982	18,820	13,679	5,527	22,453	2,740	5,174	14,539
June	2,997	8,213	17,927	18,891	13,679	5,525	22,463	2,744	5,179	14,540
July	2,988	8,206	17,904	18,935	13,655	5,530	22,502	2,750	5,193	14,559
Aug	2,984	8,196	17,854	18,997	13,639	5,526	22,514	2,748	5,210	14,556
Sept	2,978	8,173	17,789	18,993	13,587	5,530	22,495	2,750	5,206	14,539
Oct ᴾ	2,972	8,142	17,726	19,021	13,562	5,533	22,537	2,769	5,209	14,559
Nov ᴾ	2,953	8,110	17,590	19,073	13,486	5,514	22,544	2,769	5,215	14,560

ote (cont'd).—sample of the working-age population; and which count persons only once—as employed, unemployed, or not in the labor force. In the data
ı here, persons who work at more than one job are counted each time they appear on a payroll.
stablishment data for employment, hours, and earnings are classified based on the 2007 North American Industry Classification System (NAICS).
r further description and details see *Employment and Earnings.*
ɔurce: Department of Labor (Bureau of Labor Statistics).

TABLE B–47.—*Hours and earnings in private nonagricultural industries, 1960–2008* [1]

[Monthly data seasonally adjusted]

Year or month	Average weekly hours			Average hourly earnings			Average weekly earnings, total private			
	Total private	Manufacturing		Total private		Manu-facturing (current dollars)	Level		Percent change from year earlier	
		Total	Overtime	Current dollars	1982 dollars [2]		Current dollars	1982 dollars [2]	Current dollars	1982 dollars
1960	....	39.8	2.5	....	....	$2.15	....	....	....	....
1961	....	39.9	2.4	....	....	2.20	....	....	....	....
1962	....	40.5	2.8	....	....	2.27	....	....	....	....
1963	....	40.6	2.8	....	....	2.34	....	....	....	....
1964	38.5	40.8	3.1	$2.53	$7.86	2.41	$97.41	$302.52	....	....
1965	38.6	41.2	3.6	2.63	8.04	2.49	101.52	310.46	4.2	....
1966	38.5	41.4	3.9	2.73	8.13	2.60	105.11	312.83	3.5	....
1967	37.9	40.6	3.3	2.85	8.21	2.71	108.02	311.30	2.8	....
1968	37.7	40.7	3.5	3.02	8.37	2.89	113.85	315.37	5.4	....
1969	37.5	40.6	3.6	3.22	8.45	3.07	120.75	316.93	6.1	....
1970	37.0	39.8	2.9	3.40	8.46	3.23	125.80	312.94	4.2	
1971	36.8	39.9	2.9	3.63	8.64	3.45	133.58	318.05	6.2	
1972	36.9	40.6	3.4	3.90	8.99	3.70	143.91	331.59	7.7	
1973	36.9	40.7	3.8	4.14	8.98	3.97	152.77	331.39	6.2	
1974	36.4	40.0	3.2	4.43	8.65	4.31	161.25	314.94	5.6	
1975	36.0	39.5	2.6	4.73	8.48	4.71	170.28	305.16	5.6	
1976	36.1	40.1	3.1	5.06	8.58	5.09	182.67	309.61	7.3	
1977	35.9	40.3	3.4	5.44	8.66	5.55	195.30	310.99	6.9	
1978	35.8	40.4	3.6	5.88	8.69	6.05	210.50	310.93	7.8	
1979	35.6	40.2	3.3	6.34	8.41	6.57	225.70	299.34	7.2	
1980	35.2	39.7	2.8	6.85	8.00	7.15	241.12	281.68	6.8	
1981	35.2	39.8	2.8	7.44	7.89	7.86	261.89	277.72	8.6	
1982	34.7	38.9	2.3	7.87	7.87	8.36	273.09	273.09	4.3	
1983	34.9	40.1	2.9	8.20	7.96	8.70	286.18	277.84	4.8	
1984	35.1	40.7	3.4	8.49	7.96	9.05	298.00	279.55	4.1	
1985	34.9	40.5	3.3	8.74	7.92	9.40	305.03	276.55	2.4	
1986	34.7	40.7	3.4	8.93	7.97	9.59	309.87	276.42	1.6	
1987	34.7	40.9	3.7	9.14	7.87	9.77	317.16	273.18	2.4	
1988	34.6	41.0	3.8	9.44	7.82	10.05	326.62	270.60	3.0	
1989	34.5	40.9	3.8	9.80	7.75	10.35	338.10	267.27	3.5	
1990	34.3	40.5	3.9	10.20	7.66	10.78	349.75	262.77	3.4	
1991	34.1	40.4	3.8	10.52	7.59	11.13	358.51	258.67	2.5	
1992	34.2	40.7	4.0	10.77	7.55	11.40	368.25	258.24	2.7	
1993	34.3	41.1	4.4	11.05	7.54	11.70	378.91	258.47	2.9	
1994	34.5	41.7	5.0	11.34	7.54	12.04	391.22	260.29	3.2	
1995	34.3	41.3	4.7	11.65	7.54	12.34	400.07	258.78	2.3	
1996	34.3	41.3	4.8	12.04	7.57	12.75	413.28	259.92	3.3	
1997	34.5	41.7	5.1	12.51	7.69	13.14	431.86	265.60	4.5	
1998	34.5	41.4	4.9	13.01	7.89	13.45	448.56	272.18	3.9	
1999	34.3	41.4	4.9	13.49	8.01	13.85	463.15	275.03	3.3	
2000	34.3	41.3	4.7	14.02	8.04	14.32	481.01	275.97	3.9	
2001	34.0	40.3	4.0	14.54	8.12	14.76	493.79	275.71	2.7	
2002	33.9	40.5	4.2	14.97	8.25	15.29	506.75	279.20	2.6	
2003	33.7	40.4	4.2	15.37	8.28	15.74	518.06	279.13	2.2	
2004	33.7	40.8	4.6	15.69	8.24	16.14	529.09	277.88	2.1	
2005	33.8	40.7	4.6	16.13	8.18	16.56	544.33	276.17	2.9	
2006	33.9	41.1	4.4	16.76	8.24	16.81	567.87	279.19	4.3	
2007	33.8	41.2	4.2	17.42	8.32	17.26	589.72	281.82	3.8	
2007: Jan	33.8	40.9	4.1	17.12	8.35	17.02	578.66	282.13	3.9	
Feb	33.7	40.9	4.1	17.17	8.35	17.06	578.63	281.34	3.8	
Mar	33.9	41.2	4.3	17.24	8.33	17.11	584.44	282.52	4.5	
Apr	33.8	41.1	4.2	17.29	8.33	17.20	584.40	281.54	3.5	
May	33.8	41.1	4.1	17.34	8.31	17.23	586.09	280.83	4.1	
June	33.9	41.4	4.3	17.41	8.32	17.28	590.20	282.17	4.1	
July	33.8	41.4	4.2	17.47	8.33	17.30	590.49	281.65	3.7	
Aug	33.8	41.3	4.2	17.51	8.35	17.33	591.84	282.30	3.7	
Sept	33.8	41.4	4.2	17.57	8.35	17.34	593.87	282.20	4.1	
Oct	33.8	41.2	4.1	17.59	8.34	17.34	594.54	281.72	3.5	
Nov	33.8	41.3	4.1	17.64	8.27	17.40	596.23	279.67	3.8	
Dec	33.8	41.1	4.0	17.70	8.27	17.41	598.26	279.53	3.4	
2008: Jan	33.7	41.1	4.0	17.75	8.26	17.49	598.18	278.27	3.4	
Feb	33.7	41.1	4.0	17.81	8.29	17.55	600.20	279.21	3.7	
Mar	33.8	41.2	4.0	17.87	8.28	17.61	604.01	279.96	3.3	
Apr	33.8	41.0	4.0	17.89	8.27	17.62	604.68	279.62	3.5	
May	33.7	41.0	3.9	17.95	8.24	17.65	604.92	277.75	3.2	
June	33.7	41.0	3.8	18.00	8.17	17.71	606.60	275.18	2.8	
July	33.7	41.0	3.8	18.06	8.12	17.78	608.62	273.66	3.1	
Aug	33.7	40.9	3.7	18.14	8.17	17.76	611.32	275.35	3.3	
Sept	33.6	40.5	3.5	18.17	8.19	17.79	610.51	275.23	2.8	
Oct [P]	33.6	40.5	3.5	18.23	8.32	17.86	612.53	279.50	3.0	
Nov [P]	33.5	40.3	3.3	18.30	....	17.92	613.05	....	2.8	....

[1] For production or nonsupervisory workers; total includes private industry groups shown in Table B–46.
[2] Current dollars divided by the consumer price index for urban wage earners and clerical workers on a 1982=100 base.

Note.—See Note, Table B–46.

Source: Department of Labor (Bureau of Labor Statistics).

ar and month	Total private			Goods-producing			Service-providing [1]			Manufacturing		
	Total compensation	Wages and salaries	Benefits [2]	Total compensation	Wages and salaries	Benefits [2]	Total compensation	Wages and salaries	Benefits [2]	Total compensation	Wages and salaries	Benefits [2]
Indexes on SIC basis, December 2005=100; not seasonally adjusted												
ember:												
1990	59.3	62.3	52.9	59.4	63.4	52.3	59.4	61.8	53.4	59.1	63.1	52.1
1991	61.9	64.6	56.2	62.1	65.8	55.5	61.9	64.1	56.7	61.9	65.6	55.2
1992	64.1	66.3	59.1	64.5	67.6	58.7	63.9	65.7	59.4	64.3	67.6	58.3
1993	66.4	68.3	62.0	67.0	69.6	62.0	66.2	67.8	62.0	66.9	69.7	61.8
1994	68.5	70.2	64.3	69.0	71.7	64.1	68.1	69.6	64.4	69.0	71.8	63.9
1995	70.2	72.2	65.7	70.7	73.7	65.2	70.0	71.7	66.0	70.8	73.9	65.0
1996	72.4	74.7	67.0	72.7	76.0	66.4	72.3	74.2	67.3	72.9	76.3	66.5
1997	74.9	77.6	68.5	74.5	78.3	67.3	75.1	77.4	69.2	74.6	78.6	67.4
1998	77.5	80.6	70.2	76.5	81.1	68.1	78.0	80.5	71.4	76.6	81.3	67.9
1999	80.2	83.5	72.6	79.1	83.8	70.5	80.6	83.4	73.8	79.2	84.1	70.3
2000	83.6	86.7	76.7	82.6	87.1	74.3	84.2	86.6	78.1	82.3	87.1	73.6
2001	87.1	90.0	80.6	85.7	90.2	77.3	87.8	89.9	82.5	85.3	90.2	76.3
Indexes on NAICS basis, December 2005=100; not seasonally adjusted												
2001 [3]	87.3	89.9	81.3	86.0	90.0	78.5	87.8	89.8	82.4	85.5	90.2	77.2
2002	90.0	92.2	84.7	89.0	92.6	82.3	90.4	92.1	85.8	88.7	92.8	81.3
2003	93.6	95.1	90.2	92.6	94.9	88.2	94.0	95.2	91.0	92.4	95.1	87.3
2004	97.2	97.6	96.2	96.9	97.2	96.3	97.3	97.7	96.1	96.9	97.4	96.0
2005	100.0	100.0	100.0	100.0	100.0	100.0	100.0	100.0	100.0	100.0	100.0	100.0
2006	103.2	103.2	103.1	102.5	102.9	101.7	103.4	103.3	103.7	101.8	102.3	100.8
2007	106.3	106.6	105.6	105.0	106.0	103.2	106.7	106.8	106.6	103.8	104.9	101.7
3: Mar	107.3	107.6	106.5	106.1	107.1	104.0	107.7	107.7	107.6	104.7	105.9	102.3
June	108.0	108.4	107.0	106.8	108.0	104.4	108.5	108.6	108.1	105.1	106.7	102.2
Sept	108.7	109.1	107.5	107.2	108.6	104.6	109.1	109.3	108.7	105.6	107.4	102.3
Indexes on NAICS basis, December 2005=100; seasonally adjusted												
*: Mar	104.0	104.3	103.1	102.9	103.9	101.0	104.3	104.4	104.0	101.9	103.2	99.6
June	104.8	105.1	104.2	103.8	104.6	102.2	105.2	105.2	105.0	102.8	103.8	101.0
Sept	105.6	105.9	105.0	104.3	105.4	102.3	106.1	106.1	106.0	103.1	104.4	100.7
Dec	106.5	106.7	105.8	105.2	106.1	103.3	106.9	106.9	106.8	103.9	105.1	101.7
3: Mar	107.3	107.6	106.4	106.1	107.2	104.1	107.6	107.7	107.4	104.7	105.9	102.3
June	107.9	108.4	106.9	106.7	107.8	104.4	108.4	108.5	108.0	105.1	106.6	102.2
Sept	108.6	109.0	107.5	107.1	108.5	104.5	109.1	109.2	108.7	105.6	107.3	102.3
Percent change from 12 months earlier, not seasonally adjusted												
ember:												
1990	4.6	4.0	6.7	4.8	3.6	7.2	4.6	3.9	6.4	5.0	4.1	7.0
1991	4.4	3.7	6.2	4.5	3.8	6.1	4.2	3.7	6.2	4.7	4.0	6.0
992	3.6	2.6	5.2	3.9	2.7	5.8	3.2	2.5	4.8	3.9	3.0	5.6
1993	3.6	3.0	4.9	3.9	3.0	5.6	3.6	3.2	4.4	4.0	3.1	6.0
1994	3.2	2.8	3.7	3.0	3.0	3.4	2.9	2.7	3.9	3.1	3.0	3.4
1995	2.5	2.8	2.2	2.5	2.8	1.7	2.8	3.0	2.5	2.6	2.9	1.7
1996	3.1	3.5	2.0	2.8	3.1	1.8	3.3	3.5	2.0	3.0	3.2	2.3
1997	3.5	3.9	2.2	2.5	3.0	1.4	3.9	4.3	2.8	2.3	3.0	1.4
1998	3.5	3.9	2.5	2.7	3.6	1.2	3.9	4.0	3.2	2.7	3.4	.7
1999	3.5	3.6	3.4	3.4	3.3	3.5	3.3	3.6	3.4	3.4	3.4	3.5
2000	4.2	3.8	5.6	4.4	3.9	5.4	4.5	3.8	5.8	3.9	3.6	4.7
2001	4.2	3.8	5.1	3.8	3.6	4.0	4.3	3.9	5.6	3.6	3.6	3.7
cs:												
2001 [3]	4.1	3.8	5.2	3.6	3.6	3.7	4.4	3.8	5.6	3.4	3.6	3.5
2002	3.1	2.6	4.2	3.5	2.9	4.8	3.0	2.6	4.1	3.7	2.9	5.3
2003	4.0	3.1	6.5	4.0	2.5	7.2	4.0	3.4	6.1	4.2	2.5	7.4
2004	3.8	2.6	6.7	4.6	2.4	9.2	3.5	2.6	5.6	4.9	2.4	10.0
2005	2.9	2.5	4.0	3.2	2.9	3.8	2.8	2.4	4.1	3.2	2.7	4.2
2006	3.2	3.2	3.1	2.5	2.9	1.7	3.4	3.3	3.7	1.8	2.3	.8
2007	3.0	3.3	2.4	2.4	3.0	1.5	3.2	3.4	2.8	2.0	2.5	.9
: Mar	3.2	3.2	3.2	3.1	3.1	3.1	3.3	3.2	3.4	2.6	2.5	2.7
June	3.0	3.1	2.6	2.8	3.2	2.2	3.1	3.1	2.8	2.1	2.7	1.2
Sept	2.8	2.9	2.4	2.7	3.0	2.1	2.8	3.0	2.5	2.3	2.8	1.6
Percent change from 3 months earlier, seasonally adjusted												
*: Mar	0.7	1.0	-0.3	0.3	0.9	-0.8	0.8	1.0	0.0	0.0	0.7	-1.3
June	.8	.8	1.1	.9	.7	1.2	.9	.8	1.0	.9	.6	1.4
Sept	.8	.8	.8	.5	.8	.1	.9	.9	1.0	.3	.6	-.3
Dec	.9	.8	.8	.9	.7	1.0	.8	.8	.8	.8	.7	1.0
3: Mar	.8	.8	.6	.9	1.0	.8	.7	.7	.6	.8	.8	.6
June	.6	.7	.5	.6	.6	.3	.7	.7	.6	.4	.7	-.1
Sept	.6	.6	.6	.6	.4	.1	.6	.6	.6	.5	.7	.1

On Standard Industrial Classification (SIC) basis, data are for service-producing industries.
Employer costs for employee benefits.
Data on North American Industry Classification System (NAICS) basis available beginning with 2001; not strictly comparable with earlier data shown on asis.

ote.—Changes effective with the release of March 2006 data (in April 2006) include changing industry classification to NAICS from SIC and rebasing data ecember 2005=100. Historical SIC data are available through December 2005.
ata exclude farm and household workers.

ource: Department of Labor (Bureau of Labor Statistics).

TABLE B–49.—*Productivity and related data, business and nonfarm business sectors, 1959–2008*

[Index numbers, 1992=100; quarterly data seasonally adjusted]

Year or quarter	Output per hour of all persons		Output [1]		Hours of all persons [2]		Compensation per hour [3]		Real compensation per hour [4]		Unit labor costs		Implicit price deflator [5]	
	Business sector	Nonfarm business sector	Business sector	Nonfarm business sector	Business sector	Nonfarm business sector	Business sector	Nonfarm business sector	Business sector	Nonfarm business sector	Business sector	Nonfarm business sector	Business sector	Nonfarm business sector
1959	48.0	51.3	31.4	31.2	65.5	60.9	13.3	13.9	59.9	62.3	27.8	27.1	26.8	2
1960	48.9	51.9	32.0	31.8	65.6	61.2	13.9	14.5	61.3	63.9	28.4	27.9	27.1	2
1961	50.6	53.5	32.7	32.4	64.6	60.6	14.4	15.0	63.1	65.3	28.5	28.0	27.3	2
1962	52.9	55.9	34.8	34.6	65.8	61.9	15.1	15.6	65.2	67.3	28.5	27.8	27.6	2
1963	55.0	57.8	36.4	36.2	66.2	62.6	15.6	16.1	66.6	68.7	28.4	27.8	27.7	2
1964	56.8	59.6	38.7	38.7	68.1	64.9	16.2	16.6	68.3	69.9	28.5	27.9	28.1	2
1965	58.8	61.4	41.4	41.4	70.4	67.4	16.8	17.1	69.7	71.1	28.6	27.9	28.5	2
1966	61.2	63.6	44.2	44.4	72.3	69.8	17.9	18.2	72.3	73.2	29.3	28.6	29.2	2
1967	62.5	64.7	45.1	45.1	72.1	69.7	19.0	19.2	74.1	75.2	30.3	29.7	30.0	2
1968	64.7	66.9	47.3	47.5	73.2	71.0	20.5	20.7	76.9	77.8	31.7	31.0	31.2	3
1969	65.0	67.0	48.8	48.9	75.0	73.0	21.9	22.1	78.0	78.8	33.7	33.0	32.6	3
1970	66.3	68.0	48.7	48.9	73.5	71.9	23.6	23.7	79.5	79.8	35.6	34.9	34.1	3
1971	69.0	70.7	50.6	50.7	73.3	71.7	25.1	25.2	80.9	81.4	36.3	35.7	35.5	3
1972	71.2	73.1	53.9	54.1	75.6	74.0	26.7	26.9	83.3	84.0	37.4	36.8	36.8	3
1973	73.4	75.3	57.6	58.0	78.5	77.0	28.9	29.1	85.1	85.5	39.4	38.6	38.7	4
1974	72.3	74.2	56.8	57.3	78.7	77.2	31.7	31.9	84.0	84.5	43.9	43.0	42.4	4
1975	74.8	76.2	56.3	56.3	75.3	73.9	34.9	35.1	84.8	85.2	46.7	46.0	46.6	4
1976	77.1	78.7	60.0	60.2	77.8	76.5	38.0	38.1	87.1	87.4	49.2	48.3	49.0	4
1977	78.5	80.0	63.3	63.6	80.7	79.5	41.0	41.2	88.3	88.7	52.2	51.5	52.0	5
1978	79.3	81.0	67.3	67.8	84.9	83.7	44.5	44.8	89.7	90.3	56.2	55.3	55.6	5
1979	79.3	80.7	69.6	70.0	87.7	86.6	48.9	49.1	89.9	90.2	61.6	60.8	60.4	5
1980	79.2	80.6	68.8	69.2	87.0	85.9	54.1	54.4	89.6	90.0	68.4	67.5	65.8	6
1981	80.8	81.7	70.7	70.7	87.6	86.6	59.3	59.7	89.6	90.2	73.5	73.1	71.8	7
1982	80.1	80.8	68.6	68.4	85.6	84.7	63.6	63.9	90.6	91.1	79.4	79.1	75.9	7
1983	83.0	84.5	72.3	72.9	87.1	86.3	66.3	66.6	90.6	91.1	79.8	78.9	78.5	8
1984	85.2	86.1	78.6	78.9	92.2	91.6	69.1	69.5	90.8	91.2	81.1	80.7	80.8	8
1985	87.1	87.5	82.2	82.2	94.3	94.0	72.5	72.6	92.0	92.2	83.2	83.0	82.7	8
1986	89.7	90.2	85.3	85.4	95.1	94.7	76.1	76.4	94.9	95.2	84.9	84.7	84.1	8
1987	90.1	90.6	88.3	88.4	97.9	97.6	79.0	79.2	95.2	95.5	87.6	87.4	85.9	8
1988	91.5	92.1	92.1	92.4	100.6	100.4	83.0	83.1	96.5	96.7	90.7	90.2	88.6	9
1989	92.4	92.8	95.4	95.7	103.3	103.1	85.2	85.3	95.0	95.1	92.2	91.9	91.9	9
1990	94.4	94.5	96.9	97.1	102.7	102.7	90.6	90.4	96.2	96.0	96.0	95.7	95.1	9
1991	95.9	96.1	96.1	96.3	100.2	100.2	95.1	95.0	97.5	97.4	99.1	98.9	98.2	9
1992	100.0	100.0	100.0	100.0	100.0	100.0	100.0	100.0	100.0	100.0	100.0	100.0	100.0	10
1993	100.4	100.4	103.1	103.4	102.7	102.9	102.2	102.0	99.8	99.5	101.8	101.6	102.1	10
1994	101.4	101.5	108.2	108.3	106.8	106.6	103.7	103.7	99.0	99.1	102.3	102.1	103.9	10
1995	101.5	102.0	111.4	111.8	109.7	109.6	105.8	105.9	98.7	98.8	104.2	103.8	105.7	10
1996	104.5	104.7	116.5	116.8	111.5	111.5	109.5	109.4	99.5	99.5	104.8	104.5	107.4	10
1997	106.5	106.4	122.7	122.8	115.2	115.4	113.0	112.8	100.5	100.4	106.1	106.0	109.0	10
1998	109.5	109.4	128.6	128.9	117.5	117.9	119.9	119.6	105.2	104.9	109.5	109.3	109.7	10
1999	112.8	112.5	135.2	135.6	119.8	120.5	125.8	125.2	108.1	107.6	111.5	111.3	110.7	1
2000	116.1	115.7	140.5	140.8	121.0	121.7	134.7	134.2	112.0	111.6	116.0	116.0	112.7	1
2001	119.1	118.6	141.0	141.3	118.4	119.2	140.3	139.5	113.5	112.8	117.9	117.7	114.9	1
2002	123.9	123.5	143.1	143.4	115.4	116.1	145.3	144.6	115.7	115.1	117.3	117.1	116.1	1
2003	128.7	128.0	147.5	147.8	114.6	115.4	151.2	150.4	117.7	117.1	117.5	117.5	117.8	1
2004	132.4	131.6	153.7	153.9	116.1	117.0	156.9	155.9	119.0	118.2	118.5	118.5	120.8	1
2005	134.8	133.9	159.1	159.2	118.0	118.9	163.2	162.2	119.7	119.0	121.0	121.1	124.6	1
2006	136.1	135.2	163.9	164.2	120.4	121.5	169.5	168.4	120.4	119.6	124.5	124.6	128.3	1
2007	138.2	137.1	167.3	167.5	121.0	122.2	176.5	175.3	121.9	121.1	127.7	127.9	131.4	1
2004: I	131.1	130.3	151.4	151.5	115.5	116.3	153.9	152.9	118.0	117.3	117.3	117.4	119.5	1
II	132.3	131.7	153.1	153.4	115.7	116.5	155.7	154.8	118.5	117.8	117.7	117.5	120.5	1
III	132.7	132.1	154.6	154.9	116.5	117.3	157.8	156.9	119.3	118.6	118.9	118.8	121.1	1
IV	133.4	132.2	155.7	155.9	116.7	117.9	160.3	158.9	119.9	118.9	120.1	120.2	122.1	1
2005: I	134.3	133.3	157.1	157.3	117.0	118.0	161.2	160.0	120.1	119.2	120.0	120.0	123.2	1
II	134.2	133.4	158.4	158.4	118.0	118.8	161.6	160.8	119.5	118.9	120.4	120.5	123.8	1
III	135.6	134.6	160.2	160.3	118.2	119.1	164.1	163.2	119.6	118.9	121.1	121.2	125.0	1
IV	135.3	134.2	160.6	160.8	118.8	119.8	165.8	164.7	119.6	118.8	122.6	122.7	126.3	1
2006: I	136.1	135.1	162.8	163.2	119.6	120.8	168.0	166.8	120.7	119.8	123.5	123.5	127.2	1
II	136.6	135.7	164.0	164.3	120.1	121.1	168.1	167.1	119.7	118.9	123.1	123.2	128.0	1
III	135.9	135.0	164.1	164.4	120.8	121.8	169.0	167.9	119.1	118.3	124.3	124.4	128.8	1
IV	135.9	135.0	164.8	165.0	121.2	122.2	172.6	171.7	122.1	121.4	127.0	127.1	129.4	1
2007: I	135.9	135.0	164.5	164.7	121.0	122.0	174.7	173.7	122.4	121.8	128.5	128.7	130.7	1
II	137.6	136.4	166.8	167.0	121.2	122.4	175.5	174.1	121.6	120.7	127.5	127.7	131.2	1
III	139.7	138.3	169.0	169.2	121.0	122.3	177.0	175.5	121.9	120.8	126.7	126.9	131.6	1
IV	139.7	138.6	168.8	168.9	120.8	121.9	178.9	177.8	121.7	120.9	128.1	128.3	132.2	1
2008: I	140.5	139.5	169.1	169.3	120.3	121.4	180.6	179.5	121.5	120.8	128.5	128.7	132.9	1
II	141.8	140.8	170.2	170.5	120.0	121.1	181.1	179.9	120.4	119.6	127.7	127.8	133.2	1
III	142.3	141.2	169.4	169.7	119.1	120.2	182.9	181.7	119.7	118.9	128.6	128.7	134.7	1

[1] Output refers to real gross domestic product in the sector.

[2] Hours at work of all persons engaged in sector, including hours of proprietors and unpaid family workers. Estimates based primarily on establishment d

[3] Wages and salaries of employees plus employers' contributions for social insurance and private benefit plans. Also includes an estimate of wages, salaries, and supplemental payments for the self-employed.

[4] Hourly compensation divided by the consumer price index for all urban consumers for recent quarters. The trend from 1978–2007 is based on the consu price index research series (CPI-U-RS).

[5] Current dollar output divided by the output index.

Source: Department of Labor (Bureau of Labor Statistics).

[Percent change from preceding period; quarterly data at seasonally adjusted annual rates]

or quarter	Output per hour of all persons		Output [1]		Hours of all persons [2]		Compensation per hour [3]		Real compensation per hour [4]		Unit labor costs		Implicit price deflator [5]	
	Business sector	Nonfarm business sector	Business sector	Nonfarm business sector	Business sector	Nonfarm business sector	Business sector	Nonfarm business sector	Business sector	Nonfarm business sector	Business sector	Nonfarm business sector	Business sector	Nonfarm business sector
	3.8	3.8	8.1	8.6	4.2	4.6	4.1	3.9	3.4	3.2	0.3	0.1	0.8	1.3
	1.7	1.2	1.9	1.7	.2	.6	4.2	4.3	2.4	2.5	2.4	3.1	1.1	1.2
	3.5	3.1	1.9	2.0	-1.5	-1.1	3.9	3.3	2.8	2.3	.4	.2	.8	.8
	4.6	4.5	6.4	6.8	1.8	2.2	4.4	4.0	3.4	3.0	-.1	-.5	1.0	1.0
	3.9	3.5	4.6	4.7	.7	1.1	3.6	3.4	2.2	2.1	-.3	-.1	.6	.7
	3.4	3.0	6.4	6.7	2.9	3.7	3.8	3.1	2.4	1.8	.4	.2	1.1	1.3
	3.5	3.1	7.0	7.1	3.4	3.9	3.7	3.3	2.1	1.7	.2	.2	1.6	1.3
	4.1	3.6	6.8	7.1	2.6	3.5	6.7	5.9	3.8	3.0	2.6	2.3	2.5	2.3
	2.2	1.7	1.9	1.7	-.3	.0	5.7	5.8	2.5	2.7	3.4	4.0	2.7	3.2
	3.4	3.4	5.0	5.2	1.5	1.8	8.1	7.8	3.7	3.5	4.5	4.3	4.0	4.0
	.5	.2	3.0	3.0	2.5	2.9	7.0	6.8	1.4	1.3	6.5	6.7	4.6	4.5
	2.0	1.5	.0	-.1	-2.0	-1.6	7.7	7.2	1.9	1.4	5.6	5.6	4.4	4.5
	4.1	4.0	3.8	3.8	-.3	-.2	6.3	6.4	1.8	1.9	2.1	2.3	4.2	4.3
	3.2	3.3	6.5	6.7	3.1	3.2	6.3	6.5	3.0	3.2	3.0	3.1	3.6	3.2
	3.0	3.1	7.0	7.3	3.8	4.1	8.4	8.2	2.1	1.8	5.2	4.9	5.2	3.6
	-1.6	-1.5	-1.4	-1.4	.2	.1	9.6	9.8	-1.3	-1.2	11.4	11.4	9.6	10.2
	3.5	2.7	-1.0	-1.7	-4.3	-4.3	10.2	10.1	1.0	.9	6.5	7.2	9.8	10.8
	3.1	3.3	6.6	7.0	3.3	3.6	8.6	8.4	2.7	2.5	5.3	5.0	5.3	5.6
	1.7	1.6	5.6	5.6	3.8	3.9	8.0	8.1	1.4	1.5	6.2	6.4	6.0	6.3
	1.1	1.3	6.3	6.6	5.1	5.2	8.7	8.9	1.6	1.7	7.5	7.5	7.1	6.7
	.0	-.3	3.4	3.2	3.4	3.6	9.7	9.6	.1	.0	9.8	10.0	8.5	8.4
	-.2	-.2	-1.1	-1.0	-.9	-.8	10.8	10.8	-.3	-.3	11.0	11.0	8.9	9.6
	2.1	1.4	2.8	2.1	.7	.7	9.6	9.8	.1	.2	7.4	8.3	9.2	9.6
	-.8	-1.1	-3.0	-3.2	-2.3	-2.2	7.2	7.1	1.1	1.0	8.1	8.2	5.7	6.2
	3.6	4.5	5.4	6.5	1.8	1.9	4.1	4.2	-.1	.0	.6	-.3	3.4	3.1
	2.7	2.0	8.7	8.2	5.8	6.1	4.4	4.2	.2	.1	1.7	2.2	2.9	2.9
	2.2	1.6	4.6	4.2	2.3	2.6	4.8	4.6	1.3	1.1	2.5	3.0	2.4	3.0
	2.9	3.1	3.7	3.9	.8	.8	5.1	5.2	3.2	3.3	2.1	2.0	1.6	1.7
	.5	.5	3.5	3.6	3.0	3.0	3.7	3.7	.3	.3	3.2	3.2	2.2	2.2
	1.5	1.7	4.3	4.6	2.7	2.9	5.1	4.9	1.4	1.2	3.5	3.2	3.1	3.0
	1.0	.7	3.7	3.5	2.6	2.7	2.7	2.6	-1.6	-1.7	1.7	1.8	3.7	3.6
	2.1	1.9	1.5	1.5	-.6	-.4	6.3	6.1	1.3	1.0	4.1	4.1	3.6	3.7
	1.6	1.6	-.8	-.8	-2.4	-2.4	4.9	5.1	1.3	1.4	3.3	3.4	3.2	3.4
	4.3	4.1	4.0	3.9	-.2	-.2	5.2	5.3	2.6	2.7	.9	1.1	1.8	1.9
	.4	.4	3.1	3.3	2.7	2.9	2.2	2.0	-.2	-.5	1.8	1.6	2.1	2.1
	1.0	1.1	5.0	4.0	3.8	3.6	1.4	1.7	-.7	-.5	.4	.5	1.8	1.9
	.1	.5	2.9	3.2	2.8	2.8	2.1	2.1	-.3	-.3	1.9	1.6	1.8	1.7
	3.0	2.7	4.6	4.5	1.6	1.8	3.5	3.4	.8	.7	.5	.7	1.6	1.4
	1.9	1.6	5.3	5.2	3.4	3.5	3.2	3.1	1.0	.9	1.3	1.4	1.5	1.7
	2.8	2.8	4.8	5.0	2.0	2.1	6.1	6.0	4.6	4.5	3.2	3.1	.6	.7
	3.1	2.9	5.1	5.2	2.0	2.2	4.9	4.7	2.8	2.6	1.8	1.8	.9	1.1
	2.9	2.8	3.9	3.8	1.0	1.0	7.1	7.2	3.6	3.7	4.1	4.2	1.8	1.9
	2.5	2.5	.3	.4	-2.2	-2.0	4.2	4.0	1.4	1.1	1.6	1.4	2.0	1.9
	4.1	4.1	1.5	1.5	-2.5	-2.6	3.5	3.6	1.9	2.0	-.5	-.5	1.0	1.1
	3.8	3.7	3.1	3.1	-.7	-.6	4.1	4.0	1.8	1.8	.2	.3	1.5	1.3
	2.9	2.8	4.2	4.1	1.3	1.3	3.8	3.6	1.0	.9	.9	.9	2.6	2.4
	1.8	1.8	3.5	3.4	1.6	1.6	4.0	4.0	.6	.7	2.1	2.2	3.1	3.4
	.9	1.0	3.0	3.2	2.1	2.2	3.8	3.8	.5	.5	2.9	2.8	3.0	3.1
	1.5	1.4	2.0	2.0	.5	.5	4.2	4.1	1.3	1.3	2.6	2.7	2.4	2.1
I	2.4	.9	3.7	2.6	1.2	1.7	.6	-.1	-2.7	-3.4	-1.7	-1.0	3.4	3.4
II	3.7	4.5	4.4	5.0	.7	.4	4.8	5.0	1.7	1.8	1.1	.5	3.6	3.0
III	1.2	1.1	4.0	3.8	2.7	2.8	5.4	5.5	2.5	2.5	4.1	4.4	1.8	2.4
IV	2.1	.6	3.0	2.6	.9	2.1	6.4	5.3	2.2	1.1	4.3	4.7	3.5	3.8
I	2.8	3.2	3.7	3.7	.9	.5	2.3	2.8	.6	1.0	-.4	-.5	3.6	3.9
II	-.3	.3	3.2	2.9	3.5	2.6	1.0	1.9	-1.8	-.9	1.3	1.6	2.0	2.2
III	4.1	3.7	4.8	4.8	.6	1.0	6.5	6.2	.2	-.1	2.3	2.4	4.1	4.3
IV	-1.0	-1.1	1.0	1.3	1.9	2.5	4.2	3.7	.1	-.3	5.2	4.9	4.1	4.2
I	2.6	2.5	5.6	6.0	3.0	3.3	5.5	5.2	3.6	3.3	2.8	2.6	3.0	3.1
II	1.4	1.8	2.9	2.9	1.5	1.1	.2	.7	-3.3	-2.8	-1.2	-1.1	2.6	2.9
III	-2.0	-2.1	.3	.3	2.4	2.4	2.0	1.9	-1.9	-2.0	4.1	4.1	2.4	2.1
IV	.2	.2	1.7	1.4	1.5	1.2	9.0	9.3	10.6	11.0	8.8	9.1	1.9	1.5
I	-.1	.0	-.7	-.9	-.6	-.8	4.8	4.9	1.1	1.2	4.8	4.9	4.0	3.4
II	5.0	4.1	5.6	5.8	.6	1.6	1.9	.8	-2.6	-3.6	-2.9	-3.2	1.7	1.5
III	6.2	5.8	5.5	5.5	-.7	-.3	3.6	3.3	.8	.5	-2.5	-2.4	1.1	.9
IV	.1	.8	-.6	-.7	-.7	-1.6	4.4	5.3	-.6	.3	4.3	4.5	2.0	2.1
I	2.3	2.6	.7	.9	-1.6	-1.7	3.6	3.8	-.6	-.4	1.3	1.2	2.0	2.1
II	3.7	3.6	2.6	2.8	-1.0	-.8	1.2	.9	-3.7	-3.9	-2.4	-2.6	.9	.9
III	1.5	1.3	-1.7	-1.9	-3.2	-3.1	4.2	4.1	-2.4	-2.4	2.6	2.8	4.5	4.9

[1] Output refers to real gross domestic product in the sector.
[2] Hours at work of all persons engaged in the sector. See footnote 2, Table B–49.
[3] Wages and salaries of employees plus employers' contributions for social insurance and private benefit plans. Also includes an estimate of wages, salaries, and supplemental payments for the self-employed.
[4] Hourly compensation divided by a consumer price index. See footnote 4, Table B–49.
[5] Current dollar output divided by the output index.

Note.—Percent changes are based on original data and may differ slightly from percent changes based on indexes in Table B–49.

Source: Department of Labor (Bureau of Labor Statistics).

TABLE B–51.—*Industrial production indexes, major industry divisions, 1959–2008*

[2002=100; monthly data seasonally adjusted]

Year or month	Total industrial production [1]	Manufacturing				Mining	Utilities
		Total [1]	Durable	Nondurable	Other (non-NAICS) [1]		
1959	25.5	23.2					
1960	26.0	23.7					
1961	26.2	23.7					
1962	28.4	25.8					
1963	30.1	27.4					
1964	32.1	29.3					
1965	35.3	32.4					
1966	38.4	35.4					
1967	39.2	36.1					
1968	41.4	38.1					
1969	43.3	39.8					
1970	41.9	38.0					
1971	42.5	38.6					
1972	46.6	42.6	31.4	61.0	68.3	107.8	
1973	50.4	46.4	35.3	63.8	70.5	108.3	
1974	50.2	46.3	35.1	64.1	70.9	106.8	
1975	45.8	41.5	30.5	59.5	67.5	104.2	
1976	49.4	45.2	33.4	64.9	69.6	105.0	
1977	53.1	49.1	36.6	69.3	76.2	107.4	
1978	56.1	52.1	39.5	71.8	78.9	110.8	
1979	57.8	53.7	41.5	72.2	80.5	114.1	
1980	56.3	51.8	39.7	70.0	83.3	116.2	
1981	57.0	52.4	40.1	70.7	85.3	119.2	
1982	54.1	49.5	36.7	69.6	86.3	113.3	
1983	55.6	51.9	38.5	72.9	88.7	107.3	
1984	60.5	57.0	44.0	76.2	92.7	114.3	
1985	61.3	57.9	44.9	76.6	96.4	112.0	
1986	61.9	59.2	45.7	78.8	98.3	103.9	
1987	65.1	62.5	48.4	83.1	104.0	104.8	
1988	68.4	65.9	52.0	85.9	103.5	107.5	
1989	69.1	66.4	52.6	86.3	102.0	106.2	
1990	69.7	67.0	52.8	87.7	100.8	107.8	
1991	68.7	65.6	51.2	87.4	96.7	105.4	
1992	70.6	68.0	53.8	89.6	94.8	103.1	
1993	72.9	70.4	56.8	90.9	95.5	103.0	
1994	76.8	74.5	61.6	94.1	94.7	105.4	
1995	80.4	78.5	66.9	95.7	94.7	105.3	
1996	84.0	82.2	72.8	96.0	93.8	107.1	
1997	90.1	89.2	81.6	99.5	101.7	108.9	
1998	95.4	95.1	90.2	101.0	107.8	107.2	
1999	99.5	99.9	97.8	101.7	110.9	101.6	
2000	103.7	104.4	105.2	102.2	112.6	104.2	
2001	100.1	100.1	100.5	98.9	105.7	104.8	
2002	100.0	100.0	100.0	100.0	100.0	100.0	1
2003	101.2	101.3	102.7	100.1	97.1	100.2	1
2004	103.8	104.2	106.9	102.0	97.9	99.6	1
2005	107.2	108.4	112.7	104.8	98.5	98.3	1
2006	109.6	111.1	117.9	105.6	94.3	101.4	1
2007	111.4	112.9	121.0	106.6	92.9	101.4	1
2007: Jan	109.8	111.1	117.5	106.2	93.0	101.6	1
Feb	110.5	111.3	118.0	106.0	93.3	100.6	1
Mar	110.4	112.0	119.1	106.5	93.4	100.8	1
Apr	111.0	112.4	120.0	106.5	93.8	100.7	1
May	111.0	112.6	120.2	106.6	93.2	100.6	1
June	111.4	113.2	121.5	106.6	93.5	100.9	1
July	112.0	114.1	122.9	107.1	93.2	101.5	1
Aug	112.0	113.6	122.4	106.6	92.8	101.2	1
Sept	112.3	114.0	122.4	107.3	93.2	101.3	1
Oct	111.8	113.5	122.2	106.7	92.2	101.3	1
Nov	112.3	113.8	122.9	106.6	91.7	102.9	1
Dec	112.4	113.8	122.8	106.8	91.9	103.9	1
2008: Jan	112.6	113.8	122.9	106.8	91.3	103.2	1
Feb	112.3	113.1	122.2	106.0	91.2	103.6	1
Mar	112.0	113.3	122.4	106.2	91.0	103.9	1
Apr	111.4	112.3	120.7	106.0	89.1	104.0	1
May	111.2	112.3	120.6	106.2	88.5	104.1	1
June [p]	111.3	112.2	121.0	105.5	88.4	104.2	1
July [p]	111.4	112.1	121.4	105.2	87.3	105.7	1
Aug [p]	110.1	111.0	119.6	104.6	86.7	105.5	1
Sept [p]	105.9	106.9	115.9	99.8	86.3	96.5	1
Oct [p]	107.3	107.5	113.9	102.9	85.9	102.4	1

[1] Total industry and total manufacturing series include manufacturing as defined in the North American Industry Classification System (NAICS) plus those industries—logging and newspaper, periodical, book, and directory publishing—that have traditionally been considered to be manufacturing and included i the industrial sector.

Note.—Data based on NAICS; see footnote 1.

Source: Board of Governors of the Federal Reserve System.

TABLE B–52.—*Industrial production indexes, market groupings, 1959–2008*

[2002=100; monthly data seasonally adjusted]

month	Total indus- trial pro- duc- tion	Final products								Nonindustrial supplies			Materials		
		Total	Consumer goods				Equipment			Total	Con- struc- tion	Busi- ness	Total	Non- energy	Energy
			Total	Auto- motive prod- ucts	Other dur- able goods	Non- dur- able goods	Total [1]	Busi- ness	De- fense and space						
	25.5	24.4	30.9	19.1	19.6	37.2	16.5	11.9	47.2	26.4	37.5	21.6	25.5	....	51.4
	26.0	25.2	32.1	21.9	19.7	38.4	16.9	12.2	48.5	26.6	36.6	22.4	25.9	....	52.1
	26.2	25.4	32.7	20.0	20.3	39.6	16.7	11.8	49.3	27.1	36.9	23.0	25.9	....	52.5
	28.4	27.6	34.9	24.2	22.1	41.5	18.6	12.8	57.0	28.8	39.2	24.5	28.2	....	54.3
	30.1	29.2	36.9	26.5	23.8	43.4	19.7	13.5	61.5	30.4	41.0	26.1	30.0	....	57.5
	32.1	30.8	38.9	27.8	26.0	45.5	20.8	15.1	59.6	32.4	43.5	27.9	32.4	....	59.8
	35.3	33.8	42.0	34.2	29.5	47.5	23.5	17.3	65.9	34.4	46.2	29.7	36.2	....	62.6
	38.4	37.1	44.1	34.1	32.5	49.7	27.4	20.0	77.5	36.6	48.1	32.1	39.4	....	66.5
	39.2	38.6	45.2	29.9	32.9	52.3	29.2	20.4	88.4	38.1	49.4	33.7	39.0	32.2	68.8
	41.4	40.4	47.9	35.7	35.3	54.4	30.0	21.3	88.5	40.2	52.0	35.8	41.6	34.6	72.0
	43.3	41.7	49.7	35.8	37.6	56.2	30.8	22.7	84.3	42.4	54.2	38.1	44.1	36.7	75.6
	41.9	40.2	49.2	30.2	36.5	57.1	28.6	21.9	71.4	41.8	52.3	38.2	42.5	34.6	79.4
	42.5	40.6	52.0	38.4	38.6	58.8	26.8	20.8	64.1	43.1	53.9	39.4	43.2	35.2	80.1
	46.6	44.0	56.2	41.4	44.2	62.6	29.3	23.7	62.4	48.1	61.2	43.3	47.5	39.4	83.1
	50.4	47.4	58.7	45.0	47.2	64.5	33.4	27.4	68.3	51.4	66.4	46.0	51.8	43.7	85.2
	50.2	47.4	57.0	38.9	44.4	64.5	35.1	29.1	70.6	51.0	64.9	45.9	51.7	43.6	84.8
	45.8	44.7	54.8	37.5	38.8	63.4	32.1	25.9	71.2	45.8	54.9	42.4	46.0	37.4	84.0
	49.4	47.9	59.2	42.7	43.6	67.3	33.8	27.6	69.0	48.9	59.2	45.2	50.1	41.7	85.9
	53.1	51.7	62.9	48.3	48.7	69.8	37.7	31.9	61.9	53.1	64.4	48.9	53.5	45.1	88.6
	56.1	54.9	64.9	48.0	51.0	72.2	41.9	36.0	62.9	56.0	68.1	51.6	56.2	48.1	89.7
	57.8	56.7	63.9	43.2	51.3	71.8	46.8	40.6	67.5	57.7	69.8	53.4	57.7	49.4	92.1
	56.3	56.5	61.5	33.3	47.6	71.9	49.1	41.6	80.2	55.4	64.6	52.1	55.6	46.5	92.8
	57.0	57.9	61.9	34.3	48.0	72.3	51.4	42.8	86.8	56.0	65.3	53.4	55.9	46.6	93.7
	54.1	56.6	61.8	33.3	44.4	73.5	48.9	39.2	103.7	54.0	57.6	52.7	51.6	42.0	89.7
	55.6	57.7	64.1	38.7	48.2	74.3	48.6	39.4	104.6	56.9	61.7	55.2	53.0	44.9	86.9
	60.5	62.5	67.0	43.3	53.8	75.8	55.6	45.3	119.8	61.9	67.1	60.0	58.0	50.0	92.4
	61.3	64.0	67.6	43.2	53.8	76.7	58.3	46.9	134.0	63.5	68.8	61.6	57.9	50.0	91.9
	61.9	65.0	69.9	46.4	57.0	78.6	57.4	46.2	142.3	65.6	71.2	63.6	57.8	51.0	88.2
	65.1	68.0	72.9	49.6	60.0	81.4	60.6	49.4	145.3	69.6	75.7	67.4	60.9	54.4	90.3
	68.4	71.7	75.7	52.2	63.2	84.1	65.5	54.5	146.9	71.9	77.5	69.9	64.3	57.9	93.4
	69.1	72.5	76.0	54.3	63.9	83.8	67.1	56.4	147.1	72.6	77.2	70.9	64.8	58.2	94.3
	69.7	73.3	76.3	50.9	63.8	85.2	68.6	58.5	142.0	73.7	76.6	72.6	65.2	58.3	96.2
	68.7	72.4	76.2	47.5	62.0	86.4	66.3	57.5	131.5	71.9	72.4	71.6	64.2	57.1	96.3
	70.6	74.1	78.5	55.6	64.8	87.1	67.1	59.7	121.9	73.9	75.5	73.3	66.3	59.9	95.4
	72.9	76.4	81.0	61.4	69.2	88.3	69.1	62.4	115.2	76.4	78.8	75.6	68.5	62.5	95.7
	76.8	79.7	84.6	68.8	75.1	90.4	71.7	66.1	108.3	80.1	84.5	78.5	73.0	67.6	97.2
	80.4	83.0	87.2	70.9	79.7	92.6	76.5	71.8	105.4	83.1	86.4	81.8	77.1	72.2	98.7
	84.0	86.2	89.0	73.2	83.4	93.8	82.1	78.6	102.0	86.4	90.3	85.0	81.1	76.7	100.2
	90.1	91.9	92.2	78.6	88.7	96.0	92.5	90.4	100.7	92.0	94.8	91.0	87.7	84.9	100.0
	95.4	97.2	95.5	83.9	95.8	98.1	101.7	100.6	105.0	97.2	99.8	96.2	92.9	91.3	100.4
	99.5	99.9	97.5	91.9	100.9	98.0	105.9	106.5	102.1	100.8	102.4	100.3	98.6	98.4	99.9
	103.7	103.0	99.4	93.8	104.8	99.5	111.8	114.8	92.1	104.7	104.7	104.7	103.9	104.8	101.5
	100.1	101.0	98.2	90.9	98.9	99.5	107.8	108.2	100.3	104.0	100.1	100.5	99.2	98.8	100.3
	100.0	100.0	100.0	100.0	100.0	100.0	100.0	100.0	100.0	100.0	100.0	100.0	100.0	100.0	100.0
	101.2	101.2	101.3	105.6	100.7	100.5	100.9	99.7	106.3	101.1	99.6	101.7	101.3	101.8	100.0
	103.8	103.4	102.6	105.2	103.3	101.9	105.3	104.9	105.5	103.3	101.8	103.9	104.3	106.2	99.6
	107.2	107.7	105.5	102.9	106.7	105.5	113.6	112.6	116.6	107.1	106.4	107.4	106.8	110.4	98.4
	109.6	110.5	105.8	99.3	107.7	106.4	123.1	124.3	112.9	108.3	108.8	108.1	109.2	113.2	99.9
	111.4	112.8	107.5	100.9	105.4	108.8	127.1	128.4	117.1	107.9	106.0	108.7	111.3	115.5	101.6
an	109.8	111.2	106.2	95.0	105.2	108.1	124.6	125.2	116.1	107.5	105.9	108.1	109.3	113.0	100.6
±b	110.5	112.6	108.0	98.2	104.9	110.0	124.8	125.5	115.7	107.6	105.0	108.7	109.6	113.1	101.4
ar	110.4	111.9	106.9	99.2	105.0	108.4	125.2	126.5	113.1	107.8	106.0	108.4	109.9	114.1	100.3
or	111.0	112.4	107.5	101.8	106.1	108.6	125.6	126.9	114.6	108.1	106.1	108.9	110.6	114.9	100.7
ay	111.0	112.4	107.3	101.0	106.1	108.4	126.0	127.2	115.7	107.9	106.5	108.4	110.7	115.1	100.8
ne	111.4	112.9	107.6	103.7	106.2	108.3	127.2	128.3	117.4	108.2	107.3	108.5	111.0	115.7	100.5
ily	112.0	113.7	108.2	105.1	106.3	108.9	128.3	129.6	118.1	108.2	107.4	108.5	111.8	116.7	100.8
ug	112.0	113.4	107.9	103.0	106.2	108.9	128.0	129.4	117.9	108.3	107.1	108.7	112.0	116.3	102.1
ept	112.3	114.0	108.4	101.1	105.8	109.9	128.9	130.5	118.4	108.4	106.6	109.1	112.0	116.6	101.6
ct	111.8	113.0	107.3	100.0	104.8	108.8	128.1	129.9	118.3	107.9	105.4	108.8	112.2	116.4	102.5
ov	112.3	113.3	107.4	101.1	104.6	108.8	128.9	130.2	120.2	107.9	104.5	109.2	113.0	117.2	103.3
ec	112.4	113.5	107.4	101.6	103.8	108.8	129.8	131.2	119.9	107.6	104.2	108.9	113.1	116.9	104.1
an	112.6	114.0	108.0	99.6	102.5	110.1	130.0	131.4	120.9	107.7	103.6	109.3	113.0	116.7	104.2
b	112.3	113.8	107.9	98.5	101.3	110.4	129.5	131.1	119.6	107.2	102.3	109.2	112.6	116.0	104.5
lar	112.0	113.2	106.7	93.8	101.7	109.5	130.5	132.3	119.6	106.7	102.3	108.5	112.8	116.4	104.3
or	111.4	112.3	106.2	87.2	101.7	109.8	129.0	130.0	119.5	106.6	101.4	108.6	112.3	115.7	104.1
ay	111.2	112.1	105.8	87.9	101.6	109.1	129.3	130.4	119.0	106.1	101.7	107.9	112.2	115.4	104.2
ne p	111.3	112.6	106.2	92.3	101.1	109.1	129.9	130.8	120.2	105.7	101.3	107.5	112.1	115.4	104.1
ily p	111.4	112.6	106.2	93.6	101.4	108.9	129.7	130.8	119.1	105.8	102.1	107.4	112.3	115.1	105.1
ug p	110.1	111.0	104.1	83.2	99.6	108.0	129.7	130.5	119.4	104.8	101.1	106.3	111.1	113.9	103.7
ept p	105.9	108.2	102.9	84.7	96.8	106.7	122.3	121.2	116.9	102.3	99.2	103.6	105.1	108.6	96.9
ct p	107.3	108.8	104.3	81.6	96.0	109.0	120.3	118.5	118.1	102.5	98.1	104.3	107.6	109.5	101.9

...des other items not shown separately.

—See footnote 1 and Note, Table B–51.

ce: Board of Governors of the Federal Reserve System.

TABLE B–53.—*Industrial production indexes, selected manufacturing industries, 1967–2008*

[2002=100; monthly data seasonally adjusted]

Year or month	Durable manufacturing								Nondurable manufacturing					
	Primary metal		Fabricated metal products	Machinery	Computer and electronic products		Transportation equipment		Apparel	Paper	Printing and support	Chemical	Plastics and rubber products	F
	Total	Iron and steel products			Total	Selected high-technology[1]	Total	Motor vehicles and parts						
1967						0.3								
1968						.3								
1969						.3								
1970						.3								
1971						.3								
1972	122.0	129.1	69.1	67.9	1.4	.3	53.1	44.3	169.9	66.3	51.6	47.9	34.9	
1973	142.0	154.8	76.3	78.5	1.7	.4	60.7	50.6	175.1	71.7	54.2	52.4	39.2	
1974	145.5	165.4	75.0	82.4	1.9	.5	55.9	43.5	163.0	74.8	52.6	54.5	38.2	
1975	113.0	122.7	64.8	71.8	1.7	.5	50.7	38.0	159.5	64.6	49.1	47.9	32.7	
1976	120.0	127.3	69.4	74.9	2.0	.6	56.7	48.5	168.5	71.4	52.7	53.6	36.2	
1977	121.2	124.4	75.3	81.8	2.6	.8	61.7	55.1	179.1	74.5	57.1	58.3	42.6	
1978	129.0	133.6	79.0	88.1	3.1	1.0	65.6	57.4	184.3	77.9	60.4	61.2	44.1	
1979	132.1	138.3	82.5	93.0	3.9	1.3	66.3	52.6	174.6	79.0	62.2	62.6	43.4	
1980	116.1	117.3	77.8	88.5	4.7	1.6	58.8	38.8	177.2	78.8	62.7	59.2	38.6	
1981	116.2	121.6	77.3	87.6	5.5	1.9	56.6	37.8	176.2	79.9	64.3	60.2	40.9	
1982	82.2	74.7	69.2	73.3	6.1	2.2	52.1	34.1	178.5	78.6	69.1	56.3	40.2	
1983	84.2	75.4	69.8	66.1	7.1	2.6	57.5	43.5	183.7	83.7	74.3	60.2	43.7	
1984	92.3	83.0	75.9	77.2	8.7	3.4	65.3	52.2	186.3	88.0	80.9	63.7	50.5	
1985	85.2	77.1	77.0	77.4	9.3	3.6	68.7	54.2	179.0	86.2	84.2	63.2	52.5	
1986	83.2	75.2	76.5	76.2	9.6	3.7	70.3	54.1	181.1	89.8	88.4	66.0	54.7	
1987	89.7	85.7	77.9	77.8	11.0	4.5	72.9	56.1	182.3	92.7	94.9	71.1	60.6	
1988	100.2	99.7	81.9	85.6	12.3	5.4	77.4	59.9	179.1	96.4	98.0	75.2	63.3	
1989	97.9	96.2	81.3	88.8	12.7	5.7	78.9	59.3	170.2	97.5	98.4	76.6	65.4	
1990	96.7	95.1	80.3	86.7	13.8	6.4	76.5	55.8	166.8	97.4	102.1	78.4	67.2	
1991	90.8	86.9	76.6	81.3	14.3	6.9	73.4	53.3	167.7	97.6	98.9	78.1	66.5	
1992	93.0	90.9	79.0	81.1	16.1	8.2	76.1	60.7	170.9	100.0	104.3	79.3	71.6	
1993	97.5	96.4	82.0	87.1	17.7	9.6	78.3	67.0	174.9	101.1	104.6	80.2	76.7	
1994	104.9	103.9	89.1	95.4	20.7	12.1	82.0	77.0	178.4	105.5	105.7	82.2	83.0	
1995	106.0	105.6	94.6	102.2	26.7	16.9	82.1	79.3	178.6	107.0	107.3	83.6	85.1	
1996	108.6	108.1	98.0	105.8	34.5	24.1	83.5	79.9	173.6	103.7	108.0	85.3	87.9	
1997	113.3	111.4	102.4	111.6	46.1	35.4	91.1	86.1	171.6	105.9	110.2	90.3	93.4	
1998	115.2	111.2	105.8	114.4	59.2	49.1	99.2	90.6	162.5	106.8	111.5	91.8	96.7	
1999	115.1	111.9	106.4	112.0	77.2	70.0	104.5	100.5	155.6	107.6	112.4	93.6	101.9	
2000	111.4	110.8	110.7	117.7	101.3	98.4	99.7	99.9	148.0	105.3	113.1	95.0	102.9	
2001	99.4	96.8	102.6	104.2	103.6	101.7	96.2	91.4	126.9	99.3	106.3	93.3	96.9	
2002	100.0	100.0	100.0	100.0	100.0	100.0	100.0	100.0	100.0	100.0	100.0	100.0	100.0	
2003	99.1	101.2	98.7	99.7	113.8	119.7	101.0	103.5	92.8	96.8	96.2	101.3	100.3	
2004	110.0	118.2	98.9	103.8	129.0	136.5	100.7	103.7	79.8	97.6	96.9	105.6	101.5	
2005	108.0	110.1	103.5	110.2	143.5	157.2	104.6	103.9	77.0	97.5	99.0	109.3	102.3	
2006	112.4	119.5	109.1	115.5	164.6	190.6	104.2	100.2	75.4	97.5	99.5	112.6	102.8	
2007	110.3	115.7	112.0	116.0	183.4	224.4	106.2	97.2	75.7	95.8	99.8	114.2	103.4	
2007: Jan	108.0	111.8	109.6	114.2	171.7	202.2	102.6	94.2	77.7	96.2	101.2	113.3	101.6	
Feb	108.7	112.9	110.2	114.3	172.1	202.7	104.3	96.4	76.9	96.5	101.5	113.4	100.7	
Mar	109.6	113.9	111.2	115.8	173.7	206.4	104.5	96.8	75.7	96.2	101.3	114.1	101.7	
Apr	110.4	115.7	111.4	116.4	176.6	211.1	105.7	98.1	76.8	96.4	100.8	114.3	102.7	
May	110.2	116.2	111.3	117.0	177.4	213.9	105.8	97.5	76.5	96.1	99.5	114.1	103.1	
June	109.6	115.6	112.2	116.3	181.3	220.5	107.9	99.5	76.2	95.3	98.7	114.0	103.8	
July	113.2	117.6	112.6	117.4	185.6	229.2	108.9	100.8	76.2	95.9	98.4	114.5	104.5	
Aug	111.4	116.6	112.8	116.2	186.5	231.1	108.1	99.3	75.2	95.7	99.1	114.2	103.8	
Sept	109.2	112.8	113.2	118.0	188.3	234.6	106.9	96.6	74.4	95.0	99.6	115.0	105.0	
Oct	110.0	116.0	113.1	116.4	192.8	243.2	105.9	95.1	73.6	94.1	98.9	114.5	104.6	
Nov	111.0	118.3	113.7	115.4	196.2	247.5	106.9	95.8	73.4	95.4	99.4	114.7	105.4	
Dec	112.9	121.6	113.1	114.6	198.1	250.6	106.6	95.5	75.1	97.3	99.0	114.6	104.5	
2008: Jan	115.2	121.7	113.4	115.2	198.5	251.6	105.9	93.9	74.2	96.0	98.4	114.6	103.0	
Feb	114.1	124.6	113.5	114.1	202.2	257.0	104.5	93.0	73.6	93.7	97.3	113.6	102.8	
Mar	112.3	119.5	113.6	116.0	206.2	264.5	101.6	88.6	72.3	95.1	98.4	113.2	102.0	
Apr	111.5	118.2	112.4	112.4	208.9	269.5	97.8	83.1	71.7	93.8	97.4	113.2	101.3	
May	109.5	113.8	111.5	112.3	209.5	269.7	97.9	83.4	70.3	96.4	97.0	113.4	101.5	
June[p]	109.9	114.6	110.1	112.2	210.5	271.1	100.7	86.8	71.3	94.6	94.2	112.7	102.4	
July[p]	112.0	119.7	109.7	111.2	211.3	273.2	101.7	89.2	72.4	93.8	92.6	112.3	102.7	
Aug[p]	109.8	116.1	110.3	113.0	210.4	271.7	95.1	79.4	72.7	94.5	94.0	111.2	100.9	
Sept[p]	104.4	104.8	109.1	110.3	208.1	269.7	88.2	80.4	71.8	91.2	92.9	102.0	99.6	
Oct[p]	99.4	94.3	107.5	108.4	207.2	267.3	85.3	77.6	70.5	90.9	92.4	107.2	97.6	

[1] Computers and peripheral equipment, communications equipment, and semiconductors and related electronic components.

Note.—See footnote 1 and Note, Table B–51.

Source: Board of Governors of the Federal Reserve System.

[Percent [1]; monthly data seasonally adjusted]

Year or month	Total industry [2]	Manufacturing				Mining	Utilities	Stage-of-process		
		Total [2]	Durable goods	Nondurable goods	Other (non-NAICS) [2]			Crude	Primary and semi-finished	Finished
1959	....	81.6	....	....	....	....	....	....	83.0	81.1
1960	....	80.1	....	....	....	....	....	....	79.8	80.5
1961	....	77.3	....	....	....	....	....	....	77.9	77.2
1962	....	81.4	....	....	....	....	....	....	81.5	81.6
1963	....	83.5	....	....	....	....	....	....	83.8	83.4
1964	....	85.6	....	....	....	....	....	....	87.8	84.6
1965	....	89.5	....	....	....	....	....	....	91.0	88.8
1966	....	91.1	....	....	....	....	....	....	91.4	91.1
1967	87.0	87.2	87.5	86.3	....	81.2	94.5	81.1	85.0	88.2
1968	87.3	87.1	87.3	86.5	....	83.6	95.1	83.4	86.8	87.0
1969	87.4	86.6	87.0	86.2	....	86.8	96.8	85.7	88.1	85.5
1970	81.3	79.4	77.5	82.2	....	89.3	96.3	85.2	81.5	78.0
1971	79.6	77.9	75.1	81.9	....	88.0	94.7	84.4	81.6	75.4
1972	84.6	83.4	81.9	85.3	85.8	90.9	95.2	88.7	88.1	79.5
1973	88.4	87.6	88.5	86.6	84.7	91.9	94.2	90.6	92.2	83.1
1974	85.2	84.4	84.7	84.2	82.8	91.0	87.5	91.2	87.5	80.2
1975	75.6	73.5	71.5	76.0	77.3	89.1	84.7	83.9	75.1	73.5
1976	79.6	78.2	76.2	81.0	77.5	89.5	85.5	87.1	80.0	76.6
1977	83.3	82.3	81.1	84.1	83.3	89.6	86.2	89.0	84.5	79.7
1978	84.9	84.3	83.9	84.9	85.5	89.8	85.1	88.4	86.0	82.1
1979	85.0	84.2	84.4	83.7	85.7	91.1	86.3	89.3	86.0	82.0
1980	80.8	78.7	77.7	79.5	87.1	91.1	85.7	88.9	78.7	79.7
1981	79.6	77.0	75.2	78.8	87.5	90.8	84.6	89.1	77.1	77.8
1982	73.7	70.9	66.5	76.4	87.4	84.1	80.6	82.3	70.4	73.5
1983	74.9	73.5	68.7	79.6	88.1	79.7	79.6	79.8	74.2	73.5
1984	80.5	79.5	76.9	82.4	89.6	85.4	82.4	85.5	81.1	77.6
1985	79.3	78.3	75.8	80.8	90.4	83.9	82.4	83.7	79.8	77.0
1986	78.7	78.4	75.3	81.8	88.9	77.4	81.6	79.2	79.7	77.1
1987	81.2	80.9	77.6	84.7	90.7	80.4	83.4	83.2	82.8	78.6
1988	84.1	83.9	82.0	86.1	88.6	84.2	85.7	86.7	85.7	81.4
1989	83.6	83.1	81.6	84.9	85.4	85.1	86.4	87.2	84.7	81.1
1990	82.4	81.6	79.3	84.4	83.8	86.8	86.2	88.2	82.7	80.4
1991	79.6	78.3	75.0	82.2	81.1	84.8	87.2	85.4	79.7	77.9
1992	80.3	79.4	77.0	82.4	80.0	84.4	85.6	85.4	81.4	77.7
1993	81.4	80.4	78.8	82.3	81.3	85.7	87.9	85.6	83.5	77.9
1994	83.6	82.8	82.0	83.9	81.2	87.4	88.8	87.7	86.7	79.0
1995	84.0	83.2	82.7	83.9	82.0	87.7	89.9	88.5	86.8	79.6
1996	83.3	82.1	82.0	82.5	80.7	90.0	90.7	88.4	85.9	79.0
1997	84.0	83.1	82.8	83.2	84.9	91.0	89.4	90.1	86.0	80.2
1998	82.8	81.8	81.2	82.0	85.6	88.9	91.5	87.3	84.0	80.5
1999	81.9	80.1	80.5	80.4	86.1	86.0	93.0	86.6	84.1	78.4
2000	81.8	80.1	80.2	79.0	88.1	90.8	93.4	88.3	84.4	77.1
2001	76.3	73.9	71.8	75.6	83.8	90.4	89.8	85.2	77.7	72.6
2002	74.8	72.8	69.6	76.1	81.4	86.1	88.3	82.8	77.1	70.5
2003	76.0	74.0	71.1	76.7	82.9	88.0	86.5	84.6	78.4	71.4
2004	78.0	76.3	73.8	78.5	85.4	88.3	84.8	86.4	80.4	72.9
2005	80.2	78.6	76.4	80.4	86.2	88.5	85.4	86.7	82.5	75.3
2006	80.9	79.4	77.9	80.8	82.0	90.9	84.2	88.8	82.4	76.4
2007	81.0	79.4	77.7	81.2	80.1	89.3	86.2	88.5	81.7	77.5
2007: Jan	80.5	78.8	76.6	81.2	80.4	90.2	85.0	88.4	81.4	76.6
Feb	80.9	78.8	76.8	80.9	80.6	89.1	90.9	88.2	82.2	76.8
Mar	80.7	79.2	77.3	81.3	80.6	89.2	85.2	88.4	81.6	76.9
Apr	81.0	79.4	77.7	81.2	80.9	88.9	86.9	88.5	81.8	77.3
May	80.9	79.4	77.6	81.3	80.4	88.7	86.0	88.3	81.7	77.3
June	81.0	79.6	78.2	81.2	80.6	88.8	85.0	88.2	81.7	77.7
July	81.4	80.1	78.8	81.5	80.3	89.2	84.2	88.4	81.9	78.3
Aug	81.2	79.6	78.3	81.1	79.9	88.9	87.0	88.1	82.1	77.7
Sept	81.3	79.8	78.1	81.6	80.3	88.9	86.6	88.3	81.9	78.1
Oct	80.9	79.3	77.8	81.0	79.4	88.7	86.0	87.8	81.4	77.6
Nov	81.1	79.3	77.9	80.9	79.0	90.0	86.3	89.5	81.5	77.5
Dec	81.0	79.2	77.7	81.0	79.0	90.9	85.5	90.2	81.0	77.7
2008: Jan	81.0	79.1	77.5	81.0	78.5	90.2	87.4	89.5	81.3	77.5
Feb	80.7	78.5	76.9	80.3	78.4	90.5	88.6	89.4	81.0	77.0
Mar	80.4	78.5	76.8	80.4	78.2	90.7	85.4	89.6	80.4	77.0
Apr	79.9	77.7	75.6	80.2	76.6	90.7	86.5	89.2	80.2	76.0
May	79.6	77.6	75.3	80.3	76.1	90.8	84.5	89.6	79.6	75.9
June p	79.6	77.4	75.4	79.7	76.0	90.8	85.9	88.8	79.6	76.1
July p	79.6	77.2	75.5	79.5	74.9	92.1	85.2	89.7	79.3	76.0
Aug p	78.5	76.4	74.2	79.0	74.4	91.8	81.5	89.4	77.9	75.1
Sept p	75.5	73.5	71.8	75.3	74.1	84.0	83.3	80.1	75.9	73.3
Oct p	76.4	73.8	70.3	77.6	73.8	89.0	83.5	85.6	76.5	72.7

[1] Output as percent of capacity.
[2] See footnote 1 and Note, Table B–51.

Source: Board of Governors of the Federal Reserve System.

[Value put in place, billions of dollars; monthly data at seasonally adjusted annual rates]

Year or month	Total new construction	Private construction									Public construction		
		Total	Residential buildings [1]		Nonresidential buildings and other construction						Total	Federal	State and local
			Total [2]	New housing units [3]	Total	Lodging	Office	Commercial [4]	Manufacturing	Other [5]			
1964	75.1	54.9	30.5	24.1	24.4						20.2	3.7	16.5
1965	81.9	60.0	30.2	23.8	29.7						21.9	3.9	18.0
1966	85.8	61.9	28.6	21.8	33.3						23.8	3.8	20.0
1967	87.2	61.8	28.7	21.5	33.1						25.4	3.3	22.1
1968	96.8	69.4	34.2	26.7	35.2						27.4	3.2	24.2
1969	104.9	77.2	37.2	29.2	39.9						27.8	3.2	24.6
1970	105.9	78.0	35.9	27.1	42.1						27.9	3.1	24.8
1971	122.4	92.7	48.5	38.7	44.2						29.7	3.8	25.9
1972	139.1	109.1	60.7	50.1	48.4						30.0	4.2	25.8
1973	153.8	121.4	65.1	54.6	56.3						32.3	4.7	27.6
1974	155.2	117.0	56.0	43.4	61.1						38.1	5.1	33.0
1975	152.6	109.3	51.6	36.3	57.8						43.3	6.1	37.2
1976	172.1	128.2	68.3	50.8	59.9						44.0	6.8	37.2
1977	200.5	157.4	92.0	72.2	65.4						43.1	7.1	36.0
1978	239.9	189.7	109.8	85.6	79.9						50.1	8.1	42.0
1979	272.9	216.2	116.4	89.3	99.8						56.6	8.6	48.1
1980	273.9	210.3	100.4	69.6	109.9						63.6	9.6	54.0
1981	289.1	224.4	99.2	69.4	125.1						64.7	10.4	54.3
1982	279.3	216.3	84.7	57.0	131.6						63.1	10.0	53.1
1983	311.9	248.4	125.8	95.0	122.6						63.5	10.6	52.9
1984	370.2	300.0	155.0	114.6	144.9						70.2	11.2	59.0
1985	403.4	325.6	160.5	115.9	165.1						77.8	12.0	65.8
1986	433.5	348.9	190.7	135.2	158.2						84.6	12.4	72.2
1987	446.6	356.0	199.7	142.7	156.3						90.6	14.1	76.6
1988	462.0	367.3	204.5	142.4	162.8						94.7	12.3	82.5
1989	477.5	379.3	204.3	143.2	175.1						98.2	12.2	86.0
1990	476.8	369.3	191.1	132.1	178.2						107.5	12.1	95.4
1991	432.6	322.5	166.3	114.6	156.2						110.1	12.8	97.3
1992	463.7	347.8	199.4	135.1	148.4						115.8	14.4	101.5
1993	485.5	358.2	208.2	150.9	150.0	4.6	20.0	34.4	23.4	67.7	127.4	14.4	112.9
1994	531.9	401.5	241.0	176.4	160.4	4.7	20.4	39.6	28.8	66.9	130.4	14.4	116.0
1995	548.7	408.7	228.1	171.4	180.5	7.1	23.0	44.1	35.4	70.9	140.0	15.8	124.3
1996	599.7	453.0	257.5	191.1	195.5	10.9	26.5	49.4	38.1	70.6	146.7	15.3	131.4
1997	631.9	478.4	264.7	198.1	213.7	12.9	32.8	53.1	37.6	77.3	153.4	14.1	139.4
1998	688.5	533.7	296.3	224.0	237.4	14.8	40.4	55.7	40.5	86.0	154.8	14.3	140.5
1999	744.6	575.5	326.3	251.3	249.2	16.0	45.1	59.4	35.1	93.7	169.1	14.0	155.1
2000	802.8	621.4	346.1	265.0	275.3	16.3	52.4	64.1	37.6	104.9	181.3	14.2	167.2
2001	840.2	638.3	364.4	279.4	273.9	14.5	49.7	63.6	37.8	108.2	201.9	15.1	186.8
2002	847.9	634.4	396.7	298.8	237.7	10.5	35.3	59.0	22.7	110.2	213.4	16.6	196.9
2003	891.5	675.4	446.0	345.7	229.3	9.9	30.6	57.5	21.4	109.9	216.1	17.9	198.2
2004	991.6	771.4	532.9	417.5	238.5	12.0	32.9	63.2	23.7	106.8	220.2	18.3	201.8
2005	1,102.7	868.5	611.9	480.8	256.6	12.7	37.3	66.6	29.9	110.2	234.2	17.3	216.9
2006	1,167.6	912.2	613.7	468.8	298.4	17.6	45.7	73.4	35.1	126.7	255.4	17.6	237.8
2007	1,137.2	850.0	492.5	353.4	357.5	27.5	53.4	85.0	42.2	149.4	287.1	20.3	266.8
2007: Jan	1,149.1	872.3	553.3	401.1	319.0	20.7	51.7	78.4	36.6	131.6	276.8	20.5	256.3
Feb	1,149.0	875.0	545.3	390.8	329.7	21.4	51.3	80.9	38.7	137.4	274.0	18.8	255.2
Mar	1,162.4	887.3	552.1	386.0	335.1	24.0	52.1	81.7	38.0	139.4	275.1	18.5	256.6
Apr	1,148.2	869.4	528.5	381.4	340.9	25.4	50.8	83.4	41.1	140.2	278.8	18.9	259.9
May	1,154.6	868.5	520.9	373.2	347.6	26.5	50.6	84.6	40.0	145.9	286.1	19.7	266.5
June	1,149.4	863.0	508.2	367.6	354.8	27.8	51.1	85.4	40.1	150.5	286.4	20.5	265.9
July	1,139.4	852.9	493.6	358.9	359.3	29.1	52.1	84.6	42.9	150.6	286.6	20.4	266.1
Aug	1,138.8	848.5	480.2	346.9	368.3	29.3	54.1	86.5	42.6	155.7	290.3	21.5	268.8
Sept	1,134.9	837.7	465.1	334.5	372.6	30.1	55.4	87.9	42.8	156.4	297.2	20.1	277.1
Oct	1,124.2	829.9	447.0	320.5	382.9	32.1	57.6	88.6	44.8	159.9	294.3	21.3	273.0
Nov	1,115.3	816.9	428.7	305.2	388.3	32.5	57.8	89.1	47.2	161.7	298.4	21.6	276.8
Dec	1,093.5	797.5	413.9	289.2	383.7	31.2	56.1	85.1	51.2	160.0	296.0	21.9	274.1
2008: Jan	1,085.4	794.6	404.9	277.2	389.7	31.5	58.4	86.7	48.8	164.3	290.8	22.3	268.5
Feb	1,075.3	783.7	392.0	258.8	391.6	32.5	57.0	87.0	49.5	165.7	291.6	22.2	269.4
Mar	1,090.5	789.6	391.6	256.4	398.0	33.7	57.3	86.9	51.1	169.0	300.8	22.3	278.6
Apr	1,085.2	783.7	383.5	247.9	400.2	35.9	57.7	87.5	52.0	167.2	301.5	22.6	278.9
May	1,088.3	784.1	371.4	243.9	412.8	37.8	57.8	85.6	63.3	168.2	304.1	22.6	281.5
June	1,086.6	780.4	356.4	237.0	424.0	38.9	57.4	84.8	72.4	170.5	306.2	22.9	283.3
July	1,060.0	751.5	334.5	232.2	417.0	38.2	58.1	82.9	66.1	171.7	308.5	23.9	284.6
Aug	1,085.7	769.1	352.9	221.6	416.1	39.5	58.2	81.6	65.3	171.5	316.7	25.3	291.4
Sept p	1,085.7	771.9	351.2	215.1	420.6	38.8	59.4	77.6	68.3	176.4	313.8	23.7	290.1
Oct p	1,072.6	756.5	338.8	207.0	417.7	39.1	60.1	78.5	69.0	171.0	316.1	25.0	291.1

[1] Includes farm residential buildings.
[2] Includes residential improvements, not shown separately.
[3] New single- and multi-family units.
[4] Including farm.
[5] Health care, educational, religious, public safety, amusement and recreation, transportation, communication, power, highway and street, sewage and waste disposal, water supply, and conservation and development.

Note.—Data beginning with 1993 reflect reclassification.

Source: Department of Commerce (Bureau of the Census).

TABLE B–56.—*New private housing units started, authorized, and completed and houses sold, 1959–2008*

[Thousands; monthly data at seasonally adjusted annual rates]

Year or month	New housing units started				New housing units authorized [1]				New housing units completed	New houses sold
	Total	Type of structure			Total	Type of structure				
		1 unit	2 to 4 units [2]	5 units or more		1 unit	2 to 4 units	5 units or more		
1959	1,517.0	1,234.0	283.0		1,208.3	938.3	77.1	192.9		
1960	1,252.2	994.7	257.5		998.0	746.1	64.6	187.4		
1961	1,313.0	974.3	338.7		1,064.2	722.8	67.6	273.8		
1962	1,462.9	991.4	471.5		1,186.6	716.2	87.1	383.3		
1963	1,603.2	1,012.4	590.8		1,334.7	750.2	118.9	465.6		560
1964	1,528.8	970.5	108.3	450.0	1,285.8	720.1	100.8	464.9		565
1965	1,472.8	963.7	86.7	422.5	1,240.6	709.9	84.8	445.9		575
1966	1,164.9	778.6	61.2	325.1	971.9	563.2	61.0	347.7		461
1967	1,291.6	843.9	71.7	376.1	1,141.0	650.6	73.0	417.5		487
1968	1,507.6	899.4	80.7	527.3	1,353.4	694.7	84.3	574.4	1,319.8	490
1969	1,466.8	810.6	85.1	571.2	1,322.3	624.8	85.2	612.4	1,399.0	448
1970	1,433.6	812.9	84.9	535.9	1,351.5	646.8	88.1	616.7	1,418.4	485
1971	2,052.2	1,151.0	120.5	780.9	1,924.6	906.1	132.9	885.7	1,706.1	656
1972	2,356.6	1,309.2	141.2	906.2	2,218.9	1,033.1	148.6	1,037.2	2,003.9	718
1973	2,045.3	1,132.0	118.2	795.0	1,819.5	882.1	117.0	820.5	2,100.5	634
1974	1,337.7	888.1	68.0	381.6	1,074.4	643.8	64.3	366.2	1,728.5	519
1975	1,160.4	892.2	64.0	204.3	939.2	675.5	63.9	199.8	1,317.2	549
1976	1,537.5	1,162.4	85.8	289.2	1,296.2	893.6	93.1	309.5	1,377.2	646
1977	1,987.1	1,450.9	121.7	414.4	1,690.0	1,126.1	121.3	442.7	1,657.1	819
1978	2,020.3	1,433.3	125.1	462.0	1,800.5	1,182.6	130.6	487.3	1,867.5	817
1979	1,745.1	1,194.1	122.0	429.0	1,551.8	981.5	125.4	444.8	1,870.8	709
1980	1,292.2	852.2	109.5	330.5	1,190.6	710.4	114.5	365.7	1,501.6	545
1981	1,084.2	705.4	91.2	287.7	985.5	564.3	101.8	319.4	1,265.7	436
1982	1,062.2	662.6	80.1	319.6	1,000.5	546.4	88.3	365.8	1,005.5	412
1983	1,703.0	1,067.6	113.5	522.0	1,605.2	901.5	133.6	570.1	1,390.3	623
1984	1,749.5	1,084.2	121.4	543.9	1,681.8	922.4	142.6	616.8	1,652.2	639
1985	1,741.8	1,072.4	93.5	576.0	1,733.3	956.6	120.1	656.6	1,703.3	688
1986	1,805.4	1,179.4	84.0	542.0	1,769.4	1,077.6	108.4	583.5	1,756.4	750
1987	1,620.5	1,146.4	65.1	408.7	1,534.8	1,024.4	89.3	421.1	1,668.8	671
1988	1,488.1	1,081.3	58.7	348.0	1,455.6	993.8	75.7	386.1	1,529.8	676
1989	1,376.1	1,003.3	55.3	317.6	1,338.4	931.7	67.0	339.8	1,422.8	650
1990	1,192.7	894.8	37.6	260.4	1,110.8	793.9	54.3	262.6	1,308.0	534
1991	1,013.9	840.4	35.6	137.9	948.8	753.5	43.1	152.1	1,090.8	509
1992	1,199.7	1,029.9	30.9	139.0	1,094.9	910.7	45.8	138.4	1,157.5	610
1993	1,287.6	1,125.7	29.4	132.6	1,199.1	986.5	52.3	160.2	1,192.7	666
1994	1,457.0	1,198.4	35.2	223.5	1,371.6	1,068.5	62.2	241.0	1,346.9	670
1995	1,354.1	1,076.2	33.8	244.1	1,332.5	997.3	63.7	271.5	1,312.6	667
1996	1,476.8	1,160.9	45.3	270.8	1,425.6	1,069.5	65.8	290.3	1,412.9	757
1997	1,474.0	1,133.7	44.5	295.8	1,441.1	1,062.4	68.5	310.3	1,400.5	804
1998	1,616.9	1,271.4	42.6	302.9	1,612.3	1,187.6	69.2	355.5	1,474.2	886
1999	1,640.9	1,302.4	31.9	306.6	1,663.5	1,246.7	65.8	351.1	1,604.9	880
2000	1,568.7	1,230.9	38.7	299.1	1,592.3	1,198.1	64.9	329.3	1,573.7	877
2001	1,602.7	1,273.3	36.6	292.8	1,636.7	1,235.6	66.0	335.2	1,570.8	908
2002	1,704.9	1,358.6	38.5	307.9	1,747.7	1,332.6	73.7	341.4	1,648.4	973
2003	1,847.7	1,499.0	33.5	315.2	1,889.2	1,460.9	82.5	345.8	1,678.7	1,086
2004	1,955.8	1,610.5	42.3	303.0	2,070.1	1,613.4	90.4	366.2	1,841.9	1,203
2005	2,068.3	1,715.8	41.1	311.4	2,155.3	1,682.0	84.0	389.3	1,931.4	1,283
2006	1,800.9	1,465.4	42.7	292.8	1,838.9	1,378.2	76.6	384.1	1,979.4	1,051
2007	1,355.0	1,046.0	31.7	277.3	1,398.4	979.9	59.6	359.0	1,502.8	776
2007: Jan	1,382	1,106	22	254	1,585	1,138	74	373	1,815	872
Feb	1,486	1,188	30	268	1,580	1,118	73	389	1,624	820
Mar	1,492	1,196	37	259	1,578	1,135	72	371	1,620	823
Apr	1,487	1,198	36	253	1,489	1,078	61	350	1,535	907
May	1,436	1,146	34	256	1,522	1,063	64	395	1,549	857
June	1,458	1,136	38	284	1,433	1,016	56	361	1,491	793
July	1,371	1,055	40	276	1,386	997	57	332	1,515	796
Aug	1,337	968	37	332	1,343	928	55	360	1,498	702
Sept	1,185	936	29	220	1,277	870	50	357	1,378	694
Oct	1,275	884	40	351	1,182	811	48	323	1,401	723
Nov	1,179	816	21	342	1,187	767	53	367	1,404	629
Dec	1,000	779	10	211	1,111	714	56	341	1,329	600
2008: Jan	1,064	750	27	287	1,052	675	43	334	1,331	597
Feb	1,107	722	29	356	981	646	40	295	1,251	572
Mar	988	711	16	261	932	621	37	274	1,192	513
Apr	1,004	681	15	308	982	649	38	295	1,033	542
May	982	682	20	280	978	635	34	309	1,144	515
June	1,089	663	22	404	1,138	616	33	489	1,131	499
July	949	644	14	291	937	584	33	320	1,086	505
Aug	854	615	15	224	857	553	31	273	1,012	454
Sept *p*	828	549	17	262	805	538	34	233	1,161	457
Oct *p*	791	531	13	247	730	470	29	231	1,043	433

[1] Authorized by issuance of local building permits in permit-issuing places: 20,000 places beginning with 2004; 19,000 for 1994–2003; 17,000 for 1984–93; 16,000 for 1978–83; 14,000 for 1972–77; 13,000 for 1967–71; 12,000 for 1963–66; and 10,000 prior to 1963.

[2] Monthly data derived.

Note.—Data beginning with 1999 for new housing units started and completed and for new houses sold are based on new estimation methods and are not directly comparable with earlier data.

Source: Department of Commerce (Bureau of the Census).

TABLE B–57.—*Manufacturing and trade sales and inventories, 1967–2008*

[Amounts in millions of dollars; monthly data seasonally adjusted]

Year or month	Total manufacturing and trade			Manufacturing			Merchant wholesalers [1]			Retail trade			Retail and food services sales
	Sales [2]	Inventories [3]	Ratio [4]	Sales [2]	Inventories [3]	Ratio [4]	Sales [2]	Inventories [3]	Ratio [4]	Sales [2,5]	Inventories [3]	Ratio [4]	
SIC: [6]													
1967	90,820	145,681	1.60	46,486	84,646	1.82	19,576	25,786	1.32	24,757	35,249	1.42	
1968	98,685	156,611	1.59	50,229	90,560	1.80	21,012	27,166	1.29	27,445	38,885	1.42	
1969	105,690	170,400	1.61	53,501	98,145	1.83	22,818	29,800	1.31	29,371	42,455	1.45	
1970	108,221	178,594	1.65	52,805	101,599	1.92	24,167	33,354	1.38	31,249	43,641	1.40	
1971	116,895	188,991	1.62	55,906	102,567	1.83	26,492	36,568	1.38	34,497	49,856	1.45	
1972	131,081	203,227	1.55	63,027	108,121	1.72	29,866	40,297	1.35	38,189	54,809	1.44	
1973	153,677	234,406	1.53	72,931	124,499	1.71	38,115	46,918	1.23	42,631	62,989	1.48	
1974	177,912	287,144	1.61	84,790	157,625	1.86	47,982	58,667	1.22	45,141	70,852	1.57	
1975	182,198	288,992	1.59	86,589	159,708	1.84	46,634	57,774	1.24	48,975	71,510	1.46	
1976	204,150	318,345	1.56	98,797	174,636	1.77	50,698	64,622	1.27	54,655	79,087	1.45	
1977	229,513	350,706	1.53	113,201	188,378	1.66	56,136	73,179	1.30	60,176	89,149	1.48	
1978	260,320	400,931	1.54	126,905	211,691	1.67	66,413	86,934	1.31	67,002	102,306	1.53	
1979	297,701	452,640	1.52	143,936	242,157	1.68	79,051	99,679	1.26	74,713	110,804	1.48	
1980	327,233	508,924	1.56	154,391	265,215	1.72	93,099	122,631	1.32	79,743	121,078	1.52	
1981	355,822	545,786	1.53	168,129	283,413	1.69	101,180	129,654	1.28	86,514	132,719	1.53	
1982	347,625	573,908	1.67	163,351	311,852	1.95	95,211	127,428	1.36	89,062	134,628	1.49	
1983	369,286	590,287	1.56	172,547	312,379	1.78	99,225	130,075	1.28	97,514	147,833	1.44	
1984	410,124	649,780	1.53	190,682	339,516	1.73	112,199	142,452	1.23	107,243	167,812	1.49	
1985	422,583	664,039	1.56	194,538	334,749	1.73	113,459	147,409	1.28	114,586	181,881	1.52	
1986	430,419	662,738	1.55	194,657	322,654	1.68	114,960	153,574	1.32	120,803	186,510	1.56	
1987	457,735	709,848	1.50	206,326	338,109	1.59	122,968	163,903	1.29	128,442	207,836	1.55	
1988	497,157	767,222	1.49	224,619	369,374	1.57	134,521	178,801	1.30	138,017	219,047	1.54	
1989	527,039	815,455	1.52	236,698	391,212	1.63	143,760	187,009	1.28	146,581	237,234	1.58	
1990	545,909	840,594	1.52	242,686	405,073	1.65	149,506	195,833	1.29	153,718	239,688	1.56	
1991	542,815	834,609	1.53	239,847	390,950	1.65	148,306	200,448	1.33	154,661	243,211	1.54	
1992	567,176	842,809	1.48	250,394	382,510	1.54	154,150	208,302	1.32	162,632	251,997	1.52	
NAICS: [6]													
1992	540,573	836,992	1.53	242,002	378,709	1.57	147,261	196,914	1.31	151,310	261,369	1.67	168,261
1993	567,580	864,028	1.50	251,708	379,660	1.50	154,018	204,842	1.30	161,854	279,526	1.68	179,858
1994	610,253	927,330	1.46	269,843	399,910	1.44	164,575	221,978	1.29	175,835	305,442	1.66	194,638
1995	655,097	986,089	1.48	289,973	424,772	1.44	179,915	238,392	1.29	185,209	322,925	1.72	204,677
1996	687,350	1,005,497	1.46	299,766	430,446	1.43	190,362	241,041	1.27	197,222	334,010	1.67	217,463
1997	723,879	1,046,721	1.42	319,558	443,566	1.37	198,154	258,546	1.26	206,167	344,609	1.64	227,670
1998	742,837	1,078,740	1.43	324,984	449,065	1.35	202,260	272,406	1.31	215,592	357,269	1.62	238,278
1999	786,634	1,138,805	1.40	335,991	463,625	1.35	216,597	290,171	1.30	234,046	385,009	1.59	257,797
2000	834,325	1,197,597	1.41	350,715	481,673	1.35	234,546	309,071	1.29	249,063	406,853	1.59	274,518
2001	818,615	1,120,025	1.42	330,875	428,113	1.38	232,096	297,199	1.32	255,644	394,713	1.58	282,131
2002	823,714	1,140,083	1.36	326,227	423,133	1.28	236,294	300,791	1.25	261,194	416,159	1.55	288,845
2003	853,596	1,146,695	1.34	334,616	408,304	1.24	246,857	306,032	1.22	272,123	432,359	1.56	301,264
2004	923,319	1,238,037	1.30	359,081	440,697	1.19	274,710	335,935	1.17	289,528	461,405	1.56	320,526
2005	1,001,315	1,305,227	1.27	395,173	472,860	1.17	298,803	360,411	1.17	307,338	471,956	1.51	340,141
2006	1,068,026	1,390,428	1.27	418,330	511,487	1.19	325,749	390,350	1.16	323,947	488,591	1.49	358,978
2007	1,113,787	1,443,837	1.27	423,423	530,664	1.23	353,663	411,955	1.13	336,701	501,218	1.47	373,555
2007: Jan	1,069,908	1,392,163	1.30	408,610	512,189	1.25	331,772	390,950	1.18	329,526	489,024	1.48	365,610
Feb	1,080,114	1,395,913	1.29	411,584	512,706	1.25	336,263	392,674	1.17	332,267	490,533	1.48	368,271
Mar	1,093,846	1,395,099	1.28	417,629	512,948	1.23	341,337	393,980	1.15	334,880	488,131	1.46	371,322
Apr	1,103,192	1,399,680	1.27	422,726	514,686	1.22	346,315	395,470	1.14	334,151	489,524	1.46	370,568
May	1,115,541	1,405,888	1.26	426,330	516,996	1.21	349,584	396,332	1.13	339,627	492,560	1.45	376,206
June	1,110,106	1,411,042	1.27	422,938	517,956	1.22	351,429	398,126	1.13	335,739	494,960	1.47	372,603
July	1,121,298	1,416,225	1.26	431,756	518,644	1.20	352,422	398,870	1.13	337,120	498,711	1.48	374,270
Aug	1,117,717	1,420,769	1.27	423,435	518,057	1.22	357,087	400,986	1.12	337,195	501,726	1.49	374,253
Sept	1,126,455	1,428,608	1.27	422,225	521,995	1.24	363,137	405,082	1.12	341,093	501,531	1.47	378,404
Oct	1,134,373	1,430,592	1.26	427,623	522,777	1.22	364,887	405,003	1.11	341,863	502,812	1.47	379,295
Nov	1,153,365	1,435,815	1.24	435,555	526,439	1.21	373,884	407,837	1.09	343,926	501,539	1.46	381,280
Dec	1,144,800	1,443,837	1.26	433,063	530,664	1.23	371,569	411,955	1.11	340,168	501,218	1.47	377,909
2008: Jan	1,160,251	1,457,953	1.26	437,643	537,497	1.23	380,230	417,143	1.10	342,378	503,313	1.47	380,019
Feb	1,148,347	1,464,497	1.28	429,531	540,675	1.26	378,217	421,078	1.11	340,599	502,744	1.48	378,106
Mar	1,161,817	1,467,463	1.26	434,378	545,791	1.26	385,072	421,700	1.10	342,367	499,972	1.46	380,020
Apr	1,179,814	1,474,247	1.25	446,031	545,633	1.22	391,050	427,560	1.09	342,733	501,054	1.46	380,788
May	1,192,681	1,479,765	1.24	447,411	548,825	1.23	399,845	431,273	1.08	345,425	499,667	1.45	383,769
June	1,213,469	1,490,874	1.23	455,873	555,627	1.22	411,960	435,147	1.06	345,636	500,100	1.45	384,069
July	1,214,338	1,507,756	1.24	462,379	559,070	1.21	408,862	441,823	1.08	343,097	506,863	1.48	381,578
Aug	1,188,196	1,510,658	1.27	445,455	562,781	1.26	402,319	444,547	1.10	340,422	503,330	1.48	378,968
Sept [p]	1,162,953	1,506,718	1.30	431,492	558,296	1.29	396,162	444,183	1.12	335,299	504,239	1.50	374,065
Oct [p]				417,703	555,136	1.33				324,796			363,696

[1] Excludes manufacturers' sales branches and offices.
[2] Annual data are averages of monthly not seasonally adjusted figures.
[3] Seasonally adjusted, end of period. Inventories beginning with January 1982 for manufacturing and December 1980 for wholesale and retail trade are not comparable with earlier periods.
[4] Inventory/sales ratio. Monthly inventories are inventories at the end of the month to sales for the month. Annual data beginning with 1982 are the average of monthly ratios for the year. Annual data for 1967–81 are the ratio of December inventories to monthly average sales for the year.
[5] Food services included on Standard Industrial Classification (SIC) basis and excluded on North American Industry Classification System (NAICS) basis. See last column for retail and food services sales.
[6] Effective in 2001, data classified based on NAICS. Data on NAICS basis available beginning with 1992. Earlier data based on SIC. Data on both NAICS and SIC basis include semiconductors.

Source: Department of Commerce (Bureau of the Census).

TABLE B–58.—*Manufacturers' shipments and inventories, 1967–2008*

[Millions of dollars; monthly data seasonally adjusted]

Year or month	Shipments [1]			Inventories [2]								
	Total	Durable goods industries	Nondurable goods industries	Total	Durable goods industries				Nondurable goods industries			
					Total	Materials and supplies	Work in process	Finished goods	Total	Materials and supplies	Work in process	Finished goods
SIC: [3]												
1967	46,486	25,233	21,253	84,646	54,896	16,423	24,933	13,540	29,750	11,760	4,431	13,559
1968	50,229	27,624	22,605	90,560	58,732	17,344	27,213	14,175	31,828	12,328	4,852	14,648
1969	53,501	29,403	24,098	98,145	64,598	18,636	30,282	15,680	33,547	12,753	5,120	15,674
1970	52,805	28,156	24,649	101,599	66,651	19,149	29,745	17,757	34,948	13,168	5,271	16,509
1971	55,906	29,924	25,982	102,567	66,136	19,679	28,550	17,907	36,431	13,686	5,678	17,067
1972	63,027	33,987	29,040	108,121	70,067	20,807	30,713	18,547	38,054	14,677	5,998	17,379
1973	72,931	39,635	33,296	124,499	81,192	25,944	35,490	19,758	43,307	18,147	6,729	18,431
1974	84,790	44,173	40,617	157,625	101,493	35,070	42,530	23,893	56,132	23,744	8,189	24,199
1975	86,589	43,598	42,991	159,708	102,590	33,903	43,227	25,460	57,118	23,565	8,834	24,719
1976	98,797	50,623	48,174	174,636	111,988	37,457	46,074	28,457	62,648	25,847	9,929	26,872
1977	113,201	59,168	54,033	188,378	120,877	40,186	50,226	30,465	67,501	27,387	10,961	29,153
1978	126,905	67,731	59,174	211,691	138,181	45,198	58,848	34,135	73,510	29,619	12,085	31,806
1979	143,936	75,927	68,009	242,157	160,734	52,670	69,325	38,739	81,423	32,814	13,910	34,699
1980	154,391	77,419	76,972	265,215	174,788	55,173	76,945	42,670	90,427	36,606	15,884	37,937
1981	168,129	83,727	84,402	283,413	186,443	57,998	80,998	47,447	96,970	38,165	16,194	42,611
1982	163,351	79,212	84,139	311,852	200,444	59,136	86,707	54,601	111,408	44,039	18,612	48,757
1983	172,547	85,481	87,066	312,379	199,854	60,325	86,899	52,630	112,525	44,816	18,691	49,018
1984	190,682	97,940	92,742	339,516	221,330	66,031	98,251	57,048	118,186	45,692	19,328	53,166
1985	194,538	101,279	93,259	334,749	218,193	63,904	98,162	56,127	116,556	44,106	19,442	53,008
1986	194,657	103,238	91,419	322,654	211,997	61,331	97,000	53,666	110,657	42,335	18,124	50,198
1987	206,326	108,128	98,198	338,109	220,799	63,562	102,393	54,844	117,310	45,319	19,270	52,721
1988	224,619	118,458	106,161	369,374	242,468	69,611	112,958	59,899	126,906	49,396	20,559	56,951
1989	236,698	123,158	113,540	391,212	257,513	72,435	122,251	62,827	133,699	50,674	21,653	61,372
1990	242,686	123,776	118,910	405,073	263,209	73,559	124,130	65,520	141,864	52,645	22,817	66,402
1991	239,847	121,000	118,847	390,950	250,019	70,834	114,960	64,225	140,931	53,011	22,815	65,105
1992	250,394	128,489	121,905	382,510	238,105	69,459	104,424	64,222	144,405	54,007	23,532	66,866
NAICS: [3]												
1992	242,002	126,572	115,430	378,709	238,102	69,737	104,211	64,154	140,607	53,179	23,304	64,124
1993	251,708	133,712	117,996	396,580	238,737	72,657	101,999	64,081	140,923	54,289	23,305	63,329
1994	269,843	147,005	122,838	399,910	253,141	78,573	106,556	68,012	146,769	57,161	24,383	65,225
1995	289,973	158,568	131,405	424,772	267,358	85,473	106,658	75,227	157,414	60,725	25,755	70,934
1996	299,766	164,883	134,883	430,446	272,495	86,226	110,563	75,706	157,951	59,101	26,438	72,412
1997	319,558	178,949	140,610	443,566	281,074	92,292	109,960	78,822	162,492	60,160	28,478	73,854
1998	324,984	185,966	139,019	449,065	290,700	93,629	115,235	81,836	158,365	58,223	27,044	73,098
1999	335,991	193,895	142,096	463,625	296,553	97,959	114,111	84,483	167,072	61,098	28,741	77,233
2000	350,715	197,807	152,908	481,673	306,727	106,214	111,196	89,317	174,946	61,509	30,015	83,422
2001	330,875	181,201	149,674	428,113	267,829	91,291	93,924	82,614	160,284	55,726	27,073	77,485
2002	326,227	176,968	149,259	423,133	260,582	88,575	92,386	79,621	162,551	56,536	27,828	78,187
2003	334,616	178,549	156,067	408,304	246,963	82,354	88,719	75,890	161,341	56,847	27,047	77,447
2004	359,081	188,722	170,359	440,697	265,070	92,207	91,207	81,656	175,627	61,713	29,953	83,961
2005	395,173	202,070	193,103	472,860	283,598	98,271	98,929	86,398	189,262	66,394	32,889	89,979
2006	418,330	213,408	204,923	511,487	309,914	108,819	105,340	95,755	201,573	69,638	36,247	95,688
2007	423,423	213,572	209,851	530,664	320,757	109,305	113,969	97,483	209,907	72,911	38,405	98,591
2007: Jan	408,610	210,501	198,109	512,189	311,878	109,085	106,344	96,449	200,311	69,687	35,863	94,761
Feb	411,584	211,161	200,423	512,706	312,453	108,863	106,371	97,219	200,253	70,147	35,861	94,245
Mar	417,629	212,648	204,981	512,988	312,312	108,642	106,176	97,494	200,676	70,049	36,163	94,464
Apr	422,726	215,748	206,978	514,686	313,015	109,083	106,879	97,053	201,671	70,523	35,873	95,275
May	426,330	216,056	210,274	516,996	313,421	109,099	107,808	96,514	203,575	71,132	36,392	96,051
June	422,938	213,400	209,538	517,956	313,371	108,988	107,988	96,395	204,585	71,545	36,359	96,681
July	431,756	219,187	212,569	518,644	313,495	108,988	108,400	96,107	205,149	71,772	35,812	97,565
Aug	423,435	215,802	207,633	518,057	313,236	108,732	109,137	95,367	204,821	72,246	35,273	97,302
Sept	422,225	212,453	209,772	521,995	314,636	107,972	109,712	96,952	207,359	73,731	35,546	98,082
Oct	427,623	213,240	214,383	522,777	315,650	108,567	110,980	96,103	207,127	73,175	36,333	97,619
Nov	435,555	212,950	222,605	526,439	317,534	108,943	111,928	96,663	208,905	72,998	37,281	98,626
Dec	433,063	211,274	221,789	530,664	320,757	109,305	113,969	97,483	209,907	72,911	38,405	98,591
2008: Jan	437,643	215,917	221,726	537,497	322,384	110,161	115,144	97,079	215,113	75,343	40,346	99,424
Feb	429,531	211,772	217,759	540,675	323,841	110,644	116,407	96,790	216,834	75,458	41,346	100,030
Mar	434,378	209,778	224,600	545,791	327,066	111,560	118,227	97,279	218,725	75,215	41,550	101,960
Apr	446,031	213,591	232,440	545,633	328,911	112,097	119,869	96,945	216,722	75,045	40,515	101,162
May	447,411	211,049	236,362	548,825	330,426	112,275	121,109	97,042	218,399	76,167	42,033	100,199
June	455,873	212,947	242,926	555,627	333,127	113,575	122,118	97,434	222,500	76,810	41,533	104,157
July	462,379	217,549	244,830	559,070	336,185	115,462	123,189	97,534	222,885	76,685	42,641	103,559
Aug	445,455	208,339	237,116	562,781	339,033	115,897	124,479	98,657	223,748	76,770	42,683	104,295
Sept [p]	431,492	208,240	223,252	558,296	339,728	116,330	124,799	98,599	218,568	76,309	41,327	100,932
Oct [p]	417,703	202,075	215,628	555,136	341,256	116,608	126,342	98,306	213,880	73,876	39,049	100,955

[1] Annual data are averages of monthly not seasonally adjusted figures.
[2] Seasonally adjusted, end of period. Data beginning with 1982 are not comparable with earlier data.
[3] Effective in 2001, data classified based on North American Industry Classification System (NAICS). Data on NAICS basis available beginning with 1992.
Earlier data based on Standard Industrial Classification (SIC). Data on both NAICS and SIC basis include semiconductors.

Source: Department of Commerce (Bureau of the Census).

TABLE B–59.—*Manufacturers' new and unfilled orders, 1967–2008*

[Amounts in millions of dollars; monthly data seasonally adjusted]

Year or month	New orders [1]				Unfilled orders [2]			Unfilled orders to shipments ratio [2]		
	Total	Durable goods industries		Nondurable goods industries	Total	Durable goods industries	Nondurable goods industries	Total	Durable goods industries	Nondurable goods industries
		Total	Capital goods, nondefense							
SIC: [3]										
1967	47,067	25,803	....	21,265	103,711	99,735	3,976	3.66	4.37	0.73
1968	50,657	28,051	6,314	22,606	108,377	104,393	3,984	3.79	4.58	.69
1969	53,990	29,876	7,046	24,114	114,341	110,161	4,180	3.71	4.45	.69
1970	52,022	27,340	6,072	24,682	105,008	100,412	4,596	3.61	4.36	.78
1971	55,921	29,905	6,682	26,016	105,247	100,225	5,022	3.32	4.00	.76
1972	64,182	35,038	7,745	29,144	119,349	113,034	6,315	3.26	3.85	.86
1973	76,003	42,627	9,926	33,376	156,561	149,204	7,357	3.80	4.51	.91
1974	87,327	46,862	11,594	40,465	187,043	181,519	5,524	4.09	4.93	.62
1975	85,139	41,957	9,886	43,181	169,546	161,664	7,882	3.69	4.45	.82
1976	99,513	51,307	11,490	48,206	178,128	169,857	8,271	3.24	3.88	.74
1977	115,109	61,035	13,681	54,073	202,024	193,323	8,701	3.24	3.85	.71
1978	131,629	72,278	17,588	59,351	259,169	248,281	10,888	3.57	4.20	.81
1979	147,604	79,483	21,154	68,121	303,593	291,321	12,272	3.89	4.62	.82
1980	156,359	79,392	21,135	76,967	327,416	315,202	12,214	3.85	4.58	.75
1981	168,025	83,654	21,806	84,371	326,547	314,707	11,840	3.87	4.68	.69
1982	162,140	78,064	19,213	84,077	311,887	300,798	11,089	3.84	4.74	.62
1983	175,451	88,140	19,624	87,311	347,273	333,114	14,159	3.53	4.29	.69
1984	192,879	100,164	23,669	92,715	373,529	359,651	13,878	3.60	4.37	.64
1985	195,706	102,356	24,545	93,351	387,196	372,097	15,099	3.67	4.47	.68
1986	195,204	103,647	23,982	91,557	393,515	376,699	16,816	3.59	4.41	.70
1987	209,389	110,809	26,094	98,579	430,426	408,688	21,738	3.63	4.43	.83
1988	228,270	122,076	31,108	106,194	474,154	452,150	22,004	3.64	4.46	.76
1989	239,572	126,055	32,988	113,516	508,849	487,098	21,751	3.96	4.85	.77
1990	244,507	125,583	33,331	118,924	531,131	509,124	22,007	4.15	5.15	.76
1991	238,805	119,849	30,471	118,957	519,199	495,802	23,397	4.08	5.07	.79
1992	248,212	126,308	31,524	121,905	492,893	469,381	23,512	3.51	4.30	.75
NAICS: [3]										
1992	....	....	....	....	....	451,273	....	....	5.14	....
1993	246,668	128,672	40,681	....	....	425,979	....	....	4.66	....
1994	266,641	143,803	45,175	....	....	434,979	....	....	4.21	....
1995	285,542	154,137	51,011	....	....	447,411	....	....	3.97	....
1996	297,282	162,399	54,066	....	....	488,726	....	....	4.14	....
1997	314,986	174,377	60,697	....	....	512,916	....	....	4.04	....
1998	317,345	178,327	62,133	....	....	496,083	....	....	3.97	....
1999	329,770	187,674	64,392	....	....	505,498	....	....	3.76	....
2000	346,789	193,881	69,278	....	....	549,445	....	....	3.87	....
2001	322,746	173,072	58,246	....	....	514,349	....	....	4.21	....
2002	316,809	167,550	51,817	....	....	462,122	....	....	4.05	....
2003	330,369	174,302	52,894	....	....	477,608	....	....	3.92	....
2004	354,619	184,261	56,094	....	....	496,343	....	....	3.88	....
2005	395,401	202,298	65,770	....	....	572,835	....	....	3.84	....
2006	419,793	214,871	71,725	....	....	660,406	....	....	4.17	....
2007	427,597	217,746	74,288	....	....	773,297	....	....	4.80	....
2007: Jan	405,820	207,711	65,148	....	....	664,272	....	....	4.58	....
Feb	412,981	212,558	69,914	....	....	670,877	....	....	4.56	....
Mar	422,322	217,341	77,522	....	....	680,483	....	....	4.59	....
Apr	428,894	221,916	78,168	....	....	693,329	....	....	4.64	....
May	427,149	216,875	73,057	....	....	699,668	....	....	4.65	....
June	427,369	217,831	75,720	....	....	708,841	....	....	4.76	....
July	442,069	229,500	80,464	....	....	724,733	....	....	4.76	....
Aug	426,512	218,879	70,219	....	....	732,889	....	....	4.87	....
Sept	425,399	215,627	74,677	....	....	740,534	....	....	4.96	....
Oct	430,254	215,871	72,501	....	....	748,304	....	....	5.01	....
Nov	437,808	215,203	75,585	....	....	755,712	....	....	5.06	....
Dec	445,917	224,128	78,238	....	....	773,297	....	....	5.20	....
2008: Jan	435,415	213,689	73,271	....	....	777,859	....	....	5.14	....
Feb	433,860	216,101	74,408	....	....	786,860	....	....	5.24	....
Mar	440,216	215,616	75,431	....	....	797,114	....	....	5.30	....
Apr	445,915	213,475	73,609	....	....	802,972	....	....	5.27	....
May	450,033	213,671	73,639	....	....	810,293	....	....	5.33	....
June	459,576	216,650	71,958	....	....	818,023	....	....	5.30	....
July	462,993	218,163	74,498	....	....	824,232	....	....	5.25	....
Aug	443,200	206,084	68,694	....	....	826,529	....	....	5.50	....
Sept [p]	429,286	206,034	67,923	....	....	828,225	....	....	5.50	....
Oct [p]	407,370	191,742	64,851	....	....	823,094	....	....	5.69	....

[1] Annual data are averages of monthly not seasonally adjusted figures.

[2] Unfilled orders are seasonally adjusted, end of period. Ratios are unfilled orders at end of period to shipments for period (excludes industries with no unfilled orders). Annual ratios relate to seasonally adjusted data for December.

[3] Effective in 2001, data classified based on North American Industry Classification System (NAICS). Data on NAICS basis available beginning with 1992. Earlier data based on the Standard Industrial Classification (SIC). Data on SIC basis include semiconductors. Data on NAICS basis do not include semiconductors.

Note.—For NAICS basis data beginning with 1992, because there are no unfilled orders for manufacturers' nondurable goods, manufacturers' nondurable new orders and nondurable shipments are the same (see Table B–58).

Source: Department of Commerce (Bureau of the Census).

PRICES

TABLE B–60.—*Consumer price indexes for major expenditure classes, 1960–2008*

[For all urban consumers; 1982–84=100, except as noted]

Year or month	All items	Food and beverages		Apparel	Housing	Transportation	Medical care	Recreation[2]	Education and communication[2]	Other goods and services	Energy[3]
		Total[1]	Food								
1960	29.6	....	30.0	45.7	....	29.8	22.3	....	....	....	22.4
1961	29.9	....	30.4	46.1	....	30.1	22.9	....	....	....	22.5
1962	30.2	....	30.6	46.3	....	30.8	23.5	....	....	....	22.6
1963	30.6	....	31.1	46.9	....	30.9	24.1	....	....	....	22.6
1964	31.0	....	31.5	47.3	....	31.4	24.6	....	....	....	22.5
1965	31.5	....	32.2	47.8	....	31.9	25.2	....	....	....	22.9
1966	32.4	....	33.8	49.0	....	32.3	26.3	....	....	....	23.3
1967	33.4	35.0	34.1	51.0	30.8	33.3	28.2	....	....	35.1	23.8
1968	34.8	36.2	35.3	53.7	32.0	34.3	29.9	....	....	36.9	24.2
1969	36.7	38.1	37.1	56.8	34.0	35.7	31.9	....	....	38.7	24.8
1970	38.8	40.1	39.2	59.2	36.4	37.5	34.0	....	....	40.9	25.5
1971	40.5	41.4	40.4	61.1	38.0	39.5	36.1	....	....	42.9	26.5
1972	41.8	43.1	42.1	62.3	39.4	39.9	37.3	....	....	44.7	27.2
1973	44.4	48.8	48.2	64.6	41.2	41.2	38.8	....	....	46.4	29.4
1974	49.3	55.5	55.1	69.4	45.8	45.8	42.4	....	....	49.8	38.1
1975	53.8	60.2	59.8	72.5	50.7	50.1	47.5	....	....	53.9	42.1
1976	56.9	62.1	61.6	75.2	53.8	55.1	52.0	....	....	57.0	45.1
1977	60.6	65.8	65.5	78.6	57.4	59.0	57.0	....	....	60.4	49.4
1978	65.2	72.2	72.0	81.4	62.4	61.7	61.8	....	....	64.3	52.5
1979	72.6	79.9	79.9	84.9	70.1	70.5	67.5	....	....	68.9	65.7
1980	82.4	86.7	86.8	90.9	81.1	83.1	74.9	....	....	75.2	86.0
1981	90.9	93.5	93.6	95.3	90.4	93.2	82.9	....	....	82.6	97.7
1982	96.5	97.3	97.4	97.8	96.9	97.0	92.5	....	....	91.1	99.2
1983	99.6	99.5	99.4	100.2	99.5	99.3	100.6	....	....	101.1	99.9
1984	103.9	103.2	103.2	102.1	103.6	103.7	106.8	....	....	107.9	100.9
1985	107.6	105.6	105.6	105.0	107.7	106.4	113.5	....	....	114.5	101.6
1986	109.6	109.1	109.0	105.9	110.9	102.3	122.0	....	....	121.4	88.2
1987	113.6	113.5	113.5	110.6	114.2	105.4	130.1	....	....	128.5	88.6
1988	118.3	118.2	118.2	115.4	118.5	108.7	138.6	....	....	137.0	89.3
1989	124.0	124.9	125.1	118.6	123.0	114.1	149.3	....	....	147.7	94.3
1990	130.7	132.1	132.4	124.1	128.5	120.5	162.8	....	....	159.0	102.1
1991	136.2	136.8	136.3	128.7	133.6	123.8	177.0	....	....	171.6	102.5
1992	140.3	138.7	137.9	131.9	137.5	126.5	190.1	....	....	183.3	103.0
1993	144.5	141.6	140.9	133.7	141.2	130.4	201.4	90.7	85.5	192.9	104.2
1994	148.2	144.9	144.3	133.4	144.8	134.3	211.0	92.7	88.8	198.5	104.6
1995	152.4	148.9	148.4	132.0	148.5	139.1	220.5	94.5	92.2	206.9	105.2
1996	156.9	153.7	153.3	131.7	152.8	143.0	228.2	97.4	95.3	215.4	110.1
1997	160.5	157.7	157.3	132.9	156.8	144.3	234.6	99.6	98.4	224.8	111.5
1998	163.0	161.1	160.7	133.0	160.4	141.6	242.1	101.1	100.3	237.7	102.9
1999	166.6	164.6	164.1	131.3	163.9	144.4	250.6	102.0	101.2	258.3	106.6
2000	172.2	168.4	167.8	129.6	169.6	153.3	260.8	103.3	102.5	271.1	124.6
2001	177.1	173.6	173.1	127.3	176.4	154.3	272.8	104.9	105.2	282.6	129.3
2002	179.9	176.8	176.2	124.0	180.3	152.9	285.6	106.2	107.9	293.2	121.7
2003	184.0	180.5	180.0	120.9	184.8	157.6	297.1	107.5	109.8	298.7	136.5
2004	188.9	186.6	186.2	120.4	189.5	163.1	310.1	108.6	111.6	304.7	151.4
2005	195.3	191.2	190.7	119.5	195.7	173.9	323.2	109.4	113.7	313.4	177.1
2006	201.6	195.7	195.2	119.5	203.2	180.9	336.2	110.9	116.8	321.7	196.9
2007	207.342	203.300	202.916	118.998	209.586	184.682	351.054	111.443	119.577	333.328	207.723
2007: Jan	202.416	199.198	198.812	115.988	206.057	174.463	343.510	111.012	117.815	329.198	183.567
Feb	203.499	200.402	200.000	119.017	207.177	174.799	346.457	111.174	117.971	330.459	184.451
Mar	205.352	200.869	200.403	122.582	208.080	180.346	347.172	111.244	118.231	331.144	196.929
Apr	206.686	201.292	200.820	122.934	208.541	185.231	348.225	111.481	118.301	331.743	207.265
May	207.949	202.225	201.791	121.452	208.902	189.961	349.087	111.659	118.787	332.785	219.071
June	208.352	202.885	202.441	117.225	210.649	189.064	349.510	111.563	118.734	333.378	221.088
July	208.299	203.533	203.121	113.500	211.286	187.690	351.643	111.347	119.025	333.415	217.274
Aug	207.917	204.289	203.885	114.439	211.098	184.480	352.961	111.139	120.311	333.325	209.294
Sept	208.490	205.279	204.941	119.535	210.865	184.532	353.723	111.400	121.273	334.801	209.637
Oct	208.936	206.124	205.796	121.846	210.701	184.952	355.653	111.753	121.557	335.680	207.588
Nov	210.177	206.563	206.277	121.204	210.745	190.677	357.041	111.842	121.409	336.379	219.009
Dec	210.036	206.936	206.704	118.257	210.933	189.984	357.661	111.705	121.506	337.633	217.506
2008: Jan	211.080	208.837	208.618	115.795	212.244	190.459	360.459	112.083	121.762	339.052	219.465
Feb	211.693	209.462	209.166	117.839	213.026	190.520	362.155	112.365	121.766	340.191	219.311
Mar	213.528	209.692	209.385	120.881	214.389	195.189	363.000	112.731	121.832	341.827	230.505
Apr	214.823	211.365	211.102	122.113	214.890	198.608	363.184	112.874	122.073	343.410	240.194
May	216.632	212.251	212.054	120.752	215.809	205.262	363.396	112.987	122.348	344.709	257.106
June	218.815	213.383	213.243	117.019	217.941	211.787	363.616	112.991	122.828	345.885	275.621
July	219.964	215.326	215.299	114.357	219.610	212.806	363.963	113.277	123.445	346.810	280.833
Aug	219.086	216.419	216.422	116.376	219.148	206.739	364.477	113.786	124.653	346.990	266.283
Sept	218.783	217.672	217.696	121.168	218.184	203.861	365.036	114.032	125.505	348.166	258.020
Oct	216.573	218.705	218.738	122.243	217.383	192.709	365.746	114.169	125.686	349.276	231.561

[1] Includes alcoholic beverages, not shown separately.
[2] December 1997=100.
[3] Household energy—gas (piped), electricity, fuel oil, etc.—and motor fuel. Motor oil, coolant, etc. also included through 1982.

Note.—Data beginning with 1983 incorporate a rental equivalence measure for homeowners' costs.
Series reflect changes in composition and renaming beginning in 1998, and formula and methodology changes beginning in 1999.

Source: Department of Labor (Bureau of Labor Statistics).

Table B–61.—Consumer price indexes for selected expenditure classes, 1960–2008

[For all urban consumers; 1982–84=100, except as noted]

Year or month	Food and beverages — Total [1]	Food — Total	Food — At home	Food — Away from home	Housing — Total [2]	Shelter — Total [2]	Shelter — Rent of primary residence	Shelter — Owners' equivalent rent of primary residence [3]	Fuels and utilities — Total [2]	Household energy — Total [2]	Household energy — Gas (piped) and electricity
1960	....	30.0	31.5	25.4	....	25.2	38.7	....	26.0	....	23.
1961	....	30.4	31.8	26.0	....	25.4	39.2	....	26.3	....	23.
1962	....	30.6	32.0	26.7	....	25.8	39.7	....	26.3	....	23.
1963	....	31.1	32.4	27.3	....	26.1	40.1	....	26.6	....	23.
1964	....	31.5	32.7	27.8	....	26.5	40.5	....	26.6	....	23.
1965	....	32.2	33.5	28.4	....	27.0	40.9	....	26.6	....	23.
1966	....	33.8	35.2	29.7	....	27.8	41.5	....	26.7	....	23.
1967	35.0	34.1	35.1	31.3	30.8	28.8	42.2	....	27.1	21.4	23.
1968	36.2	35.3	36.3	32.9	32.0	30.1	43.3	....	27.4	21.7	23.
1969	38.1	37.1	38.0	34.9	34.0	32.6	44.7	....	28.0	22.1	24.
1970	40.1	39.2	39.9	37.5	36.4	35.5	46.5	....	29.1	23.1	25.
1971	41.4	40.4	40.9	39.4	38.0	37.0	48.7	....	31.1	24.7	27.
1972	43.1	42.1	42.7	41.0	39.4	38.7	50.4	....	32.5	25.7	28.
1973	48.8	48.2	49.7	44.2	41.2	40.5	52.5	....	34.3	27.5	29.
1974	55.5	55.1	57.1	49.8	45.8	44.4	55.2	....	40.7	34.4	34.
1975	60.2	59.8	61.8	54.5	50.7	48.8	58.0	....	45.4	39.4	40.
1976	62.1	61.6	63.1	58.2	53.8	51.5	61.1	....	49.4	43.3	44.
1977	65.8	65.5	66.8	62.6	57.4	54.9	64.8	....	54.7	49.0	50.
1978	72.2	72.0	73.8	68.3	62.4	60.5	69.3	....	58.5	53.0	55.
1979	79.9	79.9	81.8	75.9	70.1	68.9	74.3	....	64.8	61.3	61.
1980	86.7	86.8	88.4	83.4	81.1	81.0	80.9	....	75.4	74.8	71.
1981	93.5	93.6	94.8	90.9	90.4	90.5	87.9	....	86.4	87.2	81.
1982	97.3	97.4	98.1	95.8	96.9	96.9	94.6	....	94.9	95.6	93.
1983	99.5	99.4	99.1	100.0	99.5	99.1	100.1	102.5	100.2	100.5	101.
1984	103.2	103.2	102.8	104.2	103.6	104.0	105.3	107.3	104.8	104.0	105.
1985	105.6	105.6	104.3	108.3	107.7	109.8	111.8	113.2	106.5	104.5	107.
1986	109.1	109.0	107.3	112.5	110.9	115.8	118.3	119.4	104.1	99.2	105.
1987	113.5	113.5	111.9	117.0	114.2	121.3	123.1	124.8	103.0	97.3	103.
1988	118.2	118.2	116.6	121.8	118.5	127.1	127.8	131.1	104.4	98.0	104.
1989	124.9	125.1	124.2	127.4	123.0	132.8	132.8	137.4	107.8	100.9	107.
1990	132.1	132.4	132.3	133.4	128.5	140.0	138.4	144.8	111.6	104.5	109.
1991	136.8	136.3	135.8	137.9	133.6	146.3	143.3	150.4	115.3	106.7	112.
1992	138.7	137.9	136.8	140.7	137.5	151.2	146.9	155.5	117.8	108.1	114.
1993	141.6	140.9	140.1	143.2	141.2	155.7	150.3	160.5	121.3	111.2	118.
1994	144.9	144.3	144.1	145.7	144.8	160.5	154.0	165.8	122.8	111.7	119.
1995	148.9	148.4	148.8	149.0	148.5	165.7	157.8	171.3	123.7	111.5	119.
1996	153.7	153.3	154.3	152.7	152.8	171.0	162.0	176.8	127.5	115.2	122
1997	157.7	157.3	158.1	157.0	156.8	176.3	166.7	181.9	130.8	117.9	125.
1998	161.1	160.7	161.1	161.1	160.4	182.1	172.1	187.8	128.5	113.7	121.
1999	164.6	164.1	164.2	165.1	163.9	187.3	177.5	192.9	128.8	113.5	120.
2000	168.4	167.8	167.9	169.0	169.6	193.4	183.9	198.7	137.9	122.8	128.
2001	173.6	173.1	173.4	173.9	176.4	200.6	192.1	206.3	150.2	135.4	142
2002	176.8	176.2	175.6	178.3	180.3	208.1	199.7	214.7	143.6	127.2	134.
2003	180.5	180.0	179.4	182.1	184.8	213.1	205.5	219.9	154.5	138.2	145.
2004	186.6	186.2	186.2	187.5	189.5	218.8	211.0	224.9	161.9	144.4	150.
2005	191.2	190.7	189.8	193.4	195.7	224.4	217.3	230.2	179.0	161.6	166.
2006	195.7	195.2	193.1	199.4	203.2	232.1	225.1	238.2	194.7	177.1	182.
2007	203.300	202.916	201.245	206.659	209.586	240.611	234.679	246.235	200.632	181.744	186.26
2007: Jan	199.198	198.812	196.671	203.171	206.057	236.504	230.806	243.345	194.378	175.718	181.06
Feb	200.402	200.000	198.193	203.909	207.177	237.972	231.739	244.020	194.890	176.092	181.23
Mar	200.869	200.403	198.766	204.082	208.080	238.980	232.495	244.602	196.414	177.635	182.62
Apr	201.292	200.820	199.020	204.725	208.541	239.735	232.980	244.993	196.393	177.515	182.28
May	202.225	201.791	200.334	205.233	208.902	239.877	233.549	245.236	198.574	179.798	184.73
June	202.885	202.441	200.950	205.934	208.980	240.980	234.071	245.690	206.199	188.040	193.91
July	203.533	203.121	201.401	206.931	211.286	242.067	234.732	246.149	206.140	187.624	193.18
Aug	204.289	203.885	202.126	207.756	211.098	242.238	235.311	246.815	204.334	185.453	190.71
Sept	205.279	204.941	203.193	208.805	210.865	241.990	236.058	247.487	204.264	185.306	190.15
Oct	206.124	205.796	204.333	209.275	210.701	242.405	237.135	248.075	200.836	181.509	185.33
Nov	206.563	206.277	204.745	209.854	210.745	242.207	238.169	248.876	202.161	182.725	184.75
Dec	206.936	206.704	205.208	210.233	210.933	242.372	239.102	249.532	203.006	183.516	185.15
2008: Jan	208.837	208.618	207.983	211.070	212.244	243.871	239.850	250.106	204.796	185.107	186.47
Feb	209.462	209.166	208.329	211.878	213.026	244.786	240.325	250.481	205.795	185.994	187.37
Mar	209.692	209.385	208.203	212.537	214.389	245.995	240.874	250.966	209.221	189.693	190.10
Apr	211.365	211.102	210.851	213.083	214.890	246.004	241.474	251.418	213.302	194.121	194.37
May	212.251	212.054	211.863	213.967	215.809	246.069	241.803	251.576	219.881	201.212	200.99
June	213.383	213.243	213.171	215.015	217.941	247.083	242.640	252.170	231.412	213.762	213.37
July	215.326	215.299	215.785	216.376	219.610	248.075	243.367	252.504	239.039	221.742	221.80
Aug	216.419	216.422	217.259	217.063	219.148	247.985	244.181	252.957	235.650	217.455	218.65
Sept	217.672	217.696	218.629	218.225	218.184	247.737	244.926	253.493	228.450	209.501	210.95
Oct	218.705	218.738	219.660	219.290	217.383	247.844	245.855	253.902	221.199	201.176	203.50

[1] Includes alcoholic beverages, not shown separately.
[2] Includes other items not shown separately.
[3] December 1982=100.

See next page for continuation of table.

[For all urban consumers; 1982-84=100, except as noted]

Year or month	Transportation							Medical care		
	Total	Private transportation					Public trans-porta-tion	Total	Medical care com-modities	Medical care services
		Total²	New vehicles		Used cars and trucks	Motor fuel				
			Total²	New cars						
1960	29.8	30.6	51.6	51.5	25.0	24.4	22.2	22.3	46.9	19.5
1961	30.1	30.8	51.6	51.5	26.0	24.1	23.2	22.9	46.3	20.2
1962	30.8	31.4	51.4	51.3	28.4	24.3	24.0	23.5	45.6	20.9
1963	30.9	31.6	51.1	51.0	28.7	24.2	24.3	24.1	45.2	21.5
1964	31.4	32.0	50.9	50.9	30.0	24.1	24.7	24.6	45.1	22.0
1965	31.9	32.5	49.8	49.7	29.8	25.1	25.2	25.2	45.0	22.7
1966	32.3	32.9	48.9	48.8	29.0	25.6	26.1	26.3	45.1	23.9
1967	33.3	33.8	49.3	49.3	29.9	26.4	27.4	28.2	44.9	26.0
1968	34.3	34.8	50.7	50.7	....	26.8	28.7	29.9	45.0	27.9
1969	35.7	36.0	51.5	51.5	30.9	27.6	30.9	31.9	45.4	30.2
1970	37.5	37.5	53.1	53.0	31.2	27.9	35.2	34.0	46.5	32.3
1971	39.5	39.4	55.3	55.2	33.0	28.1	37.8	36.1	47.3	34.7
1972	39.9	39.7	54.8	54.7	33.1	28.4	39.3	37.3	47.4	35.9
1973	41.2	41.0	54.8	54.8	35.2	31.2	39.7	38.8	47.5	37.5
1974	45.8	46.2	58.0	57.9	36.7	42.2	40.6	42.4	49.2	41.4
1975	50.1	50.6	63.0	62.9	43.8	45.1	43.5	47.5	53.3	46.6
1976	55.1	55.6	67.0	66.9	50.3	47.0	47.8	52.0	56.5	51.3
1977	59.0	59.7	70.5	70.4	54.7	49.7	50.0	57.0	60.2	56.4
1978	61.7	62.5	75.9	75.8	55.8	51.8	51.5	61.8	64.4	61.2
1979	70.5	71.7	81.9	81.8	60.2	70.1	54.9	67.5	69.0	67.2
1980	83.1	84.2	88.5	88.4	62.3	97.4	69.0	74.9	75.4	74.8
1981	93.2	93.8	93.9	93.7	76.9	108.5	85.6	82.9	83.7	82.8
1982	97.0	97.1	97.5	97.4	88.8	102.8	94.9	92.5	92.3	92.6
1983	99.3	99.3	99.9	99.9	98.7	99.4	99.5	100.6	100.2	100.7
1984	103.7	103.6	102.6	102.8	112.5	97.9	105.7	106.8	107.5	106.7
1985	106.4	106.2	106.1	106.1	113.7	98.7	110.5	113.5	115.2	113.2
1986	102.3	101.2	110.6	110.6	108.8	77.1	117.0	122.0	122.8	121.9
1987	105.4	104.2	114.4	114.6	113.1	80.2	121.1	130.1	131.0	130.0
1988	108.7	107.6	116.5	116.9	118.0	80.9	123.3	138.6	139.9	138.3
1989	114.1	112.9	119.2	119.2	120.4	88.5	129.5	149.3	150.8	148.9
1990	120.5	118.8	121.4	121.0	117.6	101.2	142.6	162.8	163.4	162.7
1991	123.8	121.9	126.0	125.3	118.1	99.4	148.9	177.0	176.8	177.1
1992	126.5	124.6	129.2	128.4	123.2	99.0	151.4	190.1	188.1	190.5
1993	130.4	127.5	132.7	131.5	133.9	98.0	167.0	201.4	195.0	202.9
1994	134.3	131.4	137.6	136.0	141.7	98.5	172.0	211.0	200.7	213.4
1995	139.1	136.3	141.0	139.0	156.5	100.0	175.9	220.5	204.5	224.2
1996	143.0	140.0	143.7	141.4	157.0	106.3	181.9	228.2	210.4	232.4
1997	144.3	141.0	144.3	141.7	151.1	106.2	186.7	234.6	215.3	239.1
1998	141.6	137.9	143.4	140.7	150.6	92.2	190.3	242.1	221.8	246.8
1999	144.4	140.5	142.9	139.6	152.0	100.7	197.7	250.6	230.7	255.1
2000	153.3	149.1	142.8	139.6	155.8	129.3	209.6	260.8	238.1	266.0
2001	154.3	150.0	142.1	138.9	158.7	124.7	210.6	272.8	247.6	278.8
2002	152.9	148.8	140.0	137.3	152.0	116.6	207.4	285.6	256.4	292.9
2003	157.6	153.6	137.9	134.7	142.9	135.8	209.3	297.1	262.8	306.0
2004	163.1	159.4	137.1	133.9	133.3	160.4	209.1	310.1	269.3	321.3
2005	173.9	170.2	137.9	135.2	139.4	195.7	217.3	323.2	276.0	336.7
2006	180.9	177.0	137.6	136.4	140.0	221.0	226.6	336.2	285.9	350.6
2007	184.682	180.778	136.254	135.865	135.747	239.070	230.002	351.054	289.999	369.302
2007: Jan	174.463	170.562	137.603	137.204	135.257	193.900	221.403	343.510	288.088	359.757
Feb	174.799	170.775	137.340	136.844	134.597	195.377	224.061	346.457	287.703	363.908
Mar	180.346	176.468	137.228	136.589	134.382	220.515	225.893	347.172	286.940	365.164
Apr	185.231	181.478	136.963	136.400	134.363	242.944	227.567	348.225	288.349	366.070
May	189.961	186.376	136.295	135.787	134.481	265.781	228.251	349.087	288.661	367.127
June	189.064	185.175	135.820	135.479	135.067	260.655	233.389	349.510	288.508	367.758
July	187.690	183.619	135.415	135.009	136.024	252.909	235.767	351.643	290.257	370.008
Aug	184.480	180.408	135.204	134.888	137.138	238.194	233.112	352.961	291.164	371.461
Sept	184.532	180.586	134.927	134.637	137.142	239.104	230.694	353.723	291.340	372.432
Oct	184.952	180.919	135.344	135.169	136.950	239.048	232.725	355.653	292.161	374.750
Nov	190.677	186.839	136.250	136.003	136.616	262.282	233.758	357.041	293.201	376.250
Dec	189.984	186.134	136.664	136.371	136.943	258.132	233.408	357.661	293.610	376.940
2008: Jan	190.839	186.978	136.827	136.363	137.203	260.523	234.334	360.459	295.355	380.135
Feb	190.520	186.571	136.279	136.009	137.248	259.242	235.724	362.155	296.130	382.196
Mar	195.189	191.067	135.727	135.645	137.225	278.739	242.929	363.000	297.308	382.872
Apr	198.608	194.574	135.175	135.329	136.787	294.291	244.164	363.184	296.951	383.292
May	205.262	201.133	134.669	135.144	136.325	322.124	251.600	363.396	294.896	384.505
June	211.787	207.257	134.516	135.235	135.980	347.418	264.681	363.616	295.194	384.685
July	212.806	208.038	134.397	135.800	135.840	349.731	270.002	363.963	294.777	385.361
Aug	206.739	201.779	133.404	135.481	135.405	323.822	268.487	364.477	295.003	385.990
Sept	203.861	199.153	132.399	134.994	132.916	315.078	261.318	365.036	295.461	386.579
Oct	192.709	187.976	132.264	134.837	129.733	268.537	252.323	365.746	295.791	387.440

Source: Department of Labor (Bureau of Labor Statistics).

TABLE B–62.—*Consumer price indexes for commodities, services, and special groups, 1960–2008*

[For all urban consumers; 1982–84=100, except as noted]

Year or month	All items (CPI-U)[1]	Commodities		Services	Special indexes				All items		
		All commodities	Commodities less food		All items less food	All items less energy	All items less food and energy	All items less medical care	CPI-U-X1 (Dec. 1982 = 97.6)[2]	CPI-U-RS (Dec. 1977 = 100)[3]	C-CPI-U (Dec. 1999 = 100)[4]
1960	29.6	33.6	36.0	24.1	29.7	30.4	30.6	30.2	32.2	....	....
1961	29.9	33.8	36.1	24.5	30.0	30.7	31.0	30.5	32.5	....	....
1962	30.2	34.1	36.3	25.0	30.3	31.1	31.4	30.8	32.8	....	....
1963	30.6	34.4	36.6	25.5	30.7	31.5	31.8	31.1	33.3	....	....
1964	31.0	34.8	36.9	26.0	31.1	32.0	32.3	31.5	33.7	....	....
1965	31.5	35.2	37.2	26.6	31.6	32.5	32.7	32.0	34.2	....	....
1966	32.4	36.1	37.7	27.6	32.3	33.5	33.5	33.0	35.2	....	....
1967	33.4	36.8	38.6	28.8	33.4	34.4	34.7	33.7	36.3	....	....
1968	34.8	38.1	40.0	30.3	34.9	35.9	36.3	35.1	37.7	....	....
1969	36.7	39.9	41.7	32.4	36.8	38.0	38.4	37.0	39.4	....	....
1970	38.8	41.7	43.4	35.0	39.0	40.3	40.8	39.2	41.3	....	....
1971	40.5	43.2	45.1	37.0	40.8	42.0	42.7	40.8	43.1	....	....
1972	41.8	44.5	46.1	38.4	42.0	43.4	44.0	42.1	44.4	....	....
1973	44.4	47.8	47.7	40.1	43.7	46.1	45.6	44.8	47.2	....	....
1974	49.3	53.5	52.8	43.8	48.0	50.6	49.4	49.8	51.9	....	....
1975	53.8	58.2	57.6	48.0	52.5	55.1	53.9	54.3	56.2	....	....
1976	56.9	60.7	60.5	52.0	56.0	58.2	57.4	57.2	59.4	....	....
1977	60.6	64.2	63.8	56.0	59.6	61.9	61.0	60.8	63.2	....	....
1978	65.2	68.8	67.5	60.8	63.9	66.7	65.5	65.4	67.5	104.4	....
1979	72.6	76.6	75.3	67.5	71.2	73.4	71.9	72.9	74.0	114.4	....
1980	82.4	86.0	85.7	77.9	81.5	81.9	80.8	82.8	82.3	127.1	....
1981	90.9	93.2	93.1	88.1	90.4	90.1	89.2	91.4	90.1	139.2	....
1982	96.5	97.0	96.9	96.0	96.3	96.1	95.8	96.8	95.6	147.6	....
1983	99.6	99.8	100.0	99.4	99.7	99.6	99.6	99.6	99.6	153.9	....
1984	103.9	103.2	103.1	104.6	104.0	104.3	104.6	103.7	103.9	160.2	....
1985	107.6	105.4	105.2	109.9	108.0	108.4	109.1	107.2	107.6	165.7	....
1986	109.6	104.4	101.7	115.4	109.8	112.6	113.5	108.8	109.6	168.7	....
1987	113.6	107.7	104.3	120.2	113.6	117.2	118.2	112.6	113.6	174.4	....
1988	118.3	111.5	107.7	125.7	118.3	122.3	123.4	117.0	118.3	180.8	....
1989	124.0	116.7	112.0	131.9	123.7	128.1	129.0	122.4	124.0	188.6	....
1990	130.7	122.8	117.4	139.2	130.3	134.7	135.5	128.8	130.7	198.0	....
1991	136.2	126.6	121.3	146.3	136.1	140.9	142.1	133.8	136.2	205.1	....
1992	140.3	129.1	124.2	152.0	140.8	145.4	147.3	137.5	140.3	210.3	....
1993	144.5	131.5	126.3	157.9	145.1	150.0	152.2	141.2	144.5	215.5	....
1994	148.2	133.8	127.9	163.1	149.0	154.1	156.5	144.7	148.2	220.1	....
1995	152.4	136.4	129.8	168.7	153.1	158.7	161.2	148.6	152.4	225.4	....
1996	156.9	139.9	132.6	174.1	157.5	163.1	165.6	152.8	156.9	231.4	....
1997	160.5	141.8	133.4	179.4	161.1	167.1	169.5	156.3	160.5	236.4	....
1998	163.0	141.9	132.0	184.2	163.4	170.9	173.4	158.6	163.0	239.7	....
1999	166.6	144.4	134.0	188.8	167.0	174.4	177.0	162.0	166.6	244.7	....
2000	172.2	149.2	139.2	195.3	173.0	178.6	181.3	167.3	172.2	252.9	102.0
2001	177.1	150.7	138.9	203.4	177.8	183.5	186.1	171.9	177.1	260.0	104.3
2002	179.9	149.7	136.0	209.8	180.5	187.7	190.5	174.3	179.9	264.2	105.6
2003	184.0	151.2	136.5	216.5	184.7	190.6	193.2	178.1	184.0	270.1	107.8
2004	188.9	154.7	138.8	222.8	189.4	194.4	196.6	182.7	188.9	277.4	110.5
2005	195.3	160.2	144.5	230.1	196.0	198.7	200.9	188.7	195.3	286.7	113.7
2006	201.6	164.0	148.0	238.9	202.7	203.7	205.9	194.7	201.6	296.1	117.0
2007	207.342	167.509	149.720	246.848	208.098	208.925	210.729	200.080	207.342	304.5	119.948
2007: Jan	202.416	161.978	143.775	242.540	203.035	205.993	208.009	195.295	202.416	297.2	117.310
Feb	203.499	162.890	144.558	243.793	204.101	207.106	209.112	196.298	203.499	298.8	117.897
Mar	205.352	165.710	148.240	244.671	206.195	207.850	209.923	198.179	205.352	301.6	118.978
Apr	206.686	167.777	150.894	245.265	207.680	208.243	210.311	199.512	206.686	303.5	119.712
May	207.949	169.767	153.228	245.793	208.991	208.400	210.316	200.779	207.949	305.4	120.290
June	208.352	168.921	151.825	247.450	209.353	208.636	210.474	201.178	208.352	306.0	120.478
July	208.299	167.938	150.225	248.331	209.179	208.980	210.756	201.042	208.299	305.9	120.384
Aug	207.917	166.955	148.591	248.555	208.607	209.399	211.111	200.598	207.917	305.3	120.198
Sept	208.490	167.952	149.541	248.700	209.100	210.000	211.628	201.159	208.490	306.2	120.538
Oct	208.936	168.664	150.180	248.878	209.478	210.714	212.318	201.544	208.936	306.8	120.823
Nov	210.177	171.043	153.234	248.974	210.846	210.888	212.435	202.770	210.177	308.6	121.443
Dec	210.036	170.511	152.344	249.225	210.610	210.890	212.356	202.600	210.036	308.4	121.322
2008: Jan	211.080	171.179	152.531	250.648	211.512	211.846	213.138	203.569	211.080	310.0	121.895
Feb	211.693	171.530	152.799	251.527	212.136	212.545	213.866	204.136	211.693	310.9	122.251
Mar	213.528	173.884	155.881	252.817	214.236	213.420	214.866	205.992	213.528	313.6	123.204
Apr	214.823	175.838	157.870	253.426	215.462	213.851	215.059	207.317	214.823	315.5	123.845
May	216.632	178.341	160.880	254.509	217.411	214.101	215.180	209.170	216.632	318.1	124.645
June	218.815	180.534	163.385	256.668	219.757	214.600	215.553	211.408	218.815	321.3	125.582
July	219.964	181.087	163.364	258.422	220.758	215.335	216.045	212.576	219.964	323.0	126.116
Aug	219.086	179.148	160.341	258.638	219.552	215.873	216.476	211.653	219.086	321.7	125.843
Sept	218.783	179.117	159.825	258.059	218.991	216.397	216.862	211.321	218.783	321.3	125.774
Oct	216.573	175.257	154.250	257.559	216.250	216.695	217.023	209.021	216.573	318.0	124.784

[1] Consumer price index, all urban consumers.

[2] CPI-U-X1 reflects a rental equivalence approach to homeowners' costs for the CPI for years prior to 1983, the first year for which the official index incorporates such a measure. CPI-U-X1 is rebased to the December 1982 value of the CPI-U (1982–84=100) and is identical with CPI-U data from December 1982 forward. Data prior to 1967 estimated by moving the series at the same rate as the CPI-U for each year.

[3] Consumer price index research series (CPI-U-RS) using current methods introduced in June 1999. Data for 2008 are preliminary. All data are subject to revision annually.

[4] Chained consumer price index (C-CPI-U) introduced in August 2002. Data for 2007 and 2008 are subject to revision.

Source: Department of Labor (Bureau of Labor Statistics).

TABLE B–63.—*Changes in special consumer price indexes, 1960–2008*

[For all urban consumers; percent change]

Year or month	All items Dec. to Dec.[1]	All items Year to year	All items less food Dec. to Dec.[1]	All items less food Year to year	All items less energy Dec. to Dec.[1]	All items less energy Year to year	All items less food and energy Dec. to Dec.[1]	All items less food and energy Year to year	All items less medical care Dec. to Dec.[1]	All items less medical care Year to year
1960	1.4	1.7	1.0	1.7	1.3	1.7	1.0	1.3	1.3	1.3
1961	.7	1.0	1.3	1.0	.7	1.0	1.3	1.3	.3	1.0
1962	1.3	1.0	1.0	1.0	1.3	1.3	1.3	1.3	1.3	1.0
1963	1.6	1.3	1.6	1.3	1.9	1.3	1.6	1.3	1.6	1.0
1964	1.0	1.3	1.0	1.3	1.3	1.6	1.2	1.6	1.0	1.3
1965	1.9	1.6	1.6	1.6	1.9	1.6	1.5	1.2	1.9	1.6
1966	3.5	2.9	3.5	2.2	3.4	3.1	3.3	2.4	3.4	3.1
1967	3.0	3.1	3.3	3.4	3.2	2.7	3.8	3.6	2.7	2.1
1968	4.7	4.2	5.0	4.5	4.9	4.4	5.1	4.6	4.7	4.2
1969	6.2	5.5	5.6	5.4	6.5	5.8	6.2	5.8	6.1	5.4
1970	5.6	5.7	6.6	6.0	5.4	6.1	6.6	6.3	5.2	5.9
1971	3.3	4.4	3.0	4.6	3.4	4.2	3.1	4.7	3.2	4.1
1972	3.4	3.2	2.9	2.9	3.5	3.3	3.0	3.0	3.4	3.2
1973	8.7	6.2	5.6	4.0	8.2	6.2	4.7	3.6	9.1	6.4
1974	12.3	11.0	12.2	9.8	11.7	9.8	11.1	8.3	12.2	11.2
1975	6.9	9.1	7.3	9.4	6.6	8.9	6.7	9.1	6.7	9.0
1976	4.9	5.8	6.1	6.7	4.8	5.6	6.1	6.5	4.5	5.3
1977	6.7	6.5	6.4	6.4	6.7	6.4	6.5	6.3	6.7	6.3
1978	9.0	7.6	8.3	7.2	9.1	7.8	8.5	7.4	9.1	7.6
1979	13.3	11.3	14.0	11.4	11.1	10.0	11.3	9.8	13.4	11.5
1980	12.5	13.5	13.0	14.5	11.7	11.6	12.2	12.4	12.5	13.6
1981	8.9	10.3	9.8	10.9	8.5	10.0	9.5	10.4	8.8	10.4
1982	3.8	6.2	4.1	6.5	4.2	6.7	4.5	7.4	3.6	5.9
1983	3.8	3.2	4.1	3.5	4.5	3.6	4.8	4.0	3.6	2.9
1984	3.9	4.3	3.9	4.3	4.4	4.7	4.7	5.0	3.9	4.1
1985	3.8	3.6	4.1	3.8	4.0	3.9	4.3	4.3	3.5	3.4
1986	1.1	1.9	.5	1.7	3.8	3.9	3.8	4.0	.7	1.5
1987	4.4	3.6	4.6	3.5	4.1	4.1	4.2	4.1	4.3	3.5
1988	4.4	4.1	4.2	4.1	4.7	4.4	4.7	4.4	4.2	3.9
1989	4.6	4.8	4.5	4.6	4.6	4.7	4.4	4.5	4.5	4.6
1990	6.1	5.4	6.3	5.3	5.2	5.2	5.2	5.0	5.9	5.2
1991	3.1	4.2	3.3	4.5	3.9	4.6	4.4	4.9	2.7	3.9
1992	2.9	3.0	3.2	3.5	3.0	3.2	3.3	3.7	2.7	2.8
1993	2.7	3.0	2.7	3.1	3.1	3.2	3.2	3.3	2.6	2.7
1994	2.7	2.6	2.6	2.7	2.6	2.7	2.6	2.8	2.5	2.5
1995	2.5	2.8	2.7	2.8	2.9	3.0	3.0	3.0	2.5	2.7
1996	3.3	3.0	3.1	2.9	2.9	2.8	2.6	2.7	3.3	2.8
1997	1.7	2.3	1.8	2.3	2.1	2.5	2.2	2.4	1.6	2.3
1998	1.6	1.6	1.5	1.4	2.4	2.3	2.4	2.3	1.5	1.5
1999	2.7	2.2	2.8	2.2	2.0	2.0	1.9	2.1	2.6	2.1
2000	3.4	3.4	3.5	3.6	2.6	2.4	2.6	2.4	3.3	3.3
2001	1.6	2.8	1.3	2.8	2.8	2.7	2.7	2.6	1.4	2.7
2002	2.4	1.6	2.6	1.5	1.8	2.3	1.9	2.4	2.2	1.4
2003	1.9	2.3	1.5	2.3	1.5	1.5	1.1	1.4	1.8	2.2
2004	3.3	2.7	3.4	2.5	2.2	2.0	2.2	1.8	3.2	2.6
2005	3.4	3.4	3.6	3.5	2.2	2.2	2.2	2.2	3.3	3.3
2006	2.5	3.2	2.6	3.4	2.5	2.5	2.6	2.5	2.5	3.2
2007	4.1	2.8	4.0	2.7	2.8	2.6	2.4	2.3	4.0	2.8

Percent change from preceding month

Year or month	Unadjusted	Seasonally adjusted	Unadjusted	Seasonally adjusted	Unadjusted	Seasonally adjusted	Unadjusted	Seasonally adjusted	Unadjusted	Seasonally adjusted
2007: Jan	0.3	0.1	0.2	0.1	0.4	0.3	0.3	0.2	0.3	0.1
Feb	.5	.3	.5	.2	.5	.3	.5	.2	.5	.3
Mar	.9	.5	1.0	.5	.4	.1	.4	.1	1.0	.5
Apr	.6	.3	.7	.3	.2	.2	.2	.2	.7	.3
May	.6	.5	.6	.5	.1	.2	.0	.2	.6	.5
June	.2	.3	.2	.2	.1	.3	.1	.2	.2	.3
July	.0	.2	−.1	.2	.2	.2	.1	.2	−.1	.2
Aug	−.2	.0	−.3	.0	.2	.2	.2	.2	−.2	.0
Sept	.3	.4	.2	.3	.3	.3	.2	.2	.3	.4
Oct	.2	.3	.2	.3	.3	.2	.3	.2	.2	.2
Nov	.6	.9	.7	1.0	.1	.3	.1	.2	.6	.9
Dec	−.1	.4	−.1	.4	.0	.2	.0	.2	−.1	.4
2008: Jan	.5	.4	.4	.3	.5	.4	.4	.3	.5	.4
Feb	.3	.0	.3	.0	.3	.1	.3	.0	.3	.0
Mar	.9	.3	1.0	.4	.4	.2	.5	.2	.9	.4
Apr	.6	.2	.6	.1	.2	.2	.1	.1	.6	.2
May	.8	.6	.9	.7	.1	.2	.1	.2	.9	.7
June	1.0	1.1	1.1	1.1	.2	.4	.2	.3	1.1	1.1
July	.5	.8	.5	.8	.3	.4	.2	.3	.6	.9
Aug	−.4	−.1	−.5	−.3	.2	.3	.2	.2	−.4	−.2
Sept	−.1	.0	−.3	−.1	.2	.2	.2	.1	−.2	−.1
Oct	−1.0	−1.0	−1.3	−1.2	.1	.0	.1	−.1	−1.1	−1.0

[1] Changes from December to December are based on unadjusted indexes.

Source: Department of Labor (Bureau of Labor Statistics).

TABLE B–64.—*Changes in consumer price indexes for commodities and services, 1929–2007*

[For all urban consumers: percent change]

Year	All items		Commodities				Services				Medical care [2]		Energy [3]	
			Total		Food		Total		Medical care					
	Dec. to Dec. [1]	Year to year	Dec. to Dec. [1]	Year to year	Dec. to Dec. [1]	Year to year	Dec. to Dec. [1]	Year to year	Dec. to Dec. [1]	Year to year	Dec. to Dec. [1]	Year to year	Dec. to Dec. [1]	Year to year
1929	0.6	0.0	....	....	2.5	1.2	....	....	....	....	....	....	....	....
1933	.8	-5.1	....	....	6.9	-2.8	....	....	....	....	....	....	....	....
1939	.0	-1.4	-0.7	-2.0	-2.5	-2.5	0.0	0.0	1.2	1.2	1.0	0.0	....	....
1940	.7	.7	1.4	.7	2.5	1.7	.8	.8	.0	.0	.0	1.0	....	....
1941	9.9	5.0	13.3	6.7	15.7	9.2	2.4	.8	1.2	.0	1.0	.0	....	....
1942	9.0	10.9	12.9	14.5	17.9	17.6	2.3	3.1	3.5	3.5	3.8	2.9	....	....
1943	3.0	6.1	4.2	9.3	3.0	11.0	2.3	2.3	5.6	4.5	4.6	4.7	....	....
1944	2.3	1.7	2.0	1.0	.0	-1.2	2.2	2.2	3.2	4.3	2.6	3.6	....	....
1945	2.2	2.3	2.9	3.0	3.5	2.4	.7	1.5	3.1	3.1	2.6	2.6	....	....
1946	18.1	8.3	24.8	10.6	31.3	14.5	3.6	1.4	9.0	5.1	8.3	5.0	....	....
1947	8.8	14.4	10.3	20.5	11.3	21.7	5.6	4.3	6.4	8.7	6.9	8.0	....	....
1948	3.0	8.1	1.7	7.2	-.8	8.3	5.9	6.1	6.9	7.1	5.8	6.7	....	....
1949	-2.1	-1.2	-4.1	-2.7	-3.9	-4.2	3.7	5.1	1.6	3.3	1.4	2.8	....	....
1950	5.9	1.3	7.8	.7	9.8	1.6	3.6	3.0	4.0	2.4	3.4	2.0	....	....
1951	6.0	7.9	5.9	9.0	7.1	11.0	5.2	5.3	5.3	4.7	5.8	5.3	....	....
1952	.8	1.9	-.9	1.3	-1.0	1.8	4.4	4.5	5.8	6.7	4.3	5.0	....	....
1953	.7	.8	-.3	-.3	-1.1	-1.4	4.2	4.3	3.4	3.5	3.5	3.6	....	....
1954	-.7	.7	-1.6	-.9	-1.8	-.4	2.0	3.1	2.6	3.4	2.3	2.9	....	....
1955	.4	-.4	-.3	-.9	-.7	-1.4	2.0	2.0	3.2	2.6	3.3	2.2	....	....
1956	3.0	1.5	2.6	1.0	2.9	.7	3.4	2.5	3.8	3.8	3.2	3.8	....	....
1957	2.9	3.3	2.8	3.2	2.8	3.2	4.2	4.3	4.8	4.3	4.7	4.2	....	....
1958	1.8	2.8	1.2	2.1	2.4	4.5	2.7	3.7	4.6	5.3	4.5	4.6	-0.9	0.0
1959	1.7	.7	.6	.0	-1.0	-1.7	3.9	3.1	4.9	4.5	3.8	4.4	4.7	1.9
1960	1.4	1.7	1.2	.9	3.1	1.0	2.5	3.4	3.7	4.3	3.2	3.7	1.3	2.3
1961	.7	1.0	.0	.6	-.7	1.3	2.1	1.7	3.5	3.6	3.1	2.7	-1.3	.4
1962	1.3	1.0	.9	.9	1.3	.7	1.6	2.0	2.9	3.5	2.2	2.6	2.2	.7
1963	1.6	1.3	1.5	.9	2.0	1.6	2.4	2.0	2.8	2.9	2.5	2.6	-.9	.0
1964	1.0	1.3	.9	1.2	1.3	1.3	1.6	2.0	2.3	2.3	2.1	2.1	.0	-.4
1965	1.9	1.6	1.4	1.1	3.5	2.2	2.7	2.3	3.6	3.2	2.8	2.4	1.8	1.8
1966	3.5	2.9	2.5	2.6	4.0	5.0	4.8	3.8	8.3	5.3	6.7	4.4	1.7	1.1
1967	3.0	3.1	2.5	1.9	1.2	.9	4.3	4.3	8.0	8.8	6.3	7.2	1.7	2.1
1968	4.7	4.2	4.0	3.5	4.4	3.5	5.8	5.2	7.1	7.3	6.2	6.0	1.7	1.7
1969	6.2	5.5	5.4	4.7	7.0	5.1	7.7	6.9	7.3	8.2	6.2	6.7	2.9	2.5
1970	5.6	5.7	3.9	4.5	2.3	5.7	8.1	8.0	8.1	7.0	7.4	6.6	4.8	2.8
1971	3.3	4.4	2.8	3.6	4.3	3.1	4.1	5.7	5.4	7.4	4.6	6.2	3.1	3.9
1972	3.4	3.2	3.4	3.0	4.6	4.2	3.4	3.8	3.7	3.5	3.3	3.3	2.6	2.6
1973	8.7	6.2	10.4	7.4	20.3	14.5	6.2	4.4	6.0	4.5	5.3	4.0	17.0	8.1
1974	12.3	11.0	12.8	11.9	12.0	14.3	11.4	9.2	13.2	10.4	12.6	9.3	21.6	29.6
1975	6.9	9.1	6.2	8.8	6.6	8.5	8.2	9.6	10.3	12.6	9.8	12.0	11.4	10.5
1976	4.9	5.8	3.3	4.3	.5	3.0	7.2	8.3	10.8	10.1	10.0	9.5	7.1	7.1
1977	6.7	6.5	6.1	5.8	8.1	6.3	8.0	7.7	9.0	9.9	8.9	9.6	7.2	9.5
1978	9.0	7.6	8.8	7.2	11.8	9.9	9.3	8.6	9.3	8.5	8.8	8.4	7.9	6.3
1979	13.3	11.3	13.0	11.3	10.2	11.0	13.6	11.0	10.5	9.8	10.1	9.2	37.5	25.1
1980	12.5	13.5	11.0	12.3	10.2	8.6	14.2	15.4	10.1	11.3	9.9	11.0	18.0	30.9
1981	8.9	10.3	6.0	8.4	4.3	7.8	13.0	13.1	12.6	10.7	12.5	10.7	11.9	13.6
1982	3.8	6.2	3.6	4.1	3.1	4.1	4.3	9.0	11.2	11.8	11.0	11.6	1.3	1.5
1983	3.8	3.2	2.9	2.9	2.7	2.1	4.8	3.5	6.2	8.7	6.4	8.8	-.5	.7
1984	3.9	4.3	2.7	3.4	3.8	3.8	5.4	5.2	5.8	6.0	6.1	6.2	.2	1.0
1985	3.8	3.6	2.5	2.1	2.6	2.3	5.1	5.1	6.8	6.1	6.8	6.3	1.8	.7
1986	1.1	1.9	-2.0	-.9	3.8	3.2	4.5	5.0	7.9	7.7	7.7	7.5	-19.7	-13.2
1987	4.4	3.6	4.6	3.2	3.5	4.1	4.3	4.2	5.6	6.6	5.8	6.6	8.2	.5
1988	4.4	4.1	3.8	3.5	5.2	4.1	4.8	4.6	6.9	6.4	6.9	6.5	.5	.8
1989	4.6	4.8	4.1	4.7	5.6	5.8	5.1	4.9	8.6	7.7	8.5	7.7	5.1	5.6
1990	6.1	5.4	6.6	5.2	5.3	5.8	5.7	5.5	9.9	9.3	9.6	9.0	18.1	8.3
1991	3.1	4.2	1.2	3.1	1.9	2.9	4.6	5.1	8.0	8.9	7.9	8.7	-7.4	.4
1992	2.9	3.0	2.0	2.0	1.5	1.2	3.6	3.9	7.0	7.6	6.6	7.4	2.0	.5
1993	2.7	3.0	1.5	1.9	2.9	2.2	3.8	3.9	5.9	6.5	5.4	5.9	-1.4	1.2
1994	2.7	2.6	2.3	1.7	2.9	2.4	2.9	3.3	5.4	5.2	4.9	4.8	2.2	.4
1995	2.5	2.8	1.4	1.9	2.1	2.8	3.5	3.4	4.4	5.1	3.9	4.5	-1.3	.6
1996	3.3	3.0	3.2	2.6	4.3	3.3	3.3	3.2	3.2	3.7	3.0	3.5	8.6	4.7
1997	1.7	2.3	.2	1.4	1.5	2.6	2.8	3.0	2.9	2.9	2.8	2.8	-3.4	1.3
1998	1.6	1.6	.4	.1	2.3	2.2	2.6	2.7	3.2	3.2	3.4	3.2	-8.8	-7.7
1999	2.7	2.2	2.7	1.8	1.9	2.1	2.6	2.5	3.6	3.4	3.7	3.5	13.4	3.8
2000	3.4	3.4	2.7	3.3	2.8	2.3	3.9	3.4	4.6	4.3	4.2	4.1	14.2	16.9
2001	1.6	2.8	-1.4	1.0	2.8	3.2	3.7	4.1	4.8	4.8	4.7	4.6	-13.0	3.8
2002	2.4	1.6	1.2	-.7	1.5	1.8	3.2	3.1	5.6	5.1	5.0	4.7	10.7	-5.9
2003	1.9	2.3	.5	1.0	3.6	2.2	2.8	3.2	4.2	4.5	3.7	4.0	6.9	12.2
2004	3.3	2.7	3.6	2.3	2.7	3.4	3.1	2.9	4.9	5.0	4.2	4.4	16.6	10.9
2005	3.4	3.4	2.7	3.6	2.3	2.4	3.8	3.3	4.5	4.8	4.3	4.2	17.1	17.0
2006	2.5	3.2	1.3	2.4	2.1	2.4	3.4	3.8	4.1	4.1	3.6	4.0	2.9	11.2
2007	4.1	2.8	5.2	2.1	4.9	4.0	3.3	3.3	5.9	5.3	5.2	4.4	17.4	5.5

[1] Changes from December to December are based on unadjusted indexes.
[2] Commodities and services.
[3] Household energy—gas (piped), electricity, fuel oil, etc.—and motor fuel. Motor oil, coolant, etc. also included through 1982.

Source: Department of Labor (Bureau of Labor Statistics).

[1982=100]

Year or month	Total finished goods	Consumer foods			Finished goods excluding consumer foods						Total finished consumer goods
		Total	Crude	Processed	Total	Consumer goods			Capital equipment		
						Total	Durable	Nondurable			
1959	33.1	34.8	37.3	34.7	....	33.3	43.9	28.2	32.7		33.3
1960	33.4	35.5	39.8	35.2	....	33.5	43.8	28.4	32.8		33.6
1961	33.4	35.4	38.0	35.3	....	33.4	43.6	28.4	32.9		33.6
1962	33.5	35.7	38.4	35.6	....	33.4	43.4	28.4	33.0		33.7
1963	33.4	35.3	37.8	35.2	....	33.4	43.1	28.5	33.1		33.5
1964	33.5	35.4	38.9	35.2	....	33.3	43.3	28.4	33.4		33.6
1965	34.1	36.8	39.0	36.8	....	33.6	43.2	28.8	33.8		34.2
1966	35.2	39.2	41.5	39.2	....	34.1	43.4	29.3	34.6		35.4
1967	35.6	38.5	39.6	38.8	35.0	34.7	44.1	30.0	35.8		35.6
1968	36.6	40.0	42.5	40.0	35.9	35.5	45.1	30.6	37.0		36.5
1969	38.0	42.4	45.9	42.3	36.9	36.3	45.9	31.5	38.3		37.9
1970	39.3	43.8	46.0	43.9	38.2	37.4	47.2	32.5	40.1		39.1
1971	40.5	44.5	45.8	44.7	39.6	38.7	48.9	33.5	41.7		40.2
1972	41.8	46.9	48.0	47.2	40.4	39.4	50.0	34.1	42.8		41.5
1973	45.6	56.5	63.6	55.8	42.0	41.2	50.9	36.1	44.2		46.0
1974	52.6	64.4	71.6	63.9	48.8	48.2	55.5	44.0	50.5		53.1
1975	58.2	69.8	71.7	70.3	54.7	53.2	61.0	48.9	58.2		58.2
1976	60.8	69.6	76.7	69.0	58.1	56.5	63.7	52.4	62.1		60.4
1977	64.7	73.3	79.5	72.7	62.2	60.6	67.4	56.8	66.1		64.3
1978	69.8	79.9	85.8	79.4	66.7	64.9	73.6	60.0	71.3		69.4
1979	77.6	87.3	92.3	86.8	74.6	73.5	80.8	69.3	77.5		77.5
1980	88.0	92.4	93.9	92.3	86.7	87.1	91.0	85.1	85.8		88.6
1981	96.1	97.8	104.4	97.2	95.6	96.1	96.4	95.8	94.6		96.6
1982	100.0	100.0	100.0	100.0	100.0	100.0	100.0	100.0	100.0		100.0
1983	101.6	101.0	102.4	100.9	101.8	101.2	102.8	100.5	102.8		101.3
1984	103.7	105.4	111.4	104.9	103.2	102.2	104.5	101.1	105.2		103.3
1985	104.7	104.6	102.9	104.8	104.6	103.3	106.5	101.7	107.5		103.8
1986	103.2	107.3	105.6	107.4	101.9	98.5	108.9	93.3	109.7		101.4
1987	105.4	109.5	107.1	109.6	104.0	100.7	111.5	94.9	111.7		103.6
1988	108.0	112.6	109.8	112.7	106.5	103.1	113.8	97.3	114.3		106.2
1989	113.6	118.7	119.6	118.6	111.8	108.9	117.6	103.8	118.8		112.1
1990	119.2	124.4	123.0	124.4	117.4	115.3	120.4	111.5	122.9		118.2
1991	121.7	124.1	119.3	124.4	120.9	118.7	123.9	115.0	126.7		120.5
1992	123.2	123.3	107.6	124.4	123.1	120.8	125.7	117.3	129.1		121.7
1993	124.7	125.7	114.4	126.5	124.4	121.7	128.0	117.6	131.4		123.0
1994	125.5	126.8	111.3	127.9	125.1	121.6	130.9	116.2	134.1		123.3
1995	127.9	129.0	118.8	129.8	127.5	124.0	132.7	118.8	136.7		125.6
1996	131.3	133.6	129.2	133.8	130.5	127.6	134.2	123.3	138.3		129.5
1997	131.8	134.5	126.6	135.1	130.9	128.2	133.7	124.3	138.2		130.2
1998	130.7	134.3	127.2	134.8	129.5	126.4	132.9	122.2	137.6		128.9
1999	133.0	135.1	125.5	135.9	132.3	130.5	133.0	127.9	137.6		132.0
2000	138.0	137.2	123.5	138.3	138.1	138.4	133.9	138.7	138.8		138.2
2001	140.7	141.3	127.7	142.4	140.4	141.4	134.0	142.8	139.7		141.5
2002	138.9	140.1	128.5	141.0	138.3	138.8	133.0	139.8	139.1		139.4
2003	143.3	145.9	130.0	147.2	142.4	144.7	133.1	148.4	139.5		145.3
2004	148.5	152.7	138.2	153.9	147.2	150.9	135.0	156.6	141.4		151.7
2005	155.7	155.7	140.2	156.9	155.5	161.9	136.6	172.0	144.6		160.4
2006	160.4	156.7	151.3	157.1	161.0	169.2	136.9	182.6	146.9		166.0
2007	166.6	167.0	170.2	166.7	166.2	175.6	138.3	191.7	149.5		173.5
2007: Jan	160.1	161.1	164.2	160.8	159.6	166.0	138.3	177.1	148.9		164.9
Feb	161.8	163.9	178.4	162.4	161.0	167.9	138.4	180.0	149.2		167.1
Mar	164.1	166.3	187.4	164.2	163.2	171.2	138.2	185.2	149.1		170.2
Apr	165.9	166.8	182.1	165.3	165.3	174.5	137.7	190.4	149.1		172.7
May	167.5	166.8	161.7	167.4	167.4	177.6	137.7	195.0	149.1		174.8
June	167.2	166.3	147.5	168.3	167.1	177.2	137.7	194.5	149.0		174.4
July	168.5	166.4	152.9	167.9	168.8	179.7	137.6	198.1	149.1		176.2
Aug	166.1	166.3	146.5	168.4	165.8	175.3	137.2	191.8	149.0		173.0
Sept	167.4	168.4	162.5	169.1	166.9	177.0	136.7	194.6	148.9		174.8
Oct	168.6	169.7	181.9	168.6	168.1	177.9	139.8	194.5	150.6		175.9
Nov	171.4	169.5	178.0	168.8	171.6	182.9	140.2	201.5	151.0		179.4
Dec	170.4	172.2	198.7	169.6	169.6	180.1	139.5	197.9	150.7		178.2
2008: Jan	172.0	174.5	199.3	172.1	171.0	181.9	140.1	200.3	151.4		180.1
Feb	172.3	173.6	180.6	173.0	171.7	182.7	140.2	201.4	151.8		180.4
Mar	175.1	176.0	194.3	174.2	174.6	187.1	139.9	208.2	151.8		184.2
Apr	176.5	175.5	177.6	175.3	176.4	189.6	140.5	211.7	152.4		185.8
May	179.8	177.6	172.1	178.2	180.1	195.0	140.3	220.0	152.7		190.3
June	182.4	180.0	183.0	179.7	182.8	199.0	139.7	226.4	152.7		193.8
July [1]	185.0	180.9	164.1	182.6	185.9	203.2	140.3	232.5	153.6		197.1
Aug [1]	182.1	181.4	158.2	183.7	182.0	197.4	139.9	223.8	153.7		193.1
Sept [1]	182.0	182.0	168.7	183.3	181.7	196.7	140.1	222.6	154.3		192.7
Oct [1]	177.3	180.7	169.5	181.8	176.0	186.8	144.1	205.5	156.8		185.4

[1] Data have been revised through June 2008; data are subject to revision four months after date of original publication.

See next page for continuation of table.

TABLE B–65.—*Producer price indexes by stage of processing, 1959–2008*—Continued

[1982=100]

| Year or month | Intermediate materials, supplies, and components | | | | | | | | Crude materials for further processing | | | | |
| | Total | Foods and feeds [2] | Other | Materials and components | | Processed fuels and lubricants | Containers | Supplies | Total | Foodstuffs and feedstuffs | Other | | |
				For manufacturing	For construction						Total	Fuel	Other
1959	30.8	....	30.5	33.3	32.9	16.2	33.0	33.5	31.1	38.8	....	10.4	28
1960	30.8		30.7	33.3	32.7	16.6	33.4	33.3	30.4	38.4		10.5	26
1961	30.6		30.3	32.9	32.2	16.8	33.2	33.7	30.2	37.9		10.5	27
1962	30.6		30.2	32.7	32.1	16.7	33.6	34.5	30.5	38.6		10.4	27
1963	30.7		30.1	32.7	32.2	16.6	33.2	35.0	29.9	37.5		10.5	26.
1964	30.8		30.3	33.1	32.5	16.2	32.9	34.7	29.6	36.6		10.5	27.
1965	31.2		30.7	33.6	32.8	16.5	33.5	35.0	31.1	39.2		10.6	27.
1966	32.0		31.3	34.3	33.6	16.8	34.5	36.5	33.1	42.7		10.9	28.
1967	32.2	41.8	31.7	34.5	34.0	16.9	35.0	36.8	31.3	40.3	21.1	11.3	26.
1968	33.0	41.5	32.5	35.3	35.7	16.5	35.9	37.1	31.8	40.9	21.6	11.5	27.
1969	34.1	42.9	33.6	36.5	37.7	16.6	37.2	37.8	33.9	44.1	22.5	12.0	28.
1970	35.4	45.6	34.8	38.0	38.3	17.7	39.0	39.7	35.2	45.2	23.8	13.8	29.
1971	36.8	46.7	36.2	38.9	40.8	19.5	40.8	40.8	36.0	46.1	24.7	15.7	29.
1972	38.2	49.5	37.7	40.4	43.0	20.1	42.7	42.5	39.9	51.5	27.0	16.8	32.
1973	42.4	70.3	40.6	44.1	46.5	22.2	45.2	51.7	54.5	72.6	34.3	18.6	42.
1974	52.5	83.6	50.5	56.0	55.0	33.6	53.3	56.8	61.4	76.4	44.1	24.8	54.
1975	58.0	81.6	56.6	61.7	60.1	39.4	60.0	61.8	61.6	77.4	43.7	30.6	50.
1976	60.9	77.4	60.0	64.0	64.1	42.3	63.1	65.8	63.4	76.8	48.2	34.5	54.
1977	64.9	79.6	64.1	67.4	69.3	47.7	65.9	69.3	65.5	77.5	51.7	42.0	56.
1978	69.5	84.8	68.6	72.0	76.5	49.9	71.0	72.9	73.4	87.3	57.5	48.2	61.
1979	78.4	94.5	77.4	80.9	84.2	61.6	79.4	80.2	85.9	100.0	69.6	57.3	75.
1980	90.3	105.5	89.4	91.7	91.3	85.0	89.1	89.9	95.3	104.6	84.6	69.4	91.
1981	98.6	104.6	98.2	98.7	97.9	100.6	96.7	96.9	103.0	103.9	101.8	84.8	109.
1982	100.0	100.0	100.0	100.0	100.0	100.0	100.0	100.0	100.0	100.0	100.0	100.0	100.
1983	100.6	103.6	100.5	101.2	102.8	95.4	100.4	101.8	101.3	101.8	100.7	105.1	98.
1984	103.1	105.7	103.0	104.1	105.6	95.7	105.9	104.1	103.5	104.7	102.2	105.1	101.
1985	102.7	97.3	103.0	103.3	107.3	92.8	109.0	104.4	95.8	94.8	96.9	102.7	94.
1986	99.1	96.2	99.3	102.2	108.1	72.7	110.3	105.6	87.7	93.2	81.6	92.2	76.
1987	101.5	99.2	101.7	105.3	109.8	73.3	114.5	107.7	93.7	96.2	87.9	84.1	88.
1988	107.1	109.5	106.9	113.2	116.1	71.2	120.1	113.7	96.0	106.1	85.5	82.1	85.
1989	112.0	113.8	111.9	118.1	121.3	76.4	125.4	118.1	103.1	112.2	93.4	85.3	95.
1990	114.5	113.3	114.5	118.7	122.9	85.9	127.7	119.4	108.9	113.1	101.5	84.8	107.
1991	114.4	111.1	114.6	118.1	124.5	85.3	128.1	121.4	101.2	105.5	94.6	82.9	97.
1992	114.7	110.7	114.9	117.9	126.5	84.5	127.7	122.7	100.4	105.1	93.5	84.0	94.
1993	116.2	112.7	116.4	118.9	132.0	84.7	126.4	125.0	102.4	108.4	94.7	87.1	94.
1994	118.5	114.8	118.7	122.1	136.6	83.1	129.7	127.0	101.8	106.5	94.8	82.4	97.
1995	124.9	114.8	125.5	130.4	142.1	84.2	148.8	132.1	102.7	105.8	96.8	72.1	105.
1996	125.7	128.1	125.6	128.6	143.6	90.0	141.1	135.9	113.8	121.5	104.5	92.6	105.
1997	125.6	125.4	125.7	128.3	146.5	89.3	136.0	135.9	111.1	112.2	106.4	101.3	103.
1998	123.0	116.2	123.4	126.1	146.8	81.1	140.8	134.8	96.8	103.9	88.4	86.7	84.
1999	123.2	111.1	123.9	124.6	148.9	84.6	142.5	134.2	98.2	98.7	94.3	91.2	91.
2000	129.2	111.7	130.1	128.1	150.7	102.0	151.6	136.9	120.6	100.2	130.4	136.9	118.0
2001	129.7	115.9	130.5	127.4	150.6	104.5	153.1	138.7	121.0	106.1	126.8	151.4	101.5
2002	127.8	115.5	128.5	126.1	151.3	96.3	152.1	138.9	108.1	99.5	111.4	117.3	101.0
2003	133.7	125.9	134.2	129.7	153.6	112.6	153.7	141.5	135.3	113.5	148.2	185.7	116.9
2004	142.6	137.1	143.0	137.9	166.4	124.3	159.3	146.7	159.0	127.0	179.2	211.4	149.2
2005	154.0	133.8	155.1	146.0	176.6	150.0	167.1	151.9	182.2	122.7	223.4	279.7	176.7
2006	164.0	135.2	165.4	155.9	188.4	162.8	175.0	157.0	184.8	119.3	230.6	241.5	210.0
2007	170.7	154.4	171.5	162.4	192.5	173.9	180.3	161.7	207.1	146.7	246.3	236.8	238.7
2007: Jan	163.3	142.6	164.3	157.3	190.3	152.0	178.1	159.6	180.0	128.7	212.9	212.6	199.4
Feb	164.3	147.2	165.2	157.6	190.6	156.1	178.1	160.1	197.0	138.8	235.1	253.4	209.7
Mar	166.6	149.8	167.5	158.7	191.2	164.6	178.1	160.4	202.1	142.0	241.5	255.8	218.0
Apr	169.1	151.0	170.0	160.6	192.1	171.6	179.2	160.7	204.2	143.7	243.9	248.3	225.7
May	171.1	151.6	172.1	162.8	192.8	176.2	179.6	160.8	208.0	148.1	246.6	258.1	224.2
June	172.0	154.5	172.9	163.6	193.1	178.1	179.7	161.4	209.7	148.4	249.6	260.4	227.6
July	173.6	155.9	174.5	164.5	193.5	183.0	180.2	161.9	210.3	150.0	249.2	236.9	243.6
Aug	171.5	156.3	172.3	163.4	193.5	175.3	180.5	162.0	202.8	147.8	237.6	211.7	242.2
Sept	172.2	158.2	172.9	163.3	193.2	178.4	181.0	162.3	204.6	151.9	237.4	193.1	255.\
Oct	172.2	159.6	172.9	164.4	193.2	175.5	182.3	163.0	211.8	150.0	252.0	217.4	261.9
Nov	176.2	161.4	177.0	166.1	193.2	189.7	183.2	163.9	225.6	152.9	274.1	243.2	280.1
Dec	175.7	164.6	176.3	166.3	193.4	186.3	183.4	164.6	229.0	158.5	275.4	250.7	277.\
2008: Jan	177.8	170.6	178.2	168.4	194.4	188.6	185.1	166.8	235.5	162.6	283.8	253.9	288.0
Feb	179.1	175.0	179.4	170.1	195.7	189.0	185.7	168.1	245.5	165.4	299.9	283.5	295.6
Mar	184.5	180.3	184.7	173.1	197.3	206.1	185.9	170.0	262.1	169.2	327.7	306.9	324.6
Apr	187.3	180.5	187.7	175.5	200.2	211.8	187.0	171.3	274.6	168.1	352.4	329.1	349.6
May	192.8	184.5	193.3	179.1	203.3	227.3	187.6	173.1	293.1	173.2	382.4	369.2	372.4
June	197.2	186.6	197.8	182.4	206.5	238.4	189.2	174.6	301.2	178.1	393.0	378.5	383.3
July [1]	202.5	194.6	203.0	186.6	209.9	249.6	191.6	177.7	317.9	179.3	423.3	426.6	401.8
Aug [1]	200.2	194.0	200.5	190.6	213.1	224.2	194.2	179.4	280.0	170.4	360.5	335.1	358.9
Sept [1]	198.7	192.2	199.1	187.1	214.4	223.2	198.1	179.9	257.8	168.0	320.8	287.1	326.0
Oct [1]	189.8	181.1	190.3	181.8	212.8	193.2	199.4	177.9	208.8	147.9	248.2	215.9	256.1

[2] Intermediate materials for food manufacturing and feeds.

Source: Department of Labor (Bureau of Labor Statistics).

TABLE B–66.—*Producer price indexes by stage of processing, special groups, 1974–2008*

[1982=100]

Year or month	Finished goods						Intermediate materials, supplies, and components				Crude materials for further processing			
	Total	Foods	Energy	Excluding foods and energy			Total	Foods and feeds[1]	Energy	Other	Total	Foodstuffs and feedstuffs	Energy	Other
				Total	Capital equipment	Consumer goods excluding foods and energy								
74	52.6	64.4	26.2	53.6	50.5	55.5	52.5	83.6	33.1	54.0	61.4	76.4	27.8	83.3
75	58.2	69.8	30.7	59.7	58.2	60.6	58.0	81.6	38.7	60.2	61.6	77.4	33.3	69.3
76	60.8	69.6	34.3	63.1	62.1	63.7	60.9	77.4	41.5	63.8	63.4	76.8	35.3	80.2
77	64.7	73.3	39.7	66.9	66.1	67.3	64.9	79.6	46.8	67.6	65.5	77.5	40.4	79.8
78	69.8	79.9	42.3	71.9	71.3	72.2	69.5	84.8	49.1	72.5	73.4	87.3	45.2	87.8
79	77.6	87.3	57.1	78.3	77.5	78.8	78.4	94.5	61.1	80.7	85.9	100.0	54.9	106.2
80	88.0	92.4	85.2	87.1	85.8	87.8	90.3	105.5	84.9	90.3	95.3	104.6	73.1	113.1
81	96.1	97.8	101.5	94.6	94.6	94.6	98.6	104.6	100.5	97.7	103.0	103.9	97.7	111.7
82	100.0	100.0	100.0	100.0	100.0	100.0	100.0	100.0	100.0	100.0	100.0	100.0	100.0	100.0
83	101.6	101.0	95.2	103.0	102.8	103.1	100.6	103.6	95.3	101.6	101.3	101.8	98.7	105.3
84	103.7	105.4	91.2	105.5	105.2	105.7	103.1	105.7	95.5	104.7	103.5	104.7	98.0	111.7
85	104.7	104.6	87.6	108.1	107.5	108.4	102.7	97.3	92.6	105.2	95.8	94.8	93.3	104.9
86	103.2	107.3	63.0	110.6	109.7	111.1	99.1	96.2	72.6	104.9	87.7	93.2	71.8	103.1
87	105.4	109.5	61.8	113.3	111.7	114.2	101.5	99.2	73.0	107.8	93.7	96.2	75.0	115.7
88	108.0	112.6	59.8	117.0	114.3	118.5	107.1	109.5	70.9	115.2	96.0	106.1	67.7	133.0
89	113.6	118.7	65.7	122.1	118.8	124.0	112.0	113.8	76.1	120.2	103.1	111.2	75.9	137.9
90	119.2	124.4	75.0	126.6	122.9	128.8	114.5	113.3	85.5	120.9	108.9	113.1	85.9	136.3
91	121.7	124.1	78.1	131.1	126.7	133.7	114.4	111.1	85.1	121.4	101.2	105.5	80.4	128.2
92	123.2	123.3	77.8	134.2	129.1	137.3	114.7	110.7	84.3	122.0	100.4	105.1	78.8	128.4
93	124.7	125.7	78.0	135.8	131.4	138.5	116.2	112.7	84.6	123.8	102.4	108.4	76.7	140.2
94	125.5	126.8	77.0	137.1	134.1	139.0	118.5	114.8	83.0	127.1	101.8	106.5	72.1	156.2
95	127.9	129.0	78.1	140.0	136.7	141.9	124.9	114.8	84.1	135.2	102.7	105.8	69.4	173.6
96	131.3	133.6	83.2	142.0	138.3	144.3	125.7	128.1	89.8	134.0	113.8	121.5	85.0	155.8
97	131.8	134.5	83.4	142.4	138.2	145.1	125.6	125.4	89.0	134.2	111.1	112.2	87.3	156.5
98	130.7	134.3	75.1	143.7	137.6	147.7	123.0	116.2	80.8	133.5	96.8	103.9	68.6	142.1
99	133.0	135.1	78.8	146.1	137.6	151.7	123.2	111.1	84.3	133.1	98.2	98.7	78.5	135.2
00	138.0	137.2	94.1	148.0	138.8	154.0	129.2	111.7	101.7	136.6	120.6	100.2	122.1	145.2
01	140.7	141.3	96.7	150.0	139.7	156.9	129.7	115.9	104.1	136.4	121.0	106.1	122.3	130.7
02	138.9	140.1	88.8	150.2	139.1	157.6	127.8	115.5	95.9	135.8	108.1	99.5	102.0	135.7
03	143.3	145.9	102.0	150.5	139.5	157.9	133.7	125.9	111.9	138.5	135.3	113.5	147.2	152.5
04	148.5	152.7	113.0	152.7	141.4	160.3	142.6	137.1	123.2	146.5	159.0	127.0	174.6	193.0
05	155.7	155.7	132.6	156.4	144.6	164.3	154.0	133.8	149.2	154.6	182.2	122.7	234.0	202.4
06	160.4	156.7	145.9	158.7	146.9	166.7	164.0	135.2	162.8	163.8	184.8	119.3	226.9	244.5
07	166.6	167.0	156.3	161.7	149.5	170.0	170.7	154.4	174.6	168.4	207.1	146.7	232.8	282.6
07: Jan	160.1	161.1	135.6	160.6	148.9	168.5	163.3	142.6	151.8	165.5	180.0	128.7	195.9	255.5
Feb	161.8	163.9	139.0	161.2	149.2	169.2	164.3	147.2	155.7	165.5	197.0	138.8	223.9	265.6
Mar	164.1	166.3	147.4	161.0	149.1	169.0	166.6	149.8	164.0	166.2	202.1	142.0	224.7	284.5
Apr	165.9	166.8	155.4	161.0	149.1	169.0	169.1	151.0	170.5	167.7	204.2	143.7	226.5	288.4
May	167.5	166.8	161.9	161.3	149.1	169.5	171.1	151.6	176.7	168.6	208.0	148.1	233.0	282.8
June	167.2	166.3	160.9	161.3	149.0	169.6	172.0	154.5	179.2	169.0	209.7	148.4	238.0	281.5
July	168.5	166.4	166.4	161.4	149.1	169.7	173.6	155.9	184.2	169.6	210.3	150.0	236.8	284.0
Aug	166.1	166.3	155.6	161.5	149.0	170.0	171.5	156.3	177.0	168.8	202.8	147.8	221.7	284.7
Sept	167.4	168.4	159.7	161.5	148.9	170.0	172.2	158.2	179.5	168.9	204.6	151.9	219.9	289.9
Oct	168.6	169.7	159.1	163.2	150.6	171.8	172.2	159.6	177.4	169.5	211.8	150.0	237.7	292.8
Nov	171.4	169.5	170.4	163.6	151.0	172.2	176.2	161.4	191.1	170.8	225.6	152.9	267.1	289.9
Dec	170.4	172.2	163.8	163.5	150.7	172.2	175.7	164.6	187.8	170.9	229.0	158.5	268.3	291.7
08: Jan	172.0	174.5	166.6	164.4	151.4	173.2	177.8	170.6	190.5	172.5	235.5	162.6	273.6	307.3
Feb	172.3	173.6	167.2	165.0	151.8	174.0	179.1	175.0	191.5	173.7	245.5	165.4	291.7	319.7
Mar	175.1	176.0	171.3	165.1	151.8	174.1	184.5	180.3	208.6	175.8	262.1	169.2	325.4	332.1
Apr	176.5	175.5	182.4	165.7	152.4	174.8	187.3	180.5	213.4	178.3	274.6	168.1	346.1	366.7
May	179.8	177.6	194.8	166.1	152.7	175.2	192.8	184.5	228.7	181.2	293.1	173.2	386.1	372.4
June	182.4	180.0	204.6	166.0	152.7	175.2	197.2	186.6	240.3	183.8	301.2	178.1	400.4	373.8
July[2]	185.0	180.9	213.0	167.1	153.6	176.2	202.5	194.6	253.0	186.9	317.9	179.3	437.9	387.2
Aug[2]	182.1	181.4	198.2	167.3	153.7	176.6	200.2	194.0	230.3	189.9	280.0	170.4	352.7	379.1
Sept[2]	182.0	182.0	195.5	167.9	154.3	177.2	198.7	192.2	226.2	189.3	257.8	168.0	311.4	342.6
Oct[2]	177.3	180.7	167.8	170.4	156.8	179.8	189.8	181.1	196.7	186.0	208.8	147.9	233.7	283.6

[1] Intermediate materials for food manufacturing and feeds.
[2] Data have been revised through June 2008; data are subject to revision four months after date of original publication.

Source: Department of Labor (Bureau of Labor Statistics).

TABLE B–67.—*Producer price indexes for major commodity groups, 1959–2008*

[1982=100]

Year or month	Farm products and processed foods and feeds			Industrial commodities				
	Total	Farm products	Processed foods and feeds	Total	Textile products and apparel	Hides, skins, leather, and related products	Fuels and related products and power	Chemicals and allied products [1]
1959	37.6	40.2	35.6	30.5	48.1	35.9	13.7	34
1960	37.7	40.1	35.6	30.5	48.6	34.6	13.9	34
1961	37.7	39.7	36.2	30.4	47.8	34.9	14.0	34
1962	38.1	40.4	36.5	30.4	48.2	35.3	14.0	33
1963	37.7	39.6	36.8	30.3	48.2	34.3	13.9	33
1964	37.5	39.0	36.7	30.5	48.5	34.4	13.5	33
1965	39.0	40.7	38.0	30.9	48.8	35.9	13.8	33
1966	41.6	43.7	40.2	31.5	48.9	39.4	14.1	34
1967	40.2	41.3	39.8	32.0	48.9	38.1	14.4	34
1968	41.1	42.3	40.6	32.8	50.7	39.3	14.3	34
1969	43.4	45.0	42.7	33.9	51.8	41.5	14.6	34
1970	44.9	45.8	44.6	35.2	52.4	42.0	15.3	35
1971	45.8	46.6	45.5	36.5	53.3	43.4	16.6	35
1972	49.2	51.6	48.0	37.8	55.5	50.0	17.1	35
1973	63.9	72.7	58.9	40.3	60.5	54.5	19.4	37
1974	71.3	77.4	68.0	49.2	68.0	55.2	30.1	50
1975	74.0	77.0	72.6	54.9	67.4	56.5	35.4	62
1976	73.6	78.8	70.8	58.4	72.4	63.9	38.3	64
1977	75.9	79.4	74.0	62.5	75.3	68.3	43.6	65
1978	83.0	87.7	80.6	67.0	78.1	76.1	46.5	68
1979	92.3	99.6	88.5	75.7	82.5	96.1	58.9	76
1980	98.3	102.9	95.9	88.0	89.7	94.7	82.8	89.
1981	101.1	105.2	98.9	97.4	97.6	99.3	100.2	98
1982	100.0	100.0	100.0	100.0	100.0	100.0	100.0	100.
1983	102.0	102.4	101.8	101.1	100.3	103.2	95.9	100
1984	105.5	105.5	105.4	103.3	102.7	109.0	94.8	102.
1985	100.7	95.1	103.5	103.7	102.9	108.9	91.4	103
1986	101.2	92.9	105.4	100.0	103.2	113.0	69.8	102
1987	103.7	95.5	107.9	102.6	105.1	120.4	70.2	106.
1988	110.0	104.9	112.7	106.3	109.2	131.4	66.7	116.
1989	115.4	110.9	117.8	111.6	112.3	136.3	72.9	123.
1990	118.6	112.2	121.9	115.8	115.0	141.7	82.3	123.
1991	116.4	105.7	121.9	116.5	116.3	138.9	81.2	125.
1992	115.9	103.6	122.1	117.4	117.8	140.4	80.4	125.
1993	118.4	107.1	124.0	119.0	118.0	143.7	80.0	128.
1994	119.1	106.3	125.5	120.7	118.3	148.5	77.8	132.
1995	120.5	107.4	127.0	125.5	120.8	153.7	78.0	142.
1996	129.7	122.4	133.3	127.3	122.4	150.5	85.8	142.
1997	127.0	112.9	134.0	127.7	122.6	154.2	86.1	143.
1998	122.7	104.6	131.6	124.8	122.9	148.0	75.3	143.
1999	120.3	98.4	131.1	126.5	121.1	146.0	80.5	144.
2000	122.0	99.5	133.1	134.8	121.4	151.5	103.5	151.
2001	126.2	103.8	137.3	135.7	121.3	158.4	105.3	151.
2002	123.9	99.0	136.2	132.4	119.9	157.6	93.2	151.
2003	132.8	111.5	143.4	139.1	119.8	162.3	112.9	161.
2004	142.0	123.3	151.2	147.6	121.0	164.5	126.9	174.
2005	141.3	118.5	153.1	160.2	122.8	165.4	156.4	192.
2006	141.2	117.0	153.8	168.8	124.5	168.4	166.7	205.
2007	157.8	143.4	165.1	175.1	125.8	173.6	177.6	214.
2007: Jan	147.5	127.1	158.2	166.8	125.1	173.6	152.4	206.
Feb	152.9	137.5	160.6	169.1	125.4	174.1	160.2	206.
Mar	155.1	140.6	162.4	171.6	125.4	174.9	167.9	208.
Apr	156.1	141.3	163.4	173.9	125.3	176.0	174.7	210.
May	157.5	142.7	164.8	176.0	125.4	175.6	181.3	213.
June	158.0	141.8	166.2	176.4	125.7	174.7	182.4	215.
July	158.6	143.4	166.2	177.9	126.0	171.6	186.7	217.
Aug	157.8	140.4	166.6	174.9	126.2	172.6	176.3	215.
Sept	160.5	146.8	167.5	175.6	126.2	172.4	178.9	216.
Oct	161.0	148.2	167.5	176.9	126.3	172.3	180.9	218.
Nov	162.3	151.0	168.0	181.8	126.5	172.4	196.9	224.
Dec	166.0	159.6	169.4	180.7	126.6	172.6	192.6	224.
2008: Jan	169.8	164.2	172.7	182.8	126.9	172.2	195.9	229.
Feb	171.1	164.4	174.6	184.6	127.1	172.5	199.5	231.
Mar	174.5	169.6	176.9	190.2	127.2	172.5	217.1	235.
Apr	174.0	166.7	177.8	193.8	127.6	172.9	224.7	240.
May	177.1	169.7	180.8	200.0	128.2	172.9	243.2	246.
June	180.4	176.2	182.4	204.0	128.2	174.8	254.8	252.
July[2]	182.6	174.7	186.6	209.6	129.0	175.0	269.8	259.
Aug[2]	179.3	164.5	187.4	203.5	130.1	175.4	239.5	268.
Sept[2]	178.8	164.1	186.7	204.4	131.0	175.5	230.2	266.
Oct[2]	169.6	145.6	182.8	189.3	130.5	175.2	192.4	256.

[1] Prices for some items in this grouping are lagged and refer to one month earlier than the index month.
[2] Data have been revised through June 2008; data are subject to revision four months after date of original publication.

See next page for continuation of table.

[1982=100]

Year or month	Rubber and plastic products	Lumber and wood products	Pulp, paper, and allied products	Metals and metal products	Machinery and equipment	Furniture and household durables	Non-metallic mineral products	Transportation equipment Total	Motor vehicles and equipment	Miscellaneous products
59	42.6	34.7	33.7	30.6	32.8	48.0	30.3		39.9	33.4
60	42.7	33.5	34.0	30.6	33.0	47.8	30.4		39.3	33.6
61	41.1	32.0	33.0	30.5	33.0	47.5	30.5		39.2	33.7
62	39.9	32.2	33.4	30.2	33.0	47.2	30.5		39.2	33.9
63	40.1	32.8	33.1	30.3	33.1	46.9	30.3		38.9	34.2
64	39.6	33.5	33.0	31.1	33.3	47.1	30.4		39.1	34.4
65	39.7	33.7	33.3	32.0	33.7	46.8	30.4		39.2	34.7
66	40.5	35.2	34.2	32.8	34.7	47.4	30.7		39.2	35.3
67	41.4	35.1	34.6	33.2	35.9	48.3	31.2		39.8	36.2
68	42.8	39.8	35.0	34.0	37.0	49.7	32.4		40.9	37.0
69	43.6	44.0	36.0	36.0	38.2	50.7	33.6	40.4	41.7	38.1
70	44.9	39.9	37.5	38.7	40.0	51.9	35.3	41.9	43.3	39.8
71	45.2	44.7	38.1	39.4	41.4	53.1	38.2	44.2	45.7	40.8
72	45.3	50.7	39.3	40.9	42.3	53.8	39.4	45.5	47.0	41.5
73	46.6	62.2	42.3	44.0	43.7	55.7	40.7	46.1	47.4	43.3
74	56.4	64.5	52.5	57.0	50.0	61.8	47.8	50.3	51.4	48.1
75	62.2	62.1	59.0	61.5	57.9	67.5	54.4	56.7	57.6	53.4
76	66.0	72.2	62.1	65.0	61.3	70.3	58.2	60.5	61.2	55.6
77	69.4	83.0	64.6	69.3	65.2	73.2	62.6	64.6	65.2	59.4
78	72.4	96.9	67.7	75.3	70.3	77.5	69.6	69.5	70.0	66.7
79	80.5	105.5	75.9	86.0	76.7	82.8	77.6	75.3	75.8	75.5
80	90.1	101.5	86.3	95.0	86.0	90.7	88.4	82.9	83.1	93.6
81	96.4	102.8	94.8	99.6	94.4	95.9	96.7	94.3	94.6	96.1
82	100.0	100.0	100.0	100.0	100.0	100.0	100.0	100.0	100.0	100.0
83	100.8	107.9	103.3	101.8	102.7	103.4	101.6	102.8	102.2	104.8
84	102.3	108.0	110.3	104.8	105.1	105.7	105.4	105.2	104.1	107.0
85	101.9	106.6	113.3	104.4	107.2	107.1	108.6	107.9	106.4	109.4
86	101.9	107.2	116.1	103.2	108.8	108.2	110.0	110.5	109.1	111.6
87	103.0	112.8	121.8	107.1	110.4	109.9	110.0	112.5	111.7	114.9
88	109.3	118.9	130.4	118.7	113.2	113.1	111.2	114.3	113.1	120.2
89	112.6	126.7	137.8	124.1	117.4	116.9	112.6	117.7	116.2	126.5
90	113.6	129.7	141.2	122.9	120.7	119.2	114.7	121.5	118.2	134.2
91	115.1	132.1	142.9	120.2	123.0	121.2	117.2	126.4	122.1	140.8
92	115.1	146.6	145.2	119.2	123.4	122.2	117.3	130.4	124.9	145.3
93	116.0	174.0	147.3	119.2	124.0	123.7	120.0	133.7	128.0	145.4
94	117.6	180.0	152.5	124.8	125.1	126.1	124.2	137.2	131.4	141.9
95	124.3	178.1	172.2	134.5	126.6	128.2	129.0	139.7	133.0	145.4
96	123.8	176.1	168.7	131.0	126.5	130.4	131.0	141.7	134.1	147.7
97	123.2	183.8	167.9	131.8	125.9	130.8	133.2	141.6	132.7	150.9
98	122.6	179.1	171.7	127.8	124.9	131.3	135.4	141.2	131.4	156.0
99	122.5	183.6	174.1	124.6	124.3	131.7	138.9	141.8	131.7	166.6
00	125.5	178.2	183.7	128.1	124.0	132.6	142.5	143.8	132.3	170.8
01	127.2	174.4	184.8	125.4	123.7	133.2	144.3	145.2	131.5	181.3
02	126.8	173.3	185.9	125.9	122.9	133.5	146.2	144.6	129.9	182.4
03	130.1	177.4	190.0	129.2	121.9	133.9	148.2	145.7	129.6	179.6
04	133.8	195.6	195.7	149.6	122.1	135.1	153.2	148.6	131.0	183.2
05	143.8	196.5	202.6	160.8	123.7	139.4	164.2	151.0	131.5	195.1
06	153.8	194.4	209.8	181.6	126.2	142.6	179.9	152.6	131.0	205.6
07	155.0	192.4	216.9	193.5	127.3	144.7	186.2	155.0	132.2	210.3
07: Jan	154.2	192.1	213.5	185.7	127.8	143.9	185.3	155.0	132.7	207.7
Feb	154.0	192.7	214.0	187.2	127.3	144.5	185.4	155.0	132.5	211.0
Mar	153.8	193.3	215.1	191.1	127.2	144.4	185.9	154.6	132.1	210.6
Apr	153.9	193.3	215.1	195.4	127.4	144.6	186.5	154.3	131.8	209.9
May	154.2	193.1	215.8	196.3	127.2	144.9	186.3	154.2	131.6	210.3
June	154.4	193.7	216.1	195.9	127.2	144.9	186.3	154.4	131.6	210.0
July	154.8	194.4	217.2	196.6	127.1	144.8	186.0	154.4	131.3	209.7
Aug	155.7	193.2	217.6	195.5	127.0	144.5	186.3	154.2	130.9	209.7
Sept	155.6	192.3	218.2	194.5	127.1	144.7	186.4	153.7	130.0	210.7
Oct	156.0	191.1	219.5	195.0	127.1	144.9	186.4	156.9	133.9	211.2
Nov	156.5	189.8	220.1	194.3	127.2	145.3	186.7	157.3	134.3	211.7
Dec	157.5	190.0	220.2	194.1	127.4	145.4	186.9	156.6	133.2	211.3
08: Jan	159.2	189.3	222.3	197.5	127.8	145.7	188.5	157.5	133.7	212.7
Feb	159.9	189.1	223.4	201.8	128.3	146.1	188.8	157.5	133.7	213.3
Mar	160.6	189.9	224.0	208.0	128.5	146.4	189.5	156.8	132.9	214.8
Apr	161.3	190.5	224.9	217.6	128.7	147.2	191.0	157.6	133.6	214.9
May	162.8	193.8	225.2	223.4	129.2	147.3	192.1	157.5	133.3	216.4
June	164.0	194.6	225.7	226.9	129.6	148.0	194.4	156.7	132.1	217.1
July[2]	167.3	193.7	226.8	232.2	130.4	149.1	198.9	157.5	132.7	218.4
Aug[2]	169.1	193.7	230.0	232.2	130.8	149.9	203.1	157.3	132.0	219.1
Sept[2]	171.3	193.8	231.4	223.8	131.0	150.8	204.7	157.6	132.1	219.3
Oct[2]	172.9	190.9	231.0	211.5	131.2	151.4	205.1	162.2	137.5	219.2

Source: Department of Labor (Bureau of Labor Statistics).

TABLE B–68.—*Changes in producer price indexes for finished goods, 1965–2008*

[Percent change]

Year or month	Total finished goods		Finished consumer foods		Finished goods excluding consumer foods						Finished energy goods		Finished goods excluding foods and energy	
					Total		Consumer goods		Capital equipment					
	Dec. to Dec.[1]	Year to year	Dec. to Dec.[1]	Year to year	Dec. to Dec.[1]	Year to year	Dec. to Dec.[1]	Year to year	Dec. to Dec.[1]	Year to year	Dec. to Dec.[1]	Year to year	Dec. to Dec.[1]	Year to year
1965	3.3	1.8	9.1	4.0	....	....	0.9	0.9	1.5	1.2	....	....	....	....
1966	2.0	3.2	1.3	6.5	....	....	1.8	1.5	3.8	2.4	....	....	....	....
1967	1.7	1.1	-.3	-1.8	....	....	2.0	1.8	3.1	3.5	....	....	....	....
1968	3.1	2.8	4.6	3.9	2.5	2.6	2.0	2.3	3.0	3.4	....	....	....	....
1969	4.9	3.8	8.1	6.0	3.3	2.8	2.8	2.3	4.8	3.5	....	....	....	....
1970	2.1	3.4	-2.3	3.3	4.3	3.5	3.8	3.0	4.8	4.7	....	....	....	....
1971	3.3	3.1	5.8	1.6	2.0	3.7	2.1	3.5	2.4	4.0	....	....	....	....
1972	3.9	3.2	7.9	5.4	2.3	2.0	2.1	1.8	2.1	2.6	....	....	....	....
1973	11.7	9.1	22.7	20.5	6.6	4.0	7.5	4.6	5.1	3.3	....	....	....	....
1974	18.3	15.4	12.8	14.0	21.1	16.2	20.3	17.0	22.7	14.3	....	....	17.7	11.4
1975	6.6	10.6	5.6	8.4	7.2	12.1	6.8	10.4	8.1	15.2	16.3	17.2	6.0	11.4
1976	3.8	4.5	-2.5	-.3	6.2	6.2	6.0	6.2	6.5	6.7	11.6	11.7	5.7	5.7
1977	6.7	6.4	6.9	5.3	6.8	7.1	6.7	7.3	7.2	6.4	12.0	15.7	6.2	6.0
1978	9.3	7.9	11.7	9.0	8.3	7.2	8.5	7.1	8.0	7.9	8.5	6.5	8.4	7.5
1979	12.8	11.2	7.4	9.3	14.8	11.8	17.6	13.3	8.8	8.7	58.1	35.0	9.4	8.9
1980	11.8	13.4	7.5	5.8	13.4	16.2	14.1	18.5	11.4	10.7	27.9	49.2	10.8	11.2
1981	7.1	9.2	1.5	5.8	8.7	10.3	8.6	10.3	9.2	10.3	14.1	19.1	7.7	8.6
1982	3.6	4.1	2.0	2.2	4.2	4.6	4.2	4.1	3.9	5.7	-.1	-1.5	4.9	5.7
1983	.6	1.6	2.3	1.0	.0	1.8	-.9	1.2	2.0	2.8	-9.2	-4.8	1.9	3.0
1984	1.7	2.1	3.5	4.4	1.1	1.4	.8	1.0	1.8	2.3	-4.2	-4.2	2.0	2.4
1985	1.8	1.0	.6	-.8	2.2	1.4	2.1	1.1	2.7	2.2	-.2	-3.9	2.7	2.5
1986	-2.3	-1.4	2.8	2.6	-4.0	-2.6	-6.6	-4.6	2.1	2.0	-38.1	-28.1	2.7	2.3
1987	2.2	2.1	-.2	2.1	3.2	2.1	4.1	2.2	1.3	1.8	11.2	-1.9	2.1	2.4
1988	4.0	2.5	5.7	2.8	3.2	2.4	3.1	2.4	3.6	2.3	-3.6	-3.2	4.3	3.3
1989	4.9	5.2	5.2	5.4	4.8	5.0	5.3	5.6	3.8	3.9	9.5	9.9	4.2	4.4
1990	5.7	4.9	2.6	4.8	6.9	5.0	8.7	5.9	3.4	3.5	30.7	14.2	3.5	3.7
1991	-.1	2.1	-1.5	-.2	.3	3.0	-.7	2.9	2.5	3.1	-9.6	4.1	3.1	3.6
1992	1.6	1.2	1.6	-.6	1.6	1.8	1.6	1.8	1.7	1.9	-.3	-.4	2.0	2.4
1993	.2	1.2	2.4	1.9	-.4	1.1	-1.4	.7	1.8	1.8	-4.1	.3	1.4	1.2
1994	1.7	.6	1.1	.9	1.9	.6	2.0	-.1	2.0	2.1	3.5	-1.3	1.6	1.0
1995	2.3	1.9	1.9	1.7	2.3	1.9	2.3	2.0	2.2	1.9	1.1	1.4	2.6	2.1
1996	2.8	2.7	3.4	3.6	2.6	2.4	3.7	2.9	.4	1.2	11.7	6.5	.6	1.4
1997	-1.2	.4	-.8	.7	-1.2	.3	-1.5	.5	-.6	-.1	-6.4	.2	.0	.3
1998	.0	-.8	.1	-.1	-.1	-1.1	-.1	-1.4	.0	-.4	-11.7	-10.0	2.5	.9
1999	2.9	1.8	.8	.6	3.5	2.2	5.1	3.2	.3	.0	18.1	4.9	.9	1.7
2000	3.6	3.8	1.7	1.6	4.1	4.4	5.5	6.1	1.2	.9	16.6	19.4	1.3	1.3
2001	-1.6	2.0	1.8	3.0	-2.6	1.7	-3.9	2.2	.0	.6	-17.1	2.8	.9	1.4
2002	1.2	-1.3	-.6	-.8	1.7	-1.5	2.9	-1.8	-.6	-.4	12.3	-8.2	-.5	.1
2003	4.0	3.2	7.7	4.1	3.0	3.0	4.1	4.3	.8	.3	11.4	14.9	1.0	.2
2004	4.2	3.6	3.1	4.7	4.5	3.4	5.5	4.3	2.4	1.4	13.4	10.8	2.3	1.5
2005	5.4	4.8	1.7	2.0	6.4	5.6	8.8	7.3	1.2	2.3	23.9	17.3	1.4	2.4
2006	1.1	3.0	1.7	.6	1.0	3.5	.4	4.5	2.3	1.6	-2.0	10.0	2.0	1.5
2007	6.2	3.9	7.6	6.6	5.8	3.2	7.7	3.8	1.4	1.8	17.8	7.1	2.0	1.9

Percent change from preceding month

Year or month	Unadjusted	Seasonally adjusted	Unadjusted	Seasonally adjusted	Unadjusted	Seasonally adjusted	Unadjusted	Seasonally adjusted	Unadjusted	Seasonally adjusted	Unadjusted	Seasonally adjusted	Unadjusted	Seasonally adjusted
2007: Jan	-0.2	-0.1	0.6	0.9	-0.4	-0.4	-0.7	-0.6	0.2	0.1	-2.5	-2.0	0.2	0.1
Feb	1.1	1.2	1.7	1.6	.9	1.1	1.1	1.4	.2	.3	2.5	3.2	.4	.4
Mar	1.4	.9	1.5	1.5	1.4	.8	2.0	1.1	-.1	.0	6.0	3.2	-.1	-.1
Apr	1.1	.7	.3	.5	1.3	.7	1.9	1.0	.0	.1	5.4	2.6	.0	.2
May	1.0	.6	.0	-.7	1.3	.9	1.8	1.3	.0	.1	4.2	2.9	.2	.2
June	-.2	.1	-.3	-.2	-.2	.1	-.2	.1	-.1	.2	-.6	-.3	.0	.2
July	.8	.5	.1	-.1	1.0	.7	1.4	1.0	-.1	.1	3.4	2.2	.1	.2
Aug	-1.4	-.8	-.1	.0	-1.8	-1.1	-2.4	-1.4	-.1	.0	-6.5	-4.2	.1	.1
Sept	.8	.5	1.3	1.1	.7	.4	1.0	.5	-.1	.0	2.6	1.2	.0	.1
Oct	.7	.5	.8	1.3	.7	.4	.5	.5	1.1	.1	-.4	1.1	1.1	.1
Nov	1.7	2.6	-.1	-.2	2.1	3.4	2.8	4.5	.3	.4	7.1	11.7	.2	.3
Dec	-.6	-.5	1.6	1.3	-1.2	-1.0	-1.5	-1.3	-.2	-.1	-3.9	-3.5	-.1	.1
2008: Jan	.9	1.2	1.3	1.7	.8	1.0	1.0	1.2	.5	.5	1.7	2.2	.6	.6
Feb	.2	.3	-.5	-.6	.4	.6	.4	.8	.3	.4	.4	1.0	.4	.4
Mar	1.6	.9	1.4	1.4	1.7	.7	2.4	1.1	.0	.0	6.2	2.5	.1	.1
Apr	.8	.3	-.3	.0	1.0	.3	1.3	.2	.4	.6	2.8	-.1	.4	.5
May	1.9	1.4	1.2	.6	2.1	1.7	2.8	2.3	.2	.3	6.8	5.3	.2	.2
June	1.4	1.7	1.4	1.5	1.5	1.8	2.1	2.4	.0	.1	5.0	5.6	-.1	.2
July[2]	1.4	1.2	.3	.3	1.7	1.4	2.1	1.7	.6	.8	4.1	2.9	.7	.8
Aug[2]	-1.6	-.9	.3	.3	-2.1	-1.2	-2.9	-1.7	.1	.1	-6.9	-4.6	.1	.2
Sept[2]	-.1	-.4	.3	.2	-.2	-.5	-.4	-.9	.4	.5	-1.4	-2.9	.4	.4
Oct[2]	-2.6	-2.8	-.7	-.2	-3.1	-3.4	-5.0	-5.0	1.6	.5	-14.2	-12.8	1.5	.4

[1] Changes from December to December are based on unadjusted indexes.
[2] Data have been revised through June 2008; data are subject to revision four months after date of original publication.

Source: Department of Labor (Bureau of Labor Statistics).

MONEY STOCK, CREDIT, AND FINANCE

TABLE B–69.—*Money stock and debt measures, 1965–2008*

[Averages of daily figures, except debt end-of-period basis; billions of dollars, seasonally adjusted]

Year and month	M1 Sum of currency, demand deposits, travelers checks, and other checkable deposits (OCDs)	M2 M1 plus retail MMMF balances, savings deposits (including MMDAs), and small time deposits [2]	Debt [1] Debt of domestic nonfinancial sectors	Percent change From year or 6 months earlier [3] M1	Percent change From year or 6 months earlier [3] M2	From previous period [4] Debt
December:						
1965	167.8	459.2	1,008.0	....	....	....
1966	172.0	480.2	1,075.5	2.5	4.6	6.7
1967	183.3	524.8	1,151.5	6.6	9.3	7.1
1968	197.4	566.8	1,243.3	7.7	8.0	8.0
1969	203.9	587.9	1,330.4	3.3	3.7	7.1
1970	214.4	626.5	1,420.2	5.1	6.6	6.8
1971	228.3	710.3	1,555.2	6.5	13.4	9.5
1972	249.2	802.3	1,711.2	9.2	13.0	10.0
1973	262.9	855.5	1,895.5	5.5	6.6	10.7
1974	274.2	902.1	2,069.9	4.3	5.4	9.2
1975	287.1	1,016.2	2,261.8	4.7	12.6	9.3
1976	306.2	1,152.0	2,505.3	6.7	13.4	10.8
1977	330.9	1,270.3	2,826.6	8.1	10.3	12.8
1978	357.3	1,366.0	3,211.2	8.0	7.5	13.8
1979	381.8	1,473.7	3,603.0	6.9	7.9	12.2
1980	408.5	1,599.8	3,953.5	7.0	8.6	9.5
1981	436.7	1,755.5	4,361.7	6.9	9.7	10.4
1982	474.8	1,910.1	4,783.4	8.7	8.8	10.1
1983	521.4	2,126.4	5,359.2	9.8	11.3	12.0
1984	551.6	2,309.8	6,146.2	5.8	8.6	14.8
1985	619.8	2,495.5	7,123.2	12.4	8.0	15.6
1986	724.7	2,732.2	7,967.0	16.9	9.5	11.9
1987	750.2	2,831.3	8,670.7	3.5	3.6	9.0
1988	786.7	2,994.3	9,451.6	4.9	5.8	9.0
1989	792.9	3,158.6	10,152.9	.8	5.5	7.2
1990	824.7	3,277.7	10,836.7	4.0	3.8	6.5
1991	897.0	3,378.0	11,302.8	8.8	3.1	4.3
1992	1,024.9	3,431.4	11,818.3	14.3	1.6	4.5
1993	1,129.6	3,482.0	12,394.7	10.2	1.5	4.8
1994	1,150.7	3,498.1	12,979.2	1.9	.5	4.7
1995	1,127.4	3,642.1	13,673.8	−2.0	4.1	5.2
1996	1,081.3	3,820.5	14,407.6	−4.1	4.9	5.4
1997	1,072.5	4,034.1	15,219.7	−.8	5.6	5.6
1998	1,095.5	4,378.4	16,226.6	2.1	8.5	6.6
1999	1,122.5	4,633.9	17,307.7	2.5	5.8	6.4
2000	1,087.4	4,912.9	18,183.6	−3.1	6.0	5.0
2001	1,181.9	5,421.2	19,319.3	8.7	10.3	6.3
2002	1,219.7	5,766.0	20,733.8	3.2	6.4	7.3
2003	1,306.1	6,055.5	22,442.5	7.1	5.0	8.1
2004	1,376.3	6,400.7	24,456.8	5.4	5.7	8.9
2005	1,374.5	6,659.7	26,776.2	−.1	4.0	9.5
2006	1,366.5	7,012.3	29,201.4	−.6	5.3	9.1
2007	1,366.5	7,404.3	31,723.4	.0	5.6	8.6
7: Jan	1,372.5	7,058.6	....	.3	6.3	....
Feb	1,367.5	7,084.8	....	−.4	6.5	....
Mar	1,369.8	7,124.3	29,801.3	1.3	6.9	8.1
Apr	1,377.7	7,173.9	....	1.4	6.8	....
May	1,375.3	7,193.8	....	.6	6.4	....
June	1,365.9	7,210.4	30,400.5	−.1	5.7	8.0
July	1,368.5	7,233.7	....	−.6	5.0	....
Aug	1,369.9	7,286.1	....	.4	5.7	....
Sept	1,366.4	7,313.9	31,095.5	−.5	5.3	9.1
Oct	1,369.5	7,338.3	....	−1.2	4.6	....
Nov	1,365.6	7,372.3	....	−1.4	5.0	....
Dec	1,366.5	7,404.3	31,723.4	.1	5.4	8.1
8: Jan	1,367.2	7,448.9	....	−.2	5.9	....
Feb	1,372.8	7,546.8	....	.4	7.2	....
Mar	1,375.3	7,618.1	32,154.9	1.3	8.3	5.4
Apr	1,371.3	7,631.3	....	.3	8.0	....
May	1,368.0	7,640.7	....	.4	7.3	....
June	1,386.2	7,638.7	32,436.5	2.9	6.3	3.5
July	1,403.3	7,679.5	....	5.3	6.2	....
Aug	1,394.0	7,669.9	....	3.1	3.3	....
Sept	1,453.8	7,769.1	....	11.4	4.0	....
Oct	1,473.1	7,879.0	....	14.8	6.5	....

[1] Consists of outstanding credit market debt of the U.S. Government, State and local governments, and private nonfinancial sectors.
[2] Money market mutual fund (MMMF). Money market deposit account (MMDA).
[3] Annual changes are from December to December; monthly changes are from six months earlier at a simple annual rate.
[4] Annual changes are from fourth quarter to fourth quarter. Quarterly changes are from previous quarter at annual rate.

Note.—The Federal Reserve no longer publishes the M3 monetary aggregate and most of its components. Institutional money market mutual funds is ⎯lished as a memorandum item in the H.6 release, and the component on large-denomination time deposits is published in other Federal Reserve Board ⎯ases. For details, see H.6 release of March 23, 2006.

Source: Board of Governors of the Federal Reserve System.

[Averages of daily figures; billions of dollars, seasonally adjusted]

Year and month	Currency	Nonbank travelers checks	Demand deposits	Other checkable deposits (OCDs)		
				Total	At commercial banks	At thrift institutions
December:						
1965	36.0	0.5	131.3	0.1	0.0	
1966	38.0	.6	133.4	.1	.0	
1967	40.0	.6	142.5	.1	.0	
1968	43.0	.7	153.6	.1	.0	
1969	45.7	.8	157.3	.2	.0	
1970	48.6	.9	164.7	.1	.0	
1971	52.0	1.0	175.1	.2	.0	
1972	56.2	1.2	191.6	.2	.0	
1973	60.8	1.4	200.3	.3	.0	
1974	67.0	1.7	205.1	.4	.2	
1975	72.8	2.1	211.3	.9	.4	
1976	79.5	2.6	221.5	2.7	1.3	
1977	87.4	2.9	236.4	4.2	1.8	
1978	96.0	3.3	249.5	8.5	5.3	
1979	104.8	3.5	256.6	16.8	12.7	
1980	115.3	3.9	261.2	28.1	20.8	
1981	122.5	4.1	231.4	78.7	63.0	1
1982	132.5	4.1	234.1	104.1	80.5	2
1983	146.2	4.7	238.5	132.1	97.3	3
1984	156.1	5.0	243.4	147.1	104.7	4
1985	167.7	5.6	266.9	179.5	124.7	5
1986	180.4	6.1	302.9	235.2	161.0	7
1987	196.7	6.6	287.7	259.2	178.2	8
1988	212.0	7.0	287.1	280.6	192.5	8
1989	222.3	6.9	278.6	285.1	197.4	8
1990	246.5	7.7	276.8	293.7	208.7	8
1991	267.1	7.7	289.6	332.5	241.6	9
1992	292.2	8.2	340.0	384.6	280.8	10
1993	321.6	8.0	385.4	414.6	302.6	11
1994	354.5	8.6	383.6	404.0	297.4	10
1995	372.8	9.0	389.0	356.6	249.0	10
1996	394.7	8.8	402.1	275.7	172.1	10
1997	425.3	8.4	393.6	245.2	148.3	9
1998	460.5	8.5	376.6	249.9	143.9	10
1999	517.8	8.6	352.8	243.4	139.6	10
2000	531.2	8.3	309.6	238.4	133.1	10
2001	581.2	8.0	335.2	257.4	142.0	11
2002	626.3	7.8	306.2	279.4	154.3	12
2003	662.5	7.7	325.8	310.1	175.2	13
2004	697.6	7.5	343.2	328.0	186.8	14
2005	723.9	7.2	324.9	318.5	180.5	13
2006	748.9	6.7	305.9	305.0	176.8	12
2007	758.7	6.3	294.8	306.8	173.9	13
2007: Jan	750.5	6.7	307.4	308.0	178.0	13
Feb	751.0	6.6	304.6	305.3	176.5	12
Mar	752.5	6.6	302.8	307.9	176.6	13
Apr	754.4	6.6	305.9	310.9	177.3	13
May	755.4	6.6	304.2	309.2	176.3	13
June	756.0	6.5	301.5	302.0	171.7	13
July	758.0	6.5	301.0	303.0	172.0	13
Aug	758.1	6.4	302.0	303.4	171.6	13
Sept	759.2	6.4	296.1	304.7	171.7	13
Oct	761.5	6.4	296.5	305.1	173.0	13
Nov	761.1	6.3	296.2	302.0	172.3	12
Dec	758.7	6.3	294.8	306.8	173.9	13
2008: Jan	757.8	6.2	294.6	308.6	173.9	13
Feb	758.7	6.2	295.0	312.9	177.7	13
Mar	761.8	6.2	297.2	310.1	175.7	13
Apr	759.8	6.2	294.0	311.3	175.6	13
May	762.7	6.2	289.0	310.3	171.5	13
June	769.0	6.0	294.0	317.1	181.0	13
July	774.6	5.9	303.1	319.7	180.3	13
Aug	775.8	5.9	302.4	309.9	172.1	13
Sept	780.1	5.8	351.9	316.1	177.5	13
Oct	795.0	5.8	360.5	311.9	174.8	13

See next page for continuation of table.

TABLE B–70.—*Components of money stock measures, 1965–2008*—Continued

[Averages of daily figures; billions of dollars, seasonally adjusted]

Year and month	Savings deposits [1]			Small-denomination time deposits [2]			Retail money funds	Institutional money funds [3]
	Total	At commercial banks	At thrift institutions	Total	At commercial banks	At thrift institutions		
nber:								
965	256.9	92.4	164.5	34.5	26.7	7.8	0.0	0.0
966	253.1	89.9	163.3	55.0	38.7	16.3	.0	.0
967	263.7	94.1	169.6	77.8	50.7	27.1	.0	.0
968	268.9	96.1	172.8	100.5	63.5	37.1	.0	.0
969	263.7	93.8	169.8	120.4	71.6	48.8	.0	.0
970	261.0	98.6	162.3	151.2	79.3	71.9	.0	.0
971	292.2	112.8	179.4	189.7	94.7	95.1	.0	.0
972	321.4	124.8	196.6	231.6	108.2	123.5	.0	.0
973	326.8	128.0	198.7	265.8	116.8	149.0	.1	.0
974	338.6	136.8	201.8	287.9	123.1	164.8	1.4	.2
975	388.9	161.2	227.6	337.9	142.3	195.5	2.4	.5
976	453.2	201.8	251.4	390.7	155.5	235.2	1.8	.6
977	492.2	218.8	273.4	445.5	167.5	278.0	1.8	1.0
978	481.9	216.5	265.4	521.0	185.1	335.8	5.8	3.5
979	423.8	195.0	228.8	634.3	235.5	398.7	33.9	10.4
980	400.3	185.7	214.5	728.5	286.2	442.3	62.5	16.0
981	343.9	159.0	184.9	823.1	347.7	475.4	151.7	38.2
982	400.1	190.1	210.0	850.9	379.9	471.0	184.3	48.8
983	684.9	363.2	321.7	784.1	350.9	433.1	136.0	40.9
984	704.7	389.3	315.4	888.8	387.9	500.9	164.8	62.4
985	815.3	456.6	358.6	885.7	386.4	499.3	174.7	65.5
986	940.9	533.5	407.4	858.4	369.4	489.0	208.2	86.4
987	937.4	534.8	402.6	921.0	391.7	529.3	222.6	93.9
988	926.4	542.4	383.9	1,037.1	451.2	585.9	244.1	93.9
989	893.7	541.1	352.6	1,151.3	533.8	617.6	320.8	111.9
990	922.9	581.3	341.6	1,173.4	610.7	562.7	356.7	140.6
991	1,044.5	664.8	379.6	1,065.6	602.2	463.3	371.0	189.9
992	1,187.2	754.2	433.1	868.1	508.1	360.0	351.1	214.3
993	1,219.3	785.3	434.0	782.0	467.9	314.1	351.1	218.6
994	1,151.3	752.8	398.5	818.1	503.6	314.5	378.0	213.4
995	1,135.9	774.8	361.0	933.1	575.8	357.3	445.7	266.6
996	1,274.8	906.0	368.8	948.8	594.2	354.6	515.6	327.2
997	1,401.8	1,022.9	378.8	968.6	625.5	343.2	591.1	401.8
998	1,605.0	1,188.5	416.5	952.4	626.4	326.1	725.5	552.9
999	1,740.3	1,289.0	451.2	956.8	636.9	319.9	814.4	659.3
000	1,878.7	1,424.6	454.1	1,047.6	700.2	347.5	899.3	816.8
001	2,310.6	1,739.5	571.1	976.5	635.4	341.1	952.3	1,224.6
002	2,774.2	2,060.4	713.8	896.0	590.8	305.2	876.1	1,275.5
003	3,162.3	2,337.7	824.7	818.7	541.3	277.4	768.5	1,142.1
004	3,506.4	2,631.0	875.3	830.0	551.2	278.8	688.0	1,093.4
005	3,599.2	2,771.5	827.7	996.2	644.9	351.3	689.9	1,161.2
006	3,685.4	2,904.0	781.4	1,171.4	759.2	412.2	789.0	1,362.0
007	3,858.9	3,033.7	825.3	1,218.9	823.0	395.9	959.9	1,901.2
Jan	3,707.9	2,919.4	788.6	1,176.6	762.0	414.6	801.5	1,364.8
Feb	3,726.0	2,929.7	796.3	1,181.2	766.4	414.8	810.1	1,384.9
Mar	3,742.2	2,923.2	819.0	1,184.9	756.7	428.2	827.4	1,414.2
Apr	3,772.5	2,934.7	837.9	1,189.8	758.3	431.4	833.9	1,447.1
May	3,787.5	2,938.2	849.3	1,191.1	758.9	432.2	839.9	1,487.2
June	3,800.5	2,947.2	853.4	1,191.4	760.2	431.2	852.6	1,518.7
July	3,807.2	2,964.7	842.5	1,192.4	765.5	426.9	865.6	1,552.7
Aug	3,833.6	2,994.3	839.4	1,194.7	767.5	427.2	887.9	1,631.0
Sept	3,836.7	3,008.1	828.6	1,205.4	775.6	429.9	905.4	1,714.5
Oct	3,840.9	3,010.5	830.4	1,211.9	803.3	408.7	915.9	1,798.7
Nov	3,855.0	3,026.7	828.3	1,216.1	820.5	395.5	935.5	1,859.1
Dec	3,858.9	3,033.7	825.3	1,218.9	823.0	395.9	959.9	1,901.2
Jan	3,872.9	3,040.1	832.9	1,226.1	825.5	400.6	982.6	1,950.6
Feb	3,921.3	3,081.5	839.8	1,227.3	826.8	400.5	1,025.4	2,093.3
Mar	3,979.8	3,123.8	856.0	1,217.1	820.9	396.2	1,045.8	2,168.5
Apr	3,987.0	3,126.6	860.4	1,211.5	816.5	395.0	1,061.5	2,208.5
May	4,025.2	3,138.3	886.9	1,206.8	815.8	390.9	1,040.6	2,242.3
June	4,024.9	3,126.7	898.2	1,203.9	818.6	385.3	1,023.7	2,269.3
July	4,033.0	3,130.4	902.6	1,212.8	833.6	379.1	1,030.4	2,267.5
Aug	4,011.9	3,120.3	891.6	1,237.5	859.5	378.0	1,026.5	2,291.7
Sept	4,033.4	3,170.2	863.3	1,255.6	883.0	372.7	1,026.2	2,198.3
Oct	4,032.0	3,247.6	784.5	1,314.1	975.0	339.1	1,059.7	2,150.0

Savings deposits including money market deposit accounts (MMDAs); data prior to 1982 are savings deposits only.

Small-denomination deposits are those issued in amounts of less than $100,000.

Institutional money funds are not part of non-M1 M2.

ote.—See also Table B–69.

ource: Board of Governors of the Federal Reserve System.

[Averages of daily figures [1]; millions of dollars; seasonally adjusted, except as noted]

Year and month	Adjusted for changes in reserve requirements [2]					Borrowings from the Federal Reserve (NSA) [3]						
	Reserves of depository institutions				Monetary base	Total [4]	Term auction credit	Other borrowings from the Federal Reserve				
	Total	Non-borrowed	Required	Excess (NSA) [3]				Primary	Primary dealer and other broker-dealer credit [5]	Asset-backed commercial paper money market mutual fund liquidity facility	Credit extended to American International Group, Inc.	Adju mer
December:												
1966	12,223	11,690	11,884	339	51,565	532						
1967	13,180	12,952	12,805	375	54,579	228						
1968	13,767	13,021	13,341	426	58,357	746						
1969	14,168	13,049	13,882	286	61,569	1,119						1,
1970	14,558	14,225	14,309	249	65,013	332						
1971	15,230	15,104	15,049	182	69,108	126						
1972	16,645	15,595	16,361	284	75,167	1,050						1,
1973	17,021	15,723	16,717	304	81,073	1,298						1,
1974	17,550	16,823	17,292	258	87,535	727						
1975	17,822	17,692	17,556	266	93,887	130						
1976	18,388	18,335	18,115	274	101,515	53						
1977	18,990	18,420	18,800	190	110,324	569						
1978	19,753	18,885	19,521	232	120,445	868						
1979	20,720	19,248	20,279	442	131,143	1,473						1,
1980	22,015	20,325	21,501	514	142,004	1,690						1,
1981	22,443	21,807	22,124	319	149,021	636						
1982	23,600	22,966	23,100	500	160,127	634						
1983	25,367	24,593	24,806	561	175,467	774						
1984	26,913	23,727	26,078	835	187,252	3,186						
1985	31,569	30,250	30,505	1,063	203,555	1,318						
1986	38,840	38,014	37,667	1,173	223,416	827						
1987	38,913	38,135	37,893	1,019	239,829	777						
1988	40,453	38,738	39,392	1,061	256,897	1,716						
1989	40,486	40,221	39,545	941	267,754	265						
1990	41,766	41,440	40,101	1,665	293,300	326						
1991	45,516	45,324	44,526	990	317,544	192						
1992	54,421	54,298	53,267	1,154	350,912	124						
1993	60,566	60,484	59,497	1,069	386,586	82						
1994	59,466	59,257	58,295	1,171	418,339	209						
1995	56,483	56,226	55,193	1,290	434,580	257						
1996	50,185	50,030	48,766	1,418	452,051	155						
1997	46,875	46,551	45,189	1,687	479,931	324						
1998	45,170	45,053	43,658	1,512	513,921	117						
1999	42,183	41,862	40,889	1,294	593,846	[6]320						
2000	38,716	38,507	37,391	1,325	584,929	210						
2001	41,443	41,376	39,799	1,643	635,601	67						
2002	40,400	40,320	38,392	2,008	681,656	80						
2003	42,757	42,711	41,710	1,047	720,474	46		17				
2004	46,552	46,489	44,643	1,909	759,173	63		11				
2005	45,138	44,970	43,238	1,900	787,303	169		97				
2006	43,338	43,147	41,475	1,863	811,730	191		111				
2007	42,675	27,244	40,905	1,770	823,348	15,430	11,613	3,787				
2007: Jan	42,309	42,098	40,764	1,545	813,654	211		187				
Feb	42,454	42,425	41,001	1,453	813,447	30		8				
Mar	42,289	42,235	40,673	1,617	814,858	54		21				
Apr	42,576	42,497	40,989	1,587	816,973	79		32				
May	43,187	43,084	41,734	1,453	818,687	103		14				
June	43,374	43,187	41,623	1,751	819,831	187		43				
July	41,821	41,559	40,183	1,638	821,129	262		45				
Aug	45,022	44,047	40,196	4,826	824,440	975		701				
Sept	42,668	41,101	40,934	1,733	821,968	1,567		1,345				
Oct	42,436	42,182	40,977	1,459	824,647	254		126				
Nov	42,623	42,258	40,927	1,696	825,422	366		315				
Dec	42,675	27,244	40,905	1,770	823,348	15,430	11,613	3,787				
2008: Jan	42,149	−3,510	40,509	1,640	821,406	45,660	44,516	1,137				
Feb	42,804	−17,353	41,080	1,724	822,560	60,157	60,000	155				
Mar	44,292	−50,232	41,313	2,978	826,994	94,523	75,484	1,617	16,168			
Apr	43,563	−91,847	41,719	1,844	824,408	135,410	100,000	9,624	25,764			
May	44,133	−111,648	42,122	2,011	826,461	155,780	127,419	14,076	14,238			
June	43,373	−127,905	41,100	2,272	832,528	171,278	150,000	14,225	6,908			
July	43,348	−122,316	41,371	1,977	838,142	165,664	150,000	15,204	255			
Aug	44,586	−123,492	42,599	1,988	841,709	168,078	150,000	17,980	0			
Sept	102,800	−187,306	42,749	60,051	903,524	290,105	149,814	32,632	53,473	31,877	22,187	
Oct	315,525	−332,795	47,619	267,906	1,128,479	648,319	244,778	94,017	114,953	117,457	77,047	
Nov p	609,952	−88,834	50,904	559,048	1,433,092	698,786	393,088	95,839	60,655	71,009	78,070	

[1] Data are prorated averages of biweekly (maintenance period) averages of daily figures.

[2] Aggregate reserves incorporate adjustments for discontinuities associated with regulatory changes to reserve requirements. For details on aggregate reserves series see *Federal Reserve Bulletin.*

[3] Not seasonally adjusted (NSA).

[4] Includes secondary, seasonal, and other credit extensions, not shown separately.

[5] Includes credit extended through the Primary Dealer Credit Facility and credit extended to certain other broker-dealers.

[6] Total includes borrowing under the terms and conditions established for the Century Data Change Special Liquidity Facility in effect from October 1, 1999 through April 7, 2000.

Source: Board of Governors of the Federal Reserve System.

[Monthly average; billions of dollars, seasonally adjusted [1]]

Year and month	Total bank credit	Securities in bank credit			Loans and leases in bank credit							
		Total securities	U.S. Treasury and agency securities	Other securities[2]	Total loans and leases[3]	Commercial and industrial	Real estate			Consumer[5]	Security[5]	Other
							Total[4]	Revolving home equity	Commercial			
mber:												
365	297.1	96.1	64.3	31.9	201.0	69.5	48.9	....	....	45.0	8.0	29.7
366	318.6	97.2	61.0	36.2	221.4	79.3	53.8	....	....	47.7	8.3	32.4
367	350.5	111.4	70.7	40.6	239.2	86.5	58.2	....	....	51.2	9.6	33.8
368	390.5	121.9	73.8	48.1	268.6	96.5	64.8	....	....	57.7	10.5	39.2
369	401.6	112.4	64.2	48.2	289.2	106.9	69.9	....	....	62.6	10.0	39.8
370	434.4	129.7	73.4	56.3	304.6	111.6	72.9	....	....	65.3	10.4	44.5
371	485.2	147.5	79.8	67.7	337.6	118.0	81.7	....	....	73.3	10.9	53.9
372	555.3	160.6	85.4	75.2	394.7	133.6	98.8	....	....	85.4	14.4	62.5
373	638.6	168.4	89.7	78.7	470.1	162.8	119.4	....	....	98.3	11.2	78.4
374	701.7	173.8	87.9	85.9	527.9	193.0	132.5	....	....	102.1	10.6	89.6
375	732.9	206.7	117.9	88.9	526.2	184.3	137.2	....	....	104.6	12.7	87.5
376	790.7	228.6	137.3	91.3	562.1	186.3	151.3	....	....	115.9	17.7	91.0
377	876.0	236.3	137.4	98.9	639.7	205.8	178.0	....	....	138.1	20.7	97.2
378	989.4	242.2	138.4	103.8	747.2	239.0	213.5	....	....	164.6	19.1	110.9
379	1,111.4	260.7	147.2	113.4	850.7	282.2	245.0	....	....	184.5	17.4	121.6
380	1,207.1	296.8	173.2	123.6	910.3	314.5	265.7	....	....	179.2	17.2	133.6
381	1,302.7	311.1	181.8	129.3	991.6	353.3	287.5	....	....	182.7	20.2	148.0
382	1,412.3	338.6	204.7	133.9	1,073.7	396.4	303.8	....	....	188.2	23.6	161.7
383	1,566.7	403.8	263.4	140.4	1,163.0	419.1	334.8	....	....	213.2	26.5	169.4
384	1,733.4	406.6	262.9	143.7	1,326.9	479.4	380.8	....	....	253.6	34.1	179.0
385	1,922.2	455.9	273.8	182.2	1,466.3	506.5	431.0	....	....	294.5	42.9	191.4
386	2,106.6	510.0	312.8	197.2	1,596.5	544.0	499.9	....	....	314.5	38.6	199.5
387	2,255.3	535.0	338.9	196.1	1,720.2	575.0	595.7	32.2	....	327.7	34.8	187.0
388	2,445.3	561.4	365.9	195.5	1,884.0	612.0	676.6	42.6	369.6	354.9	39.7	200.8
389	2,612.0	585.5	401.0	184.6	2,026.5	642.4	769.4	53.5	414.3	375.3	40.7	198.5
390	2,757.3	635.8	457.5	178.4	2,121.5	644.8	856.7	66.4	447.5	380.8	44.7	194.5
391	2,871.2	746.2	566.5	179.7	2,125.0	622.2	882.9	74.3	445.2	363.9	51.9	204.1
392	2,989.2	842.8	666.5	176.3	2,146.4	598.0	905.9	78.5	433.7	356.2	60.0	226.3
393	3,143.2	916.9	732.7	184.2	2,226.3	588.7	946.8	78.1	426.4	387.4	80.9	222.5
394	3,317.0	940.2	722.5	217.7	2,376.9	647.9	1,010.5	80.5	437.2	447.9	70.2	200.2
395	3,598.4	984.6	702.2	282.4	2,613.8	718.6	1,091.0	84.5	458.3	491.1	78.7	234.3
396	3,740.0	975.0	699.4	275.5	2,765.1	777.0	1,141.7	90.6	482.0	511.9	69.8	264.7
397	4,080.7	1,087.4	751.9	335.5	2,993.2	846.0	1,243.3	104.6	514.2	502.7	87.7	313.6
398	4,514.1	1,225.9	795.8	430.1	3,288.2	938.8	1,333.4	103.6	559.1	497.4	134.5	384.1
399	4,742.9	1,268.8	810.4	458.4	3,474.1	990.9	1,471.9	101.1	648.0	491.5	139.6	380.1
300	5,204.2	1,337.3	790.6	546.7	3,866.9	1,079.1	1,655.9	129.7	742.2	539.8	161.0	431.1
301	5,414.6	1,482.9	852.1	630.8	3,931.7	1,018.7	1,786.1	155.4	813.6	556.2	135.0	435.6
302	5,885.0	1,714.7	1,029.4	685.3	4,170.3	955.9	2,033.8	213.1	884.5	585.9	173.8	421.0
303	6,257.9	1,853.5	1,115.6	738.0	4,404.4	896.7	2,230.2	280.3	962.0	642.3	198.1	437.1
304	6,807.6	1,947.4	1,172.0	775.4	4,860.1	918.9	2,566.1	397.9	1,083.3	696.7	197.4	481.0
305	7,523.7	2,067.5	1,162.5	905.0	5,456.2	1,036.6	2,924.4	443.7	1,274.9	707.6	245.6	542.0
306	8,353.4	2,247.7	1,218.0	1,029.8	6,105.7	1,188.3	3,357.6	467.6	1,453.6	743.3	268.6	548.0
307	9,206.3	2,424.2	1,126.2	1,298.0	6,782.2	1,434.4	3,578.6	483.2	1,604.0	809.2	287.6	672.3
Jan	8,393.9	2,248.8	1,215.4	1,033.4	6,145.1	1,195.0	3,384.5	469.0	1,465.7	746.9	267.7	551.0
Feb	8,460.1	2,246.2	1,208.1	1,038.1	6,213.9	1,208.3	3,422.4	470.8	1,481.7	750.2	276.4	556.6
Mar	8,426.2	2,256.9	1,209.1	1,047.8	6,169.3	1,220.1	3,364.1	461.5	1,488.2	747.1	279.9	558.1
Apr	8,506.1	2,264.1	1,184.0	1,080.1	6,242.0	1,229.7	3,401.2	460.8	1,496.6	751.8	280.6	578.6
May	8,563.9	2,267.7	1,163.7	1,103.9	6,296.3	1,248.0	3,431.5	462.8	1,509.3	755.5	280.4	581.0
June	8,621.4	2,290.3	1,162.8	1,127.5	6,331.1	1,266.2	3,452.8	465.1	1,525.7	764.4	266.7	581.1
July	8,705.3	2,316.7	1,166.4	1,150.4	6,388.6	1,284.7	3,460.7	465.3	1,537.0	772.2	278.2	592.8
Aug	8,842.1	2,345.9	1,175.0	1,170.9	6,496.3	1,311.2	3,498.2	468.0	1,552.0	774.0	287.5	625.4
Sept	8,956.3	2,382.7	1,172.0	1,210.8	6,573.5	1,357.1	3,507.9	472.2	1,563.0	783.1	283.5	641.9
Oct	9,057.1	2,404.5	1,138.9	1,265.5	6,652.7	1,390.2	3,539.9	475.6	1,571.8	788.5	271.9	662.2
Nov	9,180.3	2,464.5	1,129.0	1,335.5	6,715.8	1,408.5	3,562.3	478.5	1,589.5	795.9	282.0	667.1
Dec	9,206.3	2,424.2	1,126.2	1,298.0	6,782.2	1,434.4	3,578.6	483.2	1,604.0	809.2	287.6	672.3
Jan	9,274.1	2,435.2	1,104.0	1,331.2	6,838.9	1,450.7	3,594.9	486.9	1,614.3	813.2	301.5	678.7
Feb	9,334.5	2,453.3	1,094.0	1,359.4	6,881.2	1,459.7	3,622.3	492.5	1,627.6	814.7	296.0	688.5
Mar	9,455.5	2,539.3	1,105.0	1,434.3	6,916.2	1,480.1	3,649.2	498.9	1,642.7	817.9	292.3	676.6
Apr	9,408.8	2,511.1	1,093.8	1,417.3	6,897.7	1,489.4	3,654.3	506.8	1,653.7	823.4	283.6	647.1
May	9,402.5	2,481.1	1,096.0	1,385.2	6,921.4	1,495.8	3,657.2	512.2	1,663.9	827.1	292.8	648.5
June	9,374.0	2,471.3	1,112.8	1,358.5	6,902.7	1,502.9	3,648.2	518.3	1,680.0	831.7	280.8	639.1
July	9,398.3	2,490.9	1,114.3	1,376.6	6,907.4	1,509.6	3,627.1	523.5	1,667.8	839.3	295.0	636.3
Aug	9,414.5	2,477.7	1,127.7	1,350.0	6,936.8	1,509.3	3,646.0	526.2	1,674.3	845.0	305.5	630.9
Sept	9,574.2	2,533.6	1,153.8	1,379.8	7,040.6	1,536.9	3,666.7	540.4	1,680.6	852.0	331.0	654.0
Oct	9,958.1	2,717.8	1,227.4	1,490.4	7,240.3	1,601.5	3,791.5	577.8	1,717.8	870.2	302.6	674.4

Data are prorated averages of Wednesday values for domestically chartered commercial banks, branches and agencies of foreign banks, New York State ...ment companies (through September 1996), and Edge Act and agreement corporations.
...ncludes other trading assets.
...xcludes Federal funds sold to, reverse repurchase agreements (RPs) with, and loans to commercial banks in the United States.
...ncludes other residential, not shown separately.
...ncludes other items, not shown separately.
...urce: Board of Governors of the Federal Reserve System.

Table B–73.—Bond yields and interest rates, 1929–2008

[Percent per annum]

| Year and month | U.S. Treasury securities | | | | | Corporate bonds (Moody's) | | High-grade municipal bonds (Standard & Poor's)[4] | New-home mortgage yields[4] | Prime rate charged by banks[5] | Discount window (Federal Reserve Bank of New York)[5,6] | | Federal funds rate |
| | Bills (at auction)[1] | | Constant maturities[2] | | | | | | | | | | |
	3-month	6-month	3-year	10-year	30-year	Aaa[3]	Baa				Primary credit	Adjustment credit	
1929						4.73	5.90	4.27		5.50–6.00		5.16	
1933	0.515					4.49	7.76	4.71		1.50–4.00		2.56	
1939	.023					3.01	4.96	2.76		1.50		1.00	
1940	.014					2.84	4.75	2.50		1.50		1.00	
1941	.103					2.77	4.33	2.10		1.50		1.00	
1942	.326					2.83	4.28	2.36		1.50		81.00	
1943	.373					2.73	3.91	2.06		1.50		81.00	
1944	.375					2.72	3.61	1.86		1.50		81.00	
1945	.375					2.62	3.29	1.67		1.50		81.00	
1946	.375					2.53	3.05	1.64		1.50		81.00	
1947	.594					2.61	3.24	2.01		1.50–1.75		1.00	
1948	1.040					2.82	3.47	2.40		1.75–2.00		1.34	
1949	1.102					2.66	3.42	2.21		2.00		1.50	
1950	1.218					2.62	3.24	1.98		2.07		1.59	
1951	1.552					2.86	3.41	2.00		2.56		1.75	
1952	1.766					2.96	3.52	2.19		3.00		1.75	
1953	1.931		2.47	2.85		3.20	3.74	2.72		3.17		1.99	
1954	.953	1.63	2.40			2.90	3.51	2.37		3.05		1.60	
1955	1.753	2.47	2.82			3.06	3.53	2.53		3.16		1.89	1
1956	2.658	3.19	3.18			3.36	3.88	2.93		3.77		2.77	2
1957	3.267	3.98	3.65			3.89	4.71	3.60		4.20		3.12	3
1958	1.839	2.84	3.32			3.79	4.73	3.56		3.83		2.15	1
1959	3.405	3.832	4.46	4.33		4.38	5.05	3.95		4.48		3.36	3
1960	2.93	3.25	3.98	4.12		4.41	5.19	3.73		4.82		3.53	3
1961	2.38	2.61	3.54	3.88		4.35	5.08	3.46		4.50		3.00	1
1962	2.78	2.91	3.47	3.95		4.33	5.02	3.18		4.50		3.00	2
1963	3.16	3.25	3.67	4.00		4.26	4.86	3.23	5.89	4.50		3.23	3
1964	3.56	3.69	4.03	4.19		4.40	4.83	3.22	5.83	4.50		3.55	3
1965	3.95	4.05	4.22	4.28		4.49	4.87	3.27	5.81	4.54		4.04	4
1966	4.88	5.08	5.23	4.93		5.13	5.67	3.82	6.25	5.63		4.50	5
1967	4.32	4.63	5.03	5.07		5.51	6.23	3.98	6.46	5.61		4.19	4
1968	5.34	5.47	5.68	5.64		6.18	6.94	4.51	6.97	6.30		5.16	5
1969	6.68	6.85	7.02	6.67		7.03	7.81	5.81	7.81	7.96		5.87	8
1970	6.43	6.53	7.29	7.35		8.04	9.11	6.51	8.45	7.91		5.95	7
1971	4.35	4.51	5.66	6.16		7.39	8.56	5.70	7.74	5.72		4.88	4
1972	4.07	4.47	5.72	6.21		7.21	8.16	5.27	7.60	5.25		4.50	4
1973	7.04	7.18	6.96	6.85		7.44	8.24	5.18	7.96	8.03		6.44	8
1974	7.89	7.93	7.84	7.56		8.57	9.50	6.09	8.92	10.81		7.83	10
1975	5.84	6.12	7.50	7.99		8.83	10.61	6.89	9.00	7.86		6.25	5
1976	4.99	5.27	6.77	7.61		8.43	9.75	6.49	9.00	6.84		5.50	5
1977	5.27	5.52	6.68	7.42	7.75	8.02	8.97	5.56	9.02	6.83		5.46	5
1978	7.22	7.58	8.29	8.41	8.49	8.73	9.49	5.90	9.56	9.06		7.46	7
1979	10.05	10.02	9.70	9.43	9.28	9.63	10.69	6.39	10.78	12.67		10.28	11
1980	11.51	11.37	11.51	11.43	11.27	11.94	13.67	8.51	12.66	15.27		11.77	13
1981	14.03	13.78	14.46	13.92	13.45	14.17	16.04	11.23	14.70	18.87		13.42	16
1982	10.69	11.08	12.93	13.01	12.76	13.79	16.11	11.57	15.14	14.86		11.02	12
1983	8.63	8.75	10.45	11.10	11.18	12.04	13.55	9.47	12.57	10.79		8.50	9
1984	9.53	9.77	11.92	12.46	12.41	12.71	14.19	10.15	12.38	12.04		8.80	10
1985	7.47	7.64	9.64	10.62	10.79	11.37	12.72	9.18	11.55	9.93		7.69	8
1986	5.98	6.03	7.06	7.67	7.78	9.02	10.39	7.38	10.17	8.33		6.33	6
1987	5.82	6.05	7.68	8.39	8.59	9.38	10.58	7.73	9.31	8.21		5.66	6
1988	6.69	6.92	8.26	8.85	8.96	9.71	10.83	7.76	9.19	9.32		6.20	7
1989	8.12	8.04	8.55	8.49	8.45	9.26	10.18	7.24	10.13	10.87		6.93	9
1990	7.51	7.47	8.26	8.55	8.61	9.32	10.36	7.25	10.05	10.01		6.98	8
1991	5.42	5.49	6.82	7.86	8.14	8.77	9.80	6.89	9.32	8.46		5.45	5
1992	3.45	3.57	5.30	7.01	7.67	8.14	8.98	6.41	8.24	6.25		3.25	3
1993	3.02	3.14	4.44	5.87	6.59	7.22	7.93	5.63	7.20	6.00		3.00	3
1994	4.29	4.66	6.27	7.09	7.37	7.96	8.62	6.19	7.49	7.15		3.60	4
1995	5.51	5.59	6.25	6.57	6.88	7.59	8.20	5.95	7.87	8.83		5.21	5
1996	5.02	5.09	5.99	6.44	6.71	7.37	8.05	5.75	7.80	8.27		5.02	5
1997	5.07	5.18	6.10	6.35	6.61	7.26	7.86	5.55	7.71	8.44		5.00	5
1998	4.81	4.85	5.14	5.26	5.58	6.53	7.22	5.12	7.07	8.35		4.92	4
1999	4.66	4.76	5.49	5.65	5.87	7.04	7.87	5.43	7.04	8.00		4.62	4
2000	5.85	5.92	6.22	6.03	5.94	7.62	8.36	5.77	7.52	9.23		5.73	6
2001	3.44	3.39	4.09	5.02	5.49	7.08	7.95	5.19	7.00	6.91		3.40	3
2002	1.62	1.69	3.10	4.61		6.49	7.80	5.05	6.43	4.67		1.17	
2003	1.01	1.06	2.10	4.01		5.67	6.77	4.73	5.80	4.12	2.12		
2004	1.38	1.57	2.78	4.27		5.63	6.39	4.63	5.77	4.34	2.34		
2005	3.16	3.40	3.93	4.29		5.24	6.06	4.29	5.94	6.19	4.19		
2006	4.73	4.80	4.77	4.80	4.91	5.59	6.48	4.42	6.63	7.96	5.96		
2007	4.41	4.48	4.35	4.63	4.84	5.56	6.48	4.42	6.41	8.05	5.86		

[1] High bill rate at auction, issue date within period, bank-discount basis. On or after October 28, 1998, data are stop yields from uniform-price auctions. Before that date, they are weighted average yields from multiple-price auctions.

[2] Yields on the more actively traded issues adjusted to constant maturities by the Department of the Treasury. The 30-year Treasury constant maturity series was discontinued on February 18, 2002, and reintroduced on February 9, 2006.

See next page for continuation of table.

[Percent per annum]

Year and month	U.S. Treasury securities					Corporate bonds (Moody's)		High-grade muni-cipal bonds (Stand-ard & Poor's)	New-home mort-gage yields [4]	Prime rate charged by banks [5]	Discount window (Federal Reserve Bank of New York) [5, 6]			Federal funds rate [7]
	Bills (at auction) [1]		Constant maturities [2]			Aaa [3]	Baa				Primary credit	Adjust-ment credit		
	3-month	6-month	3-year	10-year	30-year									
											High-low	High-low	High-low	
2004: Jan	0.89	0.97	2.27	4.15	....	5.54	6.44	4.53	5.48	4.00–4.00	2.00–2.00	....	1.00
Feb	.92	.99	2.25	4.08	....	5.50	6.27	4.48	5.72	4.00–4.00	2.00–2.00	....	1.01
Mar	.94	.99	2.00	3.83	....	5.33	6.11	4.39	5.42	4.00–4.00	2.00–2.00	....	1.00
Apr	.94	1.06	2.57	4.35	....	5.73	6.46	4.84	5.49	4.00–4.00	2.00–2.00	....	1.00
May	1.03	1.31	3.10	4.72	....	6.04	6.75	5.03	5.77	4.00–4.00	2.00–2.00	....	1.00
June	1.27	1.58	3.26	4.73	....	6.01	6.78	5.00	5.81	4.25–4.00	2.25–2.00	....	1.03
July	1.35	1.67	3.05	4.50	....	5.82	6.62	4.82	5.96	4.25–4.25	2.25–2.25	....	1.26
Aug	1.48	1.72	2.88	4.28	....	5.65	6.46	4.65	5.88	4.50–4.25	2.50–2.25	....	1.43
Sept	1.65	1.86	2.83	4.13	....	5.46	6.27	4.49	5.72	4.75–4.50	2.75–2.50	....	1.61
Oct	1.75	1.99	2.85	4.10	....	5.47	6.21	4.43	5.82	4.75–4.75	2.75–2.75	....	1.76
Nov	2.06	2.26	3.09	4.19	....	5.52	6.20	4.48	5.91	5.00–4.75	3.00–2.75	....	1.93
Dec	2.20	2.45	3.21	4.23	....	5.47	6.15	4.40	6.02	5.25–5.00	3.25–3.00	....	2.16
2005: Jan	2.32	2.60	3.39	4.22	....	5.36	6.02	4.28	6.01	5.25–5.25	3.25–3.25	....	2.28
Feb	2.53	2.76	3.54	4.17	....	5.20	5.82	4.14	5.75	5.50–5.25	3.50–3.25	....	2.50
Mar	2.75	3.00	3.91	4.50	....	5.40	6.06	4.42	5.82	5.75–5.50	3.75–3.50	....	2.63
Apr	2.78	3.06	3.79	4.34	....	5.33	6.05	4.31	5.84	5.75–5.75	3.75–3.75	....	2.79
May	2.85	3.10	3.72	4.14	....	5.15	6.01	4.16	5.82	6.00–5.75	4.00–3.75	....	3.00
June	2.98	3.13	3.69	4.00	....	4.96	5.86	4.08	5.76	6.25–6.00	4.25–4.00	....	3.04
July	3.21	3.41	3.91	4.18	....	5.06	5.95	4.15	5.76	6.25–6.25	4.25–4.25	....	3.26
Aug	3.45	3.67	4.08	4.26	....	5.09	5.96	4.21	5.83	6.50–6.25	4.50–4.25	....	3.50
Sept	3.46	3.68	3.96	4.20	....	5.13	6.03	4.28	5.99	6.75–6.50	4.75–4.50	....	3.62
Oct	3.70	3.98	4.29	4.46	....	5.35	6.30	4.49	6.03	6.75–6.75	4.75–4.75	....	3.78
Nov	3.90	4.16	4.43	4.54	....	5.42	6.39	4.53	6.20	7.00–7.00	5.00–5.00	....	4.00
Dec	3.89	4.19	4.39	4.47	....	5.37	6.32	4.43	6.39	7.25–7.00	5.25–5.00	....	4.16
2006: Jan	4.20	4.29	4.35	4.42	....	5.29	6.24	4.31	6.12	7.50–7.25	5.50–5.25	....	4.29
Feb	4.41	4.51	4.64	4.57	4.54	5.35	6.27	4.41	6.40	7.50–7.50	5.50–5.50	....	4.49
Mar	4.51	4.61	4.74	4.72	4.73	5.53	6.41	4.44	6.53	7.75–7.50	5.75–5.50	....	4.59
Apr	4.59	4.71	4.89	4.99	5.06	5.84	6.68	4.60	6.64	7.75–7.75	5.75–5.75	....	4.79
May	4.72	4.81	4.97	5.11	5.20	5.95	6.75	4.61	6.69	8.00–7.75	6.00–5.75	....	4.94
June	4.79	4.95	5.09	5.11	5.15	5.89	6.78	4.64	6.79	8.25–8.00	6.25–6.00	....	4.99
July	4.96	5.09	5.07	5.09	5.13	5.85	6.76	4.64	6.81	8.25–8.25	6.25–6.25	....	5.24
Aug	4.98	4.99	4.85	4.88	5.00	5.68	6.59	4.43	6.87	8.25–8.25	6.25–6.25	....	5.25
Sept	4.82	4.90	4.69	4.72	4.85	5.51	6.43	4.30	6.72	8.25–8.25	6.25–6.25	....	5.25
Oct	4.89	4.91	4.72	4.73	4.85	5.51	6.42	4.32	6.69	8.25–8.25	6.25–6.25	....	5.25
Nov	4.95	4.95	4.64	4.60	4.69	5.33	6.20	4.17	6.55	8.25–8.25	6.25–6.25	....	5.25
Dec	4.84	4.87	4.58	4.56	4.68	5.32	6.22	4.17	6.37	8.25–8.25	6.25–6.25	....	5.24
2007: Jan	4.96	4.93	4.79	4.76	4.85	5.40	6.34	4.29	6.35	8.25–8.25	6.25–6.25	....	5.25
Feb	5.02	4.96	4.75	4.72	4.82	5.39	6.28	4.21	6.31	8.25–8.25	6.25–6.25	....	5.26
Mar	4.96	4.90	4.51	4.56	4.72	5.30	6.27	4.18	6.22	8.25–8.25	6.25–6.25	....	5.26
Apr	4.87	4.87	4.60	4.69	4.87	5.47	6.39	4.32	6.21	8.25–8.25	6.25–6.25	....	5.25
May	4.77	4.80	4.69	4.75	4.90	5.47	6.39	4.37	6.22	8.25–8.25	6.25–6.25	....	5.25
June	4.63	4.77	5.00	5.10	5.20	5.79	6.70	4.64	6.54	8.25–8.25	6.25–6.25	....	5.25
July	4.83	4.85	4.82	5.00	5.11	5.73	6.65	4.64	6.70	8.25–8.25	6.25–6.25	....	5.26
Aug	4.34	4.56	4.34	4.67	4.93	5.79	6.65	4.73	6.73	8.25–8.25	6.25–5.75	....	5.02
Sept	4.01	4.13	4.06	4.52	4.79	5.74	6.59	4.57	6.58	8.25–7.75	5.75–5.25	....	4.94
Oct	3.96	4.08	4.01	4.53	4.77	5.66	6.48	4.41	6.55	7.75–7.50	5.25–5.00	....	4.76
Nov	3.49	3.63	3.35	4.15	4.52	5.44	6.40	4.45	6.42	7.50–7.50	5.00–5.00	....	4.49
Dec	3.08	3.29	3.13	4.10	4.53	5.49	6.65	4.22	6.21	7.50–7.25	5.00–4.75	....	4.24
2008: Jan	2.86	2.84	2.51	3.74	4.33	5.33	6.54	4.00	6.02	7.25–6.00	4.75–3.50	....	3.94
Feb	2.21	2.09	2.19	3.74	4.52	5.53	6.82	4.35	5.96	6.00–6.00	3.50–3.50	....	2.98
Mar	1.38	1.53	1.80	3.51	4.39	5.51	6.89	4.67	5.92	6.00–5.25	3.50–2.50	....	2.61
Apr	1.32	1.54	2.23	3.68	4.44	5.55	6.97	4.43	5.98	5.25–5.00	2.50–2.25	....	2.28
May	1.71	1.82	2.69	3.88	4.60	5.57	6.93	4.34	6.01	5.00–5.00	2.25–2.25	....	1.98
June	1.89	2.15	3.08	4.10	4.69	5.68	7.07	4.48	6.13	5.00–5.00	2.25–2.25	....	2.00
July	1.72	1.99	2.87	4.01	4.57	5.67	7.16	4.88	6.29	5.00–5.00	2.25–2.25	....	2.01
Aug	1.79	1.96	2.70	3.89	4.50	5.64	7.15	4.90	6.33	5.00–5.00	2.25–2.25	....	2.00
Sept	1.46	1.78	2.32	3.69	4.27	5.65	7.31	5.03	6.09	5.00–5.00	2.25–2.25	....	1.81
Oct	.84	1.39	1.86	3.81	4.17	6.28	8.88	5.68	6.10	5.00–4.00	2.25–1.25	....	.97
Nov	.30	.86	1.51	3.53	4.00	6.15	9.22	5.28	....	4.00–4.00	1.25–1.25	....	.39

[3] Beginning with December 7, 2001, data for corporate Aaa series are industrial bonds only.

[4] Effective rate (in the primary market) on conventional mortgages, reflecting fees and charges as well as contract rate and assuming, on the average, repayment at end of 10 years. Rates beginning with January 1973 not strictly comparable with prior rates.

[5] For monthly data, high and low for the period. Prime rate for 1929–1933 and 1947–1948 are ranges of the rate in effect during the period.

[6] Primary credit replaced adjustment credit as the Federal Reserve's principal discount window lending program effective January 9, 2003.

[7] Since July 19, 1975, the daily effective rate is an average of the rates on a given day weighted by the volume of transactions at these rates. Prior to that date, the daily effective rate was the rate considered most representative of the day's transactions, usually the one at which most transactions occurred.

[8] From October 30, 1942 to April 24, 1946, a preferential rate of 0.50 percent was in effect for advances secured by Government securities maturing in one year or less.

Sources: Department of the Treasury, Board of Governors of the Federal Reserve System, Federal Housing Finance Board, Moody's Investors Service, and Standard & Poor's.

[Billions of dollars; quarterly data at seasonally adjusted annual rates]

Item	2000	2001	2002	2003	2004	2005	2006	2007
NONFINANCIAL SECTORS								
Domestic	864.8	1,152.7	1,414.5	1,676.3	1,999.4	2,319.4	2,428.4	2,515.5
By instrument	864.8	1,152.7	1,414.5	1,676.3	1,999.4	2,319.4	2,428.4	2,515.5
Commercial paper	48.1	−83.1	−57.9	−37.3	15.3	−7.7	22.4	11.3
Treasury securities	−294.9	−5.1	257.1	398.4	362.5	307.3	183.7	237.5
Agency- and GSE-backed securities [1]	−1.0	−.5	.5	−2.4	−.6	−.4	−.3	−.4
Municipal securities	23.6	122.8	159.4	137.6	130.5	195.0	177.3	215.4
Corporate bonds	164.0	343.4	133.4	152.2	75.5	56.7	215.6	311.2
Bank loans n.e.c.	95.1	−87.2	−106.6	−77.0	10.8	137.6	173.4	248.9
Other loans and advances	96.6	5.6	27.6	10.2	58.1	116.1	143.4	278.3
Mortgages	556.6	706.2	893.1	990.2	1,232.3	1,420.4	1,408.5	1,077.4
Home	427.2	551.8	758.6	800.9	1,031.0	1,105.5	1,079.5	707.6
Multifamily residential	26.9	40.3	37.1	71.2	48.3	72.5	54.6	98.4
Commercial	105.1	110.3	90.5	119.4	150.3	237.8	267.0	272.6
Farm	−2.5	3.8	6.9	−1.3	2.7	4.6	7.5	−1.3
Consumer credit	176.5	150.7	107.9	104.4	115.0	94.5	104.4	136.0
By sector	864.8	1,152.7	1,414.5	1,676.3	1,999.4	2,319.4	2,428.4	2,515.5
Household sector	583.5	672.2	832.8	983.2	1,066.8	1,180.5	1,204.6	880.6
Nonfinancial business	560.3	380.6	180.1	177.1	455.4	660.3	889.4	1,211.6
Corporate	361.9	212.7	23.1	87.1	204.8	314.5	521.1	787.0
Nonfarm noncorporate	196.4	161.5	149.8	91.6	244.5	333.0	349.9	415.9
Farm	2.0	6.4	7.1	−1.6	6.0	12.8	18.4	8.7
State and local governments	16.9	105.5	144.1	120.1	115.4	171.7	151.1	186.1
Federal Government	−295.9	−5.6	257.6	396.0	361.9	306.9	183.4	237.1
Foreign borrowing in the United States	63.0	−11.2	93.4	42.4	154.7	112.6	331.3	124.3
Commercial paper	31.7	18.3	58.8	18.3	68.7	38.2	97.1	−67.4
Bonds	21.2	−18.5	31.6	28.7	85.8	64.5	227.8	170.7
Bank loans n.e.c.	11.4	−7.3	5.3	−2.5	3.8	14.5	13.8	24.1
Other loans and advances	−1.3	−3.8	−2.3	−2.1	−3.6	−4.6	−7.4	−3.2
Nonfinancial domestic and foreign borrowing	927.8	1,141.5	1,507.9	1,718.7	2,154.2	2,432.0	2,759.8	2,639.7
FINANCIAL SECTORS								
By instrument	794.1	872.0	879.2	1,063.0	987.0	1,102.3	1,304.7	1,753.4
Open market paper	131.7	−126.9	−99.9	−62.9	22.2	214.6	197.6	−113.3
GSE issues [1]	235.2	304.1	219.8	250.9	75.0	−84.0	35.6	282.4
Agency- and GSE-backed mortgage pool securities [1]	199.7	338.5	326.8	330.6	47.9	167.3	295.4	626.3
Corporate bonds	173.0	310.1	394.2	485.6	684.4	730.7	812.7	663.3
Bank loans n.e.c.	6.9	18.7	21.1	21.4	58.1	17.0	−64.1	57.3
Other loans and advances	42.5	25.5	6.8	31.2	74.1	44.4	21.2	233.7
Mortgages	4.9	2.2	11.0	8.2	25.9	13.9	7.0	5.7
By sector	794.1	872.0	879.2	1,063.0	987.0	1,102.3	1,304.7	1,753.4
Commercial banking	60.0	52.9	49.7	48.5	78.4	85.1	177.4	263.2
U.S.-chartered commercial banks	36.8	30.2	29.9	13.2	18.7	36.9	107.5	131.8
Foreign banking offices in the United States	0.0	−.9	−.4	−.1	.1	.0	−.3	.0
Bank holding companies	23.2	23.6	20.3	35.4	59.5	48.2	70.2	131.3
Savings institutions	27.3	−2.0	−23.4	34.5	89.0	23.8	−111.9	105.2
Credit unions	0.0	1.5	2.0	2.2	2.3	3.3	4.2	13.4
Life insurance companies	−0.7	.6	2.0	2.9	3.0	.4	2.7	14.5
Government-sponsored enterprises	235.2	304.1	219.8	250.9	75.0	−84.0	35.6	282.4
Agency- and GSE-backed mortgage pools [1]	199.7	338.5	326.8	330.6	47.9	167.3	295.4	626.3
Asset-backed securities issuers	169.5	264.6	221.7	248.4	446.2	708.9	807.9	332.1
Finance companies	86.3	10.9	66.2	111.1	134.3	33.5	34.8	24.9
REITs [2]	2.6	3.2	27.3	31.5	98.3	59.8	22.9	−3.5
Brokers and dealers	15.6	1.4	−1.7	6.4	15.2	.1	6.4	−4.0
Funding corporations	−1.6	−103.6	−10.7	−2.0	−2.2	105.6	29.9	100.7
ALL SECTORS, BY INSTRUMENT								
Total	1,721.6	2,013.8	2,387.6	2,783.7	3,141.8	3,535.8	4,065.2	4,394.9
Open market paper	211.6	−191.6	−99.1	−82.0	106.2	245.1	317.1	−169.4
Treasury securities	−294.9	−5.1	257.1	398.4	362.5	307.3	183.7	237.5
Agency- and GSE-backed securities [1]	433.9	642.1	547.2	579.1	122.3	82.8	330.6	908.3
Municipal securities	23.6	122.8	159.4	137.6	130.5	195.0	177.3	215.4
Corporate and foreign bonds	358.2	635.0	559.2	665.5	845.7	851.9	1,256.1	1,145.2
Bank loans n.e.c.	113.3	−75.8	−80.2	−58.1	72.7	169.1	123.1	330.2
Other loans and advances	137.8	27.3	32.0	39.3	128.6	155.8	157.2	508.9
Mortgages	561.5	708.4	904.1	998.4	1,258.1	1,434.3	1,415.6	1,083.0
Consumer credit	176.5	150.7	107.9	104.4	115.0	94.5	104.4	136.0

[1] Government-sponsored enterprises (GSE).
[2] Real estate investment trusts (REITs).

See next page for continuation of table.

[Billions of dollars; quarterly data at seasonally adjusted annual rates]

Item	2007				2008	
	I	II	III	IV	I	II
NFINANCIAL SECTORS						
nestic	2,373.7	2,396.7	2,780.0	2,511.3	1,726.1	1,126.7
By instrument	2,373.7	2,396.7	2,780.0	2,511.3	1,726.1	1,126.7
Commercial paper	18.9	40.9	−30.6	16.0	54.6	−65.6
Treasury securities	269.1	14.6	398.6	267.5	411.4	310.1
Agency- and GSE-backed securities [1]	−1.3	−.1	−.8	.7	1.3	.3
Municipal securities	247.0	238.0	181.5	194.9	92.3	45.3
Corporate bonds	286.3	381.5	220.2	356.8	167.5	337.6
Bank loans n.e.c.	70.5	117.1	448.4	359.5	261.8	106.3
Other loans and advances	226.1	257.3	391.3	238.7	84.5	36.5
Mortgages	1,135.4	1,212.7	986.0	975.4	520.3	242.6
Home	838.1	808.3	536.0	648.1	270.2	29.5
Multifamily residential	65.0	95.2	108.1	125.2	70.3	65.2
Commercial	233.5	310.4	343.2	203.3	176.5	144.6
Farm	−1.2	−1.3	−1.3	−1.3	3.3	3.3
Consumer credit	121.8	134.8	185.4	102.0	132.4	113.6
By sector	2,373.7	2,396.7	2,780.0	2,511.3	1,726.1	1,126.7
Household sector	910.8	950.0	828.2	833.6	454.3	197.3
Nonfinancial business	975.7	1,226.1	1,401.5	1,243.2	784.7	608.0
Corporate	660.2	846.5	866.6	774.7	423.2	390.3
Nonfarm noncorporate	300.6	377.9	530.9	454.4	331.9	191.8
Farm	14.9	1.7	4.0	14.1	29.6	25.9
State and local governments	219.5	206.2	152.5	166.4	74.4	11.0
Federal Government	267.8	14.5	397.8	268.2	412.7	310.4
eign borrowing in the United States	184.4	292.9	3.3	16.4	280.9	72.1
Commercial paper	−19.8	22.4	−193.8	−78.3	214.6	40.2
Bonds	223.2	231.7	173.8	54.1	32.9	44.5
Bank loans n.e.c.	−16.0	40.7	26.3	45.3	35.4	−9.0
Other loans and advances	−3.0	−1.9	−3.0	−4.7	−1.9	−3.5
nfinancial domestic and foreign borrowing	2,558.1	2,689.6	2,783.4	2,527.7	2,006.9	1,198.8
NANCIAL SECTORS						
instrument	1,483.7	1,443.1	2,512.9	1,573.8	868.6	1,075.8
Open market paper	189.5	293.9	−607.7	−329.1	−234.2	−230.9
GSE issues [1]	66.7	161.4	556.6	344.8	119.9	655.3
Agency- and GSE-backed mortgage pool securities [1]	455.0	519.0	644.0	887.1	533.6	672.2
Corporate bonds	748.3	422.2	1,075.5	407.2	37.1	−33.5
Bank loans n.e.c.	44.9	51.1	95.9	37.2	169.6	100.3
Other loans and advances	−4.9	−11.5	738.7	212.5	223.1	−79.0
Mortgages	−15.2	9.0	12.9	16.1	19.9	−7.4
sector	1,483.7	1,443.1	2,512.9	1,573.8	868.6	1,075.8
Commercial banking	91.4	162.2	481.5	317.7	229.1	299.2
U.S.-chartered commercial banks	9.3	37.5	340.6	139.9	92.0	9.5
Foreign banking offices in the United States	−0.3	.1	−.6	.9	−.3	−.4
Bank holding companies	82.4	124.7	141.5	176.9	137.4	290.1
Savings institutions	4.5	−51.9	370.7	97.5	133.0	−120.8
Credit unions	−10.5	10.6	37.9	15.7	−15.2	27.6
Life insurance companies	4.9	12.6	26.9	13.7	9.6	9.2
Government-sponsored enterprises	66.7	161.4	556.6	344.8	119.9	655.3
Agency- and GSE-backed mortgage pools [1]	455.0	519.0	644.0	887.1	533.6	672.2
Asset-backed securities issuers	677.9	592.8	204.2	−146.5	−255.8	−342.3
Finance companies	1.9	12.6	121.1	−35.9	73.9	−39.3
REITs [2]	34.3	−23.0	−17.1	−8.3	−43.0	−21.2
Brokers and dealers	59.5	39.9	−29.4	−85.9	221.3	−21.5
Funding corporations	98.8	8.8	119.3	175.8	−137.5	−41.4
LL SECTORS, BY INSTRUMENT						
tal	4,042.4	4,134.7	5,299.2	4,103.5	2,876.0	2,275.8
Open market paper	188.7	357.3	−832.1	−391.5	34.9	−256.3
Treasury securities	269.1	14.6	398.6	267.5	411.4	310.1
Agency- and GSE-backed securities [1]	520.4	680.3	1,199.8	1,232.7	654.8	1,327.8
Municipal securities	247.0	238.0	181.5	194.9	92.3	45.3
Corporate and foreign bonds	1,257.7	1,035.4	1,469.5	818.0	237.5	348.5
Bank loans n.e.c.	99.4	208.8	570.6	442.0	466.8	197.6
Other loans and advances	218.1	243.9	1,127.0	446.5	305.7	−46.0
Mortgages	1,120.2	1,221.7	998.9	991.5	540.3	235.2
Consumer credit	121.8	134.8	185.4	102.0	132.4	113.6

Source: Board of Governors of the Federal Reserve System.

TABLE B–75.—*Mortgage debt outstanding by type of property and of financing, 1949–2008*

[Billions of dollars]

End of year or quarter	All proper-ties	Farm proper-ties	Nonfarm properties — Total	1- to 4-family houses	Multi-family proper-ties	Com-mercial proper-ties	Government underwritten — Total [1]	1- to 4-family houses — Total	FHA insured	VA guar-anteed	Conventional [2] — Total	1- to 4-family houses
1949	62.3	5.6	56.7	37.3	8.6	10.8	17.1	15.0	6.9	8.1	39.6	22.
1950	72.7	6.0	66.6	45.1	10.1	11.5	22.1	18.8	8.5	10.3	44.6	26.
1951	82.1	6.6	75.6	51.6	11.5	12.5	26.6	22.9	9.7	13.2	49.0	28.
1952	91.3	7.2	84.1	58.4	12.3	13.4	29.3	25.4	10.8	14.6	54.8	33.
1953	101.1	7.7	93.4	65.9	12.9	14.5	32.1	28.1	12.0	16.1	61.3	37.
1954	113.6	8.1	105.4	75.7	13.5	16.3	36.2	32.1	12.8	19.3	69.3	43.
1955	129.9	9.0	120.9	88.2	14.3	18.3	42.9	38.9	14.3	24.6	78.0	49.
1956	144.5	9.8	134.6	99.0	14.9	20.7	47.8	43.9	15.5	28.4	86.8	55.
1957	156.5	10.4	146.1	107.6	15.3	23.2	51.6	47.2	16.5	30.7	94.6	60.
1958	171.8	11.1	160.7	117.7	16.8	26.1	55.2	50.1	19.7	30.4	105.5	67.
1959	190.8	12.1	178.7	130.8	18.7	29.2	59.3	53.8	23.8	30.0	119.4	77.
1960	207.4	12.8	194.6	141.8	20.3	32.4	62.3	56.4	26.7	29.7	132.2	85.
1961	228.0	13.9	214.1	154.6	23.0	36.5	65.6	59.1	29.5	29.6	148.5	95.
1962	251.4	15.2	236.2	169.3	25.8	41.1	69.4	62.2	32.3	29.9	166.9	107.
1963	278.5	16.8	261.6	186.4	29.0	46.2	73.4	65.9	35.0	30.9	188.2	120.
1964	305.9	18.9	287.0	203.4	33.6	50.0	77.2	69.2	38.3	30.9	209.8	134.
1965	333.3	21.2	312.1	220.5	37.2	54.5	81.2	73.1	42.0	31.1	231.0	147.
1966	356.5	23.1	333.4	232.9	40.3	60.1	84.1	76.1	44.8	31.3	249.3	156.
1967	381.0	25.0	356.0	247.3	43.9	64.7	88.2	79.9	47.4	32.5	267.8	167.
1968	410.8	27.3	383.5	264.8	47.3	71.4	93.4	84.4	50.6	33.8	290.1	180.
1969	441.4	29.2	412.2	283.2	52.2	76.9	100.2	90.2	54.5	35.7	312.0	193.
1970	473.7	30.5	443.2	297.2	60.1	85.8	109.2	97.3	59.9	37.3	333.9	200.
1971	524.2	32.4	491.8	325.6	70.1	96.2	120.7	105.2	65.7	39.5	371.1	220.
1972	597.2	35.4	561.9	366.0	82.8	113.1	131.1	113.0	68.2	44.7	430.7	253.
1973	672.4	39.8	632.6	407.1	93.2	132.3	135.0	116.2	66.2	50.0	497.5	290.
1974	732.5	44.9	687.5	440.0	100.0	147.5	140.2	121.3	65.1	56.2	547.3	318.
1975	791.9	49.9	742.0	481.2	100.7	160.1	147.0	127.7	66.1	61.6	595.0	353.
1976	878.6	55.4	823.2	543.9	105.9	173.4	154.0	133.5	66.5	67.0	669.1	410.
1977	1,010.2	63.8	946.4	639.7	114.3	192.3	161.7	141.6	68.0	73.6	784.6	498.
1978	1,163.0	72.8	1,090.2	751.2	125.2	213.9	176.4	153.4	71.4	82.0	913.9	597.
1979	1,328.3	86.8	1,241.6	867.7	135.0	238.8	199.0	172.9	81.0	92.0	1,042.6	694.
1980	1,463.0	97.5	1,365.5	965.1	141.1	259.3	225.1	195.2	93.6	101.6	1,140.4	769.
1981	1,587.8	107.2	1,480.6	1,042.8	139.2	298.6	238.9	207.6	101.3	106.2	1,241.7	835.
1982	1,673.4	111.3	1,562.1	1,088.5	141.1	332.6	248.9	217.9	108.0	109.9	1,313.2	870.
1983	1,867.3	113.7	1,753.5	1,210.6	154.3	388.6	279.8	248.8	127.4	121.4	1,473.7	961.
1984	2,113.1	112.4	2,000.7	1,351.4	177.4	471.9	294.8	265.9	136.7	129.1	1,705.8	1,085.
1985	2,372.7	95.3	2,277.3	1,529.9	205.9	541.6	328.3	288.8	153.0	135.8	1,949.0	1,241.
1986	2,659.8	85.3	2,574.4	1,732.6	239.3	602.5	370.5	328.6	185.5	143.1	2,203.9	1,404.
1987	2,996.7	77.1	2,919.6	1,959.5	262.1	698.0	431.4	387.9	235.5	152.4	2,488.2	1,571.
1988	3,315.5	72.2	3,243.3	2,194.7	279.0	769.6	459.7	414.2	258.8	155.4	2,783.6	1,780.
1989	3,604.1	70.1	3,534.0	2,444.6	289.9	799.5	486.8	440.1	282.8	157.3	3,047.1	2,004.
1990	3,807.0	69.6	3,737.4	2,628.5	288.3	820.7	517.9	470.9	310.9	160.0	3,219.5	2,157.
1991	3,947.2	68.9	3,878.3	2,786.3	284.9	807.1	537.2	493.3	330.6	162.7	3,341.1	2,293.
1992	4,059.3	69.2	3,990.1	2,954.7	272.0	763.4	533.3	489.8	326.0	163.8	3,456.8	2,464.
1993	4,192.3	69.5	4,122.8	3,114.0	269.1	739.7	513.4	469.5	303.2	166.2	3,609.4	2,644.
1994	4,360.0	71.4	4,288.6	3,291.8	269.6	727.2	559.3	514.2	336.8	177.3	3,729.3	2,777.
1995	4,546.7	73.2	4,473.6	3,459.4	275.5	738.7	584.5	537.1	352.3	184.7	3,889.3	2,922.
1996	4,816.4	75.9	4,740.5	3,683.0	287.8	769.7	620.3	571.2	379.2	192.0	4,120.1	3,111.
1997	5,130.2	80.1	5,050.1	3,917.7	299.8	832.6	656.7	605.7	405.7	200.0	4,393.4	3,312.
1998	5,616.7	84.7	5,532.0	4,274.3	333.9	923.8	674.1	623.8	417.9	205.9	4,858.0	3,650.
1999	6,227.2	89.6	6,137.7	4,699.6	375.0	1,063.1	731.5	678.8	462.3	216.5	5,406.2	4,020.
2000	6,789.0	87.3	6,701.7	5,126.5	404.6	1,170.6	773.1	720.0	499.9	220.1	5,928.6	4,406.
2001	7,497.3	91.4	7,405.9	5,678.0	446.5	1,281.4	772.7	718.5	497.4	221.2	6,633.2	4,959.
2002	8,401.4	97.5	8,303.9	6,437.4	485.2	1,381.3	759.3	704.0	486.2	217.7	7,544.6	5,733.
2003	9,399.8	94.1	9,305.6	7,232.5	564.9	1,508.3	709.2	653.3	438.7	214.6	8,596.5	6,579.
2004	10,672.7	96.9	10,575.9	8,278.3	617.9	1,679.7	661.5	605.4	398.1	207.3	9,914.3	7,672.
2005	12,107.0	101.5	12,005.5	9,383.7	688.5	1,933.3	606.6	550.4	348.4	202.0	11,398.9	8,833.
2006	13,522.6	109.0	13,413.6	10,463.2	743.8	2,206.5	600.2	543.5	336.9	206.6	12,813.4	9,919.
2007	14,605.7	107.8	14,497.9	11,170.9	840.1	2,486.9	609.2	552.6	342.6	210.0	13,888.8	10,618.
2007: I	13,795.7	108.7	13,687.0	10,670.3	761.2	2,255.5	597.9	541.0	335.6	205.4	13,089.1	10,129.
II	14,110.9	108.4	14,002.5	10,881.3	783.5	2,337.7	598.3	541.7	335.6	206.1	13,404.2	10,339.
III	14,374.8	108.1	14,266.7	11,034.2	808.6	2,423.9	610.6	551.0	342.6	208.4	13,656.1	10,483.
IV	14,605.7	107.8	14,497.9	11,170.9	840.1	2,486.9	609.2	552.6	342.6	210.0	13,888.8	10,618.
2008: I	14,736.9	108.6	14,628.3	11,239.1	858.9	2,530.4	640.7	583.8	372.3	211.5	13,987.6	10,655.
II p	14,804.1	109.4	14,694.6	11,254.1	875.1	2,565.4	683.9	627.2	412.2	215.0	14,010.8	10,626.

[1] Includes Federal Housing Administration (FHA)–insured multi-family properties, not shown separately.
[2] Derived figures. Total includes multi-family and commercial properties with conventional mortgages, not shown separately.

Source: Board of Governors of the Federal Reserve System, based on data from various Government and private organizations.

TABLE B–76.—*Mortgage debt outstanding by holder, 1949–2008*

[Billions of dollars]

End of year or quarter	Total	Major financial institutions				Other holders	
		Total	Savings institutions [1]	Commercial banks [2]	Life insurance companies	Federal and related agencies [3]	Individuals and others [4]
9	62.3	42.9	18.3	11.6	12.9	2.0	17.5
0	72.7	51.7	21.9	13.7	16.1	2.6	18.4
1	82.1	59.5	25.5	14.7	19.3	3.3	19.3
2	91.3	66.9	29.8	15.9	21.3	3.9	20.4
3	101.1	75.0	34.8	16.9	23.3	4.4	21.7
4	113.6	85.7	41.1	18.6	26.0	4.7	23.2
5	129.9	99.3	48.9	21.0	29.4	5.3	25.3
6	144.5	111.2	55.5	22.7	33.0	6.2	27.1
7	156.5	119.7	61.2	23.3	35.2	7.7	29.1
8	171.8	131.5	68.9	25.5	37.1	8.0	32.3
9	190.8	145.5	78.1	28.1	39.2	10.2	35.1
0	207.4	157.5	86.9	28.8	41.8	11.5	38.4
1	228.0	172.6	98.0	30.4	44.2	12.2	43.1
2	251.4	192.5	111.1	34.5	46.9	12.6	46.3
3	278.5	217.1	127.2	39.4	50.5	11.8	49.5
4	305.9	241.0	141.9	44.0	55.2	12.2	52.7
5	333.3	264.6	154.9	49.7	60.0	13.5	55.2
6	356.5	280.7	161.8	54.4	64.6	17.5	58.2
7	381.0	298.6	172.3	58.9	67.4	20.9	61.4
8	410.8	319.7	184.3	65.5	70.0	25.1	66.1
9	441.4	338.9	196.4	70.5	72.0	31.1	71.4
0	473.7	355.9	208.3	73.3	74.4	38.3	79.4
1	524.2	394.2	236.2	82.5	75.5	46.3	83.6
2	597.2	449.9	273.6	99.3	76.9	54.5	92.8
3	672.4	505.3	305.0	119.1	81.3	64.7	102.4
4	732.5	542.6	324.2	132.1	86.2	82.2	107.7
5	791.9	581.2	355.8	136.2	89.2	101.1	109.6
6	878.6	647.5	404.6	151.3	91.6	116.7	114.4
7	1,010.2	745.2	469.4	179.0	96.8	140.5	124.5
8	1,163.0	848.2	528.0	214.0	106.2	170.6	144.3
9	1,328.3	938.2	574.6	245.2	118.4	216.0	174.2
0	1,463.0	996.8	603.1	262.7	131.1	256.8	209.4
1	1,587.8	1,040.5	618.5	284.2	137.7	289.4	257.9
2	1,673.4	1,021.3	578.1	301.3	142.0	355.4	296.7
3	1,867.3	1,108.1	626.6	330.5	151.0	433.3	325.8
4	2,113.1	1,247.8	709.7	381.4	156.7	490.6	374.7
5	2,372.7	1,363.5	760.5	431.2	171.8	580.9	428.2
6	2,659.8	1,476.5	778.0	504.7	193.8	733.7	449.6
7	2,996.7	1,667.6	860.5	594.8	212.4	857.9	471.2
8	3,315.5	1,834.3	924.5	676.9	232.9	937.8	543.5
9	3,604.1	1,935.2	910.3	770.7	254.2	1,067.3	601.6
0	3,807.0	1,918.8	801.6	849.3	267.9	1,258.9	629.3
1	3,947.2	1,846.2	705.4	881.3	259.5	1,422.5	678.6
2	4,059.3	1,770.4	627.9	900.5	242.0	1,558.1	730.7
3	4,192.3	1,770.1	598.4	947.8	223.9	1,682.8	739.3
4	4,360.0	1,824.7	596.2	1,012.7	215.8	1,788.0	747.3
5	4,546.7	1,900.1	596.8	1,090.2	213.1	1,878.7	768.0
6	4,816.4	1,981.9	628.3	1,145.4	208.2	2,006.1	828.4
7	5,130.2	2,084.0	631.8	1,245.3	206.8	2,111.4	934.7
8	5,616.7	2,194.6	644.0	1,337.0	213.6	2,310.9	1,111.2
9	6,227.2	2,394.3	668.1	1,495.4	230.8	2,613.3	1,219.7
00	6,789.0	2,619.0	723.0	1,660.1	235.9	2,834.4	1,335.6
01	7,497.3	2,790.9	758.0	1,789.8	243.0	3,205.0	1,501.4
02	8,401.4	3,089.3	781.0	2,058.3	250.0	3,592.2	1,719.9
03	9,399.8	3,387.3	870.6	2,255.8	260.9	4,022.1	1,990.4
04	10,672.7	3,926.3	1,057.4	2,595.6	273.3	4,079.1	2,667.3
05	12,107.0	4,396.2	1,152.7	2,958.0	285.5	4,208.5	3,502.3
06	13,522.6	4,780.8	1,074.0	3,403.1	303.8	4,525.9	4,215.9
07	14,605.7	5,067.2	1,095.3	3,645.7	326.2	5,190.0	4,348.5
07: I	13,795.7	4,810.1	1,117.3	3,386.4	306.4	4,649.6	4,336.0
II	14,110.9	4,897.3	1,112.8	3,472.1	312.3	4,778.0	4,435.6
III	14,374.8	4,989.3	1,146.9	3,525.1	317.3	4,955.9	4,429.7
IV	14,605.7	5,067.2	1,095.3	3,645.7	326.2	5,190.0	4,348.5
08: I	14,736.9	5,129.1	1,111.9	3,686.0	331.3	5,344.5	4,263.3
IIᵖ	14,804.1	5,113.6	1,115.6	3,662.2	335.8	5,517.8	4,172.7

[1] Includes savings banks and savings and loan associations. Data reported by Federal Savings and Loan Insurance Corporation–insured institutions include loans in process for 1987 and exclude loans in process beginning with 1988.

[2] Includes loans held by nondeposit trust companies but not loans held by bank trust departments.

[3] Includes Government National Mortgage Association (GNMA or Ginnie Mae), Federal Housing Administration, Veterans Administration, Farmers Home Administration (FmHA), Federal Deposit Insurance Corporation, Resolution Trust Corporation (through 1995), and in earlier years Reconstruction Finance Corporation, Homeowners Loan Corporation, Federal Farm Mortgage Corporation, and Public Housing Administration. Also includes U.S.-sponsored agencies such as Federal National Mortgage Association (FNMA or Fannie Mae), Federal Land Banks, Federal Home Loan Mortgage Corporation (FHLMC or Freddie Mac), Federal Agricultural Mortgage Corporation (Farmer Mac, beginning 1994), Federal Home Loan Banks (beginning 1997), and mortgage pass-through securities issued or guaranteed by GNMA, FHLMC, FNMA, FmHA, or Farmer Mac. Other U.S. agencies (amounts small or current separate data not readily available) included with "individuals and others."

[4] Includes private mortgage pools.

Source: Board of Governors of the Federal Reserve System, based on data from various Government and private organizations.

TABLE B–77.—*Consumer credit outstanding, 1959–2008*

[Amount outstanding (end of month); millions of dollars, seasonally adjusted]

Year and month	Total consumer credit [1]	Revolving	Nonrevolving [2]
December:			
1959	56,010.68		56,010
1960	60,025.31		60,025
1961	62,248.53		62,248
1962	68,126.72		68,126
1963	76,581.45		76,581
1964	85,959.57		85,959
1965	95,954.72		95,954
1966	101,788.22		101,788
1967	106,842.64		106,842
1968	117,399.09	2,041.54	115,357
1969	127,156.18	3,604.84	123,551
1970	131,551.55	4,961.46	126,590
1971	146,930.18	8,245.33	138,684
1972	166,189.10	9,379.24	156,809
1973	190,086.31	11,342.22	178,744
1974	198,917.84	13,241.26	185,676
1975	204,002.00	14,495.27	189,506
1976	225,721.59	16,489.05	209,232
1977	260,562.70	37,414.82	223,147
1978	306,100.39	45,690.95	260,409
1979	348,589.11	53,596.43	294,992
1980	351,920.05	54,970.05	296,950
1981	371,301.44	60,928.00	310,373
1982	389,848.74	66,348.30	323,500
1983	437,068.86	79,027.25	358,041
1984	517,278.98	100,385.63	416,893
1985	599,711.23	124,465.80	475,245
1986	654,750.24	141,068.15	513,682
1987	686,318.77	160,853.91	525,464
1988 [3]	731,917.76	184,593.12	547,324
1989	794,612.18	211,229.83	583,382
1990	808,230.57	238,642.62	569,587
1991	798,028.97	263,768.55	534,260
1992	806,118.69	278,449.67	527,669
1993	865,650.58	309,908.02	555,742
1994	997,301.74	365,569.56	631,732
1995	1,140,744.36	443,920.09	696,824
1996	1,253,437.09	507,516.57	745,920
1997	1,324,757.33	540,005.56	784,751
1998	1,420,996.44	581,414.78	839,581
1999	1,532,390.04	610,670.39	921,719
2000	1,717,652.40	683,679.12	1,033,973
2001	1,867,298.01	716,592.27	1,150,705
2002	1,974,349.73	748,837.90	1,225,511
2003	2,078,257.58	770,364.41	1,307,893
2004	2,191,612.48	799,768.16	1,391,844
2005	2,285,159.79	824,468.62	1,460,691
2006	2,387,690.52	874,620.51	1,513,070
2007	2,519,020.02	939,515.16	1,579,504
2007: Jan	2,392,788.36	876,630.35	1,516,158
Feb	2,403,133.86	881,255.52	1,521,878
Mar	2,417,041.87	888,700.09	1,528,341
Apr	2,421,816.55	889,789.77	1,532,026
May	2,438,951.37	898,790.45	1,540,160
June	2,449,501.41	903,255.47	1,546,245
July	2,462,055.98	910,097.64	1,551,958
Aug	2,480,943.75	917,150.00	1,563,793
Sept	2,493,520.04	921,882.99	1,571,637
Oct	2,501,056.39	929,246.01	1,571,810
Nov	2,513,773.66	936,078.58	1,577,695
Dec	2,519,020.02	939,515.16	1,579,504
2008: Jan	2,526,023.35	945,772.76	1,580,250
Feb	2,536,911.50	951,402.91	1,585,508
Mar	2,549,099.07	957,385.76	1,591,713
Apr	2,558,845.12	957,322.87	1,601,522
May	2,565,446.04	962,935.39	1,602,510
June	2,574,033.06	965,672.51	1,608,360
July	2,581,359.72	971,775.88	1,609,583
Aug	2,574,925.34	973,773.28	1,601,152
Sept	2,581,655.83	976,254.67	1,605,401
Oct [p]	2,578,120.53	976,073.12	1,602,047

[1] Covers most short- and intermediate-term credit extended to individuals. Credit secured by real estate is excluded.
[2] Includes automobile loans and all other loans not included in revolving credit, such as loans for mobile homes, education, boats, trailers, or vacations. These loans may be secured or unsecured. Beginning with 1977, includes student loans extended by the Federal Government and by SLM Holding Corporation.
[3] Data newly available in January 1989 result in breaks in these series between December 1988 and subsequent months.

Source: Board of Governors of the Federal Reserve System.

TABLE B–78.—*Federal receipts, outlays, surplus or deficit, and debt, fiscal years, 1940–2009*

[Billions of dollars; fiscal years]

Fiscal year or period	Total			On-budget			Off-budget			Federal debt (end of period)		Addendum: Gross domestic product
	Receipts	Outlays	Surplus or deficit (−)	Receipts	Outlays	Surplus or deficit (−)	Receipts	Outlays	Surplus or deficit (−)	Gross Federal	Held by the public	
1940	6.5	9.5	−2.9	6.0	9.5	−3.5	0.6	−0.0	0.6	50.7	42.8	96.8
1941	8.7	13.7	−4.9	8.0	13.6	−5.6	.7	.0	.7	57.5	48.2	114.1
1942	14.6	35.1	−20.5	13.7	35.1	−21.3	.9	.1	.8	79.2	67.8	144.3
1943	24.0	78.6	−54.6	22.9	78.5	−55.6	1.1	.1	1.0	142.6	127.8	180.3
1944	43.7	91.3	−47.6	42.5	91.2	−48.7	1.3	.1	1.2	204.1	184.8	209.2
1945	45.2	92.7	−47.6	43.8	92.6	−48.7	1.3	.1	1.2	260.1	235.2	221.4
1946	39.3	55.2	−15.9	38.1	55.0	−17.0	1.2	.2	1.0	271.0	241.9	222.7
1947	38.5	34.5	4.0	37.1	34.2	2.9	1.5	.3	1.2	257.1	224.3	233.2
1948	41.6	29.8	11.8	39.9	29.4	10.5	1.6	.4	1.2	252.0	216.3	256.0
1949	39.4	38.8	.6	37.7	38.4	−.7	1.7	.4	1.3	252.6	214.3	271.1
1950	39.4	42.6	−3.1	37.3	42.0	−4.7	2.1	.5	1.6	256.9	219.0	273.0
1951	51.6	45.5	6.1	48.5	44.2	4.3	3.1	1.3	1.8	255.3	214.3	320.6
1952	66.2	67.7	−1.5	62.6	66.0	−3.4	3.6	1.7	1.9	259.1	214.8	348.6
1953	69.6	76.1	−6.5	65.5	73.8	−8.3	4.1	2.3	1.8	266.0	218.4	372.9
1954	69.7	70.9	−1.2	65.1	67.9	−2.8	4.6	2.9	1.7	270.8	224.5	377.3
1955	65.5	68.4	−3.0	60.4	64.5	−4.1	5.1	4.0	1.1	274.4	226.6	394.6
1956	74.6	70.6	3.9	68.2	65.7	2.5	6.4	5.0	1.5	272.7	222.2	427.2
1957	80.0	76.6	3.4	73.2	70.6	2.6	6.8	6.0	.8	272.3	219.3	450.3
1958	79.6	82.4	−2.8	71.6	74.9	−3.3	8.0	7.5	.5	279.7	226.3	460.5
1959	79.2	92.1	−12.8	71.0	83.1	−12.1	8.3	9.0	−.7	287.5	234.7	491.5
1960	92.5	92.2	.3	81.9	81.3	.5	10.6	10.9	−.2	290.5	236.8	517.9
1961	94.4	97.7	−3.3	82.3	86.0	−3.8	12.1	11.7	.4	292.6	238.4	530.8
1962	99.7	106.8	−7.1	87.4	93.3	−5.9	12.3	13.5	−1.3	302.9	248.0	567.6
1963	106.6	111.3	−4.8	92.4	96.4	−4.0	14.2	15.0	−.8	310.3	254.0	598.7
1964	112.6	118.5	−5.9	96.2	102.8	−6.5	16.4	15.7	.6	316.1	256.8	640.4
1965	116.8	118.2	−1.4	100.1	101.7	−1.6	16.7	16.5	.2	322.3	260.8	687.1
1966	130.8	134.5	−3.7	111.7	114.8	−3.1	19.1	19.7	−.6	328.5	263.7	752.9
1967	148.8	157.5	−8.6	124.4	137.0	−12.6	24.4	20.4	4.0	340.4	266.6	811.8
1968	153.0	178.1	−25.2	128.1	155.8	−27.7	24.9	22.3	2.6	368.7	289.5	866.6
1969	186.9	183.6	3.2	157.9	158.4	−.5	29.0	25.2	3.7	365.8	278.1	948.6
1970	192.8	195.6	−2.8	159.3	168.0	−8.7	33.5	27.6	5.9	380.9	283.2	1,012.2
1971	187.1	210.2	−23.0	151.3	177.3	−26.1	35.8	32.8	3.0	408.2	303.0	1,079.9
1972	207.3	230.7	−23.4	167.4	193.5	−26.1	39.9	37.2	2.7	435.9	322.4	1,178.3
1973	230.8	245.7	−14.9	184.7	200.0	−15.2	46.1	45.7	.3	466.3	340.9	1,307.6
1974	263.2	269.4	−6.1	209.3	216.5	−7.2	53.9	52.9	1.1	483.9	343.7	1,439.3
1975	279.1	332.3	−53.2	216.6	270.8	−54.1	62.5	61.6	.9	541.9	394.7	1,560.7
1976	298.1	371.8	−73.7	231.7	301.1	−69.4	66.4	70.7	−4.3	629.0	477.4	1,736.5
Transition quarter ..	81.2	96.0	−14.7	63.2	77.3	−14.1	18.0	18.7	−.7	643.6	495.5	456.7
1977	355.6	409.2	−53.7	278.7	328.7	−49.9	76.8	80.5	−3.7	706.4	549.1	1,974.3
1978	399.6	458.7	−59.2	314.2	369.6	−55.4	85.4	89.2	−3.8	776.6	607.1	2,217.0
1979	463.3	504.0	−40.7	365.3	404.9	−39.6	98.0	99.1	−1.1	829.5	640.3	2,500.7
1980	517.1	590.9	−73.8	403.9	477.0	−73.1	113.2	113.9	−.7	909.0	711.9	2,726.7
1981	599.3	678.2	−79.0	469.1	543.0	−73.9	130.2	135.3	−5.1	994.8	789.4	3,054.7
1982	617.8	745.7	−128.0	474.3	594.9	−120.6	143.5	150.9	−7.4	1,137.3	924.6	3,227.6
1983	600.6	808.4	−207.8	453.2	660.9	−207.7	147.3	147.4	−.1	1,371.7	1,137.3	3,440.7
1984	666.5	851.9	−185.4	500.4	685.7	−185.3	166.1	166.2	−.1	1,564.6	1,307.0	3,840.2
1985	734.1	946.4	−212.3	547.9	769.4	−221.5	186.2	176.9	9.2	1,817.4	1,507.3	4,141.5
1986	769.2	990.4	−221.2	569.0	806.9	−237.9	200.2	183.5	16.7	2,120.5	1,740.6	4,412.4
1987	854.4	1,004.1	−149.7	641.0	809.3	−168.4	213.4	194.8	18.6	2,346.0	1,889.8	4,647.1
1988	909.3	1,064.5	−155.2	667.8	860.1	−192.3	241.5	204.4	37.1	2,601.1	2,051.6	5,008.6
1989	991.2	1,143.8	−152.6	727.5	932.9	−205.4	263.7	210.9	52.8	2,867.8	2,190.7	5,400.5
1990	1,032.1	1,253.1	−221.0	750.4	1,028.1	−277.6	281.7	225.1	56.6	3,206.3	2,411.6	5,735.4
1991	1,055.1	1,324.3	−269.2	761.2	1,082.6	−321.4	293.9	241.7	52.2	3,598.2	2,689.0	5,935.1
1992	1,091.3	1,381.6	−290.3	788.9	1,129.3	−340.4	302.4	252.3	50.1	4,001.8	2,999.7	6,239.9
1993	1,154.5	1,409.5	−255.1	842.5	1,142.9	−300.4	311.9	266.6	45.3	4,351.0	3,248.4	6,575.5
1994	1,258.7	1,461.9	−203.2	923.7	1,182.5	−258.8	335.0	279.4	55.7	4,643.3	3,433.1	6,961.3
1995	1,351.9	1,515.9	−164.0	1,000.9	1,227.2	−226.4	351.1	288.7	62.4	4,920.6	3,604.4	7,325.8
1996	1,453.2	1,560.6	−107.4	1,085.7	1,259.7	−174.0	367.5	300.9	66.6	5,181.5	3,734.1	7,694.1
1997	1,579.4	1,601.3	−21.9	1,187.4	1,290.7	−103.2	392.0	310.6	81.4	5,369.2	3,772.3	8,182.4
1998	1,722.0	1,652.7	69.3	1,306.2	1,336.1	−29.9	415.8	316.6	99.2	5,478.2	3,721.1	8,627.9
1999	1,827.6	1,702.0	125.6	1,383.2	1,381.3	1.9	444.5	320.8	123.7	5,605.5	3,632.4	9,125.3
2000	2,025.5	1,789.2	236.2	1,544.9	1,458.5	86.4	480.6	330.8	149.8	5,628.7	3,409.8	9,709.8
2001	1,991.4	1,863.2	128.2	1,483.9	1,516.4	−32.4	507.5	346.8	160.7	5,769.9	3,319.6	10,057.9
2002	1,853.4	2,011.2	−157.8	1,338.1	1,655.5	−317.4	515.3	355.7	159.7	6,198.4	3,540.4	10,377.4
2003	1,782.5	2,160.1	−377.6	1,258.7	1,797.1	−538.4	523.8	363.0	160.8	6,760.0	3,913.4	10,808.6
2004	1,880.3	2,293.0	−412.7	1,345.5	1,913.5	−568.0	534.7	379.5	155.2	7,354.7	4,295.5	11,499.9
2005	2,153.9	2,472.2	−318.3	1,576.4	2,070.0	−493.6	577.5	402.2	175.3	7,905.3	4,592.2	12,237.9
2006	2,407.3	2,655.4	−248.2	1,798.9	2,233.4	−434.5	608.4	422.1	186.3	8,451.4	4,829.0	13,015.5
2007	2,568.2	2,730.2	−162.0	1,933.2	2,276.6	−343.5	635.1	453.6	181.5	8,950.7	5,035.1	13,670.9
2008 (estimates)[1]	2,552.9	2,942.4	−389.4	1,896.1	2,469.8	−573.7	656.8	472.6	184.2	9,623.4	5,420.5	14,247.8
2009 (estimates)[1]	2,651.4	3,133.2	−481.8	1,969.0	2,631.7	−662.7	682.4	501.5	180.9	10,438.4	5,958.2	14,822.2

[1] Estimates from *Mid-Session Review, Budget of the U.S. Government, Fiscal Year 2009*, issued July 2008.

Note.—Fiscal years through 1976 were on a July 1–June 30 basis; beginning with October 1976 (fiscal year 1977), the fiscal year is on an October -September 30 basis. The transition quarter is the three-month period from July 1, 1976 through September 30, 1976.

See *Budget of the United States Government, Fiscal Year 2009*, for additional information.

Sources: Department of Commerce (Bureau of Economic Analysis), Department of the Treasury, and Office of Management and Budget.

TABLE B–79.—*Federal receipts, outlays, surplus or deficit, and debt, as percent of gross domestic product, fiscal years 1934–2009*

[Percent; fiscal years]

Fiscal year or period	Receipts	Outlays		Surplus or deficit (–)	Federal debt (end of period)	
		Total	National defense		Gross Federal	Held by public
1934	4.8	10.7		–5.9		
1935	5.2	9.2		–4.0		
1936	5.0	10.5		–5.5		
1937	6.1	8.6		–2.5		
1938	7.6	7.7		–.1		
1939	7.1	10.3		–3.2	54.2	46.8
1940	6.8	9.8	1.7	–3.0	52.4	44.2
1941	7.6	12.0	5.6	–4.3	50.4	42.3
1942	10.1	24.3	17.8	–14.2	54.9	47.0
1943	13.3	43.6	37.0	–30.3	79.1	70.9
1944	20.9	43.6	37.8	–22.7	97.6	88.3
1945	20.4	41.9	37.5	–21.5	117.5	106.2
1946	17.6	24.8	19.2	–7.2	121.7	108.6
1947	16.5	14.8	5.5	1.7	110.3	96.2
1948	16.2	11.6	3.6	4.6	98.4	84.5
1949	14.5	14.3	4.9	.2	93.2	79.1
1950	14.4	15.6	5.0	–1.1	94.1	80.2
1951	16.1	14.2	7.4	1.9	79.6	66.9
1952	19.0	19.4	13.2	–.4	74.3	61.6
1953	18.7	20.4	14.2	–1.7	71.3	58.6
1954	18.5	18.8	13.1	–.3	71.8	59.5
1955	16.6	17.3	10.8	–.8	69.5	57.4
1956	17.5	16.5	10.0	.9	63.8	52.
1957	17.8	17.0	10.1	.8	60.5	48.
1958	17.3	17.9	10.2	–.6	60.7	49.2
1959	16.1	18.7	10.0	–2.6	58.5	47.
1960	17.9	17.8	9.3	.1	56.1	45.
1961	17.8	18.4	9.3	–.6	55.1	44.9
1962	17.6	18.8	9.2	–1.3	53.4	43.
1963	17.8	18.6	8.9	–.8	51.8	42
1964	17.6	18.5	8.6	–.9	49.4	40.
1965	17.0	17.2	7.4	–.2	46.9	38.
1966	17.4	17.9	7.7	–.5	43.6	35.
1967	18.3	19.4	8.8	–1.1	41.9	32.
1968	17.7	20.6	9.5	–2.9	42.5	33.
1969	19.7	19.4	8.7	.3	38.6	29.
1970	19.0	19.3	8.1	–.3	37.6	28.
1971	17.3	19.5	7.3	–2.1	37.8	28.
1972	17.6	19.6	6.7	–2.0	37.0	27.
1973	17.7	18.8	5.9	–1.1	35.7	26.
1974	18.3	18.7	5.5	–.4	33.6	23.
1975	17.9	21.3	5.5	–3.4	34.7	25.
1976	17.2	21.4	5.2	–4.2	36.2	27.
Transition quarter	17.8	21.0	4.9	–3.2	35.2	27.
1977	18.0	20.7	4.9	–2.7	35.8	27.
1978	18.0	20.7	4.7	–2.7	35.0	27.
1979	18.5	20.2	4.7	–1.6	33.2	25.
1980	19.0	21.7	4.9	–2.7	33.3	26.
1981	19.6	22.2	5.2	–2.6	32.6	25.
1982	19.1	23.1	5.7	–4.0	35.2	28.
1983	17.5	23.5	6.1	–6.0	39.9	33.
1984	17.4	22.2	5.9	–4.8	40.7	34.
1985	17.7	22.9	6.1	–5.1	43.9	36.
1986	17.4	22.4	6.2	–5.0	48.1	39.
1987	18.4	21.6	6.1	–3.2	50.5	40.
1988	18.2	21.3	5.8	–3.1	51.9	41.
1989	18.4	21.2	5.6	–2.8	53.1	40.
1990	18.0	21.8	5.2	–3.9	55.9	42
1991	17.8	22.3	4.6	–4.5	60.6	45
1992	17.5	22.1	4.8	–4.7	64.1	48
1993	17.6	21.4	4.4	–3.9	66.2	49
1994	18.1	21.0	4.0	–2.9	66.7	49
1995	18.5	20.7	3.7	–2.2	67.2	49
1996	18.9	20.3	3.5	–1.4	67.3	48
1997	19.3	19.6	3.3	–.3	65.6	46
1998	20.0	19.2	3.1	.8	63.5	43
1999	20.0	18.7	3.0	1.4	61.4	39
2000	20.9	18.4	3.0	2.4	58.0	35.
2001	19.8	18.5	3.0	1.3	57.4	33.
2002	17.9	19.4	3.4	–1.5	59.7	34.
2003	16.5	20.0	3.7	–3.5	62.5	36.
2004	16.4	19.9	4.0	–3.6	64.0	37.
2005	17.6	20.2	4.0	–2.6	64.6	37.
2006	18.5	20.4	4.0	–1.9	64.9	37.
2007	18.8	20.0	4.0	–1.2	65.5	36.
2008 (estimates)	17.9	20.7	4.3	–2.7	67.5	38.
2009 (estimates)	17.9	21.1	4.6	–3.3	70.4	40.

Note.—See footnote 1 and Note, Table B–78.

Sources: Department of the Treasury and Office of Management and Budget.

TABLE B–80.—*Federal receipts and outlays, by major category, and surplus or deficit, fiscal years 1940–2009*

[Billions of dollars; fiscal years]

Fiscal year or period	Receipts (on-budget and off-budget)					Outlays (on-budget and off-budget)											Surplus or deficit (–) (on-budget and off-budget)
	Total	Individual income taxes	Corporation income taxes	Social insurance and retirement receipts	Other	Total	National defense		International affairs	Health	Medicare	Income security	Social security	Net interest	Other	
							Total	Department of Defense, military								
	6.5	0.9	1.2	1.8	2.7	9.5	1.7		0.1	0.1		1.5	0.0	0.9	5.3	–2.9
	8.7	1.3	2.1	1.9	3.3	13.7	6.4		.1	.1		1.9	.1	.9	4.1	–4.9
	14.6	3.3	4.7	2.5	4.2	35.1	25.7		1.0	.1		1.8	.1	1.1	5.4	–20.5
	24.0	6.5	9.6	3.0	4.9	78.6	66.7		1.3	.1		1.7	.2	1.5	7.0	–54.6
	43.7	19.7	14.8	3.5	5.7	91.3	79.1		1.4	.2		1.5	.2	2.2	6.6	–47.6
	45.2	18.4	16.0	3.5	7.3	92.7	83.0		1.9	.2		1.1	.3	3.1	3.1	–47.6
	39.3	16.1	11.9	3.1	8.2	55.2	42.7		1.9	.2		2.4	.4	4.1	3.6	–15.9
	38.5	17.9	8.6	3.4	8.5	34.5	12.8		5.8	.2		2.8	.5	4.2	8.2	4.0
	41.6	19.3	9.7	3.8	8.8	29.8	9.1		4.6	.2		2.5	.6	4.3	8.5	11.8
	39.4	15.6	11.2	3.8	8.9	38.8	13.2		6.1	.2		3.2	.7	4.5	11.1	.6
	39.4	15.8	10.4	4.3	8.9	42.6	13.7		4.7	.3		4.1	.8	4.8	14.2	–3.1
	51.6	21.6	14.1	5.7	10.2	45.5	23.6		3.6	.3		3.4	1.6	4.7	8.4	6.1
	66.2	27.9	21.2	6.4	10.6	67.7	46.1		2.7	.3		3.7	2.1	4.7	8.1	–1.5
	69.6	29.8	21.2	6.8	11.7	76.1	52.8		2.1	.3		3.8	2.7	5.2	9.1	–6.5
	69.7	29.5	21.1	7.2	11.9	70.9	49.3		1.6	.3		4.4	3.4	4.8	7.1	–1.2
	65.5	28.7	17.9	7.9	11.0	68.4	42.7		2.2	.3		5.1	4.4	4.8	8.9	–3.0
	74.6	32.2	20.9	9.3	12.2	70.6	42.5		2.4	.4		4.7	5.5	5.1	10.1	3.9
	80.0	35.6	21.2	10.0	13.2	76.6	45.4		3.1	.5		5.4	6.7	5.4	10.1	3.4
	79.6	34.7	20.1	11.2	13.6	82.4	46.8		3.4	.5		7.5	8.2	5.6	10.3	–2.8
	79.2	36.7	17.3	11.7	13.5	92.1	49.0		3.1	.7		8.2	9.7	5.8	15.5	–12.8
	92.5	40.7	21.5	14.7	15.6	92.2	48.1		3.0	.8		7.4	11.6	6.9	14.4	.3
	94.4	41.3	21.0	16.4	15.7	97.7	49.6		3.2	.9		9.7	12.5	6.7	15.2	–3.3
	99.7	45.6	20.5	17.0	16.5	106.8	52.3	50.1	5.6	1.2		9.2	14.4	6.9	17.2	–7.1
	106.6	47.6	21.6	19.8	17.6	111.3	53.4	51.1	5.3	1.5		9.3	15.8	7.7	18.3	–4.8
	112.6	48.7	23.5	22.0	18.5	118.5	54.8	52.6	4.9	1.8		9.7	16.6	8.2	22.6	–5.9
	116.8	48.8	25.5	22.2	20.3	118.2	50.6	48.8	5.3	1.8		9.5	17.5	8.6	25.0	–1.4
	130.8	55.4	30.1	25.5	19.8	134.5	58.1	56.6	5.6	2.5	0.1	9.7	20.7	9.4	28.5	–3.7
	148.8	61.5	34.0	32.6	20.7	157.5	71.4	70.1	5.6	3.4	2.7	10.3	21.7	10.3	32.1	–8.6
	153.0	68.7	28.7	33.9	21.7	178.1	81.9	80.4	5.3	4.4	4.6	11.8	23.9	11.1	35.1	–25.2
	186.9	87.2	36.7	39.0	23.9	183.6	82.5	80.8	4.6	5.2	5.7	13.1	27.3	12.7	32.6	3.2
	192.8	90.4	32.8	44.4	25.2	195.6	81.7	80.1	4.3	5.9	6.2	15.7	30.3	14.4	37.2	–2.8
	187.1	86.2	26.8	47.3	26.8	210.2	78.9	77.5	4.2	6.8	6.6	22.9	35.9	14.8	40.0	–23.0
	207.3	94.7	32.2	52.6	27.8	230.7	79.2	77.6	4.8	8.7	7.5	27.7	40.2	15.5	47.3	–23.4
	230.8	103.2	36.2	63.1	28.3	245.7	76.7	75.0	4.1	9.4	8.1	28.3	49.1	17.3	52.8	–14.9
	263.2	119.0	38.6	75.1	30.6	269.4	79.3	77.9	5.7	10.7	9.6	33.7	55.9	21.4	52.9	–6.1
	279.1	122.4	40.6	84.5	31.5	332.3	86.5	84.9	7.1	12.9	12.9	50.2	64.7	23.2	74.8	–53.2
	298.1	131.6	41.4	90.8	34.3	371.8	89.6	87.9	6.4	15.7	15.8	60.8	73.9	26.7	82.7	–73.7
ion quarter ..	81.2	38.8	8.5	25.2	8.8	96.0	22.3	21.8	2.5	3.9	4.3	15.0	19.8	6.9	21.4	–14.7
	355.6	157.6	54.9	106.5	36.6	409.2	97.2	95.1	6.4	17.3	19.3	61.1	85.1	29.9	93.0	–53.7
	399.6	181.0	60.0	121.0	37.7	458.7	104.5	102.3	7.5	18.5	22.8	61.5	93.9	35.5	114.7	–59.2
	463.3	217.8	65.7	138.9	40.8	504.0	116.3	113.6	7.5	20.5	26.5	66.4	104.1	42.6	120.2	–40.7
	517.1	244.1	64.6	157.8	50.6	590.9	134.0	130.9	12.7	23.2	32.1	86.6	118.5	52.5	131.3	–73.8
	599.3	285.9	61.1	182.7	69.5	678.2	157.5	153.9	13.1	26.9	39.1	100.3	139.6	68.8	133.0	–79.0
	617.8	297.7	49.2	201.5	69.3	745.7	185.3	180.7	12.3	27.4	46.6	108.2	156.0	85.0	125.0	–128.0
	600.6	288.9	37.0	209.0	65.6	808.4	209.9	204.4	11.8	28.6	52.6	123.0	170.7	89.8	121.8	–207.8
	666.5	298.4	56.9	239.4	71.8	851.9	227.4	220.9	15.9	30.4	57.5	113.4	178.2	111.1	117.9	–185.4
	734.1	334.5	61.3	265.2	73.1	946.4	252.7	245.1	16.2	33.5	65.8	129.0	188.6	129.5	131.0	–212.3
	769.2	349.0	63.1	283.9	73.2	990.4	273.4	265.4	14.2	35.9	70.2	120.6	198.8	136.0	141.4	–221.2
	854.4	392.6	83.9	303.3	74.6	1,004.1	282.0	273.9	11.6	40.0	75.1	124.1	207.4	138.6	125.3	–149.7
	909.3	401.2	94.5	334.3	79.3	1,064.5	290.4	281.9	10.5	44.5	78.9	130.4	219.3	151.8	138.8	–155.2
	991.2	445.7	103.3	359.4	82.8	1,143.8	303.6	294.8	9.6	48.4	85.0	137.4	232.5	169.0	158.4	–152.6
	1,032.1	466.9	93.5	380.0	91.7	1,253.1	299.3	289.7	13.8	57.7	98.1	148.7	248.6	184.3	202.6	–221.0
	1,055.1	467.8	98.1	396.0	93.2	1,324.3	273.3	262.3	15.9	71.2	104.5	172.5	269.0	194.4	223.6	–269.2
	1,091.3	476.0	100.3	413.7	101.4	1,381.6	298.4	286.8	16.1	89.5	119.0	199.6	287.6	199.3	172.2	–290.3
	1,154.5	509.7	117.5	428.3	99.0	1,409.5	291.1	278.5	17.2	99.4	130.6	210.0	304.6	198.7	158.0	–255.1
	1,258.7	543.1	140.4	461.5	113.8	1,461.9	281.6	268.6	17.1	107.1	144.7	217.2	319.6	202.9	171.7	–203.2
	1,351.9	590.2	157.0	484.5	120.2	1,515.9	272.1	259.4	16.4	115.4	159.9	223.8	335.8	232.1	160.3	–164.0
	1,453.2	656.4	171.8	509.4	115.5	1,560.6	265.8	253.1	13.5	119.4	174.2	229.7	349.7	241.1	167.3	–107.4
	1,579.4	737.5	182.3	539.4	120.3	1,601.3	270.5	258.3	15.2	123.8	190.0	235.0	365.3	244.0	157.4	–21.9
	1,722.0	828.6	188.7	571.8	132.9	1,652.7	268.2	255.8	13.1	131.4	192.8	237.8	379.2	241.1	189.0	69.3
	1,827.6	879.5	184.7	611.8	151.7	1,702.0	274.8	261.2	15.2	141.1	190.4	242.5	390.0	229.8	218.2	125.6
	2,025.5	1,004.5	207.3	652.9	160.9	1,789.2	294.4	281.1	17.2	154.5	197.1	253.7	409.4	222.9	239.9	236.2
	1,991.4	994.3	151.1	694.0	152.0	1,863.2	304.8	290.2	16.5	172.3	217.4	269.8	433.0	206.2	243.4	128.2
	1,853.4	858.3	148.0	700.8	146.2	2,011.2	348.5	331.9	22.4	196.5	230.9	312.7	456.0	170.9	273.3	–157.8
	1,782.5	793.7	131.8	713.0	144.1	2,160.1	404.8	387.2	21.2	219.6	249.4	334.6	474.7	153.1	302.7	–377.6
	1,880.3	809.0	189.4	733.4	148.5	2,293.0	455.8	436.5	26.9	240.1	269.4	333.1	495.5	160.2	311.9	–412.7
	2,153.9	927.2	278.3	794.1	154.2	2,472.2	495.3	474.1	34.6	250.6	298.6	345.8	523.3	184.0	339.9	–318.3
	2,407.3	1,043.9	353.9	837.8	171.6	2,655.4	521.8	499.3	29.5	252.8	329.9	352.5	548.5	226.6	393.8	–248.2
	2,568.2	1,163.5	370.2	869.6	164.9	2,730.2	552.6	529.8	28.5	266.4	375.4	366.0	586.2	237.1	318.1	–162.0
estimates [1] ..	2,523.9	1,145.7	304.3	900.4	173.4	2,978.7	624.1	594.7	28.8	280.6	390.8	432.7	617.0	248.9	355.7	–454.8
estimates [2] ..	2,651.4	1,250.4	304.1	931.5	165.5	3,133.2	682.1	656.7	39.9	301.4	411.9	431.3	656.1	237.6	382.5	–481.8

timates from *Final Monthly Treasury Statement*, issued October 2008.
timates from *Mid-Session Review, Budget of the U.S. Government, Fiscal Year 2009*, issued July 2008.
e.—See Note, Table B–78.
rces: Department of the Treasury and Office of Management and Budget.

TABLE B–81.—*Federal receipts, outlays, surplus or deficit, and debt, fiscal years 2003–2008*

[Millions of dollars; fiscal years]

Description	Actual					Estimates
	2003	2004	2005	2006	2007	2008
RECEIPTS, OUTLAYS, AND SURPLUS OR DEFICIT						
Total:						
Receipts	1,782,532	1,880,279	2,153,859	2,407,254	2,568,239	2,523,8
Outlays	2,160,117	2,293,006	2,472,205	2,655,435	2,730,241	2,978,6
Surplus or deficit (–)	–377,585	–412,727	–318,346	–248,181	–162,002	–454,"
On-budget:						
Receipts	1,258,690	1,345,534	1,576,383	1,798,872	1,933,150	1,865,8
Outlays	1,797,108	1,913,495	2,069,994	2,233,366	2,276,604	2,503,
Surplus or deficit (–)	–538,418	–567,961	–493,611	–434,494	–343,454	–638,
Off-budget:						
Receipts	523,842	534,745	577,476	608,382	635,089	658,0
Outlays	363,009	379,511	402,211	422,069	453,637	474,
Surplus or deficit (–)	160,833	155,234	175,265	186,313	181,452	183,
OUTSTANDING DEBT, END OF PERIOD						
Gross Federal debt	6,760,014	7,354,657	7,905,300	8,451,350	8,950,744	9,983,
Held by Federal Government accounts	2,846,570	3,059,113	3,313,088	3,622,378	3,915,615	4,183,
Held by the public	3,913,443	4,295,544	4,592,212	4,828,972	5,035,129	5,800,
Federal Reserve System	656,116	700,341	736,360	768,924	779,632	....
Other	3,257,327	3,595,203	3,855,852	4,060,048	4,255,497	....
RECEIPTS BY SOURCE						
Total: On-budget and off-budget	1,782,532	1,880,279	2,153,859	2,407,254	2,568,239	2,523,
Individual income taxes	793,699	808,959	927,222	1,043,908	1,163,472	1,145,
Corporation income taxes	131,778	189,371	278,282	353,915	370,243	304,
Social insurance and retirement receipts	712,978	733,407	794,125	837,821	869,607	900,
On-budget	189,136	198,662	216,649	229,439	234,518	....
Off-budget	523,842	534,745	577,476	608,382	635,089	....
Excise taxes	67,524	69,855	73,094	73,961	65,069	67,
Estate and gift taxes	21,959	24,831	24,764	27,877	26,044	28,
Customs duties and fees	19,862	21,083	23,379	24,810	26,010	27,
Miscellaneous receipts	34,732	32,773	32,993	44,962	47,794	49,
Deposits of earnings by Federal Reserve System	21,878	19,652	19,297	29,945	32,043	....
All other	12,854	13,121	13,696	15,017	15,751	....
OUTLAYS BY FUNCTION						
Total: On-budget and off-budget	2,160,117	2,293,006	2,472,205	2,655,435	2,730,241	2,978,
National defense	404,778	455,847	495,326	521,840	552,568	624,
International affairs	21,209	26,891	34,595	29,549	28,510	28,
General science, space and technology	20,873	23,053	23,628	23,616	25,566	23,
Energy	–736	–166	429	782	–860	
Natural resources and environment	29,703	30,725	28,023	33,055	31,772	30,
Agriculture	22,497	15,440	26,566	25,970	17,663	22,
Commerce and housing credit	728	5,266	7,567	6,188	488	27
On-budget	5,973	9,396	9,358	7,263	–4,605	....
Off-budget	–5,245	–4,130	–1,791	–1,075	5,093	....
Transportation	67,069	64,627	67,894	70,244	72,905	77,
Community and regional development	18,850	15,822	26,264	54,531	29,567	22,
Education, training, employment, and social services	82,603	87,990	97,567	118,560	91,676	89,
Health	219,576	240,134	250,614	252,780	266,432	280,
Medicare	249,433	269,360	298,638	329,868	375,407	390,
Income security	334,632	333,059	345,847	352,477	365,975	432
Social security	474,680	495,548	523,305	548,549	586,153	617,
On-budget	13,279	14,348	16,526	16,058	19,307	....
Off-budget	461,401	481,200	506,779	532,491	566,846	....
Veterans benefits and services	57,022	59,779	70,151	69,842	72,847	84
Administration of justice	35,340	45,576	40,019	41,016	41,244	47
General government	23,169	22,347	17,010	18,215	17,457	16
Net interest	153,073	160,245	183,986	226,603	237,109	248
On-budget	236,618	246,473	275,822	324,325	343,112	....
Off-budget	–83,545	–86,228	–91,836	–97,722	–106,003	....
Allowances	....	....	....	....	....	
Undistributed offsetting receipts	–54,382	–58,537	–65,224	–68,250	–82,238	–86
On-budget	–44,780	–47,206	–54,283	–56,625	–69,939	....
Off-budget	–9,602	–11,331	–10,941	–11,625	–12,299	....

[1] Estimates from *Final Monthly Treasury Statement*, issued October 2008.

Note.—See Note, Table B–78.

Sources: Department of the Treasury and Office of Management and Budget.

ABLE B–82.—*Federal and State and local government current receipts and expenditures, national income and product accounts (NIPA), 1959–2008*

[Billions of dollars; quarterly data at seasonally adjusted annual rates]

ar or quarter	Total government			Federal Government			State and local government			Addendum: Grants-in-aid to State and local governments
	Current receipts	Current expenditures	Net government saving (NIPA)	Current receipts	Current expenditures	Net Federal Government saving (NIPA)	Current receipts	Current expenditures	Net State and local government saving (NIPA)	
....	123.0	115.8	7.1	87.0	83.6	3.3	40.6	36.9	3.8	3.8
....	134.4	122.9	11.5	93.9	86.7	7.2	44.5	40.2	4.3	4.0
....	139.0	132.1	6.9	95.5	92.8	2.6	48.1	43.8	4.3	4.5
....	150.6	142.8	7.8	103.6	101.1	2.5	52.0	46.8	5.2	5.0
....	162.2	151.1	11.1	111.8	106.4	5.4	56.0	50.3	5.7	5.6
....	166.6	159.2	7.4	111.8	110.8	1.0	61.3	54.9	6.4	6.5
....	180.3	170.4	9.9	120.9	117.6	3.3	66.5	60.0	6.5	7.2
....	202.8	192.8	10.0	137.9	135.7	2.3	74.9	67.2	7.8	10.1
....	217.6	220.0	-2.4	146.9	156.2	-9.4	82.5	75.5	7.0	11.7
....	252.0	246.8	5.2	171.2	173.5	-2.3	93.5	86.0	7.5	12.7
....	283.4	266.7	16.7	192.5	183.8	8.7	105.5	97.5	8.0	14.6
....	286.7	294.8	-8.1	186.0	201.1	-15.2	120.1	113.0	7.1	19.3
....	303.4	325.3	-21.9	191.7	220.0	-28.4	134.9	128.5	6.5	23.2
....	346.8	355.5	-8.8	220.1	244.4	-24.4	158.4	142.8	15.6	31.7
....	390.0	385.6	4.4	250.4	261.7	-11.3	174.3	158.6	15.7	34.8
....	431.3	435.8	-4.4	279.5	293.3	-13.8	188.1	178.7	9.3	36.3
....	441.6	508.2	-66.6	277.2	346.2	-69.0	209.6	207.1	2.5	45.1
....	505.5	549.9	-44.4	322.5	374.3	-51.7	233.7	226.3	7.4	50.7
....	566.8	597.7	-31.0	363.4	407.5	-44.1	259.9	246.8	13.1	56.6
....	645.6	653.4	-7.8	423.5	450.0	-26.5	287.6	268.9	18.7	65.5
....	728.2	726.5	1.7	486.2	497.5	-11.3	308.4	295.4	13.0	66.3
....	798.0	842.8	-44.8	532.1	585.7	-53.6	338.2	329.4	8.8	72.3
....	917.2	962.9	-45.7	619.4	672.7	-53.3	370.2	362.7	7.6	72.5
....	938.5	1,072.6	-134.1	616.6	748.5	-131.9	391.4	393.6	-2.2	69.5
....	999.4	1,167.5	-168.1	642.3	815.4	-173.0	428.6	423.7	4.9	71.6
....	1,112.5	1,256.6	-144.1	709.0	877.1	-168.1	480.2	456.2	23.9	76.7
....	1,213.5	1,366.1	-152.6	773.3	948.2	-175.0	521.1	498.7	22.3	80.9
....	1,289.3	1,459.1	-169.9	815.2	1,006.0	-190.8	561.6	540.7	21.0	87.6
....	1,403.2	1,535.8	-132.6	896.6	1,041.6	-145.0	590.6	578.1	12.4	83.9
....	1,502.2	1,618.7	-116.6	958.2	1,092.7	-134.5	635.5	617.6	17.9	91.6
....	1,626.3	1,735.6	-109.3	1,037.4	1,167.5	-130.1	687.3	666.5	20.8	98.3
....	1,707.8	1,872.6	-164.8	1,081.5	1,253.5	-172.0	737.8	730.5	7.2	111.4
....	1,758.8	1,976.7	-217.9	1,101.3	1,315.0	-213.7	789.2	793.3	-4.2	131.6
....	1,843.7	2,140.4	-296.7	1,147.2	1,444.6	-297.4	845.7	845.0	.7	149.1
....	1,945.8	2,218.4	-272.6	1,222.5	1,496.0	-273.5	886.9	886.0	.9	163.7
....	2,089.0	2,290.8	-201.9	1,320.8	1,533.1	-212.3	942.9	932.4	10.5	174.7
....	2,212.6	2,397.6	-184.9	1,406.5	1,603.5	-197.0	990.2	978.2	12.0	184.1
....	2,376.1	2,492.1	-116.0	1,524.0	1,665.8	-141.8	1,043.3	1,017.5	25.8	191.2
....	2,551.9	2,568.6	-16.7	1,653.1	1,708.9	-55.8	1,097.4	1,058.3	39.1	198.6
....	2,724.2	2,633.4	90.8	1,773.8	1,734.9	38.8	1,163.2	1,111.2	52.0	212.8
....	2,895.0	2,741.0	154.0	1,891.2	1,787.6	103.6	1,236.7	1,186.3	50.4	232.9
....	3,125.9	2,886.5	239.4	2,053.8	1,864.4	189.5	1,319.5	1,269.5	50.0	247.3
....	3,113.1	3,061.6	51.5	2,016.2	1,969.5	46.7	1,373.0	1,368.2	4.8	276.1
....	2,958.7	3,240.8	-282.1	1,853.2	2,101.1	-247.9	1,410.1	1,444.3	-34.2	304.6
....	3,035.6	3,428.1	-392.5	1,879.9	2,252.1	-372.1	1,494.2	1,514.5	-20.4	338.5
....	3,254.1	3,623.2	-369.1	2,008.9	2,379.5	-370.6	1,594.3	1,592.8	1.5	349.1
....	3,620.4	3,882.6	-262.2	2,266.9	2,558.6	-291.7	1,714.4	1,684.9	29.5	360.9
....	3,963.8	4,118.8	-155.0	2,510.4	2,711.6	-201.1	1,811.4	1,765.3	46.2	358.0
....	4,177.8	4,396.7	-218.9	2,651.2	2,880.5	-229.3	1,902.8	1,892.4	10.4	376.3
I	3,553.0	3,790.4	-237.5	2,225.7	2,504.4	-278.7	1,685.7	1,644.5	41.2	358.5
II	3,614.3	3,845.5	-231.2	2,264.1	2,533.6	-269.5	1,711.3	1,673.1	38.3	361.1
III	3,571.3	3,916.8	-345.4	2,214.5	2,579.2	-364.7	1,716.5	1,697.3	19.3	359.7
IV	3,742.8	3,977.5	-234.7	2,363.3	2,617.1	-253.8	1,743.8	1,724.7	19.1	364.3
I	3,881.1	4,031.5	-150.4	2,453.6	2,661.5	-207.9	1,781.7	1,724.2	57.5	354.2
II	3,944.1	4,106.0	-161.8	2,487.6	2,712.5	-225.0	1,815.3	1,752.2	63.1	358.7
III	3,989.3	4,175.5	-186.2	2,531.9	2,750.4	-218.4	1,820.4	1,788.1	32.2	363.0
IV	4,040.8	4,162.2	-121.4	2,568.6	2,721.8	-153.2	1,828.4	1,796.6	31.8	356.2
I	4,117.4	4,319.3	-202.0	2,612.8	2,837.9	-225.2	1,877.5	1,854.3	23.2	372.9
II	4,181.1	4,356.8	-175.7	2,648.1	2,859.5	-211.4	1,909.8	1,874.0	35.8	376.8
III	4,194.4	4,434.0	-239.5	2,664.9	2,909.2	-244.3	1,905.5	1,900.7	4.7	375.9
IV	4,218.1	4,476.7	-258.6	2,679.2	2,915.6	-236.3	1,918.4	1,940.7	-22.3	379.6
I	4,215.6	4,598.7	-383.1	2,672.5	3,003.2	-330.7	1,922.9	1,975.3	-52.4	379.9
II	4,049.9	4,766.3	-716.4	2,478.8	3,128.4	-649.6	1,955.4	2,022.3	-66.9	384.4
III p	4,157.5	4,802.5	-645.0	2,597.0	3,140.2	-543.2	1,947.0	2,048.8	-101.8	386.6

te.—Federal grants-in-aid to State and local governments are reflected in Federal current expenditures and State and local current receipts. Total ment current receipts and expenditures have been adjusted to eliminate this duplication.

rce: Department of Commerce (Bureau of Economic Analysis).

TABLE B–83.—*Federal and State and local government current receipts and expenditures, national income and product accounts (NIPA), by major type, 1959–2008*

[Billions of dollars; quarterly data at seasonally adjusted annual rates]

Year or quarter	Current receipts									Current expenditures					Net govern- ment saving
		Current tax receipts				Contri- butions for govern- ment social insur- ance	Income re- ceipts on assets	Current trans- fer re- ceipts	Current surplus of govern- ment enter- prises		Con- sump- tion expen- ditures	Current trans- fer pay- ments	Interest pay- ments	Sub- si- dies	
	Total	Total[1]	Per- sonal current taxes	Taxes on produc- tion and imports	Taxes on corpo- rate income					Total[2]					
1959	123.0	107.1	42.3	41.1	23.6	13.8	0.3	0.8	1.0	115.8	80.7	26.8	7.3	1.1	
1960	134.4	113.4	46.1	44.6	22.7	16.4	2.7	.9	.9	122.9	83.3	28.0	10.4	1.1	
1961	139.0	117.1	47.3	47.0	22.8	17.0	2.9	1.1	.8	132.1	88.2	31.8	10.2	2.0	
1962	150.6	126.1	51.6	50.4	24.0	19.1	3.2	1.2	.9	142.8	96.8	32.6	11.1	2.3	
1963	162.2	134.4	54.6	53.4	26.2	21.7	3.4	1.3	1.4	151.1	102.7	34.1	12.0	2.2	
1964	166.6	137.6	52.1	57.3	28.0	22.4	3.7	1.6	1.3	159.2	108.6	34.9	12.9	2.7	
1965	180.3	149.5	57.7	60.8	30.9	23.4	4.1	1.9	1.3	170.4	115.9	37.8	13.7	3.0	
1966	202.8	163.5	66.4	63.3	33.7	31.3	4.7	2.2	1.0	192.8	132.0	41.8	15.1	3.9	
1967	217.6	173.9	73.0	68.0	32.7	34.9	5.5	2.5	.9	220.0	149.7	50.1	16.4	3.8	
1968	252.0	203.2	87.0	76.5	39.4	38.7	6.4	2.6	1.2	246.8	165.8	58.1	18.8	4.2	
1969	283.4	228.5	104.5	84.0	39.7	44.1	7.0	2.7	1.0	266.7	178.2	63.7	20.2	4.5	
1970	286.7	229.3	103.1	91.5	34.4	46.4	8.2	2.9	.0	294.8	190.2	76.8	23.1	4.8	
1971	303.4	240.4	101.7	100.6	37.7	51.2	9.0	3.1	–.2	325.3	204.7	91.6	24.5	4.7	–2
1972	346.8	274.0	123.6	108.1	41.9	59.2	9.5	3.6	.5	355.5	220.8	102.2	26.3	6.6	
1973	390.0	299.4	132.4	117.3	49.3	75.5	11.6	3.9	–.4	385.6	234.8	114.2	31.3	5.2	
1974	431.3	328.3	151.0	125.0	51.8	85.2	14.4	4.5	–.9	435.8	261.7	134.7	35.6	3.3	
1975	441.6	334.4	147.6	135.5	50.9	89.3	16.1	5.1	–3.2	508.2	294.6	169.2	40.0	4.5	–6
1976	505.5	383.8	172.3	146.6	64.2	101.3	16.3	5.8	–1.8	549.9	316.6	181.9	46.3	5.1	–4
1977	566.8	431.2	197.5	159.9	73.0	113.1	18.4	6.8	–2.6	597.7	346.6	193.3	50.8	7.1	–3
1978	645.6	485.0	229.4	171.2	83.5	131.3	23.2	8.0	–1.9	653.4	376.5	207.9	60.2	8.9	
1979	728.2	538.2	268.7	180.4	88.0	152.7	30.8	9.1	–2.6	726.5	412.3	232.6	72.9	8.5	
1980	798.0	586.0	298.9	200.7	84.8	166.2	39.9	10.7	–4.8	842.8	465.9	278.0	89.1	9.8	–4
1981	917.2	663.9	345.2	236.0	81.1	195.7	50.2	12.3	–4.9	962.9	520.6	314.2	116.7	11.5	–4
1982	938.5	659.9	354.1	241.3	63.1	208.9	58.9	14.8	–4.0	1,072.6	568.2	350.5	138.9	15.0	–1
1983	999.4	694.5	352.3	263.7	77.2	226.0	65.3	16.8	–3.1	1,167.5	610.6	378.4	156.9	21.2	–1
1984	1,112.5	763.0	377.4	290.2	94.0	257.5	74.3	19.6	–1.9	1,256.6	657.6	390.9	187.3	21.0	–1
1985	1,213.5	824.3	417.4	308.5	96.5	281.4	84.0	23.0	.8	1,366.1	720.2	415.7	208.8	21.3	–1
1986	1,289.3	869.2	437.3	323.7	106.5	303.4	89.8	25.6	1.3	1,459.1	776.1	441.9	216.3	24.8	
1987	1,403.2	966.1	489.1	347.9	127.1	323.1	86.1	26.8	1.2	1,535.8	815.2	459.7	230.8	30.2	–1
1988	1,502.2	1,019.4	505.0	374.9	137.2	361.5	90.5	28.2	2.5	1,618.7	852.8	488.8	247.7	29.4	–1
1989	1,626.3	1,109.7	566.1	399.3	141.5	385.2	94.3	32.2	4.9	1,735.6	901.4	533.1	274.0	27.2	–1
1990	1,707.8	1,161.9	592.8	425.5	140.6	410.1	98.7	35.6	1.6	1,872.6	964.4	586.1	295.3	26.8	–1
1991	1,758.8	1,180.3	586.7	457.5	133.6	430.2	98.1	44.6	5.7	1,976.7	1,014.1	622.5	312.7	27.3	–2
1992	1,843.7	1,240.2	610.6	483.8	143.1	455.0	90.5	50.5	7.6	2,140.4	1,047.8	749.5	313.2	29.9	–2
1993	1,945.8	1,318.2	646.6	503.4	165.4	477.7	87.6	55.1	7.2	2,218.4	1,072.2	796.3	313.6	36.4	–2
1994	2,089.0	1,426.1	690.7	545.6	186.7	508.2	86.6	59.5	8.6	2,290.8	1,104.1	831.2	323.4	32.2	–2
1995	2,212.6	1,517.2	744.1	558.2	211.0	532.8	92.1	59.1	11.4	2,397.6	1,136.5	872.5	354.6	34.0	–1
1996	2,376.1	1,642.0	832.1	581.1	223.6	555.2	100.2	66.0	12.7	2,492.1	1,171.1	921.4	365.3	34.3	–1
1997	2,551.9	1,780.5	926.3	612.0	237.1	587.2	103.7	67.9	12.6	2,568.6	1,216.6	947.8	371.4	32.9	
1998	2,724.2	1,911.7	1,027.0	639.8	239.2	624.2	102.4	75.5	10.3	2,633.4	1,256.0	969.6	372.4	35.4	
1999	2,895.0	2,036.2	1,107.5	674.0	248.8	661.4	106.8	80.6	10.1	2,741.0	1,334.0	1,005.5	357.3	44.2	1
2000	3,125.9	2,206.8	1,235.7	708.9	255.0	702.7	117.4	93.7	5.3	2,886.5	1,417.1	1,062.4	362.8	44.3	2
2001	3,113.1	2,168.0	1,237.3	728.6	194.9	731.1	113.7	101.8	–1.4	3,061.6	1,501.6	1,160.6	344.1	55.3	
2002	2,958.7	2,004.5	1,051.8	762.8	182.6	750.0	98.4	104.9	.9	3,240.8	1,616.9	1,270.4	315.1	38.4	–2
2003	3,035.6	2,050.3	1,001.1	807.2	233.1	778.6	95.8	109.2	1.7	3,428.1	1,736.5	1,343.2	300.6	47.9	–3
2004	3,254.1	2,213.4	1,046.3	863.8	293.3	828.8	99.1	117.0	–4.2	3,623.2	1,844.0	1,425.3	309.3	44.6	–3
2005	3,620.4	2,545.3	1,207.8	928.2	397.2	874.3	109.8	104.3	–13.4	3,882.6	1,957.5	1,520.5	345.3	59.3	–2
2006	3,963.8	2,792.4	1,353.2	976.2	449.7	925.5	120.4	134.2	–8.6	4,118.8	2,081.5	1,611.0	376.5	49.7	–1
2007	4,177.8	2,948.5	1,492.8	1,015.5	426.3	965.1	129.5	142.6	–7.9	4,396.7	2,212.0	1,721.3	411.1	52.3	–2
2005: I	3,553.0	2,470.9	1,163.8	904.5	391.2	859.6	105.2	124.3	–7.1	3,790.4	1,917.3	1,496.5	322.1	54.5	–2
II	3,614.3	2,523.1	1,192.7	924.0	396.0	866.9	109.5	124.0	–9.3	3,845.5	1,934.4	1,509.9	342.6	58.6	–2
III	3,571.3	2,543.4	1,222.3	937.4	370.2	881.1	111.4	61.3	–25.8	3,916.8	1,985.2	1,526.9	344.0	60.7	–3
IV	3,742.8	2,643.9	1,252.5	946.8	431.4	889.5	113.2	107.7	–11.4	3,977.5	1,993.0	1,548.9	372.4	63.3	–2
2006: I	3,881.1	2,726.0	1,316.0	962.7	436.5	917.1	115.9	130.0	–7.8	4,031.5	2,046.7	1,571.5	359.1	54.2	–1
II	3,944.1	2,781.7	1,341.1	973.6	456.0	918.9	118.9	133.0	–8.3	4,106.0	2,069.3	1,605.5	381.3	49.8	–1
III	3,989.3	2,815.7	1,356.2	980.1	467.7	925.5	121.6	135.6	–9.1	4,175.5	2,098.0	1,632.2	397.2	48.2	–1
IV	4,040.8	2,846.4	1,399.6	988.3	438.4	940.4	125.1	138.0	–9.2	4,162.2	2,111.8	1,635.1	368.5	46.8	–1
2007: I	4,117.4	2,901.1	1,459.5	1,002.7	426.4	959.8	126.9	140.4	–10.8	4,319.3	2,151.2	1,714.1	406.5	47.5	–2
II	4,181.1	2,959.7	1,489.4	1,012.3	445.2	959.1	128.8	142.0	–8.5	4,356.8	2,195.5	1,696.6	408.7	55.9	–1
III	4,194.4	2,959.7	1,501.6	1,019.2	426.0	966.0	130.9	143.3	–5.5	4,434.0	2,234.4	1,723.1	422.9	53.5	–2
IV	4,218.1	2,973.7	1,520.5	1,027.7	407.7	975.3	131.3	144.5	–6.7	4,476.7	2,266.8	1,751.2	406.4	52.3	–2
2008: I	4,215.6	2,951.8	1,535.0	1,025.8	375.8	992.2	132.7	145.9	–7.1	4,598.7	2,324.3	1,793.5	430.3	50.6	–3
II	4,049.9	2,779.2	1,346.1	1,039.4	378.9	995.4	135.6	147.4	–7.7	4,766.3	2,380.9	1,930.2	404.4	50.8	–7
III ᴾ ..	4,157.5	2,899.2	1,473.5	1,042.5	368.2	999.7	136.4	131.2	–8.0	4,802.5	2,440.1	1,867.1	444.8	50.4	–6

[1] Includes taxes from the rest of the world, not shown separately.
[2] Includes an item for the difference between wage accruals and disbursements, not shown separately.

Source: Department of Commerce (Bureau of Economic Analysis).

[Billions of dollars; quarterly data at seasonally adjusted annual rates]

Year or quarter	Current receipts									Current expenditures					Net Federal Government saving
	Total	Current tax receipts				Contributions for government social insurance	Income receipts on assets	Current transfer receipts	Current surplus of government enterprises	Total [2]	Consumption expenditures	Current transfer payments [3]	Interest payments	Subsidies	
		Total [1]	Personal current taxes	Taxes on production and imports	Taxes on corporate income										
9	87.0	73.3	38.5	12.2	22.5	13.4	0.0	0.4	-0.1	83.6	50.0	26.2	6.3	1.1	3.3
0	93.9	76.5	41.8	13.1	21.4	16.0	1.4	.4	-.3	86.7	49.8	27.5	8.4	1.1	7.2
1	95.5	77.5	42.7	13.2	21.5	16.5	1.5	.5	-.5	92.8	51.6	31.3	7.9	2.0	2.6
2	103.6	83.3	46.5	14.2	22.5	18.6	1.7	.5	-.5	101.1	57.8	32.3	8.6	2.3	2.5
3	111.8	88.6	49.1	14.7	24.6	21.0	1.8	.6	-.3	106.4	60.8	34.1	9.3	2.2	5.4
4	111.8	87.8	46.0	15.5	26.1	21.7	1.8	.7	-.3	110.8	62.8	35.2	10.0	2.7	1.0
5	120.9	95.7	51.1	15.5	28.9	22.7	1.9	1.1	-.3	117.6	65.7	38.3	10.6	3.0	3.3
6	137.9	104.8	58.6	14.5	31.4	30.5	2.1	1.2	-.6	135.7	75.9	44.2	11.6	3.9	2.3
7	146.9	109.9	64.4	15.2	30.0	34.0	2.5	1.1	-.6	156.2	87.1	52.6	12.7	3.8	-9.4
8	171.2	129.8	76.4	17.0	36.1	37.8	2.9	1.1	-.3	173.5	95.4	59.3	14.6	4.1	-2.3
9	192.5	146.1	91.7	17.9	36.1	43.1	2.7	1.1	-.5	183.8	98.4	65.1	15.8	4.5	8.7
'0	186.0	138.0	88.9	18.2	30.6	45.3	3.1	1.1	-1.5	201.1	98.6	80.0	17.7	4.8	-15.2
'1	191.7	138.7	85.8	19.1	33.5	50.0	3.5	1.1	-1.6	220.0	102.0	95.5	17.9	4.6	-28.4
'2	220.1	158.4	102.8	18.6	36.6	57.9	3.6	1.3	-1.1	244.4	107.7	111.9	18.8	6.6	-24.4
'3	250.4	173.1	109.6	19.9	43.3	74.0	3.8	1.3	-1.8	261.7	108.9	124.9	22.8	5.1	-11.3
'4	279.5	192.2	126.5	20.2	45.1	83.5	4.2	1.4	-1.8	293.3	118.0	145.7	26.0	3.2	-13.8
'5	277.2	187.0	120.7	22.2	43.6	87.5	4.9	1.5	-3.6	346.2	129.6	183.5	28.9	4.3	-69.0
'6	322.5	218.1	141.2	21.6	54.6	99.1	5.9	1.6	-2.2	374.3	137.2	198.5	33.8	4.9	-51.7
'7	363.4	247.4	162.2	22.9	61.6	110.3	6.7	1.9	-2.9	407.5	150.7	212.9	37.1	6.9	-44.1
'8	423.5	286.9	188.9	25.6	71.4	127.9	8.5	2.4	-2.1	450.0	163.3	232.7	45.3	8.7	-26.5
'9	486.2	326.2	224.6	26.0	74.4	148.9	10.7	2.8	-2.3	497.5	179.0	254.6	55.7	8.2	-11.3
'0	532.1	355.9	250.0	34.0	70.3	162.6	13.7	3.5	-3.6	585.7	207.5	299.1	69.7	9.4	-53.6
'1	619.4	408.1	290.6	50.3	65.7	191.8	18.3	3.8	-2.5	672.7	238.3	329.5	93.9	11.1	-53.3
'2	616.6	386.8	295.0	41.4	49.0	204.9	22.2	5.2	-2.4	748.5	263.3	358.8	111.8	14.5	-131.9
'3	642.3	393.6	286.2	44.8	61.3	221.8	23.8	6.0	-2.9	815.4	286.5	383.0	124.6	20.8	-173.0
'4	709.0	425.7	301.4	47.8	75.2	252.8	26.6	7.3	-3.4	877.1	310.0	396.5	150.3	20.6	-168.1
'5	773.3	460.6	336.0	46.4	76.3	276.5	29.1	9.4	-2.4	948.2	338.4	419.3	169.4	20.9	-175.0
'6	815.2	479.6	350.1	44.0	83.8	297.5	31.4	8.2	-1.5	1,006.0	358.2	445.1	178.2	24.5	-190.8
'7	896.6	544.0	392.5	46.3	103.2	315.9	27.9	10.0	-2.0	1,041.6	374.3	452.9	184.6	29.9	-145.0
'8	958.2	566.7	402.9	50.3	111.1	353.1	30.0	10.8	-2.3	1,092.7	382.5	481.9	199.3	29.0	-134.5
'9	1,037.4	621.7	451.5	50.2	117.2	376.3	28.6	12.4	-1.6	1,167.5	399.2	522.0	219.3	26.8	-130.1
'0	1,081.5	642.8	470.2	51.4	118.1	400.1	30.2	13.5	-5.1	1,253.5	419.8	569.9	237.5	26.4	-172.0
'1	1,101.3	636.1	461.3	62.2	109.9	418.6	30.1	17.9	-1.4	1,315.0	439.5	597.6	250.9	26.9	-213.7
'2	1,147.2	660.4	475.3	63.7	118.8	441.8	25.7	19.4	-1.1	1,444.6	445.2	718.7	251.3	29.5	-297.4
'3	1,222.5	713.4	505.5	66.7	138.5	463.6	26.2	21.1	-1.8	1,496.0	441.9	764.7	253.4	36.0	-273.5
'4	1,320.8	781.9	542.7	79.4	156.7	493.7	23.4	22.3	-.4	1,533.1	440.8	799.2	261.3	31.8	-212.3
'5	1,406.5	845.1	586.0	75.9	179.3	519.2	23.7	19.1	-.6	1,603.5	440.5	839.0	290.4	33.7	-197.0
'6	1,524.0	932.4	663.4	73.2	190.6	542.8	26.9	23.1	-1.2	1,665.8	446.3	888.3	297.3	34.0	-141.8
'7	1,653.1	1,030.6	744.3	78.2	203.0	576.4	25.9	19.9	-.3	1,708.9	457.7	918.8	300.0	32.4	-55.8
'8	1,773.8	1,116.8	825.8	81.1	204.2	613.8	21.5	21.5	.1	1,734.9	454.6	946.5	298.8	35.0	38.8
'9	1,891.2	1,195.7	893.0	83.9	213.0	651.6	21.5	22.7	.1	1,787.6	475.1	986.1	282.7	43.8	103.6
'0	2,053.8	1,313.6	999.1	87.8	219.4	691.7	25.2	25.7	-2.3	1,864.4	499.3	1,038.1	283.3	43.8	189.5
'1	2,016.2	1,252.2	994.5	85.8	164.7	717.5	24.9	27.1	-5.5	1,969.5	531.9	1,131.4	258.6	47.6	46.7
'2	1,853.2	1,075.5	830.5	87.3	150.5	734.3	20.2	24.8	-1.6	2,101.1	591.5	1,243.0	229.1	37.5	-247.9
'3	1,879.9	1,070.8	774.5	89.7	197.8	758.9	22.9	25.0	2.3	2,252.1	662.7	1,328.7	212.9	47.8	-372.1
'4	2,008.9	1,152.3	797.4	94.6	250.3	805.2	23.8	28.8	-1.2	2,379.5	723.7	1,390.6	221.0	44.2	-370.6
'5	2,266.9	1,383.0	930.7	99.2	341.0	850.0	24.0	15.0	-5.0	2,558.6	766.3	1,478.0	255.4	58.9	-291.7
'6	2,510.4	1,550.2	1,049.9	98.0	388.9	902.4	25.7	35.7	-3.6	2,711.6	811.8	1,568.1	282.3	49.4	-201.1
'7	2,651.2	1,644.5	1,167.3	97.7	365.4	942.3	29.2	37.5	-2.2	2,880.5	856.1	1,666.7	312.6	45.2	-229.3
'5: I	2,225.7	1,338.8	894.9	97.1	335.4	835.0	24.1	31.0	-3.2	2,504.4	758.2	1,458.7	233.4	54.2	-278.7
II	2,264.1	1,369.2	917.8	101.2	339.8	842.5	25.0	31.8	-4.4	2,533.6	760.3	1,461.7	253.4	58.2	-269.5
III	2,214.5	1,375.8	944.2	100.0	318.0	857.0	23.8	-35.8	-6.4	2,579.2	782.1	1,483.0	253.8	60.4	-364.7
IV	2,363.3	1,448.0	965.8	98.5	370.6	865.7	23.1	32.8	-6.2	2,617.1	764.5	1,508.7	281.0	62.9	-253.8
'6: I	2,453.6	1,504.7	1,018.8	97.8	377.3	893.6	23.7	34.7	-3.1	2,661.5	805.9	1,535.4	266.4	53.8	-207.9
II	2,487.6	1,535.1	1,031.6	98.2	394.4	895.7	24.9	35.5	-3.5	2,712.5	809.2	1,566.5	287.4	49.4	-225.0
III	2,531.9	1,570.9	1,056.0	98.6	404.6	902.6	26.0	36.0	-3.6	2,750.4	816.2	1,584.6	301.9	47.8	-218.4
IV	2,568.6	1,590.2	1,093.2	97.4	379.5	917.7	28.2	36.5	-4.0	2,721.8	816.0	1,586.0	273.3	46.5	-153.2
'7: I	2,612.8	1,615.2	1,139.5	97.7	365.6	937.1	28.4	37.0	-5.1	2,837.9	832.5	1,650.2	309.6	45.6	-225.2
II	2,648.1	1,648.2	1,157.1	96.9	381.5	936.4	29.0	37.2	-2.8	2,859.5	851.1	1,652.6	310.5	45.2	-211.4
III	2,664.9	1,654.4	1,178.1	98.2	365.1	943.3	29.8	37.6	-.2	2,909.2	869.1	1,671.4	323.9	44.8	-244.3
IV	2,679.2	1,660.0	1,194.7	98.0	349.5	952.3	29.5	38.2	-.9	2,915.6	871.6	1,692.5	306.4	45.1	-236.3
'8: I	2,672.5	1,634.9	1,201.2	95.8	322.5	968.9	29.9	39.4	-.5	3,003.2	898.0	1,729.2	329.4	46.6	-330.7
II	2,478.8	1,436.0	999.8	96.9	324.4	971.8	31.7	40.0	-.6	3,128.4	918.2	1,860.1	302.3	47.8	-649.6
III p	2,597.0	1,567.6	1,141.6	95.2	315.9	974.8	32.4	22.4	-.1	3,140.2	954.1	1,795.3	342.6	48.3	-543.2

[1] Includes taxes from the rest of the world, not shown separately.
[2] Includes an item for the difference between wage accruals and disbursements, not shown separately.
[3] Includes Federal grants-in-aid to State and local governments. See Table B–82 for data on Federal grants-in-aid.

Source: Department of Commerce (Bureau of Economic Analysis).

TABLE B–85.—*State and local government current receipts and expenditures, national income and product accounts (NIPA), 1959–2008*

[Billions of dollars; quarterly data at seasonally adjusted annual rates]

Year or quarter	Current receipts									Current expenditures					Net State and local government saving
	Total	Current tax receipts				Contributions for government social insurance	Income receipts on assets	Current transfer receipts [1]	Current surplus of government enterprises	Total [2]	Consumption expenditures	Government social benefit payments to persons	Interest payments	Subsidies	
		Total	Personal current taxes	Taxes on production and imports	Taxes on corporate income										
1959	40.6	33.8	3.8	28.8	1.2	0.4	1.1	4.2	1.1	36.9	30.7	4.3	1.8	0.0	3.8
1960	44.5	37.0	4.2	31.5	1.2	.5	1.3	4.5	1.2	40.2	33.5	4.6	2.1	.0	4.3
1961	48.1	39.7	4.6	33.8	1.3	.5	1.4	5.2	1.3	43.8	36.6	5.0	2.2	.0	4.3
1962	52.0	42.8	5.0	36.3	1.5	.5	1.5	5.8	1.4	46.8	39.0	5.3	2.4	.0	5.2
1963	56.0	45.8	5.4	38.7	1.7	.6	1.6	6.4	1.6	50.3	41.9	5.7	2.7	.0	5.7
1964	61.3	49.8	6.1	41.8	1.8	.7	1.9	7.3	1.6	54.9	45.8	6.2	2.9	.0	6.4
1965	66.5	53.9	6.6	45.3	2.0	.8	2.2	8.0	1.7	60.0	50.2	6.7	3.1	.0	6.5
1966	74.9	58.8	7.8	48.8	2.2	.8	2.6	11.1	1.6	67.2	56.1	7.6	3.4	.0	7.8
1967	82.5	64.0	8.6	52.8	2.6	.9	3.0	13.1	1.5	75.5	62.6	9.2	3.7	.0	7.0
1968	93.5	73.4	10.6	59.5	3.3	.9	3.5	14.2	1.5	86.0	70.4	11.4	4.2	.0	7.5
1969	105.5	82.5	12.8	66.0	3.6	1.0	4.3	16.2	1.5	97.5	79.9	13.2	4.4	.0	8.0
1970	120.1	91.3	14.2	73.3	3.7	1.1	5.2	21.1	1.5	113.0	91.5	16.1	5.3	.0	7.1
1971	134.9	101.7	15.9	81.5	4.3	1.2	5.5	25.2	1.4	128.5	102.7	19.3	6.5	.0	6.5
1972	158.4	115.6	20.9	89.4	5.3	1.3	5.9	34.0	1.6	142.8	113.2	22.0	7.5	.1	15.6
1973	174.3	126.3	22.8	97.4	6.0	1.5	7.8	37.3	1.5	158.6	126.0	24.1	8.5	.1	15.7
1974	188.1	136.0	24.5	104.8	6.7	1.7	10.2	39.3	.9	178.7	143.7	25.3	9.6	.1	9.3
1975	209.6	147.4	26.9	113.2	7.3	1.8	11.2	48.7	.4	207.1	165.1	30.8	11.1	.2	2.5
1976	233.7	165.7	31.1	125.0	9.6	2.2	10.4	55.0	.4	226.3	179.5	34.1	12.5	.2	7.4
1977	259.9	183.7	35.4	136.9	11.4	2.8	11.7	61.4	.3	246.8	195.9	37.0	13.7	.2	13.1
1978	287.6	198.2	40.5	145.6	12.1	3.4	14.7	71.1	.3	268.9	213.2	40.8	14.9	.2	18.7
1979	308.4	212.0	44.0	154.4	13.6	3.9	20.1	72.7	–.3	295.4	233.3	44.3	17.2	.3	13.0
1980	338.2	230.0	48.9	166.7	14.5	3.6	26.3	79.5	–1.2	329.4	258.4	51.2	19.4	.4	8.8
1981	370.2	255.8	54.6	185.7	15.4	3.9	32.0	81.0	–2.4	362.7	282.3	57.1	22.8	.4	7.6
1982	391.4	273.2	59.1	200.0	14.0	4.0	36.7	79.1	–1.6	393.6	304.9	61.2	27.1	.5	–2.2
1983	428.6	300.9	66.1	218.9	15.9	4.1	41.4	82.4	–.2	423.7	324.1	66.9	32.3	.4	4.9
1984	480.2	337.3	76.0	242.5	18.8	4.7	47.7	89.0	1.5	456.2	347.7	71.2	37.0	.4	23.9
1985	521.1	363.7	81.4	262.1	20.2	4.9	54.9	94.5	3.2	498.7	381.8	77.3	39.4	.3	22.3
1986	561.6	389.5	87.2	279.7	22.7	6.0	58.4	105.0	2.8	540.7	417.9	84.3	38.2	.3	21.0
1987	590.6	422.1	96.6	301.6	23.9	7.2	58.1	100.0	3.1	578.1	440.9	90.7	46.2	.3	12.4
1988	635.5	452.8	102.1	324.6	26.0	8.4	60.5	109.0	4.8	617.6	470.4	98.5	48.4	.4	17.9
1989	687.3	488.0	114.6	349.1	24.2	9.0	65.7	118.1	6.5	666.5	502.1	109.3	54.6	.4	20.8
1990	737.8	519.1	122.6	374.1	22.5	10.0	68.4	133.5	6.7	730.5	544.6	127.7	57.9	.4	7.2
1991	789.2	544.3	125.3	395.3	23.6	11.6	68.0	158.2	7.1	793.3	574.6	156.5	61.7	.4	–4.2
1992	845.7	579.8	135.3	420.1	24.4	13.1	64.8	180.3	7.7	845.0	602.7	180.0	61.9	.4	.7
1993	886.9	604.7	141.1	436.8	26.9	14.1	61.4	197.7	9.0	886.0	630.3	195.2	60.2	.4	.9
1994	942.9	644.2	148.0	466.3	30.0	14.5	63.2	211.9	9.0	932.4	663.3	206.7	62.0	.3	10.5
1995	990.2	672.1	158.1	482.4	31.7	13.6	68.4	224.1	12.0	978.2	696.1	217.6	64.2	.3	12.0
1996	1,043.3	709.6	168.7	507.9	33.0	12.5	73.3	234.1	13.9	1,017.5	724.8	224.3	68.1	.3	25.8
1997	1,097.4	749.9	182.0	533.8	34.1	10.8	77.8	246.6	12.3	1,058.3	758.9	227.6	71.4	.4	39.1
1998	1,163.2	794.9	201.2	558.8	34.9	10.4	80.9	266.8	10.2	1,111.2	801.4	235.8	73.6	.4	52.0
1999	1,236.7	840.4	214.5	590.2	35.8	9.8	85.3	290.8	10.4	1,186.3	858.9	252.4	74.6	.4	50.4
2000	1,319.5	893.2	236.6	621.1	35.5	11.0	92.2	315.4	7.7	1,269.5	917.8	271.7	79.5	.5	50.0
2001	1,373.0	915.8	242.7	642.8	30.2	13.6	88.8	350.8	4.0	1,368.2	969.8	305.2	85.5	7.7	4.8
2002	1,410.1	929.0	221.3	675.5	32.2	15.8	78.2	384.7	2.5	1,443.3	1,025.3	332.0	86.0	.9	–34.2
2003	1,494.2	979.4	226.6	717.5	35.3	19.8	72.9	422.7	–6	1,514.5	1,073.8	353.0	87.7	.1	–20.4
2004	1,594.3	1,061.2	249.0	769.2	43.0	23.6	75.4	437.2	–3.0	1,592.8	1,120.3	383.8	88.4	.4	1.5
2005	1,714.4	1,162.3	277.1	829.0	56.3	24.2	85.9	450.3	–8.3	1,684.9	1,191.2	403.5	89.9	.4	29.5
2006	1,811.4	1,242.2	303.3	878.2	60.7	23.1	94.7	456.5	–5.0	1,765.3	1,269.6	401.0	94.3	.4	46.2
2007	1,902.8	1,304.1	325.4	917.8	60.9	22.8	100.3	481.3	–5.7	1,892.4	1,355.9	430.8	98.5	7.1	10.4
2005: I	1,685.7	1,132.1	268.9	807.4	55.8	24.6	81.1	451.7	–3.9	1,644.5	1,159.1	396.3	88.7	.4	41.2
II	1,711.3	1,153.9	274.9	822.8	56.2	24.4	84.6	453.4	–4.9	1,673.1	1,174.1	409.4	89.2	.4	38.3
III	1,716.5	1,167.6	278.0	837.4	52.2	24.1	87.6	456.7	–19.5	1,697.3	1,203.1	403.7	90.2	.4	19.3
IV	1,743.8	1,195.8	286.7	848.3	60.8	23.8	90.2	439.2	–5.2	1,724.7	1,228.4	404.5	91.3	.4	19.1
2006: I	1,781.7	1,221.2	297.2	864.9	59.2	23.5	92.2	449.6	–4.7	1,724.2	1,240.8	390.3	92.7	.4	57.5
II	1,815.3	1,246.6	309.5	875.5	61.7	23.2	94.0	456.3	–4.8	1,752.2	1,260.2	397.7	93.9	.4	63.1
III	1,820.4	1,244.8	300.2	881.5	63.1	22.9	95.2	462.6	–5.5	1,788.1	1,281.8	410.6	95.3	.4	32.2
IV	1,828.4	1,256.2	306.4	890.9	59.0	22.8	96.9	457.6	–5.2	1,796.6	1,295.8	405.3	95.2	.4	31.8
2007: I	1,877.5	1,285.9	320.0	905.0	60.8	22.7	98.5	476.3	–5.8	1,854.3	1,318.7	436.8	96.9	1.9	23.2
II	1,909.8	1,311.5	332.3	915.4	63.7	22.7	99.8	481.5	–5.7	1,874.0	1,344.4	420.7	98.2	10.7	35.8
III	1,905.5	1,305.3	323.5	921.0	60.9	22.8	101.1	481.6	–5.3	1,900.7	1,365.3	427.6	99.1	8.8	4.7
IV	1,918.4	1,313.7	325.8	929.7	58.2	22.9	101.8	485.9	–5.9	1,940.7	1,395.2	438.3	100.0	7.3	–22.3
2008: I	1,922.9	1,317.0	333.7	929.9	53.3	23.3	102.9	486.4	–6.6	1,975.3	1,426.3	444.2	100.9	4.0	–52.4
II	1,955.4	1,343.3	346.4	942.4	54.5	23.6	103.9	491.8	–7.1	2,022.3	1,462.7	454.5	102.1	3.0	–66.9
III _p_	1,947.0	1,331.6	331.9	947.3	52.3	23.9	104.0	495.4	–7.9	2,048.8	1,486.1	458.4	102.2	2.2	–101.8

[1] Includes Federal grants-in-aid. See Table B–82 for data on Federal grants-in-aid.
[2] Includes an item for the difference between wage accruals and disbursements, not shown separately.

Source: Department of Commerce (Bureau of Economic Analysis).

TABLE B–86.—*State and local government revenues and expenditures, selected fiscal years, 1938–2006*

[Millions of dollars]

Fiscal year [1]	General revenues by source [2]							General expenditures by function [2]				
	Total	Property taxes	Sales and gross receipts taxes	Individual income taxes	Corporation net income taxes	Revenue from Federal Government	All other [3]	Total [4]	Education	Highways	Public welfare [4]	All other [4,5]
38	9,228	4,440	1,794	218	165	800	1,811	8,757	2,491	1,650	1,069	3,547
40	9,609	4,430	1,982	224	156	945	1,872	9,229	2,638	1,573	1,156	3,862
42	10,418	4,537	2,351	276	272	858	2,123	9,190	2,586	1,490	1,225	3,889
44	10,908	4,604	2,289	342	451	954	2,269	8,863	2,793	1,200	1,133	3,737
46	12,356	4,986	2,986	422	447	855	2,661	11,028	3,356	1,672	1,409	4,591
48	17,250	6,126	4,442	543	592	1,861	3,685	17,684	5,379	3,036	2,099	7,170
50	20,911	7,349	5,154	788	593	2,486	4,541	22,787	7,177	3,803	2,940	8,867
52	25,181	8,652	6,357	998	846	2,566	5,763	26,098	8,318	4,650	2,788	10,342
53	27,307	9,375	6,927	1,065	817	2,870	6,252	27,910	9,390	4,987	2,914	10,619
54	29,012	9,967	7,276	1,127	778	2,966	6,897	30,701	10,557	5,527	3,060	11,557
55	31,073	10,735	7,643	1,237	744	3,131	7,584	33,724	11,907	6,452	3,168	12,197
56	34,667	11,749	8,691	1,538	890	3,335	8,465	36,711	13,220	6,953	3,139	13,399
57	38,164	12,864	9,467	1,754	984	3,843	9,252	40,375	14,134	7,816	3,485	14,940
58	41,219	14,047	9,829	1,759	1,018	4,865	9,699	44,851	15,919	8,567	3,818	16,547
59	45,306	14,983	10,437	1,994	1,001	6,377	10,516	48,887	17,283	9,592	4,136	17,876
60	50,505	16,405	11,849	2,463	1,180	6,974	11,634	51,876	18,719	9,428	4,404	19,325
61	54,037	18,002	12,463	2,613	1,266	7,131	12,563	56,201	20,574	9,844	4,720	21,063
62	58,252	19,054	13,494	3,037	1,308	7,871	13,489	60,206	22,216	10,357	5,084	22,549
63	62,890	20,089	14,456	3,269	1,505	8,722	14,850	64,816	23,776	11,136	5,481	24,423
62–63	62,269	19,833	14,446	3,267	1,505	8,663	14,556	63,977	23,729	11,150	5,420	23,678
63–64	68,443	21,241	15,762	3,791	1,695	10,002	15,951	69,302	26,286	11,664	5,766	25,586
64–65	74,000	22,583	17,118	4,090	1,929	11,029	17,250	74,678	28,563	12,221	6,315	27,579
65–66	83,036	24,670	19,085	4,760	2,038	13,214	19,269	82,843	33,287	12,770	6,757	30,029
66–67	91,197	26,047	20,530	5,825	2,227	15,370	21,198	93,350	37,919	13,932	8,218	33,281
67–68	101,264	27,747	22,911	7,308	2,518	17,181	23,599	102,411	41,158	14,481	9,857	36,915
68–69	114,550	30,673	26,519	8,908	3,180	19,153	26,117	116,728	47,238	15,417	12,110	41,963
69–70	130,756	34,054	30,322	10,812	3,738	21,857	29,973	131,332	52,718	16,427	14,679	47,508
70–71	144,927	37,852	33,233	11,900	3,424	26,146	32,372	150,674	59,413	18,095	18,226	54,940
71–72	167,535	42,877	37,518	15,227	4,416	31,342	36,156	168,549	65,813	19,021	21,117	62,598
72–73	190,222	45,283	42,047	17,994	5,425	39,264	40,210	181,357	69,713	18,615	23,582	69,447
73–74	207,670	47,705	46,098	19,491	6,015	41,820	46,542	198,959	75,833	19,946	25,085	78,095
74–75	228,171	51,491	49,815	21,454	6,642	47,034	51,735	230,722	87,858	22,528	28,156	92,180
75–76	256,176	57,001	54,547	24,575	7,273	55,589	57,191	256,731	97,216	23,907	32,604	103,004
76–77	285,157	62,527	60,641	29,246	9,174	62,444	61,125	274,215	102,780	23,058	35,906	112,472
77–78	315,960	66,422	67,596	33,176	10,738	69,592	68,435	296,984	110,758	24,609	39,140	122,478
78–79	343,236	64,944	74,247	36,932	12,128	75,164	79,822	327,517	119,448	28,440	41,898	137,731
79–80	382,322	68,499	79,927	42,080	13,321	83,029	95,467	369,086	133,211	33,311	47,288	155,276
80–81	423,404	74,969	85,971	46,426	14,143	90,294	111,599	407,449	145,784	34,603	54,105	172,957
81–82	457,654	82,067	93,613	50,738	15,028	87,282	128,925	436,733	154,282	34,520	57,996	189,935
82–83	486,753	89,105	100,247	55,129	14,258	90,007	138,008	466,516	163,876	36,655	60,906	205,080
83–84	542,730	96,457	114,097	64,529	17,141	96,935	153,571	505,008	176,108	39,419	66,414	223,068
84–85	598,121	103,757	126,376	70,361	19,152	106,158	172,317	553,899	192,686	44,989	71,479	244,745
85–86	641,486	111,709	135,005	74,365	19,994	113,099	187,314	605,623	210,819	49,368	75,868	269,568
86–87	686,860	121,203	144,091	83,935	22,425	114,857	200,350	657,134	226,619	52,355	82,650	295,510
87–88	726,762	132,212	156,452	88,350	23,663	117,602	208,482	704,921	242,683	55,621	89,090	317,527
88–89	786,129	142,400	166,336	97,806	25,926	125,824	227,838	762,360	263,898	58,105	97,879	342,479
89–90	849,502	155,613	177,885	105,640	23,566	136,802	249,996	834,818	288,148	61,057	110,518	375,094
90–91	902,207	167,999	185,570	109,341	22,242	154,099	262,955	908,108	309,302	64,937	130,402	403,467
91–92	979,137	180,337	197,731	115,638	23,880	179,174	282,376	981,253	324,652	67,351	158,723	430,526
92–93	1,041,643	189,744	209,649	123,235	26,417	198,663	293,935	1,030,434	342,287	68,370	170,705	449,072
93–94	1,100,490	197,141	223,628	128,810	28,320	215,492	307,099	1,077,665	353,287	72,067	183,394	468,916
94–95	1,169,505	203,451	237,268	137,931	31,406	228,771	330,677	1,149,863	378,273	77,109	196,703	497,779
95–96	1,222,821	209,440	248,993	146,844	32,009	234,891	350,645	1,193,276	398,859	79,092	197,354	517,971
96–97	1,289,237	218,877	261,418	159,042	33,820	244,847	371,233	1,249,984	418,416	82,062	203,779	545,727
97–98	1,365,762	230,150	274,883	175,630	34,412	255,048	395,639	1,318,042	450,365	87,214	208,120	572,343
98–99	1,434,029	239,672	290,993	189,309	33,922	270,628	409,505	1,402,369	483,259	93,018	218,957	607,134
99–2000	1,541,322	249,178	309,290	211,661	36,059	291,950	443,186	1,506,797	521,612	101,336	237,336	646,512
00–01	1,647,161	263,689	320,217	226,334	35,296	324,033	477,592	1,626,066	563,575	107,235	261,622	693,634
01–02	1,684,879	279,191	324,123	202,832	28,152	360,546	490,035	1,736,866	594,694	115,295	285,464	741,413
02–03	1,763,212	296,683	337,787	199,407	31,369	389,264	508,702	1,821,917	621,335	116,696	310,783	772,102
03–04	1,889,741	318,242	360,629	215,215	33,716	425,683	536,256	1,907,915	655,361	118,179	339,895	794,481
04–05	2,026,724	335,981	384,383	242,273	43,138	438,432	582,517	2,017,039	689,057	124,602	367,488	835,892
05–06	2,186,018	359,109	412,114	268,599	52,931	452,233	641,032	2,128,449	727,967	135,412	374,927	890,143

[1] Fiscal years not the same for all governments. See Note.

[2] Excludes revenues or expenditures of publicly owned utilities and liquor stores and of insurance-trust activities. Intergovernmental receipts and payments tween State and local governments are also excluded.

[3] Includes motor vehicle license taxes, other taxes, and charges and miscellaneous revenues.

[4] Includes intergovernmental payments to the Federal Government.

[5] Includes expenditures for libraries, hospitals, health, employment security administration, veterans' services, air transportation, water transport and minals, parking facilities, transit subsidies, police protection, fire protection, correction, protective inspection and regulation, sewerage, natural resources, rks and recreation, housing and community development, solid waste management, financial administration, judicial and legal, general public buildings, other vernment administration, interest on general debt, and other general expenditures, not elsewhere classified.

Note.—Except for States listed, data for fiscal years listed from 1962–63 to 2005–06 are the aggregation of data for government fiscal years that ended in e 12-month period from July 1 to June 30 of those years; Texas used August and Alabama and Michigan used September as end dates. Data for 1963 and rlier years include data for government fiscal years ending during that particular calendar year.

Data prior to 1952 are not available for intervening years.

Source: Department of Commerce (Bureau of the Census).

[Billions of dollars]

End of year or month	Total Treasury securities outstanding [1]	Marketable							Nonmarketable				
		Total [2]	Treasury bills	Treasury notes	Treasury bonds	Treasury inflation-protected securities			Total	U.S. savings securities [3]	Foreign series [4]	Government account series	Other [5]
						Total	Notes	Bonds					
Fiscal year:													
1969	351.7	226.1	68.4	78.9	78.8				125.6	51.7	4.1	66.8	3
1970	369.0	232.6	76.2	93.5	63.0				136.4	51.3	4.8	76.3	4
1971	396.3	245.5	86.7	104.8	54.0				150.8	53.0	9.3	82.8	5
1972	425.4	257.2	94.6	113.4	49.1				168.2	55.9	19.0	89.6	3
1973	456.4	263.0	100.1	117.8	45.1				193.4	59.4	28.5	101.7	3
1974	473.2	266.6	105.0	128.4	33.1				206.7	61.9	25.0	115.4	4
1975	532.1	315.6	128.6	150.3	36.8				216.5	65.5	23.2	124.2	3
1976	619.3	392.6	161.2	191.8	39.6				226.7	69.7	21.5	130.6	4
1977	697.6	443.5	156.1	241.7	45.7				254.1	75.4	21.8	140.1	16
1978	767.0	485.2	160.9	267.9	56.4				281.8	79.8	21.7	153.3	27
1979	819.0	506.7	161.4	274.2	71.1				312.3	80.4	28.1	176.4	27
1980	906.4	594.5	199.8	310.9	83.8				311.9	72.7	25.2	189.8	24
1981	996.5	683.2	223.4	363.6	96.2				313.3	68.0	20.5	201.1	23
1982	1,140.9	824.4	277.9	442.9	103.6				316.5	67.3	14.6	210.5	24
1983	1,375.8	1,024.0	340.7	557.5	125.7				351.8	70.0	11.5	234.7	35
1984	1,559.6	1,176.6	356.8	661.7	158.1				383.0	72.8	8.8	259.5	41
1985	1,821.0	1,360.2	384.2	776.4	199.5				460.8	77.0	6.6	313.9	63
1986	2,122.7	1,564.3	410.7	896.9	241.7				558.4	85.6	4.1	365.9	102
1987	2,347.8	1,676.0	378.3	1,005.1	277.6				671.8	97.0	4.4	440.7	129
1988	2,599.9	1,802.9	398.5	1,089.6	299.9				797.0	106.2	6.3	536.5	148
1989	2,836.3	1,892.8	406.6	1,133.2	338.0				943.5	114.0	6.8	663.7	159
1990	3,210.9	2,092.8	482.5	1,218.1	377.2				1,118.2	122.2	36.0	779.4	180
1991	3,662.8	2,390.7	564.6	1,387.7	423.4				1,272.1	133.5	41.6	908.4	189
1992	4,061.8	2,677.5	634.3	1,566.3	461.8				1,384.3	148.3	37.0	1,011.0	188
1993	4,408.6	2,904.9	658.4	1,734.2	497.4				1,503.7	167.0	42.5	1,114.3	179
1994	4,689.5	3,091.6	697.3	1,867.5	511.8				1,597.9	176.4	42.0	1,211.7	167
1995	4,950.6	3,260.4	742.5	1,980.3	522.6				1,690.2	181.2	41.0	1,324.3	143
1996	5,220.8	3,418.4	761.2	2,098.7	543.5				1,802.4	184.1	37.5	1,454.7	126
1997	5,407.5	3,439.6	701.9	2,122.2	576.2	24.4	24.4		1,967.9	182.7	34.9	1,608.5	141
1998	5,518.7	3,331.0	637.6	2,009.1	610.4	58.8	41.9	17.0	2,187.7	180.8	35.1	1,777.3	194
1999	5,647.2	3,233.0	653.2	1,828.8	643.7	92.4	67.6	24.8	2,414.2	180.0	31.0	2,005.2	198
2000	5,622.1	2,992.8	616.2	1,611.3	635.3	115.0	81.6	33.4	2,629.3	177.7	25.4	2,242.9	183
2001 [1]	5,807.5	2,930.7	734.9	1,433.0	613.0	134.9	95.1	39.7	2,876.7	186.5	18.3	2,492.1	179
2002	6,228.2	3,136.7	868.3	1,521.6	593.0	138.9	93.7	45.1	3,091.5	193.3	12.5	2,707.3	178
2003	6,783.2	3,460.7	918.2	1,799.5	576.9	166.1	120.0	46.1	3,322.5	201.6	11.0	2,912.2	197
2004	7,379.1	3,846.1	961.5	2,109.6	552.0	223.0			3,533.0	204.2	5.9	3,130.0	192
2005	7,932.7	4,084.9	914.3	2,328.8	520.7	307.1			3,847.8	203.6	3.1	3,380.6	260
2006	8,507.0	4,303.0	911.5	2,447.2	534.7	395.6			4,203.9	203.7	3.0	3,722.7	274
2007	9,007.7	4,448.1	958.1	2,458.0	561.1	456.9			4,559.5	197.1	3.0	4,026.8	332
2008	10,024.7	5,236.0	1,489.8	2,624.8	582.9	524.5			4,788.7	194.3	3.0	4,297.7	293
2007: Jan	8,707.6	4,347.4	932.1	2,459.7	530.7	411.0			4,360.1	201.4	3.0	3,853.8	302
Feb	8,778.1	4,408.6	982.1	2,460.5	540.5	411.5			4,369.6	200.9	3.0	3,859.4	306
Mar	8,849.7	4,468.8	1,033.1	2,468.5	540.5	412.7			4,380.9	200.3	3.5	3,859.2	317
Apr	8,840.2	4,412.4	944.1	2,482.7	540.5	431.1			4,427.8	199.8	3.5	3,897.3	327
May	8,829.0	4,378.3	919.1	2,463.0	547.3	435.0			4,450.7	199.2	3.0	3,912.3	336
June	8,867.7	4,339.1	869.1	2,471.0	547.3	437.8			4,528.6	198.6	3.0	3,989.3	337
July	8,932.4	4,403.4	892.1	2,494.1	547.3	456.0			4,529.0	198.1	3.0	3,994.2	333
Aug	9,005.6	4,496.2	1,014.1	2,450.0	561.1	457.0			4,509.4	197.4	3.0	3,976.4	332
Sept	9,007.7	4,448.1	958.1	2,458.0	561.1	456.9			4,559.5	197.1	3.0	4,026.8	332
Oct	9,079.1	4,464.7	938.1	2,482.1	561.1	469.4			4,614.4	196.9	3.0	4,081.4	333
Nov	9,149.3	4,543.3	1,035.0	2,465.0	558.5	470.7			4,606.1	196.6	3.0	4,073.7	332
Dec	9,229.2	4,536.6	1,003.9	2,488.5	558.5	471.7			4,692.6	196.5	3.0	4,164.3	328
2008: Jan	9,238.0	4,532.9	984.4	2,503.9	558.5	472.0			4,705.1	195.7	5.9	4,181.7	321
Feb	9,358.1	4,661.4	1,125.4	2,478.4	571.8	471.8			4,696.7	195.6	5.3	4,175.6	320
Mar	9,437.6	4,732.4	1,158.4	2,514.1	571.8	474.1			4,705.2	195.4	4.9	4,183.7	321
Apr	9,377.6	4,642.6	1,025.7	2,540.7	571.8	490.3			4,735.0	195.3	4.9	4,213.6	321
May	9,388.8	4,685.2	1,119.2	2,476.6	581.1	494.3			4,703.6	195.2	3.3	4,190.8	314
June	9,492.0	4,696.4	1,060.5	2,543.4	581.1	497.5			4,795.6	195.0	3.1	4,288.1	309
July	9,585.5	4,822.1	1,135.8	2,574.8	581.1	516.5			4,763.4	194.8	3.0	4,266.0	299
Aug	9,645.8	4,901.9	1,227.2	2,556.4	582.9	521.4			4,743.9	194.5	3.0	4,250.9	295
Sept	10,024.7	5,236.0	1,489.8	2,624.8	582.9	524.5			4,788.7	194.3	3.0	4,297.7	293
Oct	10,574.1	5,729.4	1,909.7	2,686.6	582.9	536.2			4,844.7	194.2	4.0	4,358.4	288
Nov	10,661.2	5,822.7	2,003.7	2,674.9	594.6	535.4			4,838.5	194.2	4.0	4,353.7	286

[1] Data beginning with January 2001 are interest-bearing and non-interest-bearing securities; prior data are interest-bearing securities only.

[2] Data from 1986 to 2002 and 2005 to 2008 include Federal Financing Bank securities, not shown separately.

[3] Through 1996, series is U.S. savings bonds. Beginning 1997, includes U.S. retirement plan bonds, U.S. individual retirement bonds, and U.S. savings notes previously included in "other" nonmarketable securities.

[4] Nonmarketable certificates of indebtedness, notes, bonds, and bills in the Treasury foreign series of dollar-denominated and foreign-currency-denominated issues.

[5] Includes depository bonds; retirement plan bonds; Rural Electrification Administration bonds; State and local bonds; special issues held only by U.S. Government agencies and trust funds and the Federal home loan banks; for the period July 2003 through February 2004, depositary compensation securities; and beginning August 2008, Hope bonds for the HOPE For Homeowners Program.

Note.—Through fiscal year 1976, the fiscal year was on a July 1–June 30 basis; beginning with October 1976 (fiscal year 1977), the fiscal year is on an October 1–September 30 basis.

Source: Department of the Treasury.

End of year or month	Amount outstanding, privately held	Maturity class					Average length [1]	
		Within 1 year	1 to 5 years	5 to 10 years	10 to 20 years	20 years and over		
		Millions of dollars					Years	Months
cal year:								
1969	156,008	69,311	50,182	18,078	6,097	12,337	4	2
1970	157,910	76,443	57,035	8,286	7,876	8,272	3	8
1971	161,863	74,803	58,557	14,503	6,357	7,645	3	6
1972	165,978	79,509	57,157	16,033	6,358	6,922	3	3
1973	167,869	84,041	54,139	16,385	8,741	4,564	3	1
1974	164,862	87,150	50,103	14,197	9,930	3,481	2	11
1975	210,382	115,677	65,852	15,385	8,857	4,611	2	8
1976	279,782	150,296	90,578	24,169	8,087	6,652	2	7
1977	326,674	161,329	113,319	33,067	8,428	10,531	2	11
1978	356,501	163,819	132,993	33,500	11,383	14,805	3	3
1979	380,530	181,883	127,574	32,279	18,489	20,304	3	7
1980	463,717	220,084	156,244	38,809	25,901	22,679	3	9
1981	549,863	256,187	182,237	48,743	32,569	30,127	4	0
1982	682,043	314,436	221,783	75,749	33,017	37,058	3	11
1983	862,631	379,579	294,955	99,174	40,826	48,097	4	1
1984	1,017,488	437,941	332,808	130,417	49,664	66,658	4	6
1985	1,185,675	472,661	402,766	159,383	62,853	88,012	4	11
1986	1,354,275	506,903	467,348	189,995	70,664	119,365	5	3
1987	1,445,366	483,582	526,746	209,160	72,862	153,016	5	9
1988	1,555,208	524,201	552,993	232,453	74,186	171,375	5	9
1989	1,654,660	546,751	578,333	247,428	80,616	201,532	6	0
1990	1,841,903	626,297	630,144	267,573	82,713	235,176	6	1
1991	2,113,799	713,778	761,243	280,574	84,900	273,304	6	0
1992	2,363,802	808,705	866,329	295,921	84,706	308,141	5	11
1993	2,562,336	858,135	978,714	306,663	94,345	324,479	5	10
1994	2,719,861	877,932	1,128,322	289,998	88,208	335,401	5	8
1995	2,870,781	1,002,875	1,157,492	290,111	87,297	333,006	5	4
1996	3,011,185	1,058,558	1,212,258	306,643	111,360	322,366	5	3
1997	2,998,846	1,017,913	1,206,993	321,622	154,205	298,113	5	5
1998	2,856,637	940,572	1,105,175	319,331	157,347	334,212	5	10
1999	2,728,011	915,145	962,644	378,163	149,703	322,356	6	0
2000	2,469,152	858,903	791,540	355,382	167,082	296,246	6	2
2001	2,328,302	900,178	650,522	329,247	174,653	273,702	6	1
2002	2,492,821	939,986	802,032	311,176	203,816	235,811	5	6
2003	2,804,092	1,057,049	955,239	351,552	243,755	196,497	5	1
2004	3,145,244	1,127,850	1,150,979	414,728	243,036	208,652	4	11
2005	3,334,411	1,100,783	1,279,646	499,386	281,229	173,367	4	10
2006	3,496,359	1,140,553	1,295,589	589,748	290,733	179,736	4	11
2007	3,634,666	1,176,510	1,309,871	677,905	291,963	178,417	4	10
2008	4,745,256	2,042,003	1,468,455	719,347	352,430	163,022	4	1
07: Jan	3,554,471	1,124,464	1,335,480	634,734	290,298	169,494	4	10
Feb	3,613,660	1,171,311	1,332,822	640,611	298,399	170,517	4	10
Mar	3,649,732	1,220,193	1,324,286	636,049	298,554	170,648	4	9
Apr	3,611,093	1,128,525	1,357,728	655,774	298,188	170,878	4	10
May	3,573,898	1,123,310	1,305,310	682,977	286,028	176,272	4	11
June	3,514,691	1,075,672	1,296,936	679,143	286,376	176,564	4	11
July	3,598,529	1,102,053	1,349,349	677,402	292,887	176,838	4	11
Aug	3,702,458	1,215,692	1,333,432	682,935	291,975	178,425	4	10
Sept	3,634,666	1,176,510	1,309,871	677,905	291,963	178,417	4	10
Oct	3,671,046	1,171,587	1,332,632	696,633	291,857	178,337	4	10
Nov	3,749,458	1,272,770	1,309,028	692,196	310,684	164,780	4	9
Dec	3,781,877	1,295,981	1,309,642	700,562	310,814	164,878	4	9
08: Jan	3,805,408	1,315,046	1,295,456	710,580	319,185	165,140	4	9
Feb	3,933,939	1,454,105	1,294,886	691,672	319,156	174,120	4	8
Mar	4,127,033	1,607,155	1,323,534	702,527	319,481	174,336	4	5
Apr	4,079,776	1,509,658	1,366,837	709,124	338,330	155,827	4	6
May	4,162,323	1,618,739	1,329,756	718,171	333,602	162,056	4	6
June	4,203,441	1,580,568	1,396,177	730,327	334,145	162,224	4	6
July	4,328,809	1,668,784	1,439,791	716,694	341,086	162,453	4	5
Aug	4,386,440	1,774,790	1,390,479	706,395	351,906	162,870	4	5
Sept	4,745,256	2,042,003	1,468,455	719,347	352,430	163,022	4	1
Oct	5,238,827	2,462,352	1,496,698	764,782	352,076	162,919	3	10
Nov	5,312,125	2,540,826	1,490,667	761,948	355,148	163,536	3	10

[1] Treasury inflation-protected securities—notes, first offered in 1997, and bonds, first offered in 1998—are included in the average length calculation from 1997 forward.

Note.—Through fiscal year 1976, the fiscal year was on a July 1–June 30 basis; beginning with October 1976 (fiscal year 1977), the fiscal year is on an October 1–September 30 basis.

Data shown in this table are as of December 4, 2008.

Source: Department of the Treasury.

[Billions of dollars]

End of month	Total public debt [1]	Federal Reserve and Intragovernmental holdings [2]	Held by private investors									
			Total privately held	Depository institutions [3]	U.S. savings bonds [4]	Pension funds		Insurance companies	Mutual funds [6]	State and local governments	Foreign and international [7]	Other investors [8]
						Private [5]	State and local governments					
1994: Mar	4,575.9	1,476.0	3,099.9	397.4	175.0	120.1	224.3	233.4	212.8	443.4	661.1	63.
June	4,645.8	1,547.5	3,098.3	383.9	177.1	129.4	220.6	238.1	204.6	425.2	659.9	65
Sept	4,692.8	1,562.8	3,130.0	364.0	178.6	136.4	217.4	243.7	201.5	398.2	682.0	708
Dec	4,800.2	1,622.6	3,177.6	339.6	179.9	140.1	215.6	240.0	209.4	370.0	667.3	815
1995: Mar	4,864.1	1,619.3	3,244.8	352.9	181.4	142.1	225.0	244.2	210.5	350.5	707.0	831
June	4,951.4	1,690.1	3,261.3	339.9	182.6	142.9	217.2	245.0	202.4	313.7	762.5	855
Sept	4,974.0	1,688.0	3,286.0	330.8	183.5	142.3	211.3	245.2	211.5	304.3	820.4	838
Dec	4,988.7	1,681.0	3,307.7	315.4	185.0	143.0	208.2	241.5	224.9	289.8	835.2	864
1996: Mar	5,117.8	1,731.1	3,386.7	322.1	185.8	144.7	213.5	239.4	240.8	283.6	908.1	848
June	5,161.1	1,806.7	3,354.4	318.7	186.5	144.9	221.1	229.5	230.4	283.3	929.7	810
Sept	5,224.8	1,831.6	3,393.2	310.9	186.8	141.6	213.4	226.8	226.4	263.7	993.4	830
Dec	5,323.2	1,892.0	3,431.2	296.6	187.0	140.4	212.8	214.1	227.2	257.0	1,102.1	794
1997: Mar	5,380.9	1,928.7	3,452.2	317.3	186.5	141.7	211.1	181.8	221.6	248.1	1,157.6	788
June	5,376.2	1,998.9	3,377.3	300.2	186.3	142.1	214.9	183.1	216.4	243.3	1,182.7	708
Sept	5,413.1	2,011.5	3,401.6	292.8	186.2	143.0	223.5	186.8	221.3	235.2	1,230.5	682
Dec	5,502.4	2,087.8	3,414.6	300.3	186.5	144.1	219.0	176.6	232.3	239.3	1,241.6	674
1998: Mar	5,542.4	2,104.9	3,437.5	308.3	186.2	141.3	212.1	169.5	234.6	238.1	1,250.5	698
June	5,547.9	2,198.6	3,349.3	290.9	186.0	139.0	213.2	160.6	230.8	258.5	1,256.0	614
Sept	5,526.2	2,213.0	3,313.2	244.5	185.9	135.5	207.8	151.4	231.7	271.8	1,224.2	660
Dec	5,614.2	2,280.2	3,334.0	237.4	186.6	133.2	212.6	141.7	257.6	280.8	1,278.7	605
1999: Mar	5,651.6	2,324.1	3,327.5	247.4	186.5	135.5	211.5	137.5	245.0	288.4	1,272.3	603
June	5,638.8	2,439.6	3,199.2	240.6	186.5	142.9	213.8	133.6	228.1	298.6	1,258.8	496
Sept	5,656.3	2,480.9	3,175.4	241.2	186.2	150.9	204.8	128.0	222.5	299.2	1,281.4	46*
Dec	5,776.1	2,542.2	3,233.9	248.7	186.4	153.0	198.8	123.4	228.7	304.5	1,268.7	52*
2000: Mar	5,773.4	2,590.6	3,182.8	237.7	185.3	150.2	196.9	120.0	222.3	306.3	1,106.9	657
June	5,685.9	2,698.6	2,987.3	222.2	184.6	149.0	194.9	116.5	205.4	309.3	1,082.0	523
Sept	5,674.2	2,737.9	2,936.3	220.5	184.3	147.9	185.5	113.7	207.8	307.9	1,057.9	510
Dec	5,662.2	2,781.8	2,880.4	201.5	184.8	145.0	179.1	110.2	225.7	310.0	1,034.2	490
2001: Mar	5,773.7	2,880.9	2,892.8	188.0	184.8	153.4	177.3	109.1	225.3	316.9	1,029.9	508
June	5,726.8	3,004.2	2,722.6	188.1	185.5	148.5	183.1	108.1	221.0	324.8	1,000.5	363
Sept	5,807.5	3,027.8	2,779.7	189.5	186.4	149.9	166.8	106.8	234.1	321.2	1,005.5	419
Dec	5,943.4	3,123.9	2,819.5	181.5	190.3	144.6	155.1	105.7	261.9	328.4	1,051.2	400
2002: Mar	6,006.0	3,156.8	2,849.2	187.6	191.9	150.6	163.3	114.0	266.1	327.6	1,067.1	381
June	6,126.5	3,276.7	2,849.8	204.7	192.7	149.0	153.9	122.0	253.8	333.6	1,135.4	304
Sept	6,228.2	3,303.5	2,924.8	209.3	193.3	151.4	156.3	130.4	256.8	338.6	1,200.8	287
Dec	6,405.7	3,387.2	3,018.5	222.6	194.9	150.8	158.9	139.7	281.0	354.7	1,246.8	269
2003: Mar	6,460.8	3,390.8	3,069.9	153.6	196.9	162.9	162.1	139.5	296.6	350.0	1,286.3	322
June	6,670.1	3,505.4	3,164.7	145.4	199.1	167.3	161.3	138.7	302.3	347.9	1,382.8	320
Sept	6,783.2	3,515.3	3,268.0	147.0	201.5	164.6	155.5	137.4	287.1	357.7	1,454.2	362
Dec	6,998.0	3,620.1	3,377.9	153.3	203.8	169.2	148.6	136.5	280.8	364.2	1,533.0	388
2004: Mar	7,131.1	3,628.3	3,502.8	162.9	204.4	167.0	143.6	141.0	280.8	374.1	1,677.1	351
June	7,274.3	3,742.8	3,531.5	158.7	204.6	170.2	134.9	144.1	258.7	381.2	1,739.6	339
Sept	7,379.1	3,772.0	3,607.0	138.5	204.1	170.6	140.8	147.4	255.0	381.7	1,798.7	370
Dec	7,596.1	3,905.6	3,690.6	125.0	204.4	170.5	151.0	149.7	254.1	389.1	1,853.4	393
2005: Mar	7,776.9	3,921.6	3,855.4	141.8	204.2	174.3	158.0	152.4	261.1	412.0	1,956.3	395
June	7,836.5	4,033.5	3,803.0	127.0	204.2	177.5	171.3	155.0	248.7	444.0	1,879.6	395
Sept	7,932.7	4,067.8	3,864.9	125.4	203.6	180.9	164.8	159.0	244.7	467.6	1,930.6	388
Dec	8,170.4	4,199.8	3,970.6	112.2	205.1	181.2	153.8	160.4	251.3	481.4	2,036.0	384
2006: Mar	8,371.2	4,257.2	4,114.0	115.4	206.0	183.0	153.0	161.3	248.7	486.1	2,084.5	475
June	8,420.0	4,389.2	4,030.8	117.4	205.2	188.4	150.9	161.2	244.2	499.4	1,979.8	484
Sept	8,507.0	4,432.8	4,074.2	113.8	203.7	191.2	151.6	160.6	235.7	502.1	2,027.3	488
Dec	8,680.2	4,558.1	4,122.1	115.1	202.4	193.2	153.0	159.0	250.7	516.9	2,105.0	426
2007: Mar	8,849.7	4,576.6	4,273.1	119.9	200.3	198.5	155.1	150.8	264.2	535.0	2,196.7	452
June	8,867.7	4,715.1	4,152.6	110.6	198.6	202.2	156.1	142.1	267.2	550.3	2,193.9	33*
Sept	9,007.7	4,738.0	4,269.7	119.8	197.1	205.9	161.4	133.4	306.7	541.4	2,237.2	366
Dec	9,229.2	4,833.5	4,395.7	129.9	196.5	211.6	164.5	123.3	362.7	531.5	2,355.1	320
2008: Mar	9,437.6	4,694.7	4,742.9	127.9	195.4	222.1	165.0	123.4	464.7	523.6	2,515.6	405
June	9,492.0	4,685.8	4,806.2	115.4	195.0	226.0	167.3	123.4	449.8	522.2	2,647.9	355
Sept	10,024.7	4,680.8	5,343.9	....	194.3	....	....	....	....	....	2,862.0	....

[1] Face value.
[2] Federal Reserve holdings exclude Treasury securities held under repurchase agreements.
[3] Includes commercial banks, savings institutions, and credit unions.
[4] Current accrual value.
[5] Includes Treasury securities held by the Federal Employees Retirement System Thrift Savings Plan "G Fund."
[6] Includes money market mutual funds, mutual funds, and closed-end investment companies.
[7] Includes nonmarketable foreign series, Treasury securities, and Treasury deposit funds. Excludes Treasury securities held under repurchase agreements in custody accounts at the Federal Reserve Bank of New York. Estimates reflect benchmarks to this series at differing intervals; for further detail, see *Treasury Bulletin*.
[8] Includes individuals, Government-sponsored enterprises, brokers and dealers, bank personal trusts and estates, corporate and noncorporate businesses, and other investors.

Note.—Data shown in this table are as of December 4, 2008.

Source: Department of the Treasury.

CORPORATE PROFITS AND FINANCE

Table B–90.—*Corporate profits with inventory valuation and capital consumption adjustments, 1959–2008*

[Billions of dollars; quarterly data at seasonally adjusted annual rates]

Year or quarter	Corporate profits with inventory valuation and capital consumption adjustments	Taxes on corporate income	Corporate profits after tax with inventory valuation and capital consumption adjustments		
			Total	Net dividends	Undistributed profits with inventory valuation and capital consumption adjustments
59	55.7	23.7	32.0	12.6	19.4
60	53.8	22.8	31.0	13.4	17.6
61	54.9	22.9	32.0	13.9	18.1
62	63.3	24.1	39.2	15.0	24.1
63	69.0	26.4	42.6	16.2	26.4
64	76.5	28.2	48.3	18.2	30.1
65	87.5	31.1	56.4	20.2	36.2
66	93.2	33.9	59.3	20.7	38.7
67	91.3	32.9	58.4	21.5	36.9
68	98.8	39.6	59.2	23.5	35.6
69	95.4	40.0	55.4	24.2	31.2
70	83.6	34.8	48.9	24.3	24.6
71	98.0	38.2	59.9	25.0	34.8
72	112.1	42.3	69.7	26.8	42.9
73	125.5	50.0	75.5	29.9	45.6
74	115.8	52.8	63.0	33.2	29.8
75	134.8	51.6	83.2	33.0	50.2
76	163.3	65.3	98.1	39.0	59.0
77	192.4	74.4	118.0	44.8	73.2
78	216.6	84.9	131.8	50.8	81.0
79	223.2	90.0	133.2	57.5	75.7
80	201.1	87.2	113.9	64.1	49.9
81	226.1	84.3	141.8	73.8	68.0
82	209.7	66.5	143.2	77.7	65.4
83	264.2	80.6	183.6	83.5	100.1
84	318.6	97.5	221.1	90.8	130.3
85	330.3	99.4	230.9	97.6	133.4
86	319.5	109.7	209.8	106.2	103.7
87	368.8	130.4	238.4	112.3	126.1
88	432.6	141.6	291.0	129.9	161.1
89	426.6	146.1	280.5	158.0	122.6
90	437.8	145.4	292.4	169.1	123.3
91	451.2	138.6	312.6	180.7	131.9
92	479.3	148.7	330.6	187.9	142.7
93	541.9	171.0	370.9	202.8	168.1
94	600.3	193.7	406.5	234.7	171.8
95	696.7	218.7	478.0	254.2	223.8
96	786.2	231.7	554.5	297.6	256.9
97	868.5	246.1	622.4	334.5	287.9
98	801.6	248.3	553.3	351.6	201.7
99	851.3	258.6	592.6	337.4	255.3
00	817.9	265.2	552.7	377.9	174.8
01	767.3	204.1	563.2	370.9	192.3
02	886.3	192.6	693.7	399.2	294.5
03	993.1	243.3	749.9	424.7	325.1
04	1,231.2	307.4	923.9	539.5	384.4
05	1,447.9	413.7	1,034.2	577.4	456.9
06	1,668.5	468.9	1,199.6	702.1	497.5
07	1,642.4	450.4	1,192.0	788.7	403.4
05: I	1,438.2	407.2	1,031.0	553.0	478.0
II	1,472.4	412.0	1,060.4	561.6	498.8
III	1,342.6	386.4	956.2	581.4	374.8
IV	1,538.6	449.2	1,089.4	613.4	476.0
06: I	1,634.2	453.8	1,180.3	652.8	527.5
II	1,681.6	474.8	1,206.8	688.8	518.0
III	1,713.8	487.2	1,226.6	720.9	505.6
IV	1,644.5	459.8	1,184.8	745.8	439.0
07: I	1,617.8	448.5	1,169.3	761.5	407.8
II	1,672.5	468.5	1,204.0	779.2	424.8
III	1,668.3	451.1	1,217.3	797.6	419.7
IV	1,611.1	433.5	1,177.6	816.4	361.2
08: I	1,593.5	402.9	1,190.6	832.5	358.1
II	1,533.3	406.8	1,126.5	846.4	280.0
III p	1,518.7	396.9	1,121.8	841.4	280.4

Source: Department of Commerce (Bureau of Economic Analysis).

TABLE B-91.—Corporate profits by industry, 1959-2008

[Billions of dollars; quarterly data at seasonally adjusted annual rates]

Corporate profits with inventory valuation adjustment and without capital consumption adjustment

Year or quarter	Total	Domestic industries Total	Financial Total	Financial Federal Reserve banks	Financial Other	Nonfinancial Total	Nonfinancial Manufacturing[1]	Nonfinancial Transportation[2]	Nonfinancial Utilities	Nonfinancial Wholesale trade	Nonfinancial Retail trade	Nonfinancial Information	Nonfinancial Other	Rest of the world
SIC:[3]														
1959	53.5	50.8	7.6	0.7	6.9	43.2	26.5	7.1	....	2.9	3.3	....	3.4	
1960	51.5	48.3	8.4	.9	7.5	39.9	23.8	7.5	....	2.5	2.8	....	3.3	
1961	51.8	48.5	8.3	.8	7.6	40.2	23.4	7.9	....	2.5	3.0	....	3.4	
1962	57.0	53.3	8.6	.9	7.7	44.7	26.3	8.5	....	2.8	3.4	....	3.6	
1963	62.1	58.1	8.3	1.0	7.3	49.8	29.7	9.5	....	2.8	3.6	....	4.1	
1964	68.6	64.1	8.8	1.1	7.6	55.4	32.6	10.2	....	3.4	4.5	....	4.7	
1965	78.9	74.2	9.3	1.3	8.0	64.9	39.8	11.0	....	3.8	4.9	....	5.4	
1966	84.6	80.1	10.7	1.7	9.1	69.3	42.6	12.0	....	4.0	4.9	....	5.9	
1967	82.0	77.2	11.2	2.0	9.2	66.0	39.2	10.9	....	4.1	5.7	....	6.1	
1968	88.8	83.2	12.8	2.5	10.3	70.4	41.9	11.0	....	4.6	6.4	....	6.6	
1969	85.5	78.9	13.6	3.1	10.5	65.3	37.3	10.7	....	4.9	6.4	....	6.1	
1970	74.4	67.3	15.4	3.5	11.9	52.0	27.5	8.3	....	4.4	6.0	....	5.8	
1971	88.3	80.4	17.6	3.3	14.3	62.8	35.1	8.9	....	5.2	7.2	....	6.4	
1972	101.2	91.7	19.1	3.3	15.8	72.6	41.9	9.5	....	6.9	7.4	....	7.0	
1973	115.3	100.4	20.5	4.5	16.0	79.9	47.2	9.1	....	8.2	6.6	....	8.7	
1974	109.5	92.1	20.2	5.7	14.5	71.9	41.4	7.6	....	11.5	2.3	....	9.1	
1975	135.0	120.4	20.2	5.6	14.6	100.2	55.2	11.0	....	13.8	8.2	....	12.0	
1976	165.6	149.0	25.0	5.9	19.1	124.1	71.3	15.3	....	12.9	10.5	....	14.0	
1977	194.7	175.6	31.9	6.1	25.8	143.7	79.3	18.6	....	15.6	12.4	....	17.8	
1978	222.4	199.6	39.5	7.6	31.9	160.0	90.5	21.8	....	15.6	12.3	....	19.8	
1979	231.8	197.2	40.3	9.4	30.9	156.8	89.6	17.0	....	18.8	9.8	....	21.6	
1980	211.4	175.9	34.0	11.8	22.2	141.9	78.3	18.4	....	17.2	6.2	....	21.8	
1981	219.1	189.4	29.1	14.4	14.7	160.3	91.1	20.3	....	22.4	9.9	....	16.7	
1982	191.0	158.5	26.0	15.2	10.8	132.4	67.1	23.1	....	19.6	13.4	....	9.2	
1983	226.5	191.4	35.5	14.6	20.9	155.9	76.2	29.5	....	21.0	18.7	....	10.4	
1984	264.6	228.1	34.4	16.4	18.0	193.7	91.8	40.1	....	29.5	21.1	....	11.1	
1985	257.5	219.4	45.9	16.3	29.5	173.5	84.3	33.8	....	23.9	22.2	....	9.2	
1986	253.0	213.5	56.8	15.5	41.2	156.8	57.9	35.8	....	24.1	23.5	....	15.5	
1987	301.4	253.4	59.8	15.7	44.1	193.5	86.3	41.9	....	18.6	23.4	....	23.4	
1988	363.9	306.9	68.7	17.6	51.1	238.2	121.2	48.4	....	20.1	20.3	....	28.3	
1989	367.4	300.3	77.9	20.2	57.8	222.3	110.9	43.3	....	21.8	20.8	....	25.5	
1990	396.6	320.5	94.4	21.4	73.0	226.1	113.1	44.2	....	19.2	20.7	....	29.0	
1991	427.9	351.4	124.2	20.3	103.9	227.3	98.0	53.3	....	21.7	26.7	....	27.5	
1992	458.3	385.2	129.8	17.8	111.9	255.4	99.5	58.4	....	25.1	32.6	....	39.7	
1993	513.1	436.1	136.8	16.2	120.6	299.3	115.6	69.5	....	26.3	39.1	....	48.9	
1994	564.6	487.6	119.9	18.1	101.8	367.7	147.0	83.2	....	30.9	46.2	....	60.4	
1995	656.0	563.2	162.2	22.5	139.7	401.0	173.7	85.8	....	27.3	43.1	....	71.2	
1996	736.1	634.2	172.6	22.1	150.5	461.6	188.8	91.3	....	39.8	51.9	....	89.7	10
1997	812.3	701.4	193.0	23.8	169.2	508.4	209.0	84.2	....	47.6	64.2	....	103.4	1
1998	738.5	635.5	165.9	25.2	140.7	469.6	173.5	78.9	....	52.3	73.4	....	91.5	10
1999	776.8	655.3	196.4	26.3	170.1	458.9	175.2	56.8	....	52.6	74.6	....	99.7	12
2000	759.3	613.6	203.8	30.8	173.0	409.8	166.3	43.8	....	56.9	70.1	....	72.8	14
NAICS:[3]														
1998	738.5	635.5	165.4	25.2	140.2	470.1	157.0	21.0	32.7	53.2	66.4	20.1	119.8	1
1999	776.8	655.3	194.3	26.3	168.0	461.1	150.6	16.1	33.1	55.5	65.2	10.5	130.1	12
2000	759.3	613.6	200.2	30.8	169.4	413.4	144.3	14.9	24.4	59.7	59.6	−17.6	128.2	14
2001	719.2	549.5	227.6	28.3	199.3	322.0	52.6	1.3	24.7	52.1	71.0	−25.6	145.9	16
2002	766.2	610.4	276.4	23.7	252.7	334.0	48.2	−.9	10.6	49.3	79.4	−8.5	155.8	15
2003	894.5	729.0	317.3	20.1	297.2	411.8	76.0	7.3	11.6	55.2	86.8	3.2	171.7	1.
2004	1,161.6	968.2	348.9	20.0	328.9	619.3	152.7	14.1	18.6	79.2	91.1	43.9	219.7	1.
2005	1,582.8	1,343.3	425.3	26.6	398.7	918.1	243.8	29.1	28.9	97.3	120.4	79.7	318.9	2.
2006	1,834.2	1,566.7	478.8	33.8	445.0	1,087.9	304.3	42.5	55.6	107.5	132.3	91.1	354.7	2.
2007	1,835.1	1,490.5	449.9	37.7	412.2	1,040.6	316.6	42.7	58.5	102.6	132.3	103.0	284.9	3.
2006: I	1,778.7	1,528.3	470.0	31.0	439.0	1,058.3	279.2	39.3	44.9	102.3	133.5	87.2	371.8	2.
II	1,841.6	1,571.9	493.1	33.6	459.5	1,078.8	305.8	44.2	53.5	94.5	126.0	91.3	363.7	2.
III	1,887.2	1,626.7	473.3	35.8	437.5	1,153.4	333.5	42.2	62.5	128.3	132.1	95.8	359.1	2.
IV	1,829.3	1,540.0	478.8	34.9	443.8	1,061.2	298.9	44.4	61.4	104.9	137.5	89.9	324.2	2.
2007: I	1,794.7	1,496.6	454.1	38.2	415.9	1,042.5	317.0	40.7	57.2	108.2	132.8	100.8	285.8	2.
II	1,859.5	1,556.7	492.7	38.5	454.2	1,064.0	350.8	45.4	54.7	112.7	145.9	85.0	269.4	3.
III	1,866.1	1,509.7	460.3	37.5	422.8	1,049.3	306.6	47.0	58.7	109.1	126.0	108.4	293.5	3.
IV	1,820.2	1,398.9	392.4	36.5	355.9	1,006.5	292.1	37.7	63.2	80.2	124.5	117.9	290.9	4.
2008: I	1,641.5	1,243.1	412.8	35.8	377.1	830.2	240.5	24.4	46.2	49.2	112.0	106.0	252.0	3.
II	1,596.0	1,222.5	383.2	31.0	352.2	839.3	214.9	24.8	56.7	59.4	92.7	115.0	275.8	3.
III p	1,606.9	1,234.3	322.7	34.4	288.2	911.6								3.

[1] See Table B-92 for industry detail.
[2] Data on Standard Industrial Classification (SIC) basis include transportation and public utilities. Those on North American Industry Classification System (NAICS) basis include transporation and warehousing. Utilities classified separately in NAICS (as shown beginning 1998).
[3] SIC-based industry data use the 1987 SIC for data beginning in 1987 and the 1972 SIC for prior data. NAICS-based data use 1997 NAICS.

Note.—Industry data on SIC basis and NAICS basis are not necessarily the same and are not strictly comparable.

Source: Department of Commerce (Bureau of Economic Analysis).

[Billions of dollars; quarterly data at seasonally adjusted annual rates]

| | Corporate profits with inventory valuation adjustment and without capital consumption adjustment | | | | | | | | | | | |
| | Durable goods [2] | | | | | | Nondurable goods [2] | | | | |
Year or quarter	Total manufacturing	Total [1]	Fabricated metal products	Machinery	Computer and electronic products	Electrical equipment, appliances, and components	Motor vehicles, bodies and trailers, and parts	Other	Total	Food and beverage and tobacco products	Chemical products	Petroleum and coal products	Other
SIC:[3]													
1959	26.5	13.7	1.1	2.2	....	1.7	3.0	3.5	12.9	2.5	3.5	2.6	4.3
1960	23.8	11.6	.8	1.8		1.3	3.0	2.7	12.2	2.2	3.1	2.6	4.2
1961	23.4	11.3	1.0	1.9		1.3	2.5	2.9	12.1	2.4	3.3	2.3	4.2
1962	26.3	14.1	1.2	2.4		1.5	4.0	3.4	12.3	2.4	3.2	2.2	4.4
1963	29.7	16.4	1.3	2.6		1.6	4.9	4.0	13.3	2.7	3.7	2.2	4.7
1964	32.6	18.1	1.5	3.3		1.7	4.6	4.4	14.5	2.7	4.1	2.4	5.3
1965	39.8	23.3	2.1	4.0		2.7	6.2	5.2	16.5	2.9	4.6	2.9	6.1
1966	42.6	24.1	2.4	4.6		3.0	5.2	5.2	18.6	3.3	4.9	3.4	6.9
1967	39.2	21.3	2.5	4.2		3.0	4.0	4.9	18.0	3.3	4.3	4.0	6.4
1968	41.9	22.5	2.3	4.2		2.9	5.5	5.6	19.4	3.2	5.3	3.8	7.1
1969	37.3	19.2	2.0	3.8		2.3	4.8	4.9	18.1	3.1	4.6	3.4	7.0
1970	27.5	10.5	1.1	3.1		1.3	1.3	2.9	17.0	3.2	3.9	3.7	6.1
1971	35.1	16.6	1.5	3.1		2.0	5.2	4.1	18.5	3.6	4.5	3.8	6.6
1972	41.9	22.7	2.2	4.5		2.9	6.0	5.6	19.2	3.0	5.3	3.3	7.6
1973	47.2	25.1	2.7	4.9		3.2	5.9	6.2	22.0	2.5	6.2	5.4	7.9
1974	41.4	15.3	1.8	3.3		.6	.7	4.0	26.1	2.6	5.3	10.9	7.3
1975	55.2	20.6	3.3	5.1		2.6	2.3	4.7	34.5	8.6	6.4	10.1	9.5
1976	71.3	31.4	3.9	6.9		3.8	7.4	7.3	39.9	7.1	8.2	13.5	11.1
1977	79.3	37.9	4.5	8.6		5.9	9.4	8.5	41.4	6.9	7.8	13.1	13.6
1978	90.5	45.4	5.0	10.7		6.7	9.0	10.5	45.1	6.2	8.3	15.8	14.8
1979	89.6	37.1	5.3	9.5		5.6	4.7	8.5	52.5	5.8	7.2	24.8	14.7
1980	78.3	18.9	4.4	8.0		5.2	-4.3	2.7	59.5	6.1	5.7	34.7	13.1
1981	91.1	19.5	4.5	9.0		5.2	.3	-2.6	71.6	9.2	8.0	40.0	14.5
1982	67.1	5.0	2.7	3.1		1.7	.0	2.1	62.1	7.3	5.1	34.7	15.0
1983	76.2	19.5	3.1	4.0		3.5	5.3	8.4	56.7	6.3	7.4	23.9	19.1
1984	91.8	39.3	4.7	6.0		5.1	9.2	14.6	52.6	6.8	8.2	17.6	20.1
1985	84.3	29.7	4.9	5.7		2.6	7.4	10.1	54.6	8.8	6.6	18.7	20.5
1986	57.9	26.3	5.2	.8		2.7	4.6	12.1	31.7	7.5	7.5	-4.7	21.3
1987	86.3	40.7	5.5	5.4		5.9	3.7	17.6	45.6	11.4	14.4	-1.5	21.3
1988	121.2	54.1	6.5	11.1		7.7	6.2	16.5	67.1	12.0	18.6	12.7	23.7
1989	110.9	51.2	6.4	12.2		9.3	2.7	14.2	59.7	11.1	18.2	6.5	23.9
1990	113.1	43.8	6.0	11.8		8.5	-1.9	15.9	69.2	14.3	16.8	16.4	21.7
1991	98.0	34.4	5.3	5.7		10.0	-5.4	17.3	63.6	18.1	16.2	7.3	22.0
1992	99.5	40.6	6.2	7.5		10.4	-1.0	17.4	59.0	18.2	16.0	-.9	25.6
1993	115.6	55.8	7.4	7.5		15.2	6.0	19.4	59.7	16.4	15.9	2.7	24.7
1994	147.0	74.4	11.1	9.1		22.8	7.8	21.3	72.6	19.9	23.2	1.2	28.3
1995	173.7	80.9	11.8	14.8		21.5	.0	25.8	92.8	27.1	27.9	7.1	30.6
1996	188.8	90.6	14.5	16.9		20.1	4.2	29.2	98.2	22.1	26.4	15.0	34.7
1997	209.0	103.1	17.0	16.7		25.3	4.8	33.0	105.9	24.6	32.3	17.3	31.7
1998	173.5	87.3	16.4	19.5		8.9	5.9	30.1	86.2	21.9	26.5	6.7	31.1
1999	175.2	78.8	16.2	12.4		5.3	7.3	35.3	96.4	28.1	25.2	4.3	38.9
2000	166.3	64.8	15.4	16.3		4.7	-1.5	28.8	101.5	25.7	16.0	29.1	30.7
NAICS:[3]													
1998	157.0	83.4	16.7	15.6	3.9	6.1	6.4	34.6	73.6	21.8	25.1	4.9	21.8
1999	150.6	72.3	16.5	12.4	-6.5	6.3	7.3	36.4	78.3	30.7	23.0	1.8	22.7
2000	144.3	60.0	15.5	8.2	4.0	5.6	-1.0	27.7	84.3	25.4	14.2	26.9	17.8
2001	52.6	-25.4	9.9	2.7	-48.5	1.9	-9.2	17.8	78.0	28.0	12.6	29.6	7.8
2002	48.2	-9.9	8.9	1.7	-35.3	-.1	-5.0	20.0	58.1	24.9	18.4	1.6	13.2
2003	76.0	-5.9	7.9	1.5	-15.6	2.1	-12.3	10.5	81.9	23.6	19.5	23.3	15.5
2004	152.7	38.3	11.9	7.2	-4.9	.3	-7.6	31.3	114.5	24.2	25.4	48.9	16.0
2005	243.8	93.3	17.8	14.9	7.9	-1.6	.1	54.2	150.5	26.2	25.8	78.9	19.6
2006	304.3	115.9	19.2	20.0	14.1	8.4	-8.4	62.6	188.4	33.8	53.8	77.5	23.4
2007	316.6	127.4	21.7	22.3	13.5	10.9	-5.9	64.9	189.3	38.5	66.4	66.9	17.5
2006: I	279.2	110.8	20.8	19.6	10.5	4.1	-5.9	61.7	168.4	28.1	46.3	75.4	18.6
II	305.8	99.8	17.8	19.8	15.1	7.6	-9.1	48.5	206.0	31.5	59.0	91.5	24.1
III	333.5	127.0	17.6	19.7	17.6	10.2	-9.8	71.7	206.4	36.9	61.4	88.1	20.0
IV	298.9	126.1	20.7	20.8	13.3	11.8	-9.0	68.5	172.9	38.7	48.4	54.8	30.9
2007: I	317.0	127.2	21.5	22.7	16.4	11.6	-8.7	63.7	189.8	33.5	62.1	71.7	22.5
II	350.8	123.1	20.0	22.4	9.0	9.6	-2.7	64.8	227.8	42.7	64.6	106.7	13.8
III	306.6	130.9	22.5	22.2	13.2	10.7	-4.4	66.8	175.7	39.2	65.1	55.6	15.9
IV	292.1	128.3	22.8	22.0	15.4	11.5	-7.7	64.3	163.8	38.7	73.8	33.6	17.8
2008: I	240.5	85.5	18.9	19.2	14.4	6.9	-19.9	46.1	155.0	34.8	60.2	48.8	11.1
II	214.9	54.2	15.1	14.8	6.6	5.9	-27.4	39.3	160.7	40.9	78.5	36.6	4.7

[1] For Standard Industrial Classification (SIC) data, includes primary metal industries, not shown separately.

[2] Industry groups shown in column headings reflect North American Industry Classification System (NAICS) classification for data beginning 1998. For data on SIC basis, the industry groups would be industrial machinery and equipment (now machinery), electronic and other electric equipment (now electrical equipment, appliances, and components), motor vehicles and equipment (now motor vehicles, bodies and trailers, and parts), food and kindred products (now food and beverage and tobacco products), and chemicals and allied products (now chemical products).

[3] See footnote 3 and Note, Table B–91.

Source: Department of Commerce (Bureau of Economic Analysis).

[Billions of dollars]

	All manufacturing corporations				Durable goods industries				Nondurable goods industries			
Year or quarter	Sales (net)	Profits		Stock-holders' equity²	Sales (net)	Profits		Stock-holders' equity²	Sales (net)	Profits		Stock-holders' equity²
		Before income taxes¹	After income taxes			Before income taxes¹	After income taxes			Before income taxes¹	After income taxes	
1965	492.2	46.5	27.5	211.7	257.0	26.2	14.5	105.4	235.2	20.3	13.0	106.3
1966	554.2	51.8	30.9	230.3	291.7	29.2	16.4	115.2	262.4	22.6	14.6	115.1
1967	575.4	47.8	29.0	247.6	300.6	25.7	14.6	125.0	274.8	22.0	14.4	122.6
1968	631.9	55.4	32.1	265.9	335.5	30.6	16.5	135.6	296.4	24.8	15.5	130.3
1969	694.6	58.1	33.2	289.9	366.5	31.5	16.9	147.6	328.1	26.6	16.4	142.3
1970	708.8	48.1	28.6	306.8	363.1	23.0	12.9	155.1	345.7	25.2	15.7	151.7
1971	751.1	52.9	31.0	320.8	381.8	26.5	14.5	160.4	369.3	26.5	16.5	160.5
1972	849.5	63.2	36.5	343.4	435.8	33.6	18.4	171.4	413.7	29.6	18.0	172.0
1973	1,017.2	81.4	48.1	374.1	527.3	43.6	24.8	188.7	489.9	37.8	23.3	185.4
1973: IV	275.1	21.4	13.0	386.4	140.1	10.8	6.3	194.7	135.0	10.6	6.7	191.7
New series:												
1973: IV	236.6	20.6	13.2	368.0	122.7	10.1	6.2	185.8	113.9	10.5	7.0	182.1
1974	1,060.6	92.1	58.7	395.0	529.0	41.1	24.7	196.0	531.6	51.0	34.1	199.0
1975	1,065.2	79.9	49.1	423.4	521.1	35.3	21.4	208.1	544.1	44.6	27.7	215.3
1976	1,203.2	104.9	64.5	462.7	589.6	50.7	30.8	224.3	613.7	54.3	33.7	238.4
1977	1,328.1	115.1	70.4	496.7	657.3	57.9	34.8	239.9	670.8	57.2	35.5	256.8
1978	1,496.4	132.5	81.1	540.5	760.7	69.6	41.8	262.6	735.7	62.9	39.3	277.9
1979	1,741.8	154.2	98.7	600.5	865.7	72.4	45.2	292.5	876.1	81.8	53.5	308.0
1980	1,912.8	145.8	92.6	668.1	889.1	57.4	35.6	317.7	1,023.7	88.4	56.9	350.4
1981	2,144.7	158.6	101.3	743.4	979.5	67.2	41.6	350.4	1,165.2	91.3	59.6	393.0
1982	2,039.4	108.2	70.9	770.2	913.1	34.7	21.7	355.5	1,126.4	73.6	49.3	414.7
1983	2,114.3	133.1	85.8	812.8	973.5	48.7	30.0	372.4	1,140.8	84.4	55.8	440.4
1984	2,335.0	165.6	107.6	864.2	1,107.6	75.5	48.9	395.6	1,227.5	90.0	58.8	468.5
1985	2,331.4	137.0	87.6	866.2	1,142.6	61.5	38.6	420.9	1,188.8	75.6	49.1	445.3
1986	2,220.9	129.3	83.1	874.7	1,125.5	52.1	32.6	436.3	1,095.4	77.2	50.5	438.4
1987	2,378.2	173.0	115.6	900.9	1,178.0	78.0	53.0	444.3	1,200.3	95.1	62.6	456.6
1988³	2,596.2	215.3	153.8	957.6	1,284.7	91.6	66.9	468.7	1,311.5	123.7	86.8	488.9
1989	2,745.1	187.6	135.1	999.0	1,356.6	75.1	55.5	501.3	1,388.5	112.6	79.6	497.7
1990	2,810.7	158.1	110.1	1,043.8	1,357.2	57.3	40.7	515.0	1,453.5	100.8	69.4	528.9
1991	2,761.1	98.7	66.4	1,064.1	1,304.0	13.9	7.2	506.8	1,457.1	84.8	59.3	557.4
1992⁴	2,890.2	31.4	22.1	1,034.7	1,389.8	–33.7	–24.0	473.9	1,500.4	65.1	46.0	560.8
1993	3,015.1	117.9	83.2	1,039.7	1,490.2	38.9	27.4	482.7	1,524.9	79.0	55.7	557.1
1994	3,255.8	243.5	174.9	1,110.1	1,657.6	121.0	87.1	533.3	1,598.2	122.5	87.8	576.8
1995	3,528.3	274.5	198.2	1,240.6	1,807.7	130.6	94.3	613.7	1,720.6	143.9	103.9	627.0
1996	3,757.6	306.6	224.9	1,348.0	1,941.6	146.6	106.1	673.9	1,816.0	160.0	118.8	674.2
1997	3,920.0	331.4	244.5	1,462.7	2,075.8	167.0	121.4	743.4	1,844.2	164.4	123.1	719.3
1998	3,949.4	314.7	234.4	1,482.9	2,168.8	175.1	127.8	779.9	1,780.7	139.6	106.5	703.0
1999	4,148.9	355.3	257.8	1,569.3	2,314.2	198.8	140.3	869.6	1,834.6	156.5	117.5	699.7
2000	4,548.2	381.1	275.3	1,823.1	2,457.4	190.7	131.8	1,054.3	2,090.8	190.5	143.5	768.7
2000: IV	1,163.6	69.2	46.8	1,892.4	620.4	31.2	19.3	1,101.5	543.2	38.0	27.4	790.9
NAICS:⁵												
2000: IV	1,128.8	62.1	41.7	1,833.8	623.0	26.9	15.4	1,100.0	505.8	35.2	26.3	733.8
2001	4,295.0	83.2	36.2	1,843.0	2,321.2	–69.0	–76.1	1,080.5	1,973.8	152.2	112.3	762.5
2002	4,216.4	195.5	134.7	1,804.0	2,260.6	45.9	21.6	1,024.8	1,955.8	149.6	113.1	779.2
2003	4,397.2	305.7	237.0	1,952.2	2,282.7	117.6	88.2	1,040.8	2,114.5	188.1	148.9	911.5
2004	4,934.1	447.5	348.2	2,206.3	2,537.3	200.0	156.5	1,212.9	2,396.7	247.5	191.6	993.5
2005	5,411.5	524.2	401.3	2,410.4	2,730.5	211.3	161.2	1,304.0	2,681.0	312.9	240.2	1,106.5
2006	5,782.7	604.6	470.3	2,678.6	2,910.2	249.1	192.8	1,384.0	2,872.5	355.5	277.5	1,294.6
2007	6,055.2	598.0	439.5	2,912.0	3,009.1	245.3	158.3	1,492.9	3,046.1	352.7	281.3	1,419.1
2006: I	1,397.4	149.1	119.8	2,606.1	702.1	63.9	51.7	1,351.7	695.3	85.2	68.1	1,254.4
II	1,485.6	159.8	122.4	2,674.4	748.0	64.5	49.5	1,389.7	737.6	95.3	72.9	1,284.6
III	1,467.1	164.4	126.3	2,738.8	729.4	66.6	50.8	1,409.5	737.8	97.8	75.5	1,329.3
IV	1,432.5	131.4	101.8	2,695.1	730.6	54.1	40.8	1,385.1	701.9	77.3	61.0	1,310.0
2007: I	1,405.8	149.2	117.3	2,775.4	715.8	61.4	47.7	1,441.4	690.0	87.8	69.6	1,334.0
II	1,526.5	172.8	136.3	2,900.1	760.8	75.4	61.0	1,490.8	765.7	97.4	75.3	1,409.2
III	1,540.0	146.3	79.3	2,950.2	766.5	56.7	8.4	1,503.1	773.5	89.6	70.9	1,447.0
IV	1,582.9	129.7	106.7	3,022.3	766.1	51.8	41.2	1,536.2	816.9	77.9	65.4	1,486.1
2008: I	1,562.3	148.6	116.8	3,062.6	736.8	58.2	44.7	1,551.0	825.5	90.4	72.1	1,511.5
II	1,716.7	143.3	110.8	3,079.3	781.4	49.4	33.0	1,554.8	935.3	93.9	77.8	1,524.5

¹ In the old series, "income taxes" refers to Federal income taxes only, as State and local income taxes had already been deducted. In the new series, no income taxes have been deducted.

² Annual data are average equity for the year (using four end-of-quarter figures).

³ Beginning with 1988, profits before and after income taxes reflect inclusion of minority stockholders' interest in net income before and after income taxes.

⁴ Data for 1992 (most significantly 1992:I) reflect the early adoption of Financial Accounting Standards Board Statement 106 (Employer's Accounting for Post-Retirement Benefits Other Than Pensions) by a large number of companies during the fourth quarter of 1992. Data for 1993 (1993:I) also reflect adoption of Statement 106. Corporations must show the cumulative effect of a change in accounting principle in the first quarter of the year in which the change is adopted.

⁵ Data based on the North American Industry Classification System (NAICS). Other data shown are based on the Standard Industrial Classification (SIC).

Note.—Data are not necessarily comparable from one period to another due to changes in accounting principles, industry classifications, sampling procedures, etc. For explanatory notes concerning compilation of the series, see *Quarterly Financial Report for Manufacturing, Mining, and Trade Corporations,* Department of Commerce, Bureau of the Census.

Source: Department of Commerce (Bureau of the Census).

TABLE B–94.—*Relation of profits after taxes to stockholders' equity and to sales, all manufacturing corporations, 1959–2008*

Year or quarter	Ratio of profits after income taxes (annual rate) to stockholders' equity—percent [1]			Profits after income taxes per dollar of sales—cents		
	All manufacturing corporations	Durable goods industries	Nondurable goods industries	All manufacturing corporations	Durable goods industries	Nondurable goods industries
59	10.4	10.4	10.4	4.8	4.8	4.9
60	9.2	8.5	9.8	4.4	4.0	4.8
61	8.9	8.1	9.6	4.3	3.9	4.7
62	9.8	9.6	9.9	4.5	4.4	4.7
63	10.3	10.1	10.4	4.7	4.5	4.9
64	11.6	11.7	11.5	5.2	5.1	5.4
65	13.0	13.8	12.2	5.6	5.7	5.5
66	13.4	14.2	12.7	5.6	5.6	5.6
67	11.7	11.7	11.8	5.0	4.8	5.3
68	12.1	12.2	11.9	5.1	4.9	5.2
69	11.5	11.4	11.5	4.8	4.6	5.0
70	9.3	8.3	10.3	4.0	3.5	4.5
71	9.7	9.0	10.3	4.1	3.8	4.5
72	10.6	10.8	10.5	4.3	4.2	4.4
73	12.8	13.1	12.6	4.7	4.7	4.8
73: IV	13.4	12.9	14.0	4.7	4.5	5.0
New series:						
73: IV	14.3	13.3	15.3	5.6	5.0	6.1
74	14.9	12.6	17.1	5.5	4.7	6.4
75	11.6	10.3	12.9	4.6	4.1	5.1
76	13.9	13.7	14.2	5.4	5.2	5.5
77	14.2	14.5	13.8	5.3	5.3	5.3
78	15.0	16.0	14.2	5.4	5.5	5.3
79	16.4	15.4	17.4	5.7	5.2	6.1
80	13.9	11.2	16.3	4.8	4.0	5.6
81	13.6	11.9	15.2	4.7	4.2	5.1
82	9.2	6.1	11.9	3.5	2.4	4.4
83	10.6	8.1	12.7	4.1	3.1	4.9
84	12.5	12.4	12.5	4.6	4.4	4.8
85	10.1	9.2	11.0	3.8	3.4	4.1
86	9.5	7.5	11.5	3.7	2.9	4.6
87	12.8	11.9	13.7	4.9	4.5	5.2
88 [2]	16.1	14.3	17.8	5.9	5.2	6.6
89	13.5	11.1	16.0	4.9	4.1	5.7
90	10.6	7.9	13.1	3.9	3.0	4.8
91	6.2	1.4	10.6	2.4	.5	4.1
92 [3]	2.1	-5.1	8.2	.8	-1.7	3.1
93	8.0	5.7	10.0	2.8	1.8	3.7
94	15.8	16.3	15.2	5.4	5.3	5.5
95	16.0	15.4	16.6	5.6	5.2	6.0
96	16.7	15.7	17.6	6.0	5.5	6.5
97	16.7	16.3	17.1	6.2	5.8	6.7
98	15.8	16.4	15.2	5.9	5.9	6.0
99	16.4	16.1	16.8	6.2	6.1	6.4
00	15.1	12.5	18.7	6.1	5.4	6.9
00: IV	9.9	7.0	13.9	4.0	3.1	5.1
NAICS: [4]						
00: IV	9.1	5.6	14.3	3.7	2.5	5.2
01	2.0	-7.0	14.7	.8	-3.3	5.7
02	7.5	2.1	14.5	3.2	1.0	5.8
03	12.1	8.5	16.3	5.4	3.9	7.0
04	15.8	12.9	19.3	7.1	6.2	8.0
05	16.7	12.4	21.7	7.4	5.9	9.0
06	17.6	13.9	21.4	8.1	6.6	9.7
07	15.1	10.6	19.8	7.3	5.3	9.2
06: I	18.4	15.3	21.7	8.6	7.4	9.8
II	18.3	14.2	22.7	8.2	6.6	9.9
III	18.4	14.4	22.7	8.6	7.0	10.2
IV	15.1	11.8	18.6	7.1	5.6	8.7
07: I	16.9	13.2	20.9	8.3	6.7	10.1
II	18.8	16.4	21.4	8.9	8.0	9.8
III	10.7	2.2	19.6	5.1	1.1	9.2
IV	14.1	10.7	17.6	6.7	5.4	8.0
08: I	15.3	11.5	19.1	7.5	6.1	8.7
II	14.4	8.5	20.4	6.5	4.2	8.3

[1] Annual ratios based on average equity for the year (using four end-of-quarter figures). Quarterly ratios based on equity at end of quarter.
[2] See footnote 3, Table B–93.
[3] See footnote 4, Table B–93.
[4] See footnote 5, Table B–93.

Note.—Based on data in millions of dollars.
See Note, Table B–93.

Source: Department of Commerce (Bureau of the Census).

TABLE B–95.—Historical stock prices and yields, 1949–2003

Year	Common stock prices									Common stock yield (Standard & Poor's) (percent)[5]	
	New York Stock Exchange (NYSE) indexes[2]						Dow Jones industrial average[2]	Standard & Poor's composite index (1941–43=10)[2]	Nasdaq composite index (Feb. 5, 1971=100)[2]	Dividend-price ratio[6]	Earnings-price ratio[7]
	Composite (Dec. 31, 2002= 5,000)[3]	December 31, 1965=50									
		Composite	Industrial	Transportation	Utility[4]	Finance					
1949		9.02					179.48	15.23		6.59	15
1950		10.87					216.31	18.40		6.57	13
1951		13.08					257.64	22.34		6.13	11
1952		13.81					270.76	24.50		5.80	9
1953		13.67					275.97	24.73		5.80	10
1954		16.19					333.94	29.69		4.95	8
1955		21.54					442.72	40.49		4.08	7
1956		24.40					493.01	46.62		4.09	7
1957		23.67					475.71	44.38		4.35	7
1958		24.56					491.66	46.24		3.97	6
1959		30.73					632.12	57.38		3.23	5
1960		30.01					618.04	55.85		3.47	5
1961		35.37					691.55	66.27		2.98	4
1962		33.49					639.76	62.38		3.37	5
1963		37.51					714.81	69.87		3.17	5
1964		43.76					834.05	81.37		3.01	5
1965		47.39					910.88	88.17		3.00	5
1966	487.92	46.15	46.18	50.26	90.81	44.45	873.60	85.26		3.40	6
1967	536.84	50.77	51.97	53.51	90.86	49.82	879.12	91.93		3.20	5
1968	585.47	55.37	58.00	50.58	88.38	65.85	906.00	98.70		3.07	5
1969	578.01	54.67	57.44	46.96	85.60	70.49	876.72	97.84		3.24	6
1970	483.39	45.72	48.03	32.14	74.47	60.00	753.19	83.22		3.83	6
1971	573.33	54.22	57.92	44.35	79.05	70.38	884.76	98.29	107.44	3.14	5
1972	637.52	60.29	65.73	50.17	76.95	78.35	950.71	109.20	128.52	2.84	5
1973	607.11	57.42	63.08	37.74	75.38	70.12	923.88	107.43	109.90	3.06	7
1974	463.54	43.84	48.08	31.89	59.58	49.67	759.37	82.85	76.29	4.47	11
1975	483.55	45.73	50.52	31.10	63.00	47.14	802.49	86.16	77.20	4.31	9
1976	575.85	54.46	60.44	39.57	73.94	52.94	974.92	102.01	89.90	3.77	8
1977	567.66	53.69	57.86	41.09	81.84	55.25	894.63	98.20	98.71	4.62	10
1978	567.81	53.70	58.23	43.50	78.44	56.65	820.23	96.02	117.53	5.28	12
1979	616.68	58.32	64.76	47.34	76.41	61.42	844.40	103.01	136.57	5.47	13
1980	720.15	68.10	78.70	60.61	74.69	64.25	891.41	118.78	168.61	5.26	12
1981	782.62	74.02	85.44	72.61	77.81	73.52	932.92	128.05	203.18	5.20	11
1982	728.84	68.93	78.18	60.41	79.49	71.99	884.36	119.71	188.97	5.81	11
1983	979.52	92.63	107.45	89.36	93.99	95.34	1,190.34	160.41	285.43	4.40	8
1984	977.33	92.46	108.01	85.63	92.89	89.28	1,178.48	160.46	248.88	4.64	10
1985	1,142.97	108.09	123.79	104.11	113.49	114.21	1,328.23	186.84	290.19	4.25	8
1986	1,438.02	136.00	155.85	119.87	142.72	147.20	1,792.76	236.34	366.96	3.49	6
1987	1,709.79	161.70	195.31	140.39	148.59	146.48	2,275.99	286.83	402.57	3.08	5
1988	1,585.14	149.91	180.95	134.12	143.53	127.26	2,060.82	265.79	374.43	3.64	8
1989	1,903.36	180.02	216.23	175.28	174.87	151.88	2,508.91	322.84	437.81	3.45	7
1990	1,939.47	183.46	225.78	158.62	181.20	133.26	2,678.94	334.59	409.17	3.61	6
1991	2,181.72	206.33	258.14	173.99	185.32	150.82	2,929.33	376.18	491.69	3.24	4
1992	2,421.51	229.01	284.62	201.09	198.91	179.26	3,284.29	415.74	599.26	2.99	4
1993	2,638.96	249.58	299.99	242.49	228.90	216.42	3,522.06	451.41	715.16	2.78	4
1994	2,687.02	254.12	315.25	247.29	209.06	209.73	3,793.77	460.42	751.65	2.82	5
1995	3,078.56	291.15	367.34	269.41	220.30	238.45	4,493.76	541.72	925.19	2.56	6
1996	3,787.20	358.17	453.98	327.33	249.77	303.89	5,742.89	670.50	1,164.96	2.19	5
1997	4,827.35	456.54	574.52	414.60	283.82	424.48	7,441.15	873.43	1,469.49	1.77	4
1998	5,818.26	550.26	681.57	468.69	378.12	516.35	8,625.52	1,085.50	1,794.91	1.49	3
1999	6,546.81	619.16	774.78	491.60	473.73	530.86	10,464.88	1,327.33	2,728.15	1.25	3
2000	6,805.89	643.66	810.63	413.60	477.65	553.13	10,734.90	1,427.22	3,783.67	1.15	3
2001	6,397.85	605.07	748.26	443.59	377.30	595.61	10,189.13	1,194.18	2,035.00	1.32	2
2002	5,578.89	527.62	657.37	431.10	260.85	555.27	9,226.43	993.94	1,539.73	1.61	2
2003[3]	5,447.46		633.18	436.51	237.77	565.75	8,993.59	965.23	1,647.17	1.77	3

[1] Averages of daily closing prices.

[2] Includes stocks as follows: for NYSE, all stocks listed; for Dow Jones industrial average, 30 stocks; for Standard & Poor's (S&P) composite index, 500 stocks; and for Nasdaq composite index, over 5,000.

[3] The NYSE relaunched the composite index on January 9, 2003, incorporating new definitions, methodology, and base value. (The composite index based on December 31, 1965=50 was discontinued.) Subset indexes on financial, energy, and health care were released by the NYSE on January 8, 2004 (see Table B–9_ NYSE indexes shown in this table for industrials, utilities, transportation, and finance were discontinued.

[4] Effective April 1993, the NYSE doubled the value of the utility index to facilitate trading of options and futures on the index. Annual indexes prior to 1993 reflect the doubling.

[5] Based on 500 stocks in the S&P composite index.

[6] Aggregate cash dividends (based on latest known annual rate) divided by aggregate market value based on Wednesday closing prices. Monthly data are averages of weekly figures; annual data are averages of monthly figures.

[7] Quarterly data are ratio of earnings (after taxes) for four quarters ending with particular quarter-to-price index for last day of that quarter. Annual data are averages of quarterly ratios.

Sources: New York Stock Exchange, Dow Jones & Co., Inc., Standard & Poor's, and Nasdaq Stock Market.

TABLE B–96.—*Common stock prices and yields, 2000–2008*

Year or month	Common stock prices							Common stock yields (Standard & Poor's) (percent) [4]	
	New York Stock Exchange (NYSE) indexes [2,3] (December 31, 2002=5,000)				Dow Jones industrial average [2]	Standard & Poor's composite index (1941–43=10) [2]	Nasdaq composite index (Feb. 5, 1971=100) [2]	Dividend-price ratio [5]	Earnings-price ratio [6]
	Composite	Financial	Energy	Health care					
2000	6,805.89				10,734.90	1,427.22	3,783.67	1.15	3.63
2001	6,397.85				10,189.13	1,194.18	2,035.00	1.32	2.95
2002	5,578.89				9,226.43	993.94	1,539.73	1.61	2.92
2003	5,447.46	5,583.00	5,273.90	5,288.67	8,993.59	965.23	1,647.17	1.77	3.84
2004	6,612.62	6,822.18	6,952.36	5,924.80	10,317.39	1,130.65	1,986.53	1.72	4.89
2005	7,349.00	7,383.70	9,377.84	6,283.96	10,547.67	1,207.23	2,099.32	1.83	5.36
2006	8,357.99	8,654.40	11,206.94	6,685.06	11,408.67	1,310.46	2,263.41	1.87	5.78
2007	9,648.82	9,321.39	13,339.99	7,191.79	13,169.98	1,477.19	2,578.47	1.86	5.29
2004: Jan	6,569.76	6,827.35	6,323.29	6,000.57	10,540.05	1,132.52	2,098.00	1.62	
Feb	6,661.38	6,978.62	6,337.87	6,134.16	10,601.50	1,143.36	2,048.36	1.63	
Mar	6,574.75	6,914.60	6,455.53	5,908.76	10,323.73	1,123.98	1,979.48	1.68	4.62
Apr	6,600.77	6,792.05	6,638.65	6,028.53	10,418.40	1,133.08	2,021.32	1.68	
May	6,371.44	6,495.19	6,572.79	6,022.12	10,083.81	1,102.78	1,930.09	1.74	
June	6,548.06	6,683.10	6,780.86	6,063.65	10,364.90	1,132.76	2,000.98	1.70	4.92
July	6,443.45	6,569.52	6,971.57	5,823.34	10,152.09	1,105.85	1,912.42	1.77	
Aug	6,352.83	6,566.19	6,866.75	5,733.68	10,032.80	1,088.94	1,821.54	1.81	
Sept	6,551.90	6,773.95	7,270.08	5,890.05	10,204.67	1,117.66	1,884.73	1.78	5.18
Oct	6,608.98	6,792.44	7,593.71	5,668.02	10,001.60	1,118.07	1,938.25	1.79	
Nov	6,933.75	7,118.40	7,773.26	5,818.20	10,411.76	1,168.94	2,062.87	1.74	
Dec	7,134.42	7,354.73	7,843.99	6,006.46	10,673.38	1,199.21	2,149.53	1.72	4.83
2005: Jan	7,056.85	7,282.65	7,841.24	5,970.34	10,539.51	1,181.41	2,071.87	1.77	
Feb	7,241.89	7,377.10	8,646.71	6,052.78	10,723.82	1,199.63	2,065.74	1.76	
Mar	7,275.51	7,274.12	9,077.38	6,148.03	10,682.09	1,194.90	2,030.43	1.79	5.11
Apr	7,077.97	7,014.98	8,793.74	6,253.05	10,283.19	1,164.42	1,957.49	1.86	
May	7,094.02	7,092.20	8,513.39	6,432.30	10,377.18	1,178.28	2,005.22	1.86	
June	7,238.96	7,199.86	9,122.87	6,408.88	10,486.68	1,202.26	2,074.02	1.83	5.32
July	7,389.23	7,373.25	9,607.53	6,342.76	10,545.38	1,222.24	2,145.14	1.82	
Aug	7,482.93	7,374.01	10,034.26	6,383.81	10,554.27	1,224.27	2,157.85	1.82	
Sept	7,584.49	7,435.85	10,672.51	6,412.24	10,532.54	1,225.91	2,144.61	1.84	5.42
Oct	7,373.23	7,368.60	9,915.63	6,270.83	10,324.31	1,191.96	2,087.09	1.90	
Nov	7,585.75	7,800.01	9,998.62	6,297.57	10,695.25	1,237.37	2,202.84	1.85	
Dec	7,787.22	8,011.76	10,310.18	6,434.97	10,827.79	1,262.07	2,246.09	1.84	5.60
2006: Jan	8,007.35	8,187.86	10,965.30	6,604.09	10,872.48	1,278.72	2,289.99	1.83	
Feb	8,044.86	8,280.82	10,741.43	6,566.87	10,971.19	1,276.65	2,273.67	1.86	
Mar	8,174.34	8,459.04	10,702.23	6,653.63	11,144.45	1,293.74	2,300.26	1.85	5.61
Apr	8,351.28	8,572.54	11,467.85	6,519.78	11,234.68	1,302.18	2,338.68	1.85	
May	8,353.45	8,608.10	11,380.52	6,488.14	11,333.88	1,290.00	2,245.28	1.90	
June	7,985.59	8,225.13	10,690.86	6,395.87	10,997.97	1,253.12	2,137.41	1.96	5.86
July	8,103.97	8,340.25	11,360.86	6,566.19	11,032.53	1,260.24	2,086.21	1.94	
Aug	8,294.89	8,574.68	11,610.65	6,763.81	11,257.35	1,287.15	2,117.77	1.92	
Sept	8,383.29	8,789.30	10,807.75	6,910.95	11,533.60	1,317.81	2,221.94	1.87	5.88
Oct	8,651.02	9,101.77	11,020.11	6,975.17	11,963.12	1,363.38	2,330.17	1.83	
Nov	8,856.30	9,251.53	11,657.36	6,845.16	12,185.15	1,388.63	2,408.70	1.80	
Dec	9,089.55	9,461.77	12,078.39	6,931.01	12,377.62	1,416.42	2,431.91	1.79	5.75
2007: Jan	9,132.04	9,575.21	11,381.56	7,083.45	12,512.89	1,424.16	2,453.19	1.81	
Feb	9,345.98	9,732.63	11,658.11	7,174.03	12,631.48	1,444.79	2,479.86	1.82	
Mar	9,120.57	9,342.66	11,503.16	6,997.30	12,268.53	1,406.95	2,401.49	1.89	5.85
Apr	9,555.98	9,658.88	12,441.16	7,332.01	12,754.80	1,463.65	2,499.57	1.84	
May	9,822.99	9,864.01	13,031.00	7,474.48	13,407.76	1,511.14	2,562.14	1.81	
June	9,896.98	9,754.29	13,639.81	7,268.42	13,480.21	1,514.49	2,595.40	1.81	5.65
July	9,985.42	9,543.66	14,318.49	7,210.07	13,677.89	1,520.70	2,655.08	1.80	
Aug	9,440.44	8,963.67	13,250.28	6,957.87	13,239.71	1,454.62	2,539.50	1.92	
Sept	9,777.59	9,060.63	14,300.99	7,138.20	13,557.69	1,497.12	2,634.47	1.88	5.15
Oct	10,159.33	9,390.30	14,976.30	7,231.60	13,901.28	1,539.66	2,780.42	1.84	
Nov	9,741.15	8,522.71	14,622.23	7,127.40	13,200.58	1,463.39	2,662.80	1.95	
Dec	9,807.36	8,447.99	14,956.77	7,306.60	13,406.99	1,479.23	2,661.55	1.93	4.51
2008: Jan	9,165.10	7,776.77	14,222.14	7,068.98	12,538.12	1,378.76	2,418.09	2.06	
Feb	9,041.52	7,577.54	13,931.92	6,674.75	12,419.57	1,354.87	2,325.83	2.10	
Mar	8,776.21	7,155.51	14,000.91	6,318.44	12,193.88	1,316.94	2,254.82	2.17	4.57
Apr	9,174.10	7,579.73	15,159.35	6,381.98	12,656.63	1,370.47	2,368.10	2.09	
May	9,429.04	7,593.63	16,365.23	6,405.40	12,812.48	1,403.22	2,483.24	2.07	
June	8,996.98	6,798.20	16,272.67	6,243.42	12,056.67	1,341.25	2,427.45	2.15	4.01
July	8,427.37	6,207.89	14,899.86	6,412.48	11,322.38	1,257.33	2,278.14	2.27	
Aug	8,362.20	6,304.58	13,772.04	6,618.92	11,530.75	1,281.47	2,389.27	2.23	
Sept	7,886.29	6,159.18	12,562.82	6,316.05	11,114.08	1,217.01	2,205.20	2.36	p3.94
Oct	6,130.39	4,733.74	9,515.71	5,434.03	9,176.71	968.80	1,730.32	2.83	
Nov	5,527.63	3,779.86	9,262.07	5,088.99	8,614.55	873.28	1,501.11	3.11	

[1] Averages of daily closing prices.
[2] Includes stocks as follows: for NYSE, all stocks listed (in September 2008, about 2,500); for Dow Jones industrial average, 30 stocks; for Standard & Poor's (S&P) composite index, 500 stocks; and for Nasdaq composite index, in November 2008 about 3,000.
[3] The NYSE relaunched the composite index on January 9, 2003, incorporating new definitions, methodology, and base value. Subset indexes on financial, energy, and health care were released by the NYSE on January 8, 2004.
[4] Based on 500 stocks in the S&P composite index.
[5] Aggregate cash dividends (based on latest known annual rate) divided by aggregate market value based on Wednesday closing prices. Monthly data are averages of weekly figures, annual data are averages of monthly figures.
[6] Quarterly data are ratio of earnings (after taxes) for four quarters ending with particular quarter-to-price index for last day of that quarter. Annual data are averages of quarterly ratios.

Sources: New York Stock Exchange, Dow Jones & Co., Inc., Standard & Poor's, and Nasdaq Stock Market.

AGRICULTURE

TABLE B–97.—*Farm income, 1945–2008*

[Billions of dollars]

	Income of farm operators from farming							
	Gross farm income						Production expenses	Net farm income
Year	Total [1]	Cash marketing receipts			Value of inventory changes [3]	Direct Government payments [4]		
		Total	Livestock and products	Crops [2]				
1945	25.4	21.7	12.0	9.7	−0.4	0.7	13.1	12
1946	29.6	24.8	13.8	11.0	.0	.8	14.5	15
1947	32.4	29.6	16.5	13.1	−1.8	.3	17.0	15
1948	36.5	30.2	17.1	13.1	1.7	.3	18.8	17
1949	30.8	27.8	15.4	12.4	−.9	.2	18.0	12
1950	33.1	28.4	16.1	12.4	.8	.3	19.5	13
1951	38.3	32.8	19.6	13.2	1.2	.3	22.3	15
1952	37.7	32.5	18.2	14.3	.9	.3	22.8	14
1953	34.4	31.0	16.9	14.1	−.6	.2	21.5	13
1954	34.2	29.8	16.3	13.6	.5	.3	21.8	12
1955	33.4	29.5	16.0	13.5	.2	.2	22.2	11
1956	33.9	30.4	16.4	14.0	−.5	.6	22.7	11
1957	34.8	29.7	17.4	12.3	.6	1.0	23.7	11
1958	39.0	33.5	19.2	14.2	.8	1.1	25.8	13
1959	37.9	33.6	18.9	14.7	.0	.7	27.2	10
1960	38.6	34.0	19.0	15.0	.4	.7	27.4	11
1961	40.5	35.2	19.5	15.7	.3	1.5	28.6	12
1962	42.3	36.5	20.2	16.3	.6	1.7	30.3	12
1963	43.4	37.5	20.0	17.4	.6	1.7	31.6	11
1964	42.3	37.3	19.9	17.4	−.8	2.2	31.8	10
1965	46.5	39.4	21.9	17.5	1.0	2.5	33.6	12
1966	50.5	43.4	25.0	18.4	−.1	3.3	36.5	14
1967	50.5	42.8	24.4	18.4	.7	3.1	38.2	12
1968	51.8	44.2	25.5	18.7	.1	3.5	39.5	12
1969	56.4	48.2	28.6	19.6	.1	3.8	42.1	14
1970	58.8	50.5	29.5	21.0	.0	3.7	44.5	14
1971	62.1	52.7	30.5	22.3	1.4	3.1	47.1	15
1972	71.1	61.1	35.6	25.5	.9	4.0	51.7	19
1973	98.9	86.9	45.8	41.1	3.4	2.6	64.6	34
1974	98.2	92.4	41.3	51.1	−1.6	.5	71.0	27
1975	100.6	88.9	43.1	45.8	3.4	.8	75.0	25
1976	102.9	95.4	46.3	49.0	−1.5	.7	82.7	20
1977	108.8	96.2	47.6	48.6	1.1	1.8	88.9	19
1978	128.4	112.4	59.2	53.2	1.9	3.0	103.2	25
1979	150.7	131.5	69.2	62.3	5.0	1.4	123.3	27
1980	149.3	139.7	68.0	71.7	−6.3	1.3	133.1	16
1981	166.3	141.6	69.2	72.5	6.5	1.9	139.4	26
1982	164.1	142.6	70.3	72.3	−1.4	3.5	140.3	23
1983	153.9	136.8	69.6	67.2	−10.9	9.3	139.6	14
1984	168.0	142.8	72.9	69.9	6.0	8.4	142.0	26
1985	161.1	144.0	70.1	73.9	−2.3	7.7	132.6	28
1986	156.1	135.4	71.6	63.8	−2.2	11.8	125.0	31
1987	168.4	141.8	76.0	65.8	−2.3	16.7	130.4	38
1988	177.9	151.3	79.6	71.6	−4.1	14.5	138.3	39
1989	191.6	160.5	83.6	76.9	3.8	10.9	145.1	46
1990	197.8	169.3	89.1	80.2	3.3	9.3	151.5	46
1991	192.0	168.0	85.8	82.2	−.2	8.2	151.8	40
1992	200.6	171.5	85.8	85.7	4.2	9.2	150.4	50
1993	205.0	178.3	90.5	87.8	−4.2	13.4	158.3	46
1994	216.1	181.4	88.3	93.1	8.3	7.9	163.5	52
1995	210.8	188.2	87.2	101.0	−5.0	7.3	171.1	39
1996	235.8	199.4	92.9	106.5	7.9	7.3	176.9	58
1997	238.0	207.8	96.5	111.3	.6	7.5	186.7	51
1998	232.6	196.5	94.2	102.2	−.6	12.4	185.5	47
1999	234.9	187.8	95.7	92.1	−.2	21.5	187.2	47
2000	243.6	192.0	99.6	92.4	1.6	23.2	193.1	50
2001	251.8	200.0	106.7	93.3	1.1	22.4	196.9	54
2002	232.6	194.9	94.0	101.0	−3.4	12.4	193.1	39
2003	260.0	215.6	105.6	110.0	−2.4	16.5	199.6	60
2004	295.6	237.2	123.6	113.6	11.2	13.0	209.8	85
2005	301.1	240.9	124.9	116.0	.5	24.4	221.8	79
2006	292.4	240.8	118.2	122.6	−3.0	15.8	233.9	58
2007	341.1	284.8	137.9	147.0	3.7	11.9	254.4	86
2008 [p]	379.4	323.5	143.6	179.9	.5	12.5	292.5	86

[1] Cash marketing receipts, Government payments, value of changes in inventories, other farm-related cash income, and nonmoney income produced by farm, including imputed rent of operator residences.

[2] Crop receipts include proceeds received from commodities placed under Commodity Credit Corporation loans.

[3] Physical changes in beginning and ending year inventories of crop and livestock commodities valued at weighted average market prices during the year.

[4] Includes only Government payments made directly to farmers.

Note.—Data for 2008 are forecasts.

Source: Department of Agriculture (Economic Research Service).

TABLE B–98.—*Farm business balance sheet, 1950–2008*

[Billions of dollars]

		Assets									Claims			
		Physical assets						Financial assets						
			Non–real estate											
End of year	Total assets	Real estate	Live-stock and poultry [1]	Ma-chinery and motor vehicles	Crops [2]	Pur-chased inputs [3]	Total [4]	Invest-ments in coopera-tives	Other [4]	Total claims	Real estate debt [5]	Non-real estate debt [6]	Propri-etors' equity
1950	121.6	75.4	17.1	12.3	7.1		9.7	2.7	7.0	121.6	5.2	5.7	110.7
1951	136.0	83.8	19.5	14.3	8.2		10.2	2.9	7.3	136.0	5.7	6.9	123.4
1952	133.1	85.1	14.8	15.0	7.9		10.3	3.2	7.1	133.1	6.2	7.1	119.8
1953	128.7	84.3	11.7	15.6	6.8		10.3	3.3	7.0	128.7	6.6	6.3	115.8
1954	132.6	87.8	11.2	15.7	7.5		10.4	3.5	6.9	132.6	7.1	6.7	118.8
1955	137.0	93.0	10.6	16.3	6.5		10.6	3.7	6.9	137.0	7.8	7.3	121.9
1956	145.7	100.3	11.0	16.9	6.8		10.7	4.0	6.7	145.7	8.5	7.4	129.8
1957	154.5	106.4	13.9	17.0	6.4		10.8	4.2	6.6	154.5	9.0	8.2	137.3
1958	168.7	114.6	17.7	18.1	6.9		11.4	4.5	6.9	168.7	9.7	9.4	149.6
1959	172.9	121.2	15.2	19.3	6.2		11.0	4.8	6.2	172.9	10.6	10.7	151.6
1960	174.4	123.3	15.6	19.1	6.4		10.0	4.2	5.8	174.4	11.3	11.1	151.9
1961	181.6	129.1	16.4	19.3	6.5		10.4	4.5	5.9	181.6	12.3	11.8	157.5
1962	188.9	134.6	17.3	19.9	6.5		10.5	4.6	5.9	188.9	13.5	13.2	162.2
1963	196.7	142.4	15.9	20.4	7.4		10.7	5.0	5.7	196.7	15.0	14.6	167.1
1964	204.2	150.5	14.5	21.2	7.0		11.0	5.2	5.8	204.2	16.9	15.3	172.1
1965	220.8	161.5	17.6	22.4	7.9		11.4	5.4	6.0	220.8	18.9	16.9	185.0
1966	234.0	171.2	19.0	24.1	8.1		11.6	5.7	6.0	234.0	20.7	18.5	194.8
1967	246.1	180.9	18.8	26.3	8.0		12.0	5.8	6.1	246.1	22.6	19.6	203.9
1968	257.2	189.4	20.2	27.7	7.4		12.4	6.1	6.3	257.2	24.7	19.2	213.2
1969	267.8	195.3	22.8	28.6	8.3		12.8	6.4	6.4	267.8	26.4	20.0	221.4
1970	278.8	202.4	23.7	30.4	8.7		13.7	7.2	6.5	278.8	27.2	21.3	230.3
1971	301.8	217.6	27.3	32.4	10.0		14.5	7.9	6.7	301.8	28.8	24.0	248.9
1972	339.9	243.0	33.7	34.6	12.9		15.7	8.7	6.9	339.9	31.4	26.7	281.8
1973	418.5	298.3	42.4	39.7	21.4		16.8	9.7	7.1	418.5	35.2	31.6	351.7
1974 [7]	449.2	335.6	24.6	48.5	22.5		18.1	11.2	6.9	449.2	39.6	35.1	374.5
1975	510.8	383.6	29.4	57.4	20.5		19.9	13.0	6.9	510.8	43.8	39.8	427.3
1976	590.7	456.5	29.0	63.3	20.6		21.3	14.3	6.9	590.7	48.5	45.7	496.5
1977	651.5	509.3	31.9	69.3	20.4		20.5	13.5	7.0	651.5	55.8	52.6	543.1
1978	777.7	601.8	50.1	78.8	23.8		23.2	16.1	7.1	777.7	63.4	60.4	653.9
1979	914.7	706.1	61.4	91.9	29.9		25.4	18.1	7.3	914.7	75.8	71.7	767.2
1980	1,000.4	782.8	60.6	97.5	32.8		26.7	19.3	7.4	1,000.4	85.3	77.2	838.0
1981	997.9	785.6	53.5	101.1	29.5		28.2	20.6	7.6	997.9	93.9	83.8	820.2
1982	962.5	750.0	53.0	103.9	25.9		29.7	21.9	7.8	962.5	96.8	87.2	778.5
1983	959.3	753.4	49.5	101.7	23.7		30.9	22.8	8.1	959.3	98.1	88.1	773.1
1984	897.8	661.8	49.5	125.8	26.1	2.0	32.6	24.3	8.3	897.8	101.4	87.4	709.0
1985	775.9	586.2	46.3	86.1	22.9	1.2	33.3	24.3	9.0	775.9	94.1	78.1	603.8
1986	722.0	542.4	47.8	79.0	16.3	2.1	34.4	24.4	10.0	722.0	84.1	67.2	570.7
1987	756.5	563.7	58.0	78.7	17.8	3.2	35.2	25.3	9.9	756.5	75.8	62.7	618.0
1988	788.5	582.3	62.2	81.0	23.7	3.5	35.9	25.6	10.4	788.5	70.8	62.3	655.4
1989	813.7	600.1	66.2	84.1	23.9	2.6	36.7	26.3	10.4	813.7	68.8	62.3	682.7
1990	840.6	619.1	70.9	86.3	23.2	2.8	38.3	27.5	10.9	840.6	67.6	63.5	709.5
1991	844.2	624.8	68.1	85.9	22.2	2.6	40.5	28.7	11.8	844.2	67.4	64.4	712.3
1992	867.8	640.8	71.0	84.8	24.2	3.9	43.0	29.4	13.6	867.8	67.9	63.7	736.2
1993	909.2	677.6	72.8	85.4	23.3	3.8	46.3	31.0	15.3	909.2	68.4	65.9	774.9
1994	934.7	704.1	67.9	86.8	23.3	5.0	47.6	32.1	15.5	934.7	69.9	69.0	795.8
1995	965.7	740.5	57.8	87.6	27.4	3.4	49.1	34.1	15.0	965.7	71.7	71.3	822.8
1996	1,002.9	769.5	60.3	88.0	31.7	4.4	49.0	34.9	14.1	1,002.9	74.4	74.2	854.3
1997	1,051.3	808.2	67.1	88.7	32.7	4.9	49.6	35.7	13.9	1,051.3	78.5	78.4	894.4
1998	1,083.4	840.4	63.4	89.8	29.9	5.0	54.7	40.5	14.2	1,083.4	83.1	81.5	918.7
1999	1,138.8	887.0	73.2	89.8	28.3	4.0	56.5	41.9	14.5	1,138.8	87.2	80.5	971.1
2000	1,203.2	946.4	76.8	90.1	27.9	4.9	57.1	43.0	14.1	1,203.2	84.7	79.2	1,039.3
2001	1,255.9	996.2	78.5	92.8	25.2	4.2	58.9	43.6	15.3	1,255.9	88.5	82.1	1,085.3
2002	1,304.0	1,045.7	75.6	93.6	23.1	5.6	60.4	44.7	15.8	1,304.0	95.4	81.8	1,126.8
2003	1,378.8	1,111.8	78.5	95.9	24.4	5.6	62.4	45.6	16.9	1,378.8	94.1	81.0	1,203.6
2004	1,617.6	1,340.6	79.4	101.9	24.4	5.7	65.5			1,617.6	96.9	86.1	1,434.6
2005	1,835.5	1,549.2	81.1	106.9	24.3	6.5	67.5			1,835.5	101.5	91.7	1,642.2
2006	2,047.4	1,755.8	80.7	108.1	22.7	6.5	73.7			2,047.4	101.5	94.9	1,851.0
2007	2,209.9	1,912.2	80.7	108.5	22.7	7.0	78.8			2,209.9	107.8	103.7	1,998.4
2008 *p*	2,349.7	2,042.2	80.6	109.6	27.6	7.3	82.3			2,349.7	111.1	104.0	2,134.5

[1] Excludes commercial broilers; excludes horses and mules beginning with 1959 data; excludes turkeys beginning with 1986 data.
[2] Non–Commodity Credit Corporation (CCC) crops held on farms plus value above loan rate for crops held under CCC.
[3] Includes fertilizer, chemicals, fuels, parts, feed, seed, and other supplies.
[4] Beginning with 2004, data available only for total financial assets. Data through 2003 for other financial assets are currency and demand deposits.
[5] Includes CCC storage and drying facilities loans.
[6] Does not include CCC crop loans.
[7] Beginning with 1974 data, farms are defined as places with sales of $1,000 or more annually.

Note.—Data exclude operator households. Beginning with 1959, data include Alaska and Hawaii.

Data for 2008 are forecasts.

Source: Department of Agriculture (Economic Research Service).

Year	Farm output				Productivity indicators	
	Total	Livestock and products	Crops	Farm-related output	Farm output per unit of total factor input	Farm output per unit of labor input
1948	44	49	42	29	49	
1949	44	50	41	27	46	
1950	43	52	39	28	45	
1951	45	54	41	28	46	
1952	46	55	42	26	47	
1953	47	55	42	26	48	
1954	47	58	42	26	49	
1955	49	60	43	27	49	
1956	49	61	43	29	49	
1957	48	60	42	31	49	
1958	51	62	46	35	51	
1959	53	64	47	42	52	
1960	54	65	49	44	54	
1961	55	68	49	43	56	
1962	56	69	50	42	55	
1963	58	70	52	44	57	
1964	57	71	50	40	57	
1965	59	71	53	39	59	
1966	59	72	52	37	58	
1967	61	74	54	36	60	
1968	62	74	56	35	60	
1969	63	74	58	33	60	
1970	62	76	55	31	60	
1971	67	79	62	31	64	
1972	68	81	62	32	64	
1973	70	81	66	35	65	
1974	65	78	60	36	61	
1975	70	75	68	35	68	
1976	71	79	68	35	66	
1977	75	80	74	35	70	
1978	76	80	76	37	67	
1979	80	81	83	38	69	
1980	77	82	75	38	67	
1981	82	83	86	34	75	
1982	84	83	87	70	77	
1983	73	84	67	71	68	
1984	83	84	84	66	79	
1985	87	85	88	84	85	
1986	84	86	83	81	84	
1987	85	87	83	89	85	
1988	81	88	73	102	81	
1989	86	88	84	104	88	
1990	90	90	89	98	91	
1991	91	92	89	102	91	
1992	96	95	97	96	98	
1993	91	96	88	96	92	
1994	102	101	104	93	100	
1995	97	102	92	106	92	
1996	100	100	100	100	100	
1997	105	103	105	113	102	
1998	105	105	104	132	101	
1999	108	108	105	143	103	
2000	108	108	106	132	108	
2001	109	107	106	140	109	
2002	106	108	102	134	107	
2003	108	107	106	137	110	
2004	113	108	115	144	118	
2005	113	110	113	140	117	
2006	111	112	107	136	116	

Note.—Farm output includes primary agricultural activities and certain secondary activities that are closely linked to agricultural production for which information on production and input use cannot be separately observed. Secondary output (alternatively, farm-related output) includes recreation activities, the imputed value of employer-provided housing, land rentals under the Conservation Reserve, and services such as custom machine work and custom livestock feeding.

See Table B–100 for farm inputs.

Source: Department of Agriculture (Economic Research Service).

TABLE B-100.—*Farm input use, selected inputs, 1948–2007*

| Year | Farm employment (thousands)[1] | | | Crops harvested (millions of acres)[4] | Selected indexes of input use (1996=100) | | | | | | | | | | |
| | Total | Self-employed and unpaid family workers[2] | Hired workers[3] | | Total farm input | Capital input | | Labor input | | | Intermediate input | | | | |
						Total	Durable equipment	Total	Hired labor	Self-employed and unpaid family labor	Total	Feed and seed	Energy and lubricants[5]	Agricultural chemicals	Purchased services
1948	9,759	7,433	2,326	356	91	110	66	325	277	349	46	55	65	20	44
1949	9,633	7,392	2,241	360	95	113	77	317	257	347	52	58	72	21	43
1950	9,283	6,965	2,318	345	96	116	90	305	268	324	53	59	73	24	44
1951	8,653	6,464	2,189	344	98	118	100	293	259	311	56	61	76	25	48
1952	8,441	6,301	2,140	349	98	120	109	287	253	304	56	60	80	26	52
1953	7,904	5,817	2,087	348	98	121	114	275	246	289	56	61	81	26	49
1954	7,893	5,782	2,111	346	96	122	120	269	232	288	54	58	81	27	47
1955	7,719	5,675	2,044	340	99	122	122	263	228	281	58	65	83	28	49
1956	7,367	5,451	1,916	324	99	122	124	247	208	267	61	68	83	30	51
1957	6,966	5,046	1,920	324	99	121	122	229	199	244	63	71	82	29	52
1958	6,667	4,705	1,962	324	100	120	121	218	201	227	66	76	80	30	54
1959	6,565	4,621	1,944	324	102	120	121	217	196	227	69	77	81	34	73
1960	6,155	4,260	1,895	324	101	120	123	205	196	208	69	77	82	34	71
1961	5,994	4,135	1,859	302	100	120	121	200	195	201	69	76	84	37	70
1962	5,841	3,997	1,844	295	102	120	119	200	195	202	71	79	85	41	70
1963	5,500	3,700	1,800	298	102	120	119	192	195	190	73	82	86	45	69
1964	5,206	3,585	1,621	298	101	121	121	180	175	182	73	79	88	49	67
1965	4,964	3,465	1,499	298	100	121	123	176	165	181	73	79	89	50	68
1966	4,574	3,224	1,350	294	102	122	126	163	149	170	77	85	91	55	69
1967	4,303	3,036	1,267	306	102	122	131	154	138	161	79	86	90	62	72
1968	4,207	2,974	1,233	300	103	124	136	153	134	162	80	87	90	66	70
1969	4,050	2,843	1,207	290	104	124	139	150	135	158	83	91	92	74	68
1970	3,951	2,727	1,224	293	104	123	140	144	136	147	84	92	92	79	66
1971	3,868	2,665	1,203	305	104	123	142	142	134	145	86	94	90	86	67
1972	3,870	2,664	1,206	294	106	122	142	141	134	144	90	98	89	94	67
1973	3,947	2,702	1,245	321	107	122	145	140	136	141	91	97	90	110	71
1974	3,919	2,588	1,331	328	106	123	153	139	145	136	89	94	86	115	69
1975	3,818	2,481	1,337	336	103	125	159	137	147	131	84	91	102	79	76
1976	3,741	2,369	1,372	337	106	126	163	135	149	128	89	94	114	89	77
1977	3,660	2,347	1,313	345	106	128	169	131	145	124	89	94	120	88	77
1978	3,682	2,410	1,272	338	113	130	173	129	136	125	100	105	126	92	90
1979	3,549	2,320	1,229	348	115	131	179	131	141	126	103	109	115	100	93
1980	3,605	2,302	1,303	352	114	135	186	128	140	121	101	109	112	100	84
1981	3,497	2,241	1,256	366	110	134	187	127	140	121	95	103	108	94	80
1982	3,335	2,142	1,193	362	110	133	184	118	125	114	97	106	101	83	90
1983	3,282	1,991	1,291	306	109	131	176	117	138	106	96	106	98	77	90
1984	3,091	1,930	1,161	348	105	122	168	113	129	105	93	99	102	90	86
1985	2,760	1,753	1,007	342	102	120	159	105	117	98	91	99	91	83	88
1986	2,693	1,740	953	325	100	116	149	106	112	103	90	100	85	81	80
1987	2,681	1,717	964	302	100	112	138	108	115	105	90	99	95	78	82
1988	2,727	1,725	1,002	297	99	110	130	110	118	105	91	99	95	78	82
1989	2,637	1,709	928	318	98	108	125	106	111	103	90	95	94	84	88
1990	2,568	1,649	919	322	99	106	121	99	111	93	94	101	94	88	84
1991	2,591	1,682	909	318	99	106	118	100	110	94	96	101	94	93	88
1992	2,505	1,640	865	319	98	104	114	97	104	94	94	101	92	93	84
1993	2,367	1,510	857	308	99	103	110	93	104	88	99	103	93	95	94
1994	2,613	1,774	839	321	102	102	106	107	101	111	100	103	95	94	99
1995	2,597	1,730	867	314	105	101	103	108	105	110	105	109	100	94	103
1996	2,433	1,602	831	326	100	100	100	100	100	100	100	100	100	100	100
1997	2,432	1,557	875	333	102	100	98	99	105	96	105	105	102	103	106
1998	2,284	1,405	879	326	104	99	98	94	107	87	110	111	103	105	112
1999	2,239	1,326	913	327	105	99	98	93	112	84	113	116	105	104	114
2000	2,142	1,249	893	325	101	98	98	85	96	79	109	114	100	103	107
2001	2,081	1,211	870	321	100	98	98	84	94	78	108	111	98	100	111
2002	2,113	1,243	870	316	99	98	99	84	94	79	107	110	106	100	103
2003	2,067	1,181	886	324	98	97	100	81	90	76	106	114	89	93	102
2004	2,013	1,188	825	321	96	97	103	78	85	75	104	112	96	95	100
2005	1,988	1,208	780	321	97	98	107	76	79	74	107	113	89	96	106
2006	1,900	1,148	752	312	96	98	109	72	78	69	106	113	84	95	109
2007	1,829	1,082	747	321	....	....	....	....	....	....	....	....	....	....	....

[1] Persons involved in farmwork. Total farm employment is the sum of self-employed and unpaid family workers and hired workers shown here.
[2] Data from Current Population Survey (CPS) conducted by the Department of Commerce, Census Bureau, for the Department of Labor, Bureau of Labor Statistics.
[3] Data from national income and product accounts from Department of Commerce, Bureau of Economic Analysis.
[4] Acreage harvested plus acreages in fruits, tree nuts, and vegetables and minor crops. Includes double-cropping.
[5] Consists of petroleum fuels, natural gas, electricity, hydraulic fluids, and lubricants.

Source: Department of Agriculture (Economic Research Service).

TABLE B–101.—*Agricultural price indexes and farm real estate value, 1975–2008*

[1990-92=100, except as noted]

| Year or month | Prices received by farmers | | | Prices paid by farmers | | | | | | | | | | | Addendum: Average farm real estate value per acre (dollars)[3] |
| | All farm products | Crops | Livestock and products | All commodities, services, interest, taxes, and wage rates[1] | Production items | | | | | | | | | Wage rates | |
					Total[2]	Feed	Livestock and poultry	Fertilizer	Agricultural chemicals	Fuels	Farm machinery	Farm services	Rent		
1975	73	88	62	47	55	83	39	87	72	40	38	48		44	340
1976	75	87	64	50	59	83	47	74	78	43	43	52		48	397
1977	73	83	64	53	61	82	48	72	71	46	47	57		51	474
1978	83	89	78	58	67	80	65	72	66	48	51	60		55	531
1979	94	98	90	66	76	89	88	77	67	61	56	66		60	628
1980	98	107	89	75	85	98	85	96	71	86	63	81		65	737
1981	100	111	89	82	92	110	80	104	77	98	70	89		70	819
1982	94	98	90	86	94	99	78	105	83	97	76	96		74	823
1983	98	108	88	86	92	107	76	100	87	94	81	82		76	788
1984	101	111	91	89	94	112	73	103	90	93	85	86		77	801
1985	91	98	86	86	91	95	74	98	90	93	85	85		78	713
1986	87	87	88	85	86	88	73	90	89	76	83	83		81	640
1987	89	86	91	87	87	83	85	86	87	76	85	84		85	599
1988	99	104	93	91	90	104	91	94	89	77	89	85		87	632
1989	104	109	100	96	95	110	93	99	93	83	94	91		95	666
1990	104	103	105	99	99	103	102	97	95	100	96	96	96	96	683
1991	100	101	99	100	100	98	102	103	101	104	100	98	100	100	703
1992	98	101	97	101	101	99	96	100	103	96	104	103	104	105	713
1993	101	102	100	104	104	102	104	96	109	93	107	110	100	108	738
1994	100	105	95	106	106	106	94	105	112	89	113	110	108	111	798
1995	102	112	92	109	108	103	82	121	116	89	120	115	117	114	844
1996	112	127	99	115	115	129	75	125	119	102	125	116	128	117	887
1997	107	115	98	118	119	125	94	121	121	106	128	116	136	123	928
1998	102	107	97	115	113	111	88	112	122	84	132	115	120	129	974
1999	96	97	95	115	111	100	95	105	121	94	135	114	113	135	1,030
2000	96	96	97	119	115	102	110	110	120	129	139	118	110	140	1,090
2001	102	99	106	123	120	109	111	123	121	121	144	120	117	146	1,150
2002	98	105	90	124	119	112	102	108	119	115	148	120	120	153	1,210
2003	107	111	103	128	124	114	109	124	121	140	151	125	123	157	1,270
2004	119	115	122	134	132	121	128	140	121	165	162	127	126	160	1,360
2005	115	111	120	142	140	117	138	164	123	216	173	133	129	165	1,650
2006	115	120	111	150	148	124	134	176	128	239	182	139	141	171	1,900
2007	136	142	130	161	160	148	131	216	129	264	191	146	151	177	2,160
2007: Jan	123	131	113	155	152	140	122	182	129	186	145	151		180	2,160
Feb	127	138	118	157	154	148	125	186	129	222	187	147	151	180	
Mar	132	142	123	159	157	150	131	202	130	240	189	145	151	180	
Apr	134	143	127	160	160	148	134	209	130	258	189	144	151	176	
May	136	140	132	161	160	145	132	213	129	263	190	145	151	176	
June	137	141	134	161	160	147	129	217	129	263	190	146	151	176	
July	139	140	137	161	161	147	134	221	129	266	191	147	151	173	
Aug	139	142	137	161	161	145	136	221	129	263	192	147	151	173	
Sept	140	142	138	162	162	147	135	223	128	272	193	147	151	173	
Oct	141	149	131	163	163	151	133	228	130	283	194	147	151	179	
Nov	141	149	134	165	166	156	130	233	131	312	196	147	151	179	
Dec	142	150	134	164	167	160	127	253	131	308	197	147	151	179	
2008: Jan	144	157	129	171	172	168	123	275	133	307	198	152	163	187	2,350
Feb	145	162	131	173	175	176	128	291	133	311	199	152	163	187	
Mar	146	166	129	177	180	183	125	315	134	349	199	152	163	187	
Apr	145	168	127	181	187	186	122	344	135	369	202	153	163	183	
May	150	170	134	185	193	196	127	363	136	400	207	153	163	183	
June	158	183	137	188	196	198	124	390	140	423	207	156	163	183	
July	159	182	138	191	201	208	123	423	141	426	208	156	163	179	
Aug	156	177	137	192	203	205	128	467	147	390	209	157	163	179	
Sept	154	174	133	191	201	201	125	468	146	368	210	156	163	179	
Oct	151	168	127	187	194	185	118	459	150	316	212	156	163	185	
Nov [p]	139	152	125	183	189	170	120	450	154	254	213	155	163	185	

[1] Includes items used for family living, not shown separately.
[2] Includes other production items, not shown separately.
[3] Average for 48 States. Annual data are: March 1 for 1975, February 1 for 1976–81, April 1 for 1982–85, February 1 for 1986–89, and January 1 for 1990–2007.

Source: Department of Agriculture (National Agricultural Statistics Service).

Year	Exports							Imports					Agri-cultural trade balance
	Total [1]	Feed grains	Food grains [2]	Oilseeds and products	Cotton	Tobacco	Animals and products	Total [1]	Fruits, nuts, and veg-etables [3]	Animals and products	Coffee	Cocoa beans and products	
1950	2.9	0.2	0.6	0.2	1.0	0.3	0.3	4.0	0.2	0.7	1.1	0.2	−1.1
1951	4.0	.3	1.1	.3	1.1	.3	.5	5.2	.2	1.1	1.4	.2	−1.1
1952	3.4	.3	1.1	.2	.9	.2	.3	4.5	.2	.7	1.4	.2	−1.1
1953	2.8	.3	.7	.2	.5	.3	.4	4.2	.2	.6	1.5	.2	−1.3
1954	3.1	.2	.5	.3	.8	.3	.5	4.0	.2	.5	1.5	.3	−.9
1955	3.2	.3	.6	.4	.5	.4	.6	4.0	.2	.5	1.4	.2	−.8
1956	4.2	.4	1.0	.5	.7	.3	.7	4.0	.2	.4	1.4	.2	.2
1957	4.5	.3	1.0	.5	1.0	.4	.7	4.0	.2	.5	1.4	.2	.6
1958	3.9	.5	.8	.4	.7	.4	.5	3.9	.2	.7	1.2	.2	*
1959	4.0	.6	.9	.6	.4	.3	.6	4.1	.2	.8	1.1	.2	−.1
1960	4.8	.5	1.2	.6	1.0	.4	.6	3.8	.2	.6	1.0	.2	1.0
1961	5.0	.5	1.4	.6	.9	.4	.6	3.7	.2	.7	1.0	.2	1.3
1962	5.0	.8	1.3	.7	.5	.4	.6	3.9	.2	.9	1.0	.2	1.2
1963	5.6	.8	1.5	.8	.6	.4	.7	4.0	.3	.9	1.0	.2	1.6
1964	6.3	.9	1.7	1.0	.7	.4	.8	4.1	.3	.8	1.2	.2	2.3
1965	6.2	1.1	1.4	1.2	.5	.4	.8	4.1	.3	.9	1.1	.1	2.1
1966	6.9	1.3	1.8	1.2	.4	.5	.7	4.5	.4	1.2	1.1	.1	2.4
1967	6.4	1.1	1.5	1.3	.5	.5	.7	4.5	.4	1.1	1.0	.2	1.9
1968	6.3	.9	1.4	1.3	.5	.5	.7	5.0	.5	1.3	1.2	.2	1.3
1969	6.0	.9	1.2	1.3	.3	.6	.8	5.0	.5	1.4	.9	.2	1.1
1970	7.3	1.1	1.4	1.9	.4	.5	.9	5.8	.5	1.6	1.2	.3	1.5
1971	7.7	1.0	1.3	2.2	.6	.5	1.0	5.8	.6	1.5	1.2	.2	1.9
1972	9.4	1.5	1.8	2.4	.5	.7	1.1	6.5	.7	1.8	1.3	.2	2.9
1973	17.7	3.5	4.7	4.3	.9	.7	1.6	8.4	.8	2.6	1.7	.3	9.3
1974	21.9	4.6	5.4	5.7	1.3	.8	1.8	10.2	.8	2.2	1.6	.5	11.7
1975	21.9	5.2	6.2	4.5	1.0	.9	1.7	9.3	.8	1.8	1.7	.5	12.6
1976	23.0	6.0	4.7	5.1	1.0	.9	2.4	11.0	.9	2.3	2.9	.6	12.0
1977	23.6	4.9	3.6	6.6	1.5	1.1	2.7	13.4	1.2	2.3	4.2	1.0	10.2
1978	29.4	5.9	5.5	8.2	1.7	1.4	3.0	14.8	1.5	3.1	4.0	1.4	14.6
1979	34.7	7.7	6.3	8.9	2.2	1.2	3.8	16.7	1.7	3.9	4.2	1.2	18.0
1980	41.2	9.8	7.9	9.4	2.9	1.3	3.8	17.4	1.7	3.8	4.2	.9	23.8
1981	43.3	9.4	9.6	9.6	2.3	1.5	4.2	16.9	2.0	3.5	2.9	.9	26.4
1982	36.6	6.4	7.9	9.1	2.0	1.5	3.9	15.3	2.3	3.7	2.9	.7	21.3
1983	36.1	7.3	7.4	8.7	1.8	1.5	3.8	16.5	2.3	3.8	2.8	.8	19.6
1984	37.8	8.1	7.5	8.4	2.4	1.5	4.2	19.3	3.1	4.1	3.3	1.1	18.5
1985	29.0	6.0	4.5	5.8	1.6	1.5	4.1	20.0	3.5	4.2	3.3	1.4	9.1
1986	26.2	3.1	3.8	6.5	.8	1.2	4.5	21.5	3.6	4.5	4.6	1.1	4.7
1987	28.7	3.8	3.8	6.4	1.6	1.1	5.2	20.4	3.6	4.9	2.9	1.2	8.3
1988	37.1	5.9	5.9	7.7	2.0	1.3	6.4	21.0	3.8	5.2	2.5	1.0	16.1
1989	40.1	7.7	7.1	6.4	2.2	1.3	6.4	21.9	4.4	5.0	2.4	1.0	18.2
1990	39.5	7.0	4.8	5.7	2.8	1.4	6.6	22.9	4.6	5.6	1.9	1.1	16.6
1991	39.3	5.7	4.2	6.4	2.5	1.4	7.1	22.9	4.6	5.5	1.9	1.1	16.5
1992	43.1	5.7	5.4	7.2	2.0	1.7	8.0	24.8	4.7	5.7	1.7	1.1	18.3
1993	42.9	5.0	5.6	7.3	1.5	1.3	8.0	25.1	5.0	5.9	1.5	1.0	17.7
1994	46.2	4.7	5.3	7.2	2.7	1.3	9.2	27.0	5.3	5.7	2.5	1.0	19.2
1995	56.3	8.2	6.7	9.0	3.7	1.4	10.9	30.3	5.9	6.0	3.3	1.1	26.0
1996	60.3	9.4	7.4	10.8	2.7	1.4	11.1	33.5	6.6	6.1	2.8	1.4	26.8
1997	57.2	6.0	5.2	12.1	2.7	1.6	11.3	36.1	6.9	6.5	3.9	1.5	21.0
1998	51.8	5.0	5.0	9.5	2.6	1.5	10.6	36.9	7.7	6.9	3.4	1.7	14.9
1999	48.4	5.5	4.7	8.1	1.0	1.3	10.4	37.7	8.5	7.3	2.9	1.5	10.7
2000	51.3	5.2	4.3	8.6	1.9	1.2	11.6	39.0	8.6	8.4	2.7	1.4	12.3
2001	53.7	5.2	4.2	9.2	2.2	1.3	12.4	39.4	9.0	9.2	1.7	1.5	14.3
2002	53.1	5.5	4.5	9.6	2.0	1.0	11.1	41.9	9.7	9.0	1.7	1.8	11.2
2003	59.4	5.4	5.0	11.7	3.4	1.0	12.2	47.4	10.8	8.9	2.0	2.4	12.0
2004	61.4	6.4	6.3	10.4	4.3	1.0	10.4	54.0	12.2	10.6	2.3	2.5	7.4
2005	63.2	5.4	5.7	10.2	3.9	1.0	12.2	59.3	13.4	11.5	3.0	2.8	3.9
2006	70.9	7.7	5.5	11.3	4.5	1.1	13.5	65.3	14.6	11.5	3.3	2.7	5.6
2007	89.9	10.9	9.8	15.6	4.6	1.2	17.2	71.9	16.3	12.4	3.8	2.7	18.0
Jan-Sept:													
2007	61.8	7.4	6.5	9.4	3.7	.7	12.2	53.2	12.4	8.0	2.8	1.9	8.6
2008	87.3	12.2	11.2	16.6	3.9	.8	16.7	60.6	13.4	8.9	3.4	2.4	26.7

* Less than $50 million.

[1] Total includes items not shown separately.

[2] Rice, wheat, and wheat flour.

[3] Includes fruit, nut, and vegetable preparations. Beginning with 1989, data include bananas but exclude yeasts, starches, and other minor horticultural products.

Note.—Data derived from official estimates released by the Bureau of the Census, Department of Commerce. Agricultural commodities are defined as (1) nonmarine food products and (2) other products of agriculture that have not passed through complex processes of manufacture. Export value, at U.S. port of exportation, is based on the selling price and includes inland freight, insurance, and other charges to the port. Import value, defined generally as the market value in the foreign country, excludes import duties, ocean freight, and marine insurance.

Source: Department of Agriculture (Economic Research Service).

TABLE B–103.—U.S. international transactions, 1946–2008

[Millions of dollars; quarterly data seasonally adjusted. Credits (+), debits (–)]

Year or quarter	Goods[1]			Services				Income receipts and payments			Unilateral current transfers, net[2]	Balance on current account
	Exports	Imports	Balance on goods	Net military transactions[2]	Net travel and transportation	Other services, net	Balance on goods and services	Receipts	Payments	Balance on income		
1946	11,764	–5,067	6,697	–424	733	310	7,316	772	–212	560	–2,991	4,88
1947	16,097	–5,973	10,124	–358	946	145	10,857	1,102	–245	857	–2,722	8,99
1948	13,265	–7,557	5,708	–351	374	175	5,906	1,921	–437	1,484	–4,973	2,41
1949	12,213	–6,874	5,339	–410	230	208	5,367	1,831	–476	1,355	–5,849	87
1950	10,203	–9,081	1,122	–56	–120	242	1,188	2,068	–559	1,509	–4,537	–1,84
1951	14,243	–11,176	3,067	169	298	254	3,788	2,633	–583	2,050	–4,954	88
1952	13,449	–10,838	2,611	528	83	309	3,531	2,751	–555	2,196	–5,113	61
1953	12,412	–10,975	1,437	1,753	–238	307	3,259	2,736	–624	2,112	–6,657	–1,28
1954	12,929	–10,353	2,576	902	–269	305	3,514	2,929	–582	2,347	–5,642	21
1955	14,424	–11,527	2,897	–113	–297	299	2,786	3,406	–676	2,730	–5,086	43
1956	17,556	–12,803	4,753	–221	–361	447	4,618	3,837	–735	3,102	–4,990	2,73
1957	19,562	–13,291	6,271	–423	–189	482	6,141	4,180	–796	3,384	–4,763	4,76
1958	16,414	–12,952	3,462	–849	–633	486	2,466	3,790	–825	2,965	–4,647	78
1959	16,458	–15,310	1,148	–831	–821	573	69	4,132	–1,061	3,071	–4,422	–1,28
1960	19,650	–14,758	4,892	–1,057	–964	639	3,508	4,616	–1,238	3,379	–4,062	2,82
1961	20,108	–14,537	5,571	–1,131	–978	732	4,195	4,999	–1,245	3,755	–4,127	3,82
1962	20,781	–16,260	4,521	–912	–1,152	912	3,370	5,618	–1,324	4,294	–4,277	3,38
1963	22,272	–17,048	5,224	–742	–1,309	1,036	4,210	6,157	–1,560	4,596	–4,392	4,41
1964	25,501	–18,700	6,801	–794	–1,146	1,161	6,022	6,824	–1,783	5,041	–4,240	6,82
1965	26,461	–21,510	4,951	–487	–1,280	1,480	4,664	7,437	–2,088	5,350	–4,583	5,43
1966	29,310	–25,493	3,817	–1,043	–1,331	1,497	2,940	7,528	–2,481	5,047	–4,955	3,03
1967	30,666	–26,866	3,800	–1,187	–1,750	1,742	2,604	8,021	–2,747	5,274	–5,294	2,58
1968	33,626	–32,991	635	–596	–1,548	1,759	250	9,367	–3,378	5,990	–5,629	61
1969	36,414	–35,807	607	–718	–1,763	1,964	91	10,913	–4,869	6,044	–5,735	39
1970	42,469	–39,866	2,603	–641	–2,038	2,330	2,254	11,748	–5,515	6,233	–6,156	2,33
1971	43,319	–45,579	–2,260	653	–2,345	2,649	–1,303	12,707	–5,435	7,272	–7,402	–1,43
1972	49,381	–55,797	–6,416	1,072	–3,063	2,965	–5,443	14,765	–6,572	8,192	–8,544	–5,79
1973	71,410	–70,499	911	740	–3,158	3,406	1,900	21,808	–9,655	12,153	–6,913	7,14
1974	98,306	–103,811	–5,505	165	–3,184	4,231	–4,292	27,587	–12,084	15,503	–9,249	1,96
1975	107,088	–98,185	8,903	1,461	–2,812	4,854	12,404	25,351	–12,564	12,787	–7,075	18,11
1976	114,745	–124,228	–9,483	931	–2,558	5,027	–6,082	29,375	–13,311	16,063	–5,686	4,29
1977	120,816	–151,907	–31,091	1,731	–3,565	5,680	–27,246	32,354	–14,217	18,137	–5,226	–14,33
1978	142,075	–176,002	–33,927	857	–3,573	6,879	–29,763	42,088	–21,680	20,408	–5,788	–15,14
1979	184,439	–212,007	–27,568	–1,313	–2,935	7,251	–24,565	63,834	–32,961	30,873	–6,593	–28
1980	224,250	–249,750	–25,500	–1,822	–997	8,912	–19,407	72,606	–42,532	30,073	–8,349	2,31
1981	237,044	–265,067	–28,023	–844	144	12,552	–16,172	86,529	–53,626	32,903	–11,702	5,03
1982	211,157	–247,642	–36,485	112	–992	13,209	–24,156	91,747	–56,583	35,164	–16,544	–5,53
1983	201,799	–268,901	–67,102	–563	–4,227	14,124	–57,767	90,000	–53,614	36,386	–17,310	–38,69
1984	219,926	–332,418	–112,492	–2,547	–8,438	14,404	–109,073	108,819	–73,756	35,063	–20,335	–94,34
1985	215,915	–338,088	–122,173	–4,390	–9,798	14,483	–121,880	98,542	–72,819	25,723	–21,998	–118,15
1986	223,344	–368,425	–145,081	–5,181	–8,779	20,502	–138,538	97,064	–81,571	15,494	–24,132	–147,17
1987	250,208	–409,765	–159,557	–3,844	–8,010	19,728	–151,684	108,184	–93,891	14,293	–23,265	–160,65
1988	320,230	–447,189	–126,959	–6,320	–3,013	21,725	–114,566	136,713	–118,026	18,687	–25,274	–121,15
1989	359,916	–477,665	–117,749	–6,749	3,551	27,805	–93,142	161,287	–141,463	19,824	–26,169	–99,48
1990	387,401	–498,438	–111,037	–7,599	7,501	30,270	–80,864	171,742	–143,192	28,550	–26,654	–78,96
1991	414,083	–491,020	–76,937	–5,275	16,560	34,516	–31,136	149,214	–125,085	24,131	9,904	2,89
1992	439,631	–536,528	–96,897	–1,448	19,969	39,163	–39,212	133,767	–109,532	24,235	–35,100	–50,07
1993	456,943	–589,394	–132,451	1,383	19,714	41,040	–70,311	136,050	–110,741	25,316	–39,811	–84,80
1994	502,859	–668,690	–165,831	2,570	16,305	48,463	–98,493	166,521	–149,375	17,146	–40,265	–121,61
1995	575,204	–749,374	–174,170	4,600	21,772	51,414	–96,384	210,244	–189,353	20,891	–38,074	–113,56
1996	612,113	–803,113	–191,000	5,385	25,015	56,535	–104,065	226,129	–203,811	22,318	–43,017	–124,76
1997	678,366	–876,794	–198,428	4,968	22,152	63,035	–108,273	256,804	–244,195	12,609	–45,062	–140,72
1998	670,416	–918,637	–248,221	5,220	10,210	66,651	–166,140	261,819	–257,554	4,265	–53,187	–215,06
1999	683,965	–1,031,784	–347,819	2,593	7,085	73,051	–265,090	293,925	–280,037	13,888	–50,428	–301,63
2000	771,994	–1,226,684	–454,690	317	2,486	72,052	–379,835	350,918	–329,864	21,054	–58,645	–417,42
2001	718,712	–1,148,231	–429,519	–2,296	–3,254	69,943	–365,126	290,797	–259,075	31,722	–51,295	–384,69
2002	682,422	–1,167,377	–484,955	–7,158	–4,245	72,633	–423,725	280,942	–253,544	27,398	–64,948	–461,27
2003	713,415	–1,264,307	–550,892	–11,981	–11,475	77,433	–496,915	320,456	–275,147	45,309	–71,794	–523,40
2004	807,516	–1,477,094	–669,578	–13,518	–14,275	89,640	–607,730	413,739	–346,519	67,219	–84,482	–624,99
2005	894,631	–1,681,780	–787,149	–10,536	–13,006	99,124	–711,567	535,263	–462,905	72,358	–89,784	–728,99
2006	1,023,109	–1,861,380	–838,270	–13,602	–10,788	109,377	–753,283	685,150	–627,956	57,194	–92,027	–788,11
2007	1,148,481	–1,967,853	–819,373	–16,768	2,181	133,702	–700,258	817,779	–736,030	81,749	–112,705	–731,21
2007: I	270,318	–473,681	–203,363	–3,286	–1,587	28,692	–179,543	186,746	–173,959	12,787	–30,174	–196,93
II	279,488	–485,375	–205,887	–4,085	–806	31,960	–178,819	202,171	–192,492	9,679	–24,953	–194,09
III	295,494	–496,698	–201,204	–4,251	1,064	36,276	–168,114	213,520	–190,562	22,958	–27,796	–172,95
IV	303,180	–512,099	–208,919	–5,146	3,509	36,773	–173,783	215,343	–179,016	36,327	–29,784	–167,24
2008: I	317,813	–528,845	–211,032	–4,398	3,115	35,205	–177,111	199,827	–166,615	33,212	–31,742	–175,64
II p	337,312	–553,641	–216,328	–5,340	4,471	36,646	–180,551	194,873	–167,529	27,344	–29,941	–183,14

[1] Adjusted from Census data for differences in valuation, coverage, and timing; excludes military.
[2] Includes transfers of goods and services under U.S. military grant programs.

See next page for continuation of table.

[Millions of dollars; quarterly data seasonally adjusted. Credits (+), debits (−)]

Year or quarter	Capital account transactions, net	U.S.-owned assets abroad, excluding financial derivatives [increase/financial outflow (−)]				Foreign-owned assets in the U.S., excluding financial derivatives [increase/financial inflow (+)]			Financial derivatives, net	Statistical discrepancy	
		Total	U.S. official reserve assets [3]	Other U.S. Government assets	U.S. private assets	Total	Foreign official assets	Other foreign assets		Total (sum of the items with sign reversed)	Of which: Seasonal adjustment discrepancy
1946		−623									
1947		−3,315									
1948		−1,736									
1949		−266									
1950		1,758									
1951		−33									
1952		−415									
1953		1,256									
1954		480									
1955		182									
1956		−869									
1957		−1,165									
1958		2,292									
1959		1,035									
1960		−4,099	2,145	−1,100	−5,144	2,294	1,473	821		−1,019	
1961		−5,538	607	−910	−5,235	2,705	765	1,939		−989	
1962		−4,174	1,535	−1,085	−4,623	1,911	1,270	641		−1,124	
1963		−7,270	378	−1,662	−5,986	3,217	1,986	1,231		−360	
1964		−9,560	171	−1,680	−8,050	3,643	1,660	1,983		−907	
1965		−5,716	1,225	−1,605	−5,336	742	134	607		−457	
1966		−7,321	570	−1,543	−6,347	3,661	−672	4,333		629	
1967		−9,757	53	−2,423	−7,386	7,379	3,451	3,928		−205	
1968		−10,977	−870	−2,274	−7,833	9,928	−774	10,703		438	
1969		−11,585	−1,179	−2,200	−8,206	12,702	−1,301	14,002		−1,516	
1970		−8,470	3,348	−1,589	−10,229	6,359	6,908	−550		−219	
1971		−11,758	3,066	−1,884	−12,940	22,970	26,879	−3,909		−9,779	
1972		−13,787	706	−1,568	−12,925	21,461	10,475	10,986		−1,879	
1973		−22,874	158	−2,644	−20,388	18,388	6,026	12,362		−2,654	
1974		−34,745	−1,467	366	−33,643	35,227	10,546	24,682		−2,444	
1975		−39,703	−849	−3,474	−35,380	16,870	7,027	9,843		4,717	
1976		−51,269	−2,558	−4,214	−44,498	37,839	17,693	20,147		9,134	
1977		−34,785	−375	−3,693	−30,717	52,770	36,816	15,954		−3,650	
1978		−61,130	732	−4,660	−57,202	66,275	33,678	32,597		9,997	
1979		−64,915	6	−3,746	−61,176	39,554	−13,665	53,218		25,647	
1980		−85,815	−7,003	−5,162	−73,651	60,885	15,497	45,388		22,613	
1981		−113,054	−4,082	−5,097	−103,875	84,591	4,960	79,631		23,433	
1982	199	−127,882	−4,965	−6,131	−116,786	95,056	3,593	91,464		38,163	
1983	209	−66,373	−1,196	−5,006	−60,172	87,399	5,845	81,554		17,457	
1984	235	−40,376	−3,131	−5,489	−31,757	116,048	3,140	112,908		18,437	
1985	315	−44,752	−3,858	−2,821	−38,074	144,231	−1,119	145,349		18,362	
1986	301	−111,723	312	−2,022	−110,014	228,330	35,648	192,681		30,269	
1987	365	−79,296	9,149	1,006	−89,450	247,100	45,387	201,713		−7,514	
1988	493	−106,573	−3,912	2,967	−105,628	244,833	39,758	205,075		−17,600	
1989	336	−175,383	−25,293	1,233	−151,323	222,777	8,503	214,274		51,756	
1990	−6,579	−81,234	−2,158	2,317	−81,393	139,357	33,910	105,447		27,425	
1991	−4,479	−64,389	5,763	2,923	−73,075	108,221	17,388	90,833		−42,252	
1992	−557	−74,410	3,901	−1,667	−76,644	168,349	40,476	127,872		−43,304	
1993	−1,299	−200,551	−1,379	−351	−198,823	279,758	71,753	208,005		6,898	
1994	−1,723	−178,937	5,346	−390	−183,893	303,174	39,583	263,591		−902	
1995	−927	−352,264	−9,742	−984	−341,538	435,102	109,880	325,222		31,656	
1996	−735	−413,409	6,668	−989	−419,088	547,885	126,724	421,161		−8,977	
1997	−1,027	−485,475	−1,010	68	−484,533	704,452	19,036	685,416		−77,224	
1998	−766	−353,829	−6,783	−422	−346,624	420,794	−19,903	440,697		148,863	
1999	−4,939	−504,062	8,747	2,750	−515,559	742,210	43,543	698,667		68,421	
2000	−1,010	−560,523	−290	−941	−559,292	1,038,224	42,758	995,466		−59,265	
2001	−1,270	−382,616	−4,911	−486	−377,219	782,870	28,059	754,811		−14,285	
2002	−1,470	−294,645	−3,681	345	−291,310	795,161	115,945	679,216		−37,770	
2003	−3,480	−325,424	1,523	537	−327,484	858,303	278,069	580,234		−6,000	
2004	−2,369	−1,000,870	2,805	1,710	−1,005,385	1,533,201	397,755	1,135,446		95,030	
2005	−4,036	−546,631	14,096	5,539	−566,266	1,247,347	259,268	988,079		32,313	
2006	−3,880	−1,251,749	2,374	5,346	−1,259,469	2,061,113	487,939	1,573,174	29,710	−47,078	
2007	−1,843	−1,289,854	−122	−22,273	−1,267,459	2,057,703	411,058	1,646,645	6,496	−41,287	
2007: I	−543	−442,065	−72	445	−442,438	692,713	163,270	529,443	14,795	−67,970	12,192
II	−112	−523,556	26	−596	−522,985	718,112	88,822	629,290	−1,007	656	722
III	−617	−170,476	−54	623	−171,045	266,476	13,469	253,007	5,942	71,627	−21,805
IV	−571	−153,757	−22	−22,744	−130,990	380,402	145,497	234,905	−13,234	−45,600	8,892
2008: I	−600	−260,644	−276	3,265	−263,634	−459,017	173,533	285,484	−8,001	−14,131	9,271
II p	−652	110,431	−1,267	−41,265	152,963	26,301	144,417	−118,116		47,067	−3,464

[3] Consists of gold, special drawing rights, foreign currencies, and the U.S. reserve position in the International Monetary Fund (IMF).

Source: Department of Commerce (Bureau of Economic Analysis).

TABLE B–104.—U.S. international trade in goods by principal end-use category, 1965–2008

[Billions of dollars; quarterly data seasonally adjusted]

Year or quarter	Exports							Imports						
			Nonagricultural products							Nonpetroleum products				
	Total	Agricultural products	Total	Industrial supplies and materials	Capital goods except automotive	Automotive	Other	Total	Petroleum and products	Total	Industrial supplies and materials	Capital goods except automotive	Automotive	Other
1965	26.5	6.3	20.2	7.6	8.1	1.9	2.6	21.5	2.0	19.5	9.1	1.5	0.9	8.0
1966	29.3	6.9	22.4	8.2	8.9	2.4	2.9	25.5	2.1	23.4	10.2	2.2	1.8	9.2
1967	30.7	6.5	24.2	8.5	9.9	2.8	3.0	26.9	2.1	24.8	10.0	2.5	2.4	9.9
1968	33.6	6.3	27.3	9.6	11.1	3.5	3.2	33.0	2.4	30.6	12.0	2.8	4.0	11.8
1969	36.4	6.1	30.3	10.3	12.4	3.9	3.7	35.8	2.6	33.2	11.8	3.4	4.9	13.0
1970	42.5	7.4	35.1	12.3	14.7	3.9	4.3	39.9	2.9	36.9	12.4	4.0	5.5	15.0
1971	43.3	7.8	35.5	10.9	15.4	4.7	4.5	45.6	3.7	41.9	13.8	4.3	7.4	16.4
1972	49.4	9.5	39.9	11.9	16.9	5.5	5.6	55.8	4.7	51.1	16.3	5.9	8.7	20.2
1973	71.4	18.0	53.4	17.0	22.0	6.9	7.6	70.5	8.4	62.1	19.6	8.3	10.3	23.9
1974	98.3	22.4	75.9	26.3	30.9	8.6	10.0	103.8	26.6	77.2	27.8	9.8	12.0	27.5
1975	107.1	22.2	84.8	26.8	36.6	10.6	10.8	98.2	27.0	71.2	24.0	10.2	11.7	25.3
1976	114.7	23.4	91.4	28.4	39.1	12.1	11.7	124.2	34.6	89.7	29.8	12.3	16.2	31.4
1977	120.8	24.3	96.5	29.8	39.8	13.4	13.5	151.9	45.0	106.9	35.7	14.0	18.6	38.6
1978 [1]	142.1	29.9	112.2	34.2	47.5	15.2	15.3	176.0	42.6	133.4	40.7	19.3	25.0	48.4
1979	184.4	35.5	149.0	52.2	60.2	17.9	18.7	212.0	60.4	151.6	47.5	24.6	26.6	52.8
1980	224.3	42.0	182.2	65.1	76.3	17.4	23.4	249.8	79.5	170.2	53.0	31.6	28.3	57.4
1981	237.0	44.1	193.0	63.6	84.2	19.7	25.5	265.1	78.4	186.7	56.1	37.1	31.0	62.4
1982	211.2	37.3	173.9	57.7	76.5	17.2	22.4	247.6	62.0	185.7	48.6	38.4	34.3	64.3
1983	201.8	37.1	164.7	52.7	71.7	18.5	21.8	268.9	55.1	213.8	53.7	43.7	43.0	73.3
1984	219.9	38.4	181.5	56.8	77.0	22.4	25.3	332.4	58.1	274.4	66.1	60.4	56.5	91.4
1985	215.9	29.6	186.3	54.8	79.3	24.9	27.2	338.1	51.4	286.7	62.6	61.3	64.9	97.9
1986	223.3	27.2	196.2	59.4	82.8	25.1	28.9	368.4	34.3	334.1	69.9	72.0	78.1	114.2
1987	250.2	29.8	220.4	63.7	92.7	27.6	36.4	409.8	42.9	366.8	70.8	85.1	85.2	125.7
1988	320.2	38.8	281.4	82.6	119.1	33.4	46.3	447.2	39.6	407.6	83.1	102.2	87.9	134.4
1989 [1]	359.9	41.1	318.8	90.5	136.9	35.1	56.3	477.7	50.9	426.8	84.6	112.3	87.4	142.5
1990	387.4	40.2	347.2	97.0	153.0	36.2	61.0	498.4	62.3	436.1	83.0	116.4	88.2	148.5
1991	414.1	40.1	374.0	101.6	166.6	39.9	65.9	491.0	51.7	439.3	81.3	121.1	85.5	151.4
1992	439.6	44.1	395.6	101.7	176.4	46.9	70.6	536.5	51.6	484.9	89.1	134.8	91.5	169.6
1993	456.9	43.6	413.3	105.1	182.7	51.6	74.0	589.4	51.5	537.9	100.8	153.2	102.1	182.0
1994	502.9	47.1	455.8	112.7	205.7	57.5	79.9	668.7	51.3	617.4	113.6	185.0	118.1	200.6
1995	575.2	57.2	518.0	135.6	234.4	61.4	86.5	749.4	56.0	693.3	128.5	222.1	123.7	219.0
1996	612.1	61.5	550.6	138.7	254.0	64.4	93.6	803.1	72.7	730.4	136.1	228.4	128.7	237.1
1997	678.4	58.5	619.9	148.6	295.8	73.4	102.0	876.8	71.8	805.0	144.9	253.6	139.4	267.1
1998	670.4	53.2	617.3	139.4	299.8	72.5	105.5	918.6	50.9	867.7	151.6	269.8	148.6	297.7
1999	684.0	49.7	634.3	140.3	311.2	75.3	107.5	1,031.8	67.8	964.0	156.3	295.7	179.0	333.0
2000	772.0	52.8	719.2	163.9	357.0	80.4	117.9	1,226.7	120.3	1,106.4	181.9	347.0	195.9	381.6
2001	718.7	54.9	663.8	150.5	321.7	75.4	116.2	1,148.2	103.6	1,044.6	172.5	298.0	189.8	384.3
2002	682.4	54.5	627.9	147.6	290.4	78.9	110.9	1,167.4	103.5	1,063.9	164.6	283.3	203.7	412.2
2003	713.4	60.9	652.5	162.5	293.7	80.6	115.7	1,264.3	133.1	1,131.2	181.4	295.9	210.1	443.8
2004	807.5	62.9	744.6	192.2	331.4	89.2	131.7	1,477.1	180.5	1,296.6	232.5	343.6	228.2	492.4
2005	894.6	64.9	829.7	221.5	363.3	98.4	146.6	1,681.8	251.9	1,429.9	272.7	379.3	239.4	538.5
2006	1,023.1	72.9	950.2	263.2	415.0	107.0	165.1	1,861.4	302.4	1,559.0	300.1	418.3	256.6	584.0
2007	1,148.5	92.1	1,056.4	302.3	447.4	121.0	185.6	1,967.9	331.0	1,636.9	308.4	444.5	258.9	625.1
2005: I	214.9	15.8	199.1	53.7	86.2	23.7	35.4	399.9	53.5	346.3	65.0	90.8	57.9	132.6
II	223.7	16.5	207.2	56.3	90.8	23.9	36.3	412.4	57.5	354.9	65.7	95.3	58.6	135.3
III	223.6	16.0	207.6	55.4	90.6	24.7	36.9	422.8	66.7	356.1	66.4	95.4	60.0	134.3
IV	232.4	16.6	215.9	56.0	95.7	26.1	38.0	446.8	74.1	372.7	75.6	97.8	62.8	136.4
2006: I	244.7	17.5	227.2	60.8	100.3	26.4	39.8	453.3	73.3	380.0	73.7	101.0	64.5	140.8
II	253.3	18.1	235.2	65.8	103.0	26.2	40.3	465.0	78.4	386.6	74.6	103.9	64.5	143.7
III	259.3	18.5	240.8	67.8	104.0	27.1	41.8	477.9	83.3	394.6	77.4	106.6	62.9	147.7
IV	265.8	18.8	247.0	68.8	107.8	27.3	43.1	465.2	67.4	397.8	74.4	106.9	64.7	151.8
2007: I	270.3	19.9	250.4	69.5	107.5	28.4	45.0	473.7	70.8	402.9	74.3	108.9	64.2	155.5
II	279.5	21.5	258.0	74.8	108.3	29.6	45.2	485.4	78.1	407.2	78.7	109.9	63.5	155.1
III	295.5	25.0	270.5	77.4	114.4	31.6	47.2	496.7	83.0	413.7	79.1	112.4	66.2	156.0
IV	303.2	25.7	277.5	80.6	117.2	31.4	48.2	512.1	99.0	413.1	76.3	113.3	65.0	158.8
2008: I	317.8	29.5	288.4	89.3	116.5	30.6	51.9	528.8	112.2	416.7	80.5	113.6	64.3	158.3
II [p]	337.3	32.5	304.9	99.5	120.1	31.0	54.1	553.6	123.6	430.0	86.0	117.3	62.5	164.2

[1] End-use commodity classifications beginning 1978 and 1989 are not strictly comparable with data for earlier periods. See *Survey of Current Business*, June 1988 and July 2001.

Note.—Data are on a balance of payments basis and exclude military. In June 1990, end-use categories for goods exports were redefined to include reexports (exports of foreign goods); beginning with data for 1978, reexports are assigned to detailed end-use categories in the same manner as exports of domestic goods.

Source: Department of Commerce (Bureau of Economic Analysis).

TABLE B–105.—U.S. international trade in goods by area, 2000–2008

[Millions of dollars]

Item	2000	2001	2002	2003	2004	2005	2006	2007	2008 first 2 quarters at annual rate [1]
PORTS									
al, all countries	771,994	718,712	682,422	713,415	807,516	894,631	1,023,109	1,148,481	1,310,250
Europe	184,657	178,229	160,045	168,314	189,416	207,895	241,274	280,845	335,766
Euro area [2]	114,930	111,026	103,837	109,898	124,762	135,685	153,696	178,328	205,932
France	20,161	19,693	18,871	16,849	21,083	22,228	23,990	27,133	29,598
Germany	28,921	29,363	26,027	28,290	30,842	33,585	40,743	49,025	55,264
Italy	10,951	9,715	9,810	10,286	10,420	11,245	12,272	13,893	16,372
United Kingdom	40,725	39,701	32,085	32,871	35,124	37,569	44,215	48,733	57,312
Canada	178,877	163,259	160,916	169,930	189,981	212,192	230,983	249,712	272,124
Latin America and Other Western Hemisphere	170,267	158,969	148,158	148,955	171,887	192,382	222,298	243,063	281,100
Brazil	15,257	15,790	12,267	11,125	13,727	15,173	19,088	24,497	29,524
Mexico	111,172	101,181	97,242	97,224	110,697	120,264	133,892	135,962	147,910
Venezuela	5,509	5,600	3,967	2,782	4,743	6,411	8,977	10,193	10,964
Asia and Pacific	211,043	188,731	185,665	198,047	221,860	237,511	274,532	308,248	344,376
China	16,141	19,108	22,040	28,287	34,638	41,800	55,038	65,073	73,044
India	3,668	3,754	4,097	4,977	6,091	7,973	9,990	17,516	17,554
Japan	63,473	55,879	49,670	50,252	52,288	53,265	57,593	60,898	67,032
Korea, Republic of	27,150	21,203	21,756	23,481	25,730	27,136	31,418	33,646	36,240
Singapore	17,620	17,337	15,977	16,147	19,252	20,259	24,255	25,874	31,128
Taiwan	23,832	17,394	17,886	16,987	21,296	21,454	22,645	25,961	27,926
Middle East	16,984	18,141	17,867	18,047	21,594	29,765	35,795	43,646	50,382
Africa	10,165	11,383	9,771	10,122	12,778	14,886	18,228	22,966	26,504
Memorandum: Members of OPEC [3]	17,625	19,503	17,808	16,554	21,579	21,305	39,108	48,659	58,308
PORTS									
al, all countries	1,226,684	1,148,231	1,167,377	1,264,307	1,477,094	1,681,780	1,861,380	1,967,853	2,164,972
Europe	259,848	255,988	261,340	285,270	321,486	355,404	383,812	411,179	456,832
Euro area [2]	163,636	166,508	172,762	187,937	209,746	229,206	246,862	268,772	290,828
France	29,809	30,421	28,289	29,244	31,609	33,848	37,037	41,544	44,930
Germany	58,588	59,141	62,540	68,188	77,349	84,967	89,237	94,280	103,366
Italy	25,034	23,768	24,209	25,398	28,096	30,975	32,660	35,027	37,740
United Kingdom	43,379	41,185	40,597	42,610	46,087	50,800	53,187	56,367	58,652
Canada	234,084	219,243	212,225	224,955	259,871	294,080	306,066	320,323	359,764
Latin America and Other Western Hemisphere	210,186	199,660	205,193	218,526	256,746	295,914	334,876	348,378	389,190
Brazil	13,854	14,467	15,782	17,917	21,164	24,441	26,373	25,650	30,152
Mexico	136,829	132,279	135,701	139,695	158,096	173,034	201,195	213,552	226,480
Venezuela	18,623	15,251	15,093	17,136	24,921	33,978	37,134	39,910	52,168
Asia and Pacific	455,941	411,473	432,214	462,063	542,072	608,703	684,298	718,562	721,148
China	100,112	102,403	125,316	152,671	196,973	243,886	288,126	321,685	314,428
India	10,691	9,755	11,821	13,068	15,577	18,819	21,845	24,102	26,184
Japan	146,711	126,685	121,617	118,264	130,094	138,375	148,560	146,037	150,498
Korea, Republic of	40,309	35,207	35,606	37,238	46,177	43,791	45,811	47,547	49,652
Singapore	19,273	15,080	14,821	15,161	15,406	15,131	17,712	18,423	17,274
Taiwan	40,980	33,642	32,611	32,118	34,986	35,103	38,414	38,489	37,026
Middle East	38,977	36,424	34,304	41,469	51,283	62,467	71,907	77,405	114,722
Africa	27,648	25,443	22,101	32,024	45,636	65,211	80,420	92,005	123,314
Memorandum: Members of OPEC [3]	67,094	59,755	53,246	68,346	94,109	124,942	145,367	174,340	253,724
ALANCE (excess of exports +)									
al, all countries	−454,690	−429,519	−484,955	−550,892	−669,578	−787,149	−838,270	−819,373	−854,720
Europe	−75,191	−77,759	−101,295	−116,956	−132,070	−147,509	−142,538	−130,334	−121,066
Euro area [2]	−48,706	−55,482	−68,925	−78,039	−84,984	−93,521	−93,166	−90,445	−84,894
France	−9,648	−10,728	−9,418	−12,395	−10,526	−11,620	−13,047	−14,411	−15,332
Germany	−29,667	−29,778	−36,513	−39,898	−46,507	−51,382	−48,494	−45,255	−48,102
Italy	−14,083	−14,053	−14,399	−15,112	−17,676	−19,730	−20,388	−21,134	−21,368
United Kingdom	−2,654	−1,484	−8,512	−9,739	−10,963	−13,231	−8,971	−7,634	−1,338
Canada	−55,207	−55,984	−51,309	−55,025	−69,890	−81,888	−75,083	−70,611	−87,640
Latin America and Other Western Hemisphere	−39,919	−40,691	−57,035	−69,571	−84,859	−103,532	−112,579	−105,316	−108,092
Brazil	1,403	1,323	−3,515	−6,792	−7,437	−9,268	−7,285	−1,153	−628
Mexico	−25,657	−31,098	−38,459	−42,471	−47,399	−52,770	−67,302	−77,589	−78,570
Venezuela	−13,114	−9,651	−11,126	−14,354	−20,178	−27,568	−28,157	−29,717	−41,204
Asia and Pacific	−244,898	−222,742	−246,549	−264,016	−320,212	−371,192	−409,766	−410,314	−376,774
China	−83,971	−83,295	−103,276	−124,384	−162,335	−202,085	−233,087	−256,611	−241,382
India	−7,023	−6,001	−7,724	−8,091	−9,486	−10,846	−11,854	−6,586	−8,630
Japan	−83,238	−70,806	−71,947	−68,012	−77,806	−85,110	−90,967	−85,139	−83,466
Korea, Republic of	−13,159	−14,004	−13,850	−13,757	−20,447	−16,655	−14,393	−13,901	−13,412
Singapore	−1,653	2,257	1,156	986	3,846	5,127	6,543	7,451	13,854
Taiwan	−17,148	−16,248	−14,725	−15,131	−13,690	−13,650	−15,769	−12,528	−9,098
Middle East	−21,993	−18,283	−16,437	−23,422	−29,689	−32,702	−36,112	−33,759	−64,342
Africa	−17,483	−14,060	−12,330	−21,902	−32,858	−50,325	−62,192	−69,039	−96,808
Memorandum: Members of OPEC [3]	−49,469	−40,252	−35,438	−51,792	−72,530	−93,637	−106,259	−125,681	−195,416

[1] Preliminary; seasonally adjusted.
[2] Euro area consists of: Austria, Belgium, Cyprus (beginning in 2008), Finland, France, Germany, Greece (beginning in 2001), Ireland, Italy, Luxembourg, Malta ginning in 2008), Netherlands, Portugal, Slovenia (beginning in 2007), and Spain.
[3] Organization of Petroleum Exporting Countries, consisting of Algeria, Angola (beginning in 2007), Ecuador (beginning in 2007), Indonesia, Iran, Iraq, Kuwait, ya, Nigeria, Qatar, Saudi Arabia, United Arab Emirates, and Venezuela.

Note.—Data are on a balance of payments basis and exclude military. For further details, and additional data by country, see *Survey of Current Business,* y 2008.

Source: Department of Commerce (Bureau of Economic Analysis).

TABLE B–106.—*U.S. international trade in goods on balance of payments (BOP) and Census basis, and trade in services on BOP basis, 1981–2008*

[Billions of dollars; monthly data seasonally adjusted]

Year or month	Goods: Exports (f.a.s. value)[1,2]							Goods: Imports (customs value)[5]							Services (BOP basis)	
	Total, BOP basis[3]	Census basis (by end-use category)						Total, BOP basis	Census basis (by end-use category)						Exports	Imports
		Total, Census basis[3,4]	Foods, feeds, and beverages	Industrial supplies and materials	Capital goods except automotive	Automotive vehicles, parts, and engines	Consumer goods (nonfood) except automotive		Total, Census basis[4]	Foods, feeds, and beverages	Industrial supplies and materials	Capital goods except automotive	Automotive vehicles, parts, and engines	Consumer goods (nonfood) except automotive		
1981	237.0	238.7						265.1	261.0						57.4	4
1982	211.2	216.4	31.3	61.7	72.7	15.7	14.3	247.6	244.0	17.1	112.0	35.4	33.3	39.7	64.1	5
1983	201.8	205.6	30.9	56.7	67.2	16.8	13.4	268.9	258.0	18.2	107.0	40.9	40.8	44.9	64.3	5
1984	219.9	224.0	31.5	61.7	72.0	20.6	13.3	332.4	[6]330.7	21.0	123.7	59.8	53.5	60.0	71.2	6
1985	215.9	[7]218.8	24.0	58.5	73.9	22.9	12.6	338.1	[6]336.5	21.9	113.9	65.1	66.8	68.3	73.2	7
1986	223.3	[7]227.2	22.3	57.3	75.8	21.7	14.2	368.4	365.4	24.4	101.3	71.8	78.2	79.4	86.7	8
1987	250.2	254.1	24.3	66.7	86.2	24.6	17.7	409.8	406.2	24.8	111.0	84.5	85.2	88.7	98.7	9
1988	320.2	322.4	32.3	85.1	109.2	29.3	23.1	447.2	441.0	24.8	118.3	101.4	87.7	95.9	110.9	9
1989	359.9	363.8	37.2	99.3	138.8	34.8	36.4	477.7	473.2	25.1	132.3	113.3	86.1	102.9	127.1	10.
1990	387.4	393.6	35.1	104.4	152.7	37.4	43.3	498.4	495.3	26.6	143.2	116.4	87.3	105.7	147.8	11
1991	414.1	421.7	35.7	109.7	166.7	40.0	45.9	491.0	488.5	26.5	131.6	120.7	85.7	108.0	164.3	11
1992	439.6	448.2	40.3	109.1	175.9	47.0	51.4	536.5	532.7	27.6	138.6	134.3	91.8	122.7	177.3	11.
1993	456.9	465.1	40.6	111.8	181.7	52.4	54.7	589.4	580.7	27.9	145.6	152.4	102.4	134.0	185.9	12.
1994	502.9	512.6	42.0	121.4	205.0	57.8	60.0	668.7	663.3	31.0	162.1	184.4	118.3	146.3	200.4	13.
1995	575.2	584.7	50.5	146.2	233.0	61.8	64.4	749.4	743.5	33.2	181.8	221.4	123.8	159.9	219.2	14
1996	612.1	625.1	55.5	147.7	253.0	65.0	70.1	803.1	795.3	35.7	204.5	228.1	128.9	172.0	239.5	15.
1997	678.4	689.2	51.5	158.2	294.5	74.0	77.4	876.8	869.7	39.7	213.8	253.3	139.8	193.8	256.1	16
1998	670.4	682.1	46.4	148.3	299.4	72.4	80.3	918.6	911.9	41.2	200.1	269.5	148.7	217.0	262.8	18
1999	684.0	695.8	46.0	147.5	310.8	75.3	80.9	1,031.8	1,024.6	43.6	221.4	295.7	179.0	241.9	281.9	19
2000	772.0	781.9	47.9	172.6	356.9	80.4	89.4	1,226.7	1,218.0	46.0	299.0	347.0	195.9	281.8	298.6	22
2001	718.7	729.1	49.4	160.1	321.7	75.4	88.3	1,140.0	1,141.0	46.6	273.9	298.0	189.8	284.3	286.2	22
2002	682.4	693.1	49.6	156.8	290.4	78.9	84.4	1,167.4	1,161.4	49.7	267.7	283.3	203.7	307.8	292.3	23
2003	713.4	724.8	55.0	173.0	293.7	80.6	89.9	1,264.3	1,257.1	55.8	313.8	295.9	210.1	333.9	304.3	25
2004	807.5	818.8	56.6	203.9	331.4	89.2	103.2	1,477.1	1,469.7	62.1	412.8	343.6	228.2	372.9	353.1	29
2005	894.6	906.0	59.0	233.0	363.3	98.4	115.3	1,681.8	1,673.5	68.1	523.8	379.3	239.4	407.2	389.1	31
2006	1,023.1	1,036.6	66.0	276.0	415.0	107.0	129.1	1,861.4	1,853.9	74.9	602.0	418.3	256.6	442.6	433.9	34
2007	1,148.5	1,162.5	84.3	316.3	447.4	121.0	146.1	1,967.9	1,957.0	81.7	634.7	444.5	258.9	474.9	497.2	37
2007: Jan	90.3	91.5	6.1	23.8	36.8	9.2	11.7	156.5	155.9	6.5	48.7	36.1	21.1	38.5	38.1	3
Feb	89.0	90.0	6.3	23.8	35.2	9.4	11.5	155.5	155.0	6.6	45.6	36.5	21.2	40.0	38.0	3
Mar	91.1	92.4	6.1	24.9	35.5	9.8	11.9	161.8	160.3	6.8	49.8	36.3	21.9	40.5	39.1	3
Apr	91.2	92.5	6.5	25.4	35.0	9.8	11.9	160.0	158.8	6.6	50.5	36.1	21.3	39.2	39.3	3
May	93.4	94.7	6.5	25.9	36.7	9.9	12.1	161.9	160.8	6.7	52.0	36.2	20.7	39.4	40.3	3
June	94.9	96.0	6.7	27.0	36.7	9.9	11.8	163.5	162.9	6.8	52.8	37.2	21.4	39.5	40.9	3
July	97.5	98.7	6.9	26.5	38.2	10.9	12.3	165.3	164.2	6.9	53.5	37.2	22.2	39.1	42.5	3
Aug	98.5	99.6	7.5	27.4	38.1	10.3	12.4	165.2	164.2	7.0	53.5	37.3	21.9	39.2	43.6	3
Sept	99.5	100.4	8.1	27.6	38.1	10.4	12.6	166.2	165.1	7.0	53.5	37.9	22.1	39.4	43.3	3
Oct	100.4	101.4	7.7	27.6	39.0	10.5	12.5	168.1	167.2	6.9	55.1	37.7	22.2	40.0	43.7	3
Nov	101.0	102.4	8.0	28.0	38.8	10.8	12.3	172.7	172.0	7.1	59.2	37.9	22.1	40.3	44.2	3
Dec	101.8	102.9	8.0	28.7	39.4	10.1	12.8	171.4	170.5	6.9	60.3	37.7	20.7	39.7	44.3	3
2008: Jan	104.7	105.5	8.6	29.7	39.4	10.3	13.3	174.8	174.0	7.1	64.0	37.4	21.2	39.1	44.7	3
Feb	108.1	109.0	9.1	31.8	39.3	10.8	13.4	180.6	178.9	7.2	64.5	38.3	22.8	41.0	44.5	3
Mar	105.0	105.5	9.6	31.5	37.8	9.4	12.6	173.4	171.8	7.1	61.5	37.9	20.3	39.5	44.7	3
Apr	110.1	110.8	9.9	32.7	40.1	10.0	13.4	183.0	181.4	7.4	67.5	39.1	21.5	40.2	45.0	3.
May	111.0	111.5	9.7	34.2	39.4	10.2	13.4	183.1	182.4	7.6	67.1	39.8	20.5	41.8	45.9	3
June	116.3	117.0	10.4	36.7	40.6	10.8	14.1	187.5	186.8	7.5	73.4	38.4	20.5	41.3	46.5	3
July	120.8	121.7	10.4	38.3	41.5	12.2	14.9	194.9	193.9	7.5	79.9	39.0	20.4	41.1	47.3	3
Aug	117.9	119.0	10.2	37.4	42.3	10.5	14.0	188.9	188.3	7.8	73.8	38.3	19.3	43.6	47.4	3
Sept.p	108.1	108.5	9.1	33.3	38.1	10.3	13.5	177.7	176.2	7.6	65.7	38.8	18.6	40.1	47.3	3

[1] Department of Defense shipments of grant-aid military supplies and equipment under the Military Assistance Program are excluded from total exports through 1985 and included beginning 1986.

[2] F.a.s. (free alongside ship) value basis at U.S. port of exportation for exports.

[3] Beginning with 1989 data, exports have been adjusted for undocumented exports to Canada and are included in the appropriate end-use categories. For prior years, only total exports include this adjustment.

[4] Total includes "other" exports or imports, not shown separately.

[5] Total arrivals of imported goods other than in-transit shipments.

[6] Total includes revisions not reflected in detail.

[7] Total exports are on a revised statistical month basis; end-use categories are on a statistical month basis.

Note.—Goods on a Census basis are adjusted to a BOP basis by the Bureau of Economic Analysis, in line with concepts and definitions used to prepare international and national accounts. The adjustments are necessary to supplement coverage of Census data, to eliminate duplication of transactions recorded elsewhere in international accounts, and to value transactions according to a standard definition.

Data include international trade of the U.S. Virgin Islands, Puerto Rico, and U.S. Foreign Trade Zones.

Source: Department of Commerce (Bureau of the Census and Bureau of Economic Analysis).

TABLE B–107.—*International investment position of the United States at year-end, 2000–2007*

[Millions of dollars]

Type of investment	2000	2001	2002	2003	2004	2005	2006	2007 p
NET INTERNATIONAL INVESTMENT POSITION OF THE UNITED STATES	−1,330,630	−1,868,875	−2,037,970	−2,086,513	−2,245,417	−1,925,146	−2,225,804	−2,441,829
Financial derivatives, net [1]	....	....	....	....	....	57,915	59,836	83,529
Net international investment position, excluding financial derivatives	−1,330,630	−1,868,875	−2,037,970	−2,086,513	−2,245,417	−1,983,061	−2,285,640	−2,525,358
U.S.-OWNED ASSETS ABROAD	6,238,785	6,308,681	6,649,079	7,638,086	9,340,634	11,961,552	14,381,297	17,639,954
Financial derivatives, gross positive fair value [1]	....	....	....	....	....	1,190,029	1,238,995	2,284,581
U.S.-owned assets abroad, excluding financial derivatives	6,238,785	6,308,681	6,649,079	7,638,086	9,340,634	10,771,523	13,142,302	15,355,373
U.S. official reserve assets	128,400	129,961	158,602	183,577	189,591	188,043	219,853	277,211
Gold [2]	71,799	72,328	90,806	108,866	113,947	134,175	165,267	218,025
Special drawing rights	10,539	10,783	12,166	12,638	13,628	8,210	8,870	9,476
Reserve position in the International Monetary Fund	14,824	17,869	21,979	22,535	19,544	8,036	5,040	4,244
Foreign currencies	31,238	28,981	33,651	39,538	42,472	37,622	40,676	45,466
U.S. Government assets, other than official reserve assets	85,168	85,654	85,309	84,772	83,062	77,523	72,189	94,471
U.S. credits and other long-term assets [3]	82,574	83,132	82,682	81,980	80,308	76,960	71,635	70,015
Repayable in dollars	82,293	82,854	82,406	81,706	80,035	76,687	71,362	69,742
Other [4]	281	278	276	274	273	273	273	273
U.S. foreign currency holdings and U.S. short-term assets	2,594	2,522	2,627	2,792	2,754	563	554	24,456
U.S. private assets	6,025,217	6,093,066	6,405,168	7,369,737	9,067,981	10,505,957	12,850,260	14,983,691
Direct investment at current cost	1,531,607	1,693,131	1,867,043	2,054,464	2,498,494	2,651,721	2,935,977	3,332,828
Foreign securities	2,425,534	2,169,735	2,076,722	2,948,370	3,545,396	4,329,259	5,604,475	6,648,686
Bonds	572,692	557,062	702,742	868,948	984,978	1,011,554	1,275,515	1,478,087
Corporate stocks	1,852,842	1,612,673	1,373,980	2,079,422	2,560,418	3,317,705	4,328,960	5,170,599
U.S. claims on unaffiliated foreigners reported by U.S. nonbanking concerns [5]	836,559	839,303	901,946	594,004	793,556	1,018,462	1,163,102	1,176,027
U.S. claims reported by U.S. banks, not included elsewhere [6]	1,231,517	1,390,897	1,559,457	1,772,899	2,230,535	2,506,515	3,146,706	3,826,150
FOREIGN-OWNED ASSETS IN THE UNITED STATES	7,569,415	8,177,556	8,687,049	9,724,599	11,586,051	13,886,698	16,607,101	20,081,783
Financial derivatives, gross negative fair value [1]	....	....	....	....	....	1,132,114	1,179,159	2,201,052
Foreign-owned assets in the United States, excluding financial derivatives	7,569,415	8,177,556	8,687,049	9,724,599	11,586,051	12,754,584	15,427,942	17,880,731
Foreign official assets in the United States	1,030,708	1,109,072	1,250,977	1,562,564	2,011,899	2,306,292	2,825,628	3,337,030
U.S. Government securities	756,155	847,005	970,359	1,186,500	1,509,986	1,725,193	2,167,112	2,502,831
U.S. Treasury securities	639,796	720,149	811,995	986,301	1,251,943	1,340,598	1,558,317	1,697,365
Other	116,359	126,856	158,364	200,199	258,043	384,595	608,795	805,466
Other U.S. Government liabilities [7]	19,316	17,007	17,144	16,421	16,287	15,866	18,682	24,024
U.S. liabilities reported by U.S. banks, not included elsewhere	153,403	134,655	155,876	201,054	270,387	296,647	297,012	405,707
Other foreign official assets	101,834	110,405	107,598	158,589	215,239	268,586	342,822	404,468
Other foreign assets	6,538,707	7,068,484	7,436,072	8,162,035	9,574,152	10,448,292	12,602,314	14,543,701
Direct investment at current cost	1,421,017	1,518,473	1,499,952	1,580,994	1,742,716	1,905,979	2,151,616	2,422,796
U.S. Treasury securities	381,630	375,059	473,503	527,223	561,610	643,793	567,885	734,776
U.S. securities other than U.S. Treasury securities	2,623,014	2,821,372	2,779,067	3,422,856	3,995,506	4,352,998	5,372,361	6,132,438
Corporate and other bonds	1,068,566	1,343,071	1,530,982	1,710,787	2,035,149	2,243,135	2,824,879	3,299,325
Corporate stocks	1,554,448	1,478,301	1,248,085	1,712,069	1,960,357	2,109,863	2,547,482	2,833,113
U.S. currency	205,406	229,200	248,061	258,652	271,953	280,400	282,627	271,952
U.S. liabilities to unaffiliated foreigners reported by U.S. nonbanking concerns [8]	738,904	798,314	897,335	450,884	600,161	658,177	797,495	959,544
U.S. liabilities reported by U.S. banks, not included elsewhere [9]	1,168,736	1,326,066	1,538,154	1,921,426	2,402,206	2,606,945	3,430,330	4,022,195
Memoranda:								
Direct investment abroad at market value	2,694,014	2,314,934	2,022,588	2,729,126	3,362,796	3,637,996	4,454,635	5,147,952
Direct investment in the United States at market value	2,783,235	2,560,294	2,021,817	2,454,877	2,717,383	2,817,970	3,293,739	3,523,600

[1] A break in series in 2005 reflects the introduction of U.S. Department of the Treasury data on financial derivatives.

[2] U.S. official gold stock is valued at market prices.

[3] Also includes paid-in capital subscriptions to international financial institutions and resources provided to foreigners under foreign assistance programs requiring repayment over several years. Excludes World War I debts that are not being serviced.

[4] Includes indebtedness that the borrower may contractually, or at its option, repay with its currency, with a third country's currency, or by delivery of materials or transfer of services.

[5] A break in series in 2003 reflects the reclassification of assets reported by U.S. securities brokers from nonbank-reported assets to bank-reported assets, and a reduction in counterparty balances to eliminate double counting. A break in series in 2005 reflects the addition of previously unreported claims of U.S. financial intermediaries on their foreign parents associated with the issuance of asset-backed commercial paper in the U.S.

[6] A break in series in 2003 reflects the reclassification of assets reported by U.S. securities brokers from nonbank-reported assets to bank-reported assets.

[7] Primarily U.S. Government liabilities associated with military sales contracts and other transactions arranged with or through foreign official agencies.

[8] A break in series in 2003 reflects the reclassification of liabilities reported by U.S. securities brokers from nonbank-reported liabilities to bank-reported liabilities and a reduction in counterparty balances to eliminate double counting.

[9] A break in series in 2003 reflects the reclassification of liabilities reported by U.S. securities brokers from nonbank-reported liabilities to bank-reported liabilities.

Note.—For details regarding these data, see *Survey of Current Business*, July 2008.

Source: Department of Commerce (Bureau of Economic Analysis).

TABLE B–108.—*Industrial production and consumer prices, major industrial countries, 1980–2008*

Year or quarter	United States [1]	Canada	Japan	France	Germany [2]	Italy	United Kingdom
	Industrial production (Index, 2002=100) [3]						
1980	56.3	57.3	73.5	75.9	75.9	78.6	73.
1981	57.0	57.6	74.3	75.1	74.5	76.8	71.
1982	54.1	53.2	74.5	74.5	72.1	74.5	72.
1983	55.6	56.1	76.7	74.5	72.5	72.7	75.
1984	60.5	63.1	84.0	75.8	74.7	75.1	75.
1985	61.3	66.3	87.1	76.3	78.3	75.2	79.
1986	61.9	65.8	86.9	78.3	79.7	78.3	81.
1987	65.1	68.5	89.8	79.6	80.1	80.3	84.
1988	68.4	73.1	98.5	82.5	82.9	85.9	88.
1989	69.1	72.9	104.3	85.3	87.0	89.2	90.
1990	69.7	70.9	108.5	86.6	91.5	88.7	90.
1991	68.7	68.3	110.4	86.3	94.1	87.9	87.
1992	70.6	69.2	103.6	85.1	92.0	86.9	87.
1993	72.9	72.5	99.7	81.7	85.0	84.9	89.
1994	76.8	77.1	100.5	85.2	87.5	90.0	94
1995	80.4	80.6	103.8	86.8	88.1	95.3	96.
1996	84.0	81.6	106.1	86.6	88.3	93.7	97.
1997	90.1	86.2	110.1	90.3	91.0	97.4	98.
1998	95.4	89.2	102.5	93.8	94.4	98.5	99.
1999	99.5	94.4	102.7	96.0	95.5	98.4	101.
2000	103.7	102.6	108.5	100.0	100.9	102.6	103.
2001	100.1	98.4	101.2	101.3	101.1	101.4	101.
2002	100.0	100.0	100.0	100.0	100.0	100.0	100.
2003	101.2	100.1	103.0	99.7	100.4	99.5	99.
2004	103.8	101.7	108.0	102.0	103.4	99.1	100.
2005	107.2	103.5	109.4	102.3	106.9	98.4	99.
2006	109.6	103.3	114.3	102.8	113.2	100.7	99.
2007	111.4	103.2	117.5	104.3	120.1	100.5	100.
2007: I	110.2	103.4	115.8	103.4	117.8	101.7	99.
II	111.1	103.8	116.4	103.7	118.9	101.2	100.
III	112.1	103.5	118.4	105.0	121.5	101.8	100.
IV	112.2	102.0	119.5	105.1	122.3	99.7	100.
2008: I	112.3	99.9	118.6	105.2	123.8	100.2	100.
II	111.3	99.3	117.6	103.5	122.8	99.5	99.
III p	109.1	100.0	116.1	102.8	121.2	97.8	98.
	Consumer prices (Index, 1982–84=100)						
1980	82.4	76.1	91.0	72.2	86.7	63.9	78.
1981	90.9	85.6	95.3	81.8	92.2	75.5	87.
1982	96.5	94.9	98.1	91.7	97.0	87.8	95.
1983	99.6	100.4	99.8	100.3	100.3	100.8	99.
1984	103.9	104.7	102.1	108.0	102.7	111.4	104.
1985	107.6	109.0	104.2	114.3	104.9	121.7	111.
1986	109.6	113.5	104.9	117.2	104.7	128.9	114.
1987	113.6	118.4	104.9	121.1	105.0	135.1	119.
1988	118.3	123.2	105.6	124.3	106.3	141.9	125.
1989	124.0	129.3	108.0	128.7	109.2	150.7	135.
1990	130.7	135.5	111.4	132.9	112.2	160.4	148.
1991	136.2	143.1	115.0	137.2	116.7	170.5	156.
1992	140.3	145.3	117.0	140.4	122.7	179.5	162
1993	144.5	147.9	118.5	143.4	128.1	187.7	165.
1994	148.2	148.2	119.3	145.8	131.6	195.3	169.
1995	152.4	151.4	119.2	148.4	133.9	205.6	175.
1996	156.9	153.8	119.3	151.4	135.8	213.8	179
1997	160.5	156.2	121.5	153.2	138.4	218.2	185
1998	163.0	157.8	122.2	154.2	139.7	222.5	191
1999	166.6	160.5	121.8	155.0	140.5	226.2	194.
2000	172.2	164.9	121.0	157.6	142.5	231.9	200.
2001	177.1	169.0	120.1	160.2	145.3	238.3	203.
2002	179.9	172.8	119.0	163.3	147.4	244.3	207.
2003	184.0	177.6	118.7	166.7	148.9	250.9	213.
2004	188.9	180.9	118.7	170.3	151.4	256.4	219.
2005	195.3	184.9	118.3	173.2	153.7	261.3	225.
2006	201.6	188.5	118.7	176.2	156.2	266.9	232
2007	207.342	192.7	118.7	178.8	159.7	271.8	242
2007: I	203.756	190.5	118.0	176.8	158.0	269.2	238.
II	207.662	193.3	118.6	178.6	159.3	270.9	242
III	208.235	193.3	118.8	179.0	160.1	272.5	243
IV	209.716	193.3	119.3	180.7	161.5	274.4	246
2008: I	212.100	193.9	119.2	182.0	162.7	277.5	248.
II	216.757	197.9	120.2	184.5	163.9	280.6	253.
III p	219.278	199.9	121.4	184.8	165.1	283.3	255

[1] See Note, Table B–51 for information on U.S. industrial production series.
[2] Prior to 1991 data are for West Germany only.
[3] All data exclude construction. Quarterly data are seasonally adjusted.

Note.—National sources data have been rebased for industrial production and consumer prices.

Sources: National sources as reported by each country, Department of Labor (Bureau of Labor Statistics), and Board of Governors of the Federal Reserve System.

TABLE B–109.—*Civilian unemployment rate, and hourly compensation, major industrial countries, 1980–2008*

[Quarterly data seasonally adjusted]

Year or quarter	United States	Canada	Japan	France	Germany[1]	Italy	United Kingdom
			Civilian unemployment rate (Percent)[2]				
80	7.1	7.3	2.0	6.5	2.8	4.4	6.9
81	7.6	7.3	2.2	7.6	4.0	4.9	9.7
82	9.7	10.7	2.4	³8.3	5.6	5.4	10.8
83	9.6	11.6	2.7	8.6	³6.9	5.9	11.5
84	7.5	10.9	2.8	10.0	7.1	5.9	11.8
85	7.2	10.2	2.7	10.5	7.2	6.0	11.4
86	7.0	9.3	2.8	10.6	6.6	³7.5	11.4
87	6.2	8.4	2.9	10.8	6.3	7.9	10.5
88	5.5	7.4	2.5	10.3	6.3	7.9	8.6
89	5.3	7.1	2.3	9.6	5.7	7.8	7.3
90	³5.6	7.7	2.1	³8.6	5.0	7.0	7.1
91	6.8	9.8	2.1	9.1	³5.6	³6.9	9.5
92	7.5	10.6	2.2	10.0	6.7	7.3	10.2
93	6.9	10.8	2.5	11.3	8.0	³9.8	10.4
94	³6.1	³9.6	2.9	11.9	8.5	10.7	9.5
95	5.6	8.6	3.2	11.3	8.2	11.3	8.7
96	5.4	8.8	3.4	11.8	9.0	11.3	8.1
97	4.9	8.4	3.4	11.7	9.9	11.4	7.0
98	4.5	7.7	4.1	11.2	9.3	11.5	6.3
99	4.2	7.0	4.7	10.5	³8.5	11.0	6.0
00	4.0	6.1	4.8	9.1	7.8	10.2	5.5
01	4.7	6.5	5.1	8.4	7.9	9.2	5.1
02	5.8	7.0	5.4	8.8	8.6	8.7	5.2
03	6.0	6.9	5.3	9.2	9.3	8.5	5.0
04	5.5	6.4	4.8	9.6	10.3	8.1	4.8
05	5.1	6.0	4.5	9.6	³11.2	7.8	4.9
06	4.6	5.5	4.2	9.5	10.4	6.9	5.5
07	4.6	5.3	3.9	8.6	8.7	6.2	5.4
007: I	4.5	5.4	4.0	9.1	9.3	6.2	5.5
II	4.5	5.3	3.8	8.7	8.9	6.1	5.4
III	4.7	5.2	3.8	8.5	8.5	6.2	5.3
IV	4.8	5.2	3.9	8.2	8.1	6.4	5.2
08: I	4.9	5.2	3.9	8.0	7.8	6.7	5.3
II	5.3	5.3	4.0	8.0	7.6	6.8	5.4
III	6.0	5.3	4.1	8.3	7.5	....	....
			Manufacturing hourly compensation in U.S. dollars (Index, 1996=100)[4]				
380	51.2	51.1	25.8	41.9	35.9	40.6	49.8
381	56.3	56.1	28.3	37.7	30.6	36.6	50.3
382	61.5	62.7	26.3	36.9	30.2	35.9	47.7
383	63.3	67.1	28.4	35.6	30.1	37.5	44.3
384	65.5	67.8	29.2	34.1	28.2	37.6	42.0
385	68.8	67.7	30.3	36.1	28.9	38.8	44.7
386	72.1	67.7	44.9	49.1	40.8	53.0	54.9
387	74.4	72.6	53.6	58.9	51.4	65.7	68.1
388	76.9	81.8	61.6	61.5	54.8	70.3	79.0
389	79.2	89.1	60.9	60.5	53.8	73.6	77.7
390	82.7	96.3	62.3	74.1	67.3	90.8	94.7
391	87.4	105.0	71.4	75.7	67.6	95.3	105.6
392	91.5	104.3	78.6	84.9	78.6	102.2	105.6
393	93.3	98.9	92.2	82.9	78.8	83.4	92.5
394	96.3	96.0	102.2	87.9	84.1	85.8	96.8
395	98.1	97.9	114.9	100.7	100.3	89.8	101.5
396	100.0	100.0	100.0	100.0	100.0	100.0	100.0
397	102.6	100.9	92.8	90.2	88.4	94.8	109.6
398	108.6	99.0	87.9	89.9	88.4	91.3	119.3
399	112.9	100.9	101.1	88.9	86.7	89.4	123.2
00	123.3	104.3	106.1	81.2	79.0	79.5	122.6
01	126.1	102.8	95.3	80.9	79.0	79.7	121.6
02	135.2	104.7	93.1	90.6	85.5	86.6	133.9
03	144.7	122.1	98.4	111.0	104.7	107.6	153.0
04	147.7	135.3	106.5	125.8	115.7	122.3	180.5
05	150.5	152.4	105.5	130.5	117.3	126.4	186.3
06	156.7	165.9	98.5	138.1	123.3	130.0	202.0
07	162.2	182.0	97.0	155.1	136.8	144.9	224.8

[1] Prior to 1991 data are for West Germany only.

[2] Civilian unemployment rates, approximating U.S. concepts. Quarterly data for France, Germany, and Italy should be viewed as less precise indicators of unemployment under U.S. concepts than the annual data.

[3] There are breaks in the series for Canada (1994), France (1982 and 1990), Germany (1983, 1991, 1999, and 2005), Italy (1986, 1991, and 1993), and United States (1990 and 1994). For details on break in series in 1990 and 1994 for United States, see footnote 5, Table B–35. For details on break in series for other countries, see U.S. Department of Labor *International Comparisons of Annual Labor Force Statistics, 10 Countries, 1960–2007*, October 21, 2008.

[4] Hourly compensation in manufacturing, U.S. dollar basis; data relate to all employed persons (employees and self-employed workers). For details on manufacturing hourly compensation, see U.S. Department of Labor *International Comparisons of Manufacturing Productivity and Unit Labor Cost Trends, 2007*, September 26, 2008.

Source: Department of Labor (Bureau of Labor Statistics).

TABLE B–110.—*Foreign exchange rates, 1985–2008*

[Foreign currency units per U.S. dollar, except as noted; certified noon buying rates in New York]

Period	Australia (dollar)[1]	Canada (dollar)	China, P.R. (yuan)	EMU Members (euro)[1,2]	Germany (mark)[2]	Japan (yen)	Mexico (peso)	South Korea (won)	Sweden (krona)	Switzer-land (franc)	United Kingdom (pound)
March 1973	1.2716	0.9967	2.2401		2.8132	261.90	0.013	398.85	4.4294	3.2171	2.47:
1985	0.7003	1.3659	2.9434		2.9420	238.47	0.257	872.45	8.6032	2.4552	1.29
1986	.6709	1.3896	3.4616		2.1705	168.35	.612	884.60	7.1273	1.7979	1.46:
1987	.7014	1.3259	3.7314		1.7981	144.60	1.378	826.16	6.3469	1.4918	1.63
1988	.7841	1.2306	3.7314		1.7570	128.17	2.273	734.52	6.1370	1.4643	1.78
1989	.7919	1.1842	3.7673		1.8808	138.07	2.461	674.13	6.4559	1.6369	1.63
1990	.7807	1.1668	4.7921		1.6166	145.00	2.813	710.64	5.9231	1.3901	1.78
1991	.7787	1.1460	5.3337		1.6610	134.59	3.018	736.73	6.0521	1.4356	1.76
1992	.7352	1.2085	5.5206		1.5618	126.78	3.095	784.66	5.8258	1.4064	1.76:
1993	.6799	1.2902	5.7795		1.6545	111.08	3.116	805.75	7.7956	1.4781	1.50
1994	.7316	1.3664	8.6397		1.6216	102.18	3.385	806.93	7.7161	1.3667	1.53
1995	.7407	1.3725	8.3700		1.4321	93.96	6.447	772.69	7.1406	1.1812	1.57
1996	.7828	1.3638	8.3389		1.5049	108.78	7.600	805.00	6.7082	1.2361	1.56
1997	.7437	1.3849	8.3193		1.7348	121.06	7.918	953.19	7.6446	1.4514	1.63
1998	.6291	1.4836	8.3008		1.7597	130.99	9.152	1,400.40	7.9522	1.4506	1.65:
1999	.6454	1.4858	8.2783	1.0653		113.73	9.553	1,189.84	8.2740	1.5045	1.61
2000	.5815	1.4855	8.2784	.9232		107.80	9.459	1,130.90	9.1735	1.6904	1.51
2001	.5169	1.5487	8.2770	.8952		121.57	9.337	1,292.02	10.3425	1.6891	1.43
2002	.5437	1.5704	8.2771	.9454		125.22	9.663	1,250.31	9.7233	1.5567	1.50
2003	.6524	1.4008	8.2772	1.1321		115.94	10.793	1,192.08	8.0787	1.3450	1.63:
2004	.7365	1.3017	8.2768	1.2438		108.15	11.290	1,145.24	7.3480	1.2428	1.83:
2005	.7627	1.2115	8.1936	1.2449		110.11	10.894	1,023.75	7.4710	1.2459	1.82
2006	.7535	1.1340	7.9723	1.2563		116.31	10.906	954.32	7.3718	1.2532	1.84:
2007	.8391	1.0734	7.6058	1.3711		117.76	10.928	928.97	6.7550	1.1999	2.00:
2007: I	.7865	1.1718	7.7582	1.3109		119.33	11.024	938.98	7.0089	1.2330	1.95:
II	.8316	1.0983	7.6784	1.3484		120.80	10.878	928.69	6.8641	1.2221	1.98:
III	.8471	1.0456	7.5578	1.3748		117.74	10.965	927.27	6.7402	1.1986	2.02:
IV	.8898	.9811	7.4336	1.4482		113.23	10.849	921.26	6.4148	1.1468	2.04:
2008: I	.9058	1.0039	7.1590	1.5007		105.17	10.803	956.12	6.2668	1.0670	1.97:
II	.9435	1.0099	6.9578	1.5625		104.62	10.428	1,017.02	5.9862	1.0316	1.97:
III	.8879	1.0411	6.8375	1.5030		107.58	10.328	1,064.56	6.3175	1.0734	1.89:

Trade-weighted value of the U.S. dollar

	Nominal				Real [7]		
	G-10 index (March 1973=100)[3]	Broad index (January 1997=100)[4]	Major currencies index (March 1973=100)[5]	OITP index (January 1997=100)[6]	Broad index (March 1973=100)[4]	Major currencies index (March 1973=100)[5]	OITP index (March 1973=100)[6]
1985	143.0	67.16	133.55	13.14	123.04	122.05	125.:
1986	112.2	62.35	109.77	16.49	107.65	99.71	130.:
1987	96.9	60.42	97.16	19.92	98.89	89.21	127.:
1988	92.7	60.92	90.43	24.07	92.29	84.19	116.:
1989	98.6	66.90	94.29	29.61	94.04	88.52	111.:
1990	89.1	71.41	89.91	40.10	91.50	85.15	110.:
1991	89.8	74.35	88.59	46.69	89.97	83.48	109.8
1992	86.6	76.91	87.00	53.13	88.08	82.35	106.:
1993	93.2	83.78	89.90	63.37	89.43	85.59	103.:
1994	91.3	90.87	88.43	80.54	89.25	85.24	103.:
1995	84.2	92.65	83.41	92.51	86.80	81.37	103.:
1996	87.3	97.46	87.25	98.24	88.81	86.28	100.:
1997	96.4	104.43	93.93	104.64	93.54	93.56	101.8
1998	98.8	115.89	98.45	125.89	101.54	98.64	114.:
1999		116.04	96.89	129.20	100.92	98.40	113.8
2000		119.45	101.58	129.84	104.79	105.04	113.:
2001		125.93	107.67	135.91	110.82	112.50	118.:
2002		126.67	105.99	140.36	110.97	110.88	120.:
2003		119.11	92.99	143.52	104.24	97.81	122.:
2004		113.63	85.37	143.38	99.61	90.82	121.:
2005		110.71	83.71	138.89	97.98	90.63	117.:
2006		108.52	82.46	135.38	96.87	90.55	114.8
2007		103.40	77.84	130.28	92.28	86.40	109.0
2007: I		107.17	81.87	132.92	94.96	89.95	110.:
II		104.61	79.33	130.78	94.12	88.35	110.:
III		102.68	77.01	129.98	91.88	85.73	108.:
IV		99.15	73.29	127.46	88.14	81.57	105.:
2008: I		97.31	71.97	124.96	86.25	80.47	102.:
II		95.80	70.87	123.01	85.90	80.17	101.8
III		97.88	73.46	123.79	87.87	83.26	102.:

[1] U.S. dollars per foreign currency unit.
[2] European Economic and Monetary Union (EMU) members consists of Austria, Belgium, Finland, France, Germany, Greece (beginning in 2001), Ireland, Italy, Luxembourg, Netherlands, Portugal, Slovenia (beginning in 2007), and Spain.
[3] G-10 index discontinued after December 1998.
[4] Weighted average of the foreign exchange value of the dollar against the currencies of a broad group of U.S. trading partners.
[5] Subset of the broad index. Consists of currencies of the Euro area, Australia, Canada, Japan, Sweden, Switzerland, and the United Kingdom.
[6] Subset of the broad index. Consists of other important U.S. trading partners (OITP) whose currencies are not heavily traded outside their home markets.
[7] Adjusted for changes in consumer price indexes for the United States and other countries.

Source: Board of Governors of the Federal Reserve System.

TABLE B–111.—*International reserves, selected years, 1972–2008*

[Millions of special drawing rights (SDRs); end of period]

Area and country	1972	1982	1992	2002	2006	2007	2008 September	2008 October
countries	146,658	361,166	753,847	1,890,032	3,414,407	4,110,936	4,493,540	4,599,773
Industrial countries [1]	113,362	214,025	426,440	766,645	983,906	997,557	1,012,144	1,046,329
United States	12,112	29,918	52,995	59,160	45,615	46,820	48,192	48,608
Canada	5,572	3,439	8,662	27,225	23,265	25,944	27,542	27,768
Euro area (incl. ECB) [1]				195,771	143,735	148,786	153,485	160,499
Austria	2,505	5,544	9,703	7,480	4,985	7,079	6,657	6,443
Belgium	3,564	4,757	10,914	9,010	6,095	6,827	5,667	5,185
Cyprus	294	490	764	2,239	3,770	3,888	634	431
Finland	664	1,420	3,862	6,885	4,372	4,525	4,506	4,587
France	9,224	17,850	22,522	24,268	31,412	31,855	29,490	30,632
Germany	21,908	43,909	69,489	41,516	31,561	31,896	32,431	33,635
Greece	950	916	3,606	6,083	502	526	324	258
Ireland	1,038	2,390	2,514	3,989	485	499	495	528
Italy	5,605	15,108	22,438	23,798	19,817	20,721	24,909	26,542
Luxembourg			66	114	148	93	424	209
Malta			927	1,625	1,979	2,396	317	229
Netherlands	4,407	10,723	17,492	7,993	7,902	7,198	8,171	7,872
Portugal	2,130	1,179	14,474	8,889	1,802	1,226	1,335	1,423
Slovenia			520	5,143	4,683	624	596	570
Spain	4,567	7,450	33,640	25,992	7,663	7,582	7,781	7,890
Australia	5,656	6,053	8,429	15,307	35,618	15,764	17,136	18,974
Japan	16,916	22,001	52,937	340,088	585,600	603,794	626,418	645,720
New Zealand	767	577	2,239	3,650	9,352	10,914	9,411	
Denmark	787	2,111	8,090	19,924	19,833	20,663	19,001	
Iceland	78	133	364	326	1,532	1,634	2,348	
Norway	1,220	6,272	8,725	23,579	37,784	38,500	28,428	29,758
San Marino				135	318	410		
Sweden	1,453	3,397	16,667	12,807	16,649	17,281	21,995	22,373
Switzerland	6,961	16,930	27,100	31,693	26,773	29,432	30,083	30,696
United Kingdom	5,201	11,904	27,300	27,973	27,402	31,330	27,567	29,247
Developing countries: Total [2]	33,295	145,652	327,408	1,123,387	2,430,501	3,113,379	3,481,395	3,553,444
By area:								
Africa	3,962	7,737	13,069	53,996	147,879	183,729	222,759	230,201
Asia [2]	7,935	44,490	191,041	720,104	1,512,284	1,892,995	2,089,031	2,136,206
China, P.R. (Mainland)		10,733	15,441	214,815	710,920	969,055		
India	1,087	4,213	4,584	50,174	113,895	169,356	178,778	164,684
Korea	485	2,556	12,463	89,272	158,804	165,908	153,878	142,577
Europe	2,680	5,359	13,798	131,942	398,138	537,382	612,363	628,426
Russia				32,840	196,921	295,320	348,674	
Middle East	9,407	64,039	44,397	98,645	165,287	216,916	225,366	230,247
Western Hemisphere	9,089	25,563	65,102	118,700	206,913	282,358	331,876	328,363
Brazil	3,853	3,566	16,457	27,593	56,643	113,585	132,029	132,027
Mexico	1,072	828	13,800	37,223	50,702	55,128	63,415	57,035
Memoranda:								
Oil-exporting countries	9,927	67,108	46,392	110,079	236,971	313,284	341,689	349,433
Non-oil developing countries [2]	23,339	78,544	281,015	1,013,309	2,193,530	2,800,095	3,139,706	3,204,011

[1] Includes data for European Central Bank (ECB) beginning 1999. Detail does not add to totals shown.
[2] Includes data for Taiwan Province of China.

Note.—International reserves consists of monetary authorities' holdings of gold (at SDR 35 per ounce), SDRs, reserve positions in the International Monetary nd, and foreign exchange.

U.S. dollars per SDR (end of period) are: 1.08570 in 1972; 1.10310 in 1982; 1.37500 in 1992; 1.35952 in 2002; 1.50440 in 2006; 1.58025 in 2007; 1.55722 in eptember 2008; and 1.48830 in October 2008.

Source: International Monetary Fund, *International Financial Statistics.*

TABLE B–112.—*Growth rates in real gross domestic product, 1990–2009*

[Percent change]

Area and country	1990–99 annual average	2000	2001	2002	2003	2004	2005	2006	2007	2008[1]	2009
World	2.9	4.7	2.2	2.8	3.6	4.9	4.5	5.1	5.0	3.7	2
Advanced economies	2.7	4.0	1.2	1.6	1.9	3.2	2.6	3.0	2.6	1.4	-
Of which:											
United States	3.1	3.7	.8	1.6	2.5	3.6	2.9	2.8	2.0	1.4	-
Japan	1.5	2.9	.2	.3	1.4	2.7	1.9	2.4	2.1	.5	-
United Kingdom	2.2	3.9	2.5	2.1	2.8	2.8	2.1	2.8	3.0	.8	-1
Canada	2.4	5.2	1.8	2.9	1.9	3.1	2.9	3.1	2.7	.6	
Euro area[2]	....	3.8	1.9	.9	.8	2.1	1.6	2.8	2.6	1.2	-
Germany	2.3	3.2	1.2	*	-.2	1.2	.8	3.0	2.5	1.7	-
France	1.9	3.9	1.9	1.0	1.1	2.5	1.9	2.2	2.2	.8	-
Italy	1.4	3.7	1.8	.5	*	1.5	.6	1.8	1.5	-.2	-
Spain	2.8	5.1	3.6	2.7	3.1	3.3	3.6	3.9	3.7	1.4	-
Memorandum:											
Newly industrialized Asian economies[3]	6.1	7.7	1.2	5.5	3.2	5.9	4.8	5.6	5.6	3.9	2
Emerging and developing economies	3.2	5.9	3.8	4.8	6.3	7.5	7.1	7.9	8.0	6.6	5
Regional groups:											
Africa	2.3	3.5	4.9	6.2	5.4	6.5	5.8	6.1	6.1	5.2	4
Central and eastern Europe	1.2	4.9	.4	4.2	4.8	6.9	6.1	6.7	5.7	4.2	2
Commonwealth of Independent States[4]	....	9.1	6.1	5.2	7.8	8.2	6.8	8.2	8.6	6.9	3
Russia	....	10.0	5.1	4.7	7.3	7.2	6.4	7.4	8.1	6.8	3
Developing Asia	7.2	7.0	5.8	6.9	8.2	8.6	9.0	9.8	10.0	8.3	7
China	9.9	8.4	8.3	9.1	10.0	10.1	10.4	11.6	11.9	9.7	8
India	5.6	5.7	3.9	4.6	6.9	7.9	9.1	9.8	9.3	7.8	6
Middle East	4.3	5.5	2.6	3.8	7.1	5.8	5.7	5.7	6.0	6.1	5
Western Hemisphere	2.9	4.1	.7	.5	2.2	6.1	4.7	5.5	5.6	4.5	2
Brazil	1.7	4.3	1.3	2.7	1.1	5.7	3.2	3.8	5.4	5.2	3
Mexico	3.3	6.6	-.2	.8	1.7	4.0	3.1	4.9	3.2	1.9	

* Figure is zero or negligible.

[1] All figures are forecasts as published by the International Monetary Fund.

[2] Euro area consists of: Austria, Belgium, Cyprus, Finland, France, Germany, Greece, Ireland, Italy, Luxembourg, Malta, Netherlands, Portugal, Slovenia, and Spain.

[3] Consists of Hong Kong SAR (Special Administrative Region of China), Korea, Singapore, and Taiwan Province of China.

[4] Includes Mongolia, which is not a member of the Commonwealth of Independent States but is included for reasons of geography and similarities in economic structure.

Note.—For details on data shown in this table, see *World Economic Outlook* and *World Economic Outlook Update* published by the International Monetary Fund.

Sources: Department of Commerce (Bureau of Economic Analysis) and International Monetary Fund.